The Select Series: Microsoft® PowerPoint® 2002 Comprehensive Volume

Pamela R. Toliver

Prentice Hall

Upper Saddle River, New Jersey

LIBRARY OF CONGRESS CATALOGING-IN-PUBLICATION DATA

Toliver, Pamela R.
The select series. Microsoft PowerPoint 2002 : comprehensive volume / Pamela R. Toliver.
p. cm.
Includes index.
ISBN 0-13-060163-2
1. Computer graphics. 2. Microsoft PowerPoint (Computer file) 3. Business presentations—Graphic methods—Computer programs. I. Title

T385 .T654 2001
006.6'869—dc21 2001036588

Publisher and Vice President: Natalie E. Anderson
Executive Acquisitions Editor: Jodi McPherson
Managing Editor: Monica Stipanov
Assistant Editor: Jennifer Cappello
Editorial Assistant: Dayna Hilinsky
Developmental Editor: Christy Parrish and Samantha Penrod
Media Project Manager: Cathleen Profitko
Marketing Manager: Emily Williams Knight
Production Manager: Gail Steier De Acevedo
Project Manager: Tim Tate
Associate Director, Manufacturing: Vincent Scelta
Manufacturing Buyer: Barbara Miller
Design Manager: Pat Smythe
Interior Design: Lorraine Castellano and Proof Positive/Farrowlyne Associates, Inc.
Cover Design: Lorraine Castellano
Full-Service Composition: Proof Positive/Farrowlyne Associates, Inc.
Printer/Binder: Banta Book Group, Menasha

Credits and acknowledgments borrowed from other sources and reproduced, with permission, in this textbook appear on the appropriate page within the text or at the end of the respective project.

Prentice Hall

10 9 8 7 6 5 4 3 2 1
ISBN 0-13-060163-2

THE SELECT SERIES: MICROSOFT® OFFICE XP

Series Authors

Pamela R. Toliver and Yvonne Johnson

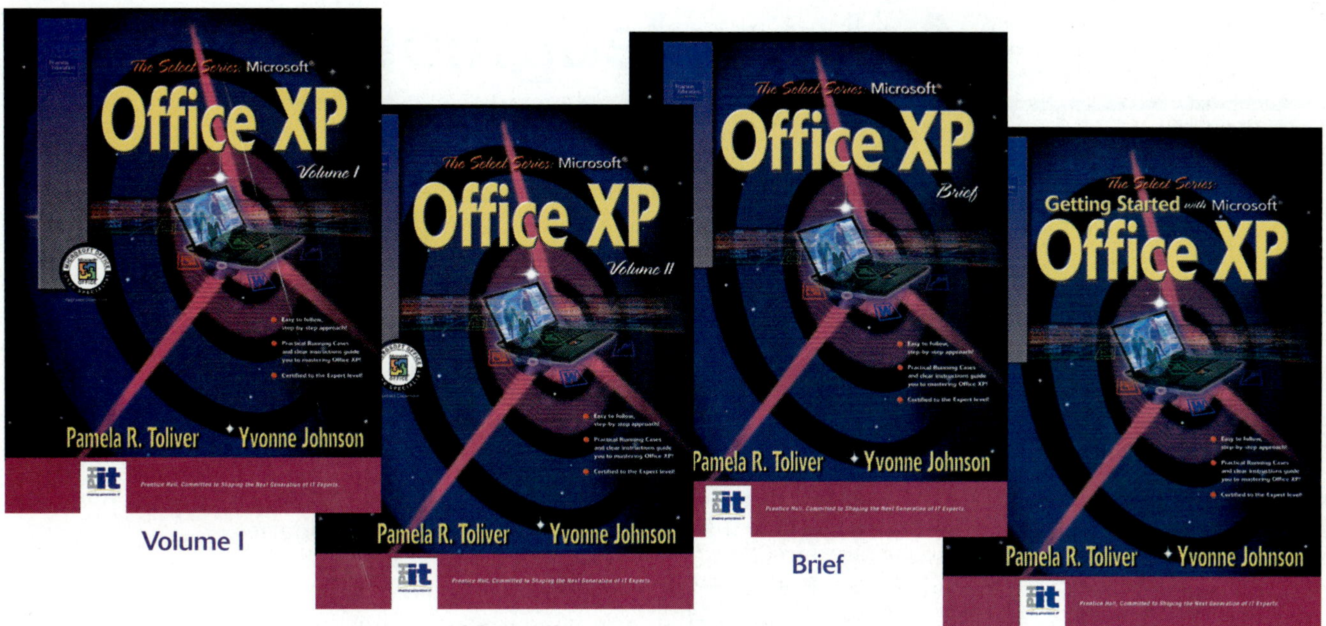

Volume I

Volume II

Brief

Getting Started

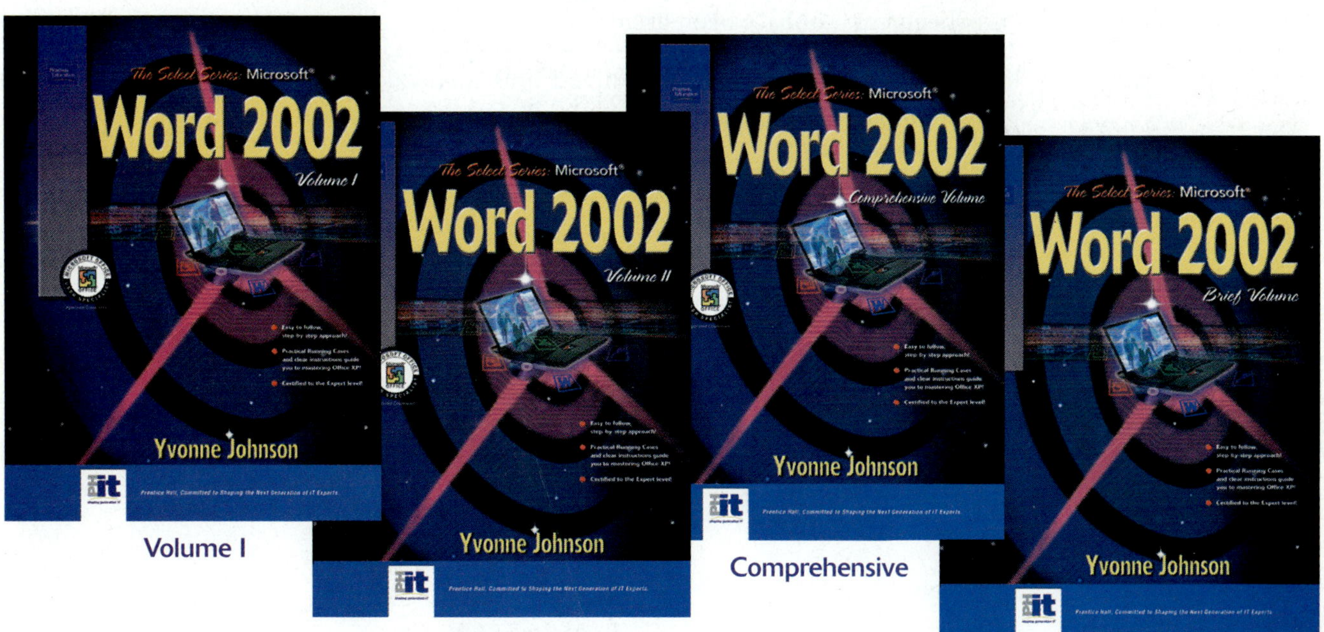

Volume I

Volume II

Comprehensive

Brief

Dedication

This book is dedicated to my husband, John, who spent so much time during the writing of this work visiting me evenings and weekends in my office. Without his love and support, this work would not have been possible.

Acknowledgments

Completing a work of this magnitude is like a snowball rolling downhill, gathering speed and picking up so much help along the way. Without the support and growth, this work would not have been completed:

To the development staff, I say thank you for keeping us on track.

To the technical reviewers, thanks for trying to keep us accurate.

To the copy editors, thanks for keeping us consistent.

To production and design, thanks for laying it all out, expanding and compressing to make it fit so beautifully within the boundaries.

But most of all, thanks to those with whom we were in almost daily contact, who kept us motivated and moving toward our accomplished goal:

To Monica—the best managing editor I have ever had—it couldn't always have been easy, but it's been great.

To Christy—the most organized and focused and easy-to-work-with project manager I have ever known—thanks for sticking with us to the end.

To Jennifer—who kept plugging for the supplemental material—thanks for pulling it together so well.

To Martha—a friend and compatriot who tested the steps and looked at the pictures so many times—someday, perhaps we can make our program installations match more completely.

And to Jodi—who came to the project later—you've done great, and guided this work in a better direction. Thanks for finessing this work to completion.

And most of all, thanks to my co-author for listening, collaborating, and picking up the pieces with me. Cheers!

Pam

Preface

About this Series

The Select Series uses a class-tested, highly visual, project-based approach that teaches students through tasks using step-by-step instructions. You will find extensive full-color figures and screen captures that guide learners through the basic skills and procedures necessary to demonstrate proficiency in their use of each software application.

The Select Series introduces an all-new design for Microsoft Office XP. The easy-to-follow design now has larger screen shots with steps listed on the left side of the accompanying screen. This unique design program, along with the use of bold color, helps reduce distraction and keeps students focused and interested as they work. In addition, selectively placed Tip boxes and Other Ways boxes enhance student learning by explaining various ways to complete a task.

Our approach to learning is designed to provide the necessary visual guidance in a project-oriented setting. Each project concludes with a review section that includes a Summary, Key Terms & Skills, Study Questions, Guided Exercises, and On Your Own Exercises. This extensive end-of-project section provides students with the opportunity to practice and gain further experience with the tasks covered in each project.

What's New in the Select Series for Office XP

The entire Select Series has been revised to include the new features found in the Office XP suite, which contains Word 2002, Excel 2002, Access 2002, PowerPoint 2002, Publisher 2002, FrontPage 2002, and Outlook 2002.

The Select Series provides students with clear, concise instruction supported by its new design, which includes bigger screen captures. Steps are now located in the margin for ease of use and readability. This instruction is further enhanced by graded exercises in the end-of-project material.

Another exciting update is that every project begins with a Running Case from Selections, Inc., a department store that has opened shop online as e-Selections.com. Students are put in an e-commerce–based business environment so that they can relate what they are learning in Office XP to a real world situation. Everything is within a scenario that puts them in the department store where they perform tasks that relate to a particular division of the store or Web site.

About the Book

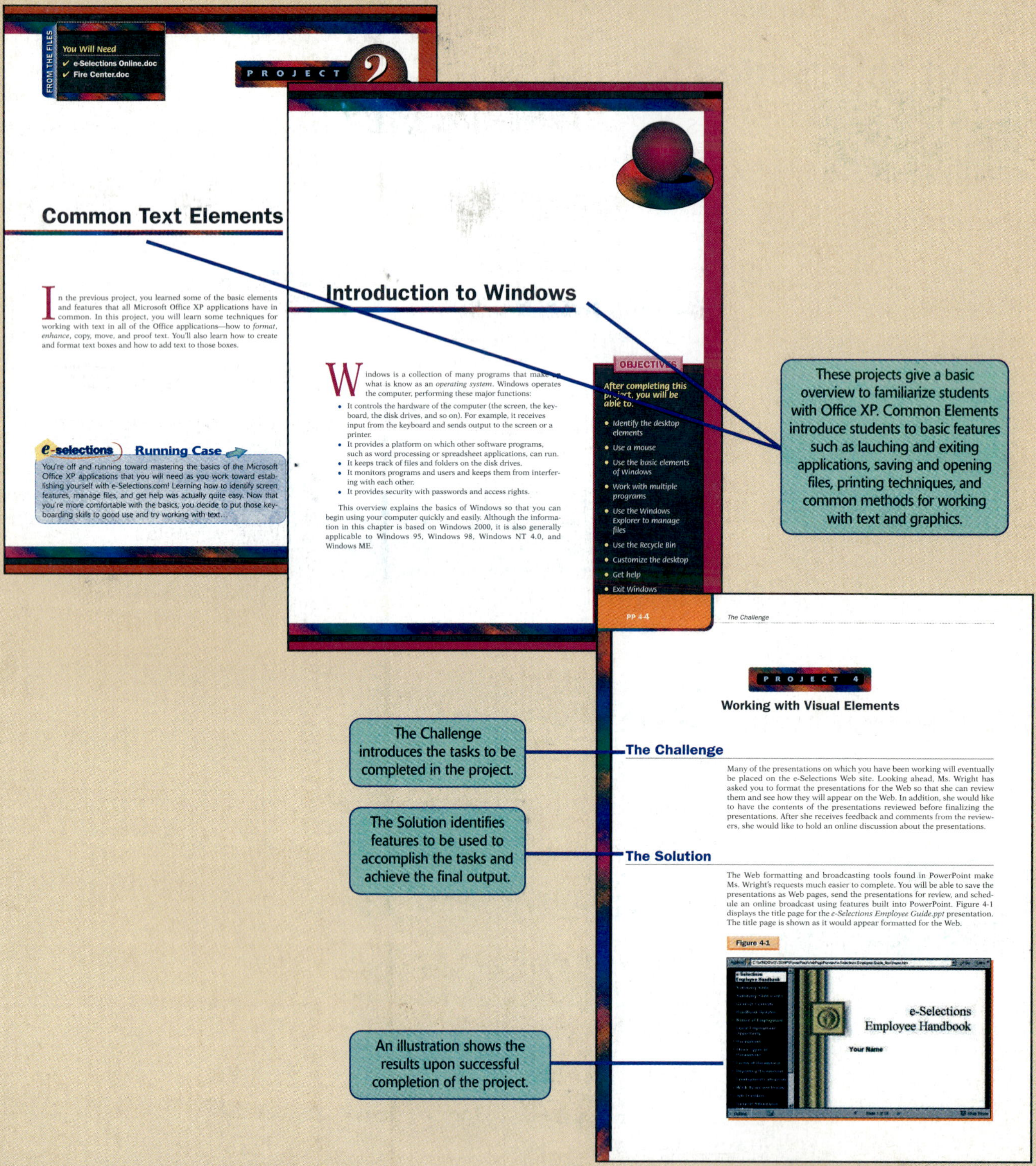

Steps have been moved into the margin next to corresponding screen captures for ease of use and readability.

New, full-color, full-size screen captures move the emphasis toward visual-based instruction.

11 Click **Play** to preview the effect of the animation.

12 Save changes to the presentation and close the task pane.

Figure 5-16

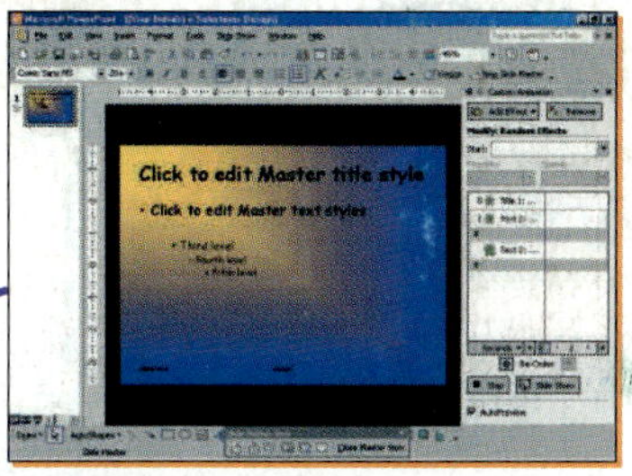

CHECK POINT

When you apply Random Effects to a placeholder on a master, PowerPoint controls the effect used to present each placeholder and bullet point. As a result, each time you show a presentation created and formatted using the template, placeholders and bullet points will appear on screen d... the presentation of random effects with the effect imm... effect used and moves through the list of available eff... result, when you use a template to create a new prese... sary to apply specific effects to slides in the presentatio... of the text or object. Since PowerPoint starts its random... immediately following the effect last used, applying a ... will control the random effect PowerPoint uses for the ...

Inserting and Formatting Graphics on Slide Mas...

You're almost finished with one of the master... Mr. Carroll requested. All you have left is to add th... to the presentation design. You can use the same p... on masters that you use to insert graphics on slide...

CHECK POINT

As you select animation schemes, you'll see a short demonstration of the scheme on the active slide. Click additional schemes to get an overview of how each scheme animates slide text.

Creating Custom Animations

The Custom Animation task pane contains options for controlling slide objects and to customize the presentation of bullet points. Using custom animation tools, you can set the order in which both text and graphic items display.

Task 10:
To Create Custom Animations

1 Display Slide 3 of the *e-Selections Online Web.ppt* presentation and then choose **Slide Show | Custom Animation**.

Figure 2-33

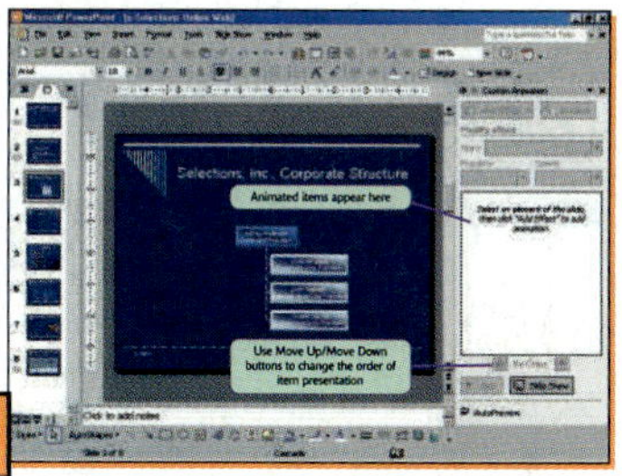

Other Ways boxes help students learn alternate methods to perform skills.

Other Ways To display the Custom Animation task pane:
- Click the task pane down arrow and select **Custom Animation**.
- Right-click a place-

Task 7:
To Schedule a Live Presentation Broadcast

1 Open the *e-Selections Web.ppt* presentation.

2 Choose **Slide Show | Online Broadcast | Schedule a Live Broadcast**.

Troubleshooting
A message box may appear informing you that the broadcast features are not currently installed on your computer. If this box appears, follow the direction of your instructor to continue.

Figure 4-20

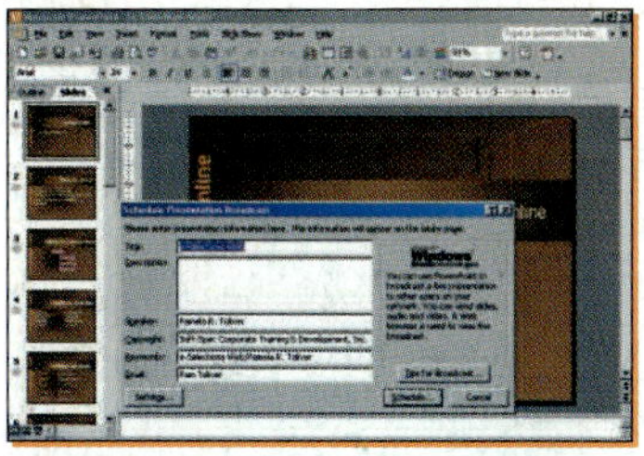

Tip Default options set on the Advanced page of the Broadcast Settings dialog box are fine for broadcasting to ten participants or fewer. Valid file locations must include a server name and follow the path structure *\\servername\foldername*.

Troubleshooting and Tip boxes appear at appropriate places throughout each project to highlight important, helpful information pertinent to the topic being discussed.

3 Click **Settings**.

4 Set the following options according to your instructor's direction:
- Select the **Audio/Video** option for the media features available on your computer.
- Select a shared location for storing the presentation you plan to broadcast and for recording the broadcast.
- Select **Full Screen** from the Slide Show mode drop-down list.

Figure 4-21

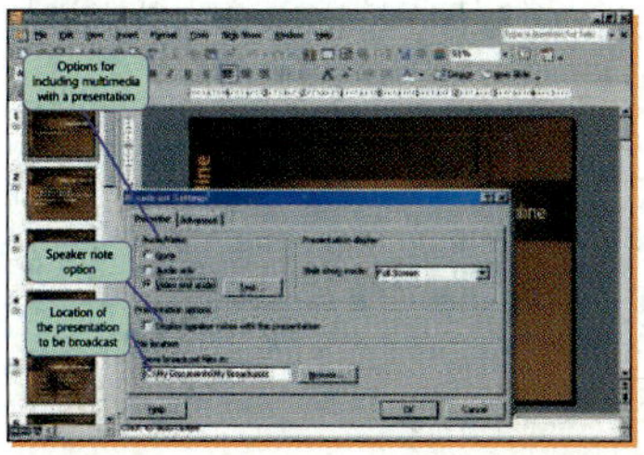

Organization of the Select Series for Office XP

The new Select Series for Office XP includes four combined Office XP texts from which to choose:

- **Microsoft Office XP Volume I** is MOUS certified in each of the major applications in the Office suite (Word, Excel, Access, and PowerPoint). Four additional supplementary modules (Introduction to Internet Explorer, Introduction to Windows, Introduction to Outlook, and Common Elements) are also included. In addition, three integrated projects are included which integrate files and data among Word, Excel, Access, and PowerPoint.
- **Microsoft Office XP Volume II** picks up where Volume I leaves off, covering advanced topics for the individual applications.
- **Microsoft Office XP Brief** provides less coverage of the individual applications than Volume I (a total of four projects as opposed to six). The supplementary modules are also included.
- A new volume, **Getting Started with Microsoft Office XP,** contains the Introduction and first chapter from each application (Word, Excel, Access, and PowerPoint) plus the four supplementary modules.

Individual texts for Word 2002, Excel 2002, Access 2002, and PowerPoint 2002 provide complete coverage of each application and are MOUS certified. They are available in Volume I and Volume II texts and also as Comprehensive texts.

This series of books has been approved by Microsoft to be used in preparation for Microsoft Office User Specialist exams.

APPROVED COURSEWARE

The Microsoft Office User Specialist (MOUS) program is globally recognized as the standard for demonstrating desktop skills with the Microsoft Office suite of business productivity applications (Microsoft Word, Microsoft Excel, Microsoft PowerPoint, Microsoft Access, and Microsoft Outlook). With MOUS certification, thousands of people have demonstrated increased productivity and have proved their ability to utilize the advanced functionality of these Microsoft applications.

Customize the Select Series with Prentice Hall's Right PHit binding program. The Select Series is part of the Right PHit Custom Binding Program, enabling instructors to create their own texts by selecting projects from Office XP to suit the needs of a specific course. An instructor could, for example, create a custom text consisting of the specific projects that he or she would like to cover from the entire suite of products. The Select Series is part of PHit's Value Pack program in which multiple books can be shrink-wrapped together at substantial savings to the student. A value pack is ideal in courses that require complete coverage of multiple applications.

Instructor and Student Resources

Instructor's Resource CD-ROM

The **Instructor's Resource CD-ROM** that is available with the Select Office XP Series contains:

- Student data files
- Solutions to all exercises and problems
- PowerPoint lectures
- Instructor's manuals in Word format that enable the instructor to annotate portions of the instructor manual for distribution to the class
- A Windows-based test manager and the associated test bank in Word format

MyPHLIP www.prenhall.com/select

This text is accompanied by a companion Web site at ***www.prenhall.com/select*** that is supported by MyPHLIP. PHLIP stands for Prentice Hall's Learning on the Internet Partnership. This enhancement brings you and your students a richer, more interactive Web experience.

Features of this new site include the ability for you to customize your homepage with real-time news headlines, current events, exercises, an interactive study guide, student data files, and downloadable supplements. This site is designed to take learning Microsoft Office XP with the Select Series to the next level.

Now you have the freedom to personalize your own online course materials! Prentice Hall provides the content and support you need to create and manage your own online course in WebCT, Blackboard, or Prentice Hall's own Course Compass. Choose "Standard" content to enhance the material from this text or "Premium" content, which provides you with even more lecture material, interactive exercises, and projects.

Training and Assessment www.prenhall.com/phit

Prentice Hall offers Performance Based Training and Assessment in one product, Train&Assess IT. The Training component offers computer-based training that a student can use to preview, learn, and review Microsoft Office application skills. Web or CD-ROM delivered, Train IT offers interactive, multimedia, computer-based training to augment classroom learning. Built-in prescriptive testing suggests a study path based not only on student test results but also on the specific textbook chosen for the course.

The Assessment component offers computer-based testing that shares the same user interface as Train IT and is used to evaluate a student's knowledge about specific topics in Word, Excel, Access, PowerPoint, Windows, Outlook, and the Internet. It does this in a task-oriented environment to demonstrate proficiency as well as comprehension of the topics by the students. More extensive than the testing in Train IT, Assess IT offers more administrative features for the instructor and additional questions for the student.

Assess IT also allows professors to test students out of a course, place students in appropriate courses, and evaluate skill sets.

CourseCompass www.coursecompass.com

CourseCompass is a dynamic, interactive online course-management tool powered exclusively for Pearson Education by Blackboard. This exciting product allows you to teach market-leading Pearson Education content in an easy-to-use, customizable format.

BlackBoard www.prenhall.com/blackboard

Prentice Hall's abundant online content, combined with Blackboard's popular tools and interface, result in robust Web-based courses that are easy to implement, manage, and use—taking your courses to new heights in student interaction and learning.

WebCT www.prenhall.com/webct

Course-management tools within WebCT include page tracking, progress tracking, class and student management, gradebook, communication, calendar, reporting tools, and more. GOLD LEVEL CUSTOMER SUPPORT, available exclusively to adopters of Prentice Hall courses, is provided free-of-charge upon adoption and provides you with priority assistance, training discounts, and dedicated technical support.

Table of Contents

FROM THE FILES

You Will Need

- ✔ e-Selections.doc
- ✔ Sample Northeast Colleges.xls

PROJECT 1

Basic Common Elements

One of the greatest advantages of using the ever-popular Microsoft Office suite is the number of features common to all programs that make up the Office suite. Microsoft Office XP takes full advantage of many common elements. The large number of common elements means that techniques you learn in one Office XP application can be used to accomplish the same task in other Office XP applications. This section introduces you to many of the features common to Office XP applications and describes some of the unique twists you'll find with these common features as you move from application to application in Microsoft Office XP.

OBJECTIVES

After completing this project, you will be able to:

- *Launch applications*
- *Work with screen elements*
- *Perform basic file management tasks*
- *Use Help*
- *Preview and print files*
- *Exit applications*

e-selections Running Case

You have recently been hired as a part-time office clerk for e-Selections.com, the online branch of Selections, Inc. Your goals are to advance in the company as you advance in your college studies and to position yourself for an upper-level position after you graduate. Because you are new to the office and unfamiliar with the software applications that are used, you decide to begin by exploring the software installed on your computer. e-Selections.com uses the most recent release of Microsoft Office.

PROJECT 1

Basic Common Elements

The Challenge

Microsoft Office applications contain numerous features that are common to the four primary Office applications. You have been asked to identify basic elements that are common to Word, Excel, Access, and PowerPoint and to develop the skills necessary for performing tasks associated with these common features.

The Solution

Because the features you have been asked to identify are common to the four primary Office applications, it's a great idea to learn the basics that apply to all applications in one centralized location. Then, when you start using each of the Microsoft Office applications, you can focus on their unique features.

Overview of Office XP Applications

Microsoft Office XP contains a number of different applications. Each application is designed to make the process of creating electronic files that contain different types of data and information more efficient. The Microsoft Office XP applications addressed in this text are listed and described in Table 1-1.

Table 1-1 Microsoft Office XP Applications and Their Uses

Application	Description
Microsoft Word 2002	The word processing program used to create, format, and save letters, manuscripts, newsletters, and other documents.
Microsoft Excel 2002	The spreadsheet program used to create, format, and save columnar data and display it graphically.
Microsoft Access 2002	The database program used to create, format, and save volumes of information (data) related to specific subjects or purposes.
Microsoft PowerPoint 2002	The presentation program used to create visual slides that present summaries of data used to enhance oral presentations.
Microsoft Outlook 2002	The e-mail, calendar, and address program used to create and store e-mail messages, list appointment and meeting dates and times, and record the names and addresses of associates.

Launching Applications

Office XP offers a variety of techniques for launching applications. The procedure you use will depend on how Office XP is installed on your computer and your personal preferences.

To *launch* Office XP applications, use one of the following procedures:

- Choose **Start | Programs,** and then select the Office XP application you want to launch.

Troubleshooting
If shortcuts to the Office XP applications do not appear on your Programs list, click the arrow button at the bottom of the Programs list and scroll until the applications appear.

Figure 1-1

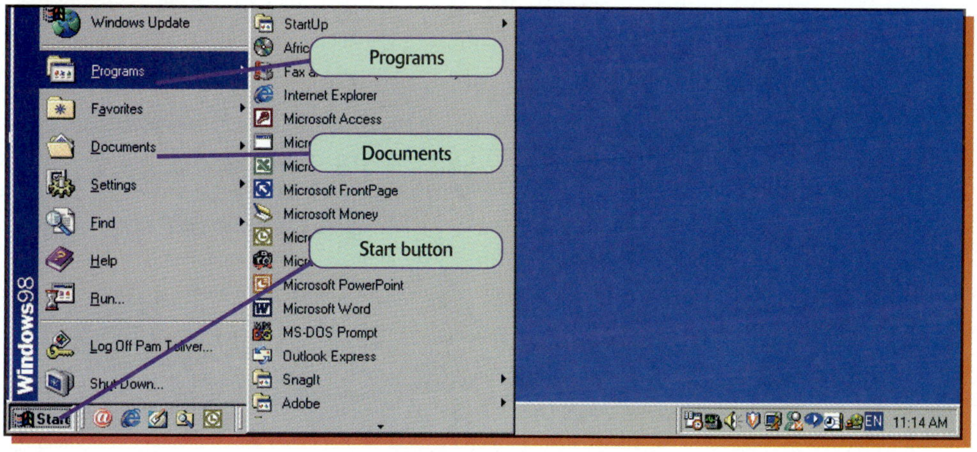

- Choose **Start | New Office Document,** and then double-click the **Blank** file type for the application you want to launch—the application required to create that type of file launches.

Figure 1-2

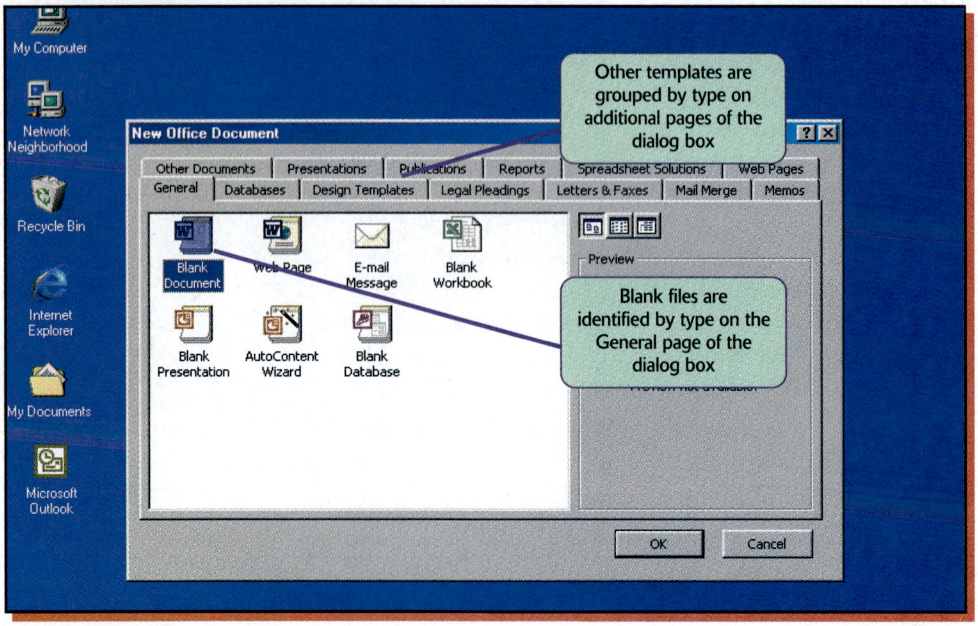

CHECK POINT

Office XP offers a series of professionally designed file formats called templates that you can choose to create a variety of different files. Click the tab for the type of file you want to create (e.g., Memos), click a template name, and view the template preview in the lower right corner of the dialog box. The templates listed depend on those installed on your computer. As a result, your templates may appear different from those listed here.

- Double-click the application shortcut icon on the desktop.
- Click the application icon on the Microsoft Office bar, if it is installed on your computer. When it is installed, the Microsoft Office bar usually appears on the right side of the computer screen. The arrangement of buttons on the bar may be different due to customizations.

> **Tip** Items shown on the desktop in Figure 1-3 represent program icons that generally appear when Microsoft Office XP is installed on a computer running Windows 95 or Windows 98 that has no additional program shortcuts placed on the desktop. Program icons and other features found on your desktop will be different from those shown here because of system customizations.

Figure 1-3

> **Tip** The Documents list shows files from all applications—not just Microsoft Office files. The icon beside each file identifies the application used to create or edit the files.

- Choose **Start | Documents** and select a recently used file to open. The application used to create the file launches. The Documents list holds the last 15 documents accessed. It may contain few items when you first start using the computer, but the list grows as you complete activities.
- Open **My Computer** or **Windows Explorer**, open the folder containing the file you want to open, and double-click the file. The application used to create the file launches.

Depending on the application you launch, the initial screen will differ:

- Word, Excel, and PowerPoint display new files: Word displays a new blank document, Excel displays a new blank workbook, and PowerPoint creates a new blank presentation.
- Access displays an empty screen and the New File task pane with a palette of tools for creating a new file or opening an existing file.

Because accessing and using most of the common elements covered in this section is easiest in Word, it will be used to introduce many common features. The procedures for launching Word 2002 described here should be accessible from all computers on which Office XP is installed.

Identifying Screen Elements

Screen elements common to all Microsoft Office XP applications are identified in Figure 1-4 and described in Table 1-2.

Task 1:

Launching Microsoft Word 2002

1 Choose **Start | Programs.**

2 Scroll to the bottom of the Programs list, if necessary.

3 Select Microsoft Word to launch Word.

Figure 1-4

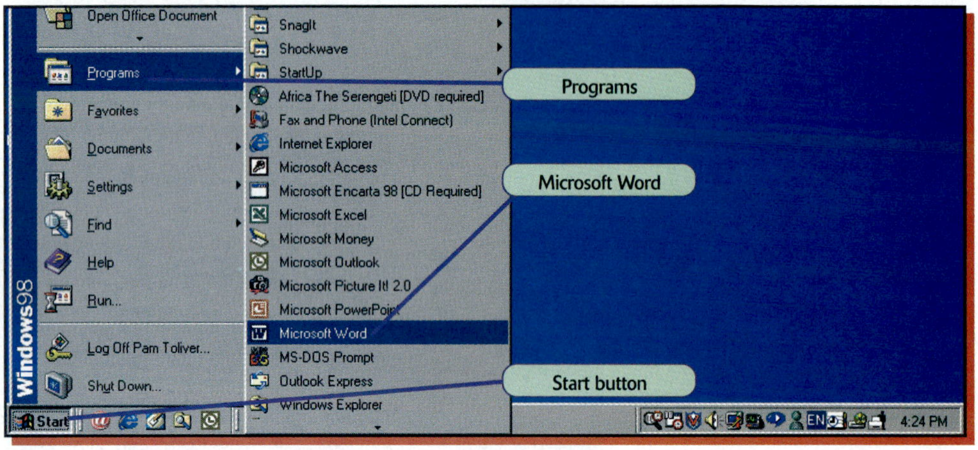

Troubleshooting The icons that appear at the right end of the task bar on your computer may be different from those shown in Figure 1-4. They represent programs that are running in the background on the active computer.

4 Review screen elements identified in Figure 1-5.

Tip Because installations and setups vary from computer to computer and set up changes from user to user, screen elements may vary from those shown here.

Figure 1-5

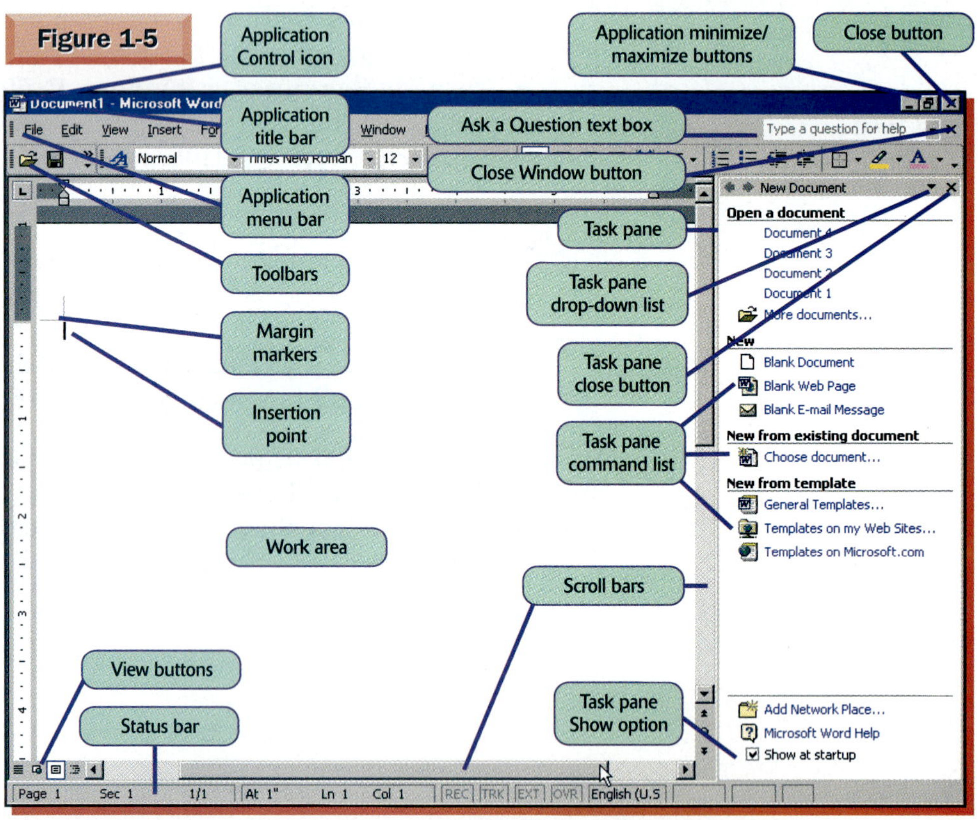

Table 1-2 Word Screen Features

Feature	Description
Application title bar	Identifies the program and file that is open.
Application menu bar	Groups task commands by type.
Application Control icon	Displays options for maximizing, minimizing, resizing, and closing the application window.
Toolbars	Provide single-click access to frequently performed tasks.
Work area	Provides room to type text.
Status bar	Identifies active application features and the insertion point position.
Insertion point	Identifies the typing position.
Application minimize/ maximize buttons	Control window size.
Close button	Exits the application.
Close Window button	Closes the active file and leaves the application running.
Scroll bars	Display different areas of the file on screen.
Task pane	Displays tools for creating and opening files and tools for performing special tasks.
Task pane Close button	Closes the task pane.
Ask a question text box	Accesses help about the topic entered.
Margin markers	Identify margin positions on screen.
Task pane command list	Displays a grouped list from which you can access the Office Clipboard and the program search feature, select a command, create a new document, open a recently edited document, or create a formatted document.
View buttons	Change the appearance of the document on screen.
Task pane drop-down list	Presents a list of different elements and features that can be displayed on the Task Pane.
Task pane Show option	Controls whether the task pane appears each time you start Word.

Working with Screen Elements

Many of the screen elements seen in Microsoft Word are common to other Office XP applications. As a result, once you learn how to navigate the screen elements in one Office application, you can apply the techniques to comparable features in other Office XP applications.

Using the Task Pane

The *task pane* is a new feature in Microsoft Office. It provides access to some of the most basic file management tools you will need as you progress through each application. You can close the task pane to increase the work area in a program and then redisplay it as needed.

The task pane is divided into distinct sections identified by the tasks to be performed. Options for performing tasks appear in blue text below each section heading. Options followed by ellipses are options that open dialog boxes; options that have no ellipses carry out a command. Task pane tools are also found on menus and *toolbars*.

Task 2:
To Close and Open the Task Pane

1. Click the task pane **Close** **X** button. The task pane closes.

2. Choose **View | Task Pane**. The task pane opens.

Figure 1-6

Other Ways

You can also display the task pane by pointing to a toolbar, right-clicking, and selecting **Task Pane** or by choosing **View | Toolbars | Task Pane**. To prevent the task pane from opening each time you launch Word, clear the **Show at startup** option at the bottom of the task pane.

Hiding and Displaying Toolbars

A variety of different toolbars can be displayed in Office XP applications, each designed to assist with specific tasks. In each application, the Standard and Formatting toolbars contain buttons for performing the most frequently completed tasks. Other toolbars appear automatically as you perform specific tasks. There will be times as you work in the different applications when you will want to display additional toolbars.

Tip

To identify the name of a toolbar button, position the mouse pointer on the button and pause. A Screen Tip will tell you what the name of the button is.

Task 3:
To Display and Hide Toolbars

1. Choose **View | Toolbars** to display a list of available toolbars.

2. Select **Formatting.** The Formatting toolbar is hidden.

Figure 1-7

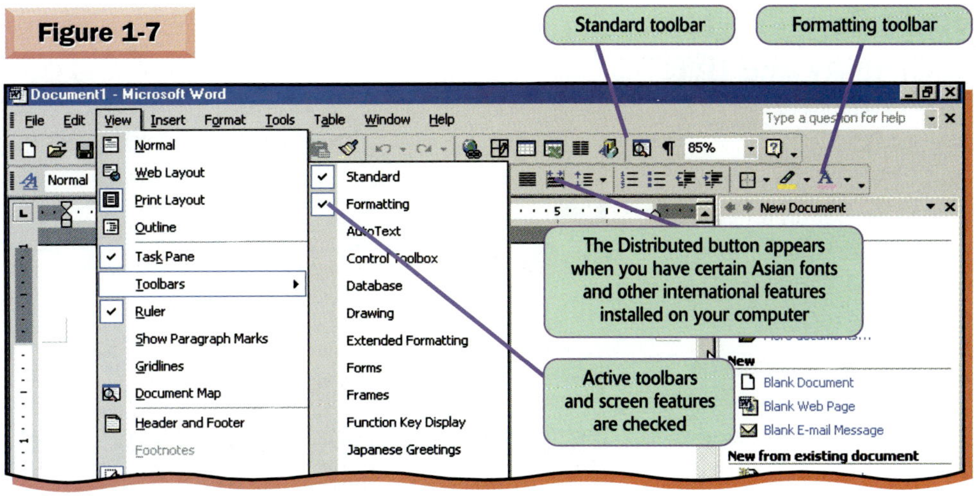

3. Point to the Standard toolbar and right-click. A list of available toolbars appears.

4. Select **Formatting.** The Formatting toolbar appears on screen in its original position.

Figure 1-8

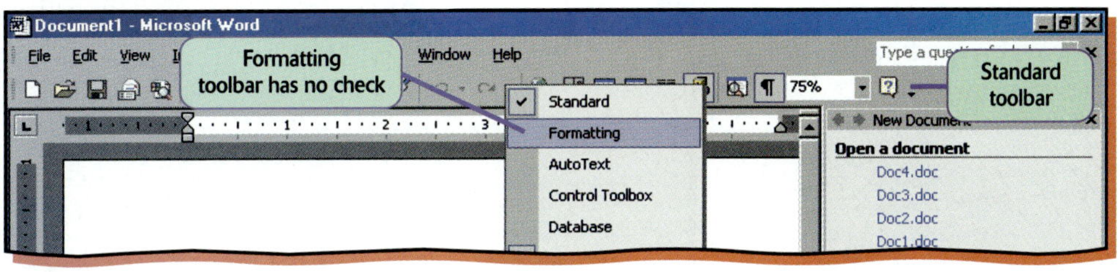

CHECK POINT

Selections, Inc., in an effort to accommodate clients worldwide through its e-Selections Online Division, has a number of International fonts, such as Asian, Japanese, and so forth, installed on some of the computers at its corporate offices. As a result, additional features are available to those who use the international workstations. You will notice additional buttons on toolbars, added menu commands, and other extra features as you work with Office XP. These features are designed to help those who develop materials for the international market to access the tools more efficiently.

Displaying and Hiding the Language Bar

The *Language bar*, when it is installed and displayed, appears as a floating toolbar in all Office XP applications. It contains tools related to the language features that are built in to Office XP. When the Language bar is closed, it appears as an icon on the taskbar tray so that it is easy to call up when you need it.

Task 4:
To Display and Hide the Language Bar

1. Click the **Language** EN button on the Windows taskbar tray and select **Show Language Bar** to open the toolbar.
2. Click the Language bar **Minimize** button. A message box displays information about how to redisplay the Language bar.
3. Click **OK**. The Language button appears on the tray of the Windows taskbar.

Troubleshooting
If the Language bar is closed, open it by choosing **Start | Settings | Control Panel | Text Services** to open the Text Services dialog box. Then click the Language Bar button and select the Show the Language bar on the desktop option. Then click OK twice and close the Control Panel dialog box.

Tip Depending on the setup on your computer, the menus and toolbars may already display on two lines.

Figure 1-9

Figure 1-10

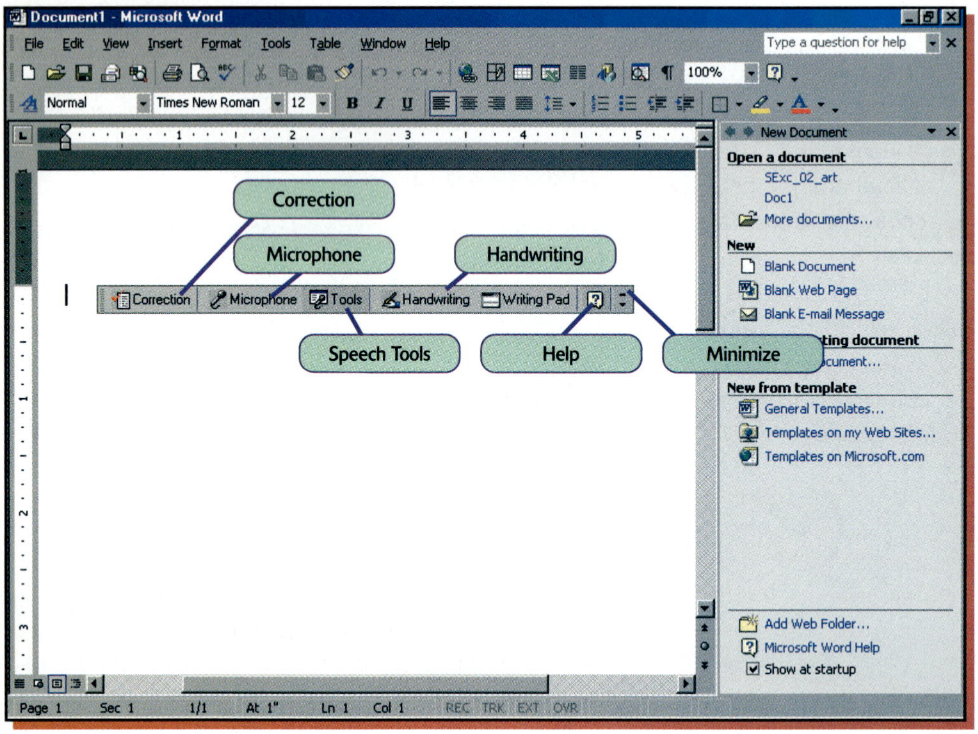

Resetting Menus and Toolbars

Menus and toolbars in Office XP are set to auto-customize as you work. Here's how they work:

- When menus in Office XP applications are displayed, only the most frequently used commands appear on the initial menu. After the menu is displayed for a few seconds, the extended menu shows additional menu commands.
- When you select a menu command from the extended menu, the command is placed on the initial menu in its standard position so that it is more readily available the next time you need it.
- The Standard and Formatting toolbars are initially displayed on one line to increase the work area on screen. Buttons for additional commands appear on a Toolbar Options drop-down list at the right end of displayed toolbars.

- When you select a button from the Toolbar Options drop-down palette, the button is placed at its standard location on the appropriate toolbar.

So that the steps presented in this book are accurate for each class working on lab computers, it is necessary to turn off this auto-customization feature.

Task 5:
To Turn Off Auto-Customization Features

1. Choose **Tools | Customize**. The Customize dialog box opens.

Other Ways

To display the Customize dialog box:

- Right-click a toolbar that is already displayed and select Customize from the shortcut menu.

Figure 1-11

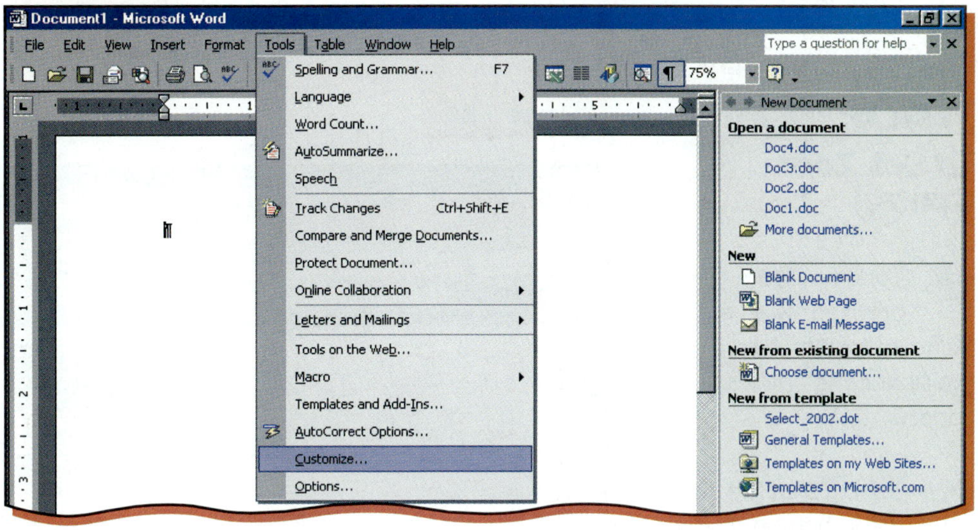

2. Click the **Options** tab, if necessary.
3. Select the **Show Standard and Formatting toolbars on two rows** option to display the full Standard and Formatting toolbars on separate rows.
4. Select the **Always show full menus** option, if necessary.
5. Click **Close**.

Figure 1-12

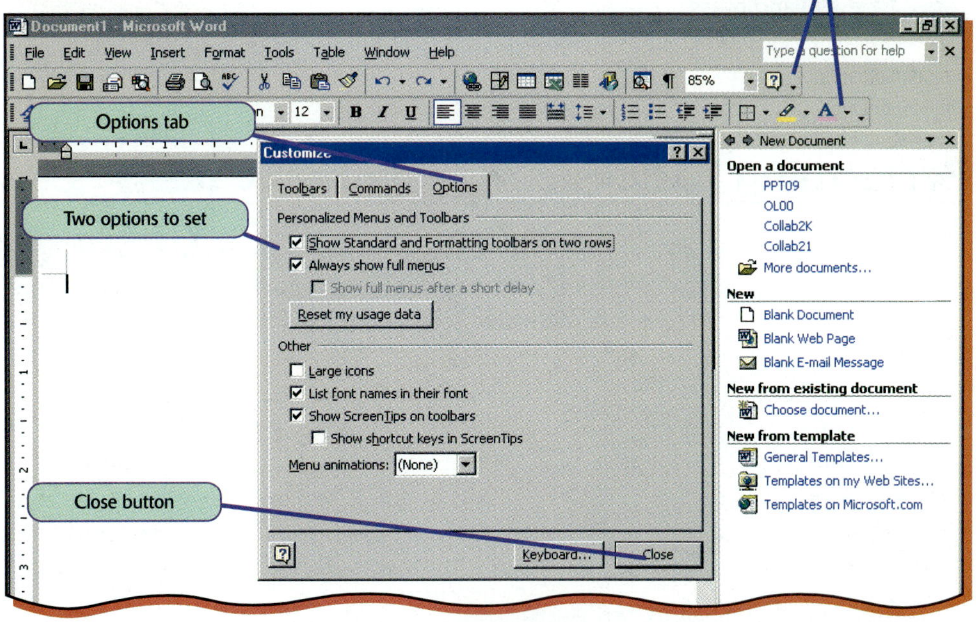

Tip

To toggle toolbars between one- and two-line displays, click the Toolbar Options button that appears as a down arrow at the end of each toolbar and select **Show Buttons on Two (or One) Row(s)**.

Changing Zoom Settings

The *Zoom* setting controls the portion of a file that appears on screen and can be used to make file text easier to read. After the auto-customization feature is turned off and the Standard and Formatting toolbars appear on separate rows, the Zoom control tool appears on the Standard toolbar.

Troubleshooting The list of Zoom values changes depending on the application and current view.

Task 6:
To Set Zoom Control

1. Click the **Zoom** 100% down arrow on the Standard toolbar. A list of available sizing options appears.
2. Select **50%**. The document shifts on screen.
3. Click in the **Zoom** box on the Standard menu.
4. Type 100 and press Enter. The document size is restored.

Figure 1-13

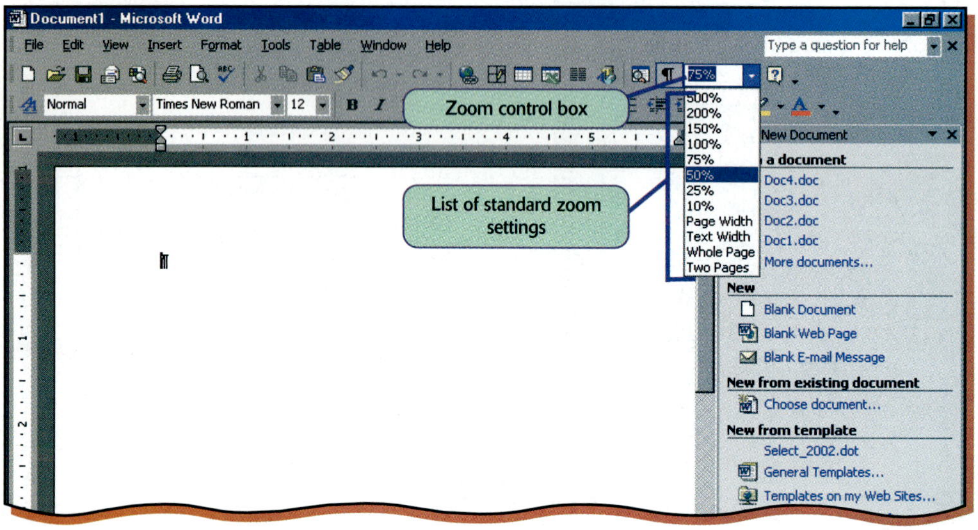

Performing Basic File Management Tasks

Basic file management tasks include opening files, creating new files, saving files, and editing file properties. The procedures for accomplishing these tasks are similar in all Office XP applications.

Opening Files

Office XP provides a number of different procedures that you can use to open an existing document, workbook, presentation, or database. The Open dialog box has been redesigned in Office XP and presents a Web-like look that even contains links to Web servers. To open a file, do one of the following:

- Choose **File | Open.**
- Click the **Open** button on the Standard toolbar.
- Press Ctrl + O.
- Choose **Start | Open Office Document.**
- Click **More Documents** in the **Open a document** area of the task pane.

Regardless of which procedure you use to open a file, an Open dialog box similar to the one shown in Figure1-14 appears. Features of the Open dialog box are described in Table 1-3.

Figure 1-14

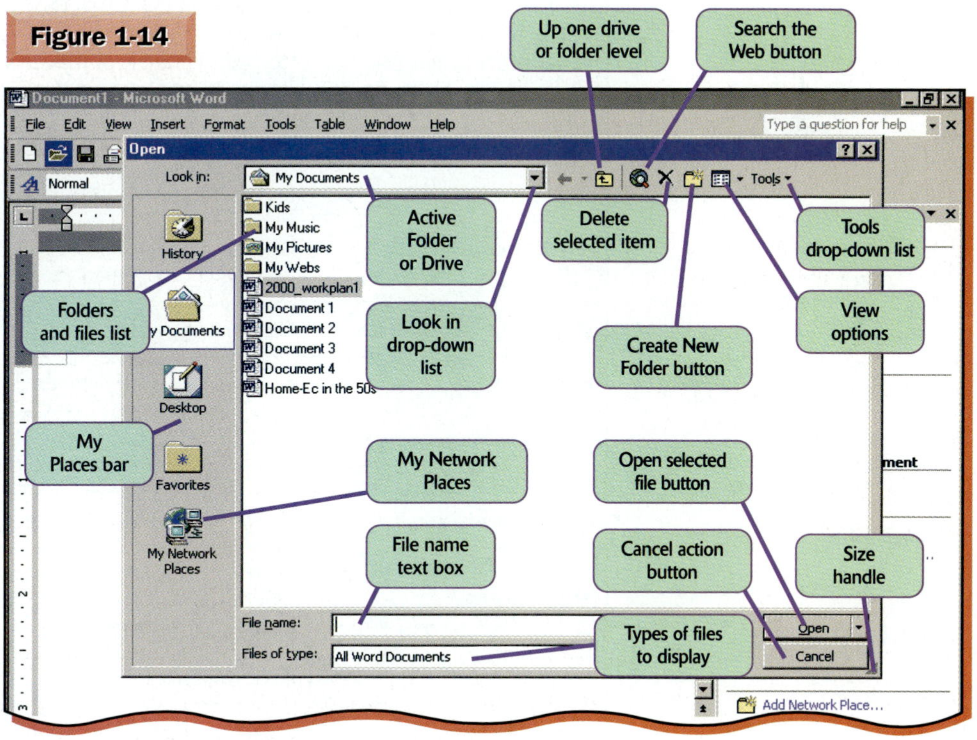

Tip A folder in Windows can contain files or additional folders.

Table 1-3 Open dialog box elements

Feature	Description
Look in drop-down list	Identifies the current drive and/or folder.
Up One Level button	Accesses the "parent" folder when a folder is active; My Computer when a drive is active; and Desktop when the My Documents folder is open.
Search the Web button	Launches Internet Explorer 5.5, or your default Web browser, to the Microsoft Homepage so that you can perform a search for the document to open.
Delete button	Removes the selected document or folder.
Create New Folder button	Creates a new folder within the active drive or folder.
View drop-down list	Displays a list of options that change the way files and folders are displayed in the dialog box.
Tools drop-down list	Contains commands that enable you to find and delete files and folders, print files, and identify properties of files and folders.
My Places bar	Contains links to folders and file storage locations so that you can open them quickly, and it can be customized to hold the folders you use most frequently.
My Network Places	Displays links to Web sites and other Network Places that you have designated on networked computers to which you have access.
Dialog box size handle	Can be dragged to change the size and shape of the dialog box.
File name text box	Enables you to type the name of the document to open.
Files of type text box	Identifies the types of files displayed. You can display other types of files by altering the file type selected.
Folders and Files list	Shows all folders and files in the active folder or on the active drive for the active application.
Open button	Opens the selected (highlighted) file or folder. It contains a drop-down list that enables you to open a copy of the file, open the file in Read-Only mode, Open and Repair, or open a Web document in a browser.
Cancel button	Closes the dialog box without opening a file or folder.

CHECK POINT

By default, the last four files opened in that application on your computer appear at the bottom of the File menu. In addition, the last fifteen files accessed appear on the Documents list displayed from the Start menu. As a result, two alternative procedures can be used to open files.

- Select the file from the bottom of the File menu.
- Choose **Start | Documents** and select the recently edited file to open.

You can change the number of files that appear at the bottom of the File menu for any application using the **Tools | Options** command and then setting the Recently used file list on the **General** page of the Options dialog box.

Task 7:
To Open a Copy of a Document

1 Launch Word, if necessary, close the task pane, and choose **File | Open**. The Open dialog box opens.

Figure 1-15

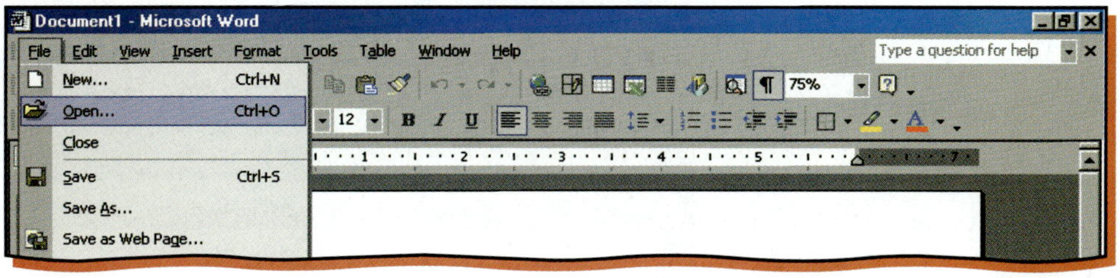

2 Click the **Look in** down arrow and open the disk drive and/or folder containing the *e-Selections.doc* file. The disk drive and/or folder name appears in the Look in text box.

3 Select the *e-Selections.doc* file. The file name appears highlighted.

4 Click the drop-down list arrow on the **Open** button and select **Open as Copy**.

Figure 1-16

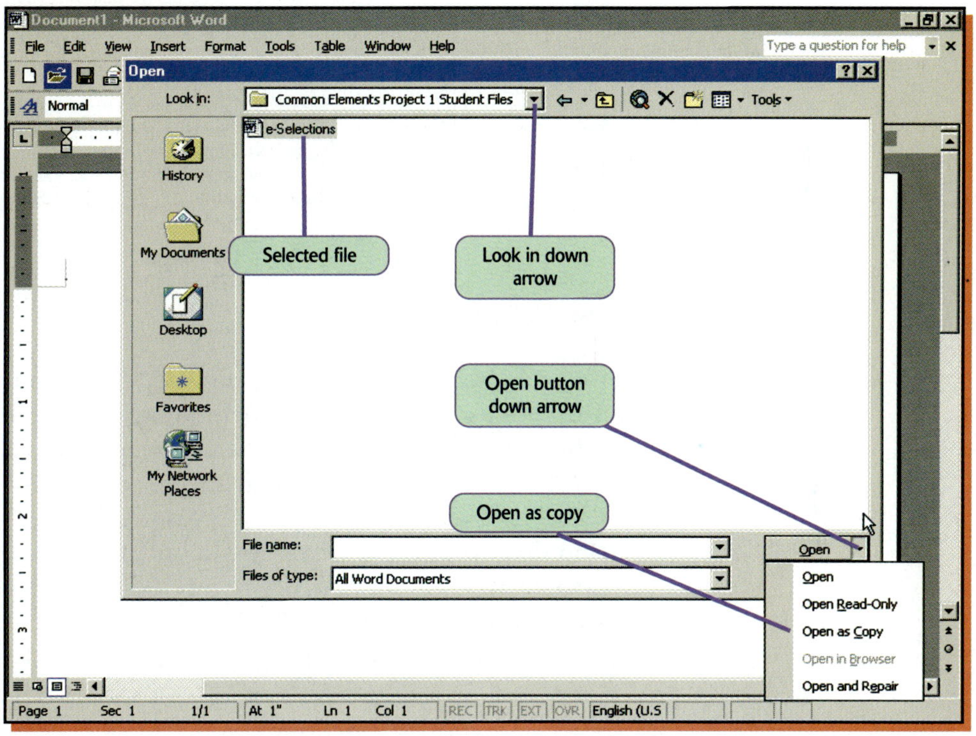

Tip You can also open a read-only copy of a document to preserve the original file. When you open a read-only copy of a document, make changes to the file, and want to save the changes, you must save the file using a new file name.

Troubleshooting The current settings on your computer control the appearance of the document on your screen. As a result, your screen may be different from the screen pictured in Figure 1-17.

5 Review the document.

Tip Opening a copy of an existing document leaves the original intact so that you can use it later, if necessary.

Figure 1-17

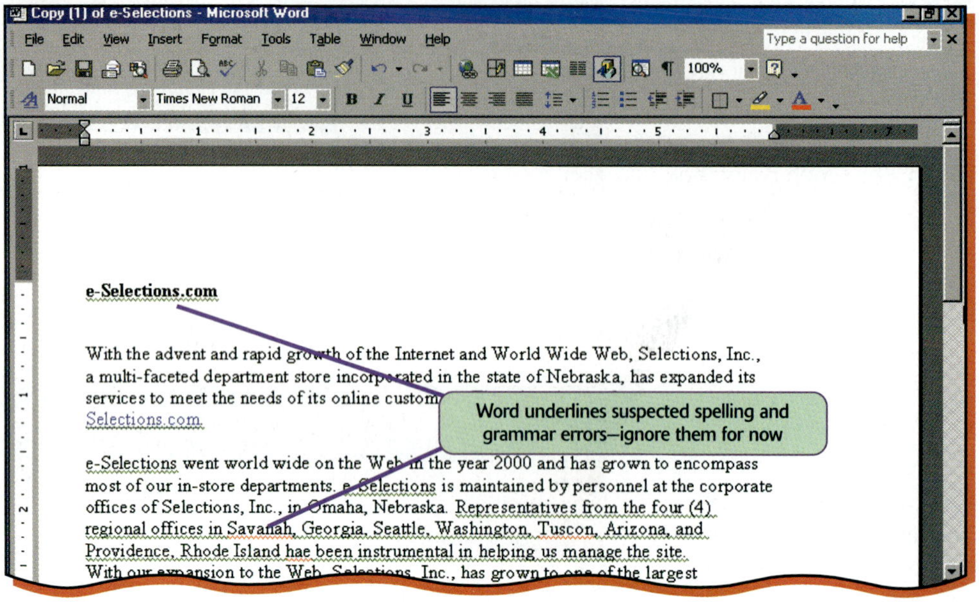

Creating New Files

As you discovered with opening files, Microsoft Office XP offers a variety of different techniques for performing tasks. Take creating new files for example; a new document appears when you launch Word, a new blank workbook is created each time you launch Excel, and a new blank presentation is created when you start PowerPoint. As you explore all Office XP applications, you'll find that options for creating and opening files are presented when you launch Access. To create a new file in any Office XP application after it is launched, you can use one of the following procedures:

- Click the **New** button on the Standard toolbar of any Office XP application. A new blank file appears if you are working in Word, Excel, and PowerPoint. In Access, clicking the New button displays the New File task pane so that you can create a blank database or a database using a template.
- Press Ctrl + N. A new blank file appears in Word, Excel, or PowerPoint. In Access, the New File task pane opens so that you can select the type of database you want to create.
- Choose **File | New**. The New dialog box opens and displays a list of templates—professionally designed, preformatted file formats specific to the application you're using—that you can use to create a specific type of file.
- Click the option for a new file from the task pane:
  - **New Blank Document** to create a new blank file;
  - **New from existing *file* | Choose *File*** to open the New from Existing File dialog box;
  - **New from template** to display the same list of templates shown using the **File | New** command.

Task 8:
To Create New Files

1. Launch Word, if necessary, and click the **New** button on the Standard toolbar to create a new blank document.

2. Display the task pane and click **Blank Document** on the task pane. Document3 appears and another document button appears on the taskbar.

3. Point to the bottom of the screen, if necessary, to display the taskbar.

Tip In addition to buttons representing different document files that are open, you may see taskbar buttons for other programs—such as e-mail programs—that are running on your computer.

Figure 1-18

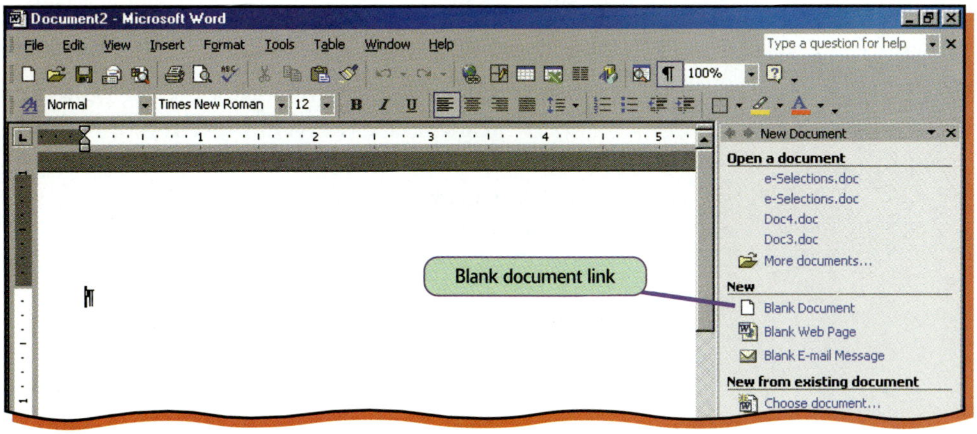

Figure 1-19

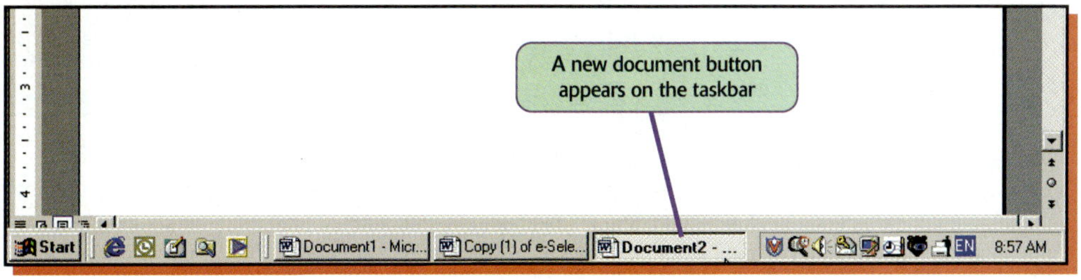

Tip When you use multiple applications in Office, more than one program may be open, but only one is active. Similarly, if you have multiple documents, workbooks, or presentations open, only one of them is actually active at any given time.

Switching Among Open Files

Word, Excel, and PowerPoint enable you to open or create multiple files without closing files that are already open. These three applications place a file button on the Windows taskbar for each file you have open. To switch from one open file to another, you can:

- Click the **Windows taskbar** button for the open file you want to access.
- Press Ctrl + F6 to browse open files for the active application.
- Press Ctrl + Shift + F6 to move backward among open files for the active application.
- Click the file name in the task pane.
- Press Alt + Tab to switch among programs and files from all open applications.
- Choose the **Window** menu and then select the file you want to access from the bottom of the menu.

Closing Files

Office XP applications provide a variety of techniques for closing files. To close the active file:

- Click the file **Close** Window **X** button at the right end of the menu bar.
- Right-click the Windows taskbar button for the file you want to close and select **Close**.
- Choose **File | Close**.
- Press Ctrl + F4.

Troubleshooting When only one file is open in Word, Excel, or Powerpoint, a Close button also appears at the right end of the title bar. This button enables you to exit the application, so be sure you click the correct Close button.

Task 9:
To Close a File

1. Switch to Document3, if necessary.
2. Click the **Close Window** **X** button.
3. Display Document2, if necessary.
4. Choose **File | Close**. The Copy of *e-Selections* appears on screen. Leave it open for the next task.

Figure 1-20

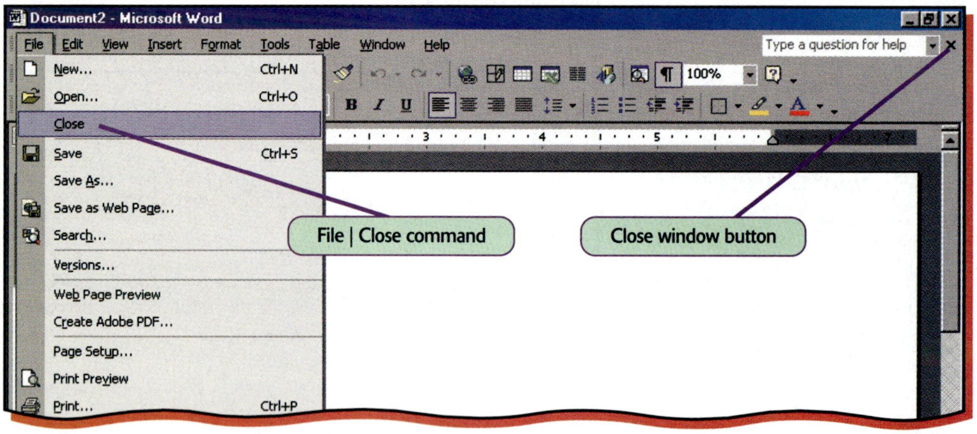

Saving Files

Each new document you create, each copy of an existing document you open, and each document you edit needs to be saved. You'll find a number of different Save commands listed on the File menu of Office XP applications. Knowing the difference between the Save commands is important. Here's how they work:

Tip The **File | Save** commands in other applications may contain different options. Be sure to review the File menu to determine different save options.

Table 1-4 Save Commands

Command	Description
Save	Automatically overwrites previously saved files that you open and edit. Opens the Save As dialog box the first time a document is saved so that you can name and select a storage location for new files. The dialog box contains text boxes where you can type a file name and select a save format. Saves copies of existing files that you open using the Open as Copy command in the same folder of the same disk using the filename *Copy (#) of xx.doc*. In Access, Save enables you to save a database object.
Save As	In Word, Excel, and PowerPoint, this command opens the Save As dialog box, which you can use to save an existing file using a different file name, save the active file in a different drive or folder, or save a file as a different file type. In Access, Save As enables you to export a selected database object to create another specific database object only.
Save as Web Page	Opens the Save As dialog box, automatically activates **Web Page** as the Save as type, and adds a page title using the first line of text in the file.

Tip Folders you create in other applications such as Windows Explorer are available for storing files from Microsoft Office XP applications.

To initiate the Save command, you can use one of the following techniques:

- Click the **Save** button on the Standard toolbar.
- Press Ctrl + S.
- Choose **File | Save**.
- Choose **File | Save As**.

Creating Folders. Because file management is so important, Office applications streamline the process by enabling you to create new folders "on the fly" from the Open and Save As dialog boxes. In addition, you can embed fonts as you save documents to ensure that the document will look the way you intended when it is opened on a different computer.

Task 10:
To Save a Copy of a File with Embedded Fonts in a New Folder

1. Click the title bar of the *Copy (1) of e-Selections.doc* file to make it active, if necessary. Active windows usually have a darker title bar than inactive windows.

2. Choose **File | Save As** to open the Save As dialog box.

Figure 1-21

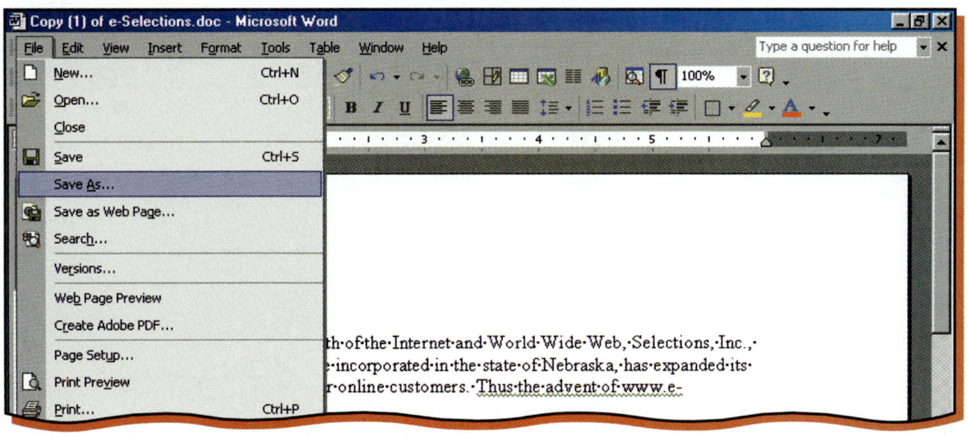

3 Click the **Save in** down arrow, select the disk drive on which you want to create a new folder, and click the **Create New Folder** button.

Figure 1-22

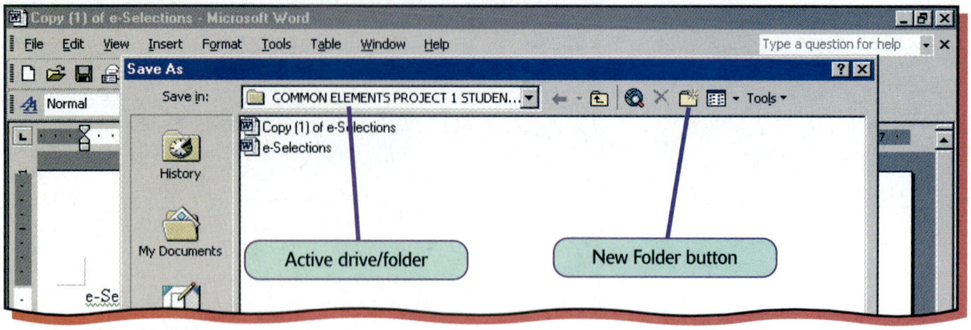

4 Type ***Your Initials*** followed by ***Your Class Name*** in the **Name** text box and click **OK**. The new folder opens and appears in the Save in text box at the top of the Save As dialog box.

Figure 1-23

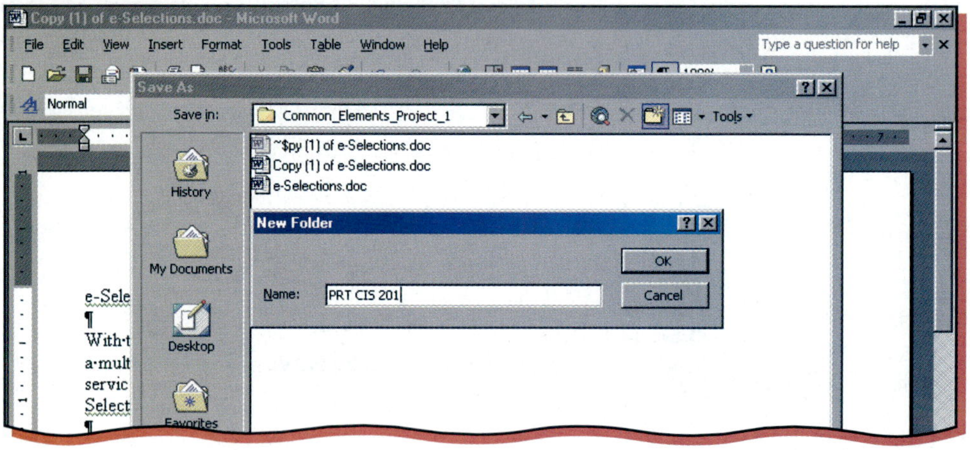

Troubleshooting If you want to create a subfolder, you must open the folder in which you want to place the subfolder.

5 Click the **Tools** down arrow and select **Save Options** to open the Save dialog box that contains save options.

Figure 1-24

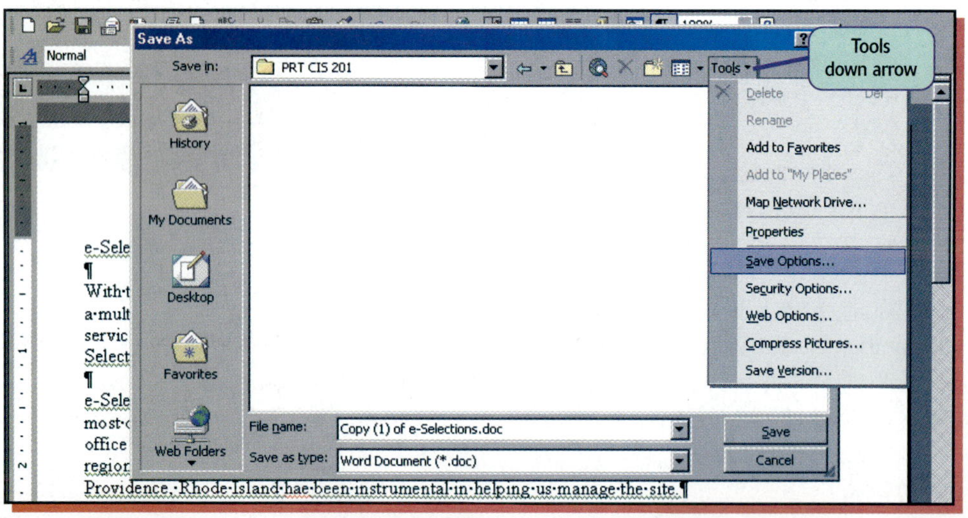

6. Select the **Embed TrueType fonts** and the **Do not embed common system fonts** options.

7. Click **OK**.

8. Click **Save**. The new file named *Copy (1) of e-Selections.doc* appears in the new folder, and the file name also appears in the title bar of the document.

Tip Be sure to review options that appear in the Save dialog box. Knowing what options are available may come in handy sometime in the future.

Figure 1-25

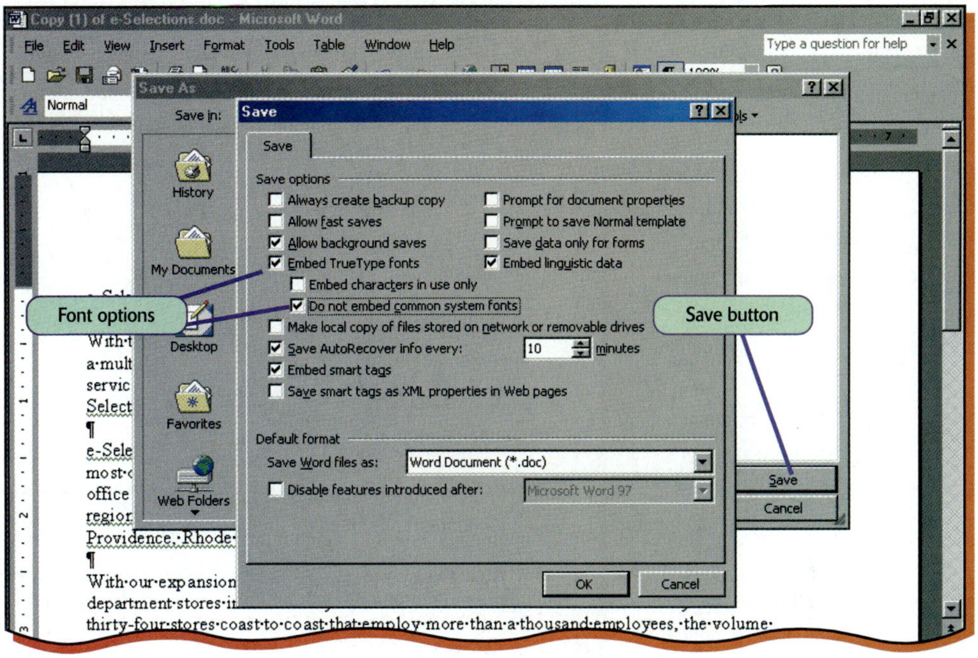

WEB TIP

You can save a Web page using the same basic save techniques used to save files in Office XP applications. Simply display the Web page in the browser and choose **File | Save As**, open the folder in which to store the file, type a file name for the file, and click **OK**.

Customizing the My Places Bar and Sizing Dialog Boxes

The *My Places bar* contains a default set of folders, Web sites, and files for the user to access—the default places on the bar may or may not be locations that you would want to access. As a result, the My Places bar can be customized to hold the folders and sites you visit most. Now that you have created a folder to hold your work, you can add the folder to My Places bar to make it more accessible.

Task 11:

To Add a Folder to the My Places Bar and Size a Dialog Box

1. Launch Word, if necessary, close the task pane, and click the **Open** button on the Standard toolbar. The Open dialog box opens.

2. Locate the personal folder you created in Task 10 and select it (but don't open it).

3. Click the **Tools** drop-down list on the dialog box toolbar and select **Add to "My Places"**.

4. Click the down arrow at the bottom of the Places bar. The new folder appears.

5. Drag the dialog box size handle to increase the size of the dialog box so that all the folders are visible. The down-arrow button disappears.

6. Click **Cancel** to close the dialog box.

Tip Adding a folder or site to the My Places bar of one dialog box adds it to all dialog boxes in all Office XP applications.

Figure 1-26

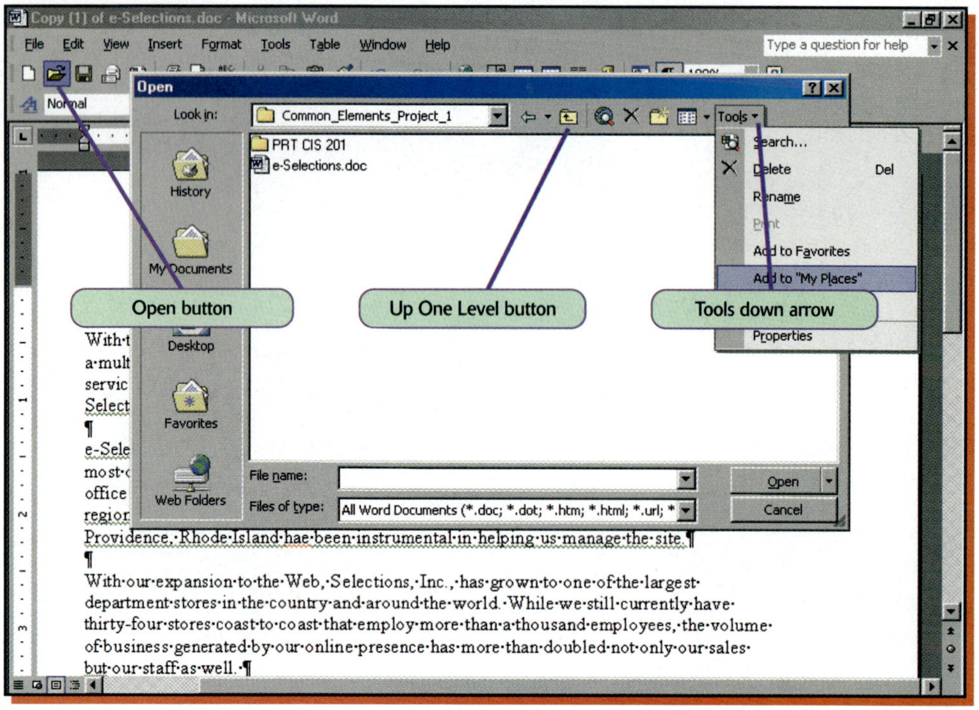

Figure 1-27

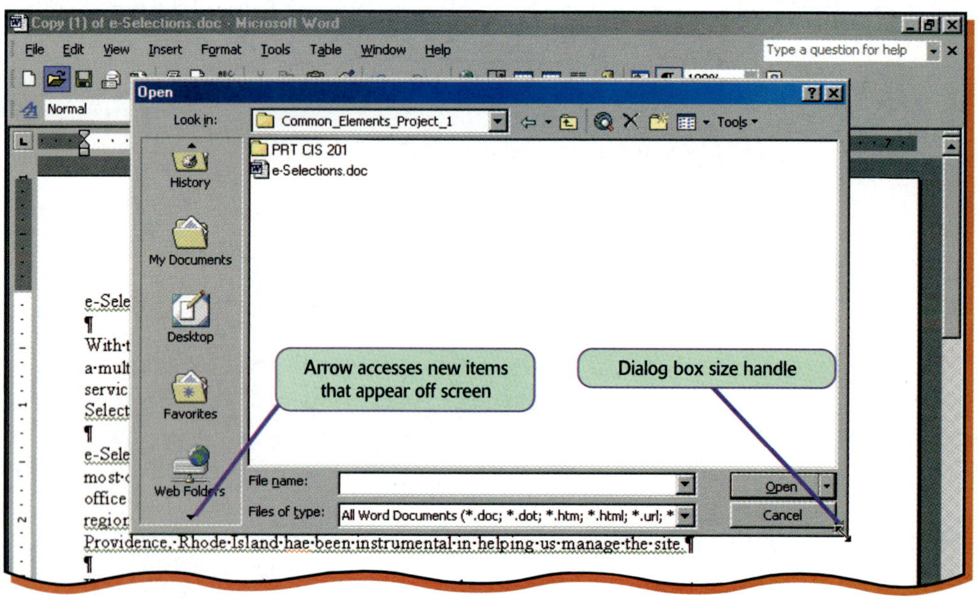

Troubleshooting Because your personal folder was the last folder you used, it may appear in the **Look in** box at the top of the dialog box and the folder will be open. Click the **Up One Level** button on the dialog box toolbar to close the folder and then select it.

Saving and Previewing Web Pages

Each Office XP application can be used to save files as Web pages and to view those files as they would appear in a Web browser. Whereas the specific steps required to save files as Web pages vary from application to application within Office XP, the basic steps for initiating the process and for viewing the files is the same for all applications.

Task 12:
To Save a File as a Web Page and View the Web File

1. Open your *Copy (1) of e-Selections.doc*, if necessary.

2. Choose **File | Save as Web Page**.

3. Click your folder in the Places bar to open the folder, if necessary.

4. Click the **Change Title** button. The Set Page Title dialog box opens.

> **Troubleshooting**
> Changing the page title has no impact on the file name or document text. The Page Title appears in the title bar of the browser when you display the document in the browser window.

5. Type ***Your Initials*** **First Web Page** in the **Page title** text box and then click **OK**.

Figure 1-28

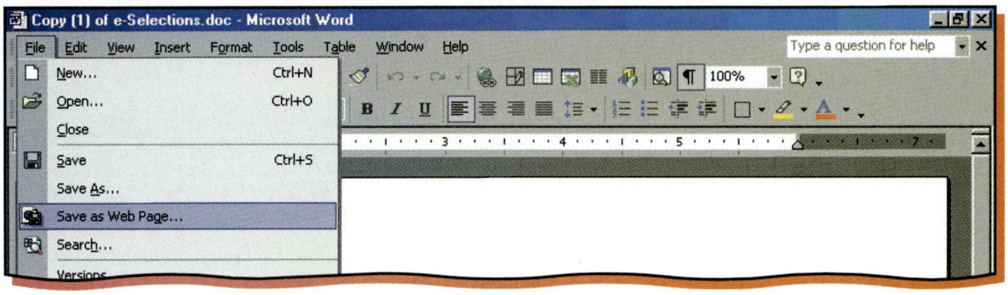

Figure 1-29

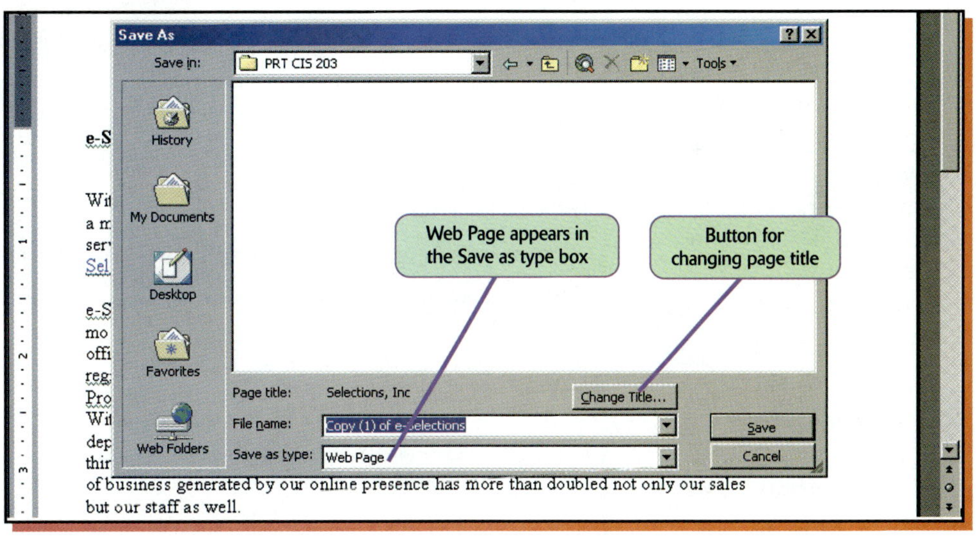

Figure 1-30

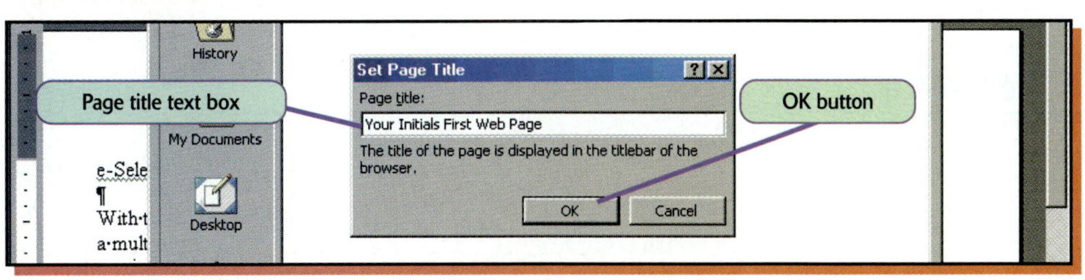

6 Type *Your Initials* **First Web Page** in the **File name** text box.

Figure 1-31

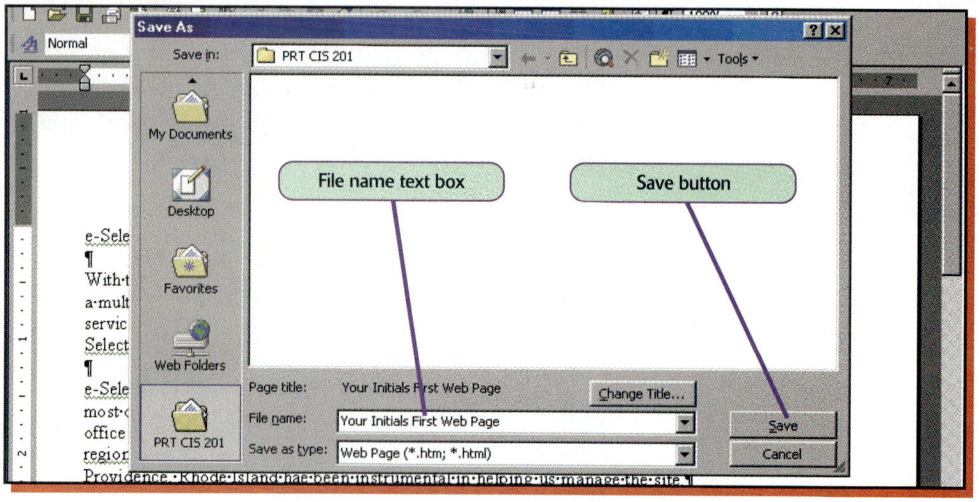

7 Click **Save**. The file is saved as a Web page and the Web Layout View becomes active.

8 Choose **File | Web Page Preview**. Your Web browser application will open and enable you to view the document as a Web page.

Figure 1-32

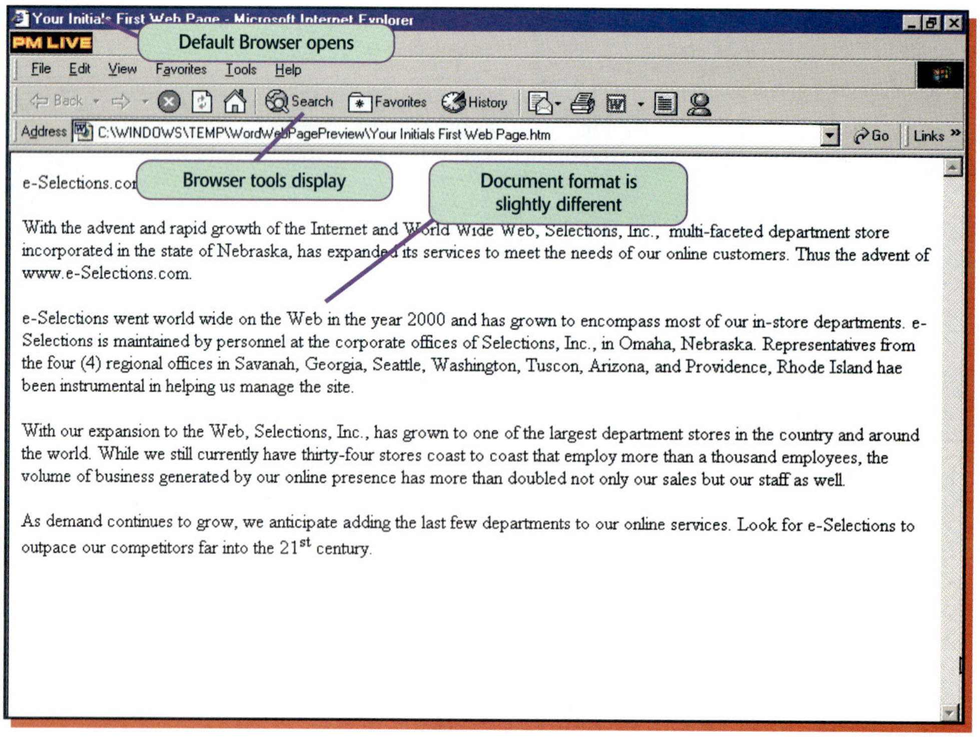

Troubleshooting The settings on your browser may be different from those shown here because of programs and other features installed on your computer.

9 Click the browser application **Close** button.

Changing File Properties

Properties, the term used to describe important information about a file, are automatically stored with each Office XP file you save. Properties are grouped into different categories and provide detailed information about the file, such as the date on which the file was created, the date on which it was last edited, the author's name, the author's company, the file size, and other application-specific information (e.g., the number of words in a Word document). In addition, the Office XP application used to create the file assigns a title for the file based on the file name assigned to the file. You can edit and check existing file information or add additional bits of information about the file.

Task 13: To Edit File Properties

1 Choose **File | Properties** to open the Properties dialog box.

Tip In Access, the name of this command on the File menu is Database Properties.

2 Select the word *first* in the Title text box.

3 Type **e-Selections** to replace *first*. The title now appears as *Your Initials e-Selections Web Page*.

4 Click **OK and close the file**.

Figure 1-33

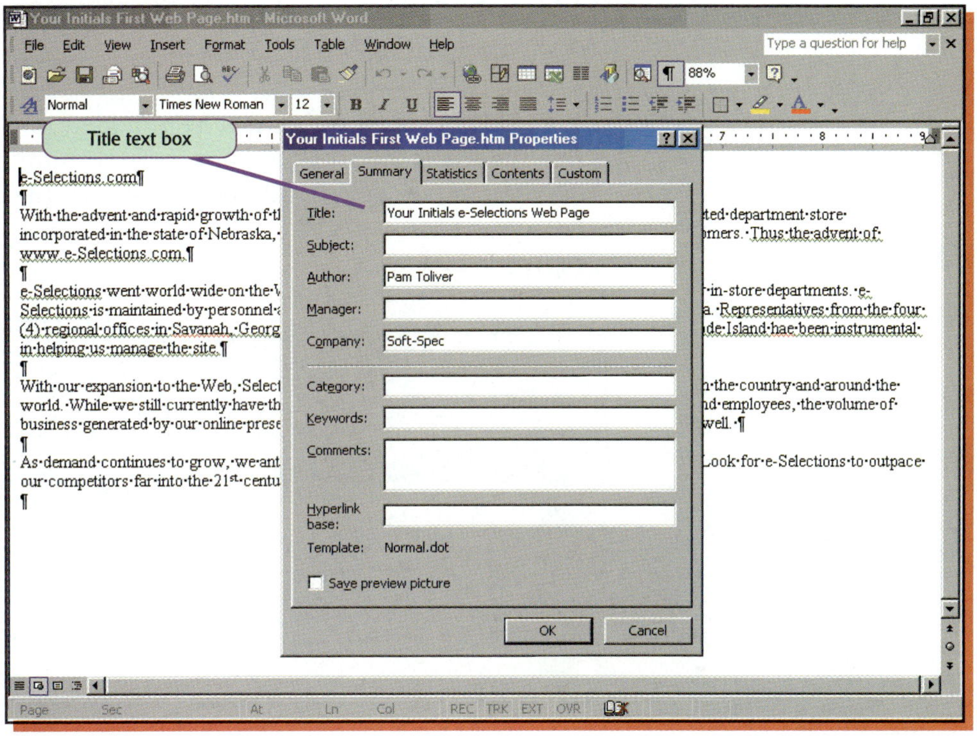

CHECK POINT

Because of the need for privacy in transmitting documents electronically, Office XP has implemented a procedure for removing personal information from a file on save. To set this option so that personal information is not transmitted with your files, follow these quick steps:

1. Choose **Tools | Options | Security.**
2. Select the **Remove personal information from this file on save** option.
3. Click **OK.**

Setting this option and then saving files prevents your name and other personal information from appearing in the Properties dialog box. It does NOT, however, prevent information about the document, such as creation date, edit date, and your company name, from appearing in the Properties dialog box.

Getting Help

In the Windows section, you learned how to use Windows Help and how to locate information about specific topics. Each Office XP application comes equipped with a variety of help features that will have you getting help from all over the world—right on your computer as you work!

Asking Questions

A new *Ask a Question* tool has been added to the right end of the menu bar. Using the Ask a Question text box, you can simply enter a question and receive a list of possible topics related to answering the question.

Task 14: To Ask a Question

1. Create a new blank document, click the **Ask a Question** text box on the menu bar to position the insertion point in the box.
2. Type **How do I display the Office Assistant?** and press Enter.
3. Click **Display tips and messages through the Office Assistant**.
4. Click the **Show** button on the Help window toolbar to display other help associated with the topic.
5. Click the Help window **Close** button. The Help window closes and Word resizes to screen size.

Troubleshooting Because the help files are updated frequently, the list you see when you search for help may be different from the lists shown in Tasks 14 and 15.

Figure 1-34

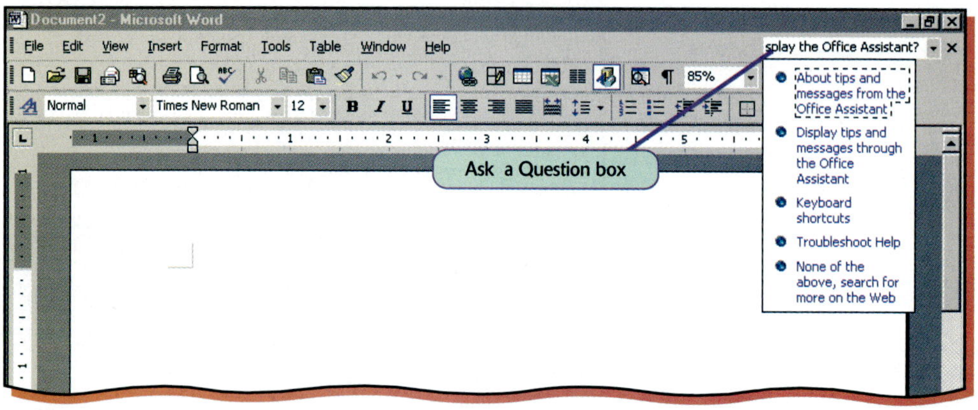

Figure 1-35

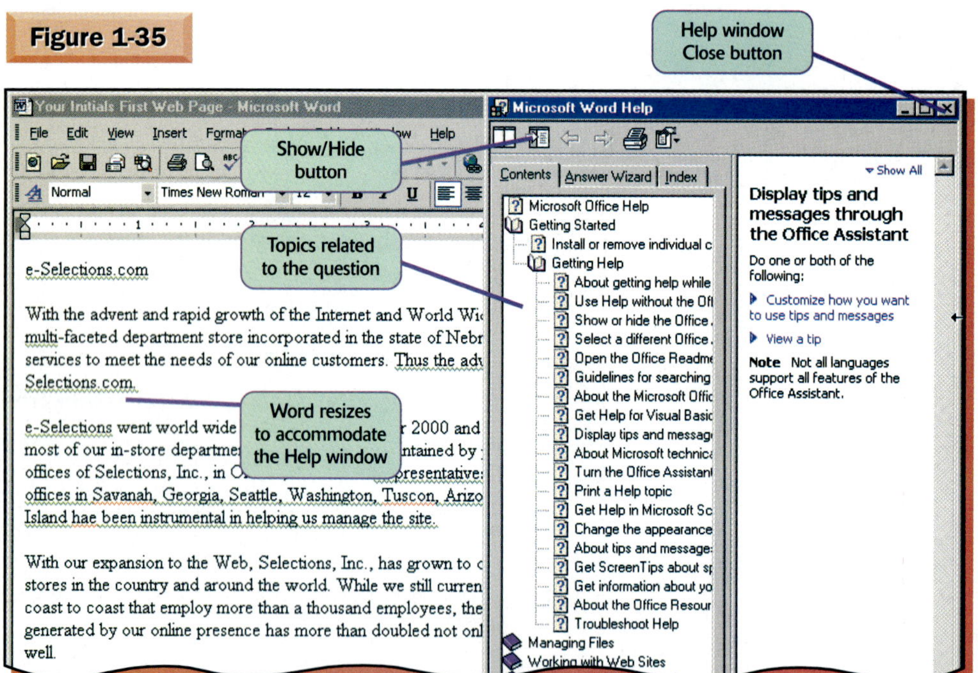

Using the Office Assistant

Tip While Clippit is the default Office Assistant, Microsoft Office applications come with a gallery of different Office Assistant shapes you can select. Search the Help files to learn how to change the Office Assistant.

The *Office Assistant* is a help feature that is growing in popularity. The Office Assistant is easy to use, is personably animated, and provides a focused list of help topics related to questions you "ask."

If the Assistant was displayed the last time one of the Office applications was used, it will appear on screen when you launch an application. When closed, the Assistant waits on the Standard toolbar and appears when you call it to look up information about topics for which you need help. After you start the Office Assistant in one application, it remains on screen until you close it—even when you open another Office application. The information it provides when you ask it a question relates to the application that is active at the time you ask a question—regardless of what application was active when you started the Office Assistant.

Task 15:
To Use the Office Assistant

1. Launch Excel using the same techniques you used to launch Word.

2. Choose **Help | Show the Office Assistant.**

Figure 1-36

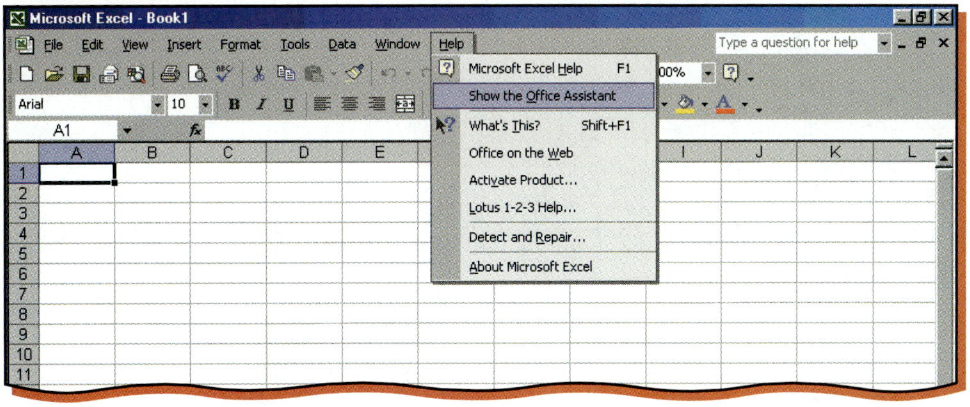

3. Click the **Office Assistant.**

Tip The Office Assistant dialog box opens in different shapes and sizes, depending on how it was last used.

Figure 1-37

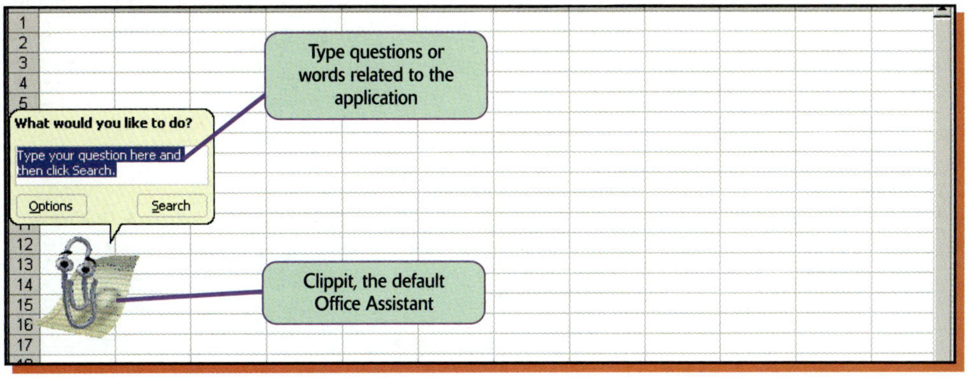

4 Type **How do I print a worksheet?** The Office Assistant takes notes as you type.

5 Click **Search** to locate associated help topics and then select **About printing**. Information and topics containing information about printing worksheets appears.

6 Close the **Help** window. The Excel window resizes to its original size.

Figure 1-38

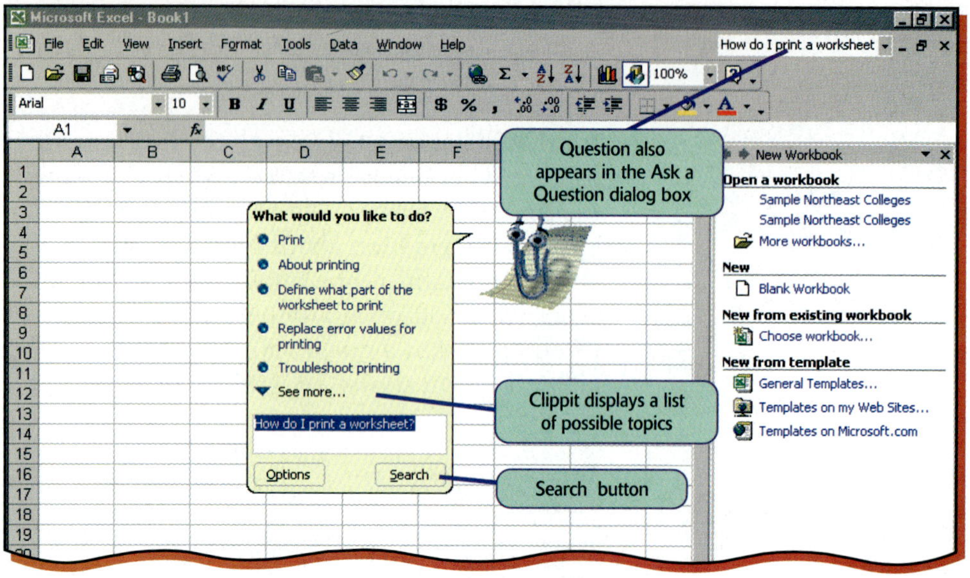

7 Right-click the **Office Assistant** and select **Hide**. The Office Assistant disappears and waits to be called again.

Figure 1-39

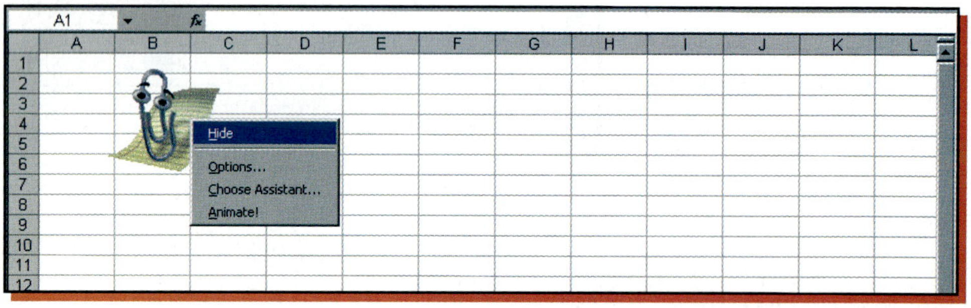

Troubleshooting After you select Hide several times, a dialog box will appear asking if you want to deactivate the Office Assistant. Read the options carefully and select the option that best represents how you want to use the Office Assistant.

Tip As you work with Help, you'll discover that the format of information displayed after you select a topic varies. In some cases, a list of step-by-step instructions appears in the Help window, and at other times, a list of further topics related to the subject you selected appears.

CHECK POINT

A number of features are available in Office XP to help you recover files. Each of these features is described in Table 1-5.

Table 1-5 Recovery Features

Feature	Description
Save on Crash	Word, Excel, and PowerPoint files that are open when a crash occurs are automatically saved so that they can be recovered after the system is restored.
Timed recovery save (AutoRecover)	An option set in Word, Excel, and PowerPoint to automatically save open files at regular intervals so that they can be recovered in case of power outages and Save on Crash failure.
Document Recovery task pane	An application pane that opens on the left side of an application window after a crash or improper shutdown, if recovery files are available. Users can choose to view both the recovery file and the original file to determine which file to use.
Hang Manager	A feature designed to "break" into a nonresponding application so that a Save on Crash action can be performed. You'll find this feature by choosing **Start** | **Programs** | **Microsoft Office Tools** | **Microsoft Office Application Recovery**.
Corrupt document recovery	An explicit corrupt document tool for recovering or repairing Word and Excel files. Simply select **Open and Repair** from the Open drop-down list as you open the file.
Office Safe Mode	Office-specific tools designed to fix and troubleshoot failed application startups. When an Office application fails to launch, a prompt should appear explaining the error and presenting start alternatives.

WEB TIP

If you're connected to the Internet, you can access one of several Web sites maintained by Microsoft to provide up-to-the-minute help online. The Web provides information directly from Microsoft support team members as well as information and helpful hints from other Office users. To access the Microsoft Web site directly from an Office XP application, choose **Help** | **Office on the Web**. Your default Web browser launches and displays the Office XP Update page.

Previewing and Printing

While each Office XP application has printing features that are specific to the application, printing basics are the same for all applications. In addition, each application has features that enable you to preview your files before printing them.

Previewing Pages

Even though most applications display files in WYSIWYG (*what you see is what you get*) format, sometimes what you see on paper is not quite what you expected. It is always a good idea to preview pages before sending them to the printer so that you can prevent some of these surprises. Each Office XP application has some type of Print Preview feature that enables you to see what the file will look like when it's printed.

- For all applications, you can display the preview by choosing **File | Print Preview,** or by clicking the **Print Preview** button on the Standard toolbar.
- In PowerPoint, you can display each slide on screen by choosing **View | Slide Show**, by pressing F5, by choosing **Slide Show | View Show**, or by clicking the **Slide Show** button at the bottom of the presentation window.

Task 16: To Preview a File

1. Launch Word, if necessary, and open your *Copy (1) of e-Selections* file.

Figure 1-40

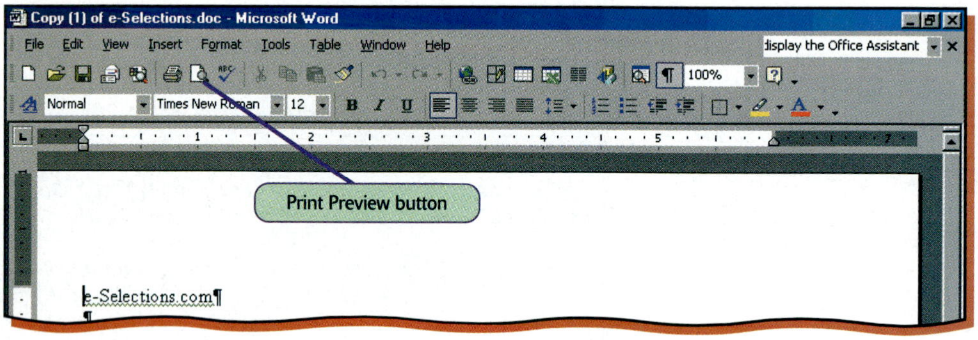

2. Click the **Print Preview** button on the Standard toolbar.

Figure 1-41

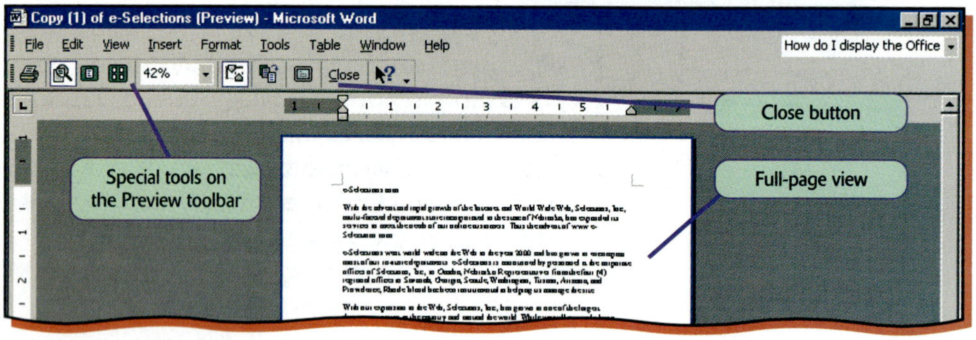

3. Click the **Close** button on the Preview toolbar.

Setting Print Options and Printing

There are three basic methods for printing documents:

- Choose **File | Print** to display the Print dialog box and set print options.
- Click the **Print** button on the Standard toolbar to print the active file using default settings.
- Press Ctrl + P to display the Print dialog box and set print options.

The options displayed in the Print dialog box vary among Office applications. There are a number of options, however, that are common to the Print dialog boxes of all the applications.

Troubleshooting If the printer you want to use is not installed on your computer, check with your instructor or the lab assistant to obtain the necessary information and disks to install the printer.

Task 17:

To Set Print Options and Print a File

1. Choose **File** | **Print**.
2. Review print options and then click **OK**.

Tip You can print comments added to documents and other file materials by selecting items from the Print what drop-down list.

Figure 1-42

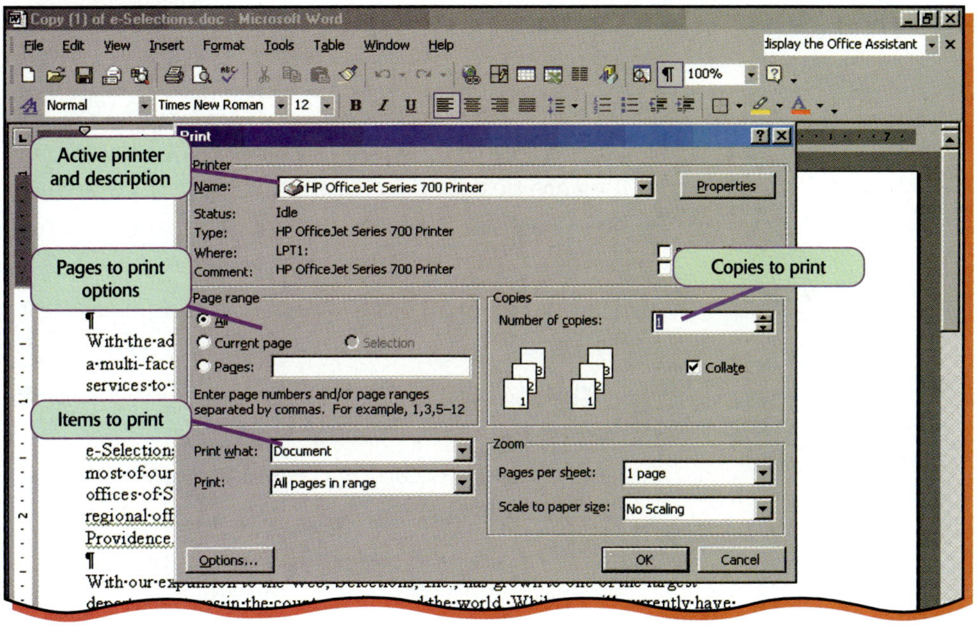

Exiting Applications

Before you exit Office XP applications, you should save work that you want to keep and close the files you have open. If you exit an application without saving changes to open files, the Office XP application prompts you to save changes to the file. Be sure to read these prompts carefully to ensure that you take the action you intend and avoid unnecessary loss of data.

To exit Office XP applications, use one of the following procedures:

- Click the application **Close** [X] button.
- Choose **File | Exit**. If multiple files are open in the application, all files close as you exit the application.
- Click the **Application Control** icon at the left end of the title bar, and select **Close**.
- Press Alt + F4.
- Right-click the **application** button on the Windows taskbar and select **Close**.

SUMMARY AND EXERCISES

SUMMARY

- The many common elements of Office XP enable you to use techniques learned in one application to accomplish the same task in other applications.
- Applications can be launched in a variety of ways, based on your preferences and how Office XP is installed on your computer.
- Screen elements appear each time you open an Office XP application; they are designed to control the way files appear in the application window, to aid in file management tasks, and to provide easy access to commonly performed tasks.
- File management tasks include opening files, creating new files, saving files, and editing file properties.
- Documents can be opened as a copy or as a read-only file to ensure that your original remains intact.
- New documents can be created as blank files or by using a predesigned template.
- Word, Excel, and PowerPoint enable you to open or create multiple files without closing files that are already open.
- When you elect to close a file that has been edited, regardless of which procedure you use, the application will prompt you to save the file.
- Files from all applications can be saved in a format recognized by the Web.
- Files saved as Web pages can be previewed from Office XP applications.
- The My Places bar, which appears in the Open and Save As dialog boxes, can be customized to hold folders and files you access frequently.
- The Open and Save As dialog boxes can be sized to display more information.
- File properties are automatically stored with each file you save unless you set options to prevent personal information from being saved with the file.
- Numerous help features are available. The Office Assistant and the Ask a Question features enable you to ask questions about the active application.
- Printing basics, such as previewing and setting print options, are basically the same for all Office XP applications.

KEY TERMS & SKILLS

KEY TERMS

corrupt document (p. 1-29)
embedded fonts (p. 1-19)
Hang Manager (p. 1-29)
Language bar (p. 1-9)
launch (p. 1-3)
My Places bar (p. 1-14)
Office Assistant (p. 1-27)
Office Safe mode (p. 1-29)
properties (p. 1-24)
Status bar (p. 1-7)
task pane (p. 1-7)
templates (p. 1-4)
toolbar (p. 1-7)
View buttons (p. 1-7)
Zoom (p. 1-12)

SKILLS

Add a folder to the My Places bar (p. 1-22)
Close a file (p. 1-18)
Close and open the task pane (p. 1-8)
Create new files (p. 1-16)
Create new folders (p. 1-19)
Display and hide toolbars (p. 1-9)
Edit file properties (p. 1-25)
Exit applications (p. 1-31)
Hide and display the Language bar (p. 1-9)
Launch applications (p. 1-3)
Launch Microsoft Word (p. 1-6)
Obtain help online (p. 1-29)
Open a copy of a document (p. 1-15)
Open a file (p. 1-13)
Preview pages (p. 1-30)
Print (p. 1-31)
Recover files (p. 1-29)
Remove personal information from a file on save (p. 1-25)
Save a copy of a file (p. 1-19)
Save a file (p. 1-18)
Save a file as a Web page (p. 1-21)
Set print options (p. 1-30)
Set Zoom control (p. 1-12)
Size a dialog box (p. 1-21)
Switch among open files (p. 1-17)
Turn off auto-customization features for menus and toolbars (p. 1-11)
Use Ask a Question (p. 1-26)
Use the Office Assistant (p. 1-27)
View the Web file (p. 1-23)

STUDY QUESTIONS

MULTIPLE CHOICE

1. Which procedures for accomplishing tasks are basically the same in all Office XP applications?
   a. presentation design
   b. file management
   c. data management
   d. toolbar options
2. Which are three options for initiating commands in Office XP?
   a. toolbar buttons, keystrokes, and mouse options
   b. taskbar buttons, menu commands, and keystrokes
   c. menu commands, keystrokes, and toolbar buttons
   d. both b and c
3. Which of the following procedures is *not* an option to open an existing document, workbook, presentation, or database?
   a. choose **Start** | **Open Office Document**
   b. choose **File** | **Open**
   c. press Ctrl + P
   d. click the **Open** button
4. The programs that display new files when you launch them are
   a. Access, PowerPoint, and Word.
   b. Excel, Access, and PowerPoint.
   c. Access and Excel.
   d. Word, Excel, and PowerPoint.
5. To change the portion of the file that appears on screen, adjust the
   a. task pane.
   b. Zoom control.
   c. toolbars.
   d. status bar.
6. Save commands include all the following *except*
   a. Save.
   b. Save As.
   c. Save as HTML.
   d. Save as Web Page.
7. To create a new file after an application is launched,
   a. press Ctrl + N.
   b. click the **New** button on the Standard toolbar.
   c. choose **File** | **New**.
   d. all of the above
8. The Ask a Question text box appears on the
   a. title bar.
   b. menu bar.
   c. toolbar.
   d. task pane.
9. Techniques for recovering files in Office XP include
   a. AutoRecover.
   b. recovering corrupt files.
   c. saving on crash.
   d. all of the above

SHORT ANSWER

1. List three different ways you can launch an application.
2. Identify several different ways to exit an application.
3. How do you open and close the task pane?
4. Regardless of the procedure you are using, what features will help prevent unwanted loss of data, and when will this option be presented to you?
5. How can you turn off the Office Assistant?
6. What is the difference between Save and Save As and when would you use each command?
7. What is Office Safe mode and when will it be used?
8. When would you remove personal information from files?
9. What are embedded fonts?
10. How do you resize a dialog box?

FILL IN THE BLANK

1. When you want to leave the original file intact but also want to use the file as a basis for a new file, you can open a(n) ____________ of the original file and save it as a new file.
2. The ____________ appears down the left side of the Open and Save As dialog boxes.
3. ____________ is the default Office Assistant.
4. Click the ____________ button to switch to a different open file.
5. ____________ enables you to see what your printout will look like before you print it.
6. Display a list of toolbars by choosing the ____________ command on the ____________menu.
7. The ____________ setting controls the portion of a file that appears on screen.
8. Files saved for Web use are saved with a(n) ____________ extension.
9. The ____________ toolbar appears to float on screen when it is active in an Office XP application.
10. Options for turning off the auto-customization feature appear in the ____________ dialog box.

FOR DISCUSSION

1. Briefly discuss when, how, and why you would use the Office Assistant.
2. Discuss the different ways to save a document and explain when and why you might choose each particular option.
3. The Word screen on one computer in the lab looks different from the Word screen on another computer in the lab. Explain the possible reasons why.
4. How do you add a folder to the My Places bar and why would you want to?

GUIDED EXERCISES

1 LAUNCHING APPLICATIONS

A good way to test the capacity of your computer system is to launch multiple applications and see if the performance speed keeps pace. You already have Word and Excel running. To test your system, you will launch various applications using a variety of different techniques.

1. Choose **Start** | **Programs** | **Accessories** | **Windows Explorer**.
2. Choose **Start** | **Programs** | **Accessories** | **Calculator**.
3. Choose **Start** | **Programs** | **Internet Explorer**.

2 SWITCHING AND EXITING APPLICATIONS

Now that you have examined the capacity of your computer, you can close all the open applications except Word.

1. Switch to Calculator and click the **Close** button.
2. Switch to Windows Explorer and choose **File** | **Close**.
3. Switch to Internet Explorer and press Alt + F4.
4. Right-click the **Excel** button on the taskbar and select **Close**.

3 PRINTING AND SAVING FILES

The e-Selections file that you opened and saved can be printed and then saved using a different file name.

1. Switch to the *Copy of e-Selections.doc* file, if necessary.
2. Choose **File** | **Print**, review print options and close the Print dialog box.
3. Click the **Print** button to print the file using default settings.
4. Choose **File** | **Save As** and open your personal folder on the My Places bar.
5. Type *Your Initials* **e-Selections** in the **File name** text box and press Enter.

4 CREATING A NEW FILE

The main purpose for creating new documents is to type text in the document work area. It's time to create your first document and type some text.

1. Switch to Word, if necessary.
2. Create a new document using the procedure you prefer.
3. Type the text shown here at the top of the document—it's okay if you make mistakes—and don't worry if your lines break at different spots from those shown here in this text.

   An apple or two for lunch on Monday is an excellent antidote to a weekend of overeating. Besides all this, the apple comes in its own packaging, travels well, and keeps indefinitely. What could be simpler?
4. Save your document in your personal folder, naming the file *An Apple on Monday*.
5. Follow your instructor's direction for placing your name on the document. Then print a copy of the document.

ON YOUR OWN

The difficulty of these case studies varies:
are the least difficult; *are more difficult; and* *are the most difficult.*

1 LAUNCHING APPLICATIONS AND WORKING WITH TOOLBARS

Launch Microsoft Excel 2002 and display the Picture toolbar. Record the names of each of the tools contained on the toolbar and identify when you would use the toolbar. Hide the toolbar.

2 CHANGING THE ZOOM SETTING

Change the Zoom setting for the blank Excel workbook to Selection using the Zoom dialog box. Record how the workbook appears. Then change the Zoom setting to 50% using the Zoom drop-down list on the Standard toolbar and record how the workbook appears on screen. Change the Zoom settings back to 100% using the preferred procedure.

3 OPENING AND SAVING AN EXCEL FILE

Open the *Sample Northeast Colleges.xls* file that you downloaded from the Prentice Hall Web site. Type **Your Name** in the active location. Then save your file as a new file in your personal folder. Name the file *Your Initials Sample Colleges*.

4 PREVIEWING AND PRINTING EXCEL FILES

Preview your *Sample Colleges* Excel file to see how it will print. Print a copy of the file.

5 SAVING, PREVIEWING, AND PRINTING AN EXCEL FILE AS A WEB PAGE

Save your *Sample Colleges* worksheet as a Web page, storing it in your personal folder. Preview the file in your default Web browser. Print a copy of the file from the Web browser.

FROM THE FILES

You Will Need

- ✓ e-Selections Online.doc
- ✓ Fire Center.doc

PROJECT 2

Common Text Elements

In the previous project, you learned some of the basic elements and features that all Microsoft Office XP applications have in common. In this project, you will learn some techniques for working with text in all of the Office applications—how to *format*, *enhance*, copy, move, and proof text. You'll also learn how to create and format text boxes and how to add text to those boxes.

e-selections Running Case

You're off and running toward mastering the basics of the Microsoft Office XP applications that you will need as you work toward establishing yourself with e-Selections.com! Learning how to identify screen features, manage files, and get help was actually quite easy. Now that you're more comfortable with the basics, you decide to put those keyboarding skills to good use and try working with text...

OBJECTIVES

After completing this project, you will be able to:

- Navigate documents
- Select text
- Insert, delete, and replace text
- Enhance, format, and align text
- Move and copy text and text format
- Use the Office Clipboard
- Undo and redo changes
- Use Office proofing tools
- Use AutoCorrect
- Use text boxes

PROJECT 2

Common Text Elements

The Setup

In Common Elements Project 1, you learned a number of screen features and other tools that control the way documents appear on screen. As you worked with these screen features, the figures in the text changed to reflect screen changes. Before starting Common Elements Projects 2 and 3, it is important that you check some of those screen settings to ensure that your screen matches the figures in the projects. The settings shown in Table 2-1 will be used in both Projects 2 and 3.

Table 2-1 Common Elements Projects 2 and 3 Screen Settings

Feature	Setting
Office Assistant	Hide the Office Assistant.
Toolbars and Menus	Set the toolbars to appear on two lines and set the Always show full menus option. Hide all toolbars except Standard and Formatting.
Task pane	Close the task pane.

Troubleshooting Because screen settings and installation options vary, you may see differences between your screens and those shown in this text.

The Challenge

Typing and formatting text is a skill required for working in all Office XP applications. The *e-Selections Online* document needs to be dressed up a bit. Formatting and text enhancements can be applied to create the document shown in Figure 2-1.

Figure 2-1

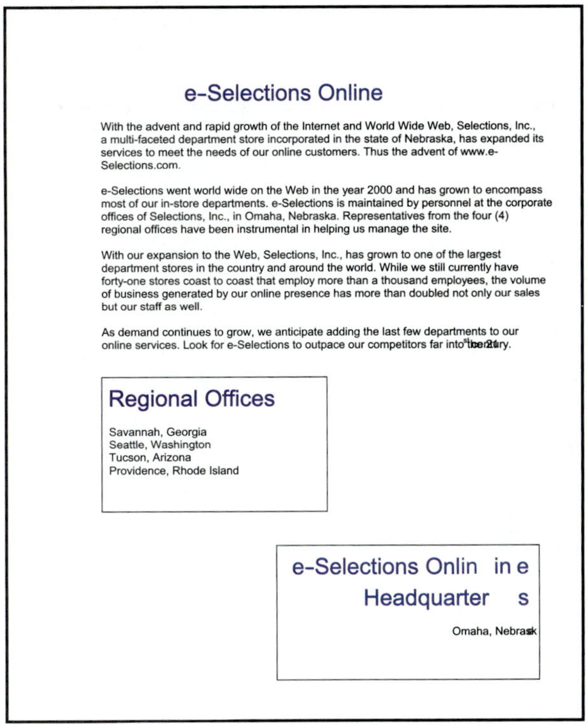

e-Selections Online

With the advent and rapid growth of the Internet and World Wide Web, Selections, Inc., a multi-faceted department store incorporated in the state of Nebraska, has expanded its services to meet the needs of our online customers. Thus the advent of www.e-Selections.com.

e-Selections went world wide on the Web in the year 2000 and has grown to encompass most of our in-store departments. e-Selections is maintained by personnel at the corporate offices of Selections, Inc., in Omaha, Nebraska. Representatives from the four (4) regional offices have been instrumental in helping us manage the site.

With our expansion to the Web, Selections, Inc., has grown to one of the largest department stores in the country and around the world. While we still currently have forty-one stores coast to coast that employ more than a thousand employees, the volume of business generated by our online presence has more than doubled not only our sales but our staff as well.

As demand continues to grow, we anticipate adding the last few departments to our online services. Look for e-Selections to outpace our competitors far into the 21st century.

Regional Offices

Savannah, Georgia
Seattle, Washington
Tucson, Arizona
Providence, Rhode Island

e-Selections Online Headquarters

Omaha, Nebraska

The Solution

Using Word, you will apply text formatting features that are common to all Office XP applications—exceptions will be noted.

Working with Text

Whether you're typing a letter in Word, entering values in an Excel worksheet, adding data to an Access table, or creating slides in PowerPoint, you'll type and edit text. Learning how to navigate, edit, enhance, format, *align*, move, and copy text now will make working with text in each application easier.

Navigating Text

Navigating text simply means moving from character to character, paragraph to paragraph, screen to screen, or page to page in a file. You can use both the keyboard and the mouse to move the insertion point within a file. Mouse techniques that are common to all Office applications include using scroll bars to display different parts of a file and clicking to position the insertion point in the paragraph, cell, or field you want to edit. Table 2-2 identifies navigation keystrokes common to Word, Excel, PowerPoint, and Access.

Table 2-2 Navigation Keystrokes	
Press	**To Move**
←	Left one character or column
→	Right one character or column
↓	Down one line or row
↑	Up one line or row
Page Up	Up one screen
PageDown	Down one screen
Home	To the beginning of a line or row
End	To the end of a line or row
Ctrl + End	To the end of a file
Ctrl + Home	To the beginning of a file

As you work with each application, you'll discover additional keystrokes specific to that application. For example: in Excel, you'll learn to move from worksheet to worksheet in a workbook; in PowerPoint, you'll learn to display presentation slides; and in Access, you'll learn to move among records in forms using the navigation controls.

Inserting, Deleting, and Typing Over Text

All Office XP applications are set with *Insert mode* active so that you simply position the insertion point where you want to insert text and start typing. Existing text moves over to make room for the new text. To *replace* existing text with new text, you can select text that you want to replace (see Table 2-3) and type the new text in its place.

Tip In Word, you can also switch to *Overtype mode* by pressing Insert on the keyboard or by double-clicking the OVR area of the status bar.

The technique used to *delete* text depends on the position of the insertion point:

- Position the insertion point immediately before the text you want to delete and press Delete once for each character and space you want to delete.
- Position the insertion point immediately after the text you want to delete and press Bksp once for each character and space you want to delete.

You can also use text selection techniques to select text and replace it with other text. Techniques for selecting text vary somewhat from application to application, but some basics are common to all applications. Table 2-3 summarizes common text selection techniques.

Table 2-3 Common Text Selection Techniques

Action	To Select
Double-click a word	The word
Triple-click a word	The paragraph or table cell
Press Shift + arrow keys	Characters, lines, or rows from the insertion point

Text appears highlighted—white text on a black background—when it is selected. Text you type and keyboard keys you press while text is selected replace selected text.

Tip The task pane also contains formatting features that are explored more thoroughly in the Microsoft Word 2002 book and the Word section of the Microsoft Office XP book.

Enhancing and Formatting Text

Word, Excel, PowerPoint, and Access datasheets share common methods for changing the appearance of text. Special features enable you to enhance and format text by changing the text *font*—the shape and size of text characters—as well as changing text *attributes*—how text characters appear. Changes you make to text that has already been typed affect the selected text only. However, you can "turn on" an enhancement or change font characteristics before typing text and it will remain active until you turn the enhancement "off" or change the font again when you are finished. Tools on the Formatting toolbar, menu commands on the Format menu, and dialog boxes can all be used to format text.

Task 1: To Navigate, Select, Enhance, and Format Text

1. Open the document *e-Selections Online.doc.*
2. Select the title *e-Selections Online.* The text appears highlighted.
3. Click the **Bold** button on the Formatting toolbar to make the text appear in bold letters.

Figure 2-2

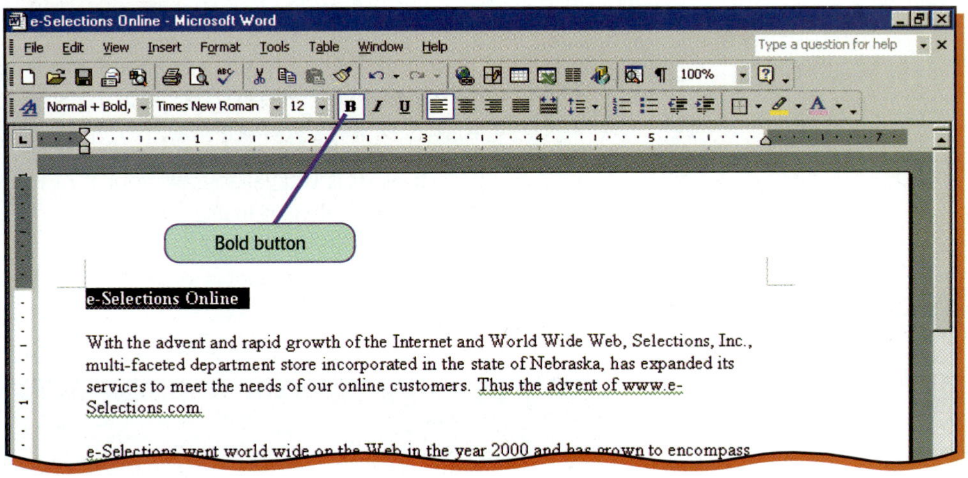

4 Click the **Font** down arrow.

5 Select **Arial Black**. The selected text reformats with the new font.

Figure 2-3

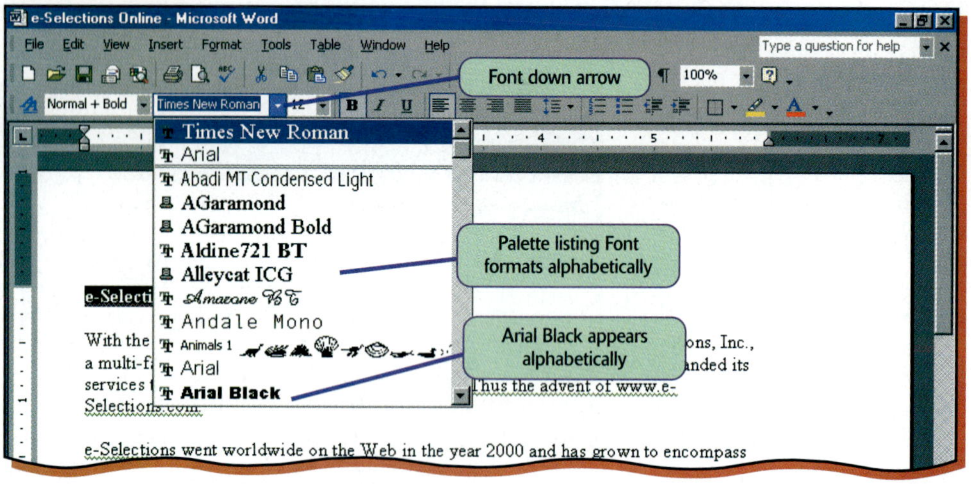

6 Click the **Font Size** down arrow. A list of numbers appears on a palette, with the current font size highlighted.

7 Select **24**. The title appears much larger.

8 Click the **Italic** button on the Formatting toolbar. The title appears slanted and the Italic button is white.

Figure 2-4

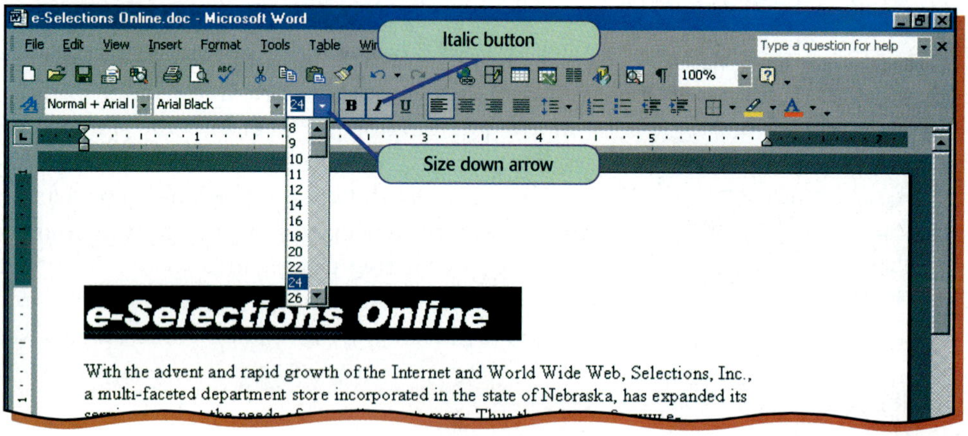

Troubleshooting The fonts installed on your computer and the printer that you are using control, to some extent, the fonts that you see listed. The fonts you see may be different from those shown here.

If Arial Black is unavailable on your font list, select a similar font or follow the direction of your instructor.

9 Choose **Format | Font** to open the Font dialog box.

Figure 2-5

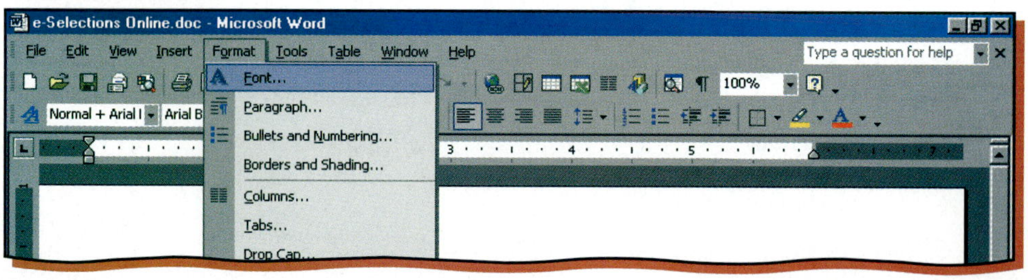

10 Click the **Font color** down arrow. A palette of colors appears.

11 Click **Blue** and click **OK**. The title text is reformatted in blue print.

Tip Notice the special effects listed in the Font dialog box. As you become more comfortable applying standard enhancements to text, you may want to try applying some of these special effects and explore options contained on other pages of this dialog box.

Figure 2-6

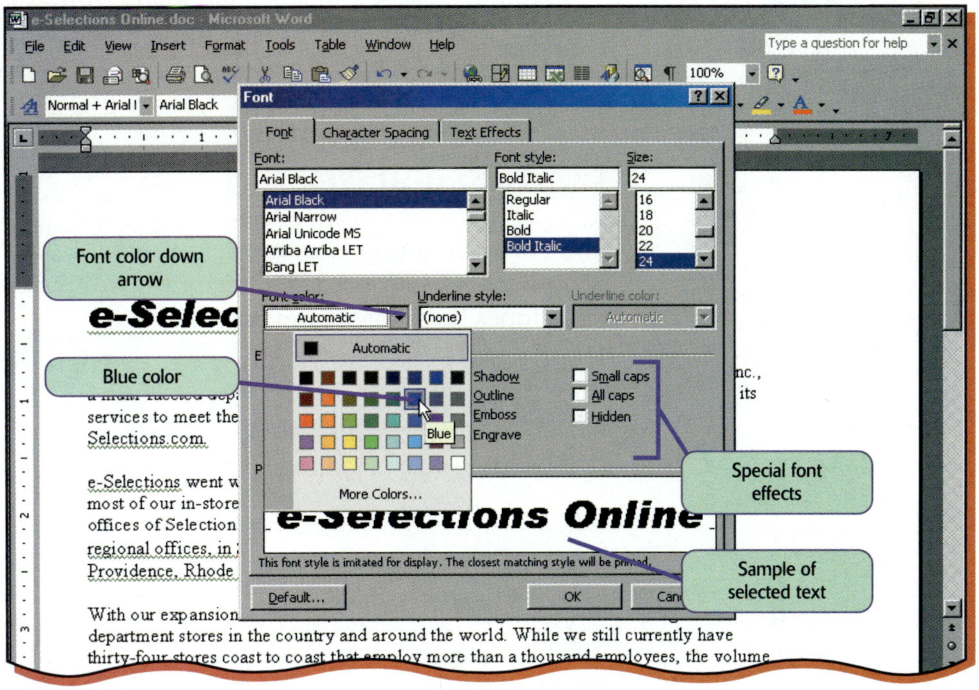

12 Press Ctrl + End to position the insertion point at the bottom of the document.

13 Choose **File | Save As** and save the file using the file name *Your Initials e-Selections Online*.

Other Ways To apply font color:

- Click the Font Color down arrow on the Formatting toolbar.

Figure 2-7

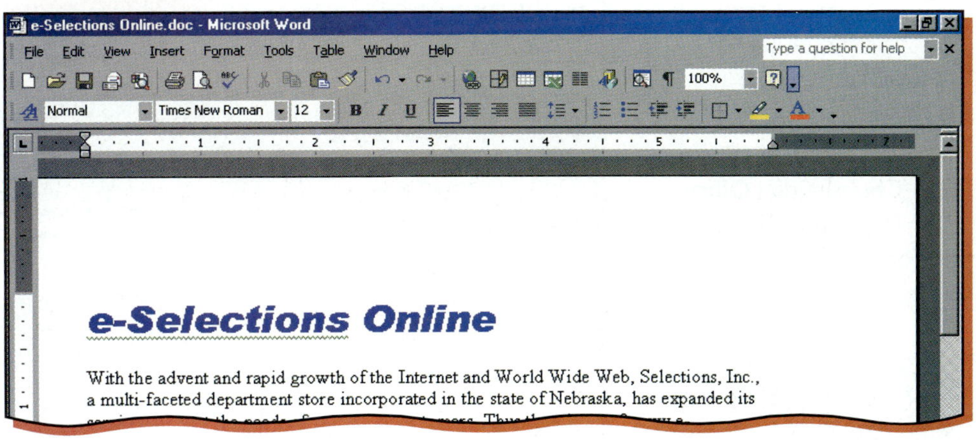

WEB TIP

Additional fonts are available online from a variety of different companies. Search the Internet for fonts to see what's available.

Copying and Moving Text

The *Cut* command is used to remove text from its current position. The *Copy* command leaves text at its current position. Office XP offers three different techniques for moving and copying text:

- Click the **Cut**, **Copy**, or **Paste** buttons on the Standard toolbar.
- Choose **Edit | Cut/Copy/Paste**.
- Press Ctrl + X to Cut; Ctrl + C to Copy; or Ctrl + V to Paste.

When you use the Cut command to move text or the Copy command to copy text, Office XP applications place the selected text or information on the Clipboard, where it stays until you *paste* it where you want it.

Although other Windows applications store only one snippet of information on the Clipboard, Office XP contains a special feature that enables you to store multiple snippets of information (up to 24) from all types of Office applications on a special Office Clipboard. You can then choose the snippet or snippets to place when you paste. The Office Clipboard appears in the task pane when it is active.

Task 2:
To Display the Office Clipboard

1 Choose **Edit | Office Clipboard**. The task pane opens and displays the Office Clipboard.

Tip To display the Office Clipboard when the task pane is already open, click the task pane down arrow and select **Clipboard**.

Figure 2-8

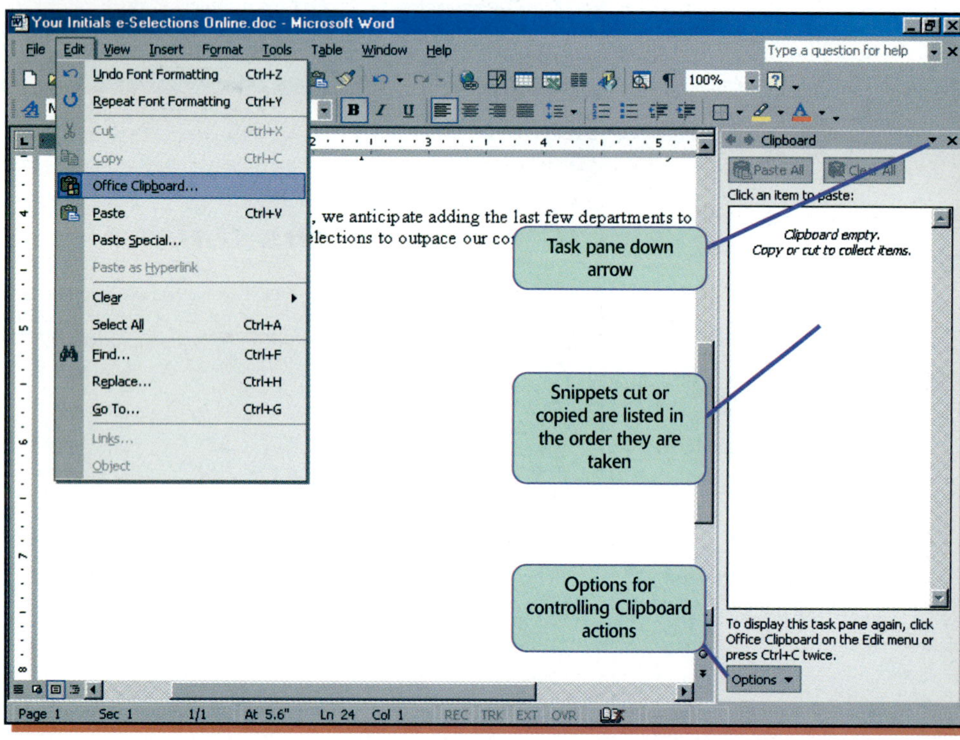

CHECK POINT

The Office Clipboard may appear automatically as you work when you cut or copy multiple snippets of information in one or more Office XP applications. Normally, items are added to the Office Clipboard only when it is active. Options that control the way the Office Clipboard acts are found on the Options drop-down list that appears at the bottom of the Clipboard task pane. These options are described in Table 2-4.

Table 2-4 Options for Controlling the Office Clipboard

Select the Option	To
Show Office Clipboard Automatically	Activate the Office Clipboard when you cut or copy the second snippet.
Collect Without Showing Office Clipboard	Places items on the Office Clipboard even when it is not open.
Show Office Clipboard Icon on Taskbar	Places an Office Clipboard icon on the tray of the Taskbar so that you can access the Office Clipboard more easily.
Show Status Near Taskbar When Copying	Displays a screen tip above the tray on the Taskbar each time you copy something to the Clipboard. The tip lets you know how many items are currently on the Office Clipboard.

In addition, you can display the Office Clipboard by pressing Ctrl + C twice. The icons that appear beside snippets on the Office Clipboard identify the application from which the snippet was taken. You can paste all snippets at the current cursor location by clicking the Paste All button. You can also click an individual snippet to insert it at the insertion point.

Task 3:

To Copy and Move Text

1. Position the insertion point at the bottom of the document, if necessary.
2. Click the **Bold** **B** button and type Regional Offices.
3. Click the **Bold** **B** button to turn bold off and then press Enter twice.

Figure 2-9

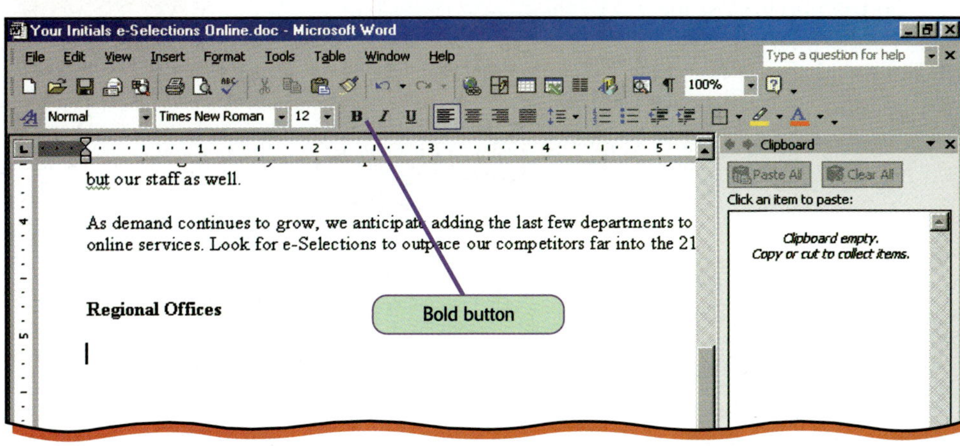

4 Select the text *Savanah, Georgia* in the second paragraph and click the **Cut** button to remove selected text from its current position and place it on the clipboard.

Figure 2-10

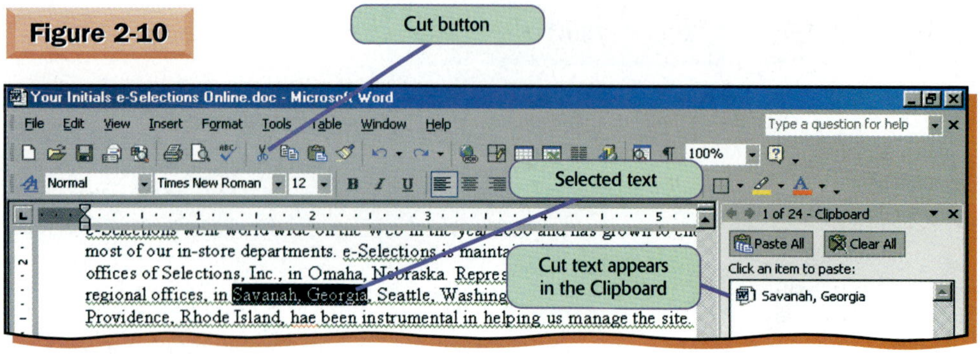

5 Move to the end of the document and click the **Paste** button to place text from the clipboard at the end of the document.

Figure 2-11

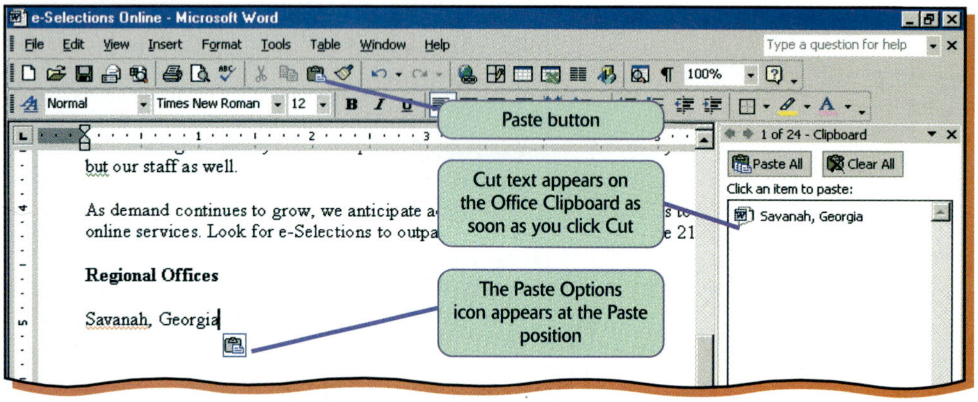

6 Click the **Paste Options** icon next to the pasted text and review the options that appear.

7 Select **Keep Source Formatting** to close the option list and then press Enter.

Figure 2-12

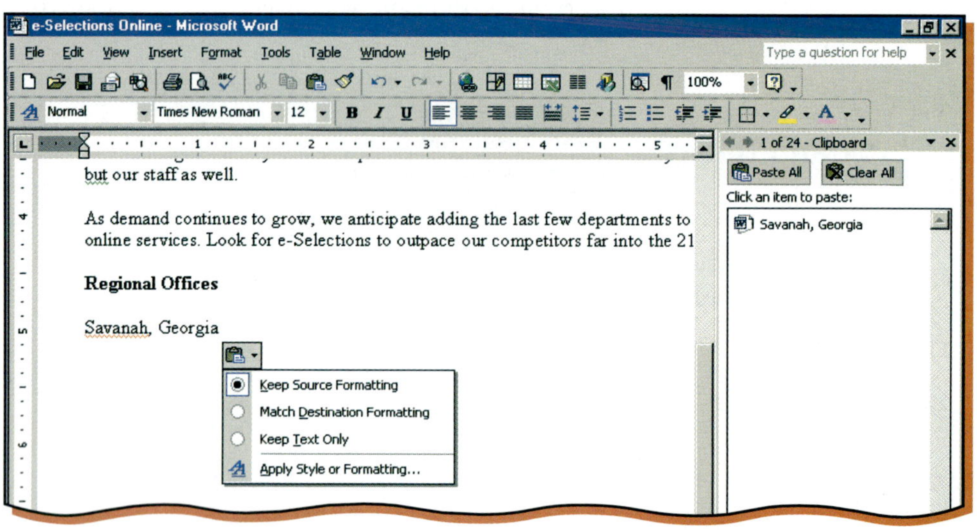

Tip

Selecting the Keep Source Formatting option tells Word to include any enhancements and special formatting that were originally applied to the text when you paste the text in the new location. To drop special formatting from the original text so that text is formatted to follow font characteristics of the paragraph in which you paste the text, you would select Match Destination Formatting from the Past Options list.

8 Repeat the procedures in Steps 4–6 to move the cities and states for the other three regional offices so that they appear as shown in Figure 2-13.

9 Select the text, *in, , , and,* that is highlighted in Figure 2-13 and delete it.

10 Save changes to the document.

Tip Snippets of information are collected on the Clipboard task pane in the order in which you cut or copy them. The most recently cut or copied snippet appears at the top of the task pane for easy access.

Figure 2-13

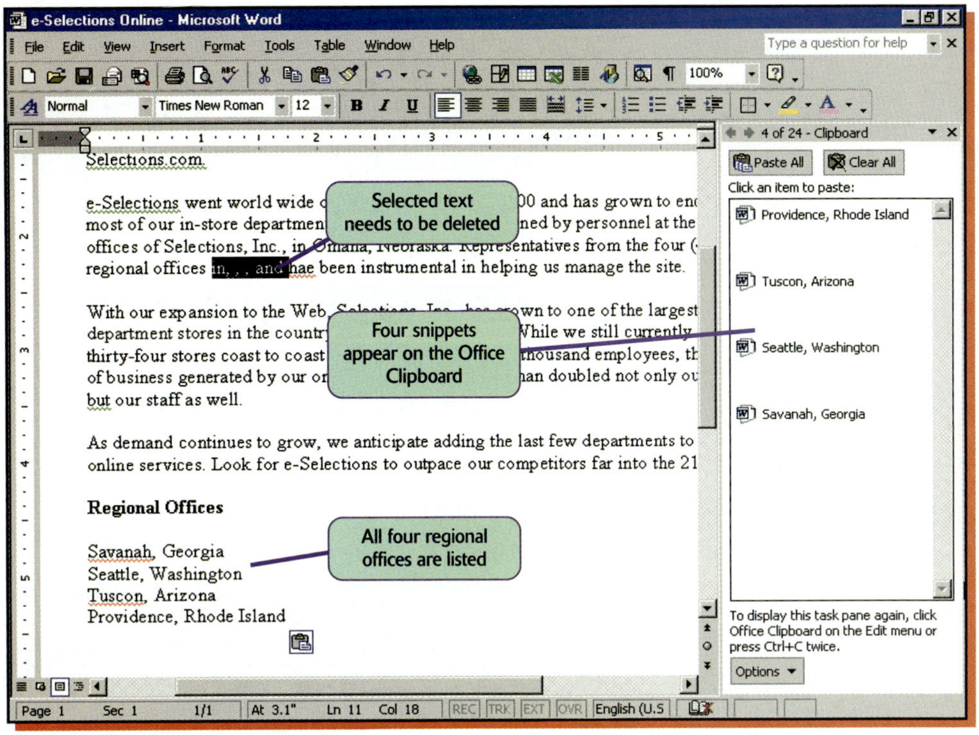

Copying Text Formats

Formatting text by applying enhancements, color, and font styles can be tedious—especially when you want to format text in several different locations and maintain consistency of format. You're in luck! Office XP applications are equipped with a *Format Painter* that's designed to help you copy text format and apply the format to other text. Using the Format Painter to copy format is basically a three-step process:

1. Select the text with the format that you want to copy.
2. Click the **Format Painter** button.
3. "Paint" the format onto the text you want to format.

Tip Double-click the Format Painter button to copy format to multiple locations. When you're finished painting all the text with the copied format, click the Format Painter button again to turn it off.

Task 4:

To Copy Text Formats Using the Format Painter

1. Close the Office Clipboard and then select the formatted title text, *e-Selections Online*.

2. Click the **Format Painter** button on the Standard toolbar to copy the format of the selected text.

3. Scroll to the bottom of the document page until the *Regional Offices* text appears on the screen.

4. Click and drag the paintbrush across the text *Regional Offices* to paint the copied format onto the text.

5. Click anywhere in the document to deselect the text.

Tip Double-click the Format Painter to apply the format to text in multiple places in a file or to text in other files.

Figure 2-14

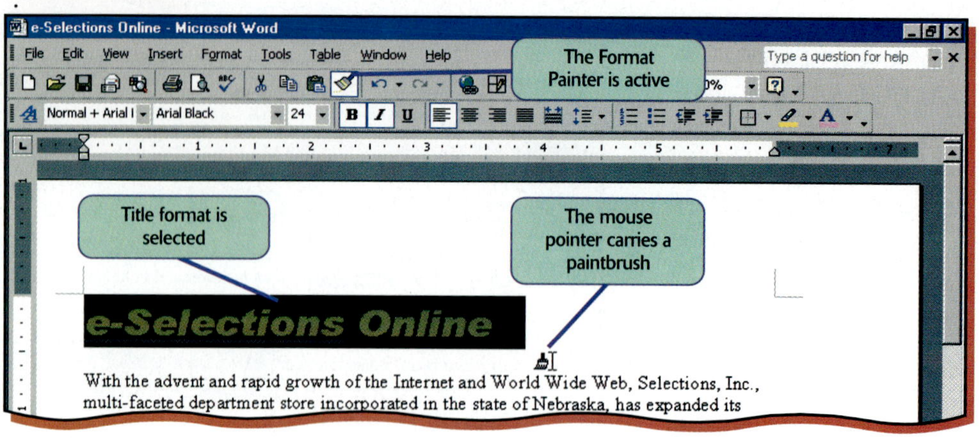

Figure 2-15

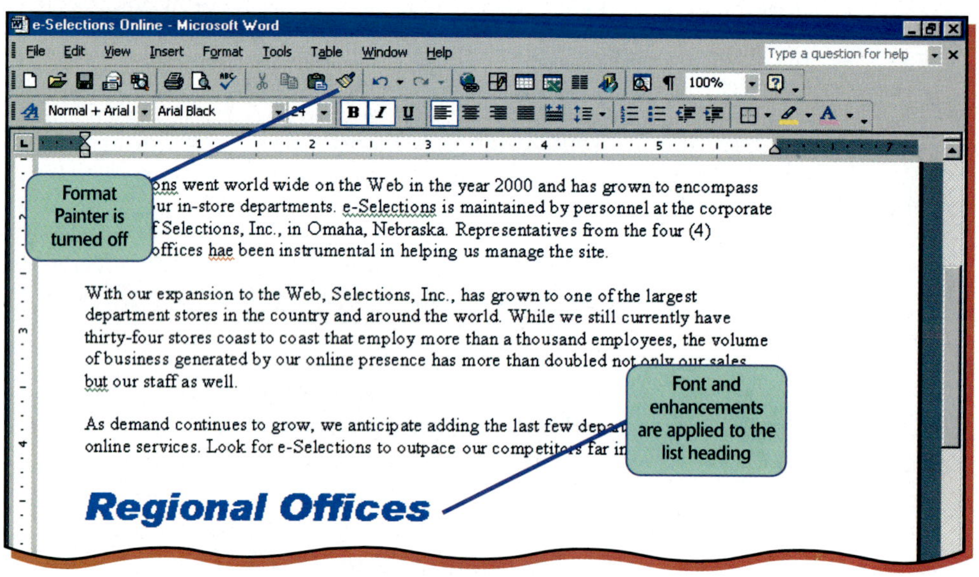

Troubleshooting Positioning the insertion point in a word is usually sufficient to copy the text format, but when multiple fonts and character settings are contained in a paragraph or in a word select the character that contains the format you want to copy.

Using Undo and Redo

The *Undo* feature in all Office XP applications reverses actions; the *Redo* feature restores actions that were reversed. Using Undo and Redo is quite simple. Office XP applications offer keyboard, mouse, and menu procedures for these two features, as shown in Table 2-5.

Table 2-5 Undo/Redo Procedures

Command	Mouse	Keyboard	Menu
Undo	Click the **Undo** button on the Standard toolbar.	Press Ctrl + Z	Choose **Edit** | **Undo**
Redo	Click the **Redo** button on the Standard toolbar.	Press Ctrl + Y	Choose **Edit** | **Redo**

Each of these actions reverses the last action, but Office XP applications enable you to reverse numerous actions in succession. In addition, you can click the down arrow beside the Undo or Redo buttons and select the action you want to reverse. All actions down to and including the action you select can be reversed.

Aligning Text

Among the buttons you'll find on the Formatting toolbars in Word, Excel, PowerPoint, and on Access Forms are buttons that control text alignment. You can use these alignment buttons to adjust the position of text in document paragraphs, table or worksheet cells, database forms, and presentation slides. You can also access alignment commands using the keyboard. The menu commands for setting alignment vary among the applications. Table 2-6 identifies common procedures for aligning text in Word, Excel, PowerPoint, and on Access Forms.

Table 2-6 Alignment Commands

Command	Mouse	Keyboard
Align Left	Click the **Align Left** button on the Formatting toolbar.	Press Ctrl + L
Center	Click the **Center** button on the Formatting toolbar.	Press Ctrl + E
Align Right	Click the **Align Right** button on the Formatting toolbar.	Press Ctrl + R
Justify	Click the **Justify** button on the Formatting toolbar.	Press Ctrl + J

Task 5:
To Align Text and Use Undo and Redo

1. Position the insertion point in the title of your *e-Selections Online.doc* document.
2. Click the **Align Right** button on the Formatting toolbar.
3. Undo the action to reposition the text at the left margin.
4. Center the title.
5. Save changes to the document.

Figure 2-16

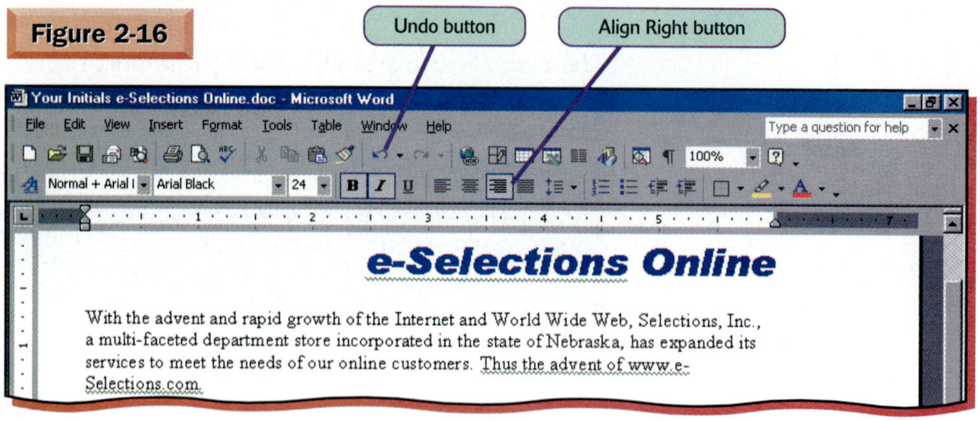

Figure 2-17

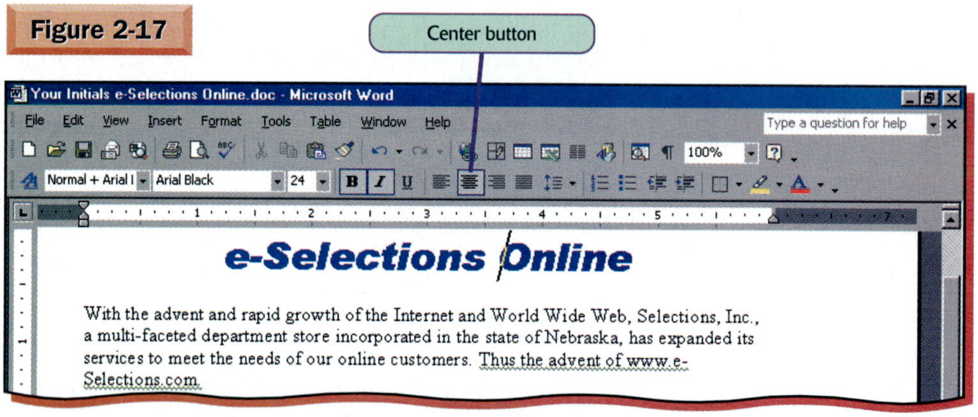

Tip If special fonts required to develop documents in different languages such as Japanese have been installed on your computer, you may see a special Distributed alignment button on the Formatting toolbar. Try aligning text using the Distributed alignment and view the results.

Using Proofing Tools

Proofing tools built into Office XP applications make it easy to locate text, replace text, and check the spelling in your files. There is also a tool that is shared by Word, Excel, Access, and PowerPoint that enables you to enter frequently mistyped text and have the Office application automatically correct your error! The procedures for using these tools are consistent among all Office XP applications.

Running the Spelling Checker

When you first opened *e-Selections Online.doc*, you saw red, wavy underlines below misspelled words in the document. Unless the spell-as-you-go feature is turned off, the *spelling checker* feature runs continuously as you work in Office XP applications. The spelling checker feature locates words that don't appear in the Office XP dictionary and highlights them for you so that you can determine whether they are correct or need to be changed.

> **Tip**
>
> Words that are underlined as you work can be corrected quite easily. Simply point to the misspelled word and right-click. A list of suggested spellings for the word that is not recognized appears at the top of the shortcut menu. Select the correct spelling of the word, click **Ignore All**, or click **Add** to add the word to the dictionary.

Task 6:
To Use Spelling Checker on a File

1. Press Ctrl + Home to move to the beginning of the document and then click the **Spelling** button on the Standard toolbar.

2. Click **Ignore Rule**—this text appears as you want it to appear. Word locates the next possible error and highlights it.

Figure 2-18

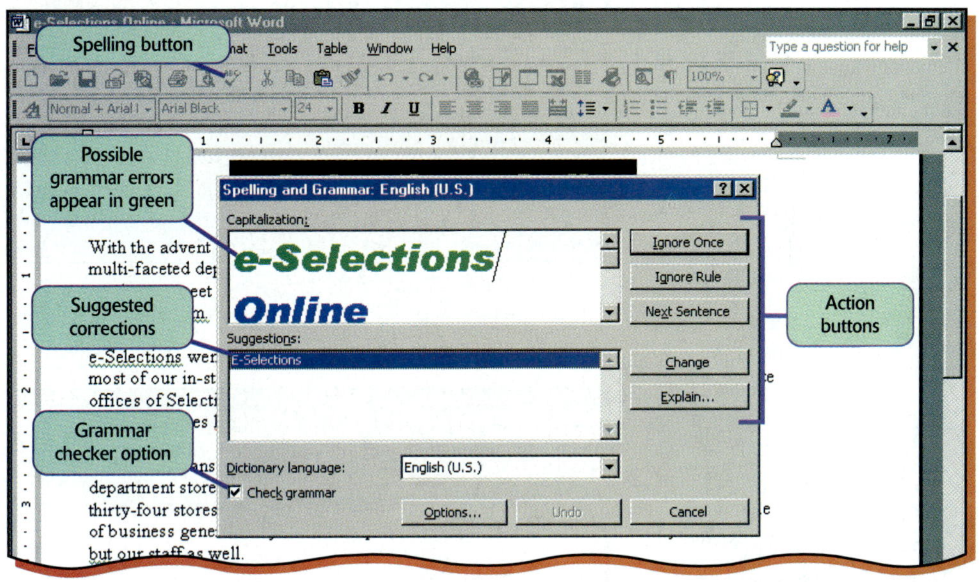

3. Click **Ignore Once**. The next possible error is highlighted.

4. Click **Ignore Rule** to ignore this rule, too.

Figure 2-19

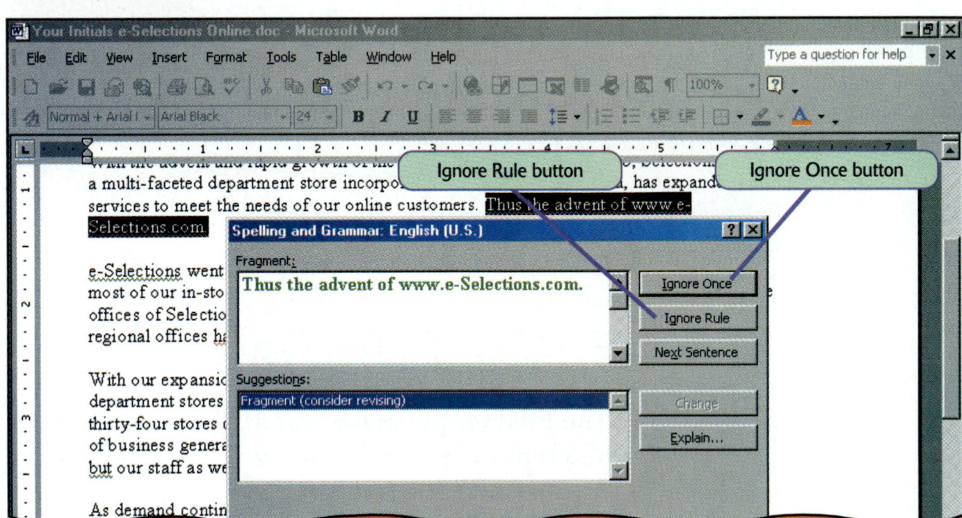

> **Troubleshooting**
>
> If you start the spelling checker in the middle of a document, a different message window may appear that asks if you want to continue proofing the document from the beginning. Click **Yes** and continue until the spelling checker is complete.

5 Select *have* from the **Suggestions** list and click **Change**. Word highlights the next possible error.

6 Continue checking the file, correcting errors that appear, until Word tells you the spelling and grammar check is complete.

Figure 2-20

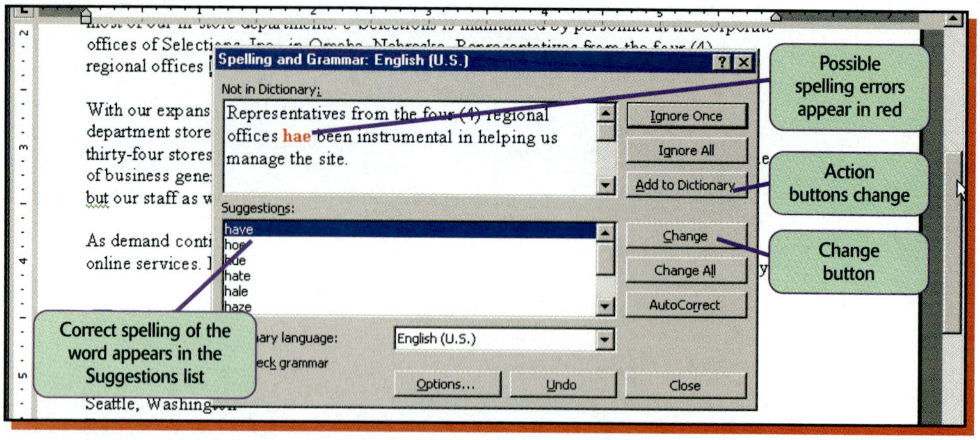

Tip If Word fails to present the correct spelling in the list of suggested words, you can correct the spelling of the word in the Not in Document area of the Spelling and Grammar dialog box and then click Change.

7 Click **OK** and save changes to the file.

Tip It is often tempting to click the Replace All button to replace all occurrences of a misspelled in a document with another spelling of the word. Carefully consider whether replacing all occurrences of a word with the selected replacement is the correct action—Word follows your directive explicitly—sometimes with unexpected results!

Figure 2-21

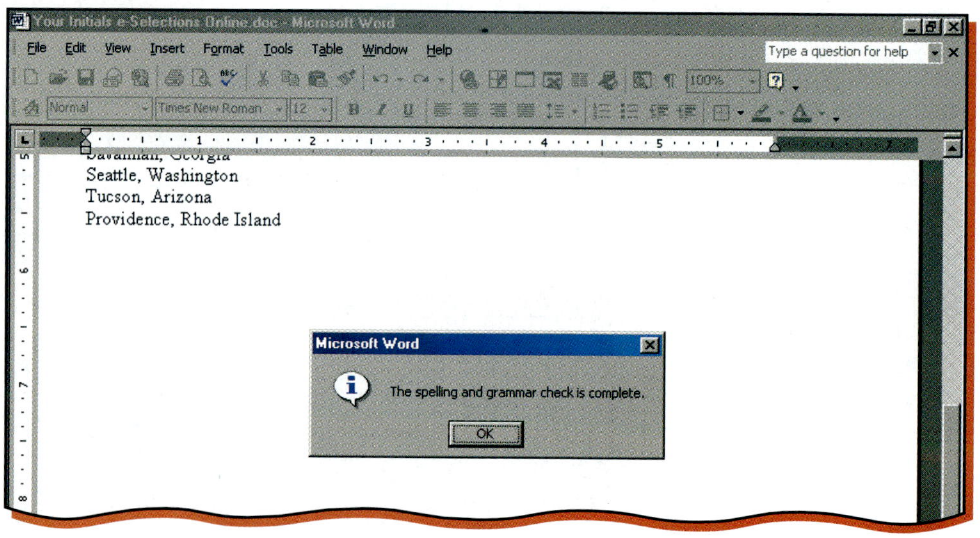

Finding and Replacing Text

The Find and Replace features enable you to locate text if it appears in a file and replace text with substitute text. These features are powerful tools for navigating and editing large files.

Task 7:
To Find and Replace Text

1. Press Ctrl + Home to position the insertion point at the top of the document and then choose **Edit | Find**. The Find and Replace dialog box opens.

2. Type **thirty-four** in the **Find what** text box and click **Find Next**.

Troubleshooting Word searches the document for the phrase beginning at the insertion point. As a result, you may find a different occurrence of the phrase.

Figure 2-22

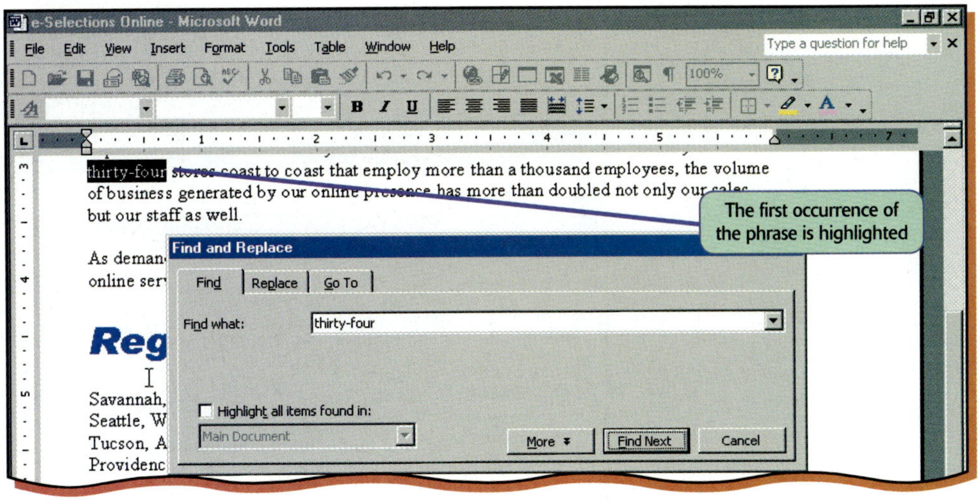

Troubleshooting In Access, the Find command is available only when an object is open. Find does not appear on the Edit menu when the database window is active.

3. Click the **Replace** tab.

4. Type **forty-one** in the **Replace with** text box and click **Replace All**. Word replaces all occurrences of the number thirty-four with the number forty-one. A message window tells you how many replacements were made.

Figure 2-23

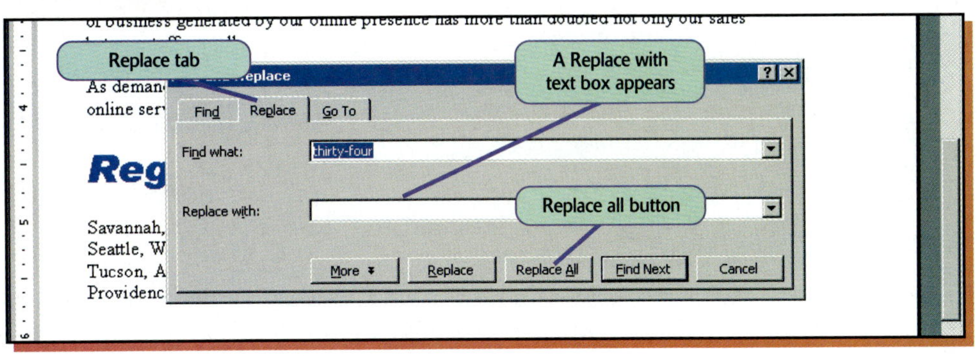

5 Click **OK**, close the dialog box, and save your changes to the document.

Figure 2-24

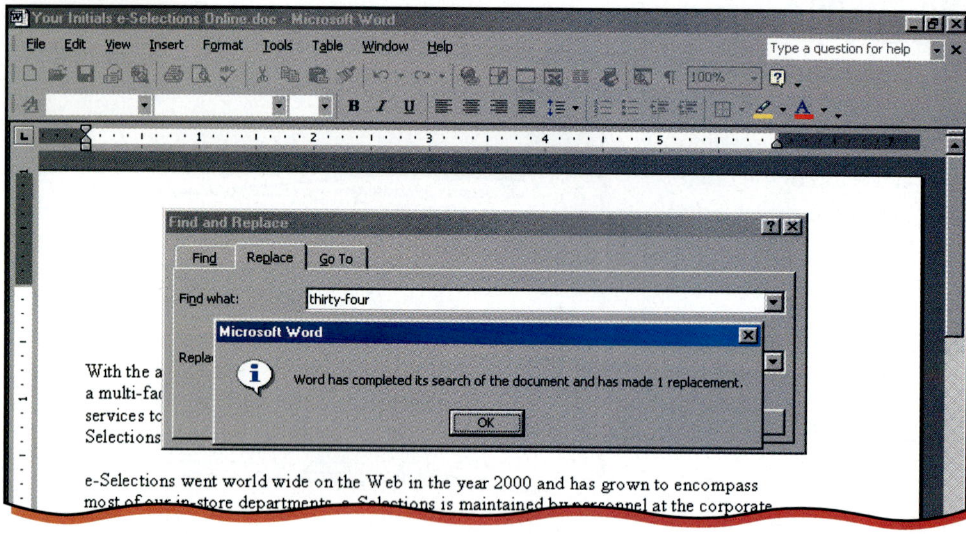

CHECK POINT

The Find command is a useful tool for locating text in the active document. But what about those times when you want to locate information contained in another file or in an e-mail message?

The **Search** command is a feature new to Office XP applications. It makes it possible to locate text contained in files stored on your computer (including all disk drives), on a network, or in an e-mail message. When you become more comfortable with the basic Find and Replace functions, you'll want to explore this new Search feature using the Microsoft documentation and online Help features.

Creating and Using AutoCorrect Entries

Each of the Office XP applications comes equipped with an *AutoCorrect* feature that is designed to automatically correct the most frequently misspelled or mistyped words. When you type *t-e-h* or *a-h-v-e*, for example, the Office application automatically changes the words to *t-h-e* and *h-a-v-e* to correct the spelling. Office comes with a built-in set of commonly mistyped words that can be edited. You can also add the words *you* most frequently mistype to the AutoCorrect list and use AutoCorrect to create entries that will substitute frequently used phrases for abbreviations. Mistyped or abbreviated text is replaced after you press the spacebar, an end-of-sentence punctuation mark, or Enter.

Task 8:
To Create AutoCorrect Entries

1. Open *e-Selections Online.doc*, if necessary.
2. Select the word *e-Selections*.
3. Choose **Tools | AutoCorrect Options** to open the AutoCorrect dialog box.

Troubleshooting The AutoCorrect entries you see may be different from those shown here.

4. Type **esel** in the **Replace** text box.
5. Click **Add**. The entry *esel* appears alphabetically on the AutoCorrect list.
6. Click **OK**. The dialog box closes.

Tip Other options that appear on the AutoCorrect page of the AutoCorrect dialog box control how Word corrects typing errors as your work. For example, you can ensure that Word automatically capitalizes the days of the week when you forget to capitalize them, have Word correct two initial capital letters at the beginning of a word, or capitalize the first letter of each sentence when you fail to do so.

Figure 2-25

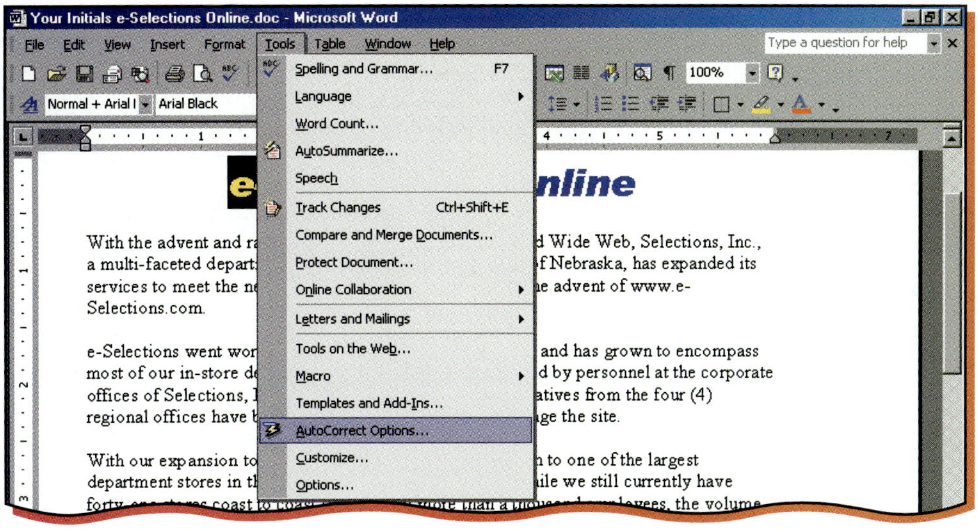

Figure 2-26

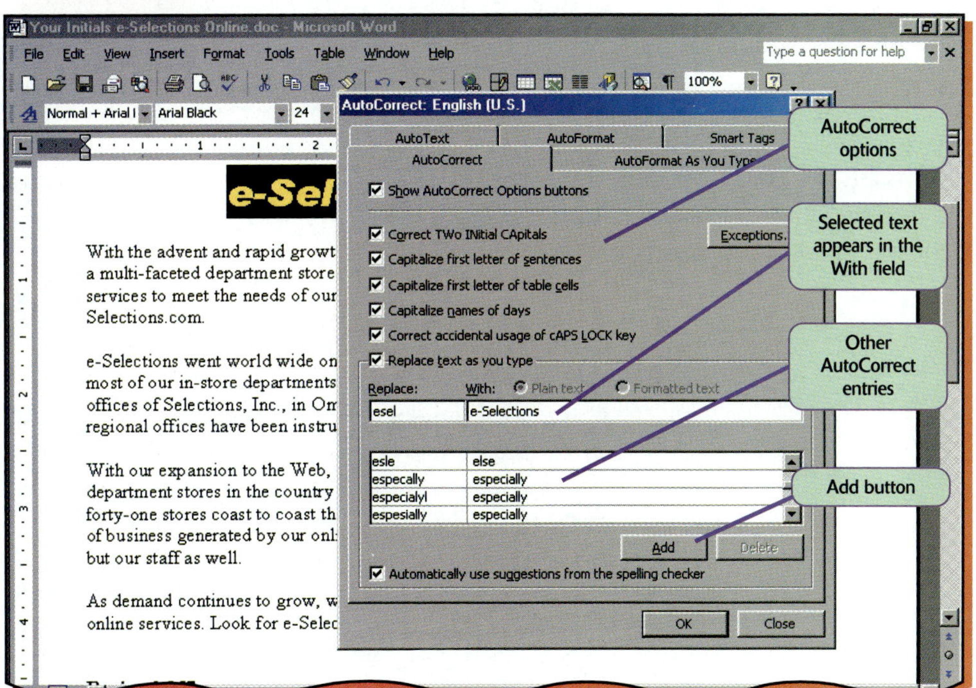

7 Move to the end of the document, press Enter twice, type **esel**, and press Spacebar. AutoCorrect expands the text and substitutes e-Selections for the abbreviation.

8 Point to the replacement text. A small blue rectangle appears below the first character of the replacement text.

9 Point to the blue rectangle.

Figure 2-27

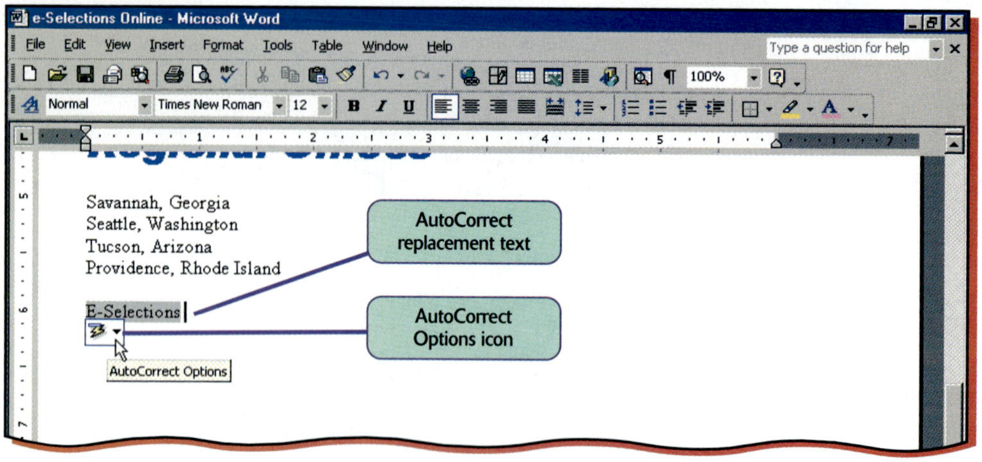

Troubleshooting The AutoCorrect Options button appears only when you point to the blue rectangle.

10 Click the **AutoCorrect Options** icon.

11 Press Esc to close the AutoCorrect Options list.

12 Delete the line added using AutoCorrect and then save the changes to the file.

Figure 2-28

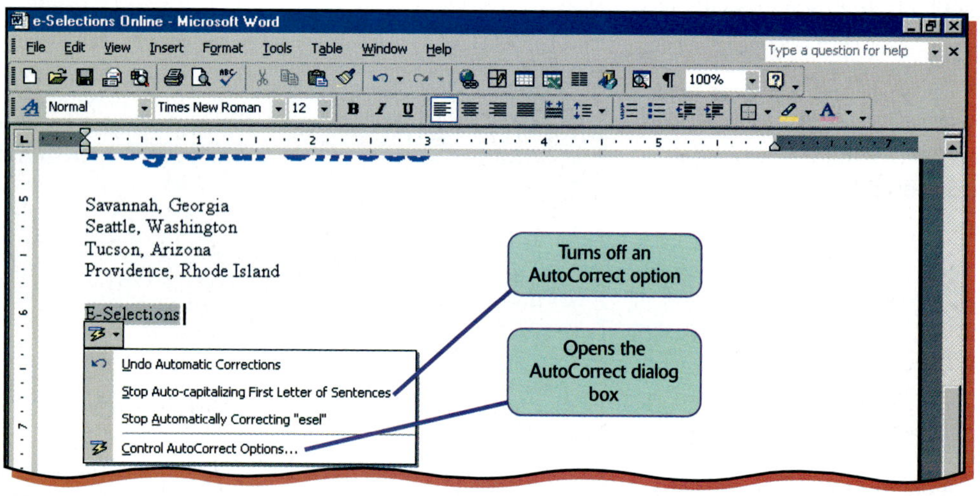

Tip Options displayed on the AutoCorrect Options list enable you to undo an AutoCorrect action, turn off the AutoCorrect entry you just typed, or set AutoCorrect Options. Additional options appear on the AutoCorrect Options list when Word takes an AutoCorrect action such as capitalizing the first word of a sentence or correcting two initial capital letters in a word.

Creating Text Boxes

Most text added to Office XP files appears within the basic file structure; between margins of documents, within cells of spreadsheets, within placeholders of presentation slides, and within database objects. Text boxes enable you to add text outside the parameters of the file structure. Text boxes are drawn on screen and text is typed within the text box. Text boxes can be repositioned within the file as needed.

Task 9:
To Create a Text Box

1 Open *e-Selections Online.doc*, if necessary, and position the insertion point at the end of the document.

2 Click the **Drawing** button on the Standard toolbar to open the Drawing toolbar at the bottom of the window.

3 Select the *Regional Offices* title and list text at the bottom of the document.

4 Click the **Text Box** tool on the Drawing toolbar. The mouse pointer changes to a crosshair pointer that looks like a plus (+) sign.

Tip The crosshair pointer is used to draw text boxes and other shapes identified in Common Elements Project 3. The center of the crosshair pointer marks the position of the box or object start point.

Figure 2-29

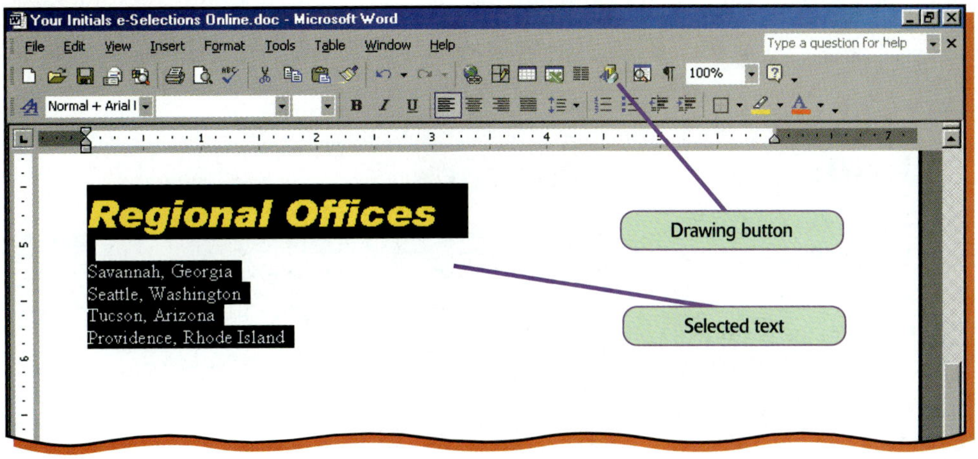

Figure 2-30

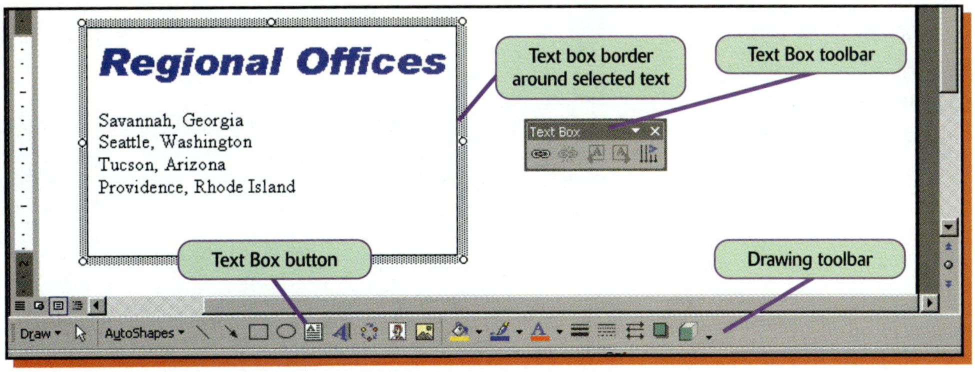

Troubleshooting In Word, a Drawing Canvas appears if you click the Text Box tool before selecting text. You can draw the text box anywhere on the document, either inside or outside the Drawing Canvas, or press Esc to close the Drawing Canvas.

Adding Text to Text Boxes and Repositioning the Text Box

You can also create a new text box and type text directly into the text box. Then change the shape and format of the text box and reposition the text box wherever you want it in the document. Document text will automatically adjust to appear around the text box.

Task 10: To Add Text to Text Boxes

1. Scroll to the bottom of the document and position the insertion point to the right of the existing text box.
2. Click the **Text Box** tool and then press Esc to close the Drawing Canvas, if necessary.
3. Position the mouse pointer on the document page where the upper left corner of the text box should be and drag the mouse diagonally to draw a second text box beside the existing text box.

Figure 2-31

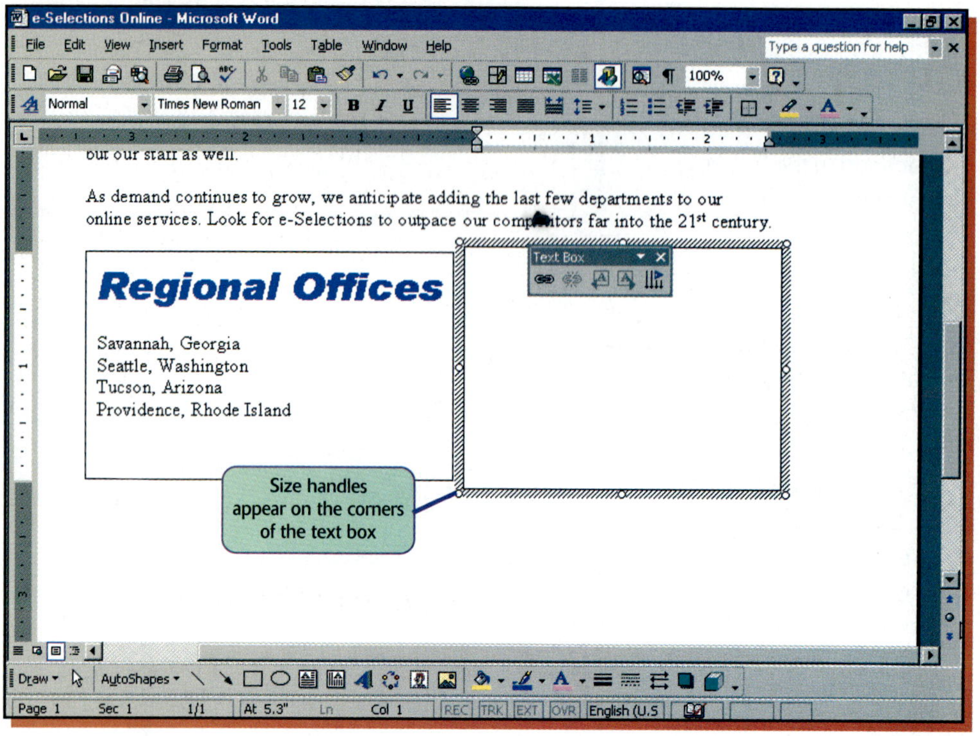

4 Type the text shown in Figure 2-32 in the new text box.

Tip Typing text in text boxes requires basically the same skills used to type text in the document outside the text boxes. Text wraps within the confines of the text box. Press Enter to start new lines when necessary.

Figure 2-32

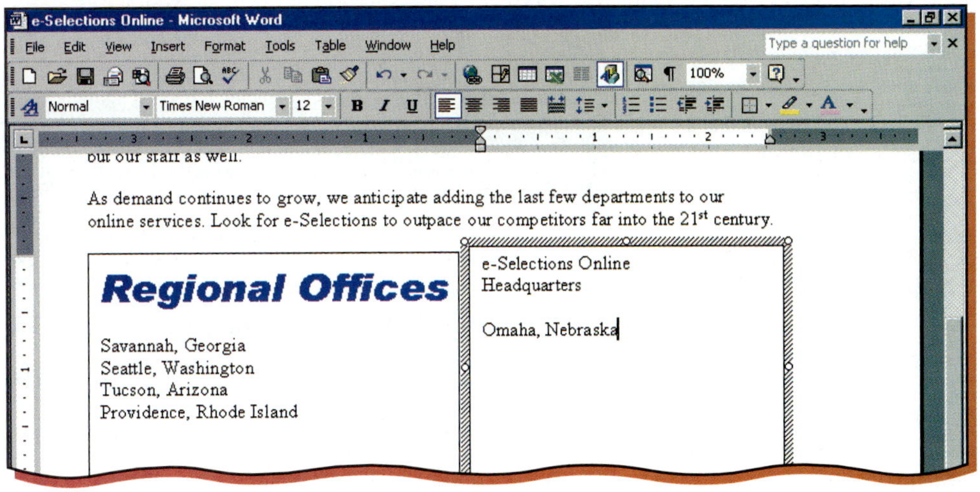

5 Copy the format from the *Regional Offices* title to the *e-Selections Online Headquarters* title using the Format Painter.

Troubleshooting If you paint the format onto the city and state shown in the text box, undo the action and try again.

Figure 2-33

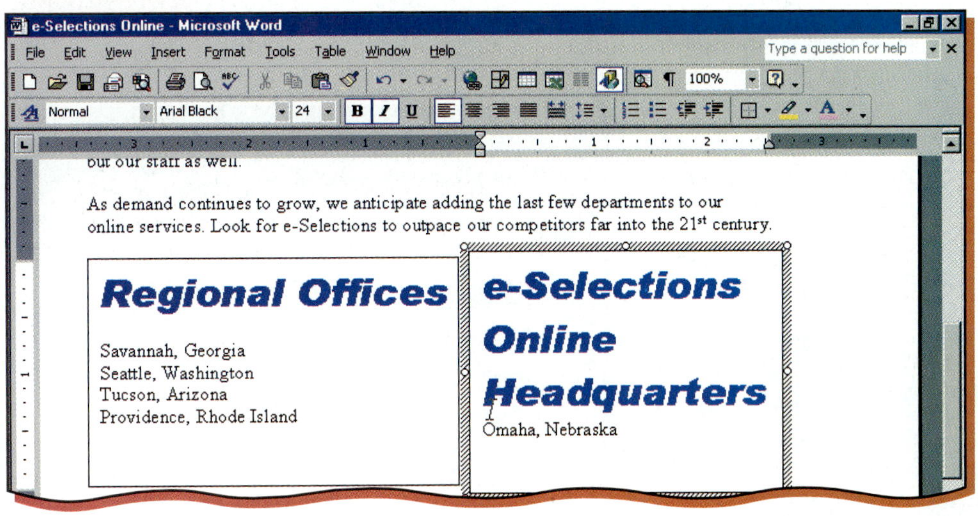

6 Select the new text box, position the mouse pointer on the lower right corner size handle, and then click and drag the handle to resize the text box as shown in Figure 2-34.

Troubleshooting If you accidentally drag the side of the text box off the page, you can undo the action and try again. It often takes several tries to get the hang of box sizing.

Figure 2-34

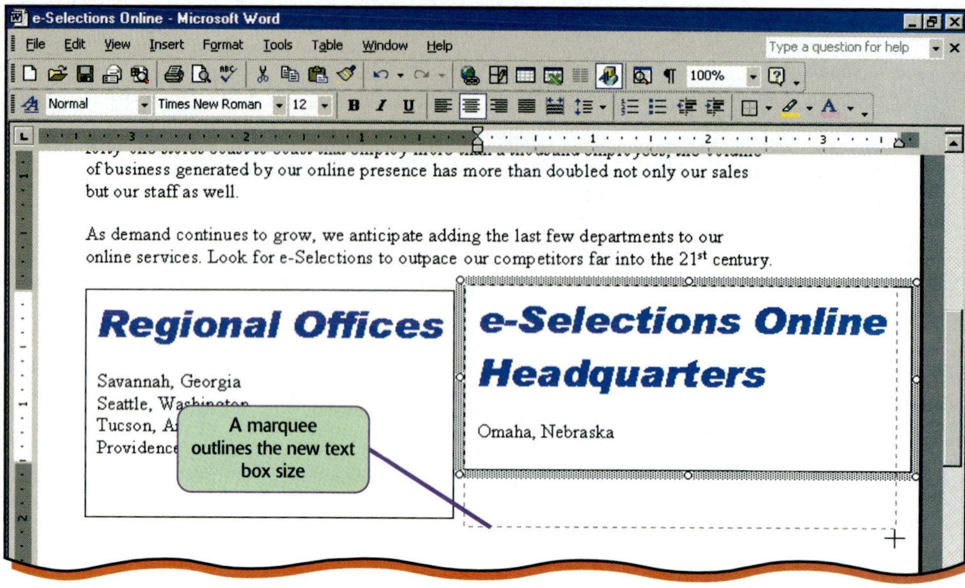

7 Press Shift and click the text box, position the insertion point on a border of the text box until you see a four-headed mouse pointer, and then click and drag the new text box to position it as shown in Figure 2-35.

Tip Pressing Shift while clicking drawn objects selects the whole object rather than positioning the insertion point in the text within the text box.

8 Right align text in the new text box and then save changes and close the file.

Figure 2-35

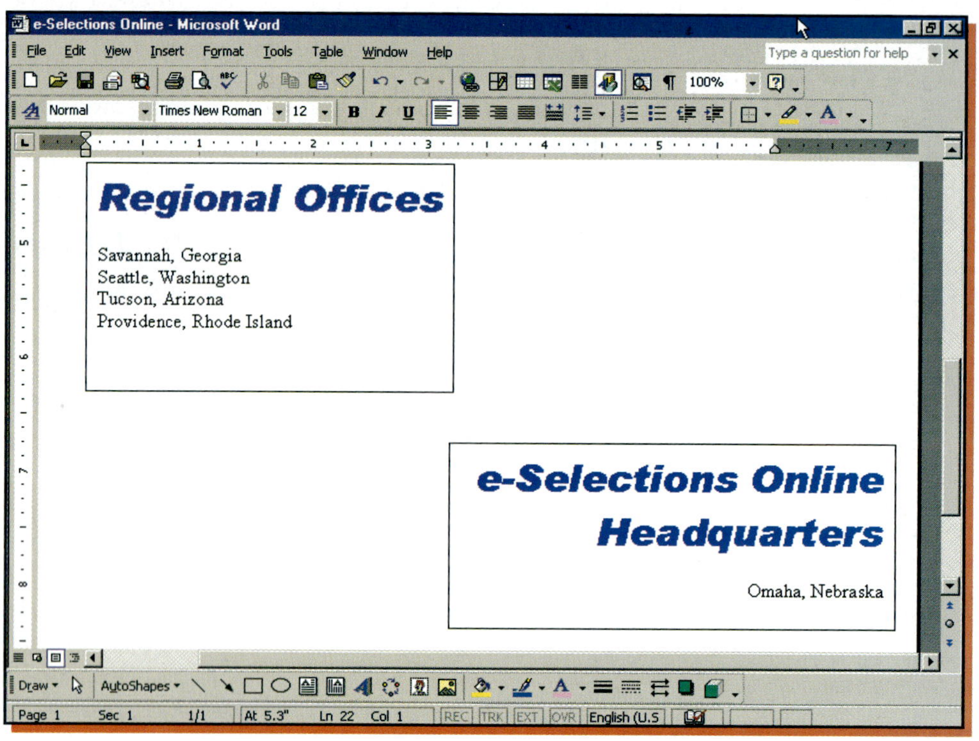

SUMMARY AND EXERCISES

SUMMARY

- Navigating text enables you to move from character to character, paragraph to paragraph, screen to screen, or page to page.
- By selecting text, you can apply enhancements to text, change fonts, or move and copy text.
- Inserting and deleting text is the same in all Office XP applications. Word enables you to switch to Overtype mode to replace text as you type.
- Enhancing and formatting text is made easy using the buttons on the Formatting toolbar.
- Text can be cut, copied, and moved within or among all Office XP applications.
- The Office Clipboard can hold up to 24 snippets of information and can be displayed at any time an Office application is open.
- Office XP makes it easy to maintain text format consistency by using Format Painter.
- Using the Undo feature enables you to reverse the last action, and using the Redo feature enables you to restore actions that were reversed using the Undo feature. In Office XP you can also reverse multiple actions.
- Text can be aligned left or right, centered, or justified on the left or right.
- Proofing tools are used to locate text, replace text, and check the spelling of text in files.
- The AutoCorrect feature corrects commonly misspelled words and enables you to enter your own words to be automatically corrected.
- Text boxes can be drawn on screen and can be used to hold text and position the text more precisely in a file.

KEY TERMS & SKILLS

KEY TERMS

align (p. 2-3)
attributes (p. 2-5)
delete (p. 2-4)
enhance (p. 2-1)
font (p. 2-5)
format (p. 2-1)
Insert mode (p. 2-4)
justify (p. 2-13)
Overtype mode (p. 2-4)
paste (p. 2-8)
Redo (p. 2-13)
replace (p. 2-4)
spelling checker (p. 2-14)
Undo (p. 2-13)

SKILLS

Add text to text boxes (p. 2-22)
Align text (p. 2-13)
Copy and move text (p. 2-9)
Copy text format (p. 2-11)
Create and use AutoCorrect (p. 2-18)
Create text boxes (p. 2-21)
Display and use the Office Clipboard (p. 2-8)
Enhance and format text (p. 2-5)
Find and replace text (p. 2-16)
Insert, delete, and replace text (p. 2-4)
Navigate text (p. 2-3)
Spelling checker used in files (p. 2-15)
Use Undo and Redo (p. 2-13)

STUDY QUESTIONS

MULTIPLE CHOICE

1. Moving from character to character, paragraph to paragraph, screen to screen, or page to page is called
a. scrolling.
b. skipping.
c. navigating.
d. keystroking.

2. You can change the appearance of text by changing the font, size, and
a. art.
b. attributes.
c. paragraph.
d. selection.

3. To move up one screen, the key that is used in all applications is
a. PrtScr.
b. ↑.
c. Ctrl + Home.
d. Page Up.

4. To move to the end of a file, press
a. End.
b. Ctrl + End.
c. PageDown.
d. none of the above

5. Which application contains numerous objects but enables text formatting in only one type of object?
   a. Word
   b. Excel
   c. Access
   d. PowerPoint

6. All of the following are text attributes, *except*
   a. font face.
   b. superscript.
   c. emboss.
   d. hidden.

7. To remove text to the left of the insertion point, press
   a. Del.
   b. Bksp.
   c. Shift + ←.
   d. Insert.

8. The feature that holds multiple snippets of information in Office XP is
   a. the Clipboard.
   b. AutoCorrect.
   c. the Office Clipboard.
   d. the shortcut menu.

9. To remove selected text from its current location, click
   a. Cut.
   b. Copy.
   c. Paste.
   d. Italic.

10. To reverse the last action, click
   a. Cut.
   b. Undo.
   c. Redo.
   d. Format Painter.

SHORT ANSWER

1. What must you do before you can apply, enhance, or change the text font of existing text?
2. List three ways to delete text.
3. Which buttons can you use to reverse the last action or selected actions?
4. List the four basic alignments that can be applied to text in Office XP applications.
5. Identify the three-step process required to copy text formats using the Format Painter.
6. What are the keyboard shortcuts for Cut, Copy, and Paste?
7. Describe the difference between right alignment and justified alignment.
8. How do you turn off the grammar checker after starting the spelling checker?
9. How does formatting text contained in text boxes differ from formatting text contained in files?
10. What menu do you access to create an AutoCorrect entry from selected text?

FILL IN THE BLANK

1. You can use the keyboard or the _____________ to move within a file.
2. _____________ mode enables you to replace existing text as you type new text in Word.
3. Double-click the _____________ button to copy a text format to multiple places.

4. Misspelled words are located and corrected using ____________.
5. After clicking the Format Painter button, the mouse pointer appears to carry a ____________.
6. The ____________ ____________ is automatically activated when you start the spelling checker.
7. ____________ can be used to store frequently used, long phrases so that you can type an abbreviation and automatically enter the expanded text.
8. The ____________ feature helps you move swiftly to a particular word or phrase in an Office XP file.
9. To be able to move text to specific positions in files, place the text in a ____________ ____________.
10. The Office Clipboard can hold ____________ pieces of information.

DISCUSSION

1. Discuss several different ways of enhancing and formatting text.
2. Discuss the advantages of placing text in text boxes rather than within document margins, within spreadsheet cells, or in other locations.
3. Identify the different ways that the Office Clipboard can be used and how the Office Clipboard is accessed.

GUIDED EXERCISES

1 FORMATTING TEXT AND CREATING TEXT BOXES

Figure 2-36 contains two text boxes that appear side by side on the document page.

Figure 2-36

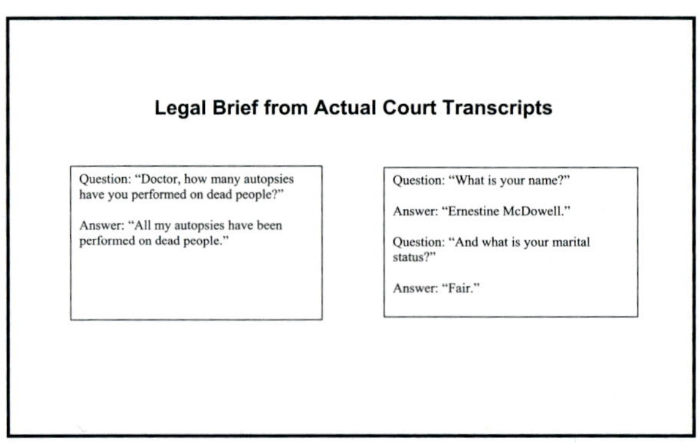

To ensure that the text boxes are the same size, you can create the first text box and then copy it before adding text to the text boxes. To create the text boxes, follow these steps.

1. Launch Word, if necessary, and create a new blank document.
2. Change the Zoom setting to **Page Width**.

3 Create the title:

- Type the title text **Legal Brief from Actual Court Transcripts.**
- Center the title.
- Format the title text using an Arial 18-point type.

4 Display the Drawing toolbar and create a new text box on the left side of the document, ensuring that the text box does not extend beyond the approximate center point on the page.

5 Press Shift and click the text box border to select it.

6 Copy the first text box:

- Click the **Copy** button.
- Click the white area on screen to clear the existing text box.

Troubleshooting If the text box remains selected, the new text box will appear within the existing text box when you paste.

- Click the **Paste** button to paste a second text box on the screen.
- Drag the copy of the text box so that it appears to the right of the first text box and align the text boxes as precisely as possible.

7 Click inside the text box on the left and type the following text:

Question: "Doctor, how many autopsies have you performed on dead people?"

Answer: "All my autopsies have been performed on dead people."

8 Click inside the text box on the right and type the following text:

Question: "What is your name?"
Answer: "Ernestine McDowell."

Question: "And what is your marital status?"
Answer: "Fair."

9 Save the document using the file name *Legal Briefs*, print a copy of the document, and then close the file.

2 CREATING AN AUTOCORRECT ENTRY

One of the most effective uses of AutoCorrect is to expand your name by simply typing your initials. Follow these instructions to create an AutoCorrect entry that enters your name.

1. Launch Word, if necessary, and create a new blank document.
2. Type *Your Name* at the top of the document and then select *Your Name*.
3. Choose **Tools** | **AutoCorrect Options** and type *Your Initials* in the **Replace** field; click OK.
4. Press Enter and then type *Your Initials* followed by the Spacebar to test your AutoCorrect entry.
5. Close the file without saving it.

WEB TIP

Government Web addresses generally have a .gov extension. Search for Government Web sites to locate the official site for the Interagency Fire Center.

ON YOUR OWN

The difficulty of these case studies varies:
are the least difficult; *are more difficult; and* *are the most difficult.*

1 FORMATTING TEXT

Open the file Fire Center. Format text contained in the file as follows:

- Title: 18 point Arial, Small Caps, centered
- Bulleted list: 14 point Arial

Replace the text Your Name at the bottom of the file by typing *Your Name* and then right align the text. Check the spelling in the file. Save the file using the file name Your Initials Fire Center.

2 ADDING A TEXT BOX TO AN EXISTING FILE

Open the file *Fire Center* (Substitute *Your Initials Fire Center* if you completed On Your Own Exercise 1) and add the following text to a new text box below the bulleted list:

Visit the National Interagency Fire Center Online.

Center the text, change the font size to 17 points, and format the text using Arial font. Then print a copy of the file and save changes to the file using the file name *Your Initials Fire Center*.

3 CREATING A FUN NOTICE

Create the notice shown in Figure 2-37 using a font and font size similar to the font shown in the figure. Save the file using the file name *Phantom Ghost*, print a copy of the document, and then close the document.

Figure 2-37

Good . . . Evening!

If you do not wish a curse on this house,
you must make two treats
and deliver them to two houses
in the neighborhood.
You have only two days.
Post the picture of the Phantom Ghost on
your door 'til Halloween.
This will ward off any other phantoms
that may visit!

Copy this letter and the Phantom Ghost
twice and give it with treats
to two homes that do not have
a Phantom Ghost posted.

Share the Spirit!
Have a Happy Halloween!

FROM THE FILES

You Will Need

- ✔ e-Selections Online Graphics.doc
- ✔ e-Selections Logo.jpg
- ✔ Stars.wmf
- ✔ Phantom Ghosties.doc

PROJECT 3

Common Graphics Elements

Adding art to Office XP files dresses them up and makes them more inviting. Each Office XP application offers such a wide variety of methods for adding art to your files that it's sometimes difficult to decide which feature to use. You can add *clip art* images, *scanned images*, picture files, *WordArt*, and manual drawings to files in all Office XP applications. Each art type has a complete set of tools for editing and manipulating the art object. As a result, this project is designed to get you started on your artistic journey—you can explore the features that you will need to use the most on your own.

e-selections Running Case

With the advent of e-Selections.com, managers plan to start publishing information from different Office applications on the Web site. The graphics design specialist assigned to e-Selections.com has asked you to explore some of the graphics capabilities available in Office XP applications so that these capabilities can be reported to those who are in charge of the different e-Selections.com divisions. You will begin your explorations using Word.

OBJECTIVES

After completing this project, you will be able to:

- *Insert and edit clip art*
- *Display the Clip Organizer*
- *Insert graphic images*
- *Create and format WordArt*
- *Create and manipulate drawings*

PROJECT 3

Common Graphics Elements

The Challenge

As you explore the Internet and specific Web pages, you will notice that graphics have been used extensively to create Web page designs. As you begin working with Office XP applications, you will be expected to know how to add graphics and drawings to the files you create using the different applications.

The Solution

Office XP applications share many of the same graphics and art elements. As a result, introducing the basic concepts of adding art images and drawing provides a base on which to build additional skills as you move through the different applications. Because you are already more familiar with Word than any of the other Office XP applications, you will continue to use Word as you develop your artistic talents.

Troubleshooting Be sure to review the setup section of Common Elements Project 2 for screen features and other settings that affect this project.

Working with Clip Art

All Office XP applications share a common *Clip Organizer* that contains a variety of different images that you can add to files. The first time you access the Clip Organizer, the Office XP application takes a few moments to build the gallery and then presents *thumbnails*—very small copies—of the images.

Inserting Clip Art Images

Clip art images appear at the insertion point when you add them to most Office XP files. After you get the image in the file, you can position and size the image so that it appears in the file where you want it.

Task 1:
To Insert Clip Art Images

1 Launch Word, if necessary, and create a new blank document.

2 Choose **Insert | Picture | Clip Art** to open the Insert Clip Art task pane.

Figure 3-1

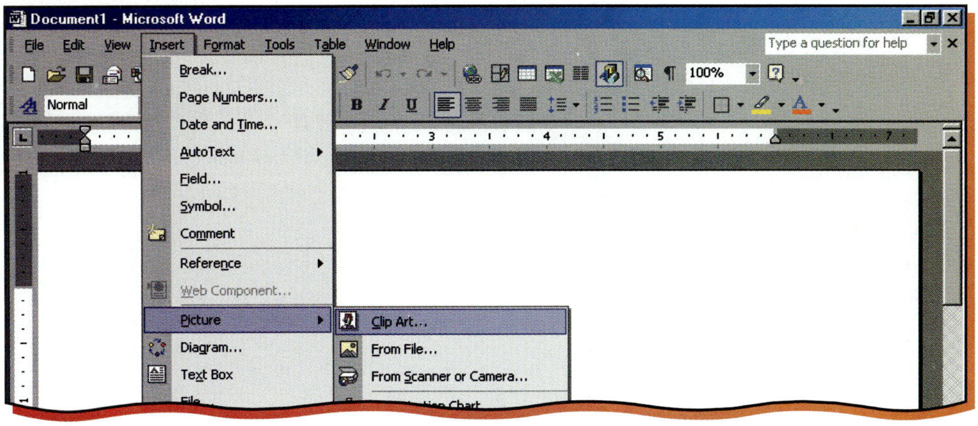

3 Type **People** in the **Search text** box and click **Search**.

Troubleshooting
Depending on the clip art that is installed on your computer, the graphics you see may be different from those displayed here.

Figure 3-2

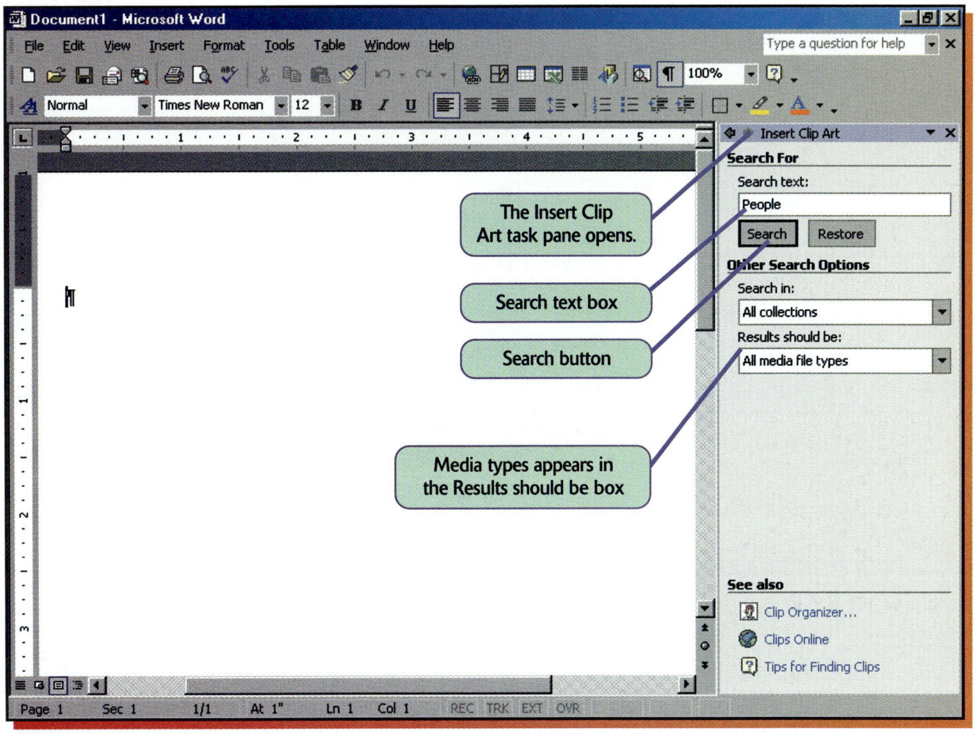

Tip
If Office XP has been installed more than one time on your computer, it is possible that you will see two sets of the same clip art images. If a previous version of Microsoft Office has been upgraded to Office XP, some image duplication may occur.

4 Point to one of the thumbnail images.

Troubleshooting

Screen tips may require several seconds to appear when you point to an image. Be careful to hold the mouse pointer still to see the screen tip.

Figure 3-3

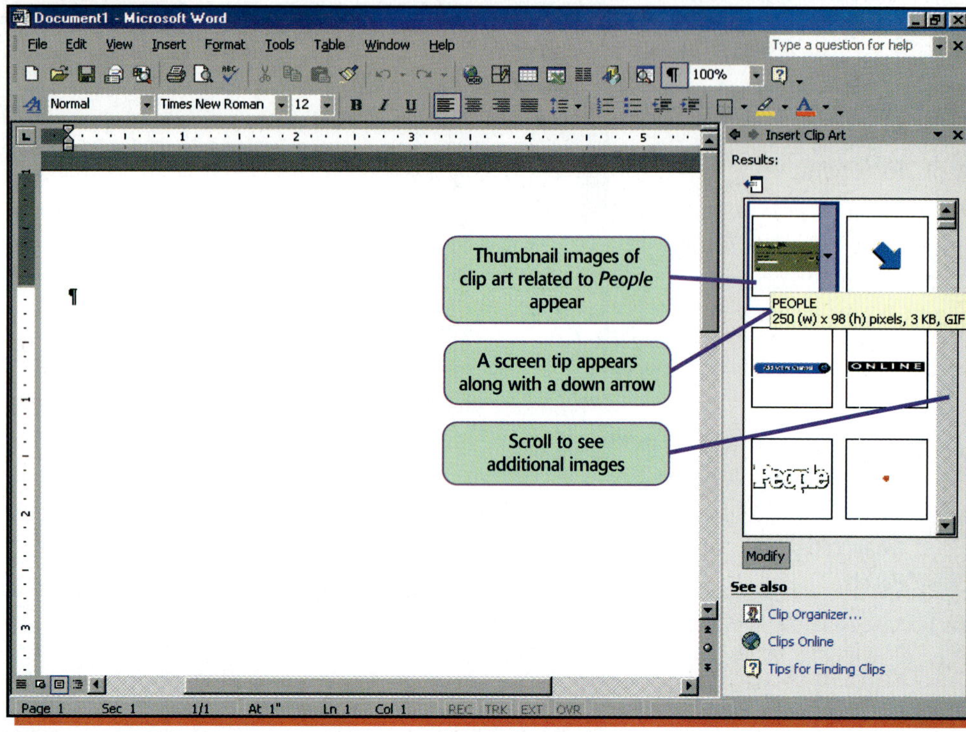

5 Scroll to locate the image of the golfer similar to the image shown in Figure 3-4.

Tip

The down arrow appears on the right side of the image to which you are pointing. Other images will not display a down arrow.

Figure 3-4

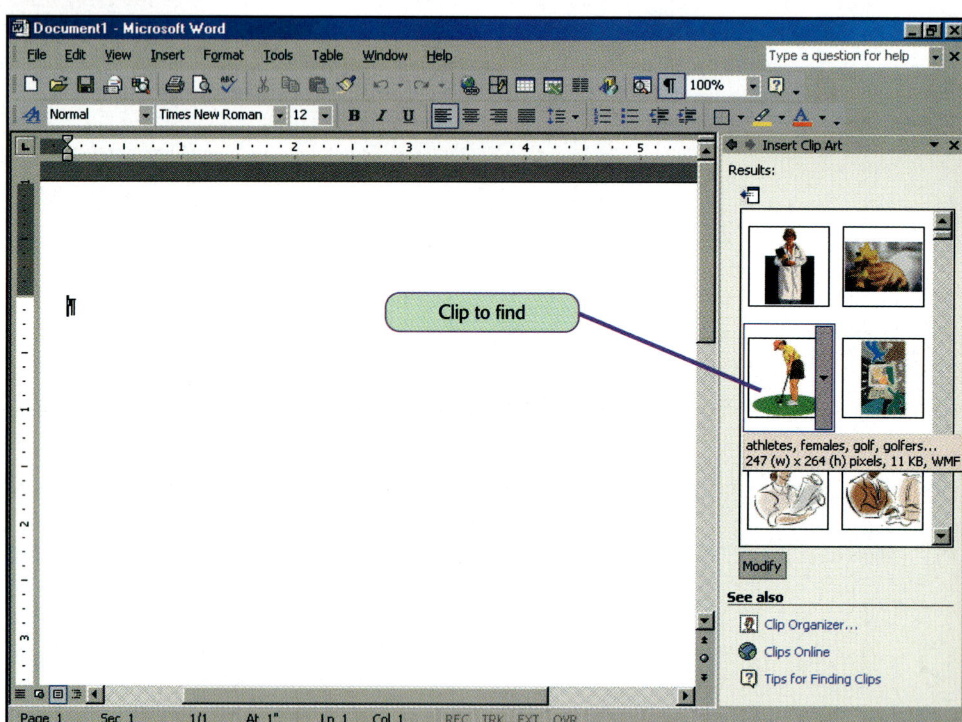

6 Click the thumbnail image in the task pane and save your file using the name *Your Initials Golfing.*

7 Close the task pane.

Tip When you close the task pane, the image will appear slightly larger.

Troubleshooting
Clip art image size and position may appear distorted in Normal view. To view the images in better format, choose **View | Print Layout.**

Figure 3-5

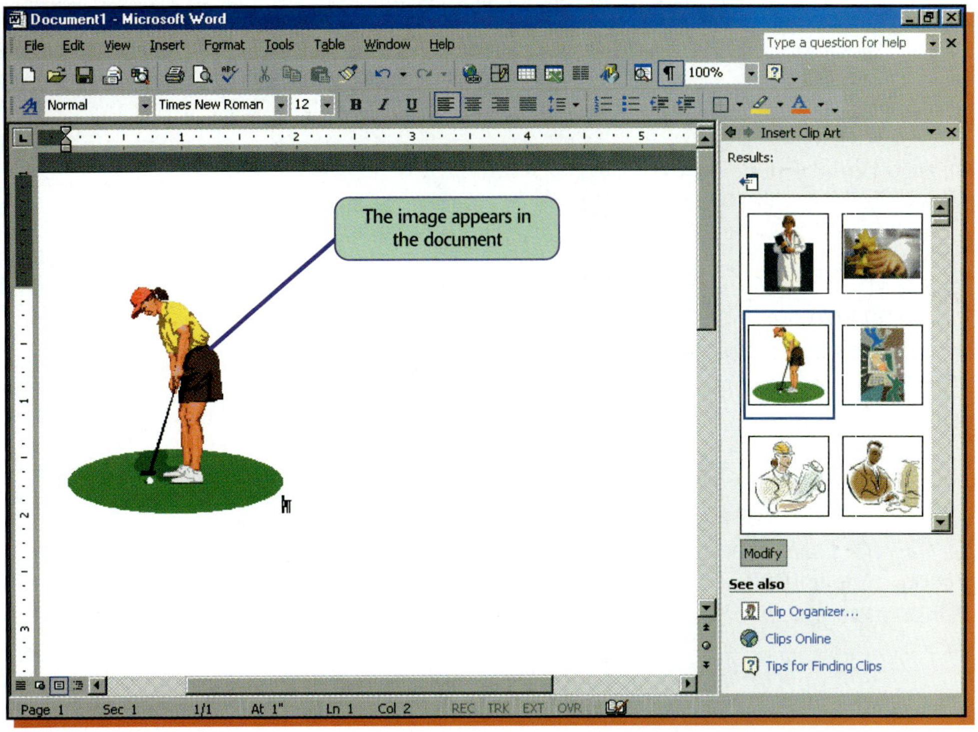

WEB TIP

The Internet is a great source for locating clip art to add to your files. You can search for sites containing clip art and download clips. In addition, Microsoft has set up a special site from which users can download new clips. Access the Microsoft Design Gallery Live from the task pane by clicking the Clips Online link or display the Clip Organizer and click the Clips Online toolbar button.

Tip Before you can move or size a clip art image that appears on a document, you must select it. The easiest way to select an image is to click it.

Moving and Sizing Clip Art Images

After you insert a clip art image into a file, you can size the image so that it fits the space you want it to occupy and move the image to position it more precisely. However, before you can move most clip art images, you have to change the image layout settings.

Task 2:

To Move and Size Clip Art Images

1 Launch Word and open the *Your Initials Golfing.doc* document, if necessary.

2 Click the golfer image and then position the insertion point on the black square in the lower right corner of the image.

Troubleshooting

If the rulers are hidden, choose **View | Ruler** to display them.

Figure 3-6

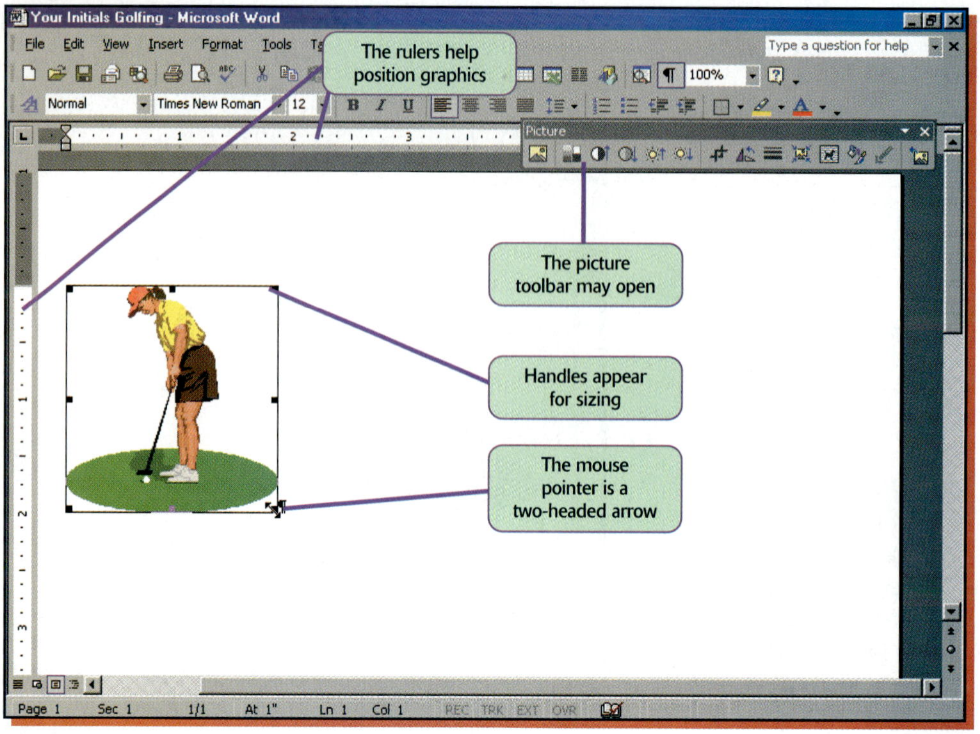

3 Drag the corner handle until the right edge of the graphic appears at about the 4" mark on the horizontal ruler and to about the 4 1/2" mark on the vertical ruler.

4 Point to the center of the selected image and right-click. The shortcut menu appears.

5 Select **Format Picture**. The Format Object dialog box appears.

Figure 3-7

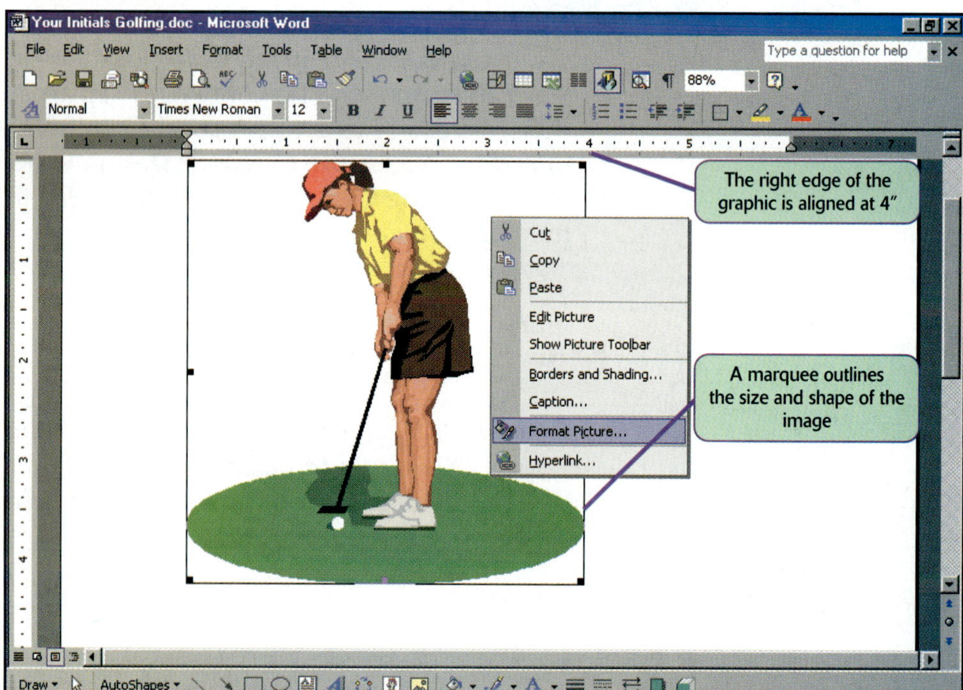

Tip

Options available in the Format Object dialog box vary depending on the type of object that is active. In addition, the page of the dialog box that appears is controlled, to some extent, by the type of object selected.

6 Click the **Layout** tab.

7 Select **Square** and then click **Advanced** to display the Advanced Layout dialog box.

Tip The default layout places clip art images and other pictures in line with text. In this case, it lines up the image at the left margin because text in the document is left-aligned by default.

Figure 3-8

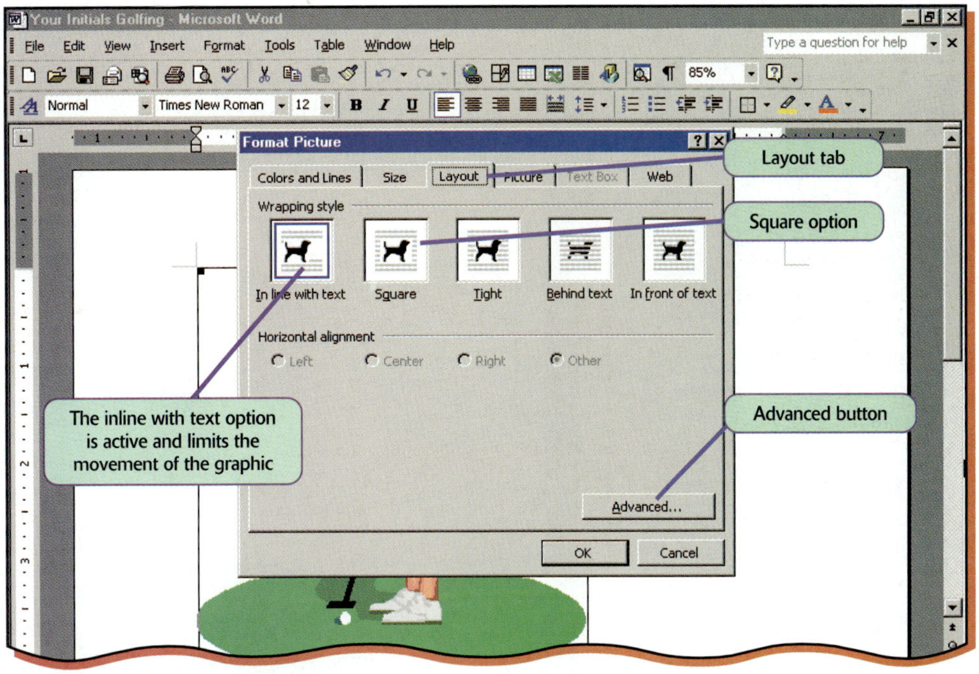

8 Clear the **Move object with text** option and click **OK** twice.

Tip Word normally attaches clip art you add to files to the text in the paragraph closest to the image. In this document, the picture is attached to the empty paragraph marker that appears on each new blank document you create. Because the paragraph is left-aligned, the clip art image appears left-aligned. Clearing the Move object with text option removes the invisible connection between the clip art image and the paragraph so that you can position the image anywhere on the page.

Figure 3-9

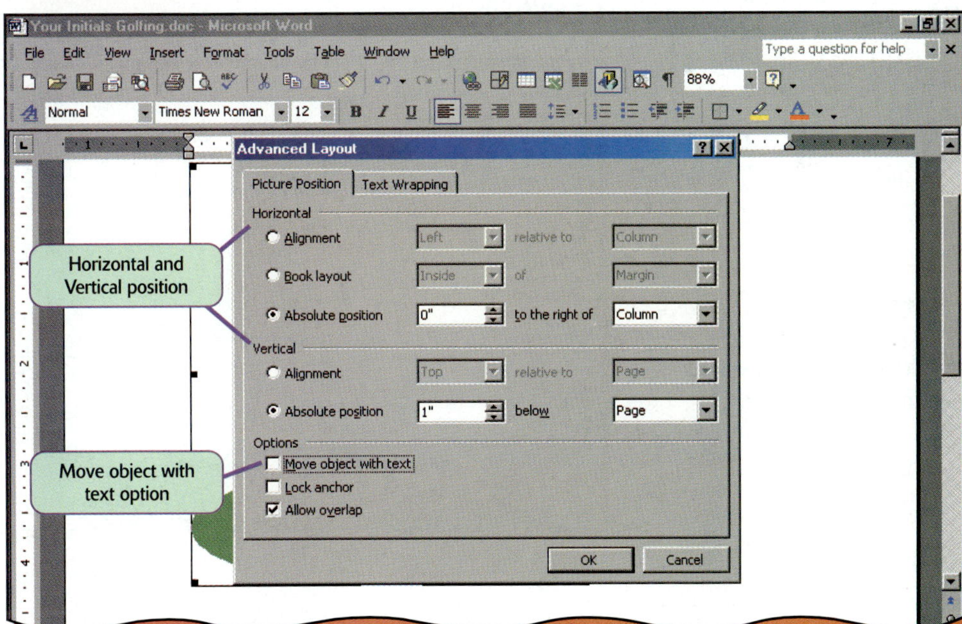

9 Point to the center of the image and click.

Tip Most clip art images can be rotated freely to position them at just the angle you want to display. To rotate an image, position the mouse pointer on the green circle that appears above the image. When you see a circular black arrow as the mouse pointer, drag the green circle to rotate the image.

Figure 3-10

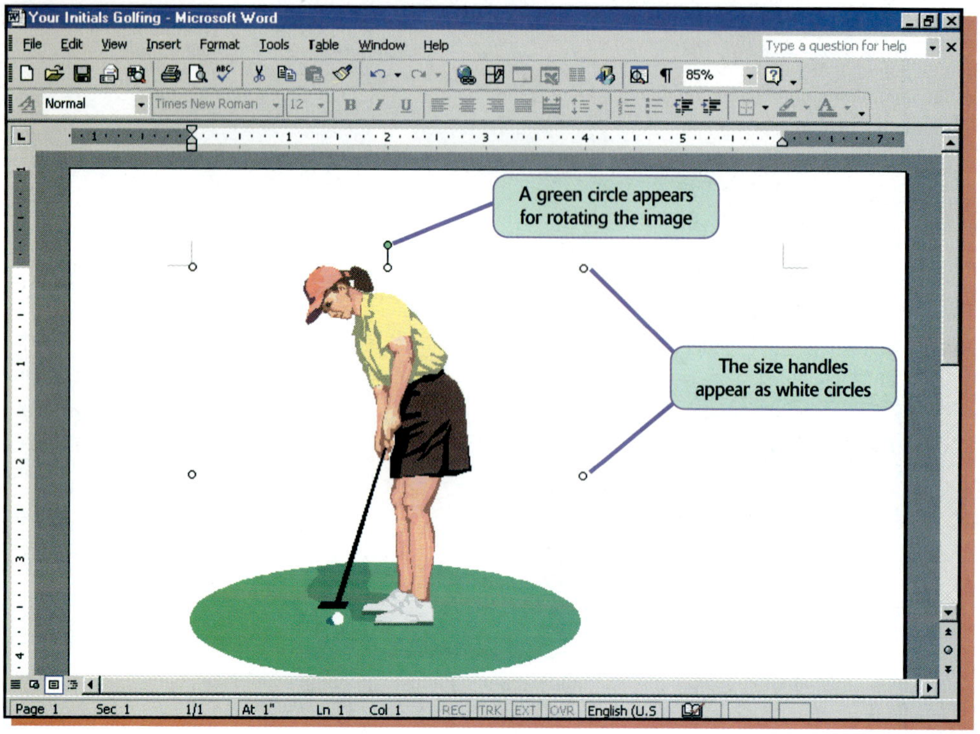

10 Drag the picture to a different location on the page.

11 Save changes to the file.

Troubleshooting Be sure to position the mouse pointer in the middle of the figure you want to move rather than on a sizing handle. Dragging a size handle changes the figure size but leaves the left edge of the figure in its original position.

Figure 3-11

Manipulating Clip Art Images

The white handles that appear on clip art images can be used to size the image, just as the black squares were used to adjust the image layout. After the image layout is adjusted so that you can move the graphic, the Rotate tool enables you to change the angle of the graphic. Clip art images can also be ungrouped so that different parts of the image can be edited, regrouped, flipped, and rotated.

Task 3:
To Ungroup Clip Art Images

1 Launch Word and open the *Your Initials Golfing.doc* document, if necessary.

2 Select the clip art image and click the **Drawing** button on the Standard toolbar.

> **Tip** The Drawing button on the Standard toolbar opens the Drawing toolbar. The Drawing toolbar appears anchored at the bottom of the Word window by default. However, you can float or reposition the toolbar just as you can other toolbars.

3 Click the **Draw** Draw button on the Drawing toolbar to display the Draw menu.

4 Click **Ungroup** to break the image into individual pieces.

Figure 3-12

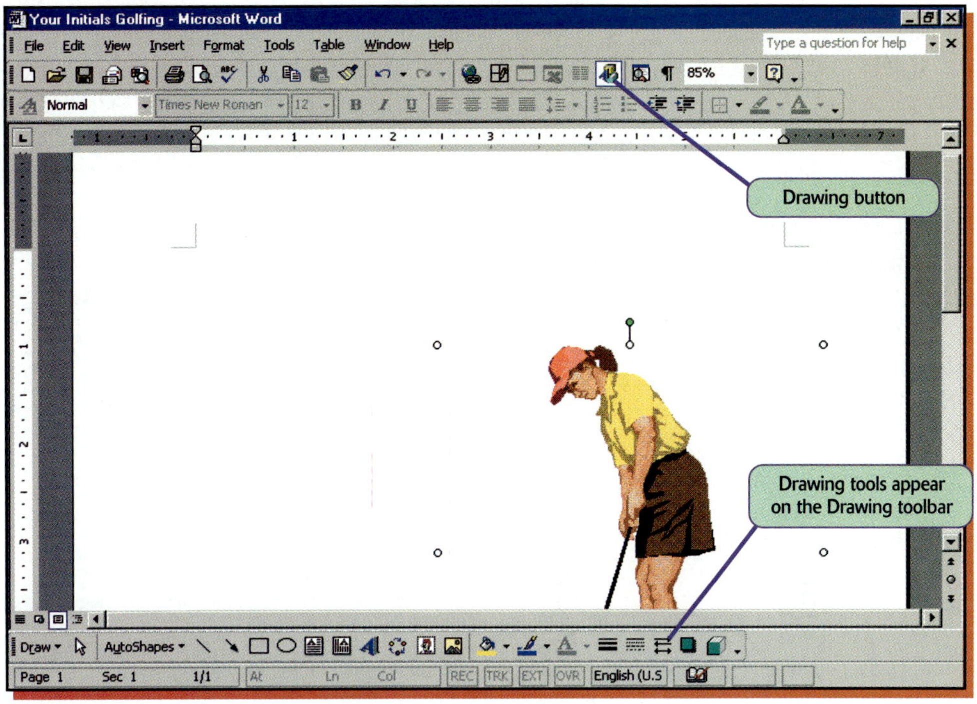

Figure 3-13

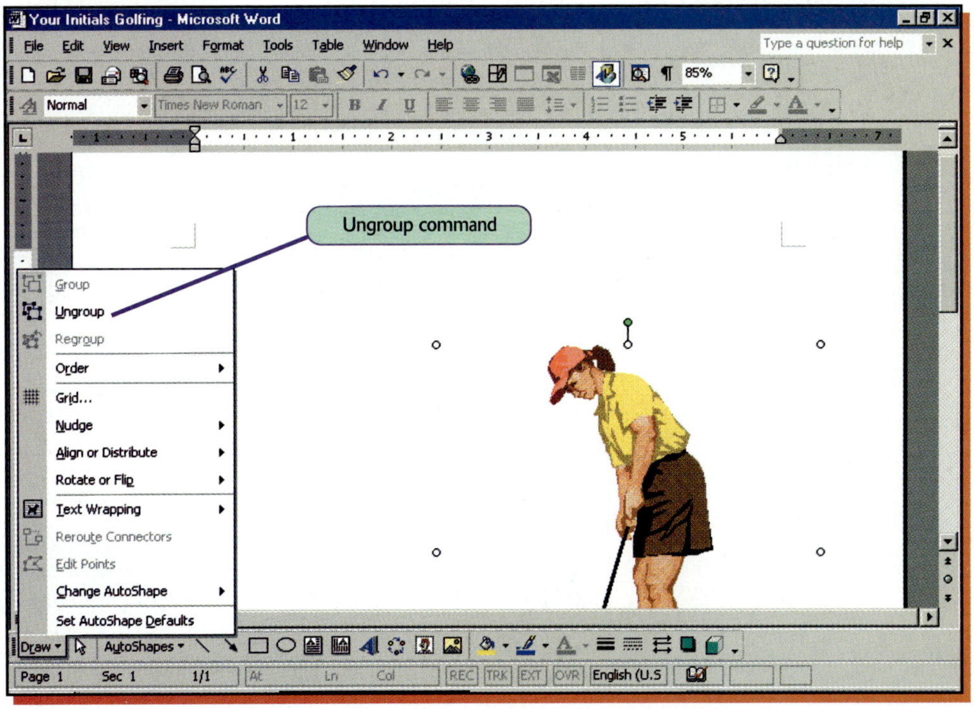

Tip

Each clip art image is compiled of numerous lines and shapes grouped together so that you can move and size the whole image. To change the color of a piece of the image, you must first ungroup it. When you ungroup a clip art image, handles appear on all the individual pieces that make up the image. In some cases, an image is made up of smaller groups images that can also be ungrouped.

5. Click **Yes** to convert the image to an Office object.

Figure 3-14

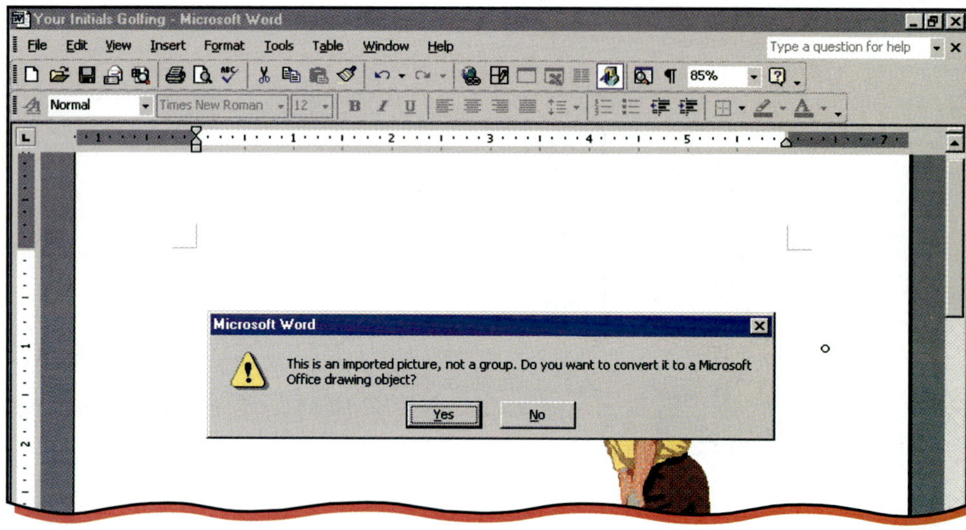

Tip

Right-click on the Canvas edge and select **Show Drawing Canvas Toolbar**, if necessary, to display the *Drawing Canvas* toolbar.

6. Save changes to your work.

Figure 3-15

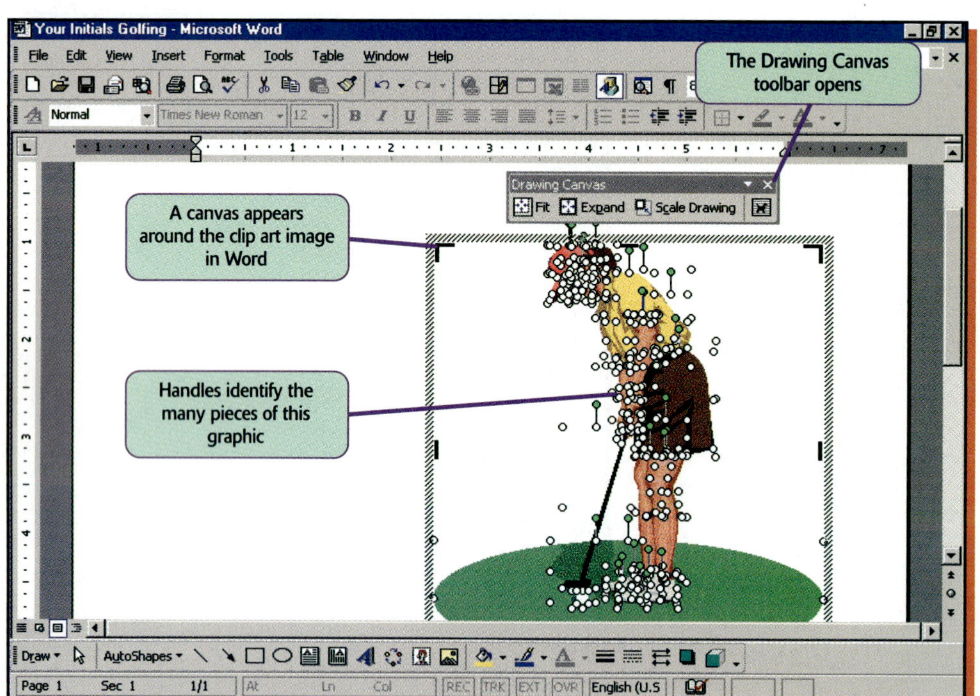

Task 4:
To Edit Clip Art Images

1. Click a white area away from the selected pieces, but inside the canvas border. All selection handles disappear.

2. Click the golfer's shorts to select the individual piece of the graphic.

3. Click the **Fill Color** down arrow on the Drawing toolbar and select the **Red** fill color. The shorts change color.

4. Click the **Expand** button on the Drawing Canvas toolbar two or three times to move the canvas border away from all parts of the graphic.

5. Position the mouse pointer below and to the right of the putting green, and then drag a marquee around all pieces of the clip art image.

6. Choose **Draw | Group** on the Drawing toolbar. The clip art image is reformed to a single object.

Figure 3-16

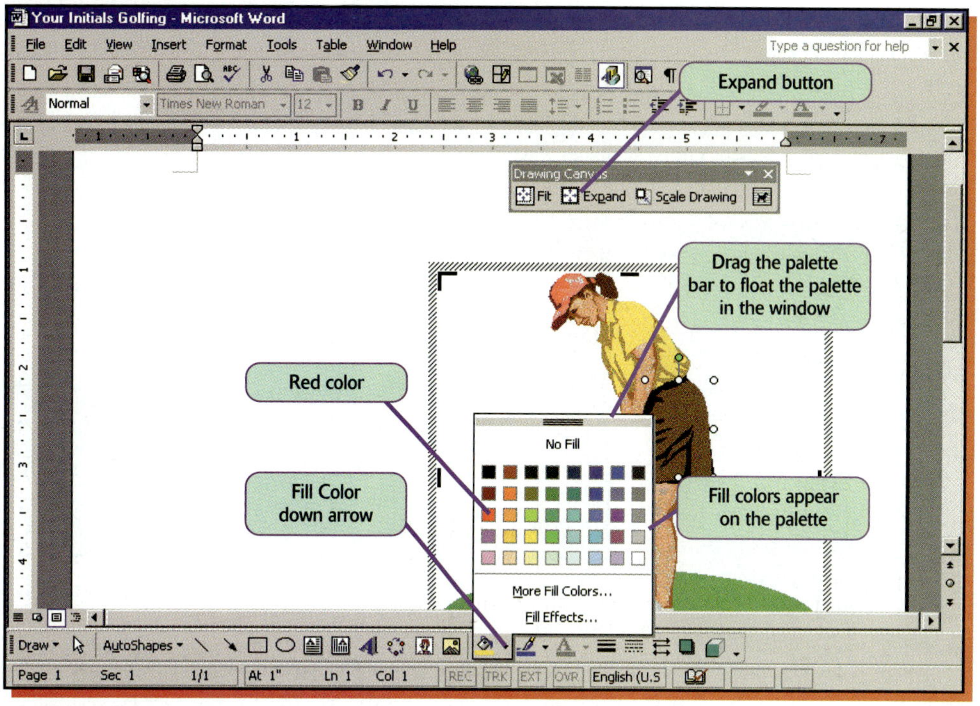

Figure 3-17

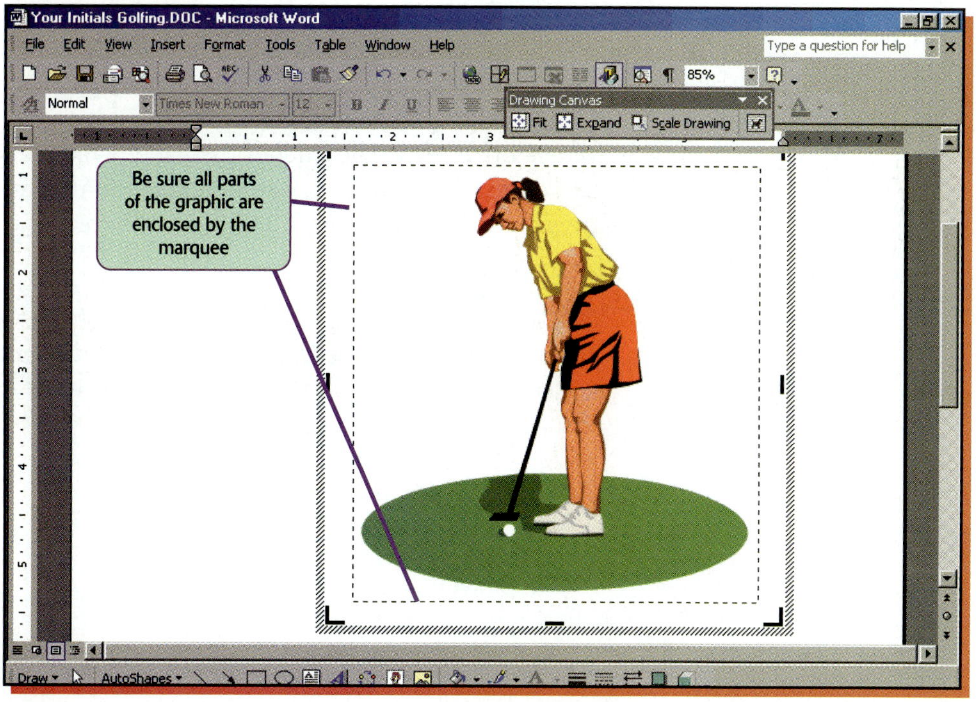

Troubleshooting The Drawing Canvas is a feature unique to Word. As you work with clip art in other applications, you will not see the Drawing Canvas.

7 Choose **Draw | Rotate or Flip | Flip Horizontal**. The golfer faces the opposite direction.

8 Save changes to your work and close the file.

> **Tip** Design specialists often recommend that clip art and pictures added to documents be positioned so that they face toward the middle of the page. Flipping a clip art image is a great way to make the image conform to good design recommendations.

Figure 3-18

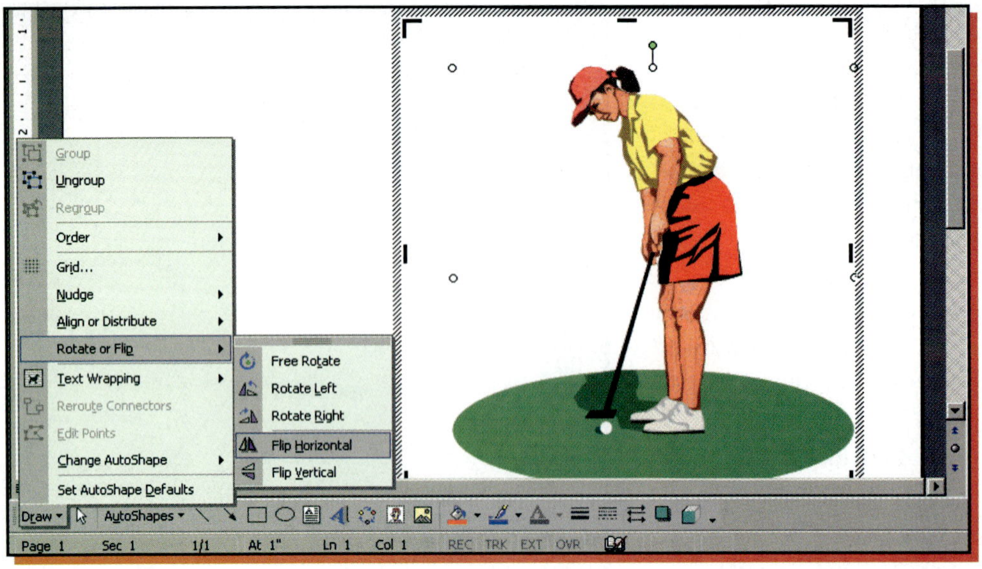

Displaying the Clip Organizer

In the previous tasks, you have worked with clip art that you inserted from the task pane. The Clip Organizer displays a list of folders containing the clip art that is available on your computer as well as other media clips, such as movies, sounds, and so forth. Images are grouped by type and placed in appropriate folders. Opening the folder related to the topic you are addressing displays thumbnails of the clip art that is available in the folder. Until you add images to the Favorites folder and download graphics from other sources, many of the folders are empty. The images displayed when you searched for banner clips are part of a set of standard clip art images that come with Office XP. These images are grouped by type into numerous folders in the Office Collection.

CHECK POINT

Do you recall how you displayed clips in the task pane that relate to a specific topic? You typed the topic in the search box and then clicked Search.

Task 5:

To Display and Use the Clip Organizer

1 Launch Word, if necessary, and create a new blank document.

2 Choose **Insert | Picture | Clip Art**. The task pane opens.

3 Click the **Clip Organizer** link at the bottom of the task pane.

> **Troubleshooting**
> If this is the first time the Clip Organizer has been started on your machine, a Microsoft Clip Organizer message may appear. Check the **Don't show this message again** option and click **OK**. The system will build the Clip Organizer for you.

4 Click the **Expansion** button beside the **Office Collections** folder to display collection subfolders.

Figure 3-19

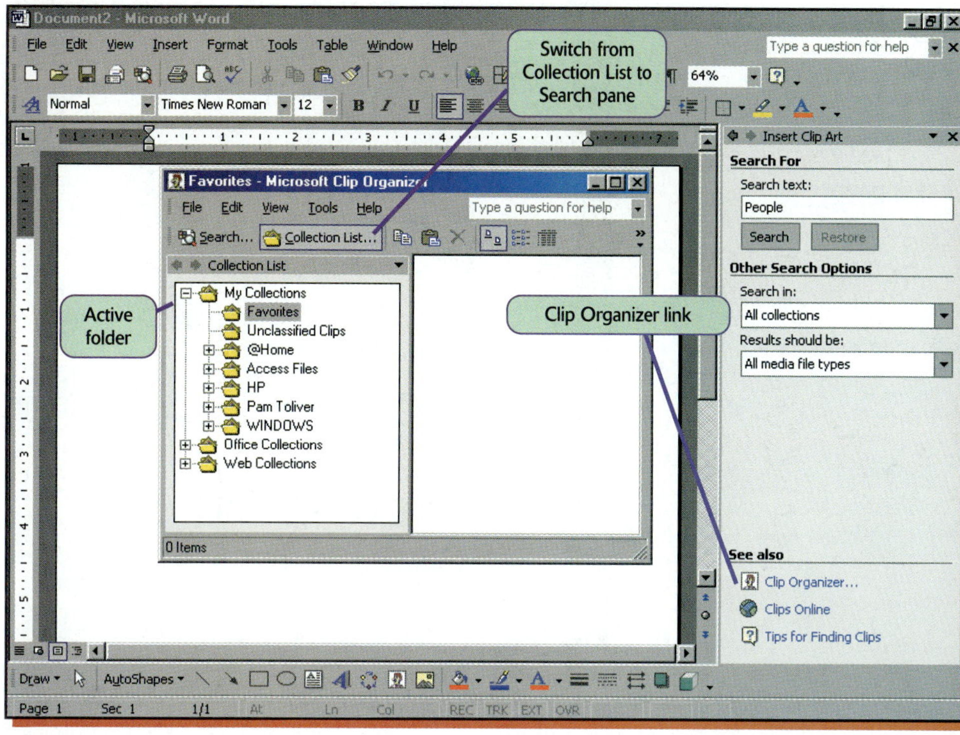

Figure 3-20

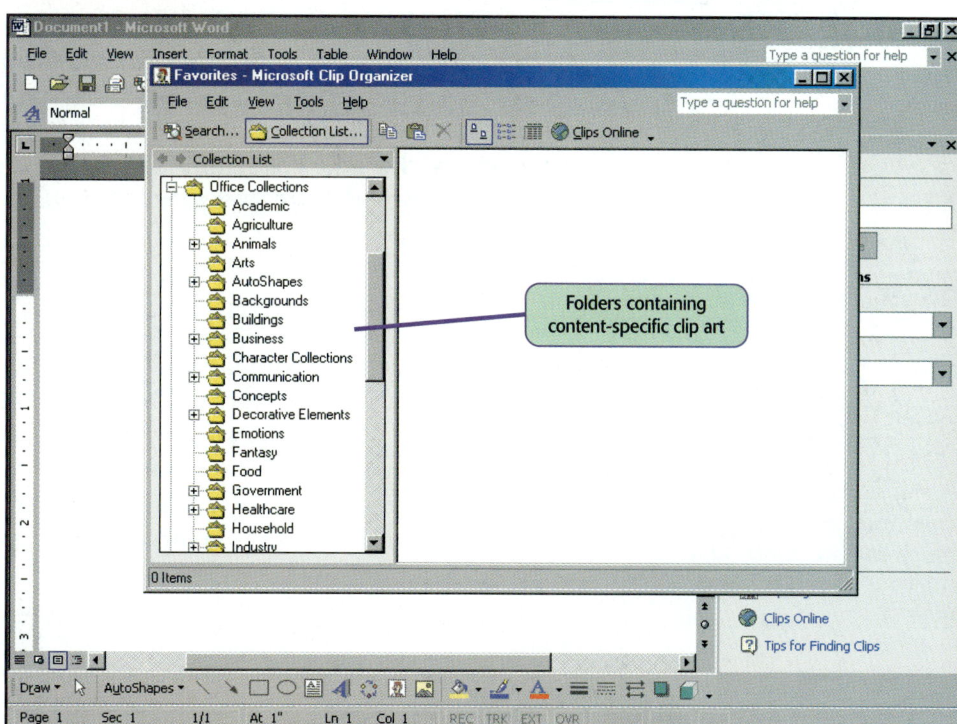

5 Select **Buildings** to open the folder and display thumbnail images contained in the folder.

6 Close the Clip Organizer and close the task pane.

Figure 3-21

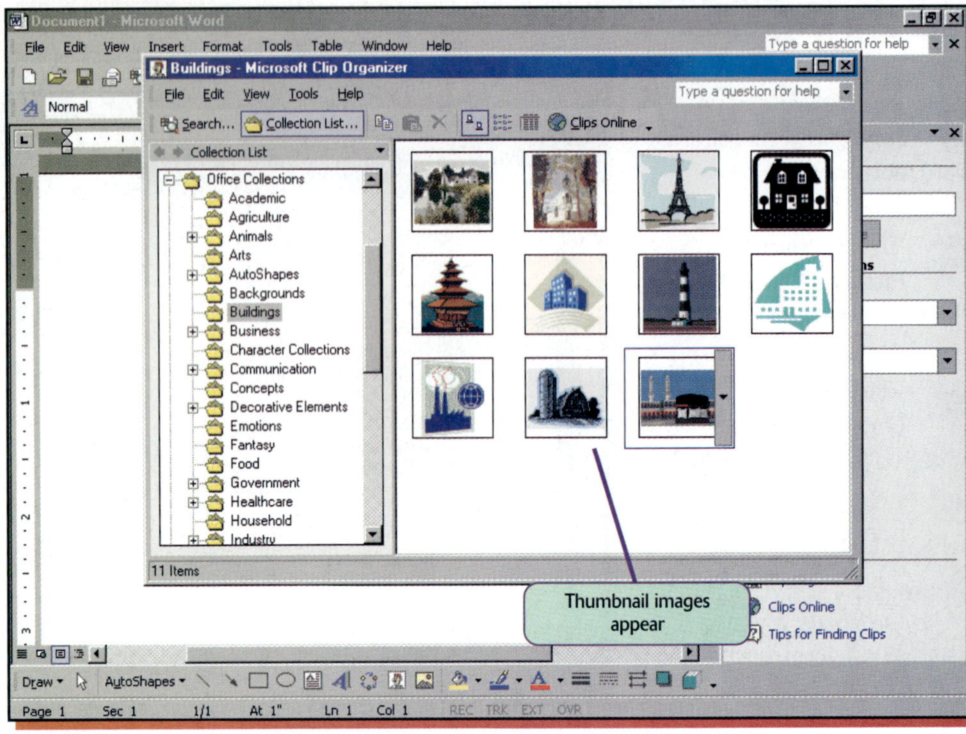

WEB TIP

As you locate clips on the Internet, you can download the clips and store them in the My Collections folders found in the Clip Organizer. You can also create new collection folders in My Collections. Simply select the My Collections folder, choose **File | New Collection,** type the name of the new collection folder, and click OK.

Inserting Graphic Images

Tip Graphic images are easy to identify by their extensions. Look for files with extensions such as .jpg, .bmp, .tif, .wmf, and .pcx.

As you continue to work with Office XP applications, you will begin to acquire images from a variety of sources—from the Internet, from scanned images from friends and relatives, and from graphics collections that you purchase. As you accumulate these images, you will often want to insert them into Office XP files. The procedure for inserting graphic images basically uses the same techniques you used to insert clip art images.

Task 6:
To Insert Graphic Files

1. Open the *e-Selections Online Graphics.doc* file.

2. Position the insertion point at the top of the document and choose **Insert | Picture | From File** to open the Insert Picture dialog box.

3. Open the disk and folder containing the *e-Selections Logo.jpg*

4. Select **e-Selections Logo** and then click **Insert** to place the figure in the document.

Figure 3-22

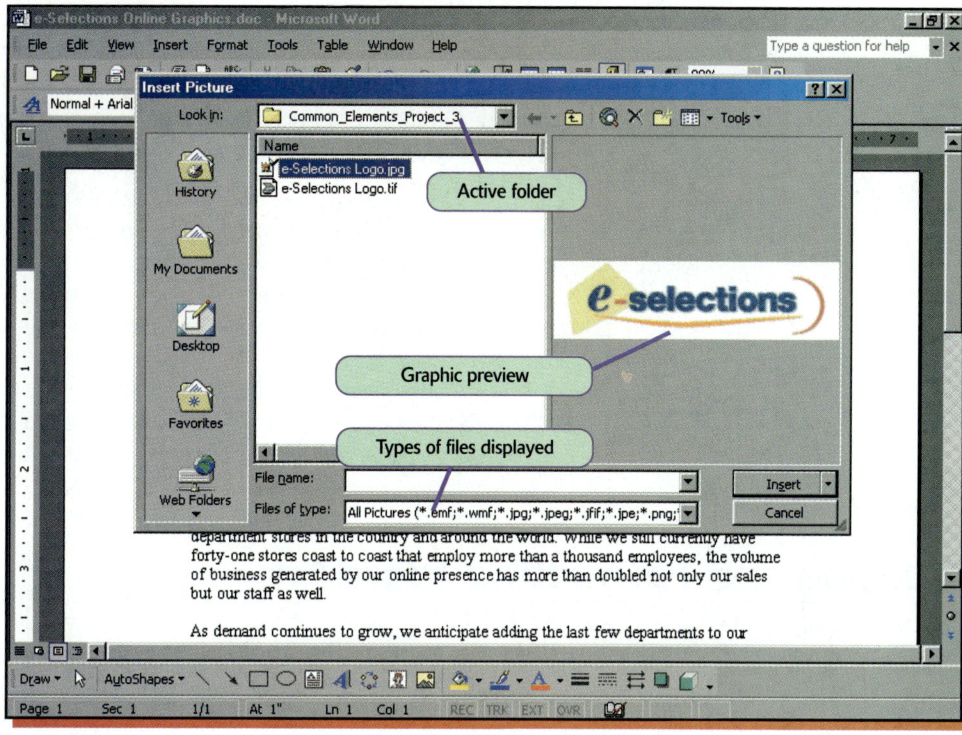

5. Change the layout of the graphic so that you can reposition it freely on screen and then size and position the graphic so that it appears in the upper left corner outside the margin area, as shown in Figure 3-23.

6. Save changes to the file and print a copy of the document.

Figure 3-23

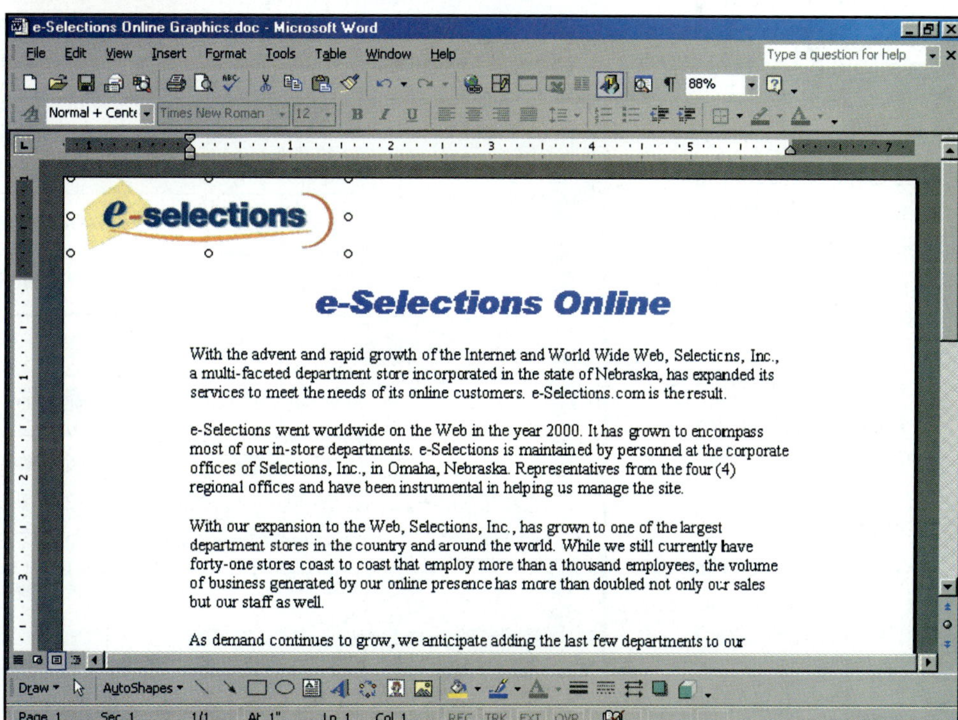

> **Tip** While most clip art images can be ungrouped and edited, pictures you insert into files usually require a graphics editing program to edit.

CHECK POINT

Have you received pictures of your relatives attached to an e-mail message? Have you been impressed by photos that appear in newsletters? Perhaps you've even seen family photos on personal Web pages. If you have, you may have wondered how your family and friends converted their pictures to electronic files that can be sent with messages and posted on the Web.

Microsoft Office contains features that enable you to scan photographs and save them as graphics. Then it's simply a matter of inserting the files in e-mail messages or positioning the file in newsletter documents. You will, of course, need a scanner or a *digital camera* and you will also need to know the basics of how to use this equipment. Once you've got the equipment under control, you can get graphics directly from a scanner or camera using Microsoft Office XP applications. From any Microsoft Office Application, choose **Insert | Picture | From Scanner or Camera** and follow the screen prompts to capture the picture. Then use the skills you've learned in this project to manipulate the graphic.

Creating and Formatting WordArt

WordArt is a feature that enables you to dress up your files by creating graphic text—shaping text on curves and flows. WordArt is easy to create and can be positioned in a file to fit the size and shape you need. You can use WordArt to create a letterhead for your e-Selections stationery.

Task 7: To Create WordArt

1. Launch Word, if necessary, display the Drawing toolbar, if necessary, and open a copy of *e-Selections Online Graphics.doc*.
2. Delete the logo graphics, select the title text, and then click the **Cut** button to place the text on the clipboard.
3. Click the **Bold** and **Italic** buttons to turn them off, if necessary.
4. Click the **Insert WordArt** button on the Drawing toolbar to open the WordArt Gallery.
5. Double-click the WordArt style identified in Figure 3-24.

Figure 3-24

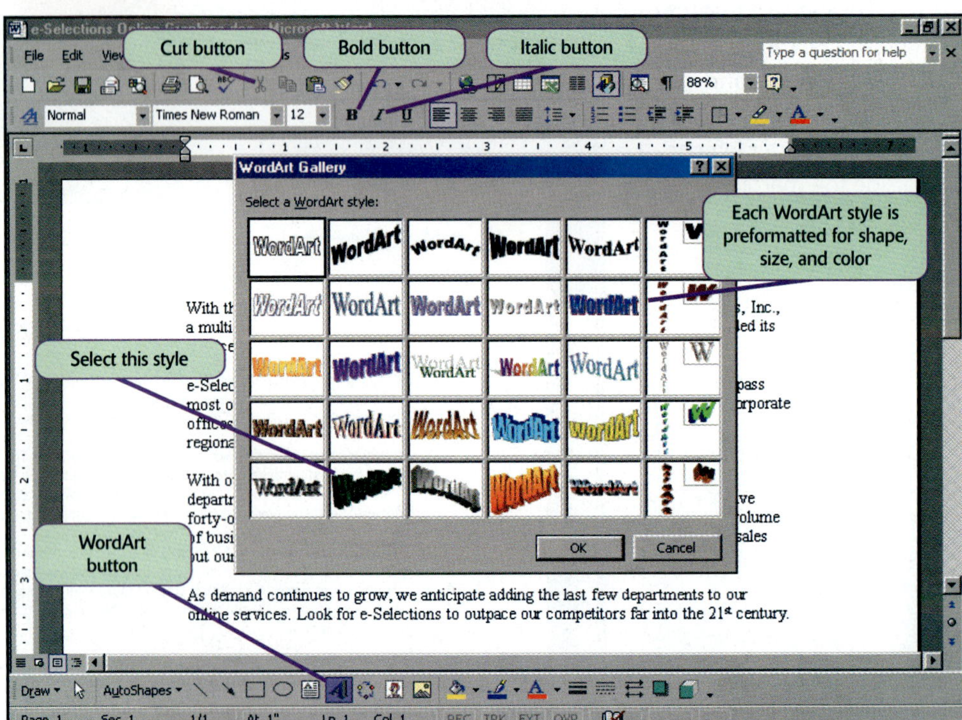

6 Press Ctrl + V to insert the title text and then click **OK**.

Tip When the Drawing toolbar is hidden, you can choose **Insert | Picture | WordArt** to create WordArt.

Figure 3-25

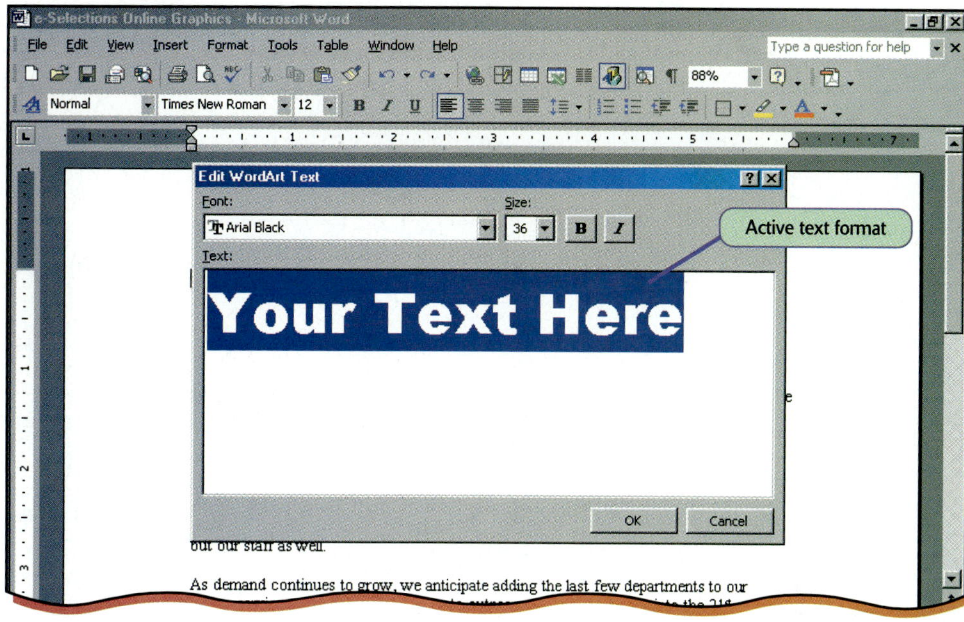

7 Save the document using the file name *Your Initials WordArt* and then close all open files.

WEB TIP

If you've purchased a book, a CD, a movie, or a video game lately, you know how quickly costs associated with these purchases can add up. Search the Web for online companies that act as resellers of these popular media items. You'll find that you can save more than half the cost by buying previously owned items!

Figure 3-26

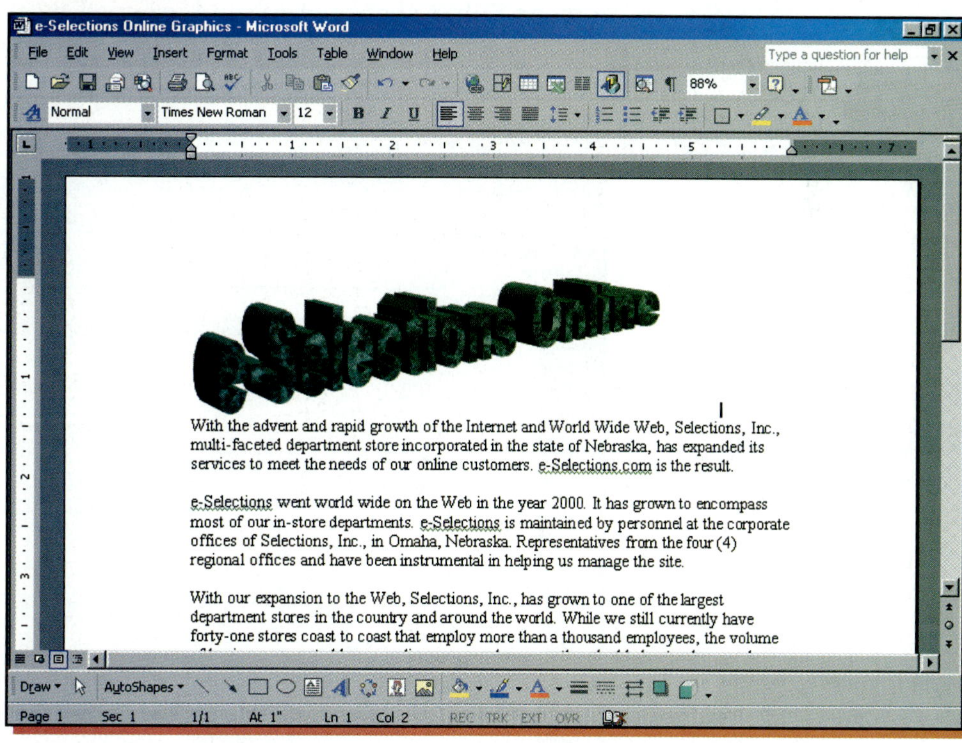

Creating and Manipulating Drawings

When you want to add shapes, lines, text boxes, and arrows to your Office XP files, you will find a sophisticated set of drawing tools that enable you to enhance files with original freehand creations. Even if you're no artist, you'll find the tools on the Drawing toolbar easy to use. Drawing is basically a three-step process:

1. Select the tool that represents the shape you want to draw.
2. Position the pointer where you want to start the drawing.
3. Click and drag the pointer to the shape ending point.

Then, while the shape is still selected, you can move, size, and edit the shape as needed.

Creating Basic Shapes and AutoShapes

Buttons for the shapes that are drawn most frequently appear on the Drawing toolbar. Other shapes are found grouped by type on the *AutoShapes* menu found on the Drawing toolbar.

Task 8:
To Create Shapes

1. Launch Word, if necessary, and create a new blank document.

2. Display the Drawing toolbar, if necessary, and click the **Rectangle** button.

Figure 3-27

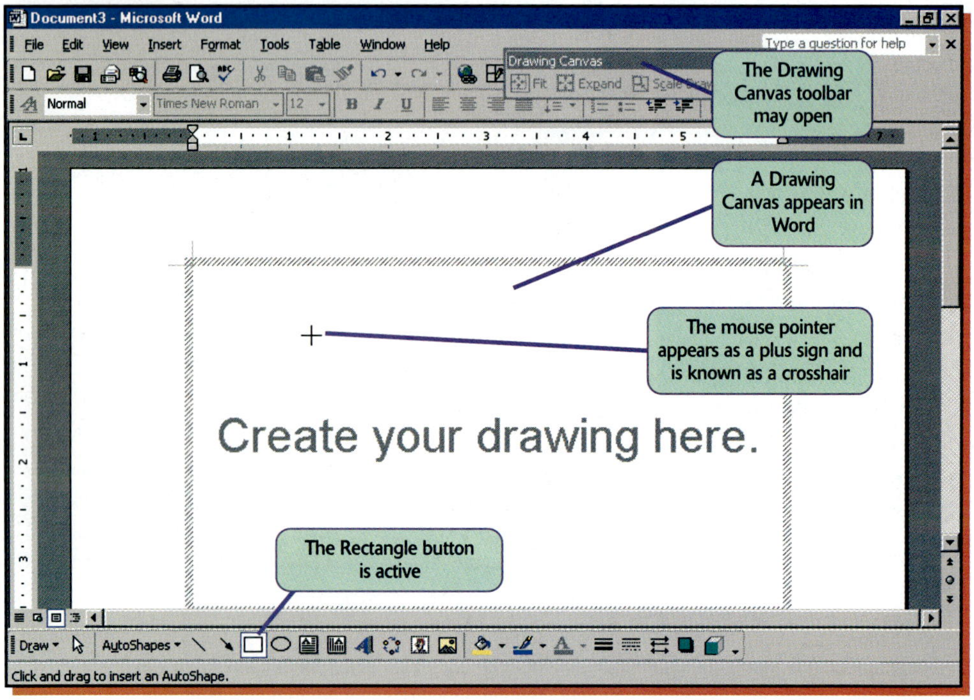

3 Position the *crosshair* mouse pointer on the left side of the Drawing Canvas and then click and drag the crosshair diagonally to form a rectangle.

Tip You can set different colors for shape fills and border. In addition, you can change the line size to add weight to shape borders. Experiment with drawing tools to create different types of custom effects.

Figure 3-28

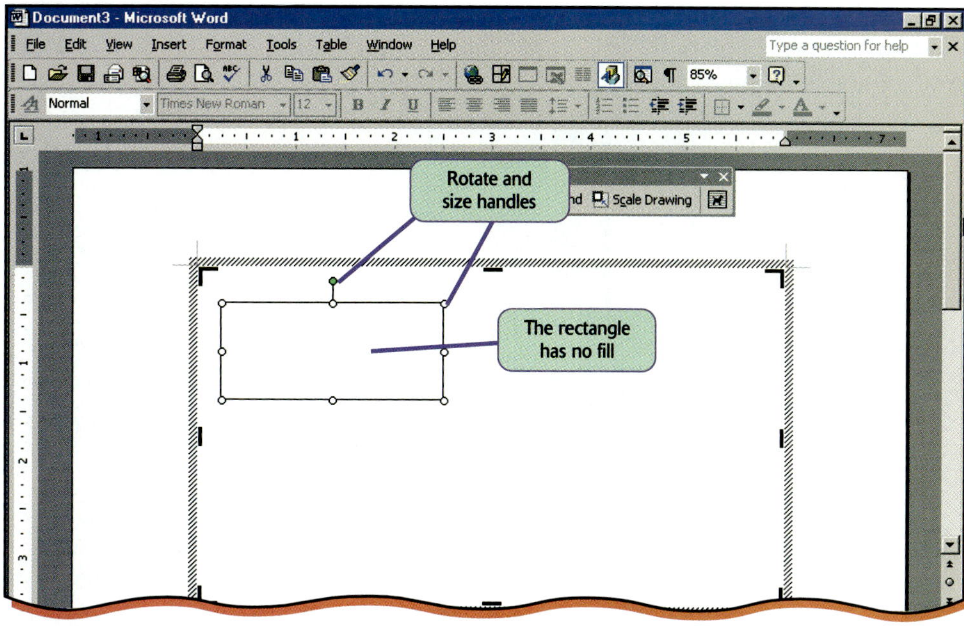

4 Click the **Fill Color** button to fill the rectangle with the default fill color.

5 Click the **AutoShapes** menu on the Drawing toolbar.

6 Select **Basic Shapes** to open the Basic Shapes palette and select the **Lightning Bolt** shape.

Tip Point to each shape on the Basic Shapes palette to identify the different shapes available. Screen tips help locate specific shapes.

Figure 3-29

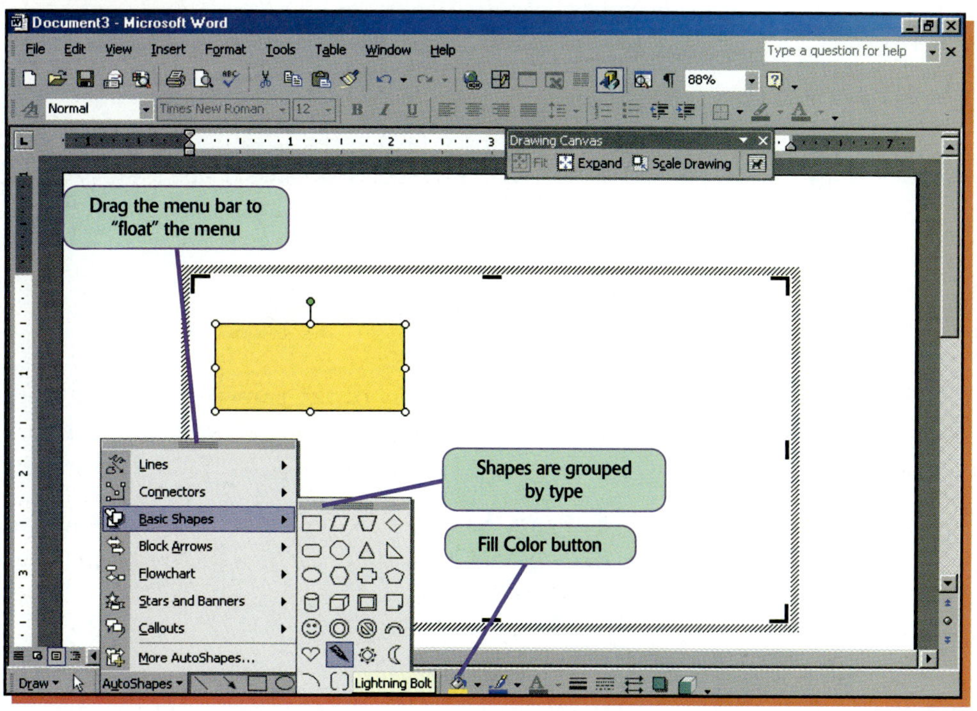

7 Repeat the procedures outlined in Steps 3 and 4 to create a lightning bolt shape to the right of the rectangle and fill it with color.

Figure 3-30

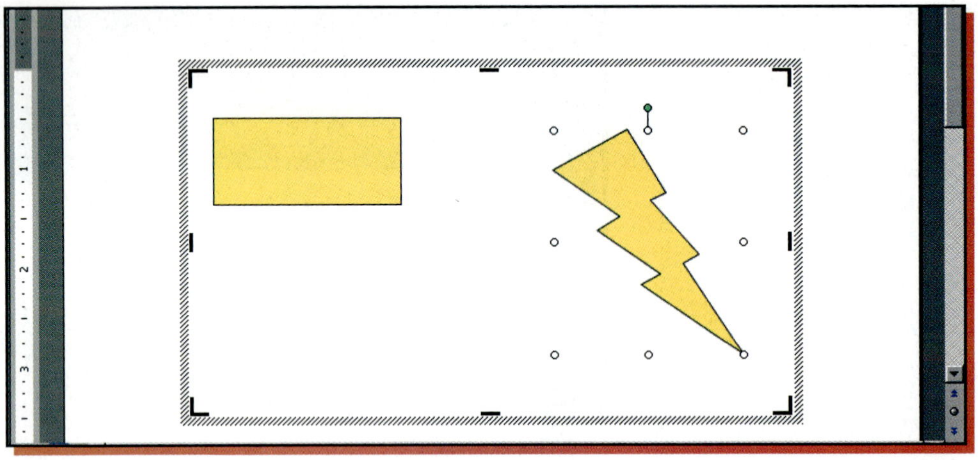

CHECK POINT

As you become more comfortable with the drawing tools available in Microsoft Office Applications, you'll find yourself wanting to be more precise in drawing shapes. Here are some tips to get you started and help you position and size both clip art and drawn objects:

- Press and hold the Ctrl key as you size objects to size the object from the center point out.
- Press and hold the Shift key while you draw lines to make them straight and while you draw shapes to make them symmetrical—rectangles become squares, ovals become circles, and triangles are equilateral.
- Press and hold the Alt key to release the "snap to" feature so that you can move a boundary or size a shape more precisely.

Formatting Shapes

You can use many of the same techniques that you used to format clip art to format drawn objects. You can size, flip, rotate, and change the color of drawn objects just as you can edit and manipulate clip art.

Setting Wrap Text Options. Text can be added to most drawn objects. After adding text, you will often need to change the text wrap option so that text appears properly on the drawn object.

Task 9:
To Set Text Wrap Options

1 Right-click the **lightning bolt** and select **Add Text**. The insertion point appears within the lightning bolt.

Figure 3-31

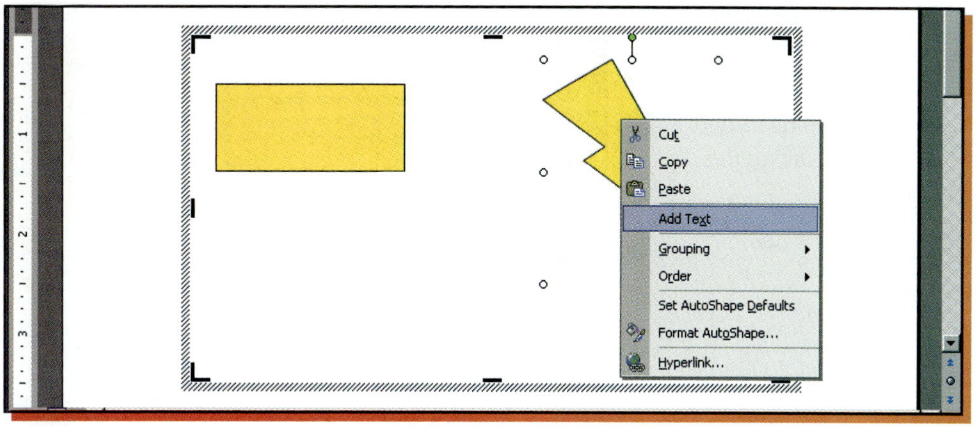

2 Type **Lightning Strikes Again!**

Troubleshooting
Text may be hidden as you type. Don't worry—we're about to fix it.

Figure 3-32

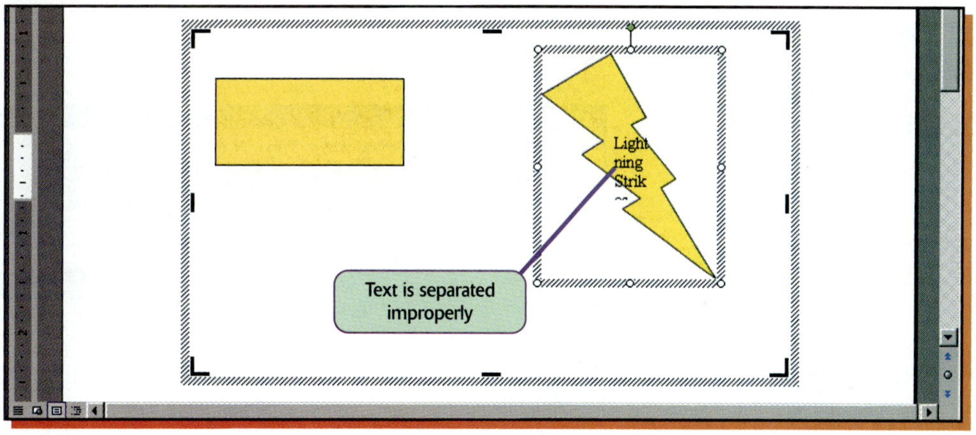

3 Right-click a blank area of the lightning bolt and select **Format AutoShape** to open the Format AutoShape dialog box.

4 Click the **Text Box** tab, select the **Resize AutoShape to fit text** option, and then click **OK**. The lightning bolt changes size to accommodate the text.

Figure 3-33

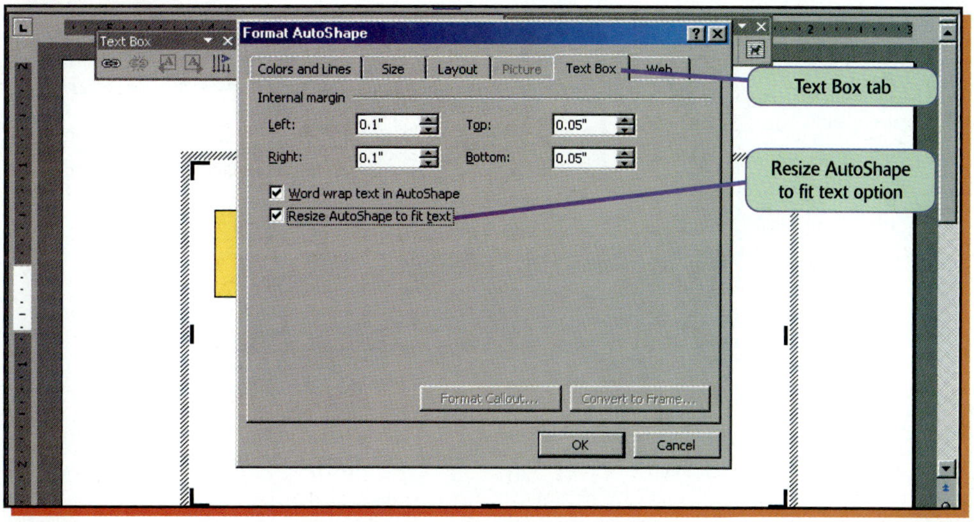

5 Manually drag handles to size the lightning bolt so that the text is within the bolt boundaries.

6 Close the document without saving the changes.

Figure 3-34

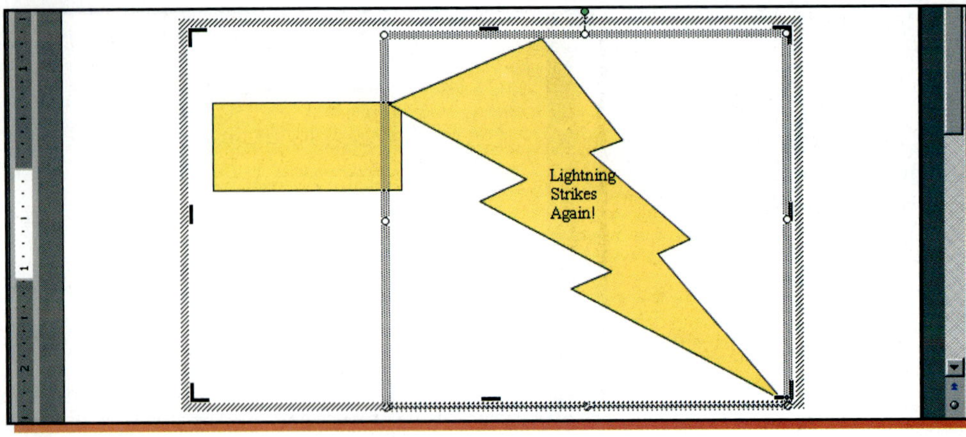

Changing the Fill and Line Color. Fill and line color can be changed to format drawn objects. In addition, special fill effects can be used to create special visual effects.

Task 10:
To Create Special Effects Using Fill and Line Color

1 Create a new blank document in Word.

2 Double-click the **Oval** button on the Drawing toolbar and create the drawing shown in Figure 3-35.

> **Tip** Double-clicking a drawing button enables you to draw multiple shapes using the same drawing tool without having to continually click the shape.

Figure 3-35

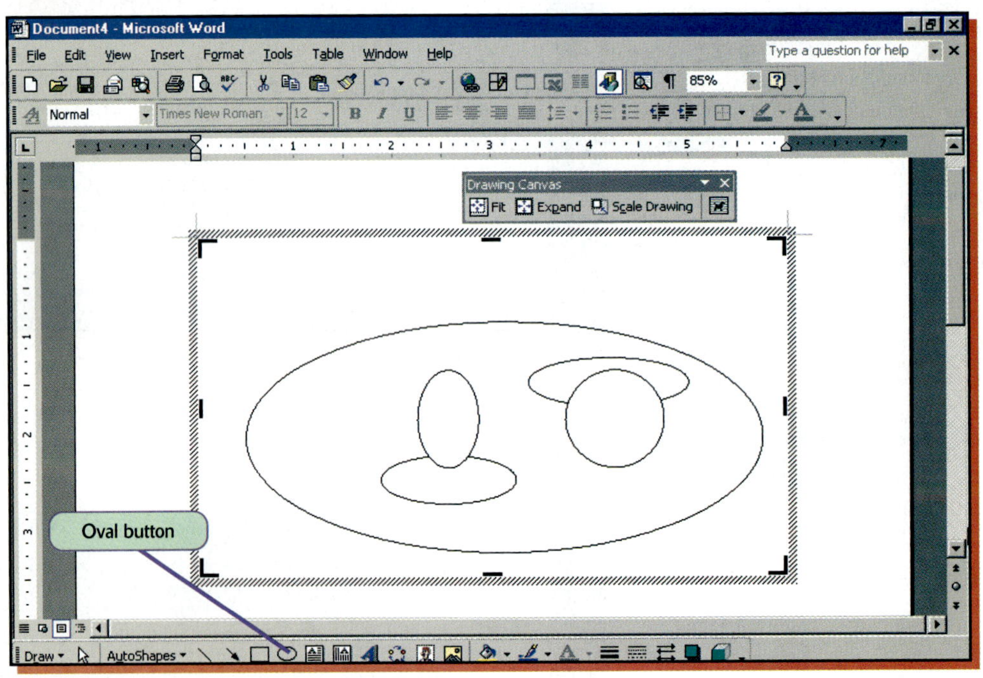

3 Press Esc, select the largest oval in the Drawing Canvas, click the **Fill Color** down arrow, and select **Fill Effects** to open the Fill Effects dialog box.

Tip The Fill Effects dialog box contains tabbed pages that display a number of different fill effect options. Explore these effects as time permits.

Figure 3-36

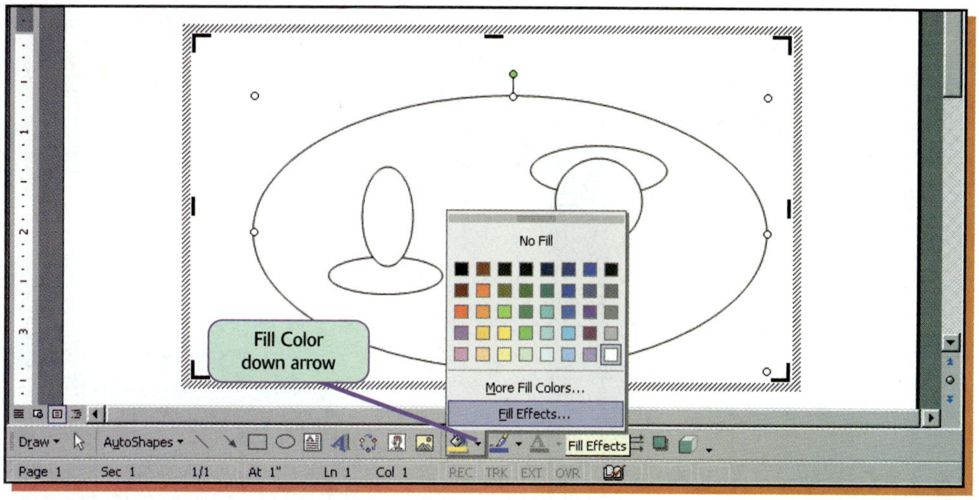

4 Click the **Gradient** tab and set the following options:

- Two colors
- Color 1: Light Blue
- Color 2: Dark Blue
- Shading Styles: Diagonal up

Troubleshooting After you select a shading style, the Variants palette displays different shading angles. The active variant appears with a darker border that is sometimes easy to miss.

Figure 3-37

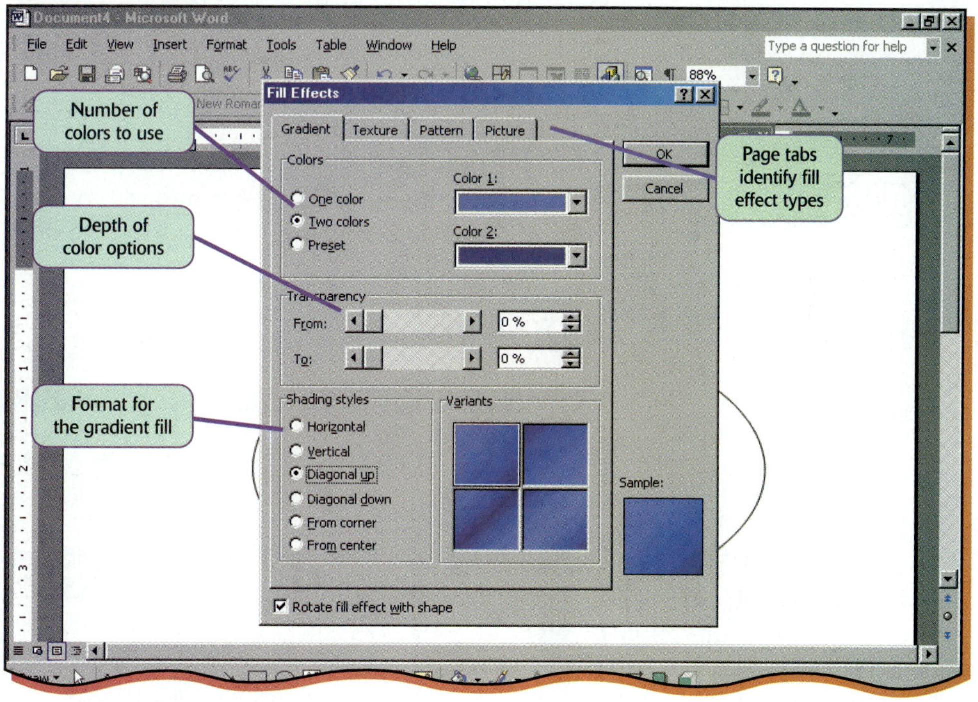

5 Click **OK** and then select the vertical oval on the left.

6 Display the **Fill Effects** dialog box and set the options listed in Step 4, changing the Shading Styles to **Diagonal Down**; then click **OK**.

7 Click the **Line Color** drop-down list arrow and select **No Line**.

8 Save the file using the file name *Your Initials Floating Circles*.

Tip Removing the line from drawn objects makes them appear to blend in with other drawn objects or with file background colors.

Figure 3-38

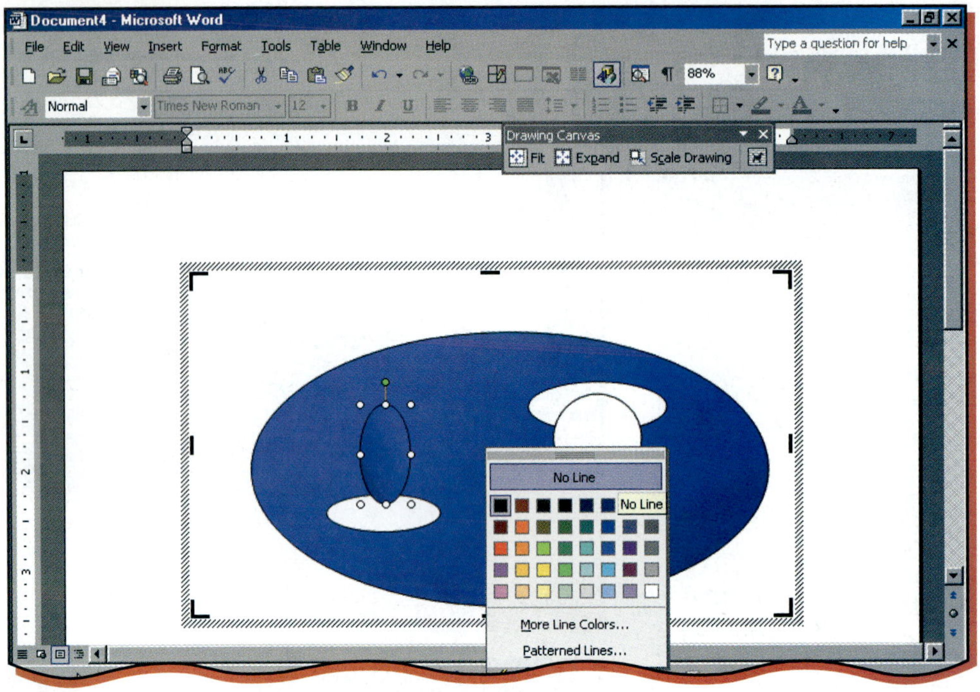

Changing Shapes

After a shape is created and formatted, you can change the shape just as you change the line and fill colors. The format you apply to drawn shapes can create special effects.

Task 11: To Change a Drawn Shape

1 Launch Word and open the *Your Initials Floating Circles.doc* document, if necessary.

2 Select the oval on the right to select it.

Figure 3-39

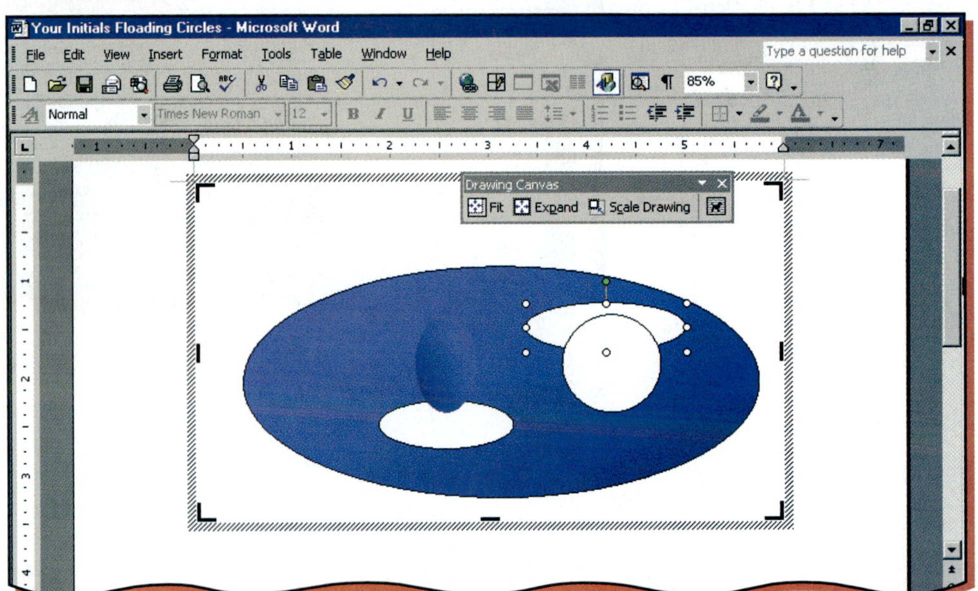

3 Choose **Draw | Change AutoShape | Basic Shapes**.

4 Select the **Change Shape to Rectangle** shape on the Basic Shapes palette.

Tip Notice that the screen tip that appears when you point to different shapes on the palette includes the "Change Shape to" text to let you know that you are changing an existing shape to a different shape. When no drawn shape is selected, the screen tip simply identifies the shape.

Figure 3-40

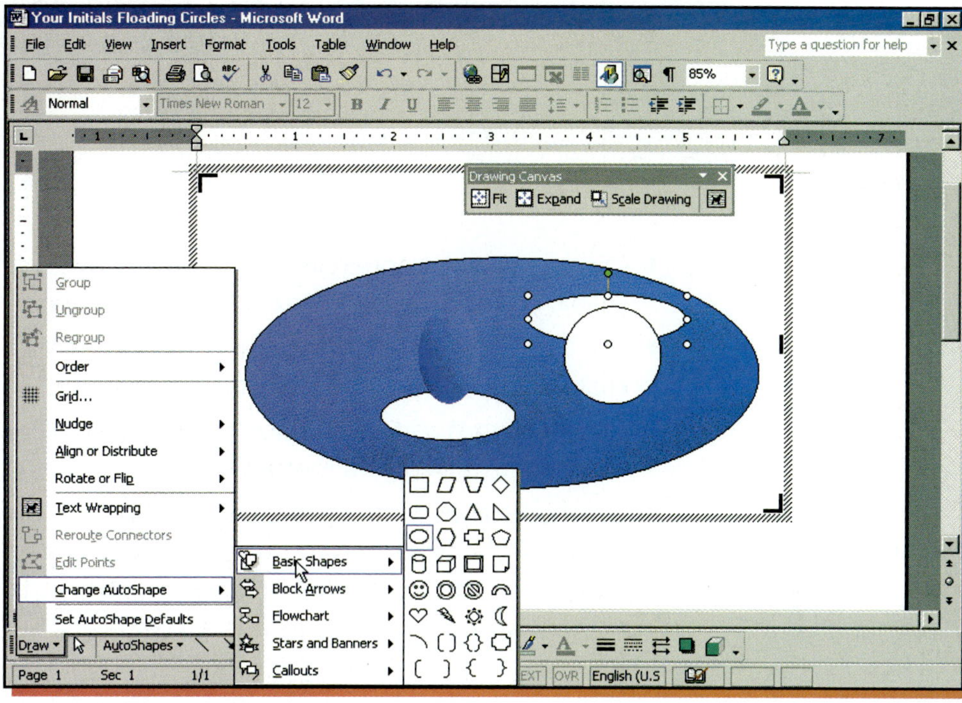

5 Save and close the document and exit Word.

Troubleshooting You will work with this diagram in the exercises at the end of Project 3, so be sure to save it.

Figure 3-41

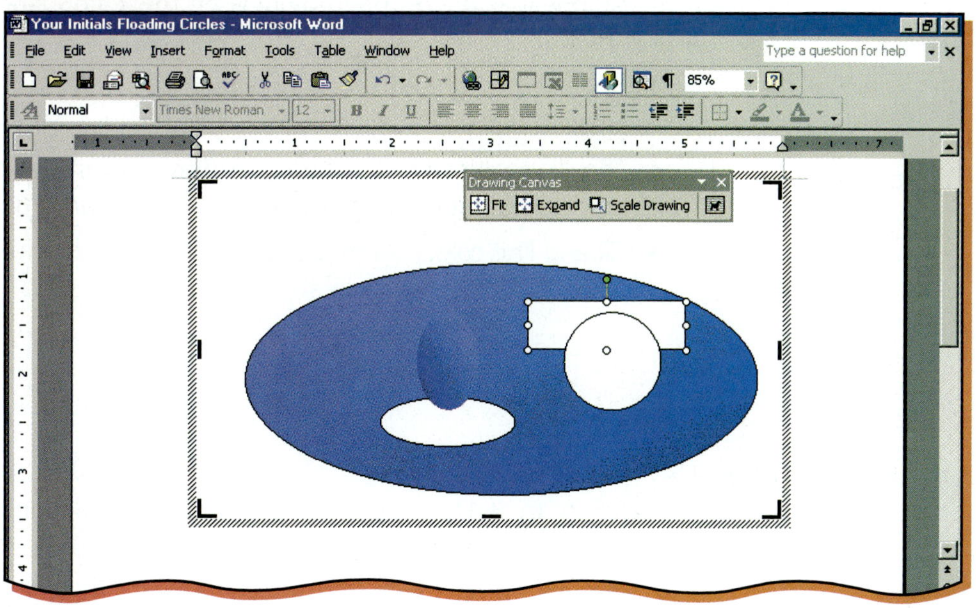

SUMMARY AND EXERCISES

SUMMARY

- Clip art images, scanned images, WordArt, and manual drawings enable you to dress up files in all Office XP applications.
- The Clip Organizer contains graphics on a number of topics and enables you to search by topic for related images.
- Clip art images added to Office XP files can be flipped, rotated, ungrouped, edited, and regrouped.
- Graphics scanned into computers or input from digital cameras as well as files of graphics received from other sources or downloaded from the Internet can be inserted in Office XP files.
- WordArt enables you to graphically format text to enhance Office XP files.
- The sophisticated set of drawing tools on the Drawing toolbar enables you to create original freehand art.
- When a shape or object is inserted, you can move, size, and edit the selected item.
- AutoShapes are grouped by type on the AutoShapes menu of the Drawing toolbar.
- Text can be added to most drawn shapes as well as to clip art and graphic items inserted into files.
- The shape chosen for a particular drawing can be changed to different shapes without deleting the original shape and redrawing it.
- Fill and line color can be changed for drawn shapes as well as for pieces of ungrouped clip art objects.

KEY TERMS & SKILLS

KEY TERMS

AutoShapes (p. 3-18)
clip art (p. 3-1)
Clip Organizer (p. 3-2)
crosshair (p. 3-19)
digital camera (p. 3-16)
Drawing Canvas (p. 3-10)
fill (p. 3-11)
gradient (p. 3-23)
scanned images (p. 3-1)
thumbnails (p. 3-2)
WordArt (p. 3-1)

SKILLS

Change a drawn shape (p. 3-24)
Create special effects using fill and line color (p. 3-22)
Create WordArt (p. 3-16)
Display and use the Clip Organizer (p. 3-13)
Draw shapes (p. 3-18)
Edit clip art images (p. 3-11)
Insert clip art images (p. 3-2)
Insert graphics from scanners and digital cameras (p. 3-14)
Move and size clip art images (p. 3-5)
Set text wrap options (p. 3-21)
Ungroup clip art images (p. 3-9)

STUDY QUESTIONS

MULTIPLE CHOICE

1. The dialog box that displays clip art images is the
   a. Format Object.
   b. Clip Organizer.
   c. Drawing Palette.
   d. Edit Picture.

2. When you search for clip art images that are related to a particular topic, possible images that meet your needs appear in the
   a. task pane.
   b. active file.
   c. status bar.
   d. toolbars.

3. All of the following are different types of graphic images *except*
   a. .tif.
   b. .pcx.
   c. .jpg.
   d. .xfx.

4. The button on the Standard toolbar that displays the Drawing toolbar is
   a. Tables and Borders.
   b. Insert Hyperlink.
   c. Drawing.
   d. Insert Chart.

5. Before you can move most clip art images, you must change which settings?
   a. Picture Layout
   b. Graphic Format
   c. Image Size
   d. Object Format

6. To create a letterhead that arches over the top of a page, you would choose which feature?
   a. Headers
   b. Clip Art
   c. TextFont
   d. WordArt

7. Clearing which option restores free placement of a graphic?
   a. enable overlapping
   b. lock anchor
   c. move object with text
   d. none of the above

8. The toolbar that contains tools for drawing free shapes is the
   a. Standard toolbar.
   b. Picture toolbar.
   c. Drawing toolbar.
   d. Web toolbar.

9. The Change AutoShape command is found on what menu?
   a. Format
   b. Insert
   c. AutoShapes
   d. Draw

10. To view all text added to drawn shapes, it is sometimes necessary to set the
   a. wrap text options.
   b. shape format.
   c. fill color.
   d. line color.

SHORT ANSWER

1. What are the first three steps of adding a clip art picture to a file?
2. What commands do you use to fill a drawn object with two different colors and where are the commands located?
3. Which feature would you use to draw lines, arrows, and boxes?
4. What steps would you follow to insert a graphic from the Internet?
5. Where is the AutoShapes menu located?
6. How are shapes organized on the AutoShapes menu?
7. What are the very small copies of images in the Clip Gallery called?
8. How do you add text to drawn objects?
9. What is the difference between flipping an object and rotating it?
10. What are some additional sources for graphics that you can add to files?

FILL IN THE BLANK

1. ______________ is a feature that enables you to dress up files by creating graphic text.
2. Office XP applications share a common ______________ that contains a variety of different images you can add to your files.
3. ______________ appear on selected images, which enable you to resize or drag the object.
4. Clip art images are stored in collection ______________ that sort images by type.
5. Before you can change the color of a piece of a clip art image, you must first ______________ it.
6. The Drawing Canvas for drawing shapes appears only in the ______________ application.
7. Color added to the center of drawn objects is called ______________.
8. Small copies of clip art images are called ______________.
9. Commands for adding graphics to Office XP files appear on the ______________ menu.
10. Graphics can be captured as electronic files from printed pictures using a ______________.

DISCUSSION

1. Describe the steps you would follow to move and resize a clip art image.
2. How do the procedures for adding clip art differ from the procedures for adding other graphics to Office XP files?
3. When would you use the Clip Organizer instead of the task pane for adding items to Office XP files?
4. Explain the procedures you would follow to put a clip art image back together.

GUIDED EXERCISES

1 FLOATING OBJECTS

The ovals and rectangles you added to the *Your Initials Floating Circles.doc* document are not yet complete. The finished graphic is pictured in Figure 3-42.

Figure 3-42

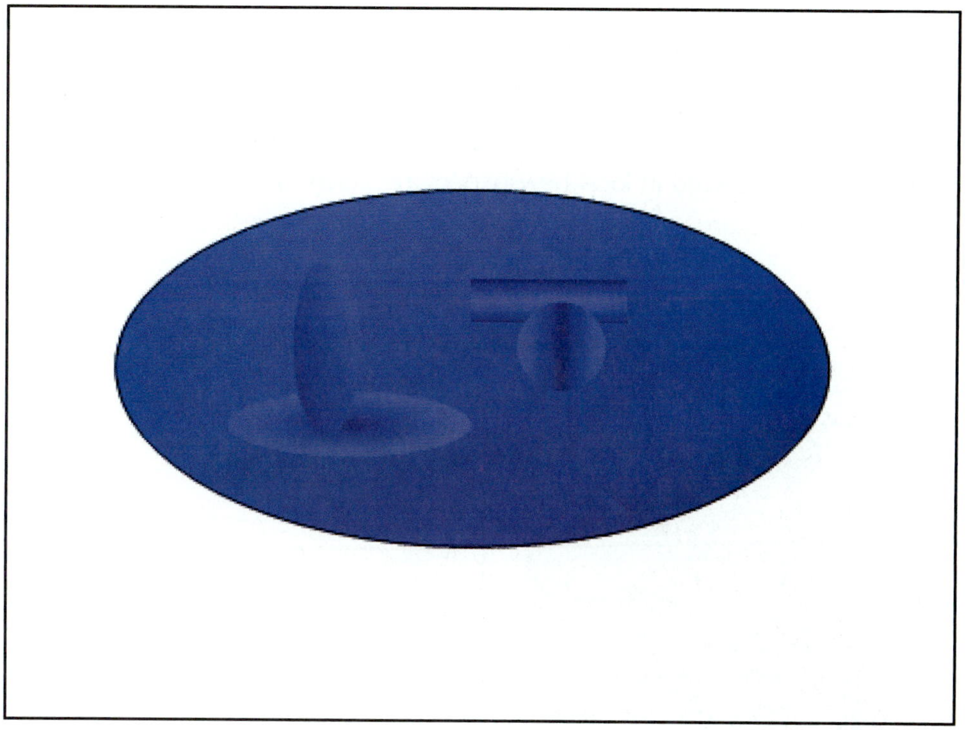

You can complete this task before moving on to other tasks. Follow these instructions:

1. Launch Word and open *Your Initials Floating Circles.doc*, if necessary.
2. Display the Drawing toolbar, if necessary.
3. Select one of the unfilled ovals.
4. Click the **Fill Color**  button on the Drawing toolbar and select **Fill Effects**.
5. Set the following options on the Gradient page of the Fill Effects dialog box:
   - Colors: Two colors
   - Color 1 Light Blue
   - Color 2 Dark Blue

- Shading styles A different style from other shapes
- Variants A different variant from other shapes

6. Remove the border line from the shape.
7. Repeat the procedures outlined in Steps 3–6 for all other shapes.
8. Save changes to the file and print a copy of the drawing.

2 CREATING A GRAPHIC FLYER

Store hours for Selections, Inc., are changing in the fall. You have been asked to create the flyer pictured in Figure 3-43 so that it can be distributed to customers and placed in local newspapers to inform the public of the new hours.

Figure 3-43

Follow these steps to complete the flyer:

1. Create a new blank document.
2. Insert the picture file **Stars.wmf** and size it appropriately on the page.

Right-click the graphic and select **Format Picture**. Click the **Layout** tab and select the **Behind text** wrapping style and the **Right** Horizontal alignment option; then click OK.

4. Change the font for the flyer to Lucida Handwriting or a similar script or writing font and change the size to 36 points.
5. Click the **Align Right** button on the Formatting toolbar.
6. Type the text as shown and make adjustments as necessary to reposition the graphic or text on the page.
7. Save the document using the file name *New Store Hours Flyer* and print a copy of the flyer.
8. Close the document.

3 CREATING BUILDING BLOCKS

e-Selections personnel have decided to promote healthy eating habits. The flyer they want to distribute is shown in Figure 3-44.

Figure 3-44

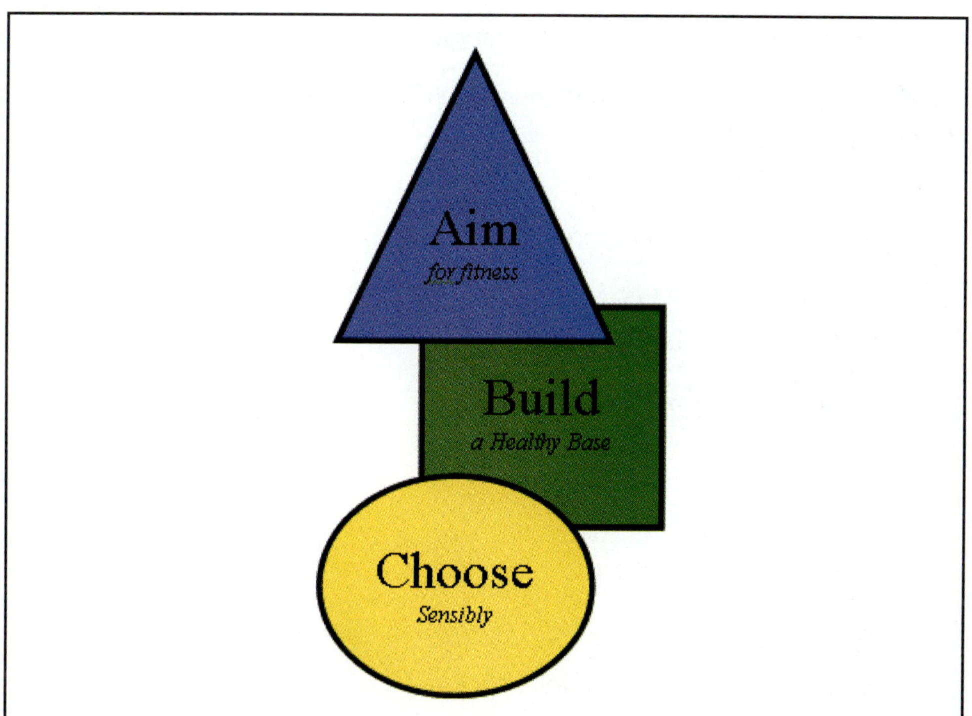

Create the graphic for the flyer by following these steps:

1. Launch Word, if necessary, and create a new blank document.
2. Create the square in the center of the building blocks and set the following options:
   - Change the fill color to green.
   - Click the **Line Style** button on the Drawing toolbar and select **3 pt**.
3. Choose **AutoShapes** | **Basic Shapes** | **Isosceles Triangle**, draw and position the triangle as shown in Figure 38, and set the following format:
   - Change the fill color to blue.
   - Change the line style to 3 pt.
4. Draw the ellipse, position it as shown, and set the following format:
   - Change the fill color to yellow.
   - Change the line style to 3 pt.
5. Right-click each of the drawn objects separately, type the text shown, and format the text as follows:
   - Center the text in all shapes.
   - Change the size of text in the first line to 28 pts.
   - Italicize text on the second line.
6. Adjust the size of the objects to accommodate the text.
7. Save your file using the file name *Your Initials Building Blocks* and print a copy of the file.

ON YOUR OWN

The difficulty of these case studies varies:
are the least difficult; *are more difficult; and* *are the most difficult.*

1 ADDING A TEXT BOX

Open the file *Phantom Ghosties.doc*. Insert a text box below the existing text on the second page and type **Phantom Ghost** in the text box. Center the text box and arrange the text so that it appears on one line. Size and format the text in the text box using the same font and size as text in the document but change the text color to black and fill the text box with orange background. Save changes to the file and print a copy of the document.

2 LOCATING LICENSE AGREEMENTS FOR CLIP ART USAGE

Search the Internet for clip art. Visit numerous sites and locate at least two different license agreements for downloading the clip art collections that you find. Print copies of the license agreements.

3 CREATING A FUN NOTICE GRAPHIC

Open the file *Phantom Ghosties.doc*. Access Clips Online to locate a clip of a ghost. Insert the clip art of a ghost below the text box. Format the graphic so that it is centered on the page and size the graphic so that it covers a large portion of the page. Save changes to the file and print a copy of the file.

FINDING CLIP ART ONLINE, INSERTING CLIP ART, AND ADDING TEXT

Search the Microsoft Design Gallery Live site for clip art graphics of apples. Download the apple you like best. Then create a new blank document in Word and add the clip art image of the apple to the document. Size the graphic so that it encompasses most of the page and position the apple in the center of the page. Then add the following text to a text box in the center of the apple:

An apple or two for lunch on Monday is an excellent antidote to a weekend of overeating. Apples travel well, come in their own packaging, and keep for a long time. What could be simpler?

Center the text in the text box and size and format the text as desired. Then change the fill color of the text box to the color of the apple. Save your file using the file name *Your Initials An Apple a Day* and print a copy of the file.

5 CREATING STATIONERY USING WORDART

Create personal stationery that contains each of the following features:

- WordArt containing your name.
- A text box containing your address and phone number—formatted using a unique font.
- A graphic that represents your personality.

Size and arrange the features attractively on the page in such a way that there is room to type letters on the stationery. Save the document using the file name *Your Initials Personal Stationery*.

6 CREATING FAMILIAR LOGOS

Many logos are quite popular and easily recognized by the general population. However, how easy are these logos to duplicate? Locate at least three logos that appear relatively simple in their construction and try to recreate these logos altogether on the same page of a document. Then download a copy of the logo from the Internet and insert the graphic logo beside your reconstructed logo. Save the file using the file name *Your Initials Logos* and print a copy of the file.

FROM THE FILES

You Will Need

✔ Slide Samples.pps

Introducing PowerPoint 2002

Microsoft PowerPoint 2002 is a presentation graphics program that enables you to prepare slide shows and present them with style and impact. In addition, you can use PowerPoint to:

- Print handouts for the audience and include slide miniatures and lines on the handouts for note taking.
- Create notes for yourself to aid in your presentation delivery.
- Create an interactive presentation that runs automatically, as well as a presentation containing slides timed to coincide with your talk.
- Jazz up your presentation using animation, graphics, and other multimedia components.

OBJECTIVES

After completing this project, you will be able to:

- *Launch PowerPoint*
- *Identify PowerPoint screen features*
- *Identify PowerPoint terminology*
- *Add text to slide placeholders*
- *Preview and print presentation materials*
- *Create presentations using the AutoContent Wizard*

e-selections Running Case

Welcome to the graphics department of e-Selections! You have been temporarily assigned to the graphics department to help Amber Wright, Administrative Manager of e-Selections, prepare two presentations for the e-Selections Web site. You will be using PowerPoint 2002, the presentation graphics program that is part of Office XP, to create the presentation. It's time to start learning the ins and outs of PowerPoint!

Introducing PowerPoint 2002

The Challenge

The title slides for each presentation you will create are shown in Figure O-1. As you can see, these slides only contain basic information to get the presentation started.

Figure O-1

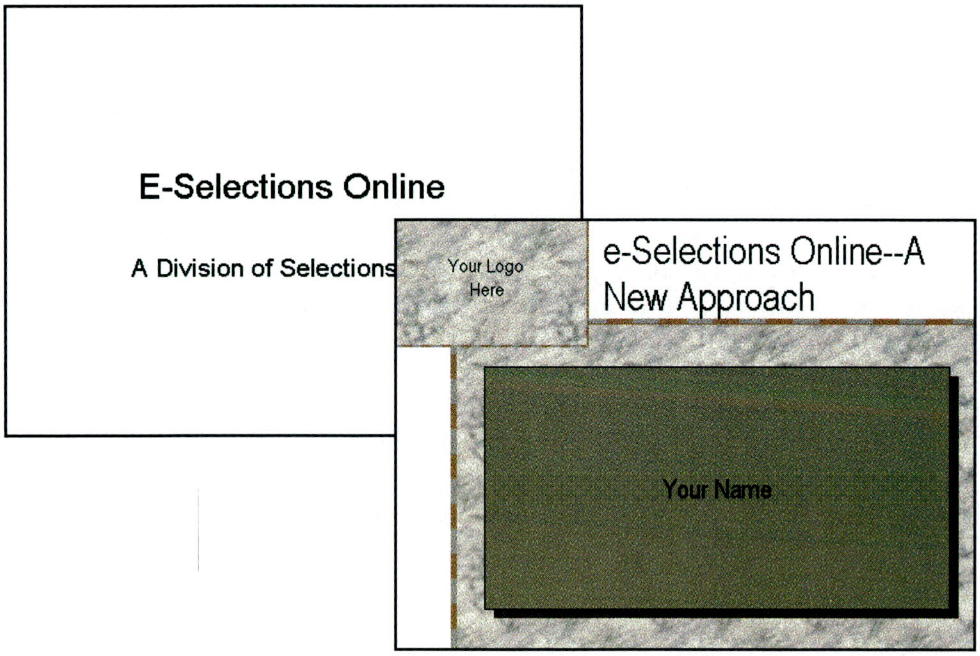

The Solution

Although Ms. Wright has given you a starting point for the presentations, you will need to follow basic design strategy as you develop each presentation. Before you can actually begin the task, however, it's important to learn all you can about PowerPoint so that you can incorporate special features into your presentation design.

Launching PowerPoint

After powering up your computer, logging on to the required networks, and responding to messages that are built in to your computer system, Windows starts automatically. You can launch PowerPoint 2002 using the same techniques you use to launch other programs. Upon launching PowerPoint, a new blank presentation appears.

Task 1:
To Launch PowerPoint

1 Choose **Start** | **Programs** and point to PowerPoint.

Troubleshooting
If you accidentally close the pane on the left side of the PowerPoint window, you can restore it by choosing **View** | **Normal (Restore Panes).**

Figure 0-2

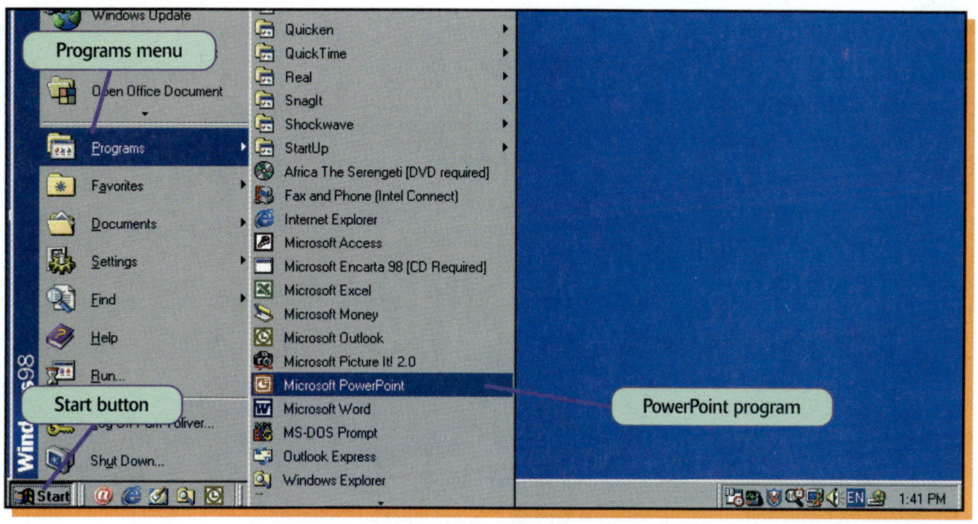

2 Click PowerPoint.

Figure 0-3

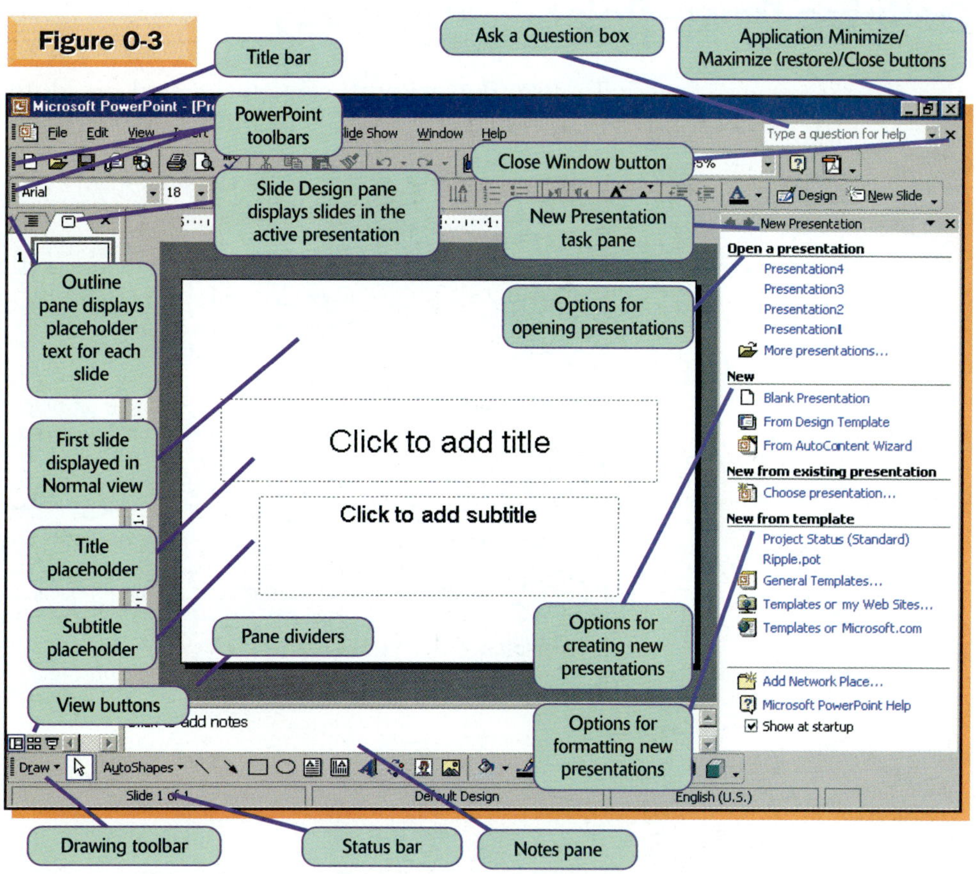

Other Ways

To launch PowerPoint:

- Double-click the PowerPoint shortcut icon on the desktop.
- Choose Start | New Office Document, and double-click the Blank Presentation template.
- Click the PowerPoint icon on the Microsoft Office Manager toolbar.

The Setup

Options set in other Office XP applications affect the way PowerPoint appears when you launch it. As a result, the features displayed in the PowerPoint window on your computer may be different from those in Figure O-3. Table O-1 shows the settings that are used throughout this PowerPoint project. Please change your settings to reflect those in the table. As you progress through the tasks in this section, you will display and hide additional screen elements as needed.

WEB TIP

Search the Internet using the term *presentations* as the search topic. You'll find lots of good ideas for developing dynamic presentations!

Table O-1 PowerPoint Settings

Feature	Setting
Office Shortcut bar	Close the **Office Shortcut** bar.
Office Assistant	Hide the **Office Assistant.**
Toolbars	Close all toolbars except the Standard, Formatting, and Drawing toolbars. Choose **Tools | Customize | Options** and check the **Show Standard and Formatting toolbars on two rows** option.
Menus	Choose **Tools | Customize | Options** and check the **Always show full menus** option.
Task pane	Choose **View | Task Pane.**

Defining PowerPoint Terminology

To use PowerPoint effectively, you need to become familiar with the PowerPoint terminology identified in Table O-2.

Table O-2 PowerPoint Terminology

Term	Description
Slides	Basic units of a presentation. Presentations typically consist of numerous slides. Each slide in a presentation is equivalent to a page of a document, a worksheet in a workbook, or a database record.
Placeholders	Predefined areas outlined on slides that are designed to hold slide text, bulleted lists, graphs, tables, charts, and so forth.
Slide layouts	Preformatted slide layouts that contain specific object placeholders to identify the types of items placed on the slides.
Masters	Layouts that contain the text, bullets, alignment, header/footer text, and background format for all slides in a presentation.
Templates	Professionally developed slide designs that you can apply to your presentations to give a consistent look to all slides in a presentation.

Adding Text to Placeholders

The title slide appears in the Slide pane of the Normal view window and contains two *placeholders*. Each placeholder provides instructions for adding text. Text you type in the placeholders automatically appears in the Outline pane of the PowerPoint window when the Outline pane is active.

Task 2:

To Add Text to Slide Placeholders

1 Click the **Outline** tab on the Outline/Slide Design pane and then click the title placeholder.

Figure 0-4

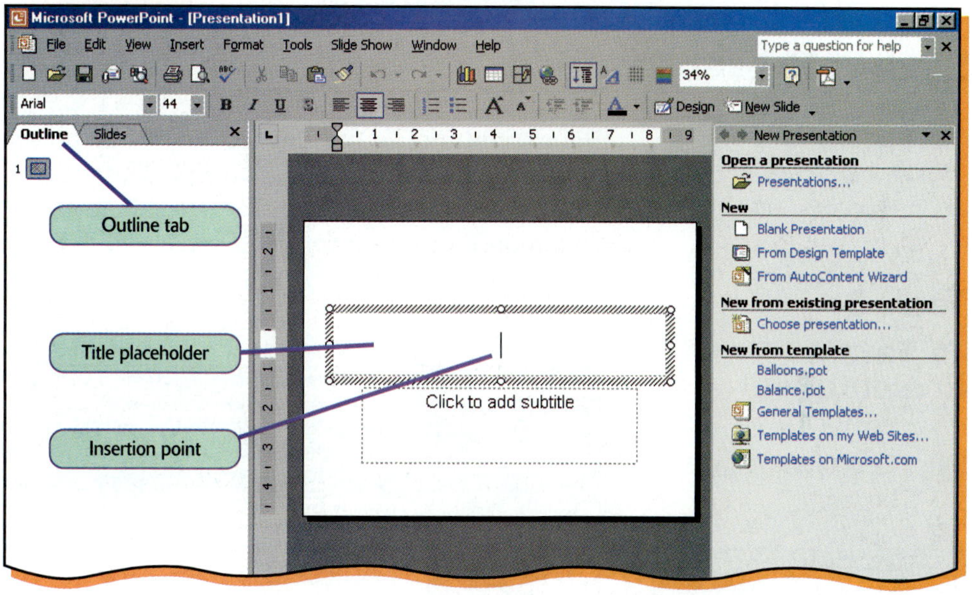

2 Type **e-Selections Online.**

3 Press Ctrl + Enter to move to the subtitle placeholder.

Other Ways

To select a placeholder:

- Click the subtitle placeholder to make it active.

4 Type **A Division of Selections, Inc.**

Figure 0-5

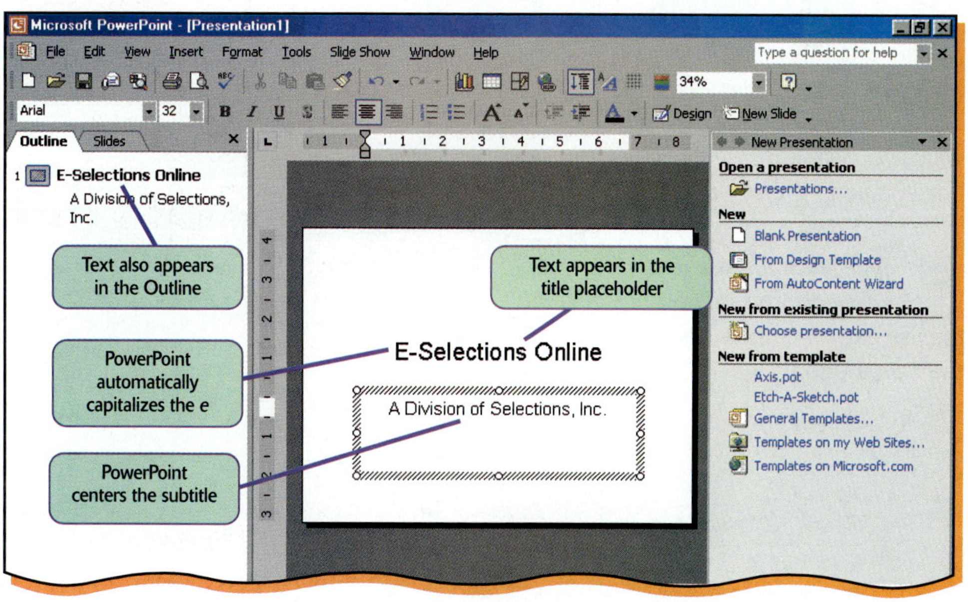

CHECK POINT

PowerPoint contains a feature called *AutoFit* that is active by default. The AutoFit feature is designed to automatically resize text in text placeholders to ensure that the text fits neatly within the placeholder borders. When PowerPoint adjusts font size in a placeholder, the AutoFit Options button appears on the left side of the placeholder. Point to the down arrow on the button and select the AutoFit option you want PowerPoint to use for adjusting the text in the placeholder.

Saving Presentations

Before continuing, it's time to save your presentation. The basic procedures and techniques required to save presentations in PowerPoint are the same as the procedures used to save files in other Office XP applications. (See Common Elements Project 1 for detailed information.)

Task 3:
To Save a Presentation

1. Click the Save button.

Other Ways To save a new presentation:

- Press Ctrl + S
- Choose **File** | **Save**.

2. Open the folder and/or disk drive in which you want to save the presentation.

3. Type ***Your Initials* e-Selections Online** in the File name text box. Click the **Save** button.

Figure 0-6

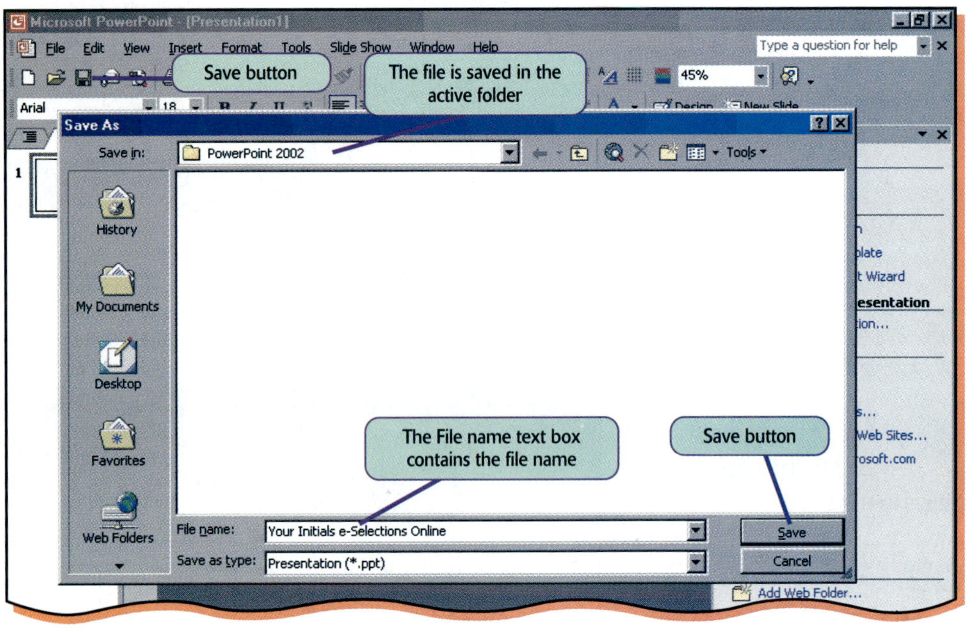

Previewing and Printing Presentation Materials

The Print dialog box contains options that are unique to PowerPoint and to the types of presentation materials that you need to print. You'll find options that enable you to print each slide individually on a sheet of paper or transparency film, handouts containing multiple slides on the same page, the Outline view of your presentation, or notes pages. It is always a good idea to preview your materials before printing them to ensure that they are both properly formatted and appear as you planned.

Task 4:

To Preview and Print Presentation Materials

1. Choose **File | Print**.

Figure 0-7

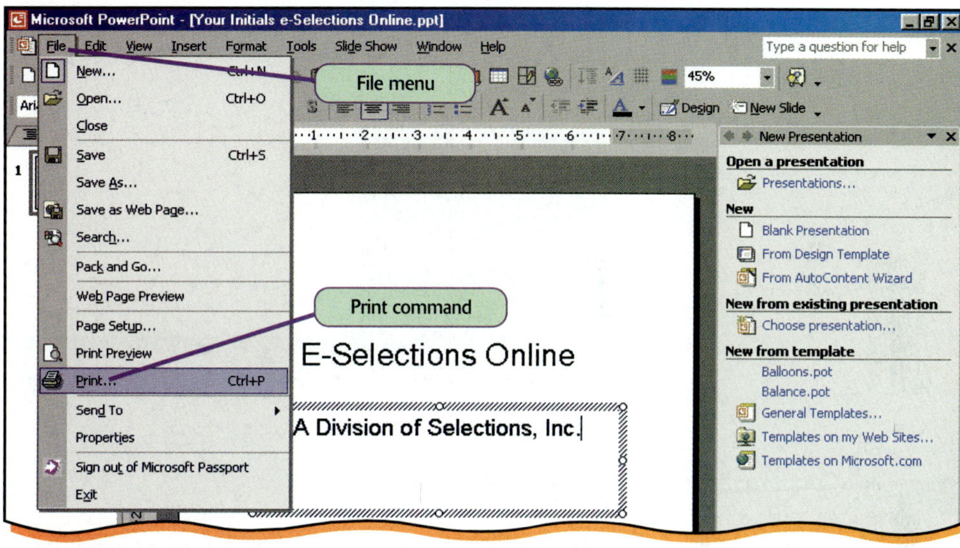

2. Click the **Print what** down arrow.

3. Select **Handouts** and then select **2** from the **Slides per page** drop-down list.

4. Check the **Frame slides** option. Click the **Preview** button.

Figure 0-8

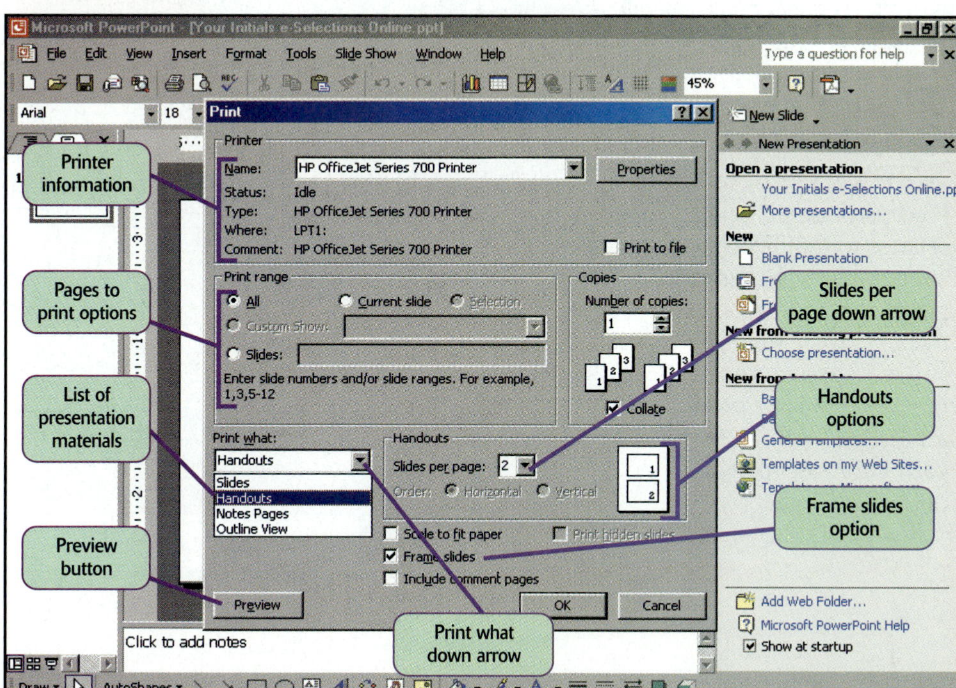

Other Ways

To preview and print a presentation:

- Press Ctrl + P.
- Click the Print Preview button on the Standard toolbar.
- Click the Print button to bypass the Print dialog box.

5 Click **Print** on the Preview toolbar.

Figure 0-9

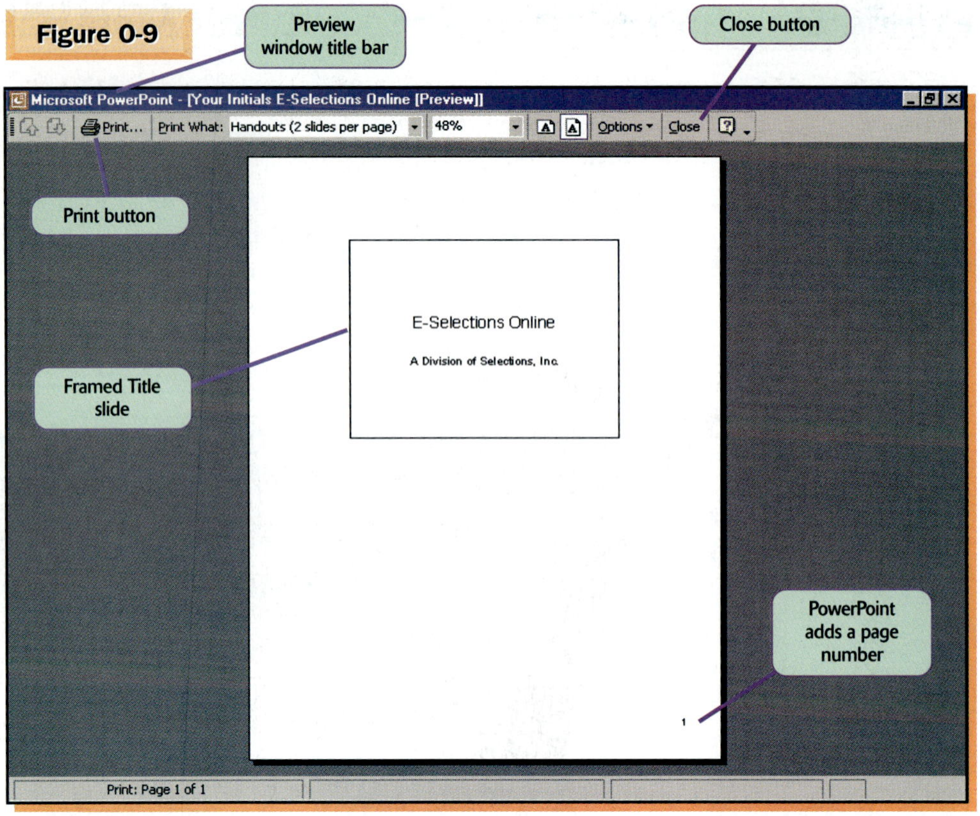

6 Click **Cancel** to cancel the Print dialog box, and then click **Close** on the Preview toolbar.

7 Click the file Close ☒ button. The presentation closes.

Troubleshooting
PowerPoint resets print settings to the default after you print a presentation or presentation materials. As a result, you will need to reselect the presentation materials that you want to print each time you open and print a presentation.

Figure 0-10

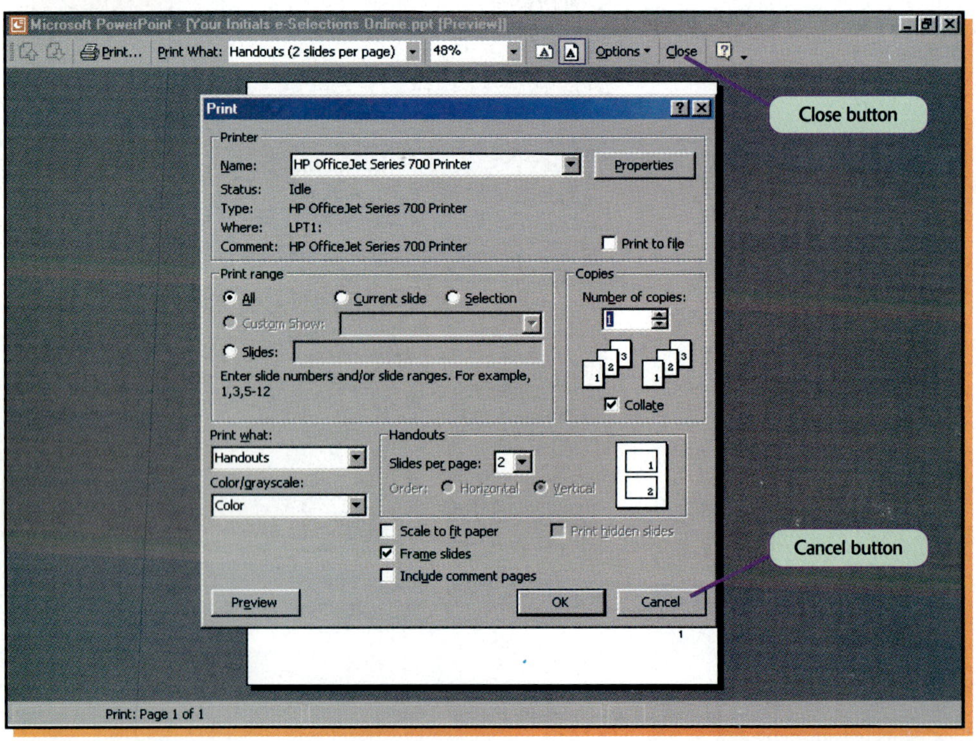

Creating Presentations Using the AutoContent Wizard

The PowerPoint *AutoContent Wizard* helps you build generic outlines for specific types of presentations. The wizard enables you to choose the type of presentation to create and then presents a series of dialog boxes that will guide you through the process. After the outline is complete, you can edit the presentation and substitute your specific text for the generic text the wizard provides.

Task 5:
To Create an AutoContent Presentation

1. Click the **From AutoContent Wizard** link under the **New** section of the task pane.

Figure 0-11

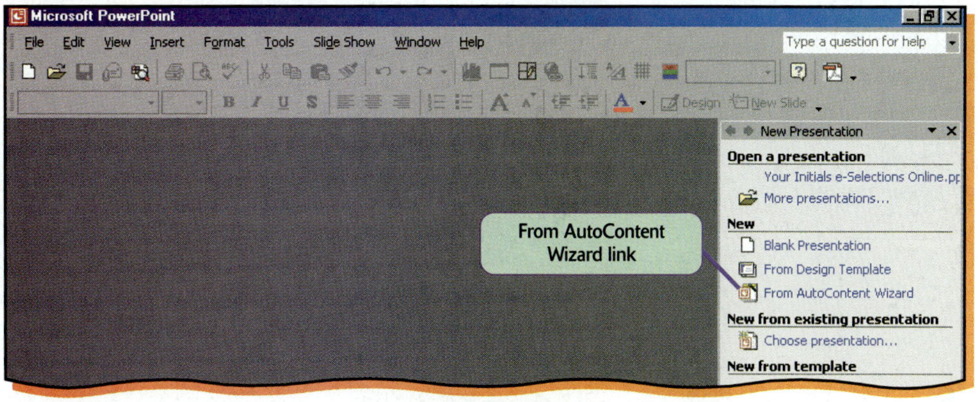

2. Click **No, don't provide help now.** The Office Assistant closes.

3. Click **Next.**

Figure 0-12

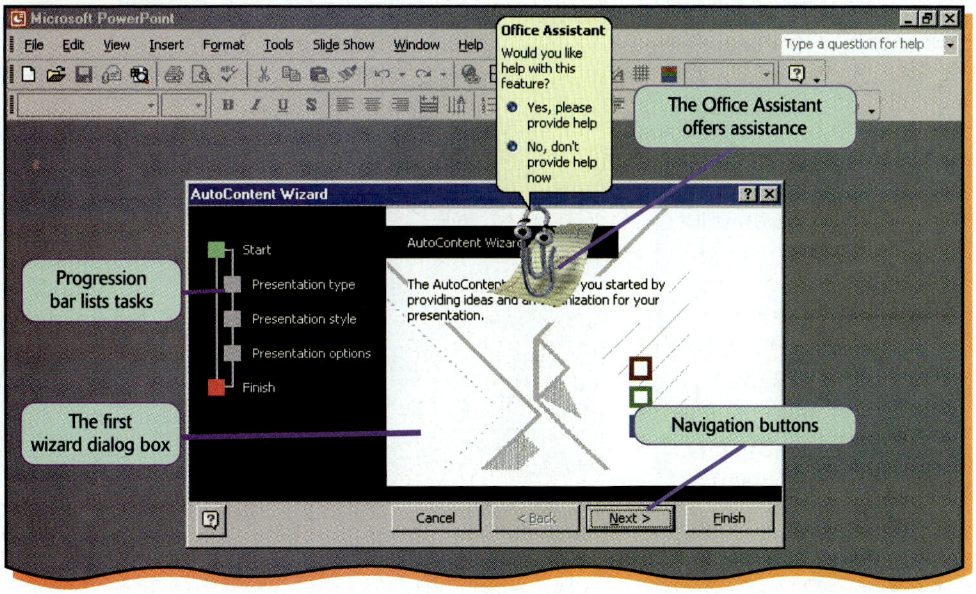

Tip The panel on the left side of the AutoContent Wizard dialog box identifies the number of Wizard pages required to complete the new presentation. As you move through the different Wizard pages, the square beside the active page in the panel changes from grey to green.

4 Click the **Sales/Marketing** button, select **Product/ Services Overview**, and click **Next**.

Tip The types of presentations available for each category—Corporate, Sales/Marketing, etc.—varies. For future reference, you might want to review the AutoContent presentations available in each group.

Figure 0-13

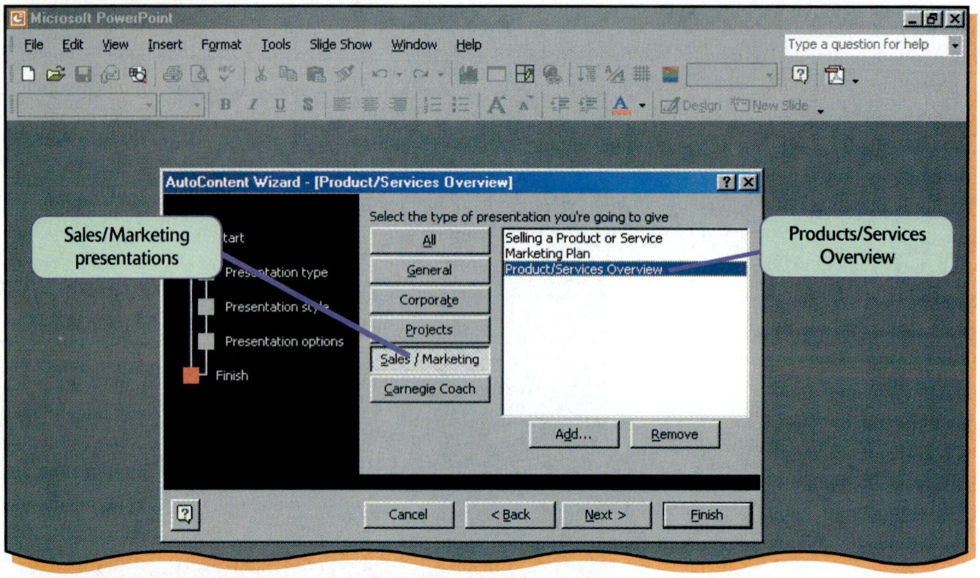

5 Select the **Web presentation** option and click **Next**.

Tip The type of output you select is determined by the equipment you plan to use to show the presentation. If you select one of the overheads options, you will need the transparency film required by your printer available for printing the presentations. To print 35mm slides of the presentation, you will need a special device attached to your computer that is specifically designed to produce the slides.

Figure 0-14

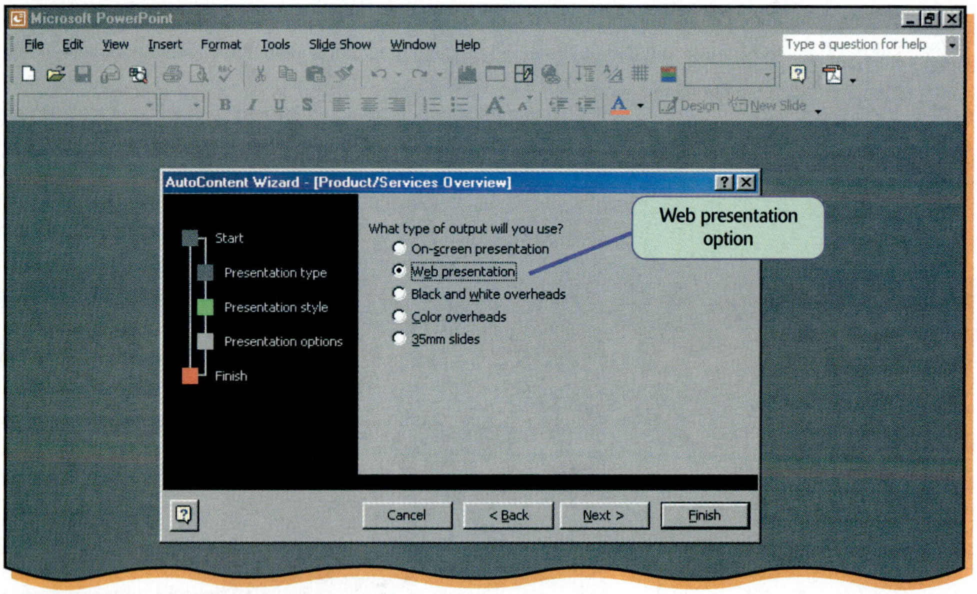

6 Type **e-Selections Online—A New Approach** in the **Presentation title** text box, clear the check marks in the **Footer** options, and click **Finish**.

> **Tip** If you change your mind about adding the date and slide number to the footer area of each slide, you can add the items later using the **View | Header and Footer** command.

Figure 0-15

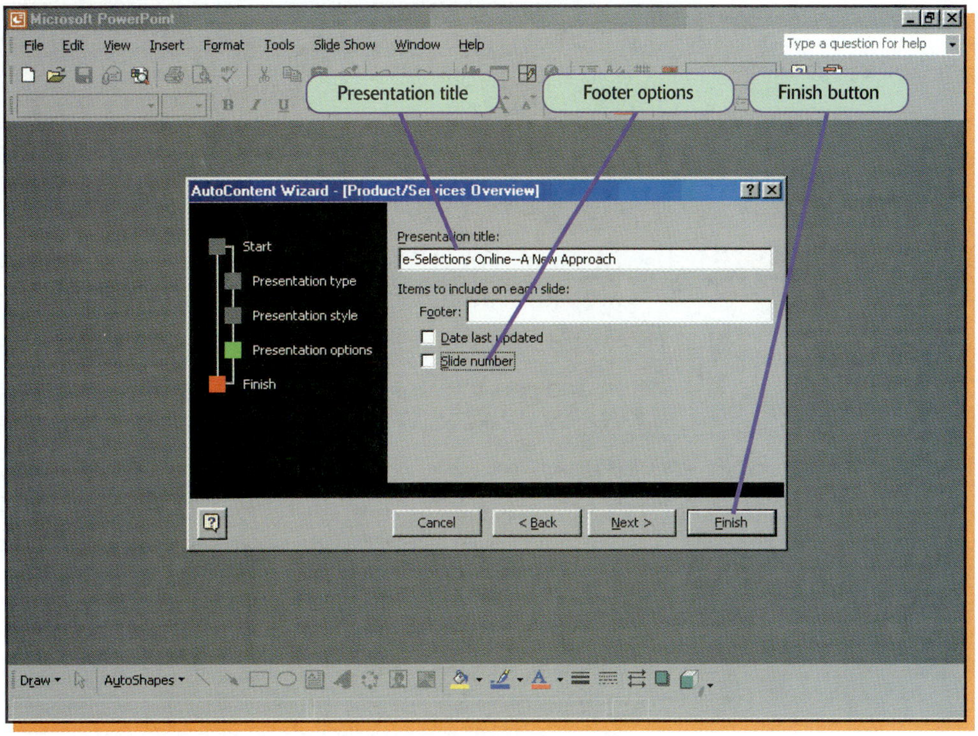

7 Save the presentation using the file name *Your Initials—A New Approach* and then close it.

Figure 0-16

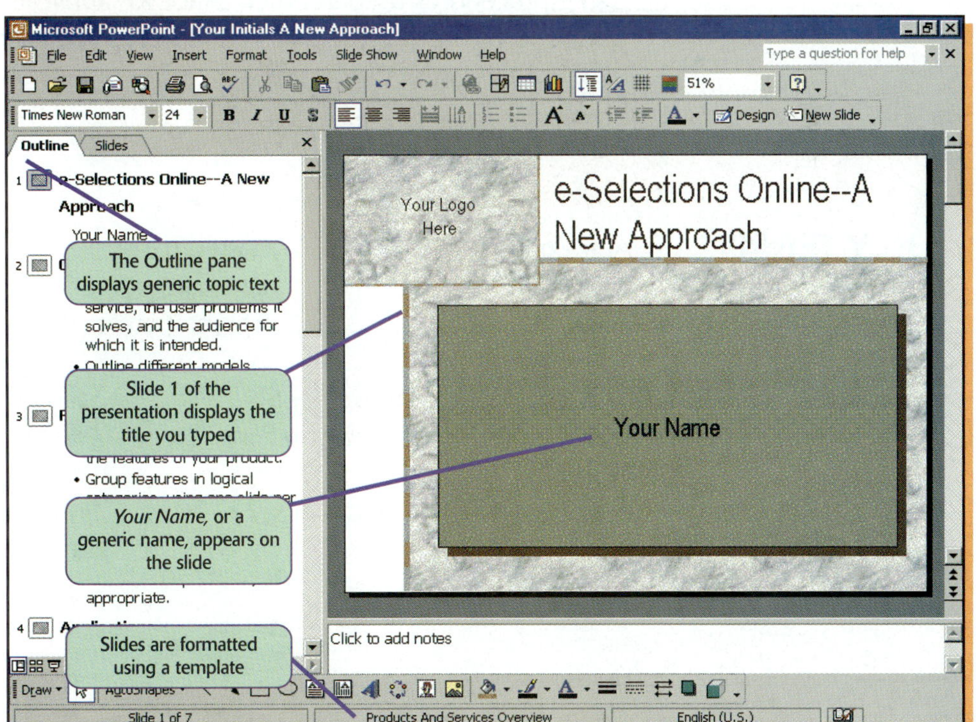

SUMMARY AND EXERCISES

SUMMARY

- Microsoft PowerPoint is a presentation graphics program designed to prepare slide shows and other materials to aid in presentation delivery.
- Presentations may include handouts, slides, speaker's notes, and outlines.
- In addition to blank presentations that have no special formatting, presentations can be created using an AutoContent Wizard and design templates.
- Each presentation may contain numerous slides, each designed to focus on a particular aspect of the broad presentation theme.
- PowerPoint displays presentations in different views using a variety of tools: View buttons, the Outline pane, Slide Design task pane, the Notes Pages pane, and the Slide pane. Each view is designed to help you accomplish specific tasks.
- Toolbars appear automatically as you work in PowerPoint. As a result, tools needed to accomplish specific tasks are available when you need them.
- You can save, open, close, and print presentations using many of the same procedures used in other Office XP applications; you can print a variety of different presentation materials by selecting the desired format from the Print dialog box.

KEY TERMS & SKILLS

KEY TERMS

AutoContent Wizard (p. 9)
AutoFit (p. 6)
master (p. 4)
placeholder (p. 4)
presentation (p. 1)
slide layout (p. 4)
slide (p. 4)
template (p. 4)

SKILLS

Add text to placeholders (p. 5)
Create AutoContent presentations (p. 9)
Identify PowerPoint terminology (p. 4)
Identify screen features (p. 3)
Launch PowerPoint (p. 3)
Preview presentations (p. 7)
Print presentations (p. 7)
Save presentations (p. 6)

STUDY QUESTIONS

MULTIPLE CHOICE

1. A collection of related slides that summarizes key points and acts as a visual aid for a report is called a
   a. summary report.
   b. presentation.
   c. placeholder.
   d. template.

2. Normal view displays
   a. all slide objects.
   b. the slide title and body text only.
   c. small slide images.
   d. slide images, notes about the slide, and the Slide Design/Outline pane.

3. Most slides contain
   a. slide tables.
   b. pictures.
   c. slide titles.
   d. slide names.

4. To launch PowerPoint,
   a. double-click the **Outlook** icon.
   b. open **My Computer**.
   c. start Office XP and press Ctrl + N.
   d. choose **Start | Programs | PowerPoint**.

5. The term that refers to the layout of objects on slides is
   a. slide layouts.
   b. Master.
   c. template.
   d. slide.

6. To create a new, blank presentation,
   a. launch **PowerPoint**—a new presentation automatically appears.
   b. choose **New Presentation** from the PowerPoint dialog box.
   c. select **Blank** presentation from the PowerPoint dialog box.
   d. select **Template** from the PowerPoint dialog box.

7. After launching PowerPoint, the task pane displays options for
   a. creating and opening presentations.
   b. only a list of the most recently edited presentations.
   c. small slide images.
   d. slide designs.

8. The pane on the left side of the PowerPoint window displays
   a. placeholders.
   b. a toolbar.
   c. the Slide Design/Outline pane.
   d. slide layouts.

9. View buttons appear
   a. on the Standard toolbar.
   b. on the task pane.
   c. on the status bar.
   d. at the bottom of the presentation window.

10. All the toolbars listed below appear when you launch PowerPoint except
   a. Standard.
   b. Drawing.
   c. Formatting.
   d. Picture.

SHORT ANSWER

1. What are slide layouts?
2. What six things should you consider as you plan your presentation?
3. What supporting materials can you generate from a presentation?
4. What are the panes of the Normal view and when should you use each pane?
5. What is a template?
6. How do you create a new presentation if PowerPoint is already running?
7. How do you print handouts?
8. How do you move from one placeholder on a slide to another without using the mouse?
9. What button do you click to preview a presentation?

FILL IN THE BLANK

1. PowerPoint can be used to generate slides, handouts, _____________, and notes pages.
2. Professional designs that contain graphics and background color schemes you can use to dress up a presentation are called _____________.
3. The _____________ is the basic unit of a presentation.
4. The _____________ replaces instruction text in a placeholder when you begin typing.
5. The title slide contains two _____________ that contain instructions for adding text.
6. The _____________ button is selected to view the tri-pane window.
7. The _____________ _____________ task pane appears on the left side of the PowerPoint window.
8. The _____________ _____________ helps you develop a presentation designed for a specific purpose.
9. The preview feature enables you to see how presentation materials will _____________.
10. _____________ are prepared and distributed to the audience for note taking during your presentation delivery.

DISCUSSION

1. How are slide layouts, templates, and masters different?
2. How do you identify the material you want to print?
3. What are the advantages of formatting a presentation by using the AutoContent Wizard?
4. What kinds of presentations could you create with PowerPoint for your other classes?

GUIDED EXERCISES

1 A SEASON OF VALUES AT SELECTIONS

Different seasons of the year control, to some extent, the products that e-Selections will offer online shoppers. Ms. Wright has asked you to create the first slide in a new presentation that will eventually identify products specific to each season. Follow these instructions to complete your task.

1. Launch **PowerPoint**, if necessary, or click **Blank Presentation** from the **New** area of the task pane.

> **Troubleshooting** If the task pane is hidden or displays different features, choose **File | New** to display the New Presentation task pane.

2. Type **e-Selections Online** in the title placeholder and type **A store for all seasons** in the subtitle placeholder.
3. Save the presentation using the file name *Your Initials A Season of Values*, print a copy of the title slide, and close the file.

2 PRINTING A NEW APPROACH OUTLINE

The presentation you created using the AutoContent Wizard contains valuable sample text that you can use to identify the type of information you should include in a marketing presentation. You can print the presentation outline rather than printing slides or handouts and conserve paper. Follow these instructions:

1. Click the *Your Initials—A New Approach* file in the Open a presentation section of the task pane.
2. Choose **File | Print**, click the **Print what** down arrow, select **Outline View,** and click **Preview** to view the outline before printing.
3. Click **Print** on the Preview toolbar to print the outline and then close the file.

3 SELECTIONS NEW HIRE OVERVIEW

New employees at Selections, Inc., could benefit from a presentation that provides an overview of the company. You can use the AutoContent Wizard to outline a new presentation for Selections, Inc., to use for new employee hires. Follow these instructions to get started.

1. Launch **PowerPoint**, if necessary, and choose **From AutoContent Wizard** from the New section of the task pane.

2. Click **Next**, click **Corporate**, select **Employee Orientation** from the corporate list, click **Next**. Select the **On-screen presentation** option and click **Next**.
3. Type **Selections, Inc., New Employee Overview** in the title placeholder.
4. Clear the check marks in the Footer options and click **Finish**.
5. Save the presentation using the file name *Your Initials New Employee Overview* and print a copy of the outline.

4 ANALYZING PRESENTATION SLIDES

As you become more comfortable with designing and building presentations, you will become aware of some of the do's and don'ts associated with developing presentation slides. Additional tips are stored in the PowerPoint *Slide Samples* show. In addition, the show contains slides that will give you practice analyzing slide format and content. You'll need pencil and paper for this activity. Then follow these instructions:

1. Choose **File | Open** and locate the file *Slide Samples.pps*.
2. Double-click the file name. The title slide appears on screen for review.
3. Press Enter to advance to the next slide and review the information it contains.
4. Repeat the procedures contained in Step 3 for the first nine slides.
5. When the slide titled Slide 1 appears on screen, review the slide, identify the positive and negative features of the slide, and then jot down suggestions for improvement.
6. Repeat the procedures outlined in Step 5 for slides 2 through 5.
7. After the last slide, press Enter twice to display the show in PowerPoint and then print a copy of the show as black-and-white handouts with six slides per page.
8. Create a new Word document and type the list of positive and negative aspects you identified for each slide. Also, include some suggestions for improvement.
9. Save the Word document using the file name *Analysis of Slide Samples*. Print a copy of the document to submit to your instructor.

ON YOUR OWN

The difficulty of these case studies varies:
are the least difficult; *are more difficult; and* *are the most difficult.*

1 A NEW TELEVISION SEASON

With the advent of the new television season each fall, networks and local television stations publicize their new shows in a variety of different ways. The manager of the local television station has asked that you design and outline a plan for promoting the new shows that will debut on the local station. Create a new blank presentation for JPLD-TV's new season; preview and enter appropriate information in the title slide. Save the presentation using the file name *Your Initials JPLD,* print a copy of the title slide, and close the presentation.

2 FOREST RESEARCH IN THE ROCKY MOUNTAINS

The Rocky Mountain Research Station for the U. S. Forest Service Research Branch is one of seven different research stations located across the country. It conducts research in the territory between the Mississippi River and California. You've been asked by the director of the research station to create a presentation outlining the status of research scientists and the research goals of the station. Create a new blank presentation that contains the title slide shown in Figure O-17. Save the presentation using the file name *Your Initials RMRS* and print a copy of the slide.

Figure 0-17

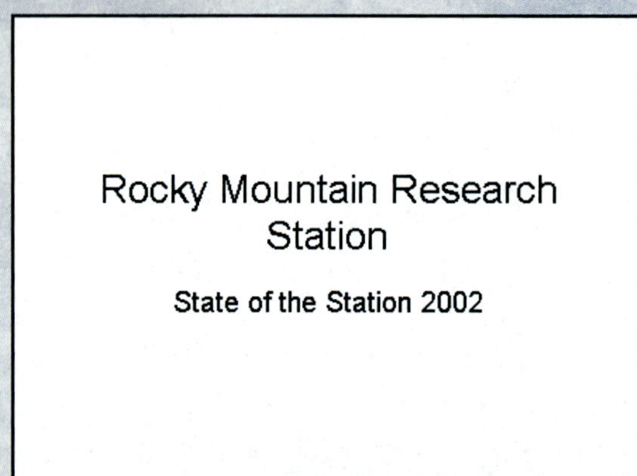

3 YOUR MAJOR AREA OF STUDY

Many educational disciplines are having difficulty meeting the demands of today's consumer market. College students often wait until the last minute to determine what their major is going to be. A professor in your area of study (or one in which you are interested) has asked that you prepare an outline for a presentation that identifies the requirements for completing a degree in that area of study, some of the benefits to be derived from the discipline, job opportunities in the field, and potential salaries for different regions of the country. The professor plans to use the presentation to encourage others to enter the discipline. To get started, print a copy of the presentation *Your Initials—A New Approach* outline. Use the presentation outline as a guide for designing the new presentation about your major area of study. Then launch PowerPoint and create a new blank presentation entitled *Your Initials Major Study Area*. Enter text in placeholders on the title slide, save changes to the presentation, and print a copy of the title slide.

4 A FAMILY AFFAIR

Keeping track of family affairs can be a very tedious business. Keeping track of your relatives can be quite challenging! Create an outline of at least three generations of your family tree. Include in the outline as many names, birth dates, and birth places as you can find for yourself, your siblings, your parents (or guardians), and your grandparents. Then create a new presentation containing the title slide of the presentation and save the presentation using the file name *Your Initials Family Tree*.

5 PRESENTING YOUR RESUME

Ms. Amber Wright likes the format and design of your resume. She asks you to create an outline of the resume, including text, in a format that would be appropriate for a PowerPoint presentation. Use Roman numerals to identify each slide for the presentation and identify the format (table, bulleted list, etc.) that would be appropriate for information you want to place on each slide.

6 REVIEWING PRESENTATIONS ON THE INTERNET

The Internet is full of presentations that provide great examples on which to base the presentations you create. You'll also find a number of presentations posted on the Web that aren't so great—they have design flaws and are poorly organized. Search the Internet for presentations related to something of interest to you. Review at least two different presentations and evaluate each presentation for the following items:

- Target audience
- Content
- Design
- Format
- Graphics
- Color

Download the presentation from the Internet for viewing. Then create a report that identifies your opinion of the items listed above.

WEB TIP

Having trouble locating information about your family lineage? Try searching the Web for genealogy sites such as The Family Tree. Is your family name listed on any of the sites? If not, find out how you can post your family tree on one of the Web sites for others to view.

FROM THE FILES

You Will Need

- ✔ e-Selections Web.ppt
- ✔ A Novel Approach.ppt
- ✔ Seasons of Values.ppt
- ✔ JPLD-TV.ppt
- ✔ New Employee Overview.ppt
- ✔ Rocky Mountain Research.ppt

PROJECT 1

Building Presentations

Now that you have designed and created a number of different presentations using some of the techniques provided in PowerPoint, it's time to start building those presentations. In this project, you will add slides to presentations, edit presentation text, format presentation materials, proof presentations, learn to navigate presentations, and explore PowerPoint views.

OBJECTIVES

After completing this project, you will be able to:

- Open presentations
- Add slides to presentations
- Apply slide layouts
- Create table slides
- Insert, view, and print comments
- Navigate presentations
- Add text to outlines and slide notes
- Edit and format slide text
- Proof presentations
- Set up pages
- Pack a presentation to go

e-selections Running Case

So far, you've made great progress in your PowerPoint exploration. You have started both presentations that Ms. Wright wants you to complete and can now begin building and formatting the presentations.

Plotting and Planning a Presentation

Jim Endicott, Owner/Manager of Distinction, a consulting business focused on how to help companies communicate their important messages more effectively, has learned that people seem to learn best by what they see, not by what they're told. Based on this premise, he formulated three basic lessons for communicating that he relates in an article entitled Ho, Ho, Ho, Hum:

- **Lesson One:** How well we qualify our target audience can mean the difference between success and failure. Well-illustrated presentations lose their effectiveness if they are too long. "Time is clearly relative but for the attention span of a six year-old (or a Board of Directors) a message that doesn't move briskly to a compelling conclusion can leave your audience checking out the exits. I much prefer creating presentations that conclude slightly prematurely. First of all, it's a rare experience for an audience. Secondly, you will exhaust the planned topic before you've exhausted your audience—equally rare."

- **Lesson Two:** Make time your ally, not your enemy. "As you craft your presentation content, the level of confidence in the message you're creating will be directly related to the sum of your experiences, education and intuition. Think twice about addressing an audience on a topic where you'll need to 'wing it.' You can be assured that savvy audiences will see through the veneer and you will not only lose their respect but their attention as well."

- **Lesson Three:** The best presentation content flows from your experiences, observations, and passion.

Careful planning will enable you to develop a presentation targeted to your audience, design a look that best conveys the purpose of the presentation, and determine the method you plan to use to deliver the presentation. Consider the following as you plan each presentation:

- **Why are you giving the presentation?** *Determining the message you want to communicate and the action you want the audience to take helps ensure that the focus of the material will be on target.*

- **What materials do you want to use with the presentation?** *Deciding whether slides, handouts, notes, and/or overhead transparencies would be most effective allows you to be more efficient as you create the presentation materials.*

- **Who will be in the audience and how many people will attend?** *Categorizing the attendees as managers, corporate executives, salespeople, peers, and so forth enables you to develop a presentation geared to the proper level.*

- **When will the presentation occur?** *Identifying the time of day, placement of the presentation in relation to other presentations, and so on helps to determine presentation strategy and length.*

- **Where is the presentation to be given?** *Considering the size of the room, acoustics of the room, location of the speaker platform, and other factors helps you determine the size of slide and screen elements to include in a presentation. Keep in mind the old adage that "Less is more." Small printed characters are difficult to see from the back of the room, and information is often lost on crowded slides. Limit lists to short statements rather than complete sentences, make the font larger, and keep graphics and other components simple.*

- **How will the presentation materials be delivered—on screen or as handouts?** *Presentation design is affected by the way the presentation is delivered. Adding color to slides can be more effective in on-screen presentations, while color used for handouts and transparencies might be too dark.*

After you have considered each of these questions and outlined your presentation, you're ready to launch PowerPoint and put it to work for you.

PROJECT 1

Building Presentations

The Challenge

Ms. Wright has asked you to continue the presentation you started designing for the Web. You have already devised several slides that you want to add to the presentation for the Web and have also developed an outline for the Marketing/Sales presentation. The slides and outline appear in Figure 1-1.

Figure 1-1

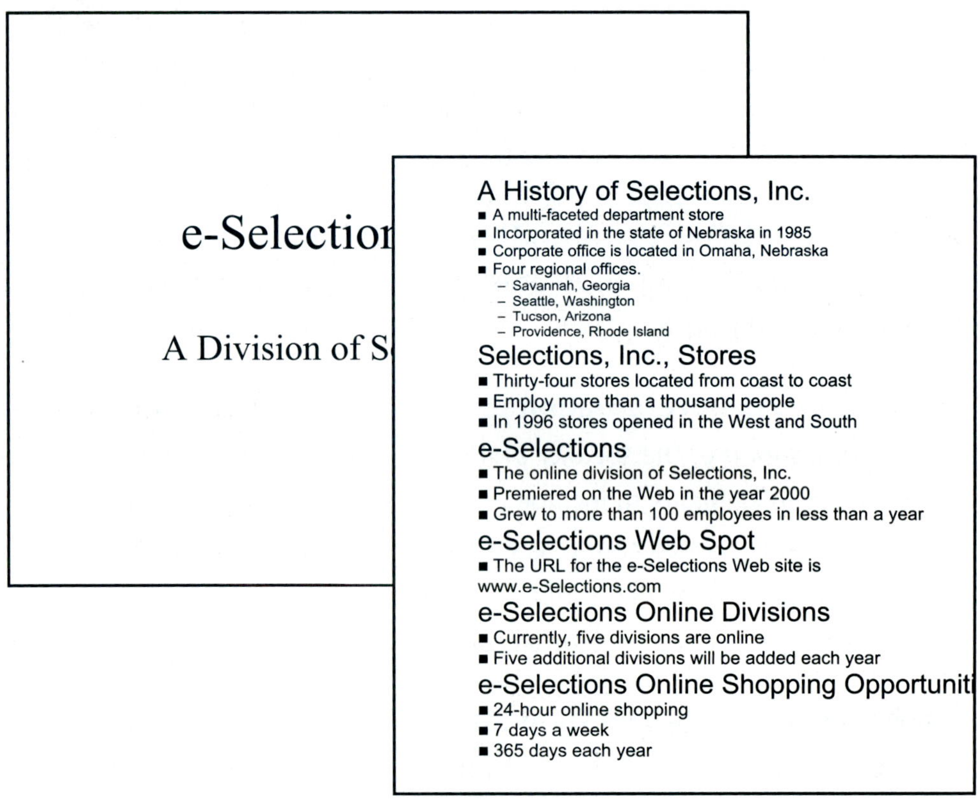

The Solution

Before getting too far along in the presentation, you want to be sure that Ms. Wright approves the direction you are taking with both presentations. You will add several slides to the Web presentation, type the outline for the Marketing/Sales presentation, and then ask Ms. Wright to review them before continuing.

Creating New Slides

Presentations generally consist of numerous slides, all related to the same topic. Behind each title slide, you often need to add slides to provide explanatory information or supporting documentation. When you add slides to a presentation, they follow the active slide. PowerPoint offers a variety of techniques for adding new slides:

- Click the New Slide [New Slide] button on the Formatting toolbar.
- Click a slide layout down arrow on the task pane and then select **Insert New Slide.**
- Choose **Insert | New Slide** from the menus.
- Press [Ctrl] + [M].
- Press [Ctrl] + [Enter] from the last placeholder on the active slide to create a new bulleted-list slide.

Task 1:
To Create a New Slide

1 Launch **PowerPoint** and click **More Presentations** in the Open a presentation area of the New Presentation task pane.

Troubleshooting
If the New Presentation task pane is hidden or other features appear in the task pane, choose **File | New** to display the New Presentation task pane

2 Open the drive and folder containing the *e-Selections Web.ppt* presentation and double-click the presentation name.

Figure 1-2

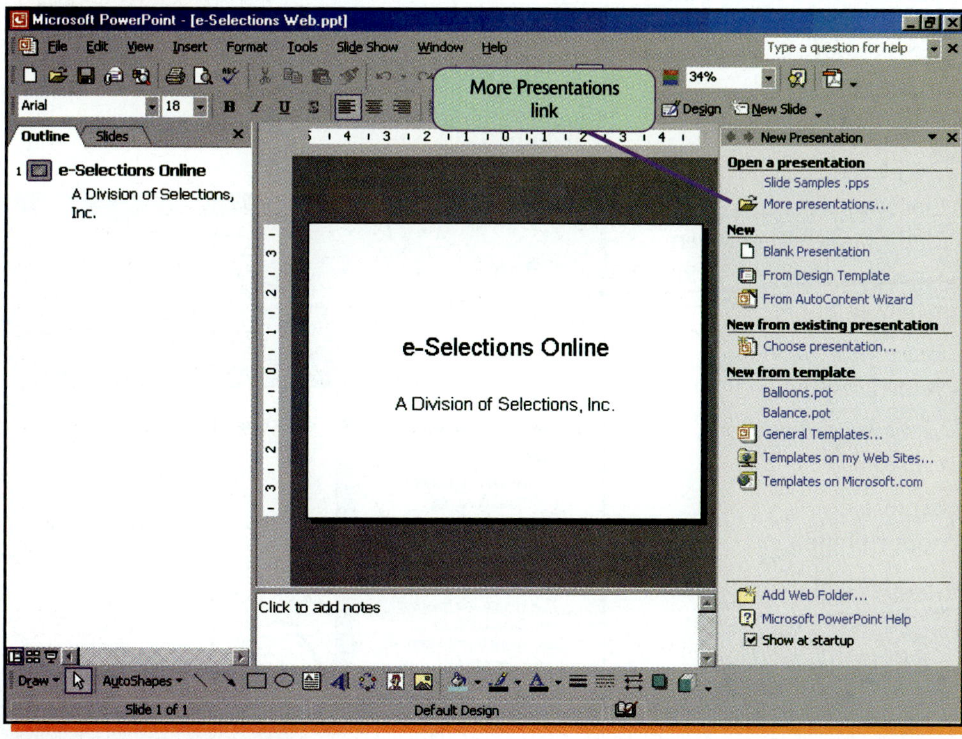

Tip For detailed information about opening files, refer to Common Elements Project 1.

3 Click the New Slide **New Slide** button on the Formatting toolbar and set the **Zoom** to 33%, if necessary.

4 Click the title placeholder and type **What do you want to do?**

Tip Each time you click the New Slide button on the Formatting toolbar, the Slide Layout task pane opens.

Figure 1-3

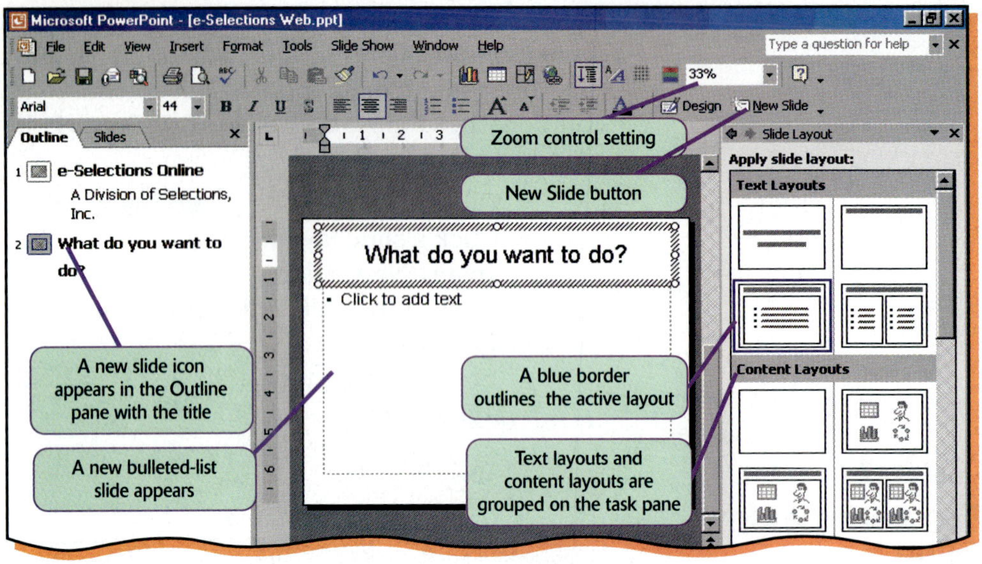

5 Click the bulleted-list placeholder and type the following list items exactly as they appear here (even misspelled words), pressing Enter between bulleted items:

- **Learn more about Selections, Inc.**
- **View the e-Selections Catalog**
- **Explore employement opportunities**
- **Locate the nearest Selections, Inc., department store**
- **Contact us**

6 Save changes to the presentation.

Figure 1-4

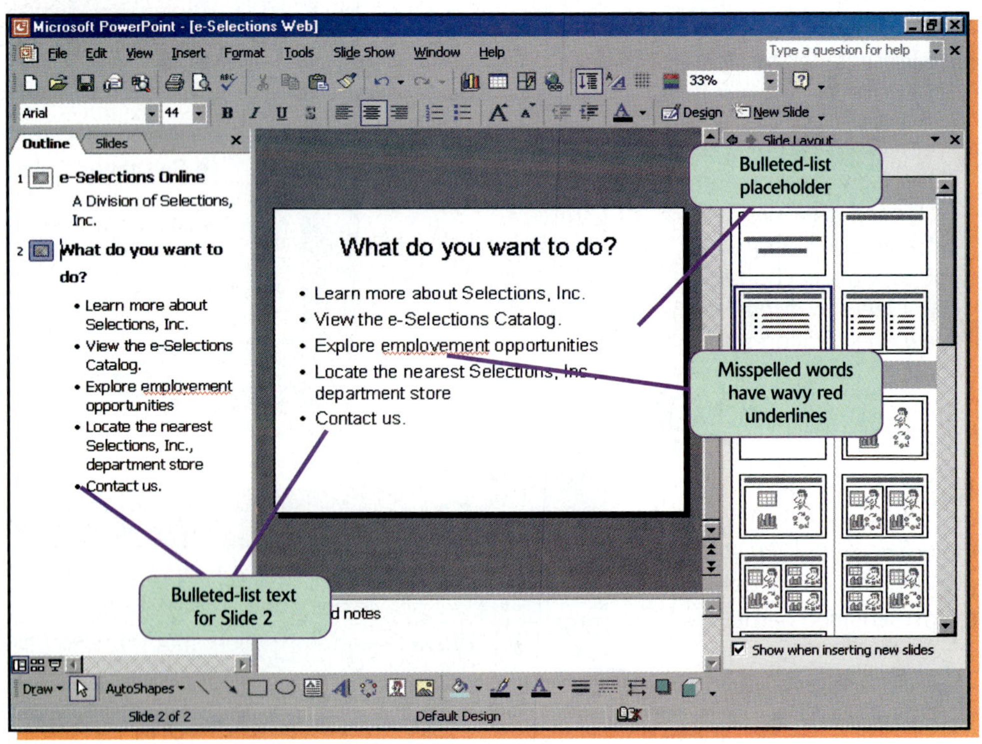

Applying Slide Layouts

Slide layouts contain placeholders that are preformatted for the different types of objects that you can place on slides. The Slide Layout task pane displays slide formats grouped by type: Text, Content, Text and Content, and Other Layouts. Selecting an appropriate slide layout as you create a new slide makes creating, inserting, and formatting slide objects more efficient. As you build presentations, you will use a variety of different slide layouts.

Formatting Text Slides

PowerPoint offers a variety of different Text Layouts containing placeholders of different sizes and arrangements. You can select the format and arrangement of text placeholders as you create slides or you can apply a different layout to existing slides.

Task 2:
To Create a New Slide and Format it Using a Slide Layout

1. Point to the **Title and 2-Column Text** icon in the **Text Layouts** portion of the Slide Layout task pane.
2. Click the down arrow on the **Title and 2-Column Text** slide layout.
3. Select **Insert New Slide**.

Figure 1-5

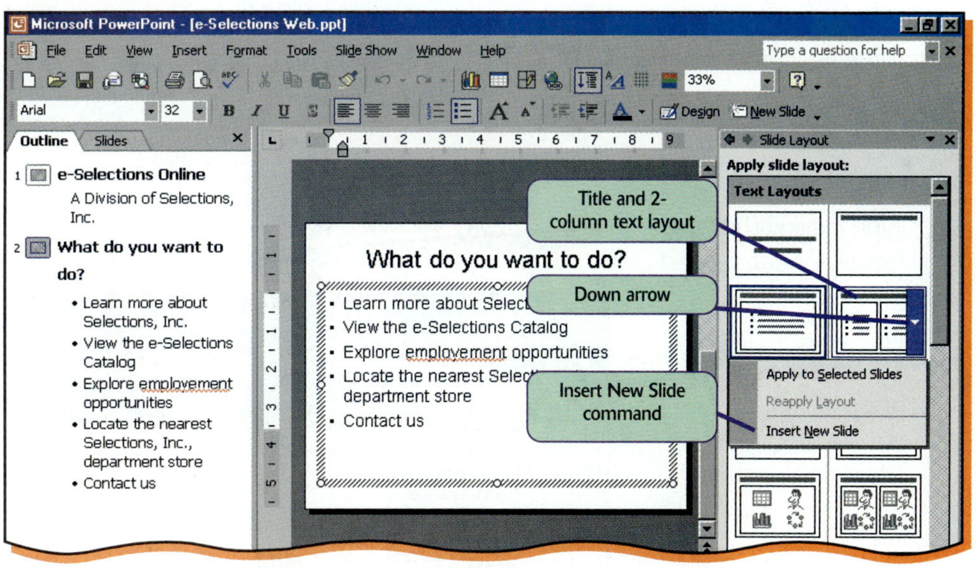

Troubleshooting If the Slide Layout task pane is hidden, choose **View | Task Pane** to display it. Then select **Slide Layout** from the task pane title bar drop-down list, if necessary.

4 Close the task pane, set the **Zoom** to 50%, if necessary.

Troubleshooting
Each pane of the Normal view window can be set to display a different Zoom setting. Be sure the Slide pane is active when you adjust the Zoom setting.

Figure 1-6

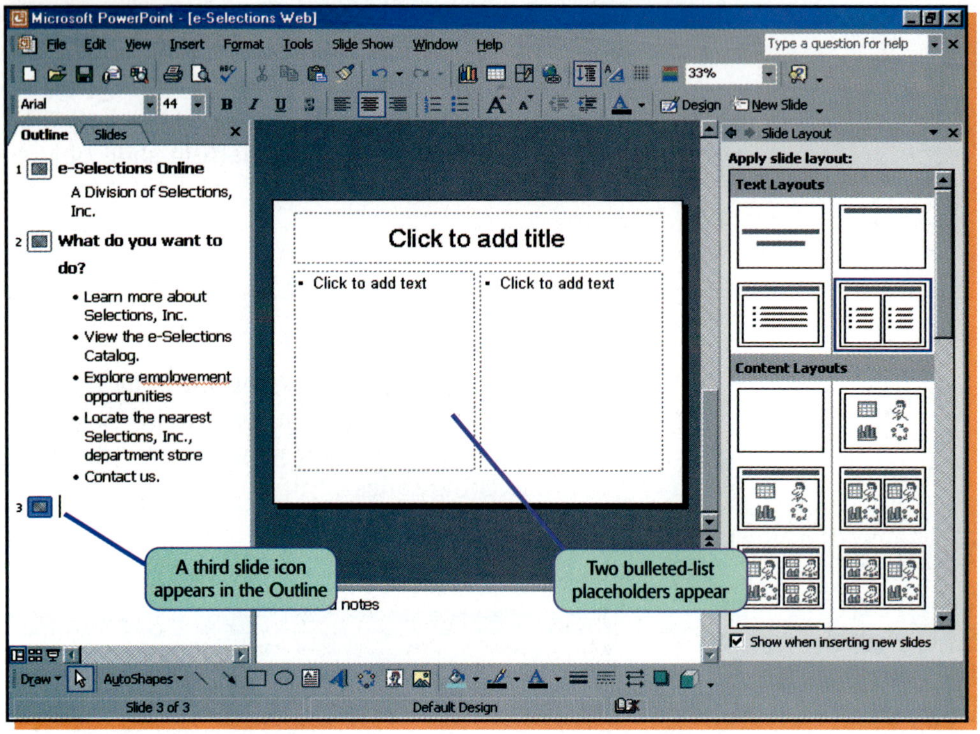

5 Type the text shown in Figure 1-7 into the text boxes on the new slide.

6 Save changes to the presentation.

Figure 1-7

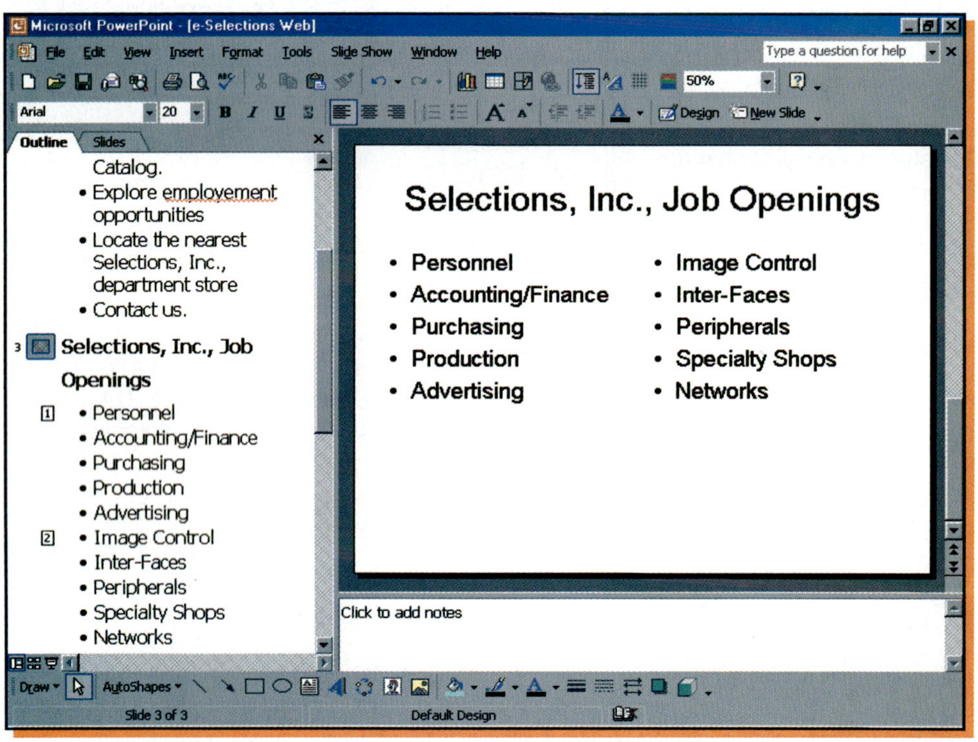

Creating Table Slides

The slides you have created thus far have contained placeholders designed to hold text. The Slide Layout task pane also displays additional groups of layouts formatted with placeholders that hold objects other than, or in addition to, text. By selecting one of the Content Layout formats, you can easily select the item in the placeholder that you want to add to the slide.

Task 3: To Create a Table Slide

1. Choose **View | Task Pane**

> **Tip** Displaying the task pane when a presentation is active automatically displays the slide layouts on the task pane.

2. Scroll down the **Slide Layout** task pane until the Content Layouts group appears.

3. Locate the **Title and Content** layout identified in Figure 1-9.

4. Select **Insert New Slide** from the drop-down list.

> **Troubleshooting** Be careful to click the down arrow that appears when you point to the Title and Content slide layout. If you click the Title and Content slide layout rather than the down arrow, the layout of the active slide changes.

Figure 1-8

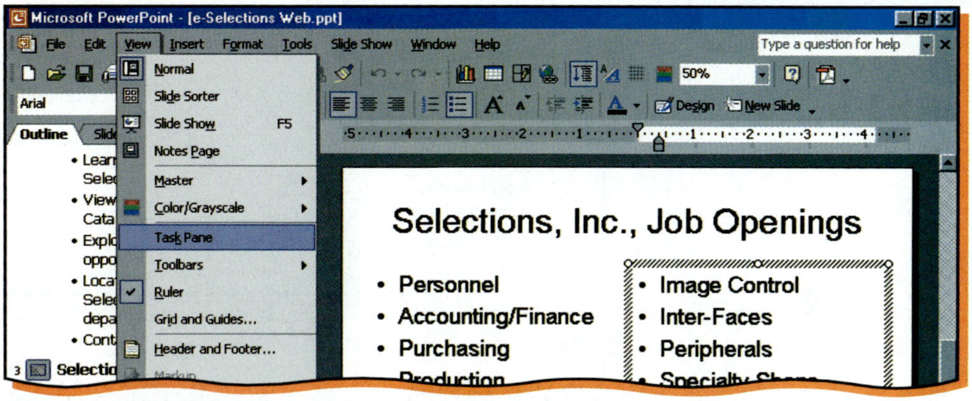

Figure 1-9

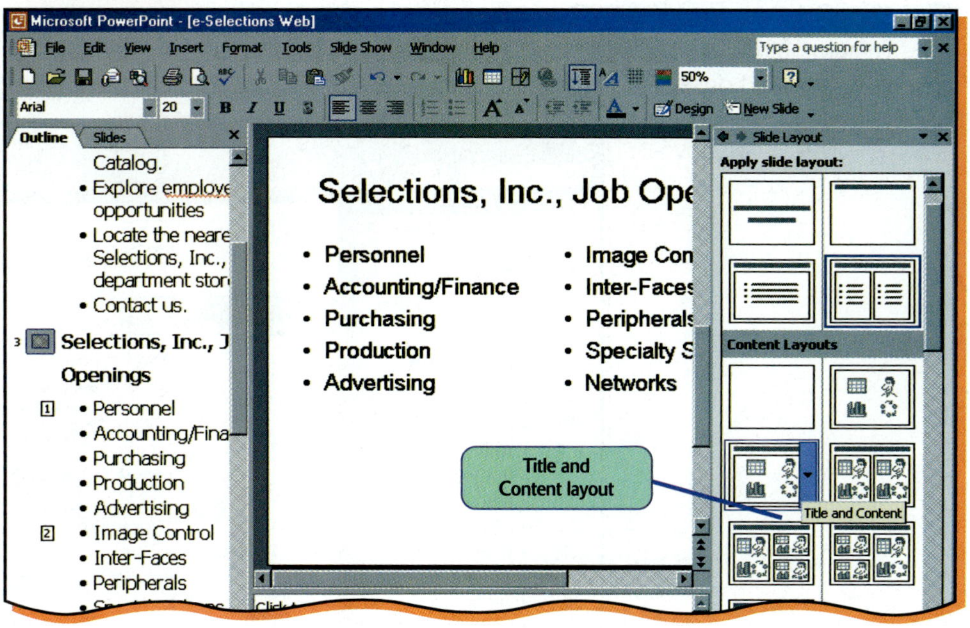

5 Click the Insert Table icon in the Content placeholder to open the Insert Table dialog box.

Other Ways

To insert a table:

- Choose **Insert** | **Table.**

Figure 1-10

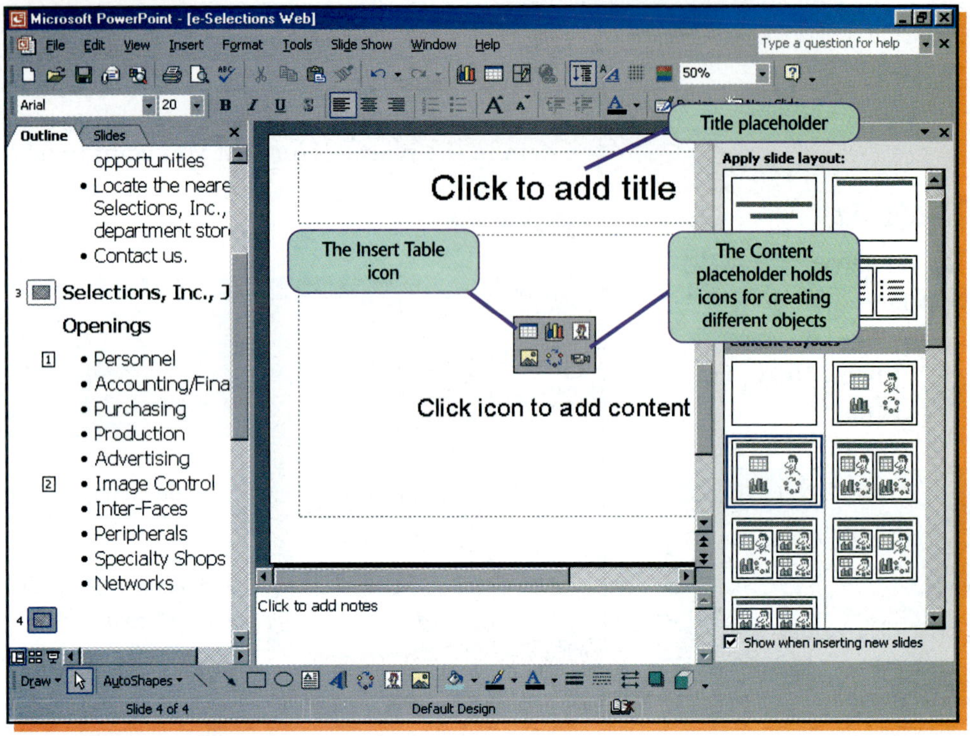

6 Click **OK** to accept the defaults of the Insert Table dialog box and close the Task Pane.

Figure 1-11

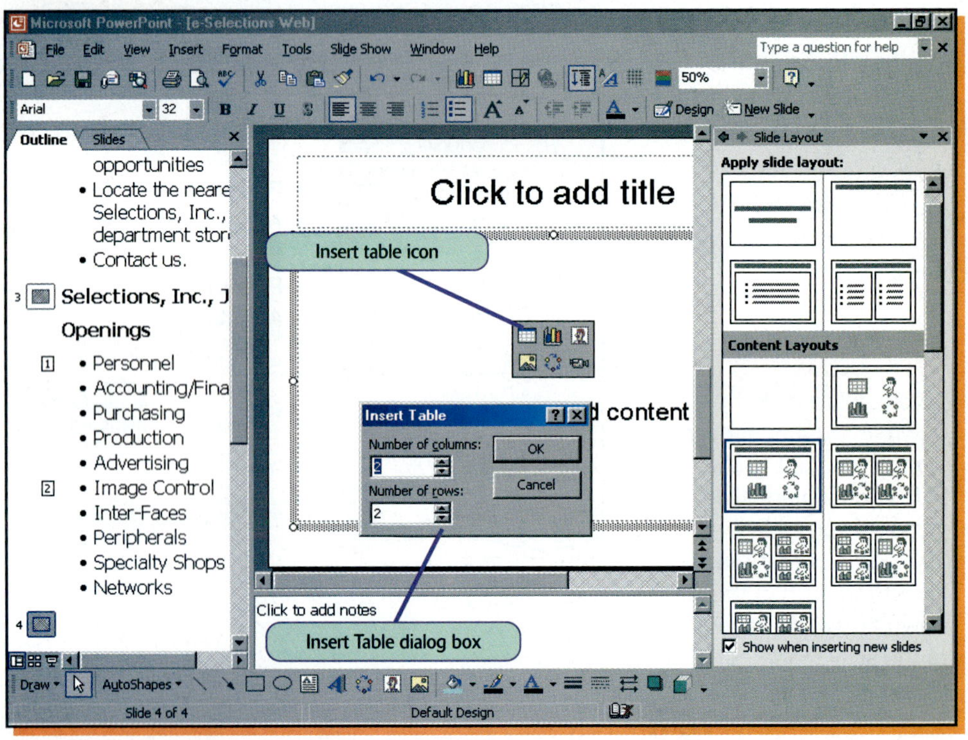

> **Tip** The Tables and Borders toolbar may appear. Simply move the toolbar out of the way or close it.

7 Type the text shown in Figure 1-12 in the new slide's title and table cells, pressing [Tab] to move to the next cell in the table.

8 Save changes to the presentation.

Figure 1-12

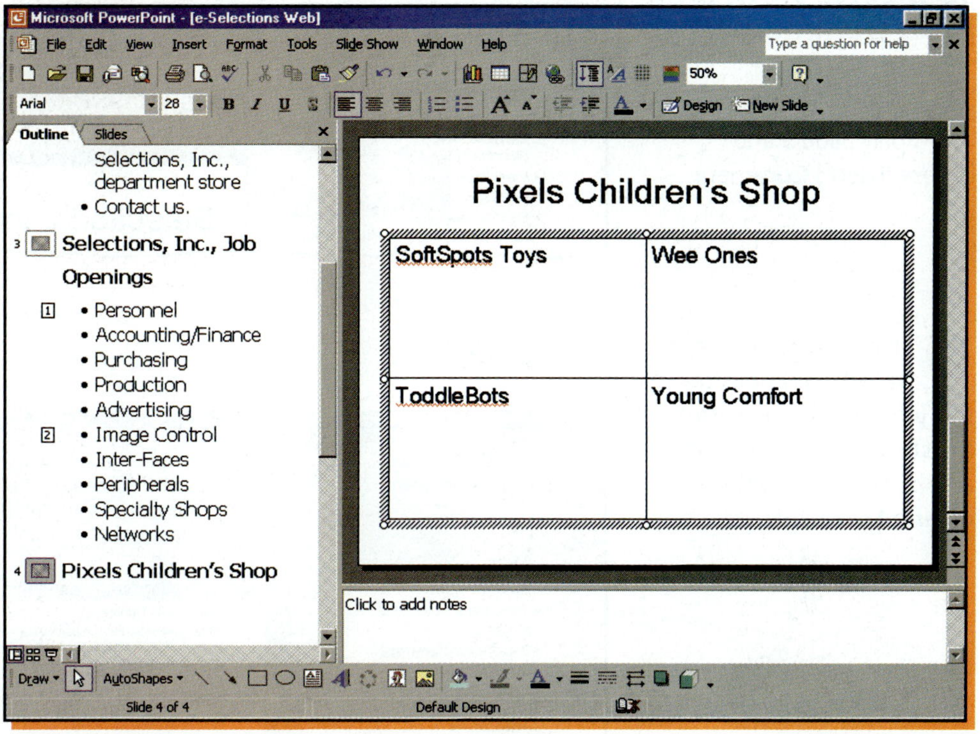

CHECK POINT

Electronic presentations are usually created to supplement and enhance oral presentations. The PowerPoint presentation displays in the PowerPoint application window after you have shown the last presentation slide, leaving the audience with a slightly diminished impression. To end a presentation smoothly, PowerPoint places a blank, *black slide* at the end of the presentation by default. When this last slide appears, you know the presentation is complete. To check that this option is set, choose **Tools** | **Options** | **View** and ensure that the **End with black slide** option is selected.

Inserting, Viewing, and Printing Comments

Electronic *comments* can be added to PowerPoint 2002 files to insert text in a presentation without making it part of the actual presentation. Adding comments to the presentation is a great way to record reminders, enter additional information, or make suggestions about the file. Comments that have been added to presentations can be printed along with presentation materials and appear on separate pages immediately following the slide containing the comment.

Task 4:

To Insert, View, and Print Comments

1 Press [Page Up] to display Slide 3 and choose **Insert | Comment**.

Figure 1-13

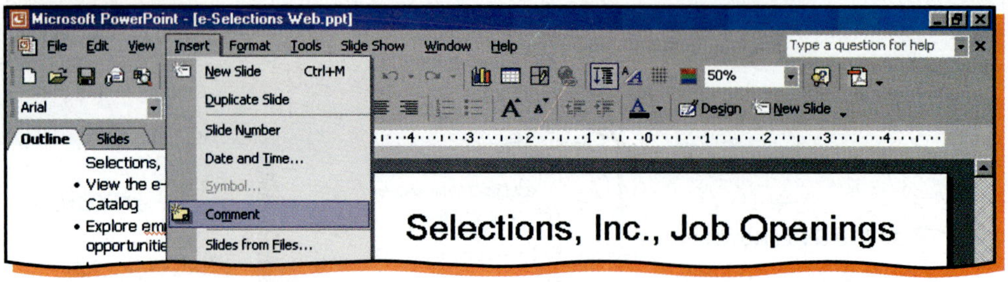

2 Type **Should we separate the administrative job opportunities from the store job opportunities and place each type on a different slide?**

Figure 1-14

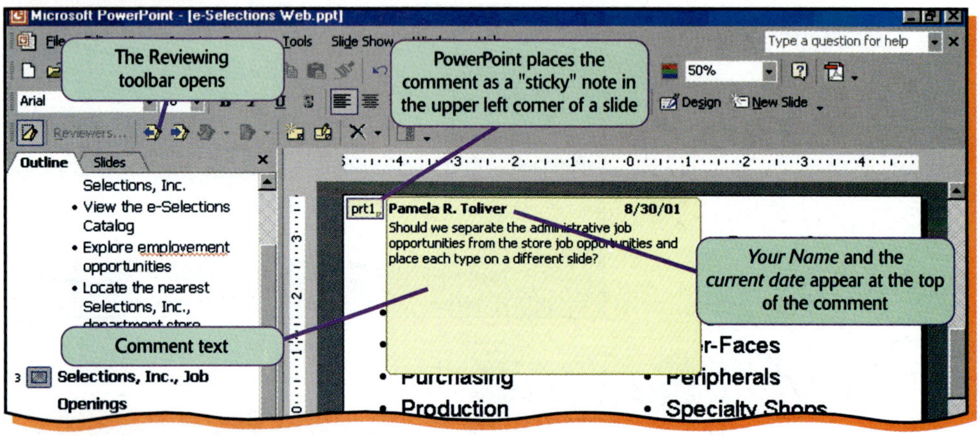

3 Click a blank area of the slide.

4 Point to the **Comment** icon in the upper left corner of the slide to see the full comment text.

5 Save changes to the presentation and close the **Reviewing** toolbar.

Tip Right-click a button on any toolbar and select Reviewing to close the toolbar.

Figure 1-15

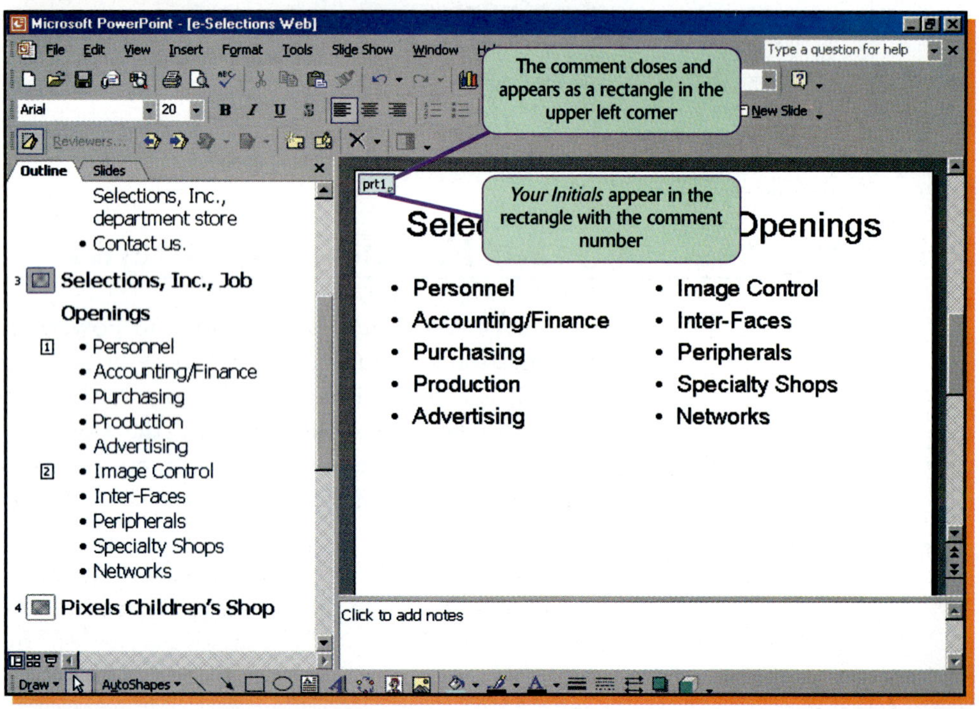

6 Press Ctrl + P to open the Print dialog box.

Other Ways
To display the Print dialog box
- Choose **File | Print**.

7 Select the **Include comment pages** option and click **Preview**.

Figure 1-16

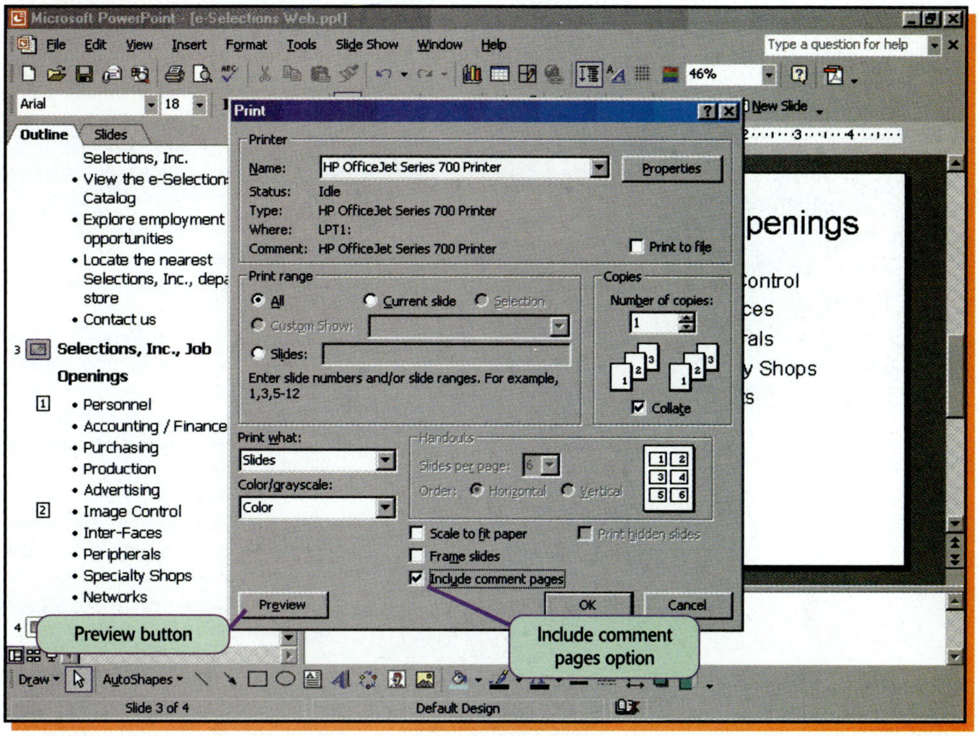

8 Click the Next Page button on the toolbar three times to display the comments page following Slide 3 and then click on the text at the top of the page.

9 Click **Close** on the Preview toolbar, save changes to the presentation, and then close the presentation.

Figure 1-17

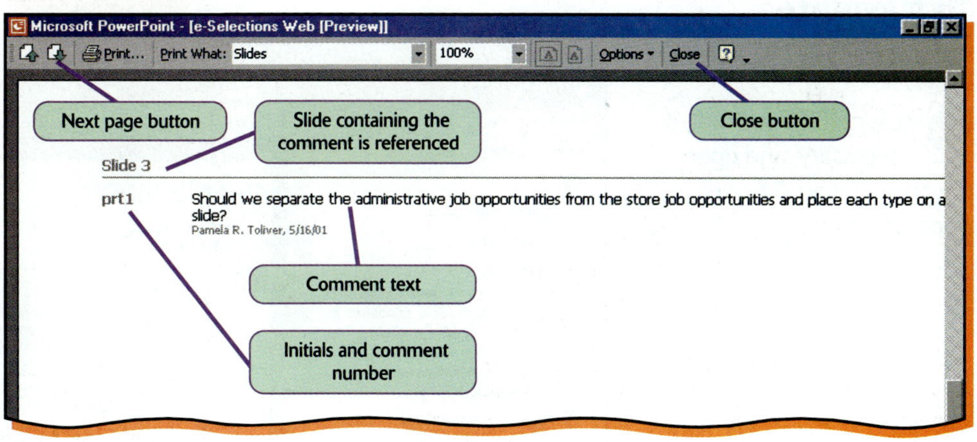

Navigating Presentations

You've already discovered that placeholder text not only appears in the placeholder on the slide, but also displays in the presentation outline. A quick glance at the Outline pane helps you to determine how many slides the presentation contains. It also provides a quick overview of the presentation contents. As you add more slides to your presentation, the outline will often extend beyond the screen. You can determine the number of presentation slides by glancing at the status bar. As your presentation grows, navigating slides in the presentation becomes important. Using a variety of keyboard and mouse navigation techniques, you can display different slides in the presentation for editing or review. Navigation techniques are identified in Table 1-1.

Tip If a slide placeholder is active when you press Ctrl + Home or Ctrl + End, PowerPoint moves to the beginning or end of the placeholder.

Table 1-1 Presentation Slide Navigation Techniques

To Display/Access	Mouse Technique	Keyboard Shortcut
Next slide	Click the Next Slide button at the bottom of the vertical scroll bar.	Press PageDown.
Previous slide	Click the Previous Slide button at the bottom of the vertical scroll bar.	Press Page Up.
Specific slides	Drag the scroll box in the **Slide** pane until the title or slide number you want to display appears.	
First slide	Click the **Slides** tab on the **Slide Design** pane and then click Slide 1.	Press Ctrl + Home.
Last slide	Click the **Slides** tab on the **Slide Design** pane and then click the last slide.	Press Ctrl + End.
Normal view panes	Click the appropriate pane.	Press F6 until the pane is active.

Task 5: To Navigate Presentations

1. Launch **PowerPoint,** if necessary, and open the presentation *A Novel Approach.ppt*.

Figure 1-18

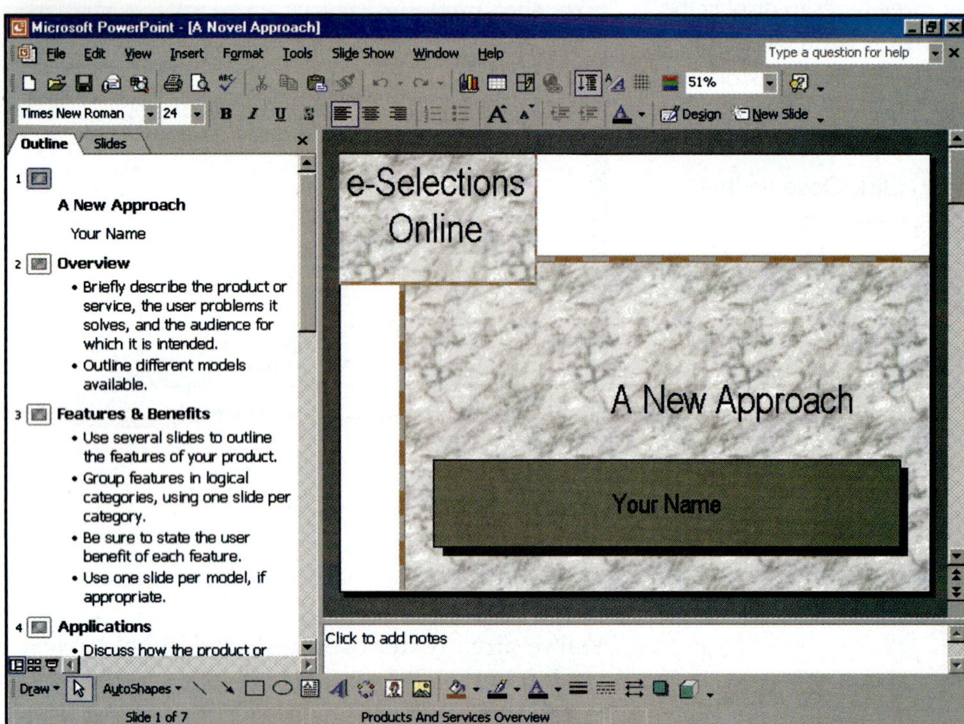

2 Click the title text for Slide 2 in the Outline pane.

3 Press PageDown to display Slide 3. Press Ctrl + Home to display Slide 1.

4 Click the Next Slide button to display Slide 2. Drag the scroll box in the vertical scroll bar to display Slide 5.

Figure 1-19

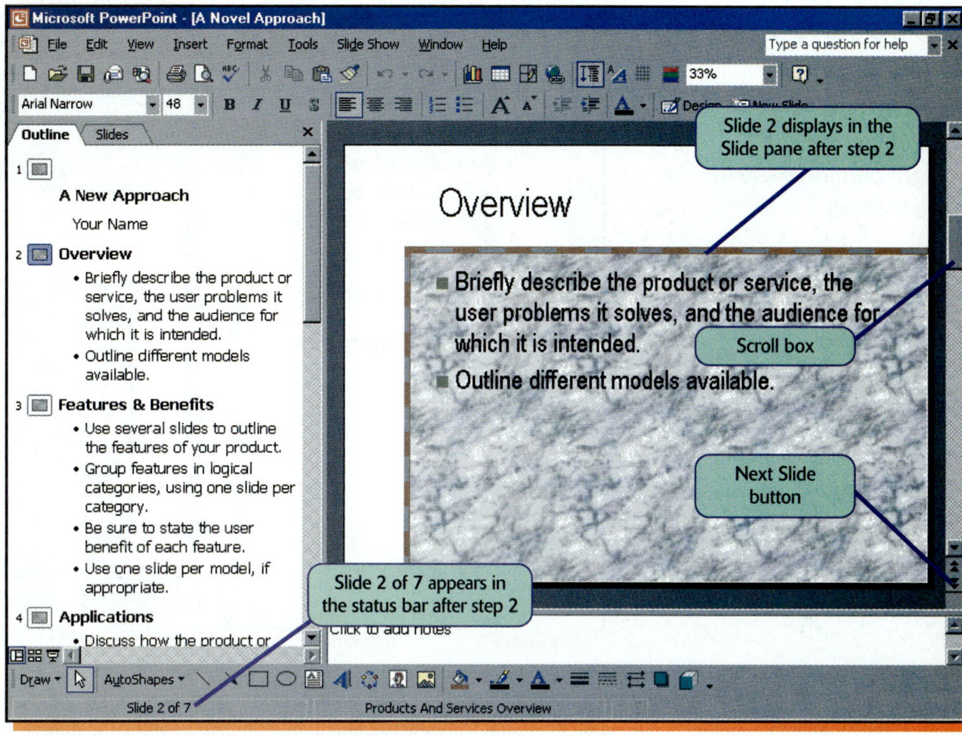

WEB TIP

New online Web technology has doctors treating patients from a distance. While this new technology has a limited prognosis, it is improving. However, if you're looking for medical advice or trying to figure out what's wrong with you, it's easy to find information about your symptoms on the Web. Search for Internet medical resources and see how many different sites you find.

Using PowerPoint Views

So far, you have typed text into text placeholders directly onto the slide in the Slide pane of Normal view. As you've already discovered, Normal view displays three panes: Slide pane, Slide Design/Outline pane, and the Notes pane. You can type text in all three panes.

Adding Text to Outlines

When you want to create a series of bulleted-list slides quickly, use the Outline pane.

Task 6:
To Type Text in the Outline Pane

1 Click the **Outline** tab on the **Slide Design/Outline** pane to make it active.

2 Press Ctrl + End to move to the last item in the outline and then press Ctrl + Enter to create a new slide.

3 Type the list displayed in Figure 1-20, pressing Enter between items. Save changes to the presentation.

Figure 1-20

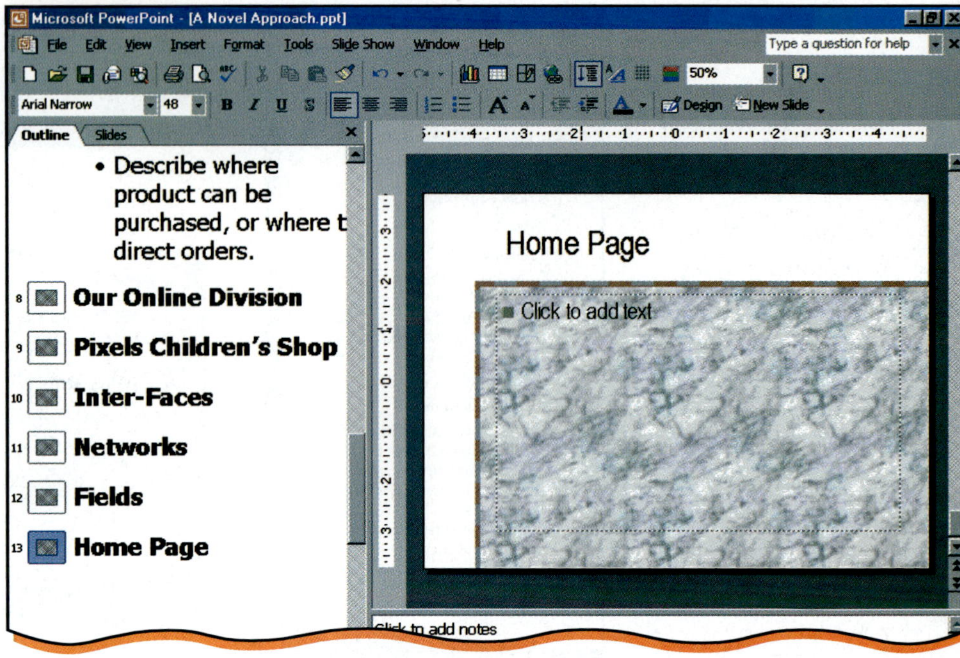

Other Ways

To create a new slide in Outline view:

- Press Ctrl + M.
- Click the New Slide button.
- Choose **Insert | New Slide.**

Promoting and Demoting Text

When you work in the Outline pane, you can easily *promote* and *demote* text using both the keyboard and mouse.

- Promoting items moves them from bullet points to slide titles or higher-level bullet points.
- Demoting items moves them from slide titles to bullet points or to lower-level bullet points.

Task 7:

To Promote and Demote Text

1 Click the slide icon for Slide 8 and press Tab to demote the text to a bullet point.

2 Repeat the procedure found in Step 1 to demote the renumbered Slides 8 through 12.

Other Ways

To promote and demote text:

- Click the Decrease Indent button to promote an item.
- Click the Increase Indent button to demote an item.

Figure 1-21

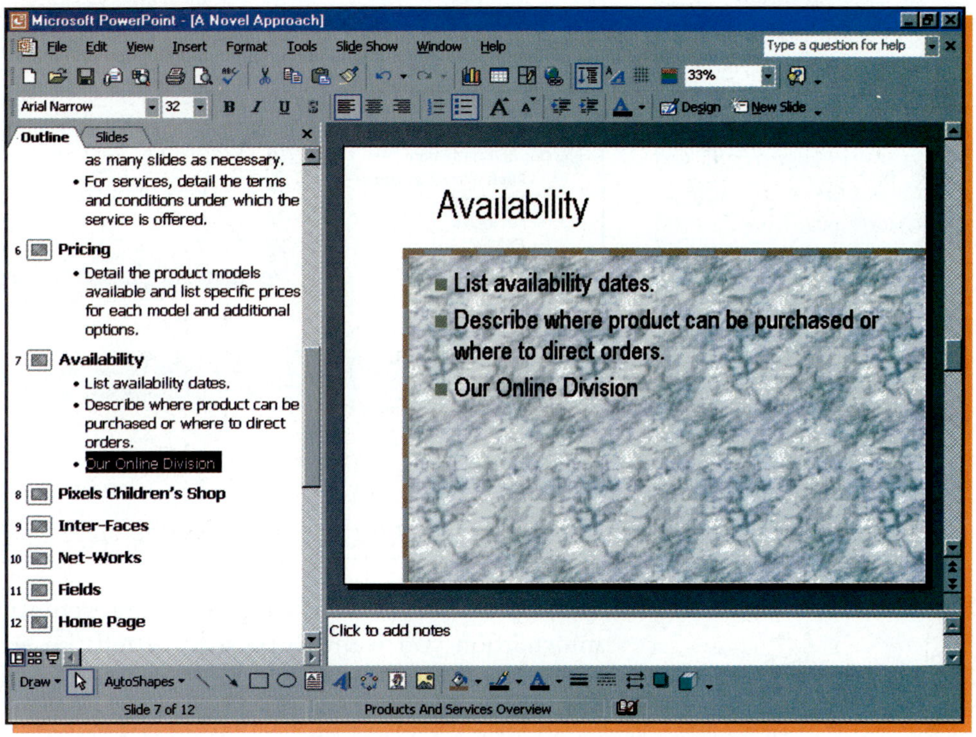

3. Click anywhere in the Outline pane text *Our Online Division* and press Shift + Tab to promote this bullet point to a slide title.

4. Save changes to the file.

Tip You can use the same techniques to promote and demote text in the bulleted list placeholder of the Slide pane that you used to promote and demote text in the Outline pane. Simply press Tab and Shift + Tab to demote or promote text or use the Increase Indent and Decrease Indent buttons on the Formatting toolbar.

Figure 1-22

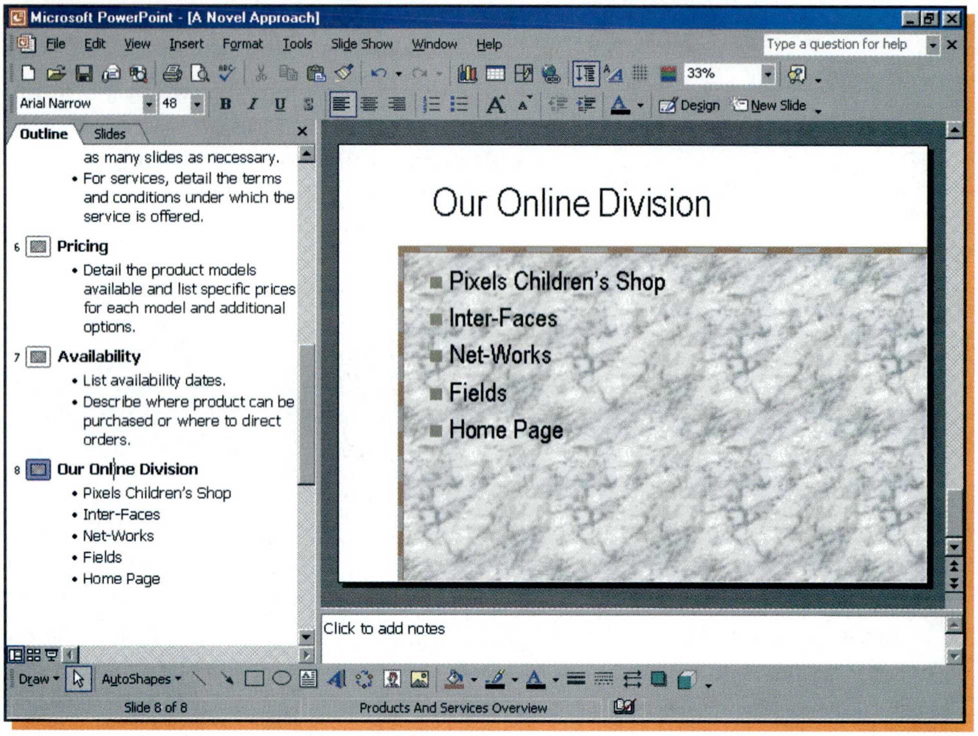

Adding Notes to Notes Pages

You can use *slide notes* during an oral presentation to remind you of important information you want to be sure to tell the audience. Type notes about the active presentation slide in the Slide Notes pane of the window and use the notes as you deliver your oral presentation.

Task 8:
To Add Text to Notes Pages

1. Press Ctrl + Home to display Slide 1 and press F6 until the insertion point appears in the Notes Pages pane.

2. Type **Test equipment to ensure that the projection device connects to my laptop.**

3. Save changes to the presentation.

Figure 1-23

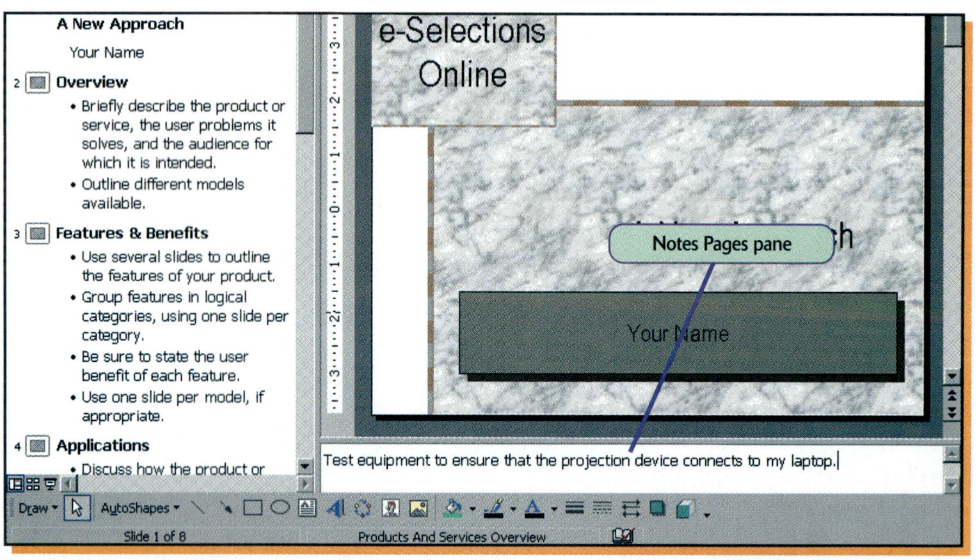

Editing Presentations

Presentation-editing techniques range in scope from simple text selection and editing to formatting and aligning placeholders. Because of the graphic nature of PowerPoint, there are a number of unique formatting techniques.

Selecting and Editing Slide Text

For the most part, the procedures for selecting and formatting text in PowerPoint are the same as those used to select and format text in other Office XP applications. However, PowerPoint does provide some special techniques for selecting specific units of text. You'll use text-editing techniques to replace the generic text with content-specific text in the Sales/Marketing presentation.

Task 9:
To Select and Edit Presentation Text

1. Display Slide 2 in the presentation *A Novel Approach.ppt* and click the **Outline** tab in the **Slide Design/Outline** pane, if necessary.

2. Double-click *Overview* in the **Outline** pane and type **A History of Selections, Inc.**

3. Click the bullet beside the first bulleted-text item in the Outline pane and Type **A multi-faceted department store** to replace existing text.

Tip The shape of the mouse pointer changes as you point to slide icons or bullets and text. To select specific text, the mouse should appear as an I-beam. To select all slide or bullet point text, the mouse pointer should appear as a four-headed arrow.

Figure 1-24

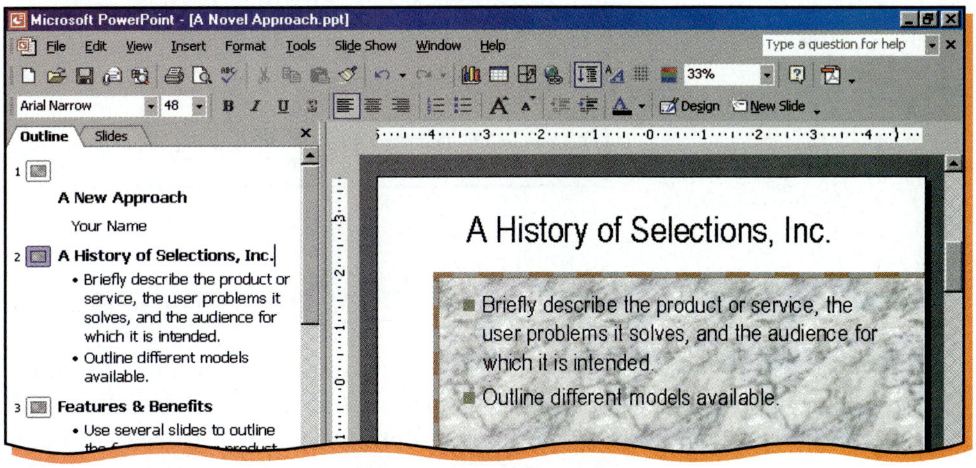

Figure 1-25

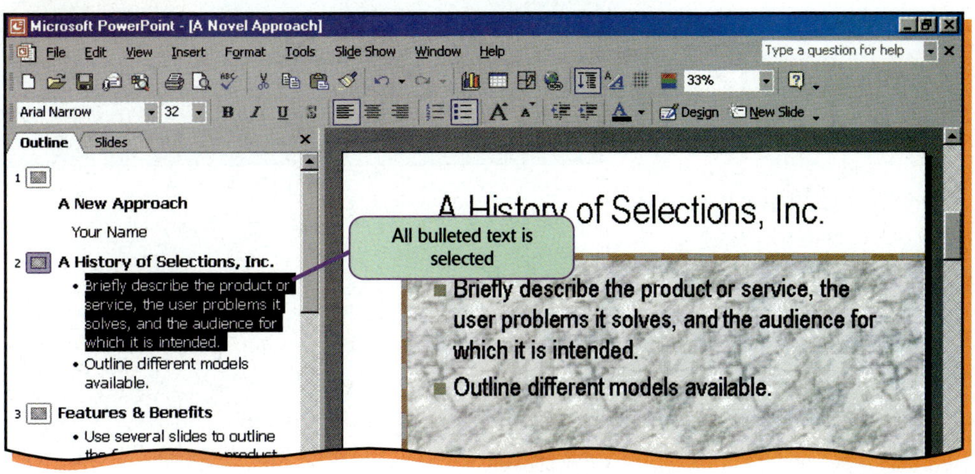

5 Repeat the procedures outlined in Steps 2 and 3 to replace the generic text in the Outline with the text shown in Figure 1-26.

Tip Clicking a slide icon on the Outline/Slide Design pane selects all slide placeholder text—the title and all bulleted list text.

6 Save changes to the presentation.

Figure 1-26

A History of Selections, Inc.
- A multi-faceted department store
- Incorporated in the state of Nebraska in 1985
- Corporate office is located in Omaha, Nebraska
- Four regional offices.
  - Savannah, Georgia
  - Seattle, Washington
  - Tucson, Arizona
  - Providence, Rhode Island

Selections, Inc., Stores
- Thirty-four stores located from coast to coast
- Employ more than a thousand people
- In 1996 stores opened in the West and South

e-Selections
- The online division of Selections, Inc.
- Premiered on the Web in the year 2000
- Grew to more than 100 employees in less than a year

e-Selections Web Spot
- The URL for the e-Selections Web site is www.e-Selections.com

e-Selections Online Divisions
- Currently, five divisions are online
- Five additional divisions will be added each year

e-Selections Online Shopping Opportunitie
- 24-hour online shopping
- 7 days a week
- 365 days each year

Replacing Presentation Fonts

The presentation template that you use for your presentation sets font format. The AutoContent Wizard automatically applied a template to the Sales/Marketing presentation when you created the presentation. The *Replace Fonts* feature in PowerPoint enables you to change the font for text in the entire presentation and eliminates the need to select text on each slide to change it.

Tip Using the Replace Fonts command to replace presentation fonts has no effect on text enhancements. As a result, if you have applied bold or other enhancements to specific placeholder text, those enhancements will be applied to the new font.

Task 10:

To Replace Presentation Fonts

1. Choose **Format | Replace Fonts**.

Figure 1-27

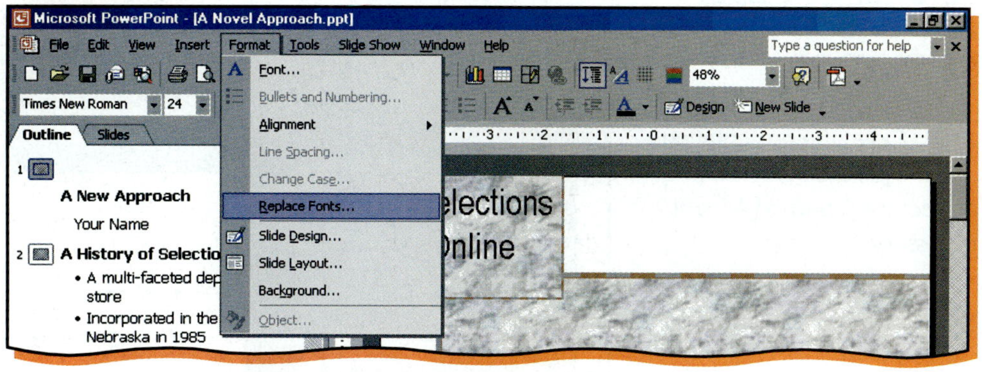

2. Click the **With** down arrow and select **Mistral**.

Troubleshooting If Mistral is unavailable on your computer, select the font identified by your instructor.

3. Click **Replace** and then click **Close**.

4. Save changes to the presentation and then close the presentation.

Figure 1-28

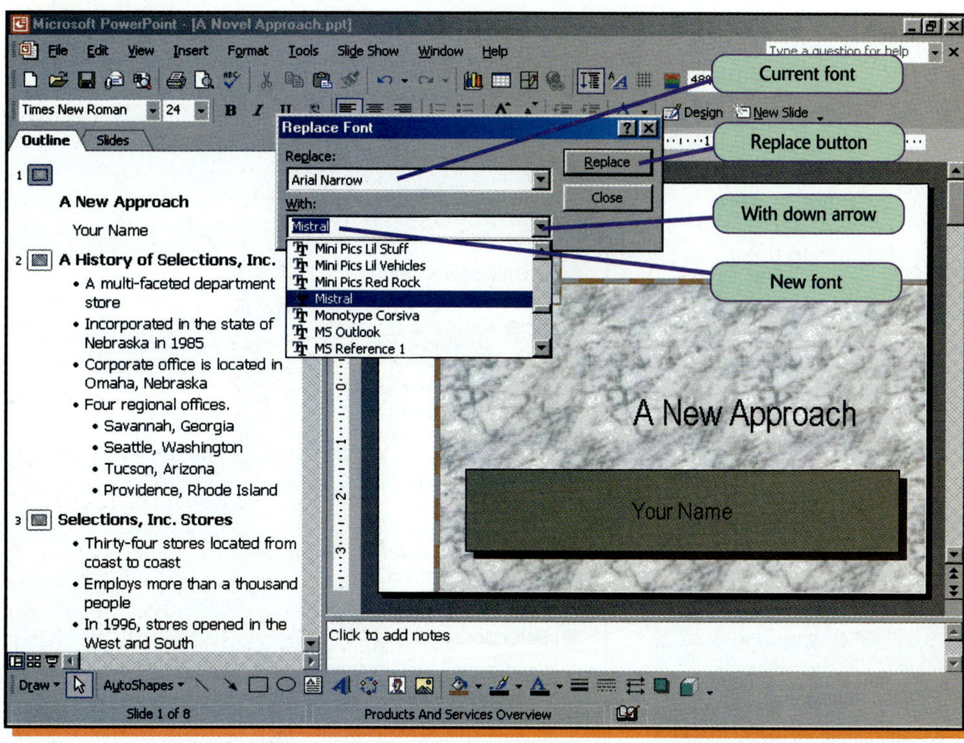

Tip Font changes appear in slide placeholders; however, the font displayed in the Outline pane does not change.

Setting up Pages

Most presentation materials can be printed on a variety of different paper sizes using either *portrait* or *landscape* orientation. The Page Setup dialog box contains options for setting the paper size and orientation for the particular material you are printing—slides, handouts, or slide notes.

Task 11:
To Change Paper Size and Orientation

1. Open the presentation *e-Selections Web.ppt* and set the **Zoom** to 46%, if necessary.

2. Choose **File | Page Setup**.

Figure 1-29

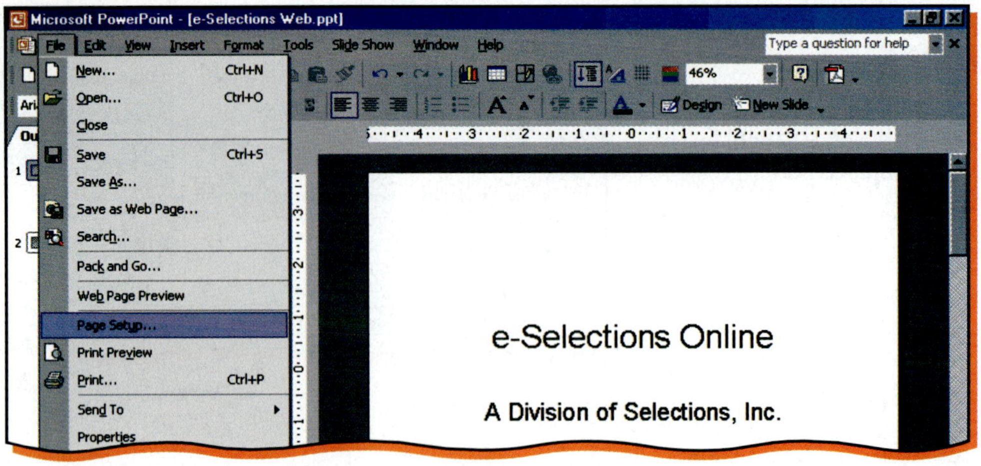

3. Select **Letter Paper (8.5x11 in)** from the **Slides sized for** drop-down list.

4. Click **OK** and save changes to the presentation.

> **Tip** You can change the number for the first slide in the presentation by adjusting the number in the Number slides from value box. When you change the number of the first slide in the presentation, numbers on all presentation slides adjust sequentially.

Figure 1-30

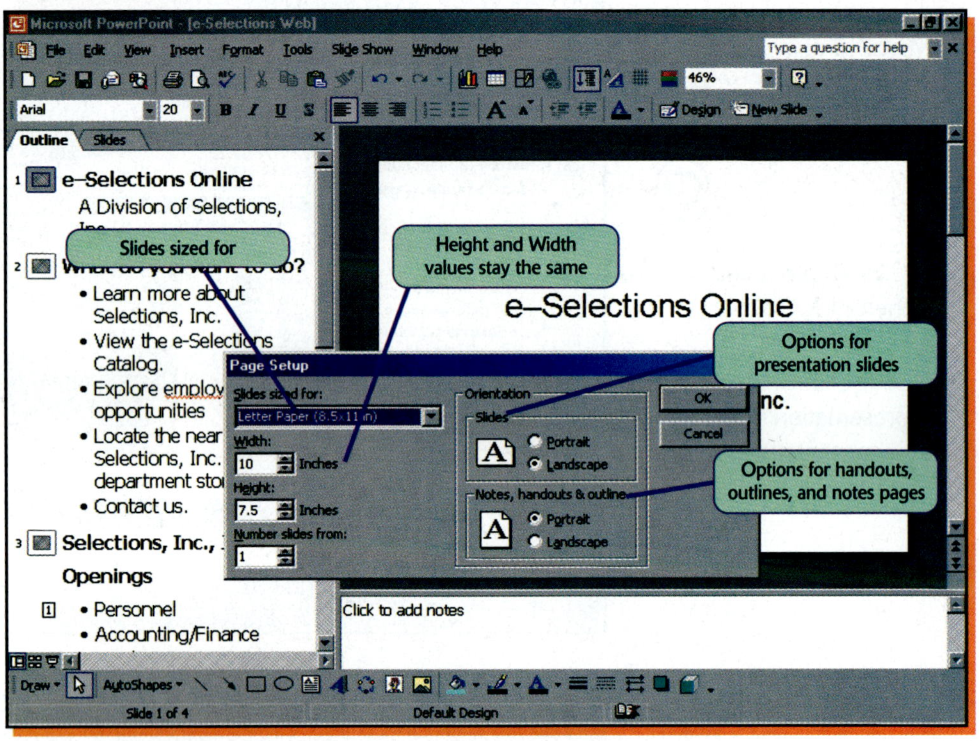

Formatting Text Placeholders

Changing the orientation or page size for presentations often affects the placement of placeholders on those slides. You can select, size, and move placeholders using the same techniques that you use to size and move graphic objects. In PowerPoint, however, sizing and positioning text placeholders enables you to adjust the position of slide text the way setting margins adjusts the placement of text on word processing documents.

Task 12: To Format Text Placeholders

1 Display Slide 1 in the presentation *e-Selections Web.ppt*, close the task pane, if necessary, and choose **View | Ruler** to display the ruler, if necessary.

Troubleshooting
Displaying the ruler may affect the size of the panes displayed in Normal view. Adjust the Zoom control setting for the Slide pane or Outline/Slide Design pane, if necessary.

Figure 1-31

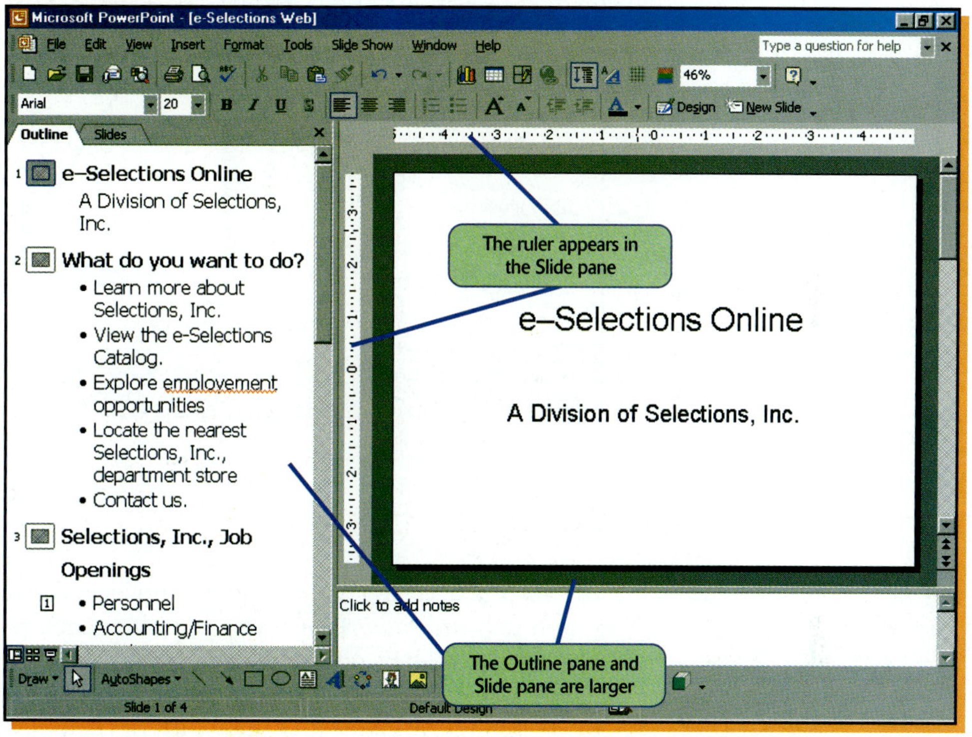

2. Press Shift and click the title placeholder.

3. Drag the placeholder border to position it in the upper left corner of the slide and save changes to the presentation.

Figure 1-32

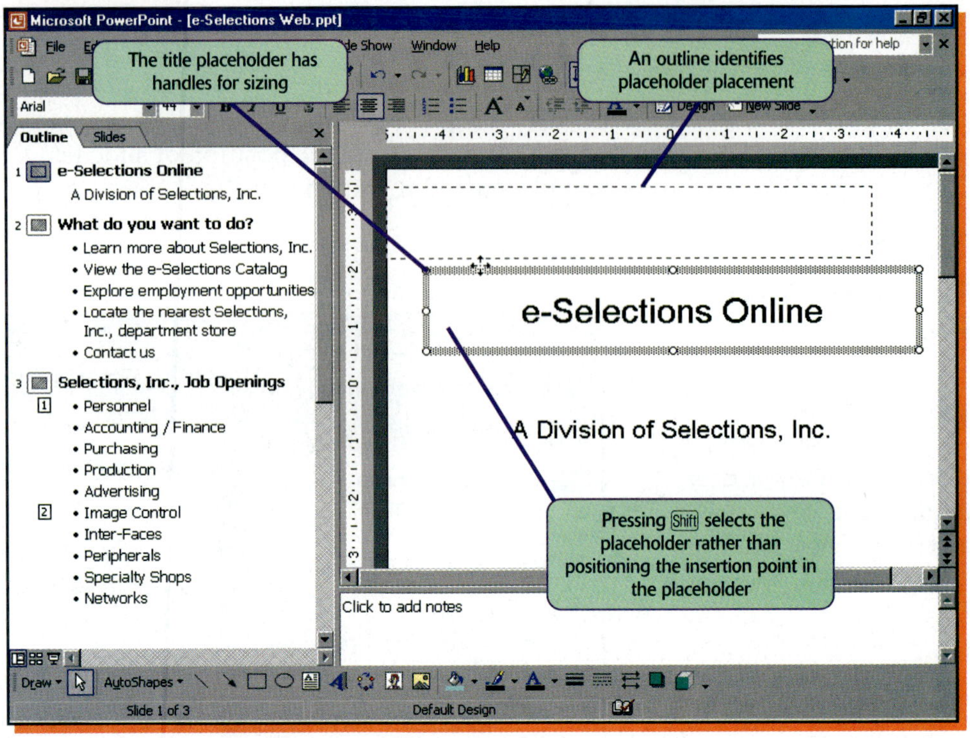

Aligning Placeholder Text

In word-processing applications, such as Word, text alignment affects paragraph text. In PowerPoint, you can align each paragraph within a placeholder separately or align all paragraphs within a placeholder by simply selecting the placeholder. Moreover, a special alignment button is available in PowerPoint to stretch placeholder text the width of the placeholder.

Task 13:
To Align Placeholder Text

1. Press Shift and select the title placeholder for Slide 1, if necessary.

2. Click the Align Left button on the Formatting toolbar and save changes to the presentation.

Tip A Distributed button appears on the Formatting toolbar when certain international fonts such as Japanese are installed on your computer. If you see the button on your workstation, you may want to select it rather than the Align Left button to change text alignment.

Figure 1-33

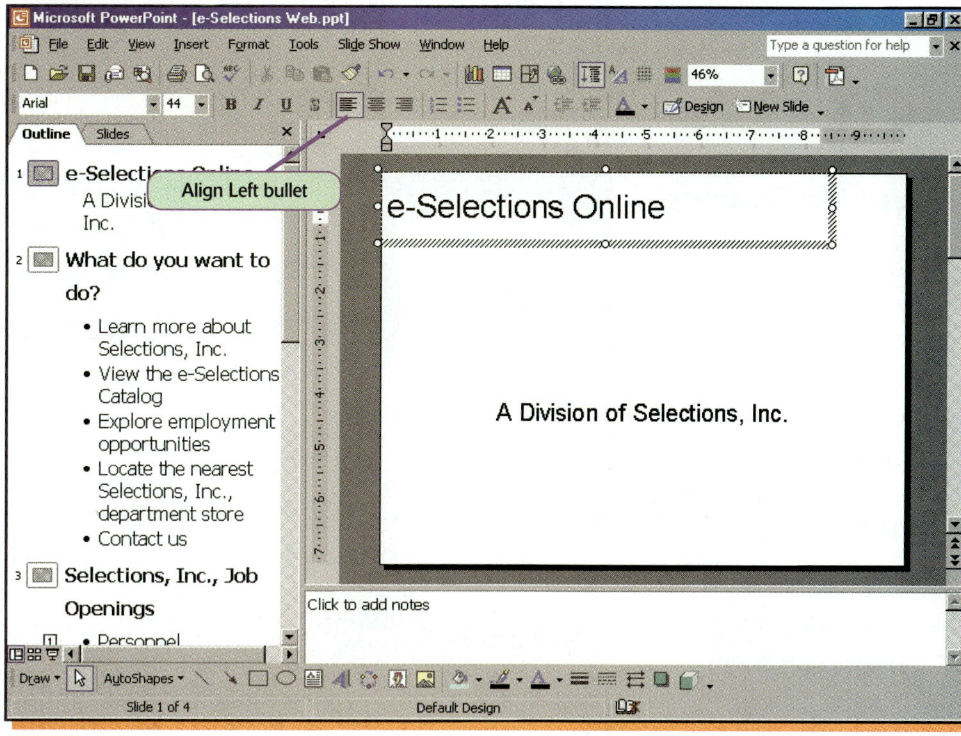

Changing Line Spacing

PowerPoint controls the spacing between lines of text within each text placeholder individually.

Task 14: To Change Placeholder Line Spacing

1. Display Slide 2 in the presentation *e-Selections Web.ppt*.
2. Press Shift, click the bulleted-list placeholder, and choose **Format** | **Line Spacing**.
3. Select the value in the **Before paragraph** value box and type .5.
4. Click **OK** and save changes to the presentation. Bulleted-list points spread out vertically within the placeholder.

Figure 1-34

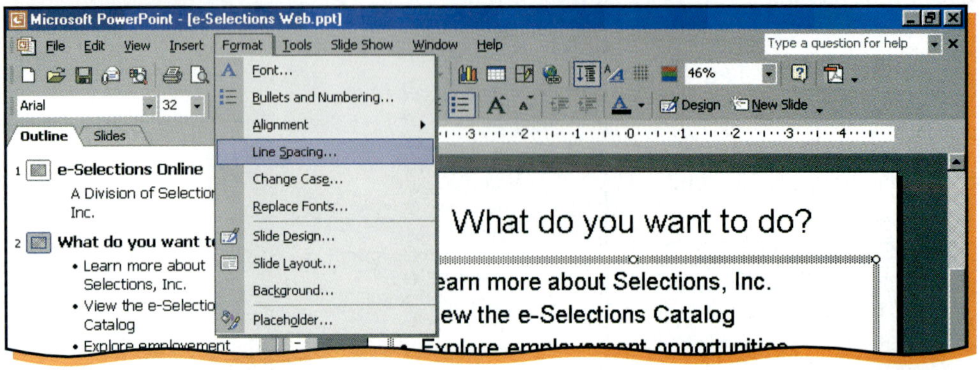

Figure 1-35

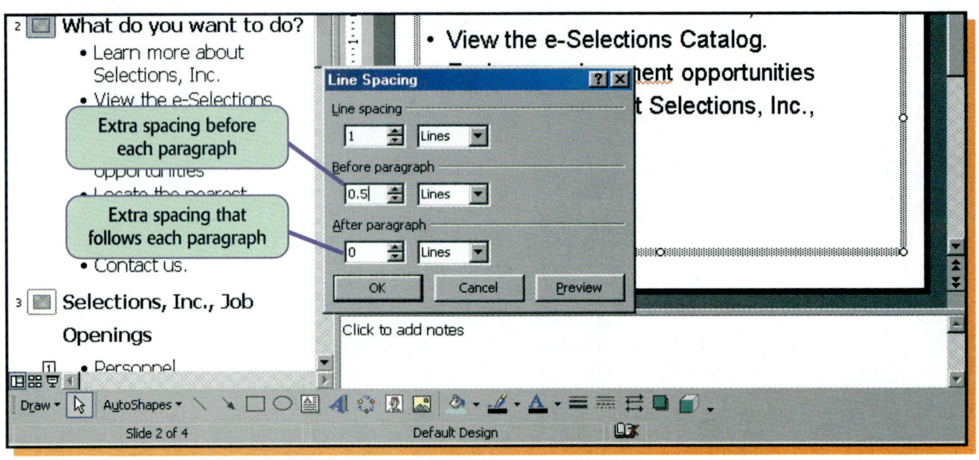

Tip To set the line spacing for multiple placeholders on a slide at the same time, press Shift and click each placeholder you want to format and then set the line spacing.

Proofing Presentations

Proofing tools in PowerPoint include the spelling checker and the Find and Replace features found in other Office XP applications. They also include a feature that enables you to quickly and efficiently proof your presentation for consistency of style. Using the *style checker,* you can check placeholder text for consistency of end punctuation and capitalization and check spelling at the same time. *Visual Clarity* options help ensure that presentation information will be easily seen and read. When the style checker is turned on, PowerPoint checks format as you work and little light bulbs appear each time a style inconsistency is found. As a result, the style checker is turned off by default.

Task 15:
To Check Presentations for Spelling, Style, and Clarity

1 Display Slide 1 of the presentation *e-Selections Web.ppt* and click the Spelling button on the Standard toolbar.

Other Ways

To display the Spelling dialog box:

- Choose **Tools | Spelling.**
- Press F7.

2 Spell check the file, correcting any errors you find.

3 Choose **Tools | Options.**

Figure 1-36

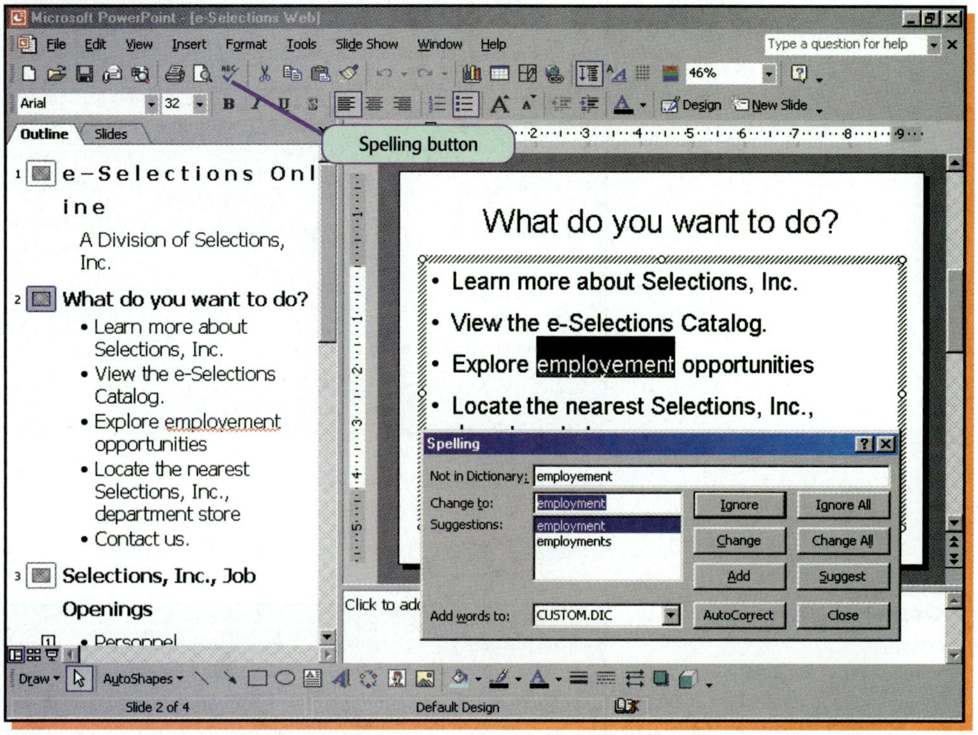

Figure 1-37

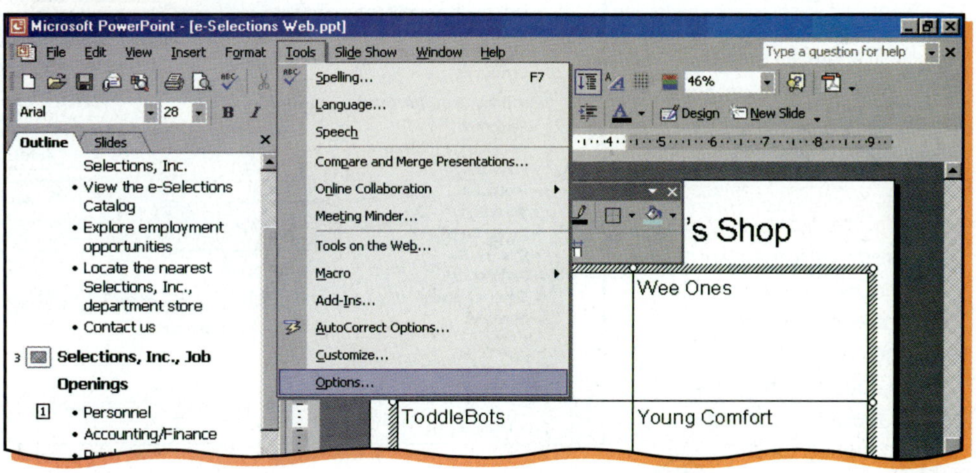

4 Click the **Spelling and Style** tab in the Options dialog box.

5 Select the **Check style** option and then click **Style Options**.

Figure 1-38

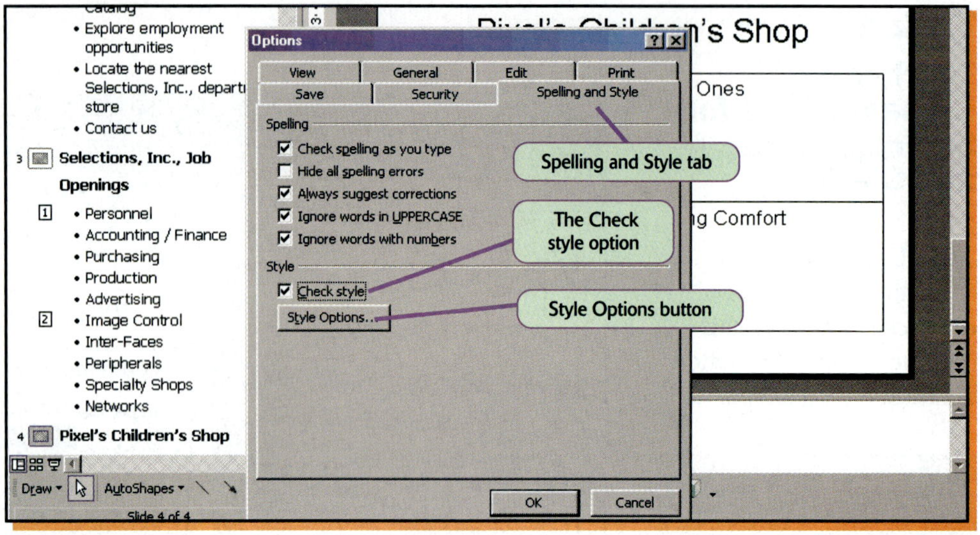

6 Select the **Slide title punctuation** and **Body punctuation** options, if necessary.

7 Select **Paragraphs do not have punctuation** from both the **Slide title punctuation** and **Body punctuation** drop-down lists.

8 Click **OK** to turn on the style checker and display Slide 2.

Figure 1-39

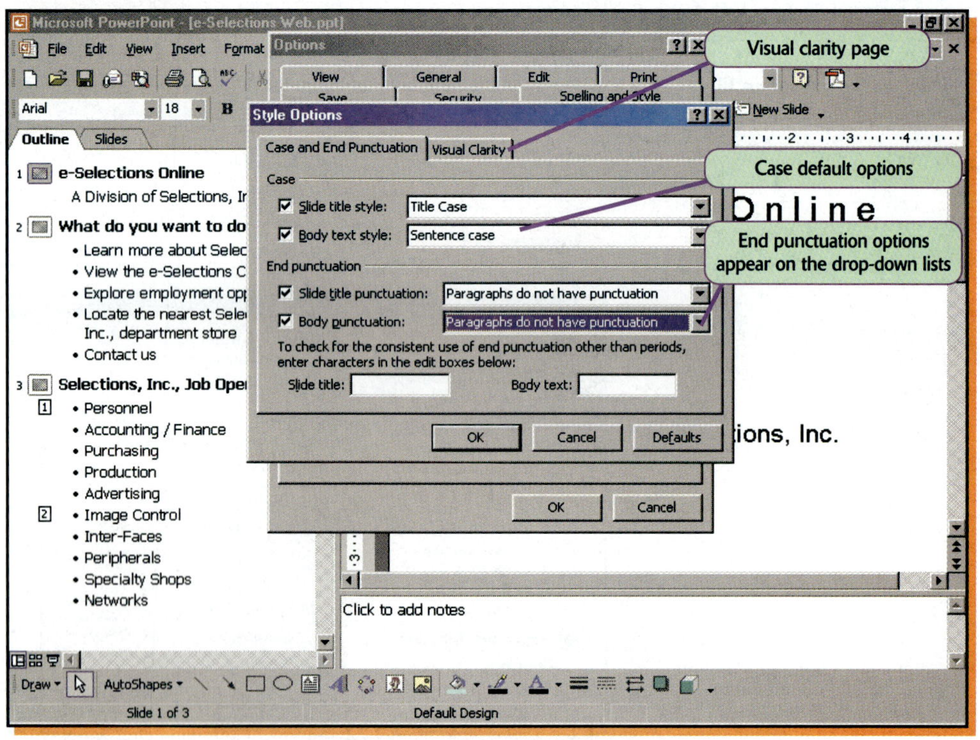

Troubleshooting

Be sure to click the appropriate down arrow for the option you want to change. Settings in the Style Options dialog box make it easy to select the correct option for the wrong item!

9 Click the **light bulb**.

> **Tip** To turn off the style checker, repeat the instructions in steps 3 and 4 and clear the check mark from the Check style option.

Figure 1-40

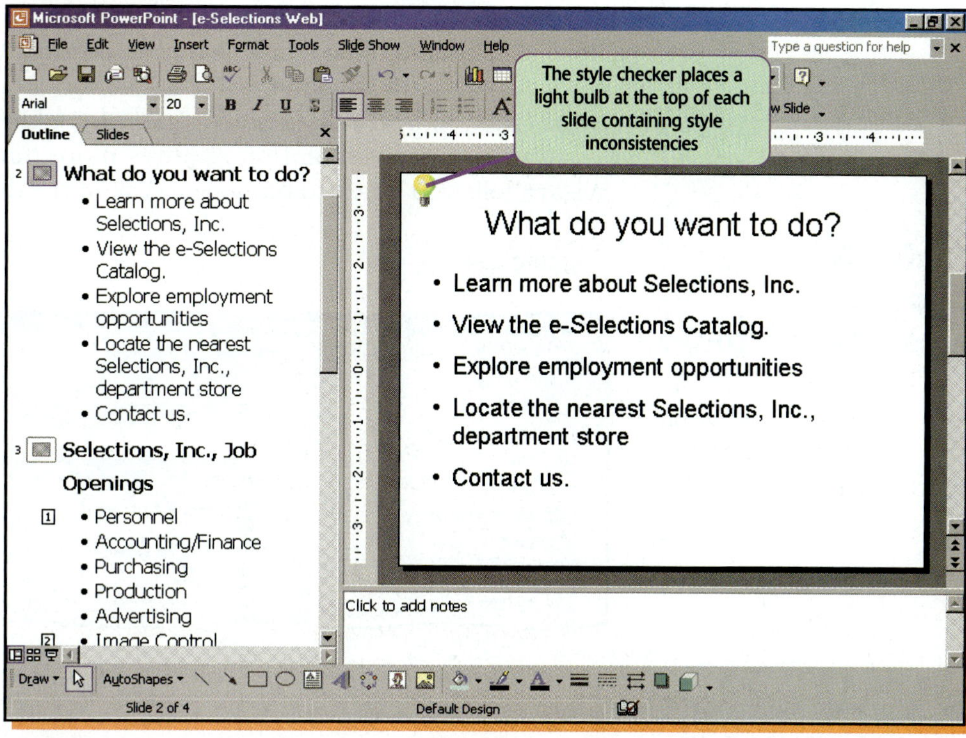

10 Click **Ignore this style rule for this presentation only**.

11 Display each slide in the presentation and make style corrections to ensure uniformity, save changes, and close the presentation.

Figure 1-41

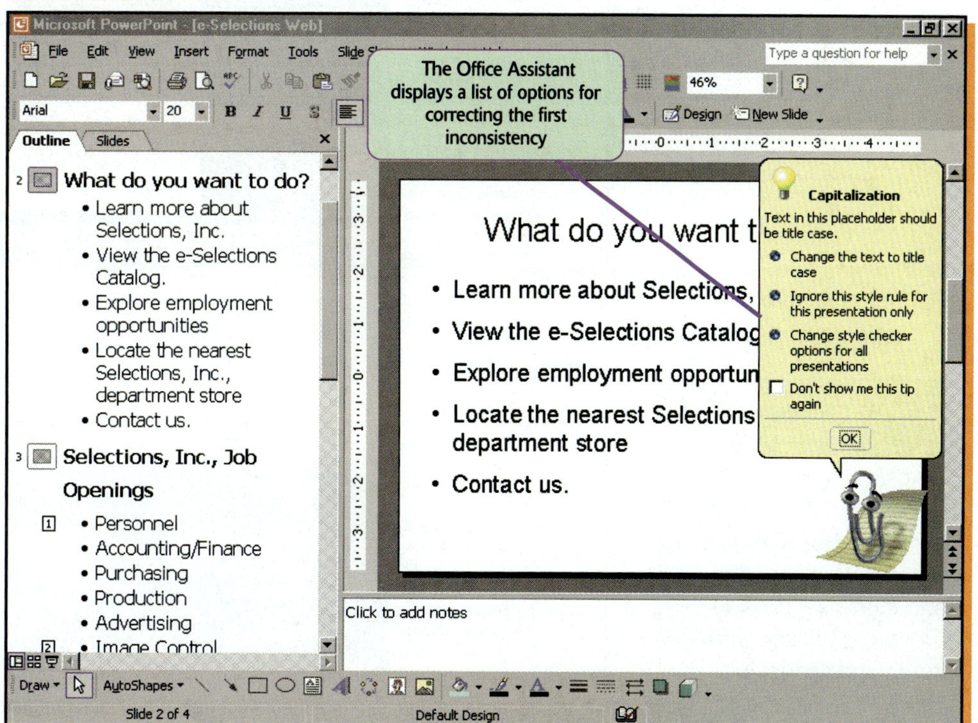

Packing a Presentation to Go

As your presentations grow, they become huge files that are often difficult to store on a single floppy disk. Graphics, templates, and animation effects all increase the size of presentations. Luckily, PowerPoint has a *Pack and Go Wizard* that compresses the presentation, making it more compact and easier to store. If your presentation requires more than one disk, the Pack and Go Wizard tells you when to put a new disk in the disk drive.

Task 16:
To Pack a Presentation to Go

1. Open the presentation *A Novel Approach.ppt* and choose **File | Pack and Go**.

Figure 1-42

2. Click **No, don't provide help now** in the **Office Assistant** list and click **Next**.

Figure 1-43

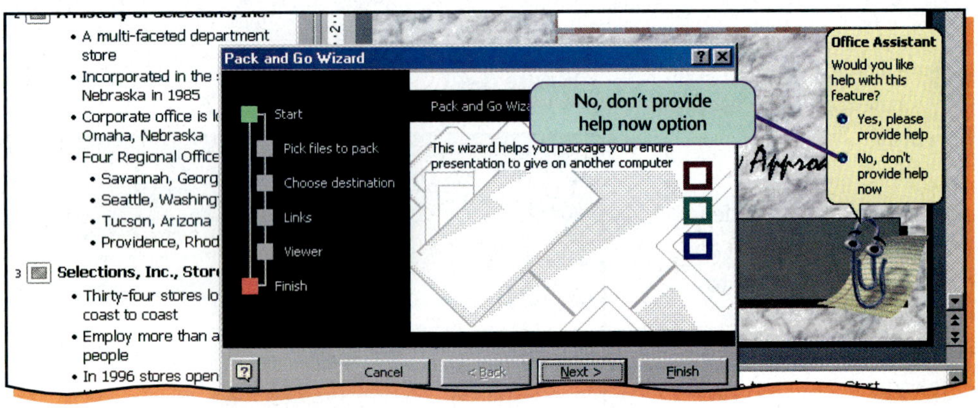

3. Select **Active presentation** and click **Next**.

Tip To package multiple presentations together in one Pack and Go operation, select the **Other presentation(s)** option and then click **Browse**. Open the folder containing the presentations you want to package, press Ctrl, and click the name of each presentation you want to pack.

Figure 1-44

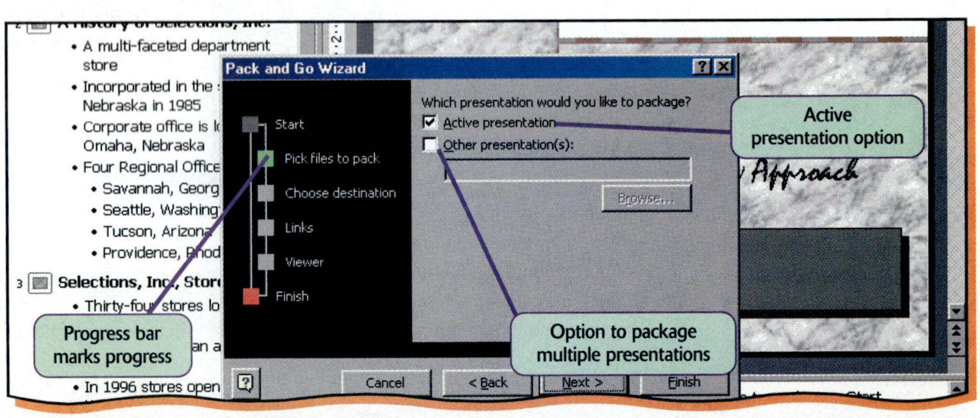

4 Select the **A:\ drive** option, place a formatted disk in the floppy drive, and click **Next**.

Figure 1-45

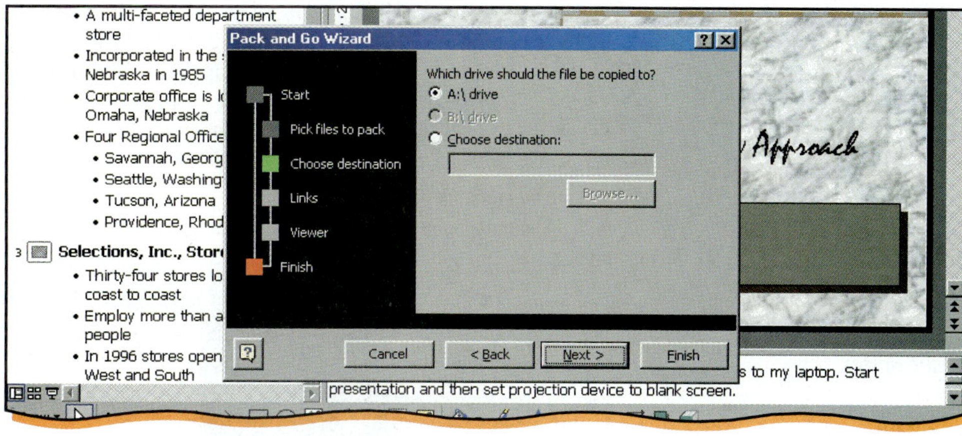

5 Clear the **Include linked files** option, select **Embed TrueType fonts**, and then click **Next**.

Figure 1-46

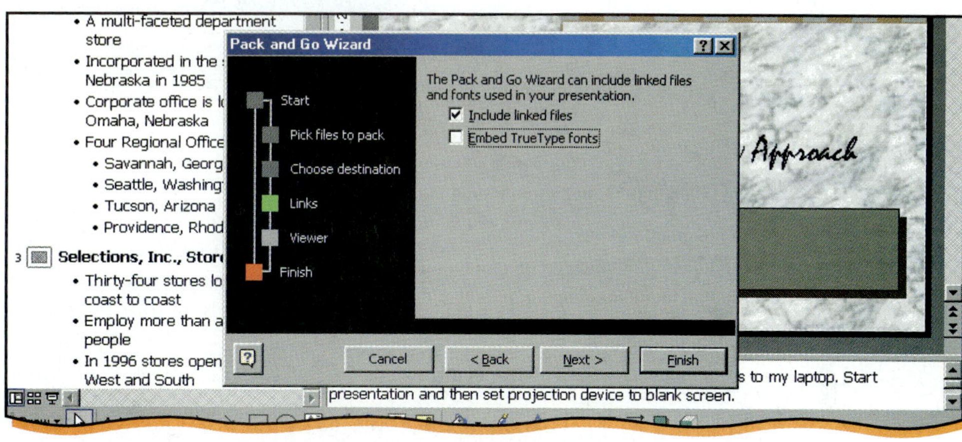

6 Click **Don't include the Viewer** and click **Next**.

Tip Packing linked files and TrueType fonts with a presentation ensures that the presentation will display properly on other computers.

Figure 1-47

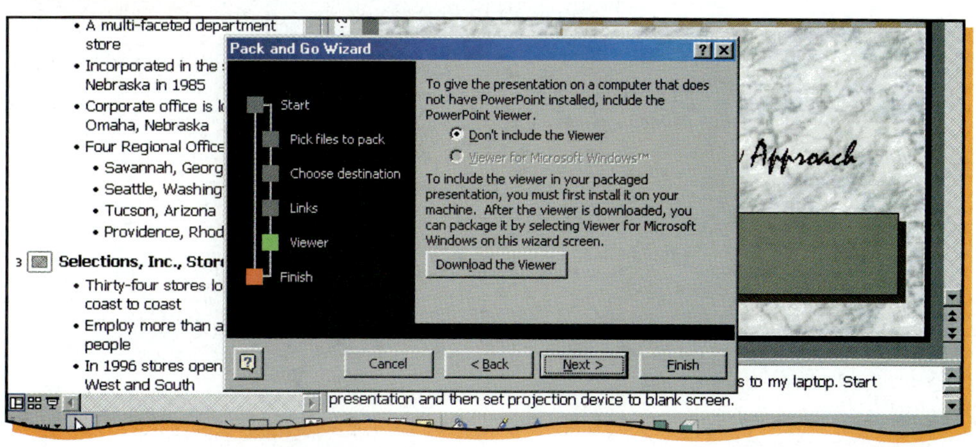

7 Click **Finish**. PowerPoint whirs and burps a bit as it packages the presentation on the disk. If the presentation is too large to fit on one disk, you may be asked to insert another disk. When the presentation is packaged, a message window may appear that tells you that Pack and Go successfully packed the presentation.

8 Click **OK** to acknowledge the message, if necessary.

Troubleshooting The viewer is required to show a presentation on a computer that does not have PowerPoint installed on it. If the Pack and Go feature has not yet been used on your computer, instructions for downloading the viewer appear. Obtain instructions from the lab assistant or your instructor on how to proceed.

Figure 1-48

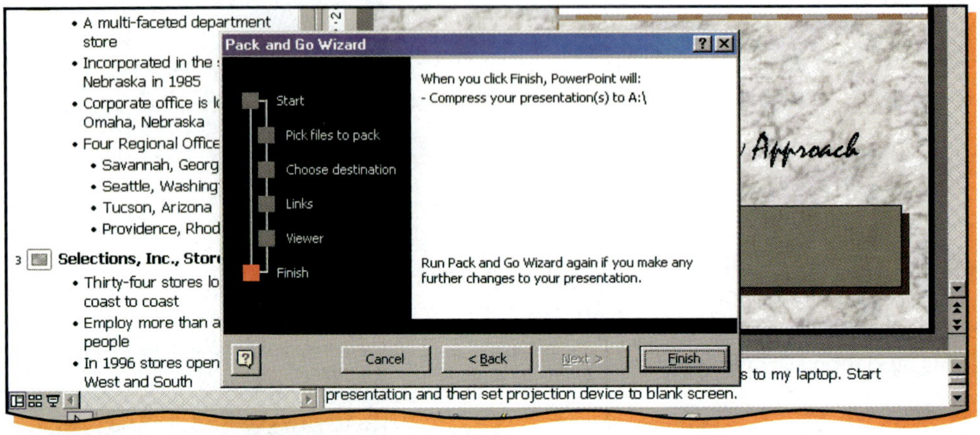

CHECK POINT

Packing a presentation to go automatically creates two files on your disk: *pngsetup.exe* and *pres0.ppz*. The pngsetup.exe file can be used to install, setup, and show the presentation on any computer that has enough memory and disk space. The *pres0.ppz* file contains slides and other important information about the presentation. To show a presentation that you have packed to go:

1. Display the contents of the disk in My Computer or in Windows Explorer.
2. Double-click the *pngsetup.exe* file. A Pack and Go Setup dialog box opens.
3. Click **Browse** and open the drive and folder from which you want to show the presentation.
4. Click **OK** twice. A warning message may appear telling you that the presentation will overwrite files with the same name as the presentation is unpacked.
5. Click **Yes** to continue. A message window asks if you would like to show the presentation.
6. Click **Yes** to start the presentation.

SUMMARY AND EXERCISES

SUMMARY

- PowerPoint offers a variety of techniques for creating new slides.
- The Slide Layout task pane displays slide formats grouped by type: Text, Content, Text and Content, and Other Layouts.
- PowerPoint offers a variety of different Text Layouts, containing placeholders of different sizes and arrangements.
- Select the format and arrangement of text placeholders as you create slides or apply a different layout to existing slides.
- To end a presentation smoothly, PowerPoint places a blank, black slide at the end of the presentation by default.
- A quick glance at the Outline pane helps you determine how many slides the presentation contains. It also provides a quick overview of slide contents.
- Using a variety of keyboard and mouse navigation techniques, you can display different slides in the presentation for editing or review.
- Normal view displays three panes: Slide pane, Slide Design/Outline pane, and the Notes Pages pane.
- When you want to create a series of bulleted-list slides quickly, use the Outline pane.
- Promoting items moves them from bullet points to higher-level bullet points or to slide titles.
- Demoting items moves them from slide titles to bullet points or from bullet points to lower-level bullet points.
- You can use slide notes during an oral presentation to remind you of important information you want to be sure to tell the audience.
- A special alignment option, called Distributed, is available when certain international fonts are installed on a computer and is used to stretch placeholder text the width of the placeholder.
- In PowerPoint, you can align each paragraph within a placeholder separately or align all paragraphs within a placeholder by simply selecting the placeholder.
- You can also select all slide text by clicking a slide icon in the Outline pane or select bulleted-list text by clicking the bullet in the Outline pane.

- PowerPoint's Replace Fonts feature enables you to change the font of the text in the entire presentation and eliminates the need to select and change text on each slide.
- The Page Setup dialog box contains options for setting the paper size and orientation for the particular material you are printing—slides, handouts, or slide notes.
- You can select, size, and move placeholders using the same techniques that you use to size and move graphic objects.
- Sizing and positioning text placeholders enables you to adjust the position of slide text the way setting margins adjusts the placement of text on word processing documents.
- Using the style checker, you can check placeholder text for consistency of end punctuation and capitalization and check spelling at the same time.
- The Pack and Go Wizard compresses presentations, making them more compact and easier to store.

KEY TERMS & SKILLS

KEY TERMS

black slide (p. 1-11)
comments (p. 1-11)
demote (p. 1-17)
Distributed (p. 1-33)
landscape (p. 1-21)
Pack and Go Wizard (p. 1-30)
portrait (p. 1-21)
promote (p. 1-17)
Replace Fonts (p. 1-20)
slide layouts (p. 1-7)
slide notes (p. 1-18)
style checker (p. 1-26)
table slides (p. 1-9)
Visual Clarity (p. 1-26)

SKILLS

Add text to notes pages (p. 1-18)
Align placeholder text (p. 1-24)
Change paper size and orientation (p. 1-22)
Change placeholder line spacing (p. 1-26)
Check presentations for spelling, style, and clarity (p. 1-27)
Create a table slide (p. 1-9)
Create new slides (p. 1-5)
Format text placeholders (p. 1-23)
Format text slides (p. 1-7)
Insert and view comments (p. 1-11)
Navigate presentations (p. 1-13)
Pack a presentation to go (p. 1-30)
Print comments (p. 1-12)
Promote and demote text (p. 1-17)
Replace presentation fonts (p. 1-20)
Select, edit, and format presentation text (p. 1-19)
Type text in the Outline Pane (p. 1-16)
Use a slide layout (p. 1-7)

STUDY QUESTIONS

MULTIPLE CHOICE

1. Slides added to a presentation are formatted using
   a. slide layouts.
   b. text and title boxes.
   c. blank slides that resemble blank pieces of paper.
   d. outlines.

2. New slide layouts contain
   a. fields.
   b. placeholders.
   c. tables.
   d. templates.

3. Placeholders identify
   a. slide names.
   b. slide fields.
   c. slide titles.
   d. slide objects.

4. To add a new slide to a presentation, use any of the following techniques except
   a. double-clicking the active slide.
   b. clicking the New Slide 

button on the toolbar.
   c. pressing Ctrl + M.
   d. choosing **Insert | New Slide** from the menu.

5. The Outline pane displays
   a. all slide objects.
   b. the slide title and body text only.
   c. small slide images.
   d. slide images and notes about the slide.

6. Normal view displays
   a. all slide objects.
   b. the slide title and body text only.
   c. small slide images.
   d. slide images, notes about the slide, and an outline.

7. Which case would you use if you would like all letters in your placeholder to appear capitalized?
   a. sentence case
   b. lowercase
   c. title case
   d. uppercase

8. What allows you to adjust the position of text the way setting a margin does in Word?
   a. margin control
   b. ruler
   c. slide placement
   d. sizing and positioning placeholder
9. Slide Layouts are grouped by type into all the following categories except
   a. Text
   b. Content
   c. Miscellaneous Layouts
   d. Text and Content
10. To add a table slide to a presentation, create a new slide formatted using the Content layout and then click
    a. the Insert Table button on the slide.
    b. the **Insert | Table** menu command.
    c. the table placeholder.
    d. none of the above

SHORT ANSWER

1. How do you create a new presentation if PowerPoint is already running?
2. What are the panes of the Normal view and when should you use each pane?
3. How do you switch from one pane to the next?
4. How can you use the vertical scroll bar to display a specific slide?
5. How does the mouse pointer appear when you point to a bullet or slide icon in the outline?
6. How can you display the ruler in PowerPoint?
7. Which feature compresses your presentation for easy storage on disk?
8. Why would you include the Viewer when you pack your presentation to go?
9. What different techniques can you use to create a new slide?
10. How do you add a comment to a slide?

FILL IN THE BLANK

1. Select the ____________ ____________ button to view the tri-pane window.
2. To list a number of key points on a single slide, select the ____________ ____________ slide layout.
3. You can type text in the ____________ pane of a window when you want to create a series of bulleted-list slides.
4. To check spelling, find, search for and replace words, and check your presentation for consistency of style, use ____________ tools.
5. Displaying the ____________ helps to position and size placeholders.

6. To change the distance between lines of type within a placeholder, adjust the ______________.
7. To ensure your presentation displays properly when you Pack and Go, you would include ______________ in the Pack and Go Wizard.
8. If the computer you are using for a presentation does not have PowerPoint installed, you will need to include the ______________ when you Pack and Go.
9. Change the font for all slides in the presentation using the ______________ ______________ dialog box.
10. ______________ text in an outline moves the text to a higher bulleted level; ______________ text in an outline moves the text to a lower bulleted level.

DISCUSSION

1. How do you check the presentation style to ensure consistency of the presentation?
2. Discuss why you would use the Pack and Go feature instead of saving your presentation as you normally would on a disk.
3. How do you display the New Presentation task pane if it is not displayed?
4. Describe how comments added to presentation slides appear, how you can view comment text, and how to print comments.

GUIDED EXERCISES

1 BUILDING THE JPLD-TV PRESENTATION SLIDE

The JPLD-TV presentation contains only a title slide, so it needs to have additional slides added to the presentation. Follow the steps below to add a new bulleted-list slide to the presentation.

1. Open the *JPLD-TV.ppt* presentation.
2. Click the New Slide [New Slide] button on the Formatting toolbar to create a new bulleted list slide.
3. Type **Monday's Lineup** in the title placeholder of the new slide.
4. Type the following bulleted list in the bulleted list placeholder:
   - **The Gizmo**
   - **Ridgewood Square**
   - **Blind Alley**
5. Save changes to the presentation and print a copy of the new slide.

2 PROOFING A NOVEL APPROACH PRESENTATION

The presentation *A Novel Approach.ppt* that you have created and are developing needs to be checked for spelling and style. Follow these instructions to proof your presentation.

1. Open the presentation *A Novel Approach.ppt*.
2. Click the Spelling and Grammar button to locate errors and correct the presentation.
3. Choose **Tools | Options | Spelling and Style** and set the following style options:
   - Slide title style: **Title Case**
   - Body text style: **Sentence case**
   - Slide title punctuation: **Paragraphs do not have punctuation**
   - Body punctuation: **Paragraphs have consistent punctuation**
4. Click **OK** twice and then display each slide in the presentation, click any **light bulbs** that appear, and respond appropriately to the style errors.
5. Choose **Tools | Options | Spelling and Style** and clear the **Check style** option.
6. Save changes to the presentation and print a copy of the presentation as handouts with four slides per page.

3 TRACKING RESTAURANTS

Traveling to different cities and countries provides an excellent opportunity to experience the foods unique to different cultures. However, finding great places to eat can be a challenge. On a recent trip to New Orleans, you identified a number of different restaurants that served quite a variety of dishes that you'd like to remember. After jotting down the names of the restaurants and some of the special attractions each restaurant featured, you have decided to create a presentation to keep track of eating establishments in the different cities you visit. The outline of the restaurants you found in New Orleans appears in Figure 1-49.

Figure 1-49

I. **The Cosmopolitan Cuisine of New Orleans**
   A Taste of Something for Everyone by *Your Name*

II. **Thibodeaux's Crawfish Pot**
   A. The best cajun restaurant this side of Mardi Gras!
   B. Authentic gumbo, fried alligator, crawfish etouffee, and blackened steak
   C. Featuring Brunet's attic - Louisiana specialty items so you can take the bayou home with you

III. **Catch of the Day**
   A. Fresh fish flown in twice daily to give you the freshest selection possible
   B. New England lobster, crabs, scallops, and over 30 different fishes every day
   C. Lobster bisque, clam chowder, and seafood gumbo made from scratch

Follow these steps to create the presentation.

1. Click the New button on the Standard toolbar to create a new blank presentation that contains a title slide.
2. Click the **Outline** tab on the **Slide Design/Outline** pane to make it active.
3. Type the text that appears beside the Roman numeral I on Figure 1-49 into the space beside the first slide icon in the Outline pane.
4. Press Enter, press Tab to indent the subtitle text, and then type the text that appears below Roman numeral I.
5. Press Ctrl + Enter to create a new bulleted-list slide.
6. Type the text for the next Roman numeral beside the new slide icon.

7. Press Enter and Tab, type the text beside the letter A of the second item in the outline, and press Enter to type the next bulleted-list item.

8. Repeat this procedure to create three slides from the outline, promoting and demoting text as necessary to produce the desired result.

9. Check the spelling in the file and save the presentation using the file name *New Orleans Cuisine*, and then print a copy of the presentation as black-and-white handouts with three slides per page.

WEB TIP

Locate restaurants in the city you are visiting on the Web! Search for restaurant guides and then enter the city you are visiting. Some guides even let you narrow the search to a particular area and provide maps with directions for getting to the restaurants.

4 SELECTIONS SEASONS OF VALUES

Poetic quips have been written to identify sale items to be featured during the year. These quips need to be added as new slides in the *Seasons of Values* presentation. The presentation currently contains only a title slide. New slides are shown in Figure 1-50.

Figure 1-50

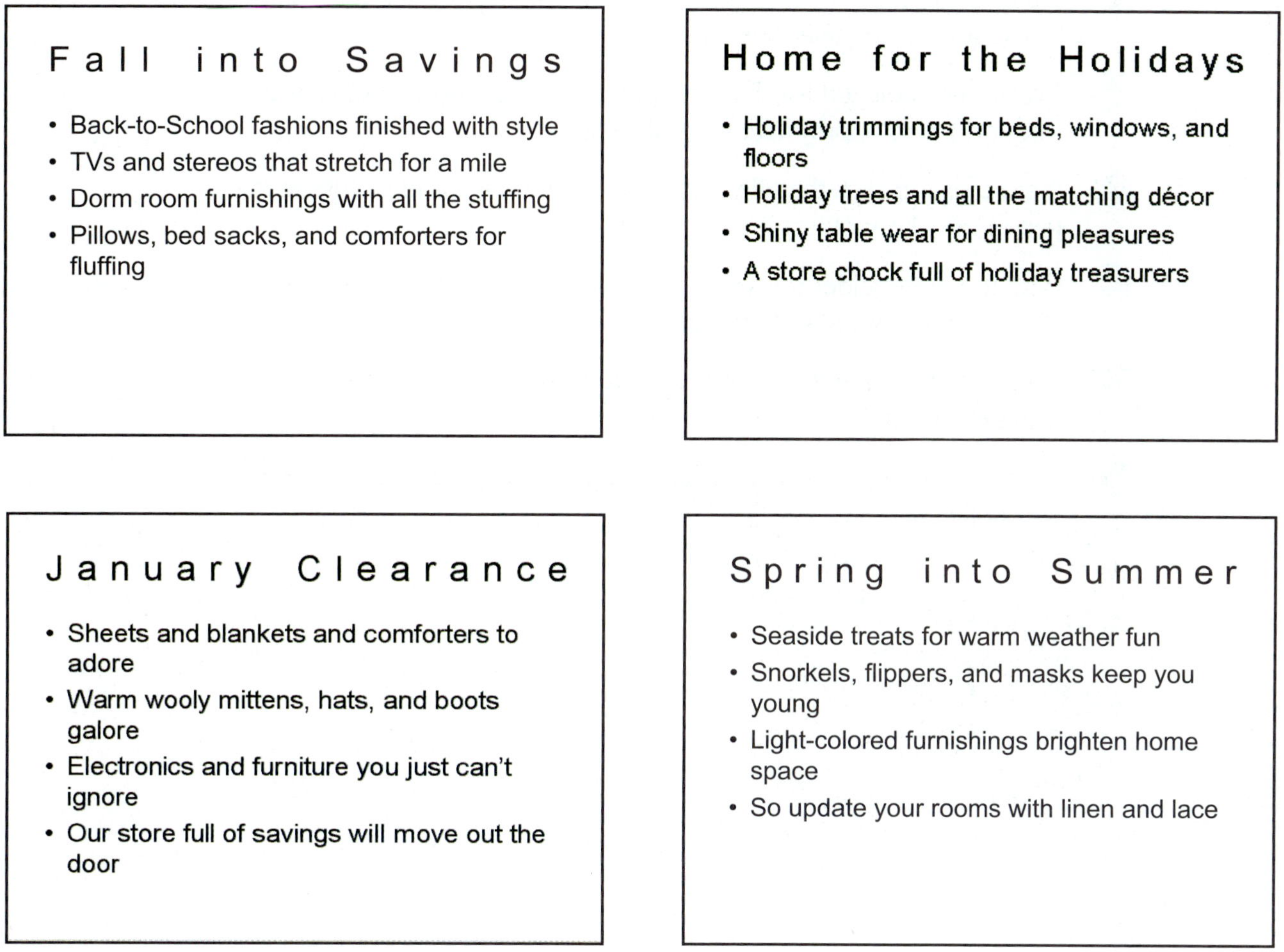
Fall into Savings
• Back-to-School fashions finished with style
• TVs and stereos that stretch for a mile
• Dorm room furnishings with all the stuffing
• Pillows, bed sacks, and comforters for fluffing
Home for the Holidays
• Holiday trimmings for beds, windows, and floors
• Holiday trees and all the matching décor
• Shiny table wear for dining pleasures
• A store chock full of holiday treasurers
January Clearance
• Sheets and blankets and comforters to adore
• Warm wooly mittens, hats, and boots galore
• Electronics and furniture you just can't ignore
• Our store full of savings will move out the door
Spring into Summer
• Seaside treats for warm weather fun
• Snorkels, flippers, and masks keep you young
• Light-colored furnishings brighten home space
• So update your rooms with linen and lace

Follow these steps to add the slides to the presentation.

1. Open the presentation *Seasons of Values.ppt* and replace the Your Name text on the title slide with your name.
2. Create new bulleted list slides and type the data shown in Slides 2 through 5 into appropriate slide placeholders.
3. Press Shift and click the title placeholder on Slide 2 and distribute the text in the placeholder.
4. With the placeholder still selected, double-click the Format Painter button on the Standard toolbar.
5. Paint the titles of Slides 3 through 5 to format the placeholders with the text format.
6. Save changes to the presentation and print a copy of the presentation outline.

ON YOUR OWN

The difficulty of these case studies varies:
are the least difficult; *are more difficult; and* *are the most difficult.*

1 SELECTIONS NEW EMPLOYEE OVERVIEW

Add the slide pictured in Figure 1-51 to the presentation *New Employee Overview.ppt*.

Figure 1-51

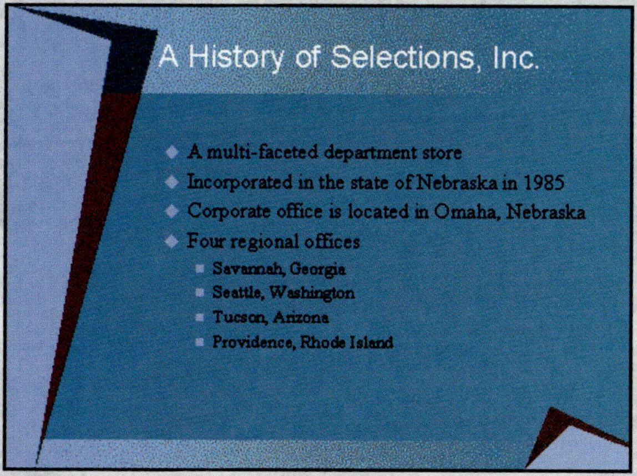

Save changes to the presentation and print a copy of the new slide.

2 TV FROM THE 60S, 70S, AND 80S

For the last few generations, television has had a major influence on our lives. Search the Internet for the following names and then create a new presentation that identifies the shows associated with the characters and the years the show appeared.

- Jed Clampett
- Alf
- Buffalo Bob
- Rod Brown
- Diane Chambers
- Mork
- Fred Mertz

Your presentation should consist of a title slide containing your name, an appropriate title, and at least two bulleted-list slides. Format the bulleted list text with the character name left-aligned and the show in which the character appeared and the years the show appeared right-aligned immediately below the character name. Add the name of the actor who played the character or other interesting pieces of information about each character. Save your presentation using the file name *Characters from the Tube* and print a copy of the presentation as black-and-white handouts with three slides per page.

3 ROCKY MOUNTAIN RESEARCH

Open the presentation *Rocky Mountain Research.ppt*. Add the table slide pictured in Figure 1-52 to the presentation using the Content Over Text slide layout. Adjust the size of the placeholders to accommodate the contents and reposition the placeholders on screen when necessary. Save changes to the presentation and print a copy of the new slide.

Figure 1-52

Scientists – FY 2000

Rank	Number
GS-11	1
GS-12	14
GS-13	41
GS-14	42
GS-15	13
SS-16	1

- **400+ Employees**
- **167 Temps**

4 DRESSING FOR SUCCESS

Candidates for jobs are now showing up in jeans, purple sweat suits, and spike heels or sneakers. Other applicants show up with pierced body parts and spiked hair. Still others chew gum or arrive with rumpled clothes or with their pants falling down. Such outlandish dress often costs candidates the job. Does the way you dress and act really make a difference? In many cases, it does. Create a presentation using the following tips for effective job interview dress. Then go online and see if you can find additional topics of interest to add to the presentation. Save the presentation using the file name *Dressing for Success* and print a copy of the presentation as handouts.

Tips for Women	Tips for Men
Solid color, conservative suit	Solid color, conservative suit
Coordinated blouse	White long-sleeve shirt
Moderate shoes	Conservative tie
Limited jewelry	Dark socks, professional shoes
Neat, professional hairstyle	Very limited jewelry
Tan or light hosiery	Neat, professional hairstyle
Sparse make-up & perfume	Go easy on the aftershave
Manicured nails	Neatly trimmed nails
Portfolio or briefcase	Portfolio or briefcase

5 THE WORKS OF SHAKESPEARE

William Shakespeare is debatably one of the world's most renowned writers. During his life, he wrote many works that varied greatly—from historical plays to humorous works that bordered on the ridiculous. Connect to the Internet and locate works of Shakespeare that would fit into the different periods of his life. Then create a presentation that contains a title slide and bulleted-list slides that represent the different periods of his writing. Type at least four entries in the bulleted-list placeholder of each slide. Apply a different Text Layout to one of the slides so that the slide contains two bulleted-list placeholders and type four entries into each of the placeholders. Save your presentation using the file name *The Works of Shakespeare* and print a copy of the presentation as black-and-white handouts with six slides per page.

6 PACKING MULTIPLE PRESENTATIONS TO GO

The Pack and Go Wizard not only enables you to pack up the active presentation, but also contains settings for selecting multiple presentations and packing them together on a single disk. Use the settings to package up all the presentations you have used in this project onto a single disk and submit the disk to your instructor.

Photospread credits pages 1-2 & 1-3

©Masterfile: ©MTPA Stock; ©Tony Stone: ©Chuck Keeler; ©Pearson Education; ©Lorraine Castellano

FROM THE FILES

-You Will Need

- ✔ Arizona Gov.avi
- ✔ e-Selections Online Web.ppt
- ✔ e-Selections Marketing.ppt
- ✔ Gizmo.jpg
- ✔ JPDL-TV Stars.ppt
- ✔ Poinsettia.gif
- ✔ Rocky Mountain Station.ppt
- ✔ Seasons of Savings.ppt
- ✔ Skiing.avi
- ✔ So They Say.ppt
- ✔ Sugarplum.mid

PROJECT 2

Enhancing Presentations

OBJECTIVES

After completing this project, you will be able to:

- *Apply presentation templates*
- *Create a new template-formatted presentation*
- *Display presentation masters*
- *Create headers and footers*
- *Apply slide masters to presentations*
- *Customize slide back-grounds*
- *Create and apply cus-tom slide templates*
- *Format slide tables*
- *Create an organization chart*
- *Add art, music, and video to slides*
- *Animate slide text*
- *E-mail a presentation*

PowerPoint contains a variety of tools that you can use to enhance presentation slides. You learned how to add and manipulate art objects in Office XP applications in Common Elements Project 3. In this project, you will learn how to add music, video, and new charts to your presentations. You'll also learn how to use special PowerPoint techniques to dress up presentation slides using professionally designed layouts, how to customize these designs to better meet your needs, and how to make your text dance!

e-selections Running Case

The progress you've made during the short time you've been working with Ms. Amber Wright, the Administrative Manager of the e-Selections Online division of Selections, Inc., is amazing! Because you've done such an outstanding job designing presentations and seem to have a knack for working with PowerPoint, Ms. Wright has asked that you be permanently assigned to the e-Selections team! This is exciting, because you will be able to complete the work she's assigned to you, and you've just discovered some new features in PowerPoint that make dressing up a presentation a snap.

Techno-calities for Ensuring Smooth Presentation Delivery

Wouldn't it be wonderful if the best presentation technology were no technology at all—just you, your audience, and a story to tell? In the real world, bright, compelling images orchestrated by a laptop computer, a projection system, and a darkened room are required to assist in sharing a story with others.

Because visuals make up such an important part of presentations, it's important to ensure that the technology required for the presentation does not sabotage the continuity and flow of a presentation. Short of dressing up in a Halloween costume and tap-dancing on the podium, it's a good idea to plan ahead to divert technology failures. Here are a few tips from Jim Endicott, Owner/Manager of Distinction, for working through the techno-calities to ensure that your presentation is a success.

- **Plan Ahead:** *Complete the "Request for AV" form as soon as it arrives—equipment is being reserved and rooms are being set up based on your answers to the questions on that form—and include all details.*
- **Know who to contact in case equipment fails:** *A quick call to the conference center or conference producers will provide the name(s) to call for technical assistance during your presentation.*
- **Create presentation backups:** *Whenever possible, print a paper copy of the presentation, burn a CD ROM of your presentation (with embedded fonts), and travel with your own laptop and electronic projector as well.*
- **Bring all the right stuff:** *Bring your own peripherals, such as docking bars, accessories, component bars, cables that require proprietary connectors, power supplies, and remote devices.*
- **Arrive early:** *Whenever possible, arrive at least 60 minutes early or set up the day before your presentation.*

When all is said and done, it is also important to know the equipment you'll be using. That way you can fix things or improvise "on the fly" as the presentation progresses. Here are some things to know about each piece of equipment:

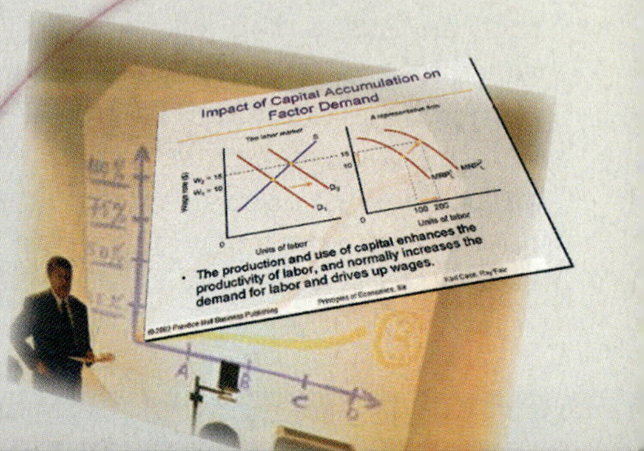

1 About the laptop/computer you're using, you need to know

- How to change screen resolution
- How much RAM you have—this affects the speed of presentation delivery
- How to quickly toggle between laptop/computer, projector, or dual mode displays
- Where and how to adjust external volume
- How to "wake" the computer if it goes to sleep

2 About the electronic projector, you need to know

- How to connect the cables to the laptop/computer
- The menu items for adjusting the image and position and how to adjust them
- How to adjust the brightness of the projector to work with room lighting
- How to "wake" the projector from standby mode

3 About the mouse or remote pointing device, be sure to

- Keep a fresh set of batteries handy
- Learn how to use your remote without the audience knowing—avoid blatant pointing
- Know your angle and distance limitations for line-of-sight
- Identify the lighting conditions that can affect the remote's performance
- Practice using it to point to small items and clicking

Moreover, remember—if disaster strikes, a five-minute coffee break is usually all that's needed to get you ready to roll again.

PROJECT 2

Enhancing Presentations

The Challenge

Ms. Wright has reviewed the presentation slides you created in previous projects and has approved the direction you are taking with the presentations. She would now like you to dress up the presentations you've started and create a general design for the presentation so that she can circulate the design to the other e-Selections managers for feedback. In addition, Ms. Wright has received a request from the Personnel Division at Selections, Inc., for a presentation design that will contain information from the employee handbook. Each of the designs that you have formulated for the presentations appears in Figure 2-1.

Figure 2-1

The Solution

Because you already know the basics of working with art objects in Office XP applications, you know that you can increase the impact of the presentation by adding art objects to the slides you've developed. You can also use music and video to enhance slides, but you'll have to determine how to add those features. After reviewing the stash of template designs available in PowerPoint, you decide to modify an existing design to meet the needs of the company. Organizing information on some slides is a simple matter after you discover organization charts!

Applying Presentation Templates

If you have worked with word processing programs, such as Word, you are already familiar with the concept of *templates*—preformatted layouts that hold text font format and alignment, color combinations, layout, and design elements. In PowerPoint, presentation templates provide style and color and add the pizzazz your presentation needs to attract the attention of your audience. Applying a template to your presentation helps maintain consistency among the slides in the presentation. PowerPoint provides a variety of techniques that you can use to open the Slide Design task pane and display a list of templates:

- Click the Design button on the Formatting toolbar.
- Double-click the template name area of the status bar at the bottom of the presentation window.
- Choose **Format | Slide Design.**
- Click the task pane down arrow and select **Slide Design—Design Templates.**
- Click the **From Design Template** link in the **New** area of the New Presentation task pane.

Task 1:

To Apply Templates to Presentation Slides

1 Launch **PowerPoint** and open the presentation *e-Selections Online Web.ppt*.

2 Click the Design button on the Formatting toolbar.

> **Tip** Clicking the Design button opens the Slide Design task pane if the task pane is hidden. If the task pane is displayed, clicking the Design button displays the Slide Design task pane.

3 Click the **Browse** link at the bottom of the Slide Design task pane and open the **Presentation Designs** folder.

Figure 2-2

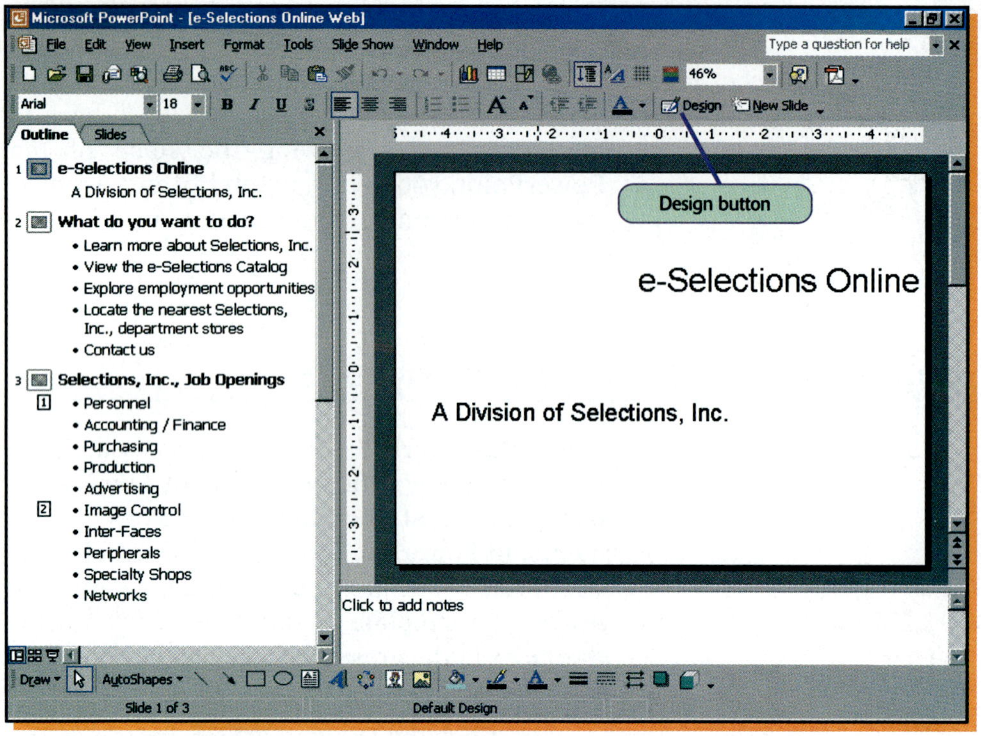

Figure 2-3

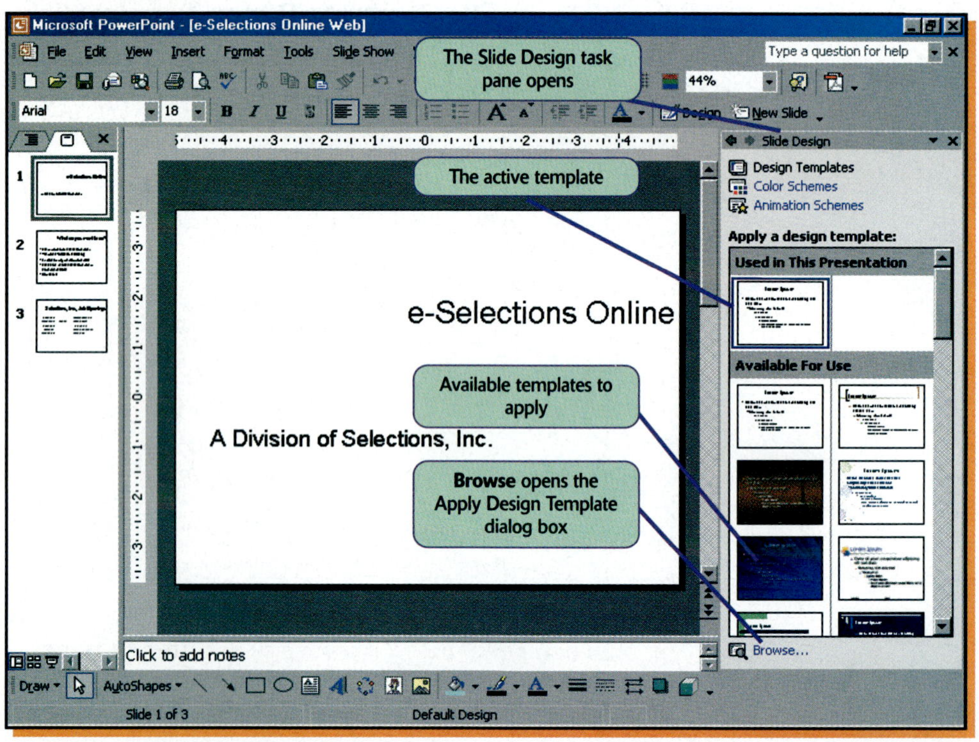

4 Click the **Cascade** template name.

Troubleshooting
Select a template identified by your instructor if Cascade is unavailable.

Figure 2-4

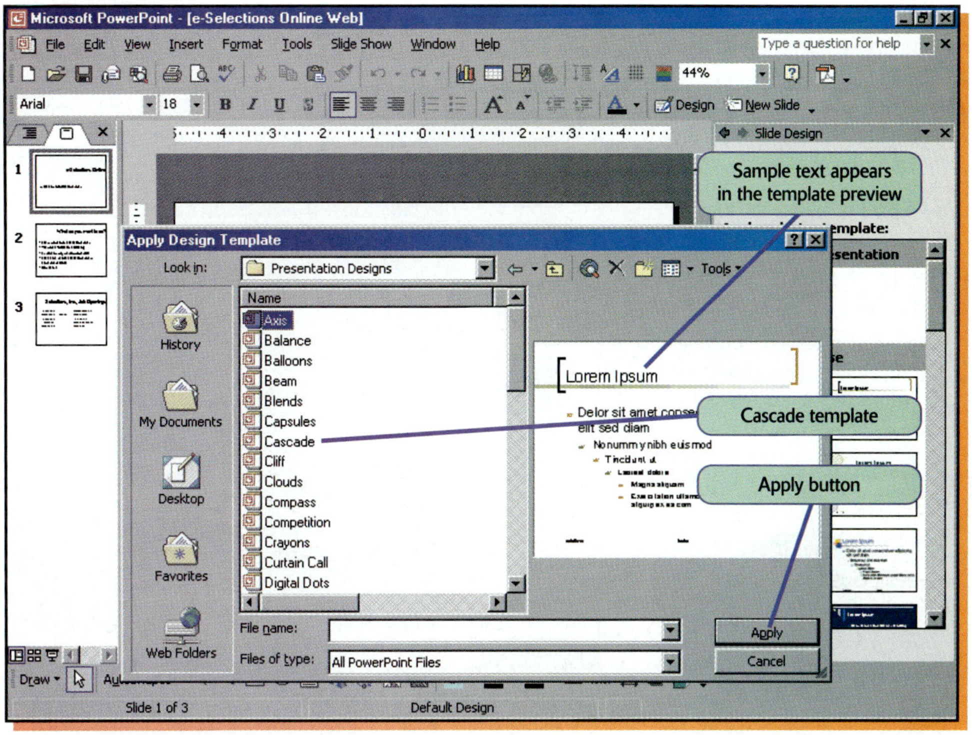

5 Click **Apply**.

Figure 2-5

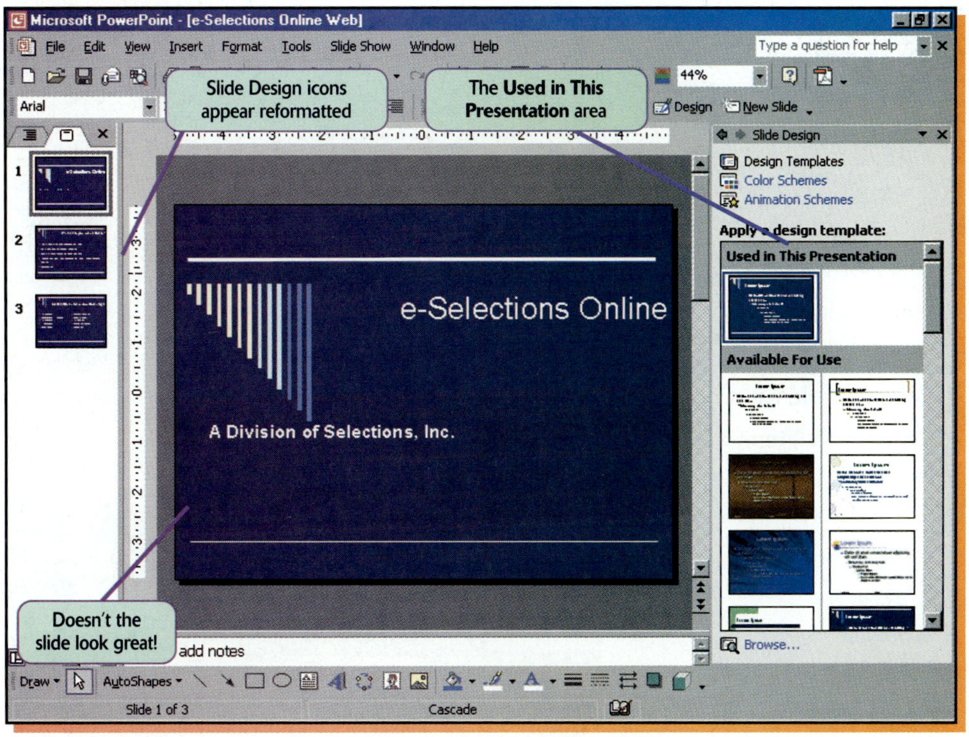

6 Create a bulleted-list slide at the end of the presentation and then scroll the templates in the Slide Design task pane until you find the *Digital Dots* template.

Troubleshooting

You may have to scroll the list of available templates to locate Digital Dots. If you don't see the Digital Dots template, use the template identified by your instructor.

Figure 2-6

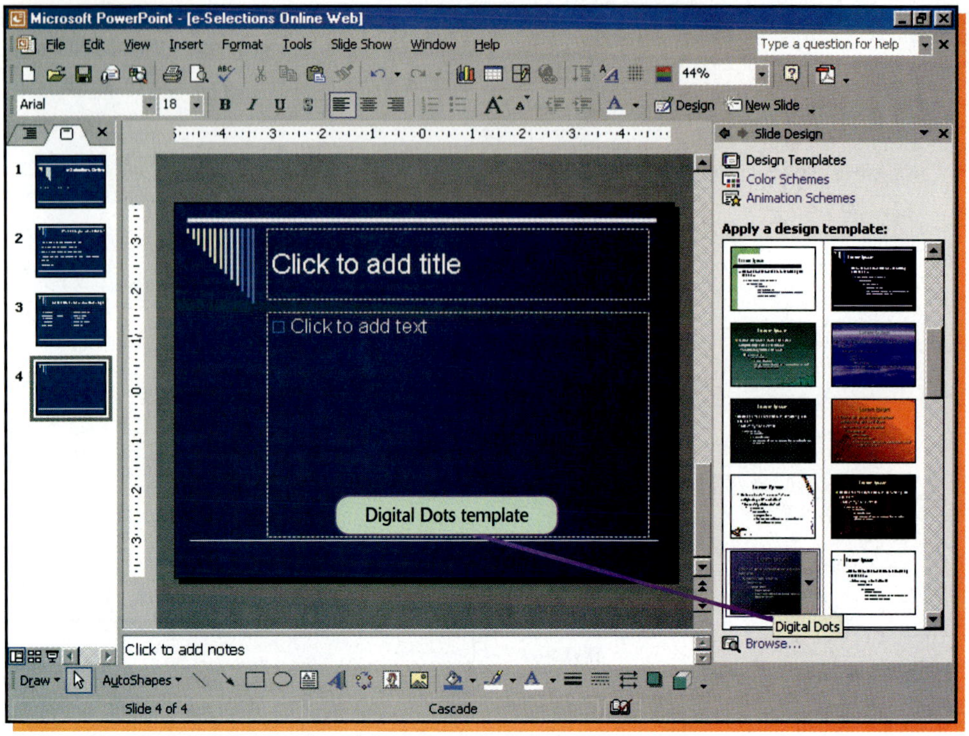

7 Click the down arrow on the *Digital Dots* template icon and select **Apply to Selected Slides.**

8 Type the text shown in Figure 2-7 into text boxes on Slide 4 and save changes to the presentation.

Digital Networks
- Networking Software
- Interface Cards
- Digital Cable Modems
- Digital Satellites
- Digital Cellular Communication Devices
  - Telephones
  - Pagers
  - Personal Digital Assistants

Figure 2-7

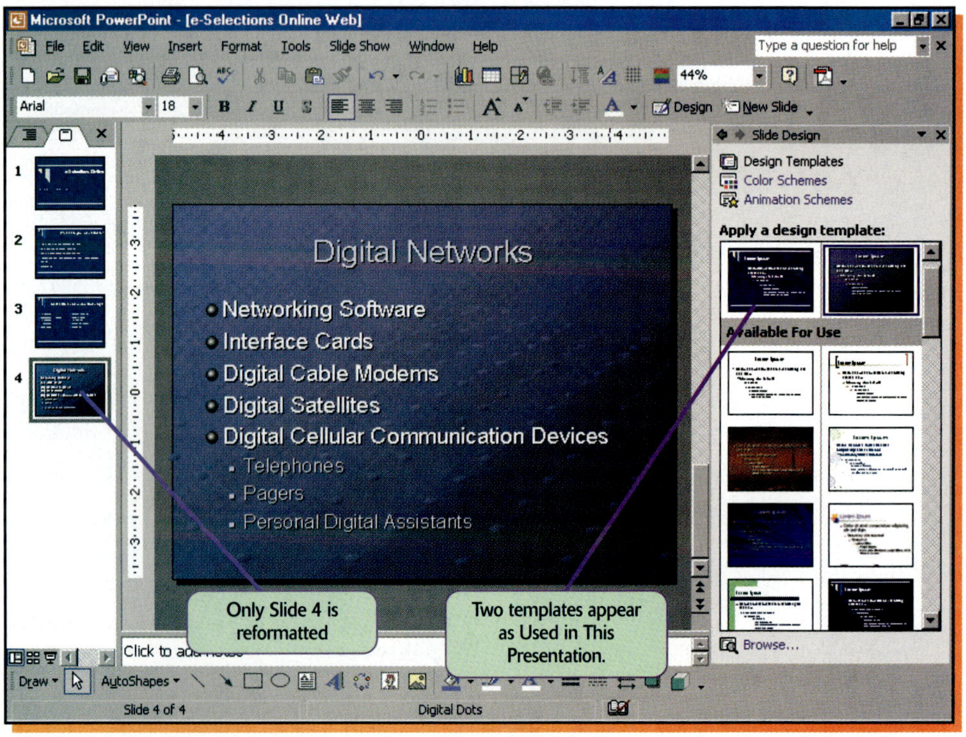

> **Tip** The file size of a presentation formatted using a template is significantly higher than the file size of a blank presentation. If you notice a delay in screen element display when you work with presentations formatted with a template, you may want to add text and other items to the presentation first and then apply a template.

Creating New Template-Formatted Presentations

You've already discovered that PowerPoint applies an appropriate template to presentations created using the AutoContent Wizard. You can also create new, preformatted presentations with a template instead of working with blank templates and applying a template after the presentation is complete. By selecting a template before building the presentation, you get a better perspective for how slide items blend with the template colors and design. You can also adjust the size and placement of objects so that they fit within the confines of template objects.

Task 2:
To Create a New Template-Formatted Presentation

1. Close all open presentations and choose **File | New** to open the New Presentation task pane. Click the **From Design Template** link on the task pane.

2. Click the **Browse** link at the bottom of the task pane, open the **Presentation Designs** folder, if necessary, and double-click the template of your choice for the new presentation.

3. Type Selections, Inc., Employee Handbook in the title placeholder of the title slide and adjust the placeholder so that *Employee Handbook* appears on the second title line.

4. Type *Your Name* in the subtitle placeholder. Save the presentation using the file name *Selections Employee Handbook* and close the file.

Figure 2-8

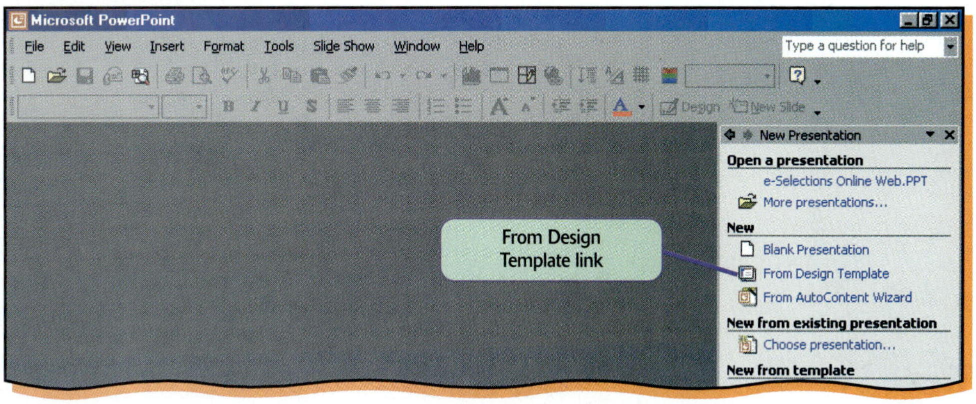

Figure 2-9

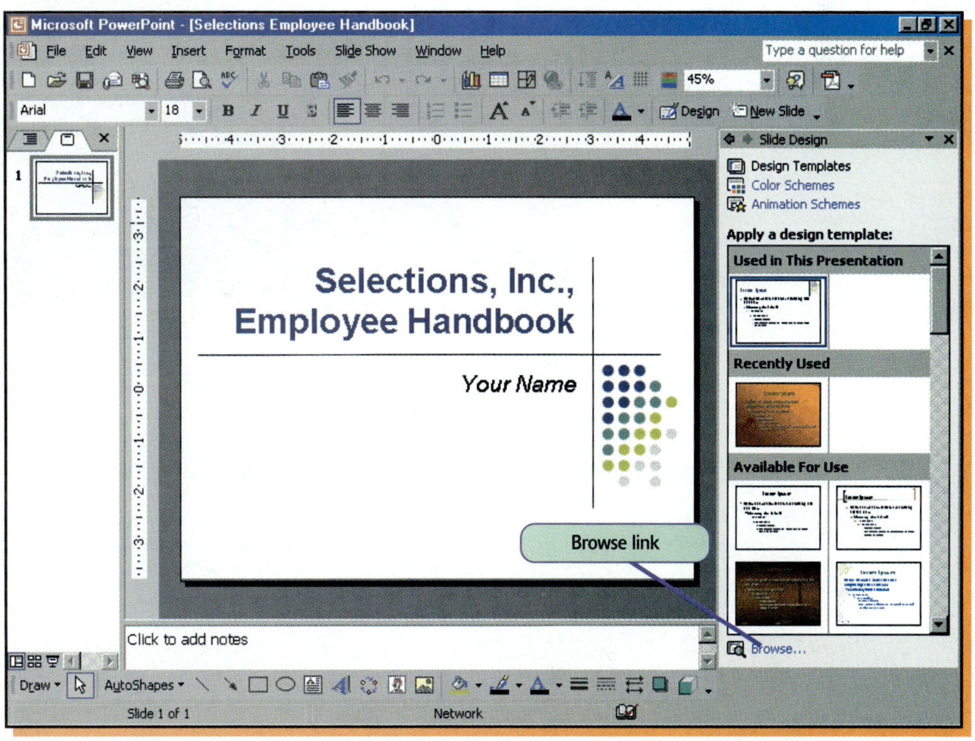

WEB TIP

Search the Internet for additional templates to add to your template collection. The Microsoft PowerPoint Web site is a great place to start. Microsoft frequently adds new dynamic template designs.

Working the Masters

Each presentation you create contains slides formatted with a template that contains design elements, such as background color, text placeholder format, and graphics. These design elements are stored in layouts called *masters*. Each template contains separate masters for each type of presentation material (slides, notes, and handouts).

Creating Headers and Footers

You can add *header* and *footer* information to presentation slides, notes, and handouts by selecting options in the Header and Footer dialog box. Header and footer items added in the dialog box automatically appear on the masters.

Task 3: To Add Footer Items

1 Display Slide 4 of *e-Selections Online Web.ppt* in Normal view and choose **View | Header and Footer**.

Figure 2-10

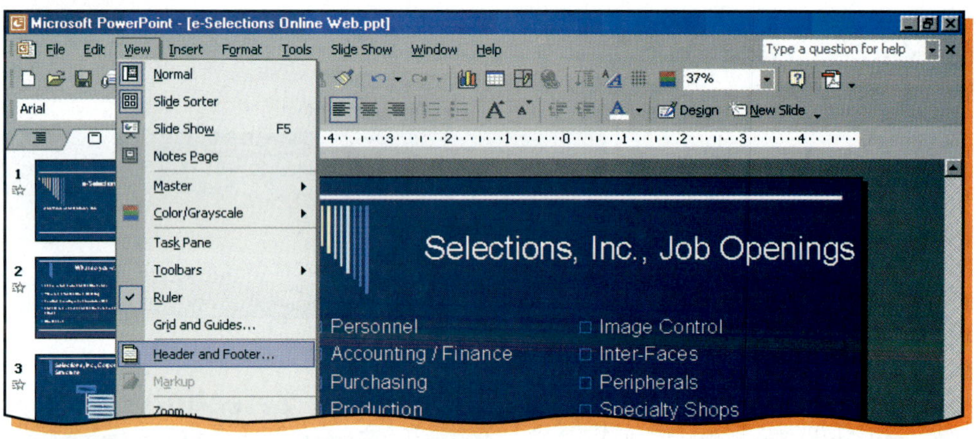

Tip When you create a new presentation using the AutoContent Wizard, you can select footer options on the last page of the AutoContent Wizard.

2 Set the following options in the Header and Footer dialog box:

- Click **Update automatically** for the date and time.
- Select the **Slide number** option.
- Clear the **Footer** option.

3 Click **Apply to All**. All slides appear with the slide number and date in the footer area. Save changes to the presentation.

Figure 2-11

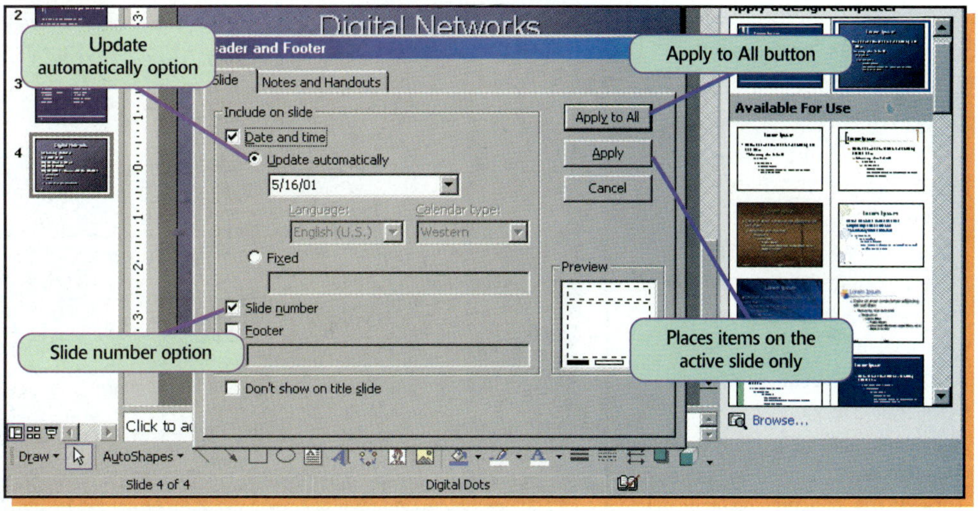

Displaying Presentation Masters

All presentation templates contain at least two different masters for formatting slides:

- PowerPoint applies the Slide Master design to slides formatted using all slide layouts except the Title slide layout.
- PowerPoint applies the Title Master design to slides formatted using the Title slide layout.

If you use multiple templates to format the slides in a presentation, you can see the masters for each of the templates used by displaying the masters.

Task 4:
To Display Slide Masters

1 Display Slide 1 of *e-Selections Online Web.ppt* and close the task pane.

2 Choose **View** | **Master** | **Slide Master**.

Tip If you are working with a blank presentation, only the master for bulleted-list slides appears.

Figure 2-12

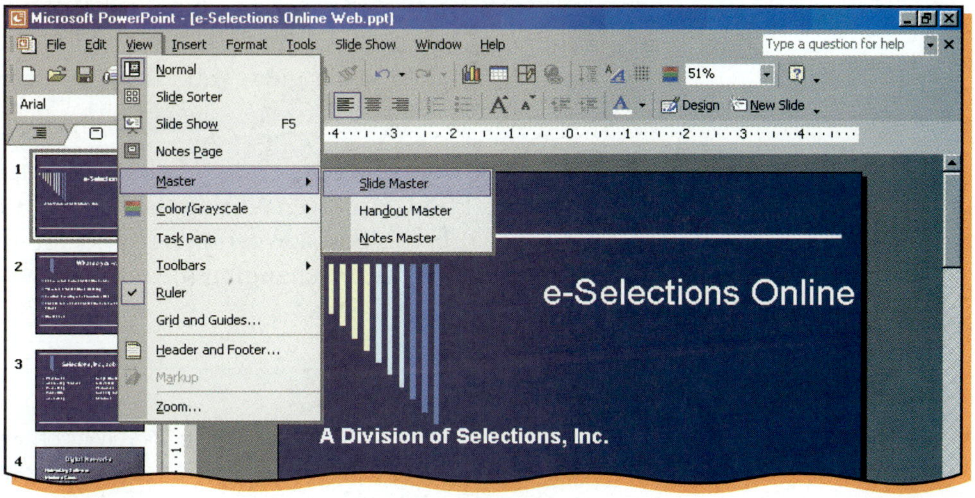

3 Click the **Cascade Title Master** icon in the masters pane on the left. Bullet formats for different bullet levels appear in the placeholder.

Troubleshooting
Cascade was the name of the template you applied to this presentation, remember? If you're having trouble locating it, point to the icons in the masters pane on the left and review the screen tips. If the masters pane is hidden, click the Normal view button at the bottom of the presentation window twice to restore the panes and then press Shift and click the Normal view button again to redisplay the masters.

Figure 2-13

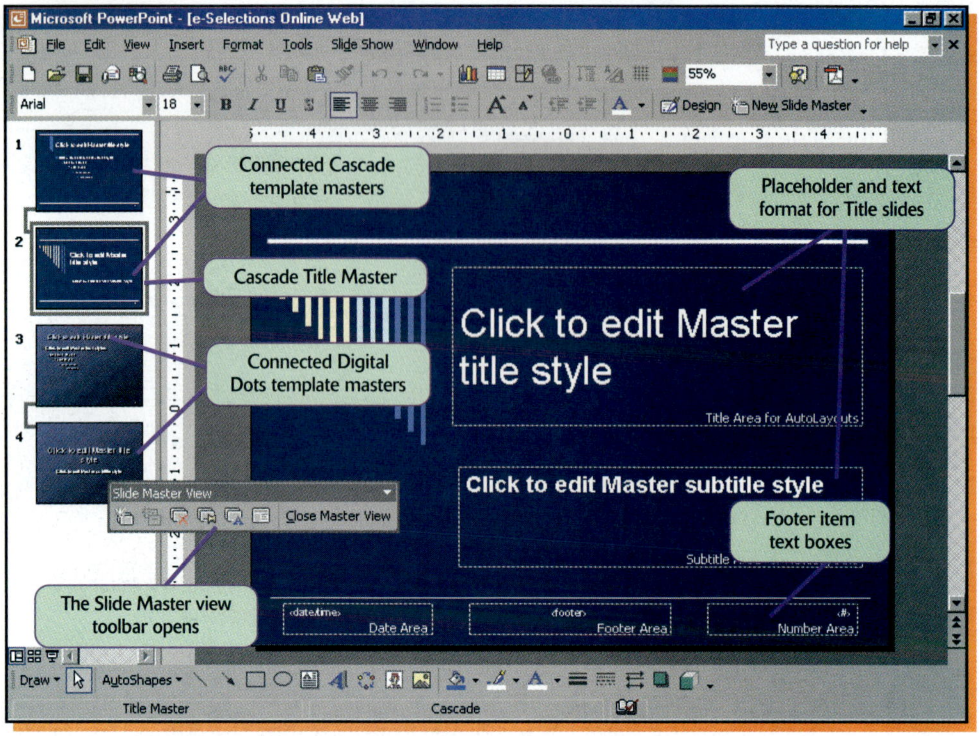

Creating Custom Slide Templates

Although templates come equipped with both slide and title masters, you can create new slide masters as well as new title masters. Customizing existing masters is the most efficient way to create your own custom-designed templates. From the Master view, you can customize slide masters and save them as new masters.

The Digital Dots template contains the elements you want to see on Slide 4 in the presentation. However, editing the color of the template will make it blend in better with the Cascade template used for the other slides. You can customize the template by changing the background color and saving the changes as a new custom master.

Tip
To design a completely new slide master, click the Insert New Slide Master button on the Slide Master View toolbar. A blank slide master appears and you can build the master from scratch.

Task 5:

To Customize Slide Backgrounds and Create a New Slide Master

1. Display the **Master** view, if necessary, and click the Design **Design** button to open the task pane.

Other Ways

To display the Design task pane:

- Choose **Format | Slide Design**.

2. Click the **Digital Dots** slide master icon in the masters pane on the left.

Figure 2-14

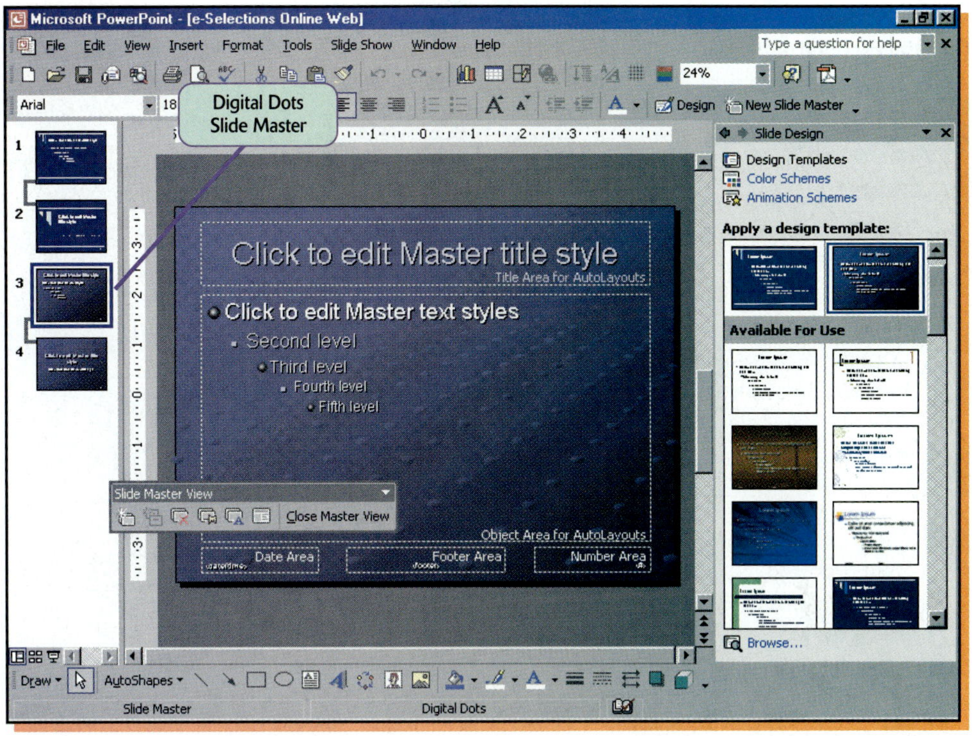

3. Click the **Color Schemes** link at the top of the Slide Design task pane.

4. Click the color scheme icon identified in Figure 2-15. The background changes on the Digital Dots slide template.

Figure 2-15

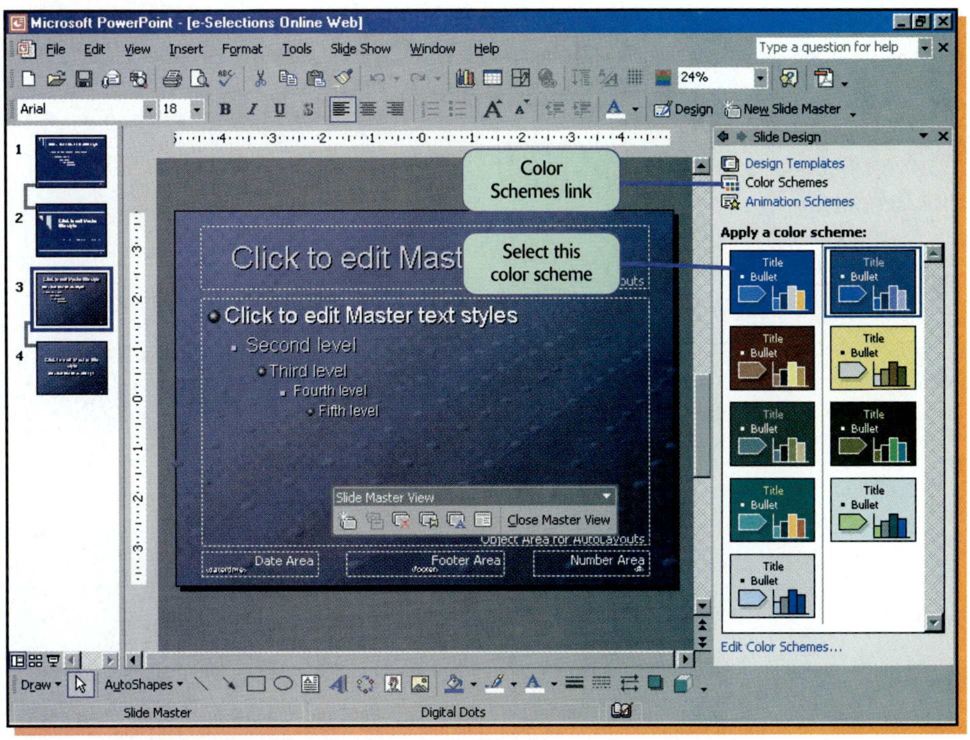

5 Press Shift, click the title placeholder, and click the Align Right button on the Formatting toolbar.

Other Ways

To select a placeholder:

- Point to the border area of the placeholder until the mouse pointer appears as a four-headed arrow and then click to select the placeholder.

Figure 2-16

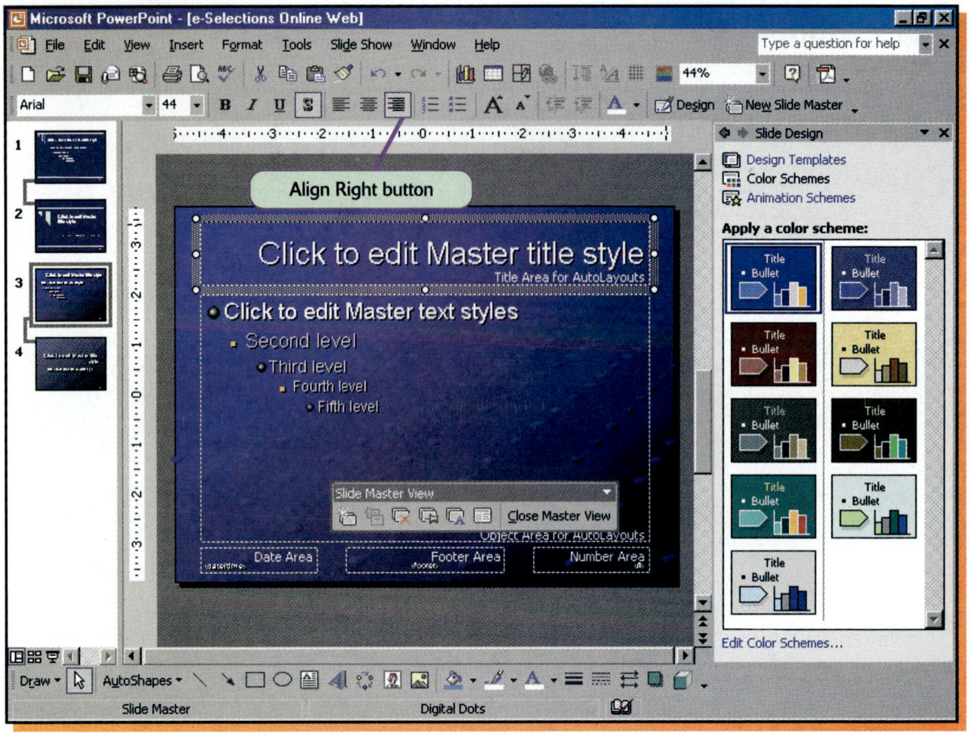

6 Click the Rename Master button on the **Slide Master View** toolbar.

7 Type *Your Initials* e-selections and click Rename.

8 Click **Close Master View** Close Master View and save changes to the presentation.

Figure 2-17

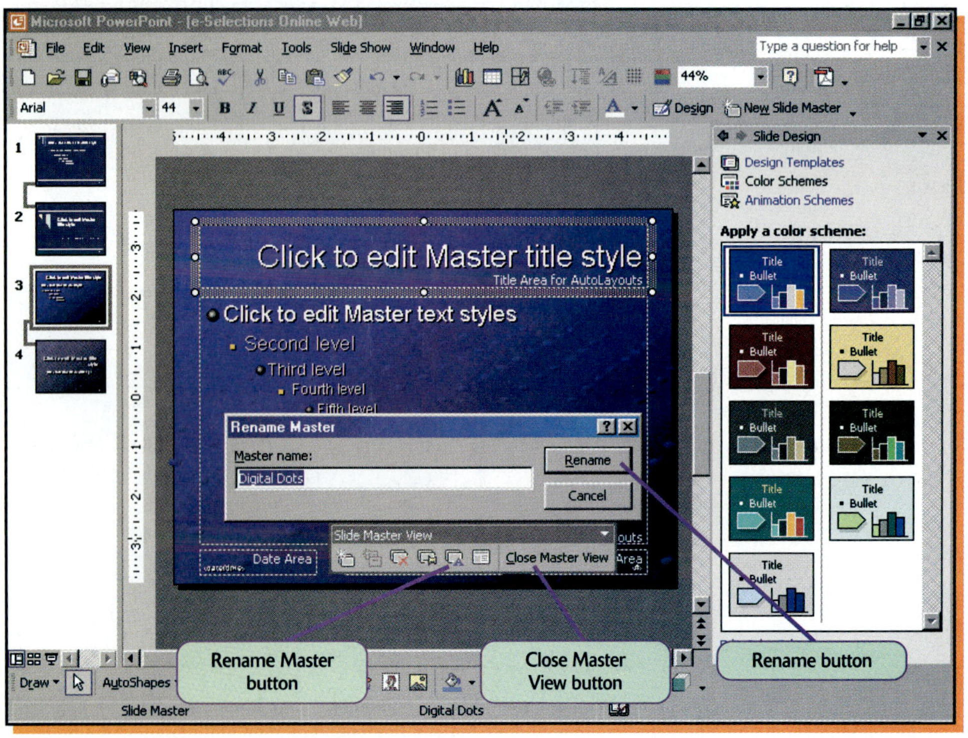

Creating and Formatting Custom Tables

When you created the tables on slides in other projects, you used the Content slide layout tools. You can format the tables you create using tools contained on the Tables and Borders toolbar.

Task 6:

To Create and Format a Table

1. Display Slide 4 of *e-Selections Online Web.ppt*, create a new slide, and apply the **Title and Content** slide layout to the slide.
2. Apply the **Cascade** template to the new slide.

Figure 2-18

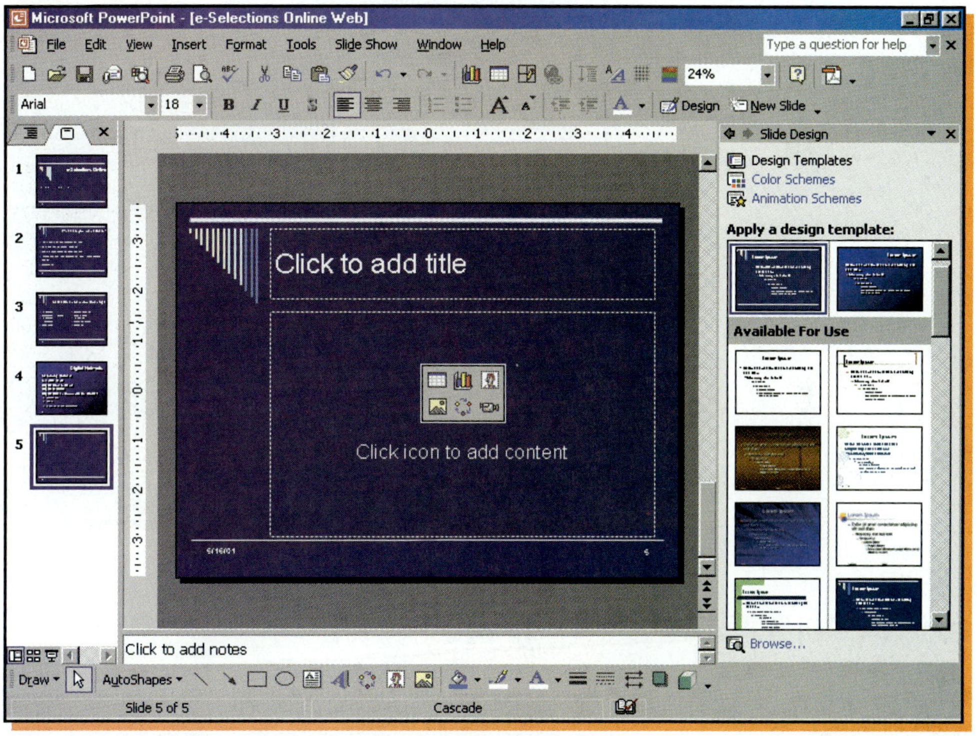

Tip

The Title and Content slide layout contains icons that represent a number of different content items. Point to each icon and view the screen tips that identify each content item.

3 Create a new two-column, five-row table in the Content placeholder.

4 Close the task pane and click the Tables and Borders button on the Standard toolbar to display the Tables and Borders toolbar, if necessary.

Figure 2-19

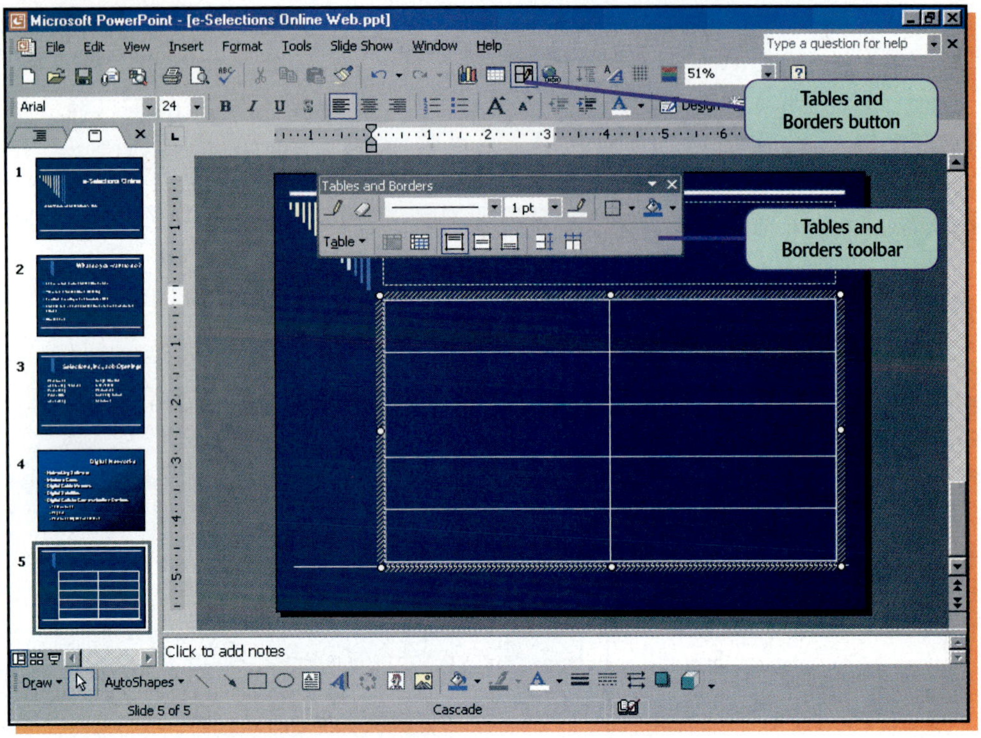

5 Press Esc to deactivate the Draw Table tool and then click and drag to select all table cells.

Other Ways

To format a table:

- Create the table and then choose **Format** | **Table**. Then set the appropriate format options and click **OK**.

6 Click the Border Color button on the Tables and Borders toolbar.

7 Click the **Follow Fills Scheme Color** on the color palette. The mouse pointer becomes a pencil.

Figure 2-20

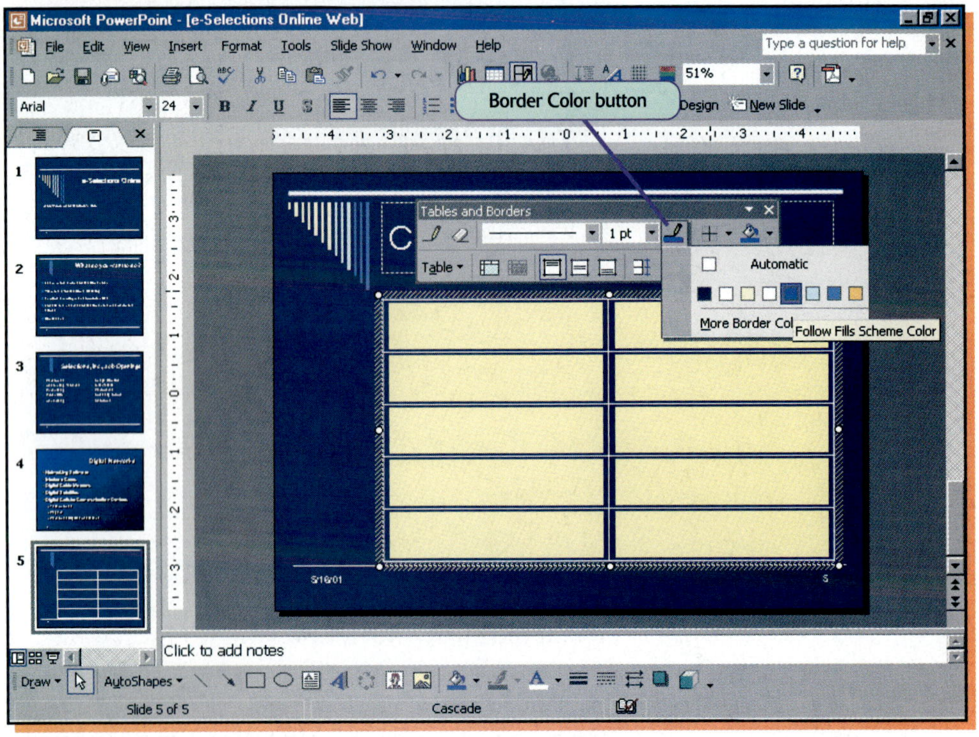

8 Click the Borders down arrow on the Tables and Borders toolbar and click the No Border button.

9 Click the Borders down arrow again and click the Inside Borders button.

Tip As you point to each button on the borders palette, a screen tip identifies the border type.

10 Type the text displayed in Figure 2-22 into the title placeholder and table, and change the font size for all table cells to 20.

11 Select the cells in the first column and click the Center Vertically button on the Tables and Borders toolbar. Save changes to the presentation.

Figure 2-21

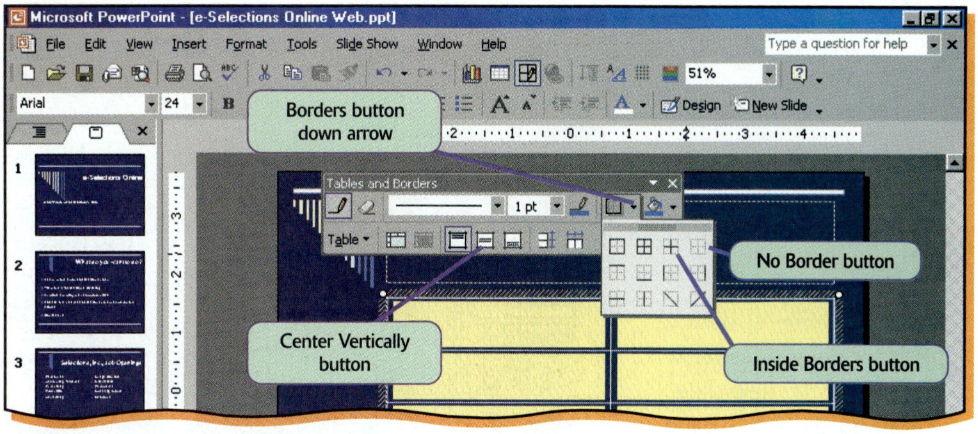

Figure 2-22

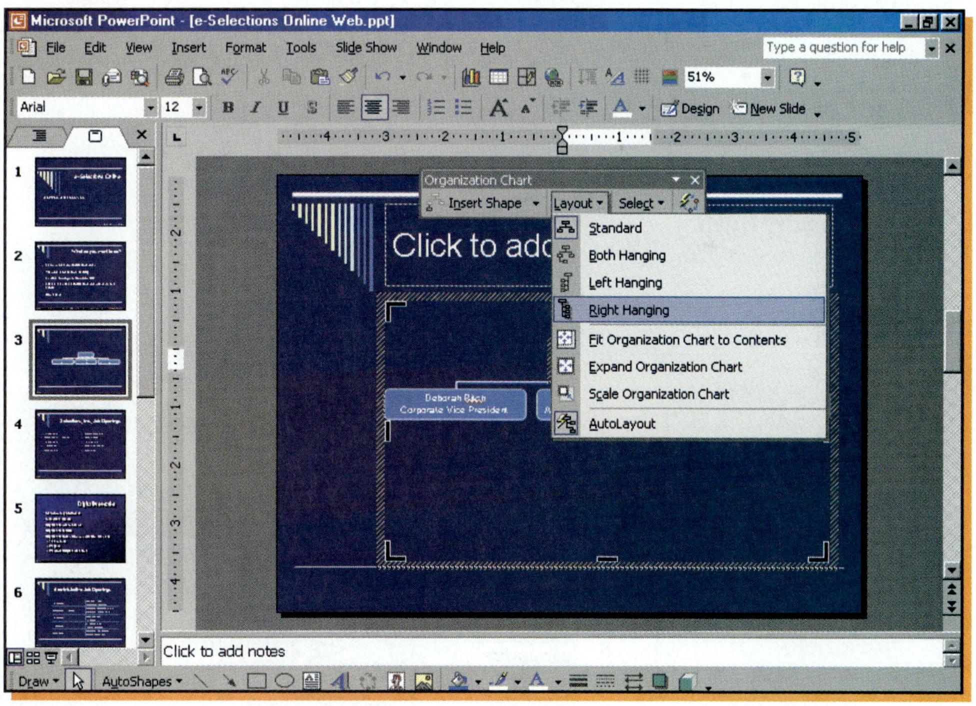

Creating Organization Charts

The table structure enables you to format data in columns. When you want to display a *hierarchical structure* that outlines the management levels of individuals within an organization, you can use PowerPoint's Organization Chart program. An organization chart contains boxes interconnected in a way that represents the relationships between the boxes.

Task 7: To Create an Organization Chart

1. Open the presentation *e-Selections Online Web.ppt* in PowerPoint, if necessary, and display Slide 2.

2. Click the New Slide [New Slide] button, apply the **Title and Content** slide layout to the new slide, and then close the task pane.

Tip New slides appear immediately following the slide that is active when you create a new slide. As a result, the new slide is Slide 3.

Figure 2-23

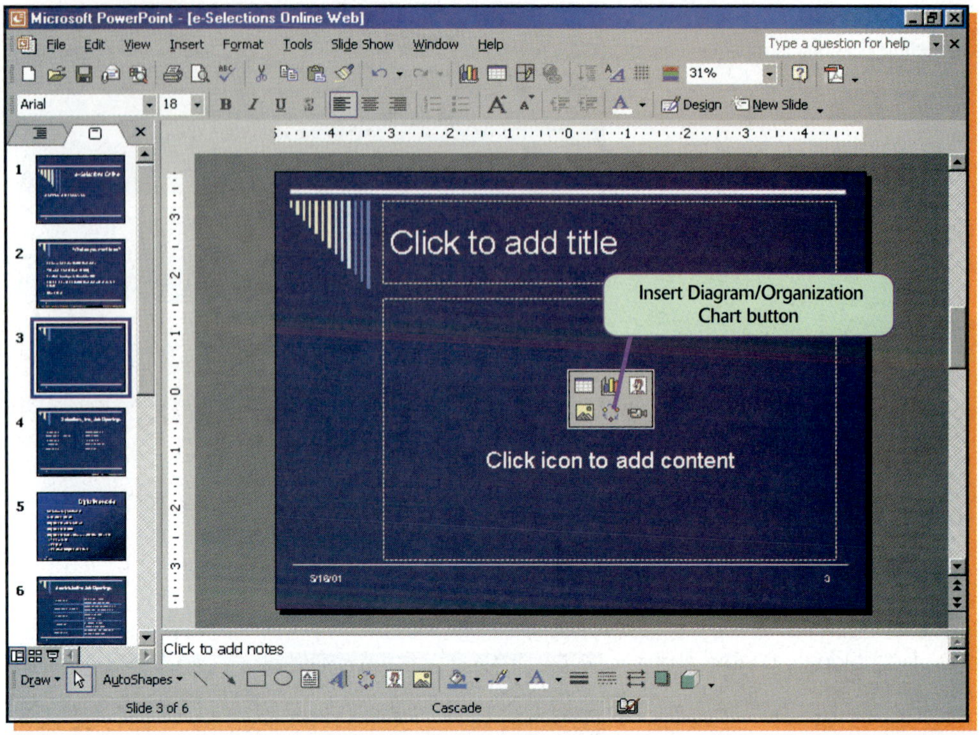

3. Click the Insert Diagram or Organization Chart icon in the content placeholder.

Other Ways To display the Diagram Gallery dialog box:
- Choose **Insert | Diagram.**
- Click the Insert Diagram or Organization Chart button on the Drawing toolbar.

4. Click the organization chart graphic and then click **OK**.

Figure 2-24

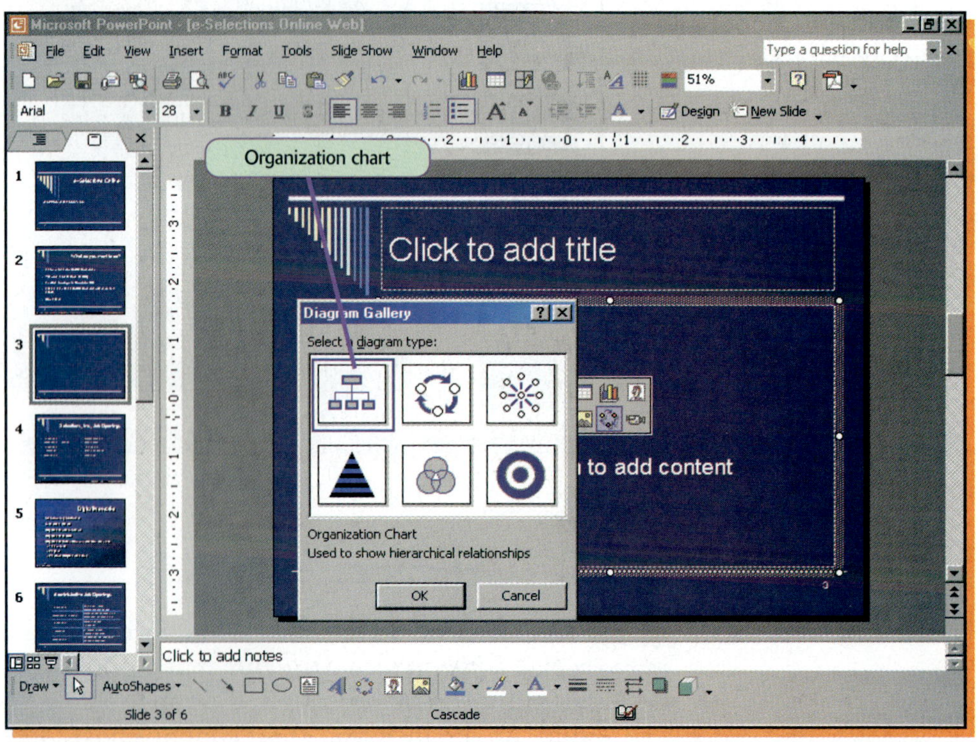

5 Click the top box on the organization chart, type **Jeffrey Anderson**, press Enter, and type **Owner and President.**

Troubleshooting
The text, as you type in each box, may become difficult to read. That's okay—you'll fix it later.

Figure 2-25

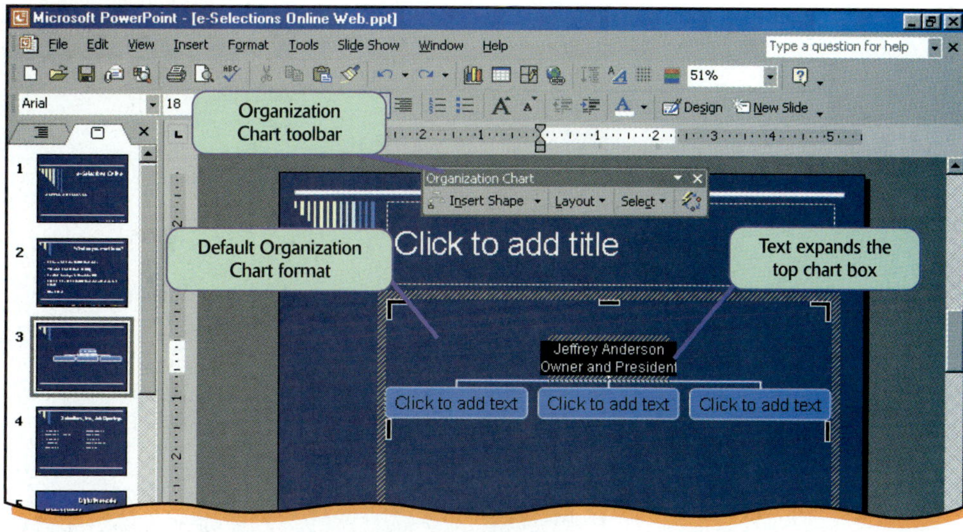

6 Click each of the boxes on the second level and type the following text:

- **Deborah Ritch, Corporate Vice President**
- **John Vincenti, Administrative Vice President**
- **Ronald Carroll, e-Selections Vice President**

7 Click the top box on the chart, click the **Layout** down arrow on the Organization Chart toolbar, and select **Right Hanging**.

8 Click the AutoFormat button on the Organization Chart toolbar.

Figure 2-26

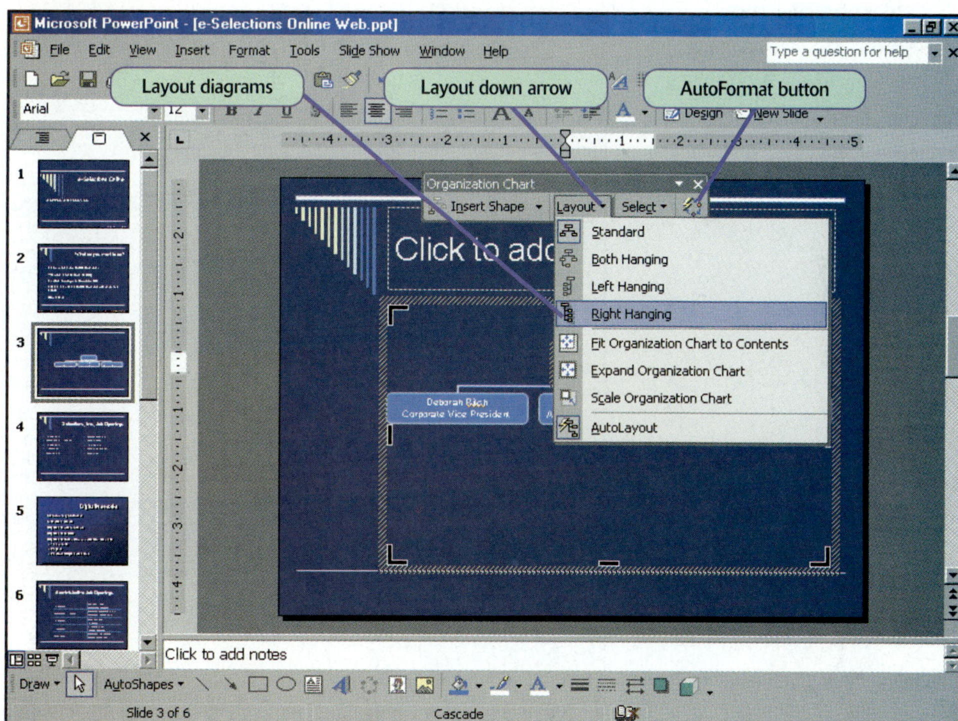

9 Click **Beveled Gradient** in the Select a Diagram Style list and then click **Apply**.

Figure 2-27

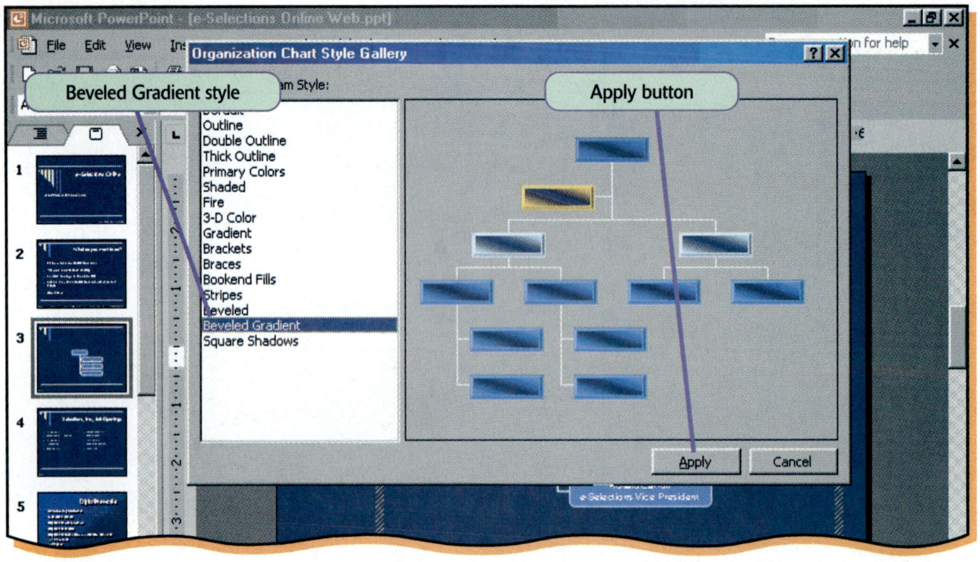

10 Click the title placeholder, type **Selections, Inc., Corporate Structure**, and save changes to the presentation.

Figure 2-28

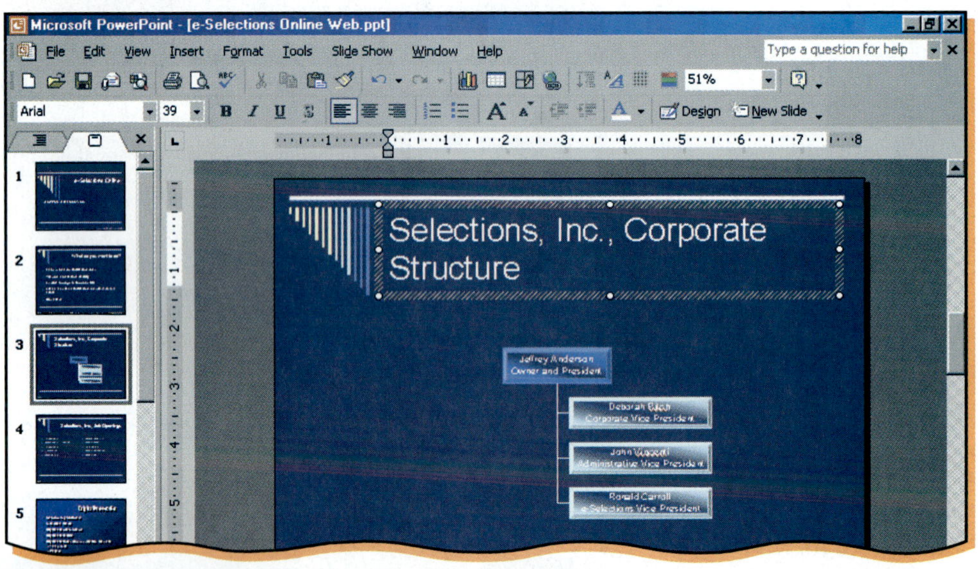

CHECK POINT

You can save organization charts that you add to presentation slides and use them again. Because PowerPoint saves organization charts as pictures, you can insert them in most Office XP files—Word documents, Excel workbooks, and Access data sheets—as well as in other presentations. To save the chart, right-click on the organization chart that appears on the slide and choose **Save as Picture.** Save it on the drive and in the folder of your choice; just be sure you remember where you put it.

Adding Art, Music, and Videos to Slides

The Clip Organizer holds pictures, music, and videos that make dressing up your presentations quick and easy. In addition, you can use media from other sources and download media from the Internet to add to your presentations. The WordArt feature that you explored in Common Elements Project 3 is also available in PowerPoint. It helps you to change text into "words of art." PowerPoint contains features that streamline the process of adding media to presentation slides.

Task 8:
To Add Media Clips to Slides

1. Display the last slide in the *e-Selections Online Web.ppt* presentation and click the New Slide **New Slide** button.

2. Apply the **Title, Text, and Content** slide layout to the new slide.

3. Click the Insert Clip Art icon in the Content placeholder.

Figure 2-29

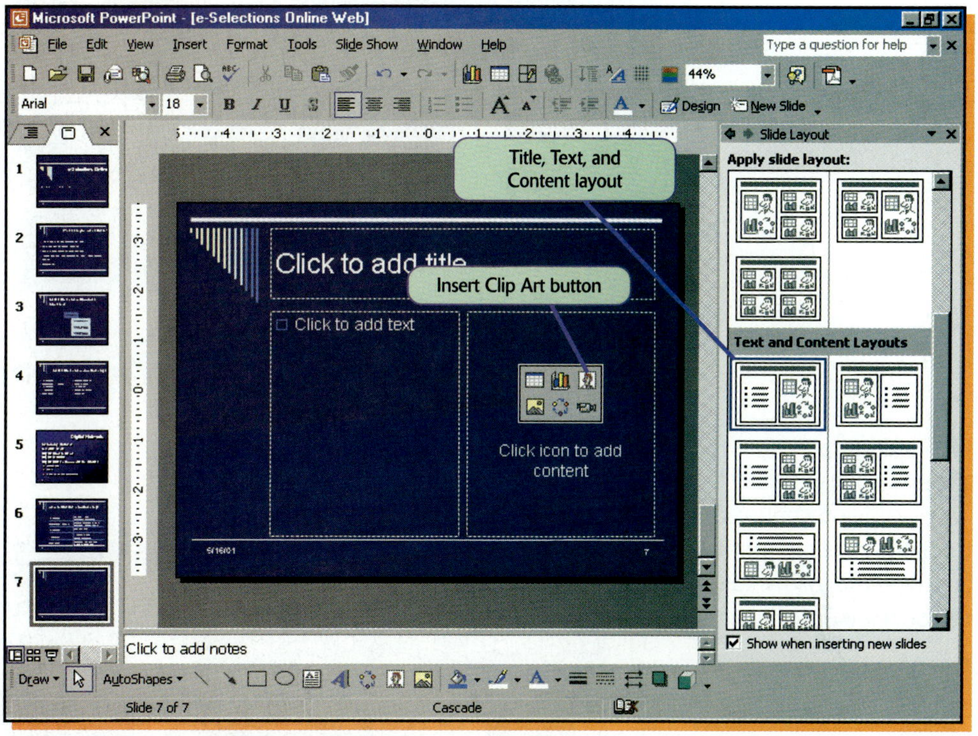

Tip As the number of different placeholders contained on a slide increases, the size of each placeholder gets smaller. PowerPoint adjusts the size of text and other items in each placeholder to maintain consistency.

4 Type **sports** in the Search text field and click **Search**.

Troubleshooting
The graphics displayed on your screen might be different from those shown in Figure 2-30 depending on the collections installed on your computer.

Figure 2-30

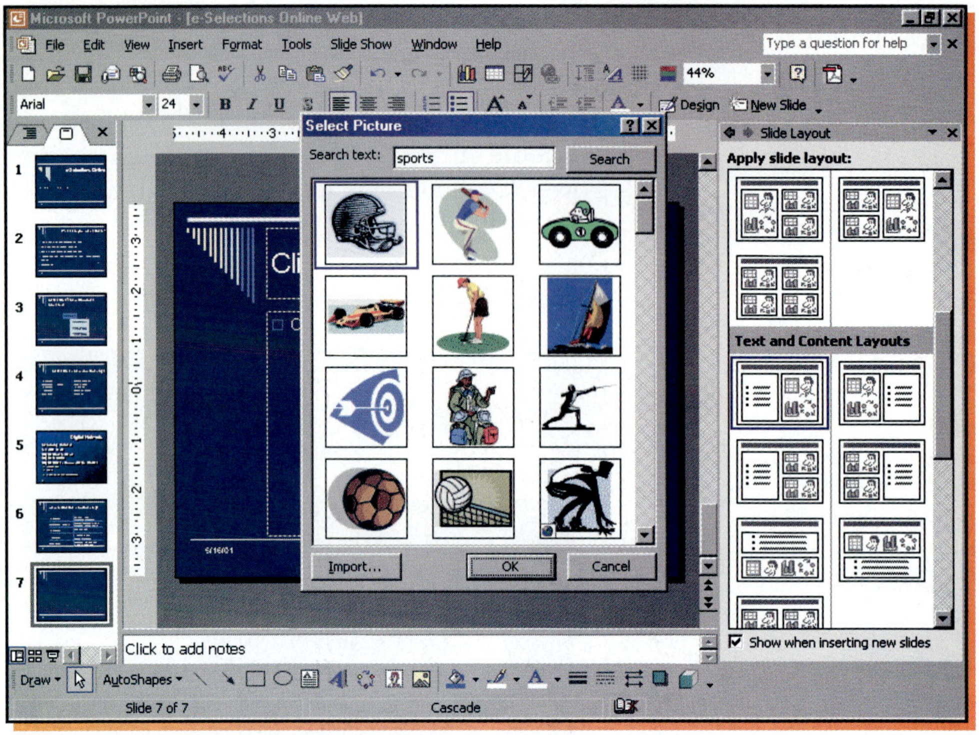

5 Click the **soccer ball** clip and choose **OK**; then close the task pane and type the following text in the bulleted-list placeholder:

- Soccer Equipment
- Tennis Rackets
- Archery Supplies
- Golf Clubs
- Baseball Bats
- Ski Equipment
- Biking Tools
- Balls of All Types

Figure 2-31

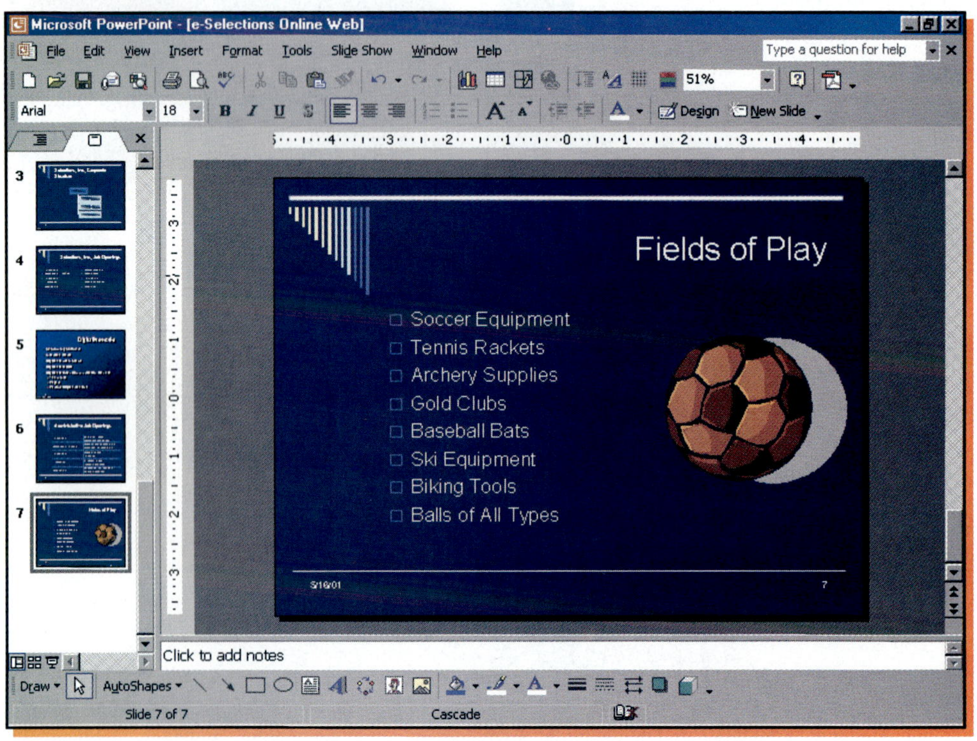

6 Choose **Insert | Movies and Sounds | Sound from Clip Organizer**.

Troubleshooting
The same Clip Organizer that holds clip art images also contains sound and movie clips. Depending on the installation procedures used to set up PowerPoint on your computer, clip libraries may need to be installed the first time you access them. Follow the direction of your instructor to set up clip libraries, if necessary.

Figure 2-32

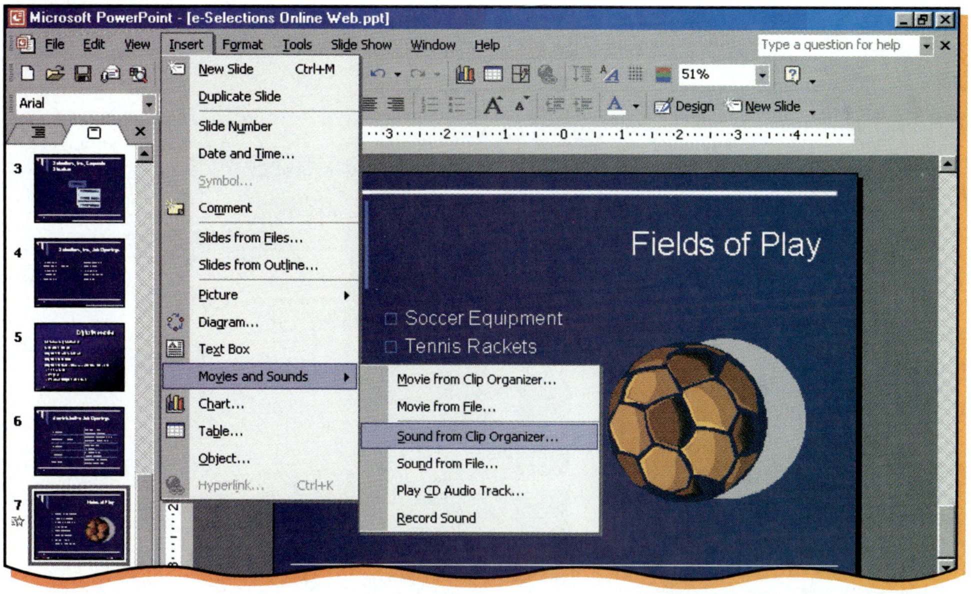

7 Locate the **Claps Cheers** sound clip, click it, and choose **Yes** to play the sound automatically. A speaker icon appears on the slide.

Troubleshooting
Select the sound clip identified by your instructor if the Claps Cheers sound clip is unavailable.

8 Move the speaker icon to the lower left corner of the slide and save changes to the presentation.

Figure 2-33

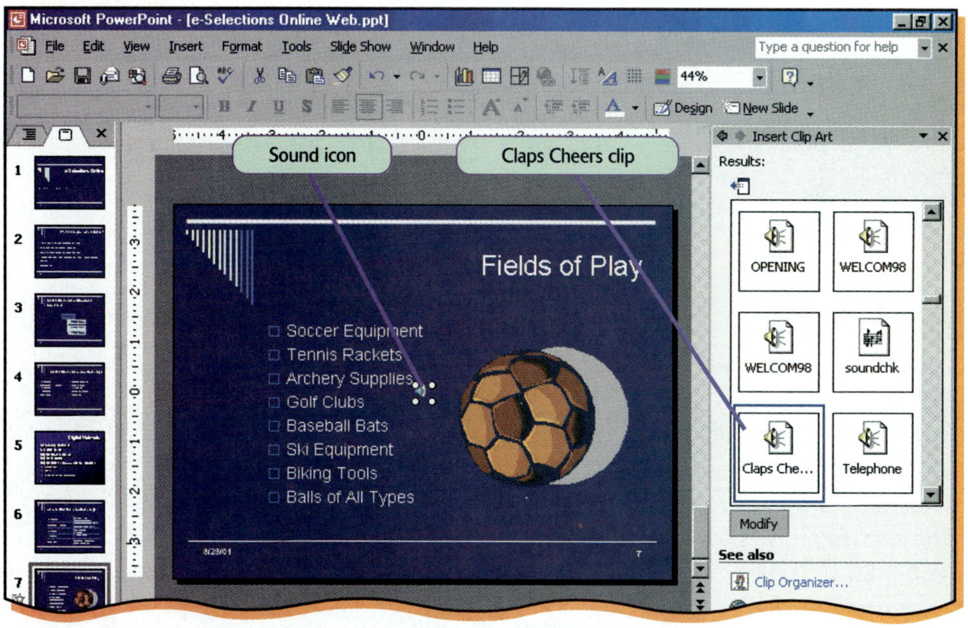

Tip You can easily identify sound files by their extensions. The most popular file name extensions for sound files are .wav and .mid.

9 Create another new slide and apply the **Title Only** slide layout to the new slide.

10 Choose **Insert | Movies and Sounds | Movie from File**.

11 Open the drive and folder containing the *Skiing.avi* file, highlight the file, click **OK**, and click **Yes** to play the movie automatically.

> **Tip**
> Movie files are also easy to identify. Most movie files have .avi, .rm, or .mpeg extensions. A Real Media player must be installed on computers to run .rm files.

12 Complete the slide pictured in Figure 2-35 and save changes to the presentation.

> **WEB TIP**
> The Internet is a great source for locating sound and movie clips. Search for .avi files and .wav files and jot down the names of the sites you find.

Figure 2-34

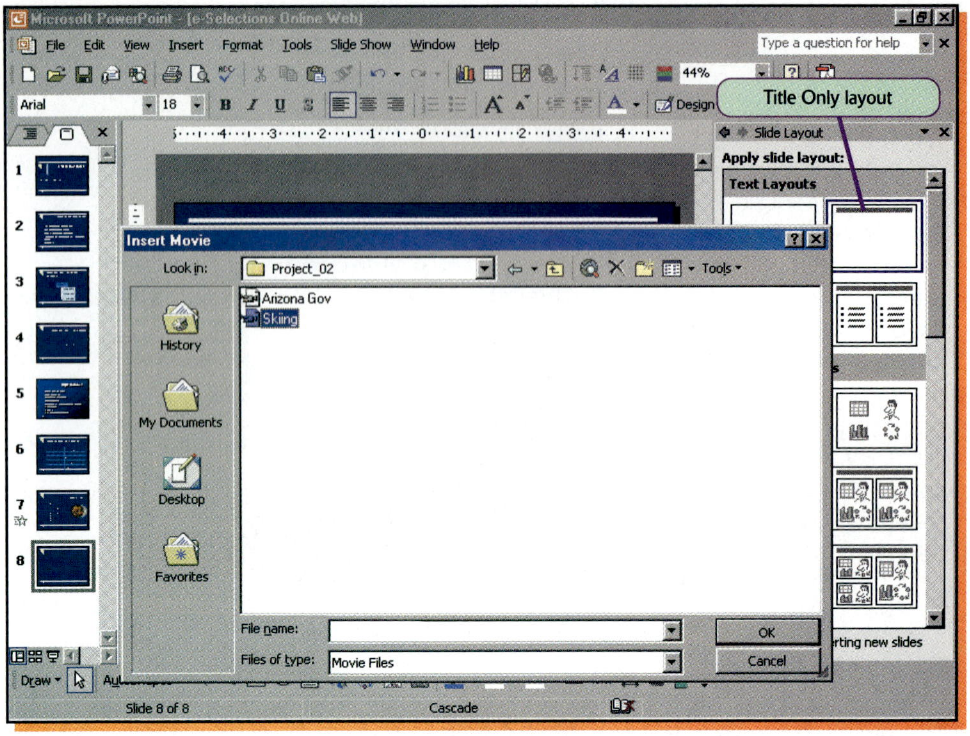

Figure 2-35

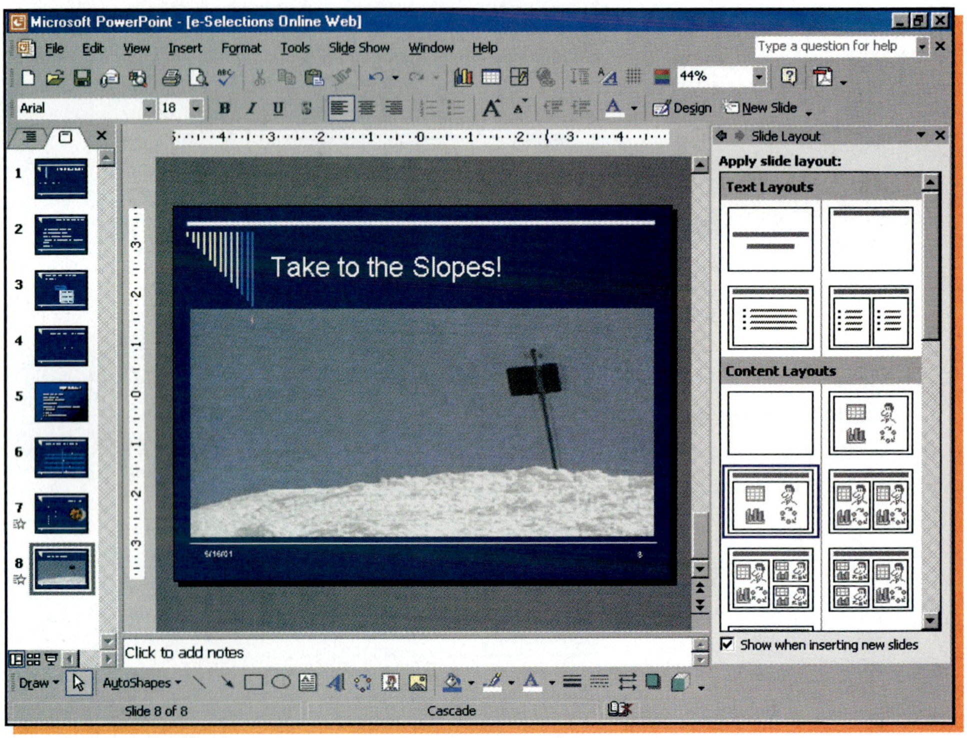

Animating Slide Text

PowerPoint is equipped with *animation schemes* that make "animating" slide placeholder text a snap! Applying an animation scheme to a slide in PowerPoint 2002 animates all placeholders on the slide using the same effect. Animated placeholders appear on screen individually when you apply an animation scheme. You can also create *custom animations* that enable you to set the animation of the title and then animate bulleted-list text to present each bulleted item individually. Setting animation schemes helps focus the attention of your audience on each individual bulleted item as you discuss it and removes the distractions of presenting all bulleted points at once.

Setting Animation Schemes

The Animation Schemes task pane contains a basic set of animation tools that enable you to control text presentation. Use these tools to apply schemes to placeholders on selected slides or to apply the effects to all slides or the Slide Master.

Task 9:
To Apply Animation Schemes

1. Display Slide 1 in the *e-Selections Online Web.ppt* presentation, click the Design **Design** button, and then click the **Animation Schemes** link at the top of the task pane.
2. Click the **Fade in one by one** scheme.
3. Display Slide 2, scroll the task pane, and click the **Dissolve in** scheme. Save changes to the presentation.

Figure 2-36

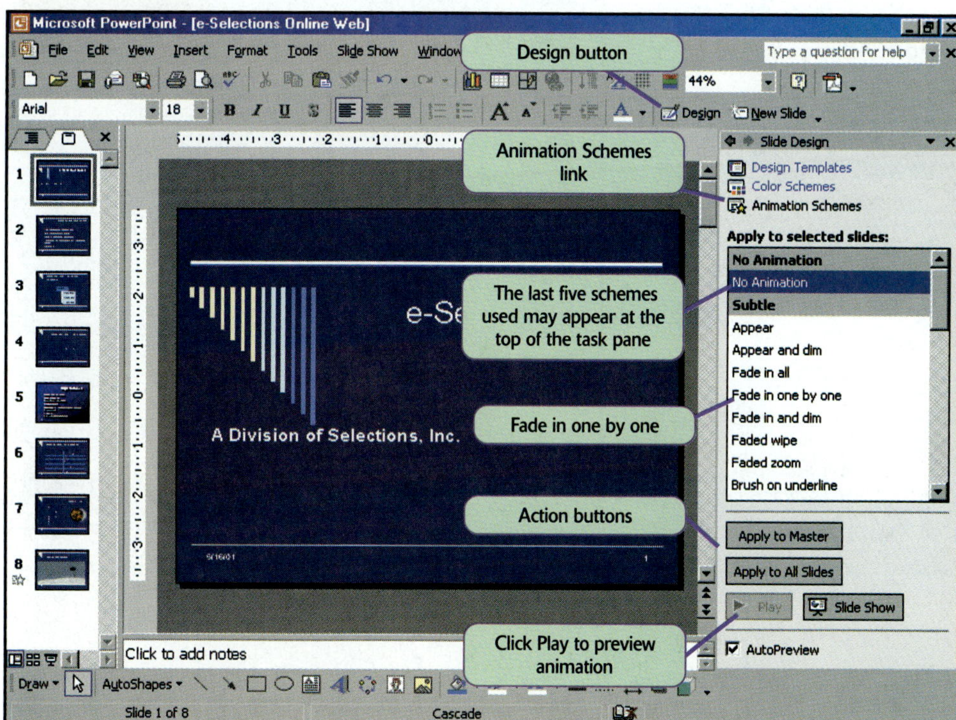

Troubleshooting The schemes listed in the Recently Used area may be different from those displayed in Figure 2-31. Listed items change as you explore different schemes.

CHECK POINT

As you select animation schemes, you'll see a short demonstration of the scheme on the active slide. Click additional schemes to get an overview of how each scheme animates slide text.

Creating Custom Animations

The Custom Animation task pane contains options for controlling slide objects and to customize the presentation of bullet points. Using custom animation tools, you can set the order in which both text and graphic items display.

Task 10:
To Create Custom Animations

1. Display Slide 3 of the *e-Selections Online Web.ppt* presentation and then choose **Slide Show | Custom Animation**.

Other Ways

To display the Custom Animation task pane:

- Click the task pane down arrow and select **Custom Animation**.
- Right-click a placeholder and select **Custom Animation** from the shortcut menu.

Figure 2-37

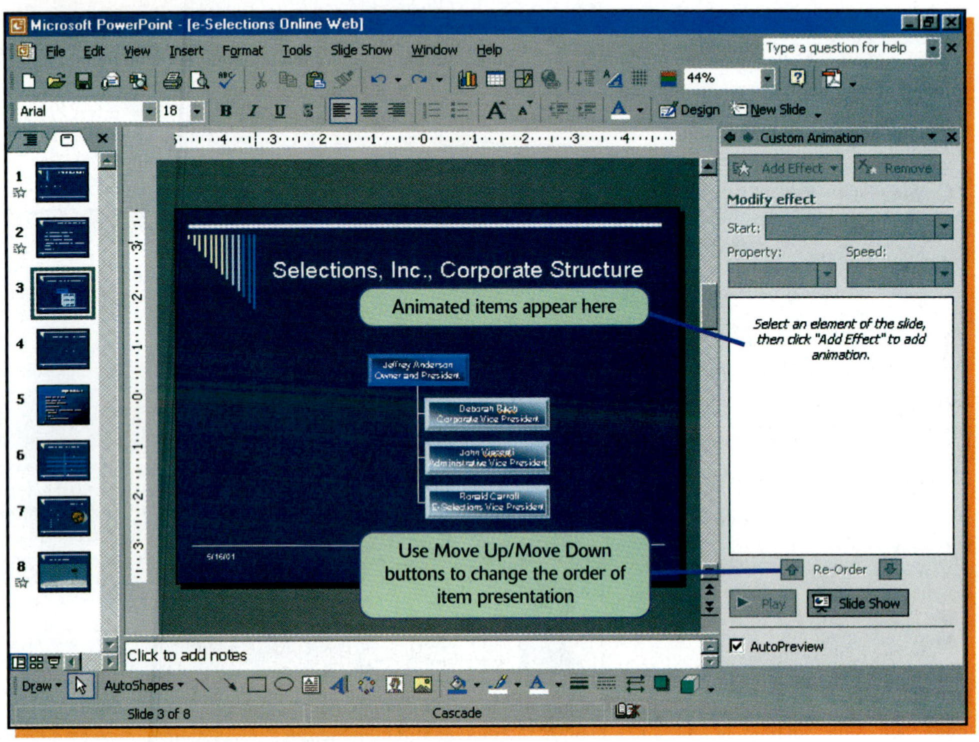

2 Click the organization chart in the center of the slide, click **Add Effect**, and click **Entrance**.

Figure 2-38

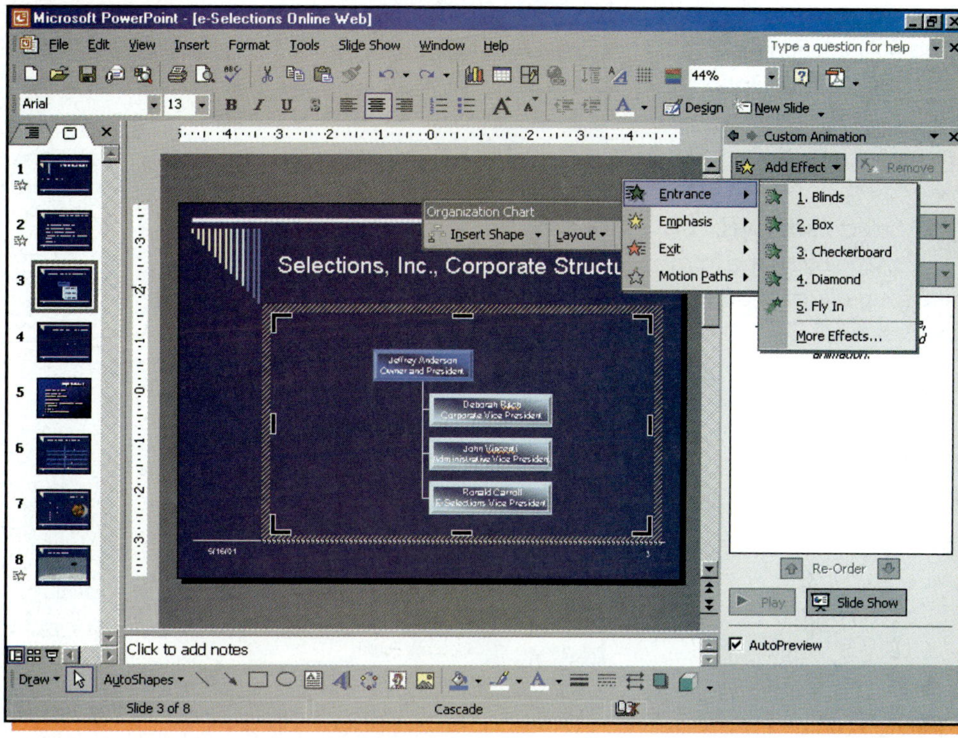

3 Select **Blinds** and then click the **Start** down arrow and select **With Previous**.

Tip PowerPoint considers each box of the organization chart a separate element within the slide object. As a result, you can animate each box individually so that the chart appears one box at a time on the slide.

Figure 2-39

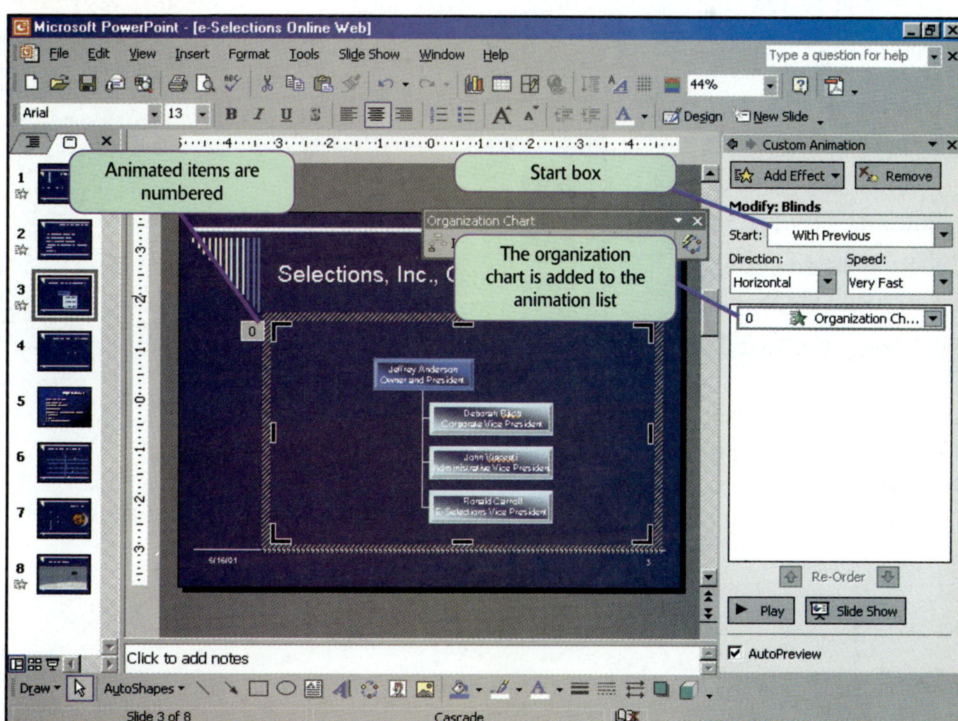

4 Click the **Organization Chart** item down arrow in the Custom Animation task pane, select **Effect Options**, and click the **Diagram Animation** tab.

5 Select **Each level, shape by shape** from the **Group diagram** drop-down list. Click **OK**.

Figure 2-40

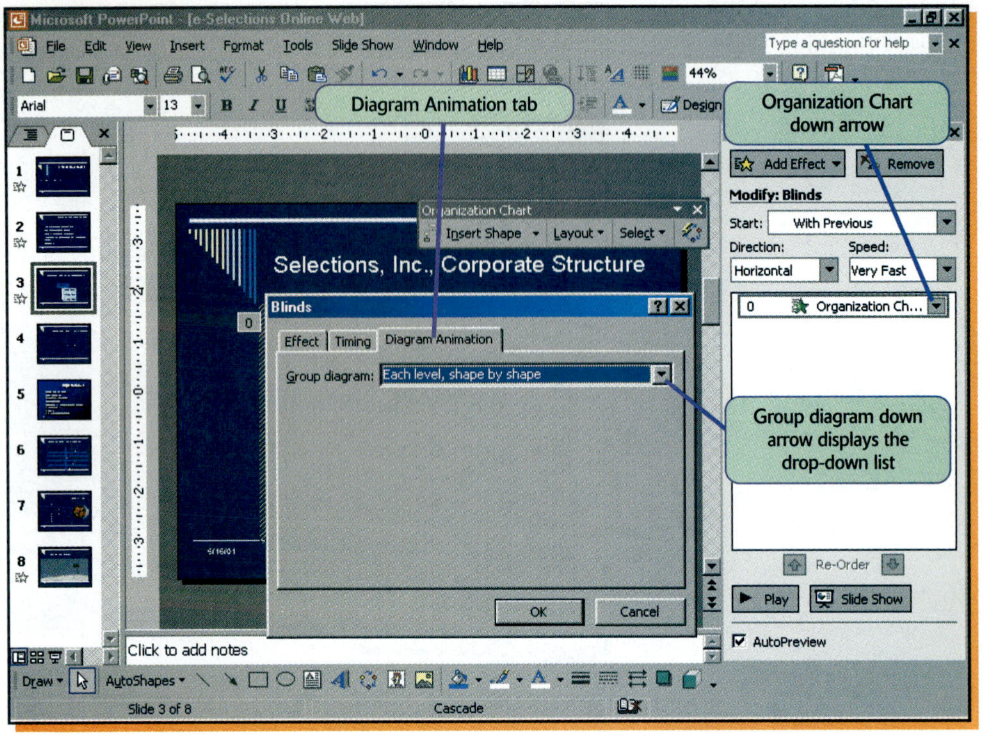

6 Display Slide 4, and add these effects to slide placeholders:

- Title: **Entrance | Checkerboard**
- Left Bulleted List: **Entrance | Fly In**
- Right Bulleted List: **Entrance | Fly In**

7 Select the **Text 2** item in the Custom Animation task pane and select **From Left** from the **Direction** drop-down list.

Figure 2-41

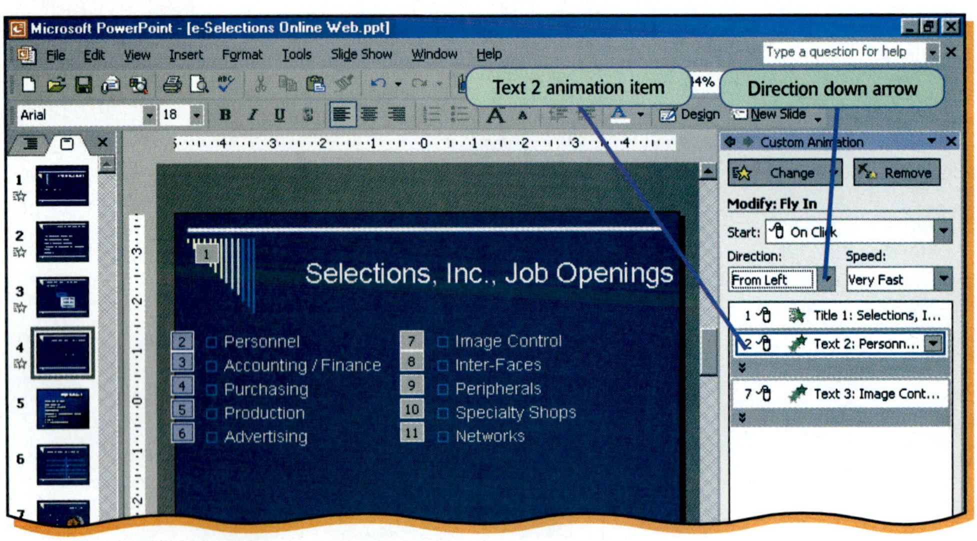

8 Select the **Text 3** item in the Custom Animation task pane and select **From Right** from the **Direction** drop-down list.

Figure 2-42

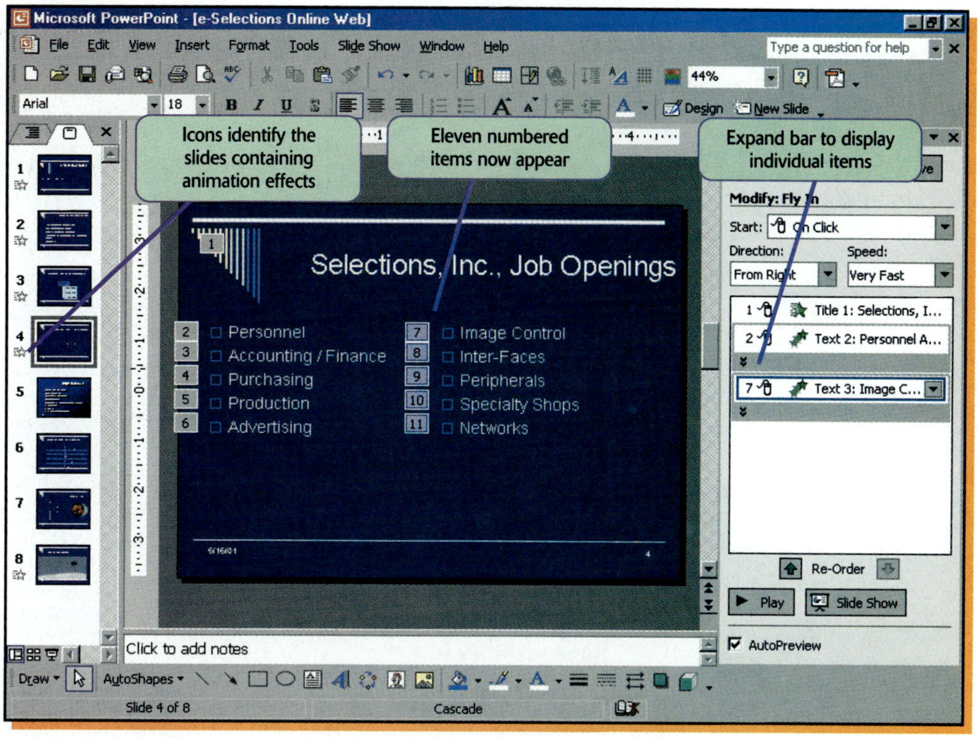

CHECK POINT

Each animated object on a slide appears in the Custom Animation task pane. By clicking the Expand bar, you can display each element of the animated object. When you click an individual item in the task pane, a down arrow appears so that you can select Start, Effect, and timing options for the item. You can also remove animation from individual items from the drop-down list.

9 Click **Play** to preview the effect of the animation.

10 Click the Outline tab on the Outline/Design pane and save changes to the presentation.

Figure 2-43

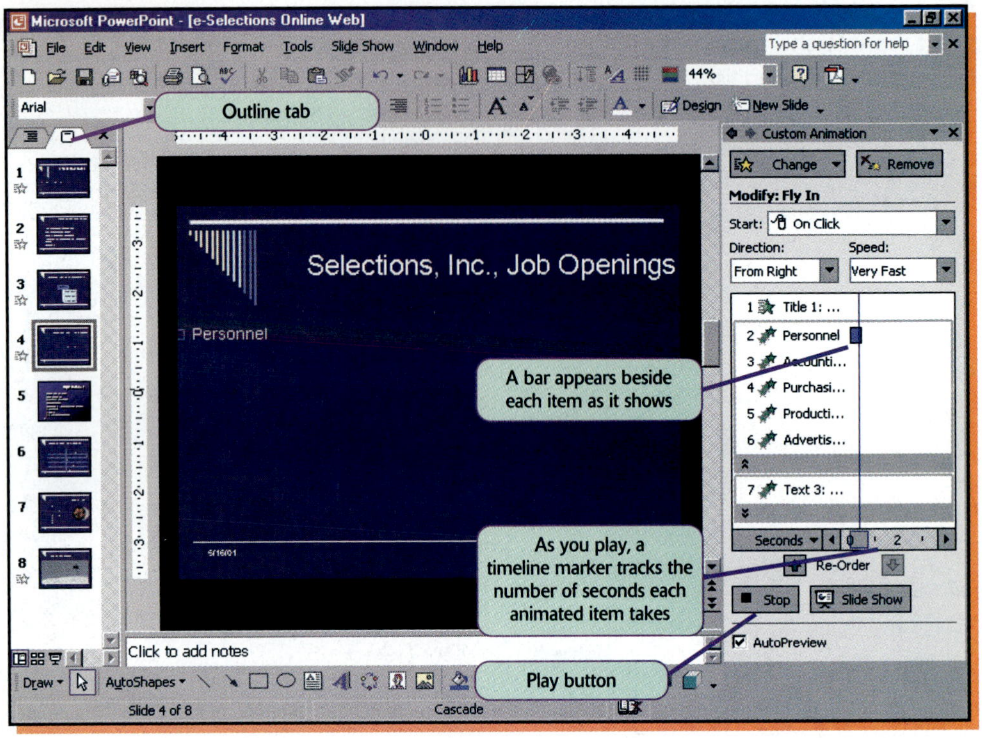

WEB TIP

Microsoft has provided a number of animated graphics on its Web site. Check them out and see if there are any you would like to download into your clip organizer.

CHECK POINT

Icons that appear beside animated objects listed at the bottom of the Custom Animation task pane identify the different types of *animation effects* applied to the objects. Each type of animation effect you use controls the point at which the effect occurs during a slide show.

Icon	Effect Type	Description
	Entrance effect	Animates slide text or objects as they move onto the screen.
	Emphasis	Animates slide text or objects after they are already displayed.
	Exit	Animates slide text or objects as they move off the screen.

Mailing Presentations

The Pack and Go Wizard introduced earlier in this application showed you how to compress your presentation on a disk so that you could show it on another computer. Another way to distribute your presentation is by e-mailing it to someone. When you e-mail a presentation to a friend or coworker (or to yourself at your home e-mail address), you are essentially saving the file on another machine. To open and view the presentation, you would need to have PowerPoint installed on the computer.

Task 11: To E-Mail a Presentation

1. Display Slide 1 of the *e-Selections Online Web.ppt* presentation.

2. Choose **File | Send To | Mail Recipient (as Attachment)**.

Figure 2-44

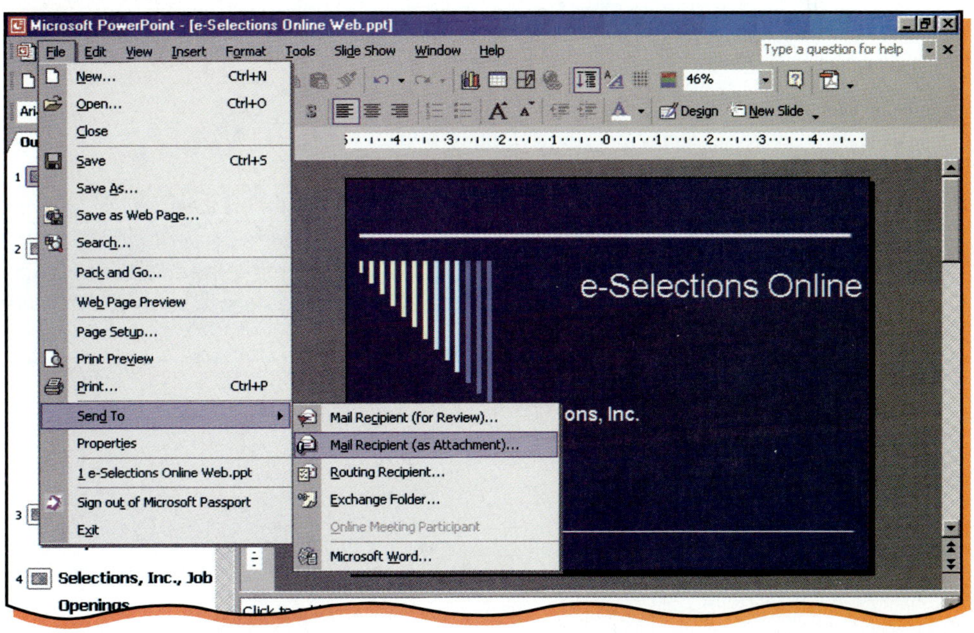

3 Address the mail message to your instructor and to yourself, type a message asking your instructor to review the presentation and return it, and then send the message.

Figure 2-45

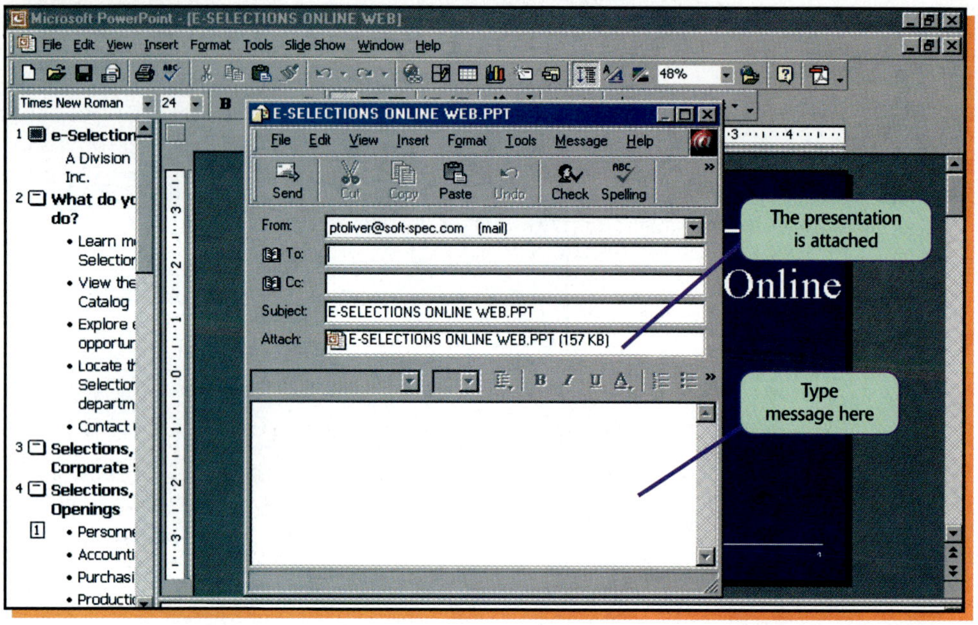

Troubleshooting The **Send To | Mail Recipient** commands are compatible with 32-bit e-mail programs that are Messaging Application Programming Interface (MAPI) compliant. If you are using an electronic mail program that is incompatible with PowerPoint, an error message occurs.

Troubleshooting A new mail message opens automatically in the default e-mail program you are using. As a result, the message window you see may be different from the one pictured in Figure 2-45.

Tip Sending a presentation to a mail recipient for review enables others to add comments to the presentation and send them back to you electronically. You can also flag the message for follow-up, if you're using Outlook, and set a deadline date to remind the reviewer to complete the task before the deadline.

SUMMARY AND EXERCISES

SUMMARY

- Templates are preformatted layouts that hold text font format and alignment, color combinations, layout, and design elements.
- Applying a template to your presentations helps maintain consistency among the slides in the presentation.
- Design elements are stored in layouts called masters.
- All presentation templates contain at least two different masters for formatting slides: Title Master and Slide Master.
- If you use multiple templates to format the slides in a presentation, you can see the masters for each of the templates used by displaying the masters.
- From the Master view, you can customize slide masters and save them as new masters.
- Table formatting tools appear on the Tables and Borders toolbar.
- An organization chart contains boxes interconnected in a way that represents the relationships between the boxes.
- New slides added to presentations appear immediately following the active slide.
- You can save organization charts as pictures and insert the organization chart in most Office XP files.
- PowerPoint contains features that streamline the process of adding media clips to presentation slides.
- PowerPoint is equipped with animation schemes that you can apply to slides.
- In PowerPoint 2002, you can set placeholders on each slide to animate individually or set all slides to animate using the same scheme.
- Custom animations enable you to set the animation of the title and then animate bulleted-list text to present each bulleted item individually using different effects.
- The Animation Schemes task pane contains a basic set of animation tools for controlling text presentation.

- The Custom Animation task pane contains options for controlling slide objects and for customizing the presentation of bullet points.
- You can identify different types of animation effects by the icons that appear beside the animated object in the Custom Animation task pane. The type of animation effect you use controls the point at which the effect occurs during a slide show.

KEY TERMS & SKILLS

KEY TERMS

animation (p. 2-25)
animation effects (p. 2-31)
animation schemes (p. 2-25)
custom animation (p. 2-25)
footer (p. 2-10)
header (p. 2-10)
hierarchical structure (p. 2-17)
masters (p. 2-10)
organization chart (p. 2-17)
templates (p. 2-5)

SKILLS

Add footer items (p. 2-10)
Add media clips to slides (p. 2-21)
Apply a color scheme (p. 2-13)
Apply animation schemes (p. 2-25)
Apply templates to presentation slides (p. 2-6)
Create a new slide master (p. 2-13)
Create a new template-formatted presentation (p. 2-9)
Create a table (p. 2-15)
Create an organization chart (p. 2-17)
Create custom animations (p. 2-26)
Customize slide background (p. 2-13)
Display slide masters (p. 2-11)
E-mail a presentation (p. 2-31)
Format a table (p. 2-15)

STUDY QUESTIONS

MULTIPLE CHOICE

1. To help maintain consistency of appearance among presentation slides, apply a
   a. slide layout.
   b. template.
   c. master.
   d. color scheme.

2. You can use all the following techniques to apply a template to an existing presentation except
   a. click the Design button and then click the template.
   b. choose **Format | Design**.
   c. click the template name on the status bar.
   d. click the task pane down arrow and select **Slide Design—Design Template**.

3. The Clip Organizer holds all the following except
   a. clip art.
   b. sounds.
   c. movies.
   d. templates.

4. To animate placeholder text on all slides, apply
   a. animation schemes.
   b. slide masters.
   c. animation clips.
   d. templates.

5. Presentation design features are stored in
   a. templates.
   b. masters.
   c. the Clip Organizer.
   d. the task pane.

6. To set different animation effects for objects on a slide, apply a(n)
   a. animation scheme.
   b. template.
   c. master.
   d. custom animation.

7. To insert a media clip on a slide, apply a(n)
   a. master layout.
   b. animation effect.
   c. Content slide layout.
   d. custom layout.

8. To display masters, click the
   a. Format menu.
   b. Insert menu.
   c. View menu.
   d. Tools menu.

9. Each presentation design template has
   a. one master.
   b. two masters.
   c. three masters.
   d. at least four masters.

10. One way to edit a template design is to change the
   a. animation scheme.
   b. slide format.
   c. background color.
   d. view.

GUIDED EXERCISES

SHORT ANSWER

1. What are two different ways to distribute presentations?
2. What file name extension do movie files often have?
3. What file name extensions might sound clips have?
4. Where do tools for formatting tables appear?
5. What different animation effect features can you control after you apply the effect?
6. How do you set an organization chart to display one box at a time?
7. How can you quickly preview animation effects applied to a slide?
8. What three types of animation effects can you apply to slide objects?
9. Where do new slides added to presentations appear?
10. Name two ways to change the background color of slides.

FILL IN THE BLANK

1. Pictures, sounds, and movies are examples of ____________.
2. Preformatted layouts that hold text font formats, color schemes, layouts, and other design elements are called ____________.
3. To apply an animation effect to an object, you must first ____________ it.
4. Design elements are stored in ____________ layouts.
5. The two masters included with each template are the ____________ and ____________.
6. An ____________ ____________ is a type of diagram that you can add to slides to show the hierarchical structure.
7. To change the arrangement of boxes on an organization chart, change the chart ____________.
8. Separate master layouts are available for ____________ and ____________.
9. When you click Play on the Animation task pane, a ____________ tracks the progression of the animation.
10. You can use the ____________ feature to change the color of organization chart boxes.

DISCUSSION

1. What is the difference between animation schemes and custom animations?
2. What are the advantages of applying different templates to presentation slides.
3. Discuss when you would create a new slide master.
4. When would you choose to e-mail a presentation instead of packing it to go.

GUIDED EXERCISES

1 NARROWING CUSTOM ANIMATION ON *E-SELECTIONS ONLINE WEB*

You aren't quite finished with the *e-Selections Online Web.ppt* presentation. Because Ms. Wright will be using the presentation as she talks about the new division of Selections, Inc., she would like each bullet point on most slides presented individually and only when she clicks the mouse. She would also like previously discussed bullet points to dim when the next bullet point appears. Finally, she wants animation effects applied to all slides in the presentation. Follow these directions to complete the presentation.

1. Open the *e-Selections Online Web.ppt* presentation, if necessary, and choose **Slide Show | Custom Animation** to open the Custom Animation task pane.
2. Display Slide 2, click Learn more about Selections, Inc., in the Outline task pane, and select Effect Options from the item drop-down list in the task pane.
3. Click the **After animation** down arrow, click the medium blue color from the color palette, and then click **OK**.
4. Click the **Image Control** bullet point and select On Click from the Start drop-down list in the task pane.
5. Display Slide 5, apply the **Unfold** animation scheme, and apply the following **Effects Options** to each main bullet point:
   - Sound: **Laser**
   - Animate text: **By letter**
   - Text Animation tab Group text: **By 2nd level paragraphs**
6. Display Slide 6 and animate the table.
7. Display Slide 7, animate the bulleted-list placeholder, and set the graphic to **fly in from the right**.
8. Click the double-down arrow on the grey bar in the task pane to expand the animation list in the task pane, click the soccer ball graphic item and then click the Move Up  button at the bottom of the task pane until the graphic appears just below the Soccer Equipment item.

9. Play the animation to ensure that the soccer ball appears just after the first bullet point.

10. Save changes to the presentation and close it.

2 DRESSING UP SEASONAL SALES

The seasonal sales presentation is pretty blasé in appearance. To make it more appealing to the general public, you need to dress it up a bit so that slides appear as shown in Figure 2-46.

Figure 2-46

Follow these steps to update the format of the presentation.

1. Open the presentation *Seasons of Savings.ppt*.
2. Display the **Slide Design** task pane and apply the **Curtain Call** template to the presentation.
3. Apply the **Crayons** template to Slide 2 only.
4. Apply the **Cliff** template to Slide 5 only.
5. Display the **Slide Master** and click the Insert New Slide Master button.
6. Choose **Format | Background** and select Fill Effects from the Background fill drop-down list and format the slide background to contain a gradient fill using red and green.
7. Click the Rename button on the Slide Master View toolbar, name the master Christmas, and close the master view.
8. Display Slide 3, click the Design button on the Formatting toolbar to display the Slide Design task pane, click the Christmas design down arrow, and select Apply to Selected Slides.
9. Choose **Insert | Picture | From File** and insert the *Poinsettia.gif* graphic on Slide 3, size, position, and format the graphic; then add the *Sugarplum.mid* music file to the slide by choosing **Insert | Movies** and **Sounds | Sound from File.**

> **Tip** Search for the sound clip *America the Beautiful.mid* in the Clip Organizer to locate the file, if necessary.

10. Save changes to the presentation and print a copy of the presentation as handouts with six slides per page and close the file.

3 POLISHING *E-SELECTIONS MARKETING.PPT*

You've worked hard on the marketing presentation requested by Ms. Wright. It's time now to apply the finishing touches to the presentation. Ms. Wright prefers a different template from the current one. In addition, she would like to see the slide number and date in the footer area of the presentation. Of course, animation schemes will help polish the presentation. The finished presentation appears in Figure 2-47.

Figure 2-47

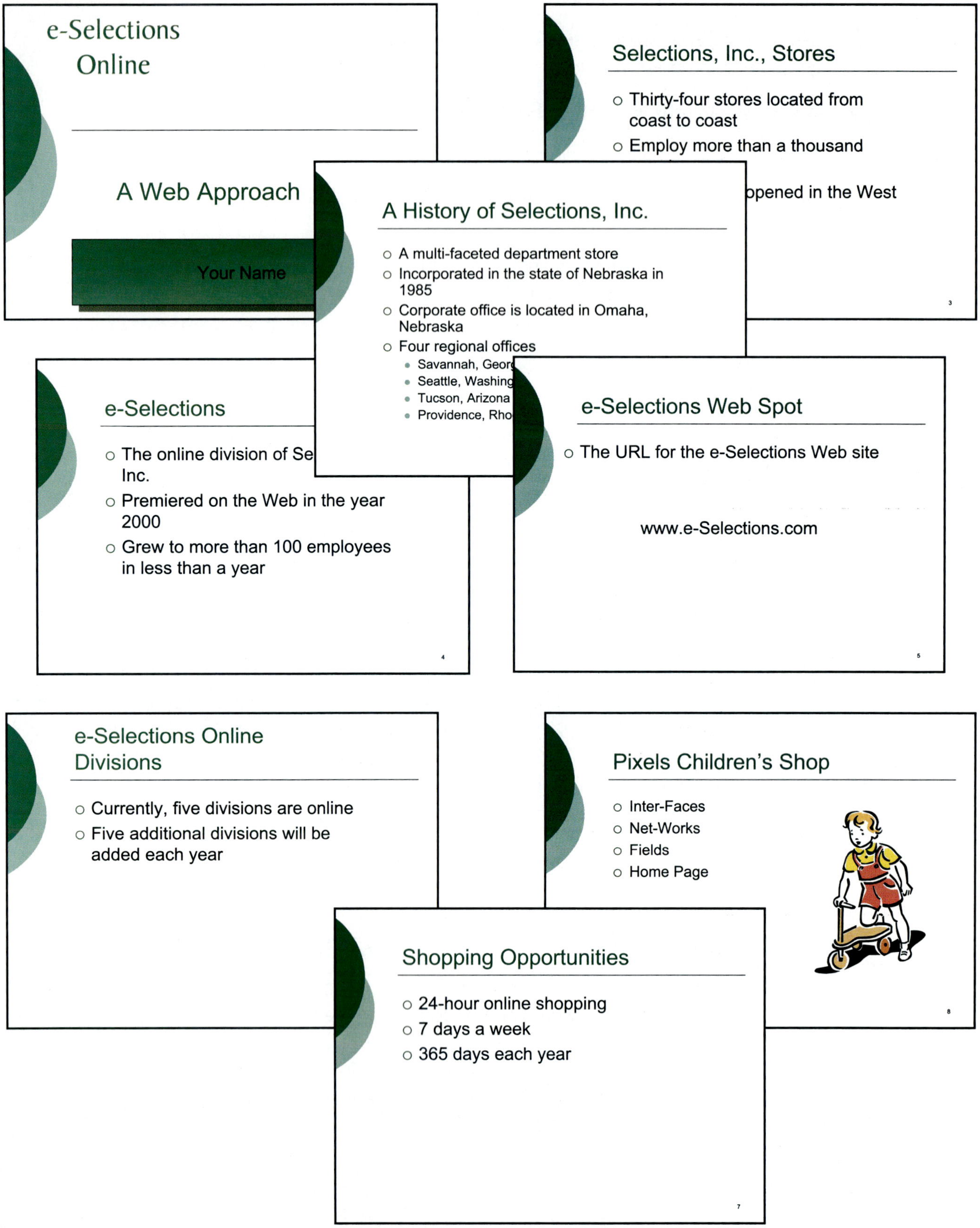
e-Selections Online
A Web Approach
Your Name
Selections, Inc., Stores
Thirty-four stores located from coast to coast
Employ more than a thousand
pened in the West
3
A History of Selections, Inc.
A multi-faceted department store
Incorporated in the state of Nebraska in 1985
Corporate office is located in Omaha, Nebraska
Four regional offices
Savannah, Georg
Seattle, Washing
Tucson, Arizona
Providence, Rho
e-Selections
The online division of Se
Inc.
Premiered on the Web in the year 2000
Grew to more than 100 employees in less than a year
4
e-Selections Web Spot
The URL for the e-Selections Web site
www.e-Selections.com
5
e-Selections Online Divisions
Currently, five divisions are online
Five additional divisions will be added each year
Pixels Children's Shop
Inter-Faces
Net-Works
Fields
Home Page
8
Shopping Opportunities
24-hour online shopping
7 days a week
365 days each year
7

Follow these instructions to complete the presentation.

1. Open the copy of *e-Selections Marketing.ppt*.
2. Apply the **Eclipse** template to the presentation or the template identified by your instructor.
3. Display the **Slide Master**, select the drawn rectangles in the bulleted-list and title areas. Press Del then close the master.
4. Display the **Header and Footer** dialog box and select the appropriate options to set the date without automatic update and slide number on each slide.
5. Apply animation schemes to each slide and add clip art, if desired.
6. Save changes to the presentation and print a copy of the presentation as handouts with four slides per page.

4 STAR POWER

The star of one of the new programs introduced this season by the JPLD-TV station has finally sent you a picture. You can add the picture to the *JPLD-TV Stars.ppt* presentation and format the presentation to create the presentation pictured in Figure 2-48.

Figure 2-48

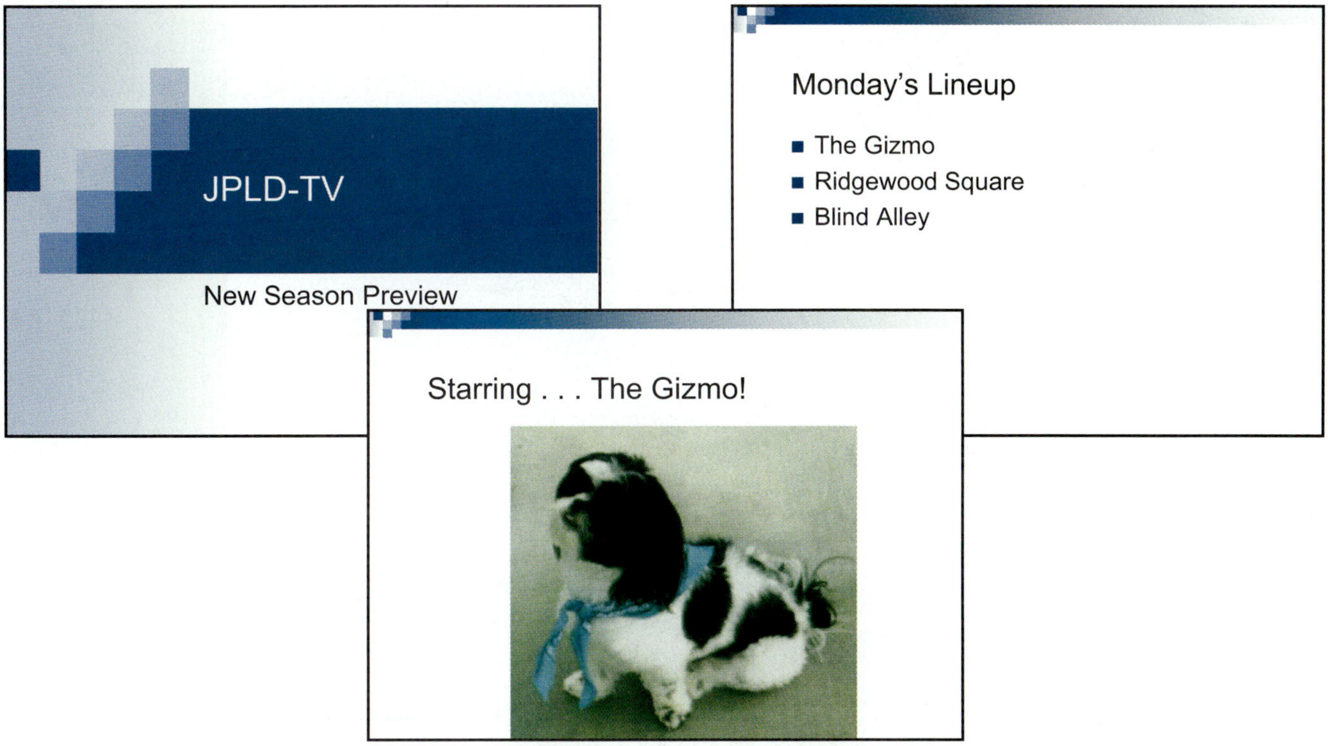

Follow these directions:

1. Open the *JPLD-TV Stars.ppt* presentation and create a new slide containing a title only.
2. Type **Starring...The Gizmo!** in the title placeholder.
3. Choose **Insert | Picture | From File**, open the folder containing the *Gizmo.jpg* graphic, and insert the graphic.
4. Apply a suitable template to the presentation, save changes, and print a copy of the presentation as black-and-white handouts with four slides per page.
5. Close the presentation.

ON YOUR OWN

The difficulty of these case studies varies:
are the least difficult; are more difficult; and are the most difficult.

1 PLAYING POLITICS

Each year, voters go to the polls to elect officials to local, state, and national positions. The last gubernatorial race for the state of Arizona called on a popular television game show of the time. Create a new two-slide presentation, format it with the template of your choice, and insert the video file Arizona Gov.avi on Slide 2. Add appropriate title and subtitle placeholder text after viewing the video file. Save the presentation using the file name *Arizona Goes Primetime.ppt* and e-mail the file to your instructor.

2 ADDING TABLES TO PRESENTATIONS

The organization chart provides a great way to present an overview of information about a business or organization. Because many government agencies contain many different divisions, it's often hard to keep track of how each division fits in to the general scope of the agency. Creating an organization chart in the *Rocky Mountain Station.ppt* presentation could provide a valuable overview. Add a slide to the presentation that outlines the organizational structure shown in Figure 2-49. Then format the table on Slide 2 of the presentation and apply an appropriate template to the presentation. Finally, add the sound file "America the Beautiful" to the title slide. Save changes to the presentation and print a copy of the presentation as handouts with three slides per page.

Figure 2-49

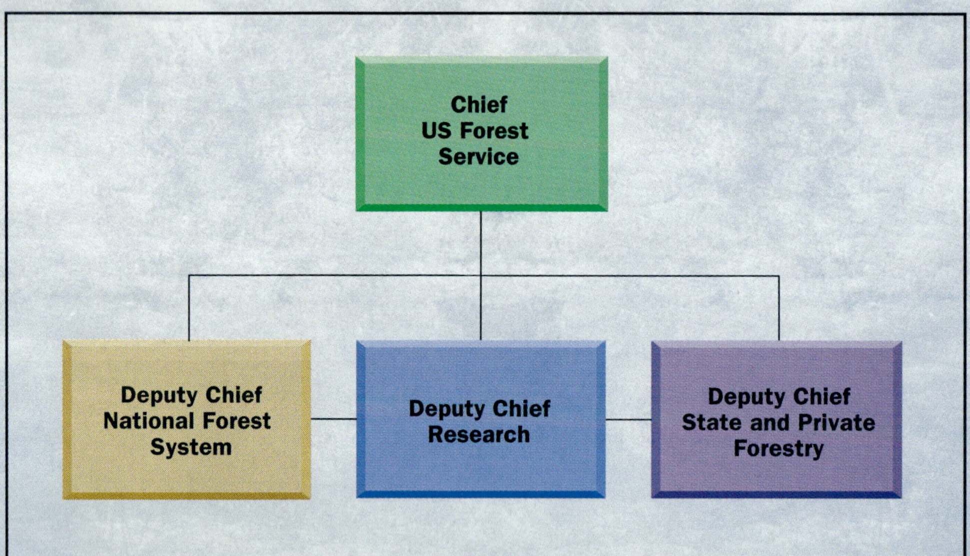

Tip

Search for the sound clip *America the Beautiful.mid* in the Clip Organizer to locate the file, if necessary or follow the direction of your instructor to insert an appropriate clip.

3 CUSTOMIZING THE HANDBOOK

The basic format and design of the template used for the *Selections Employee Handbook.ppt* presentation is what Ms. Wright would like to use for the *e-Selections Employee Handbook.ppt* presentation—with a few modifications. She would like you to edit the template masters and develop the design for the *e-Selections Employee Handbook.ppt* so that the design appears as shown in Figure 2-50.

Figure 2-50

Be sure to create a new presentation using the template of your choice and edit masters in the new presentation. When you're finished, add a blank bulleted-list slide to the presentation, save the presentation using the file name *e-Selections Employee Handbook*, and print a copy of the two slides.

4 DRAWING OUT YOUR WORDS

The WordArt feature available in Office XP applications helps you create text designs that add special visual effects to slides. Change the *e-Selections Employee Handbook.ppt* title slide by removing the title textbox and creating a WordArt object for the words *Employee Handbook*. Save changes to the presentation and print a copy of the title slide

5 SAY IT WITH PICTURES

Most people have special sayings that others automatically associate with them. You've heard them all your life—from friends, relatives, and especially from Grandma and Grandpa! Some of these sayings have been captured in a presentation titled *So They Say.ppt*. Your task is to graphically depict these sayings by adding clip art to the placeholders and arranging the graphics in such a way that they represent the saying identified in the title placeholder of each slide. Be sure to replace the name on the title slide with your name, save your presentation, and then print a copy of the presentation slides.

6 PERSONALIZING A TEMPLATE

One of the most effective ways to provide an overview of your accomplishments is to develop and format a presentation. Such a presentation could summarize not only your accomplishments but could also serve as an introduction to your qualifications for employment. Placed on a disk, the presentation becomes something you could leave with potential employers after job interviews. Connect to the Internet and search for presentation templates. After you locate a template that you like, download the template, create a new slide master as well as a new title master, and customize it so that it is uniquely yours. Then save the edited designs using *Your Name* as the design name. Print a copy of both designs.

7 COLORING YOUR WORLD

Children everywhere seem to enjoy coloring. Finding just the right coloring book, however, can sometimes be a challenge. Create a ten-slide presentation containing graphics that children can color. Size and center the graphics to cover a large portion of the slide. Ungroup each image, remove the fill color, and format the line of each graphic so that it defines different graphic parts. Type the graphic name in the title placeholder of each slide. Add a title page to the presentation and save the presentation using the file name *Coloring Your World*. Then print a copy of each slide.

Tip For information on ungrouping images, see Common Elements Project 3.

8 GOING HOME

Most everyone has a hometown. But do you know your city officials, where or who to call in case of a crisis, or how to obtain help in an emergency? The proverbial "911" is great in most emergencies, but knowing more direct lines of communication can ease the frustration of finding help in less extreme circumstances. Your hometown has asked you to create an electronic presentation that contains source information to help the public contact the people who can help them in different situations. They will display and discuss the presentation at town council meetings, public information seminars, and community activities. An outline of the presentation appears in Figure 2-51. Fill in the necessary names and contact numbers for officials in your hometown. Then create a presentation to contain the information. Use a variety of different slide layouts and include sound for at least two slides in the presentation. Apply a template to the presentation and then animate each slide. Save the presentation using the file name *At Your Fingertips*, then e-mail the presentation to your instructor.

Figure 2-51

I. Contacting the Law Enforcement
   A. Sheriff
   B. Police Department
II. Contacting Emergency Services
   A. Fire Department
   B. Ambulance Service
   C. Drunken Driver Reporting
III. Contacting Medical Facilities
   A. Hospital
   B. Clinic
   C. Doctor
   D. Dentist
IV. Contacting the City Council
   A. Mayor
   B. District 1 Council Person
   C. District 2 Council Person
   D. Additional Council Persons for Your Hometown
V. Contacting the School Board
   A. School Board President
   B. School Board Member 1
   C. School Board Member 2
   D. Additional Board Persons for Your Hometown

VI. Connecting with City Hall
   A. Driver's License Bureau
   B. Department of Motor Vehicles
   C. Voter Registration
   D. Alcohol, Tobacco, and Firearms
VII. Crisis Connections
   A. Mental Health Services
   B. Homeless Help
   C. Poison Control
   D. Stranger Danger Precautions

Photospread credits pages 2-2 & 2-3

©Masterfile: ©MTPA Stock, ©Bill Frymire-3 Dimensional Graphics; ©CORBIS; ©Pearson Education, ©Lorraine Castellano

FROM THE FILES

You Will Need

- ✓ e-Selections Marketing Division.ppt
- ✓ e-Selections Media.ppt
- ✓ e-Selections Web Online.ppt
- ✓ e-Selections Notebook.ppt
- ✓ Southern Cuisine.ppt
- ✓ Making Lemonade.ppt

PROJECT 3

Viewing and Arranging Slide Shows

As you create PowerPoint presentations, you design them to provide powerful visuals to enhance oral presentations. You can format slides in a presentation for on-screen viewing or for use with a projector or other audiovisual screen or flat surface as you present a report to an audience.

Showing your presentations with style has a positive impact on your audience. The PowerPoint slide show feature enables you to show your presentation on a computer screen. Seeing your presentation "live" for the first time can be quite satisfying and exciting. In this project, you learn how to dress up your presentation for on-screen viewing and how to use the Slide Sorter view to rearrange slides within a presentation.

e-selections Running Case

Since your position in the e-Selections division became permanent, a number of different divisions have noticed the dynamic presentations you created for Ms. Wright. As a result, a number of requests have come from these divisions asking for your assistance in completing presentations for employees and managers throughout Selections, Inc. As you develop presentations for some of these divisions, you will discover some of the unique features available in PowerPoint!

OBJECTIVES

After completing this project, you will be able to:

- Start a slide show
- Use the Slide Show Navigator
- Annotate slides
- Use the Slide Sorter view to move, copy, duplicate, and delete slides
- Hide slides
- Create summary slides
- Create hyperlinks
- Apply slide transitions
- Rehearse presentation timings
- Set up slide shows

Template, Graphics, ClipArt, Movies, and Sound Clip Sources… and a bit about plagiarism!

Connecting with your audience is vital to the success of any presentation. One way to connect is by enhancing your presentation content with visual aids. Finding just the right visual for the information you are presenting can be a real challenge. Enter the Internet…and open up a world of supplements just ripe for the picking. Here are some tips and techniques to get you started:

- **Use Internet search engines** (such as Yahoo.com, Excite.com, and GoTo.com) to locate charts, graphs, and other statistics related to your topic.
- **Browse different Web sites** related to your topic to locate visual aids. Then download the aids you want to use. You'll find anything from hot tips to sophisticated animation tools to use in the presentation.
- **Check out "Shareware"**—software specifically designed to provide samples of presentation graphics, sound bites, or videos. Try a product and if you like it, send a "donation" to the Shareware developer—it's an unspoken rule.
- **Look for interesting audio files** on Web sites that you can incorporate into slide shows.
- **Search for "presentation templates"** to locate free samples and CDs containing jazzed up PowerPoint templates. PresentationPro, and PhotoGraphic Specialties are just a few of the companies and organizations on the Web that offer templates.
- Visit Microsoft's Web site regularly for additional clips to add to the Clip Gallery, designs for bullets and borders, and to download graphics, sound clips, and movies into the Clip Gallery on your computer. That way they will be available when you need them.

Don't go overboard with graphics!

Of course, the Internet is not the only source from which you can obtain effective visuals. Visit any store that sells CDs and/or computer equipment and browse the aisles of software available. Where you used to find clip-art books (books with all sorts of different drawings that you could clip out and paste on newsletters, posters, and other materials), you'll now find CDs stocked full of clip art that can be electronically placed in documents, presentations, and other files. These CDs are reasonably priced and store images related to specific topics such as business, sports, and so forth. You'll also find program supplements containing presentation templates and utility programs designed to make creating and editing clip art and templates easier.

Once you've found the visuals you want to add to your presentation, use the visuals with discretion. Tad Simons, editor of *Presentations* magazine says, "It's all too easy to go overboard on the nifty graphic options that come with PowerPoint. The key to using presentation software in a sophisticated way is to boil down key concepts into an arresting visual image—one that communicates what you are trying to say without creating a lot of excess visual noise."

Caution…Caution…Caution…

Copyright laws protect information—graphics, pictures, audio files, and articles—available on the Internet! Just because it's on the Web doesn't mean it's free for the taking. Get permission from the copyright holder before using it.

PROJECT 3

Viewing and Arranging Slide Shows

The Challenge

Mr. Steve McGuffee, the Selections, Inc., Marketing division manager, has requested that you help in finalizing a presentation that marketing representatives can use across the country to "sell" Selections. He plans to send the presentation to store managers and marketing representatives for review, but wants to ensure that it is as dressed up as possible so that marketing reps will be able to test the presentation fully. He would like the marketing reps to be able to navigate to different parts of the presentation smoothly, to include additional information in the presentation in case someone asks for more-detailed information, and to set up the presentation so that it can be viewed by individuals at trade shows. He also wants slides in the presentation rearranged so that it flows more smoothly. Because his knowledge of PowerPoint is limited, he turns to Ms. Wright for help. Ms. Wright, of course, turns the project over to you.

The Solution

PowerPoint contains some powerful tools that will enable you to get the presentation set up for Mr. McGuffee very quickly. Setting *action buttons* that *hyperlink* to specific slides will enable presenters and viewers to display slides containing just the information they want to view, and you can activate special settings to set up the presentation for viewing at trade shows. Slide Sorter view provides tools for organizing presentations. Figure 3-1 shows the first few slides in the presentation as they appear in Slide Sorter view.

Tip You can change the number of slides that appear in the Slide Sorter view window by changing the Zoom setting.

Figure 3-1

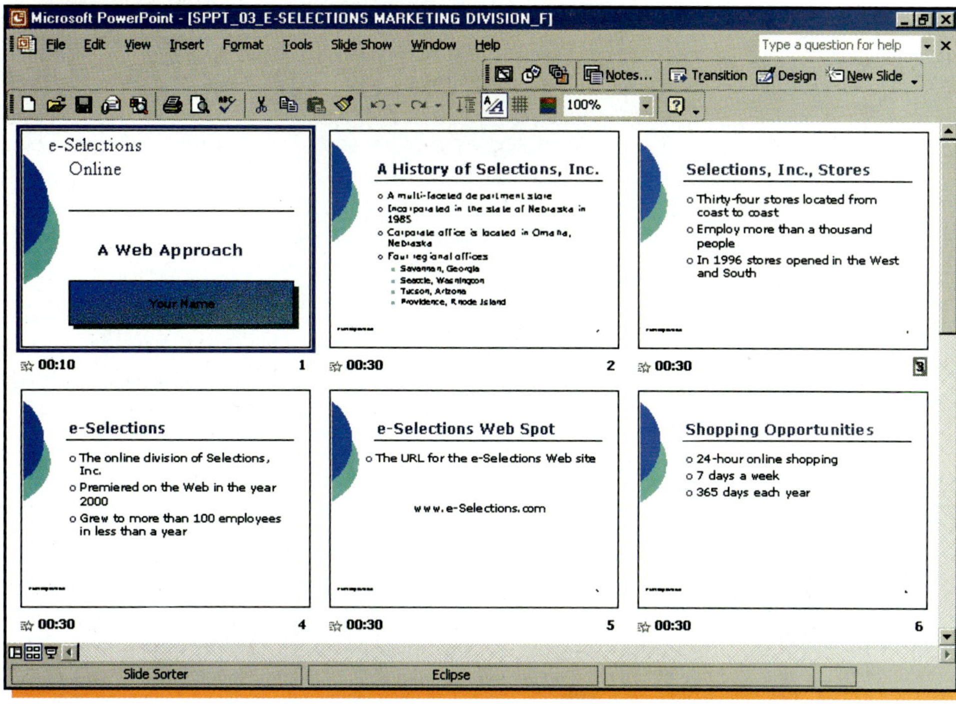

Of course, before deciding what you need to do to the presentation, you must first view the presentation as it currently exists.

Starting a Slide Show

Viewing your presentation as a slide show can make it come to life. Slide shows display slides in the presentation window without the PowerPoint toolbars, title bar, and status bar. During a slide show, each slide literally fills the screen and you can focus on slide content to determine their impact. PowerPoint offers a number of ways to launch a slide show.

To start the slide show with Slide 1 regardless of what slide is active:

- Choose **View | Slide Show**.
- Choose **Slide Show | View Show**.
- Press F5.

To start a slide show with the active slide:

- Click the Slide Show button at the bottom of the presentation window.

CHECK POINT

Some people use the slide show as a way to preview the information on their slides before printing them. Of course, on screen, slides appear in living color. If you print them on a black-and-white printer, however, the effect may be something less than you had hoped. To view your slides as they will appear when printed on a black-and-white printer, click the Color/Grayscale button on the Standard toolbar and select the color option you want to see or choose **View | Color/Grayscale** and then select the appropriate color option: **Color**, **Grayscale**, or **Pure Black and White**.

For those times when you may not have a computer on which to view or display your presentation, print the presentation on transparency film and show the presentation using an overhead projector. Be sure you have the correct transparency film that is safe to use with your printer to avoid ruining the printer with melting transparency film!

Task 1: To View a Presentation as a Slide Show

1. Open the *e-Selections Marketing Division.ppt* presentation and display the first slide in Normal view.

2. Press F5 to start the slide show.

Figure 3-2

Navigating Slide Shows

PowerPoint offers three basic techniques for navigating slides during slide shows:

- Keyboard commands
- Mouse techniques
- Slide Show shortcut menu commands

Tip When slides are animated, clicking the left mouse button may present the next bullet point or the next object rather than the next slide.

Using Keyboard Shortcuts and Mouse Techniques

You can use both the keyboard and mouse to move through the slides during a slide show. Table 3-1 compares the actions for using both techniques. Practice the techniques to determine which ones you like best.

Table 3-1 Slide Show Navigation Techniques

Movement	Mouse Action	Keyboard Action(s)
Advance to next slide	Click the left mouse button.	Press N, Enter, Spacebar, PageDown, ↓, or →.
Return to previous slide	Right-click and select **Previous**.	Press P, Bksp, Page Up, ↑, or ←.
Specific slide number		Type the slide number and then press Enter. For example, type 5 and then press Enter.
Stop show	Right-click and select **End Show.**	Press Esc.

Using the Slide Show Shortcut Menu

The Slide Show shortcut menu provides an additional tool for navigating presentation slides during a slide show. The menu contains commands for navigating the slide show as well as for controlling on-screen features, such as the mouse pointer and slide meter.

Task 2:
To Use the Slide Show Shortcut Menu

1. Press F5. Right-click anywhere on the screen. Click **Screen | Black Screen**. A blank, black screen appears.

2. Click the left mouse button to return to the slide.

Figure 3-3

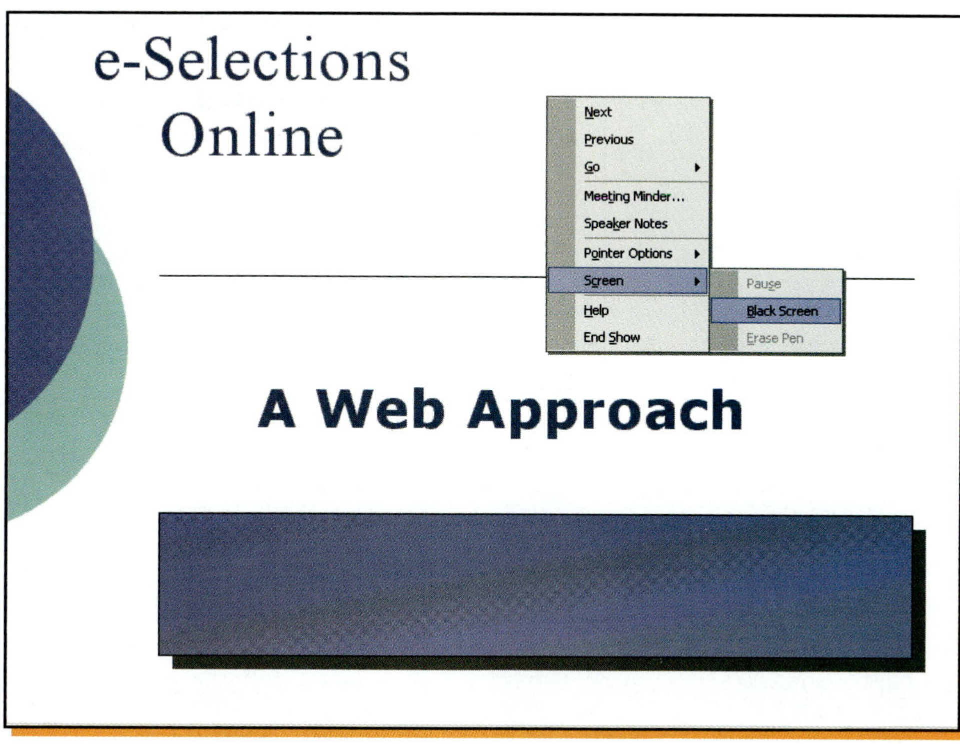

3 Right-click and select **Next** to display the subtitle text.

4 Right-click and select **End Show**.

Other Ways

To display the Slide Show shortcut menu:

- Move the mouse pointer on screen until a Shortcut Menu button appears in the lower-left corner of the slide. Then click the Shortcut button to display the shortcut menu.

Annotating Slides

One great advantage of displaying presentations as slide shows is that you can *annotate*—actually draw on presentation slides—during the show. Annotations enable you to underscore items for emphasis, draw circles around on-screen features to direct the audience focus, or simply create a diagram as you answer audience questions. Annotation markings disappear when you advance to the next slide and have no affect on slide contents. As a result, you can erase annotations and start the annotations over when necessary.

Task 3:
To Annotate Slides during a Slide Show

1 Display Slide 3 of the *e-Selections Marketing Division.ppt* presentation and click the Slide Show button.

2 Right-click and then choose **Pointer Options | Pen**. The mouse pointer looks like a pen.

Figure 3-4

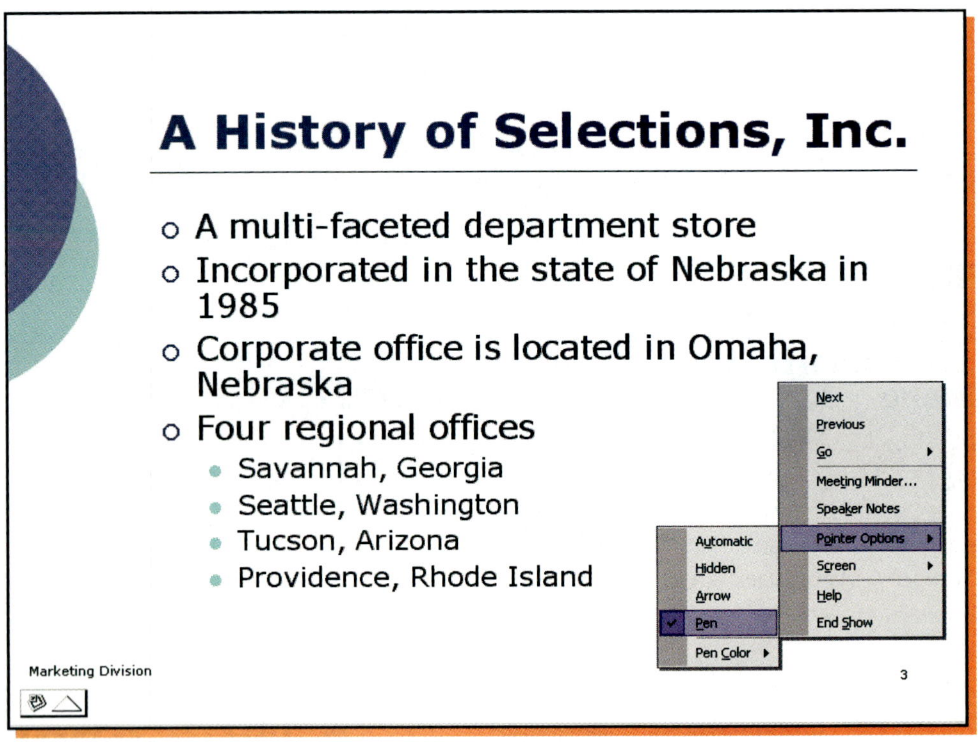

3 Position the mouse pen below *1985* in the second bulleted-list point, press the left mouse button, and drag the mouse to draw a circle around the year.

4 Press [E] to erase the annotation. Press [Esc] twice to drop the pencil and end the slide show.

Figure 3-5

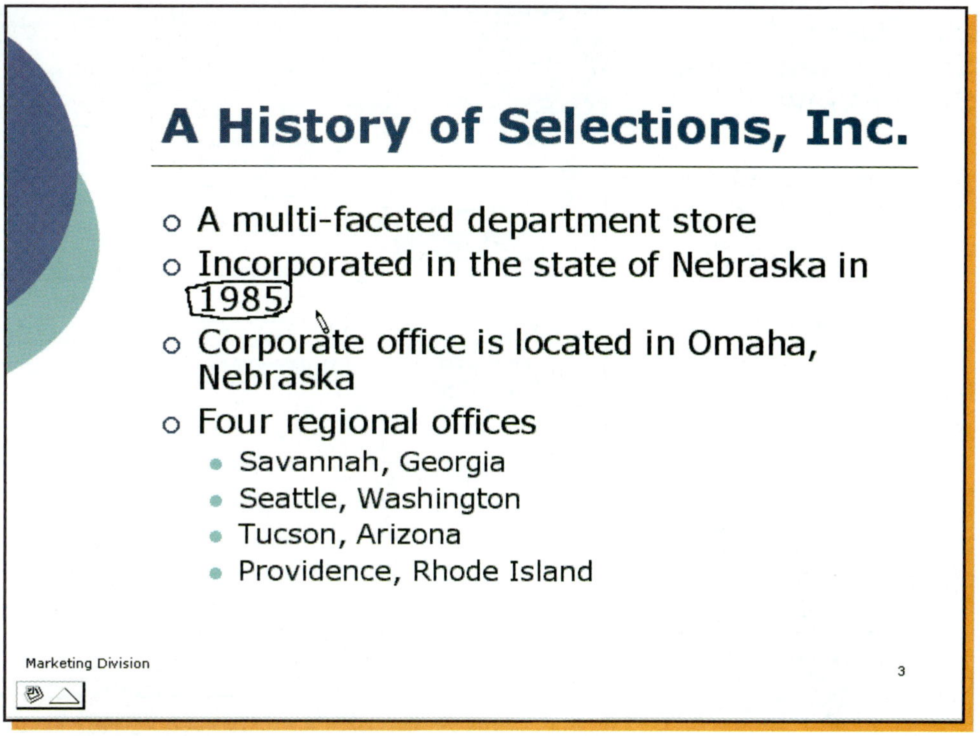

Tip Moving an annotated slide off screen and then back on screen also erases annotations.

Using the Slide Sorter View

After viewing the presentation as a slide show, you might find that you need to rearrange the slides so that the flow is smoother or to match changes in the oral presentation. Slide Sorter view displays *thumbnails*—miniature images—of presentation slides. You can reorder the slides by dragging the thumbnails to new positions. Slide Sorter view prevents slide editing; as a result, you must return to Normal or Slide view to edit slide text and graphics.

Moving, Copying, and Duplicating Slides

In Slide Sorter view, moving slides is as simple as dragging and dropping a slide to a new position in the presentation. Copying and duplicating slides is an easy way to create additional slides that contain the same information to prevent having to reconstruct them. You can move, copy, and duplicate slides to get them in the order Mr. McGuffee outlined.

Task 4:

To Move, Copy, and Duplicate Slides Using Slide Sorter View

1 Open the *e-Selections Marketing Division.ppt* presentation, if necessary.

2 Click the Slide Sorter view button at the bottom of the presentation window.

> **Other Ways**
> To switch to Slide Sorter view:
> - Choose **View | Slide Sorter**.

3 Click Slide 3 to make it active and then click and drag the slide so that a bar appears between Slides 1 and 2, as shown in Figure 3-7; then drop the slide.

4 Repeat the procedures outlined in Step 3 to move the following slides into the proper position:
- Slide 7 (Selections, Inc., Stores) to Slide 3
- Slide 6 (e-Selections) to Slide 4
- Slide 6 (e-Selections Web Spot) to Slide 5
- Slide 7 (Shopping Opportunities) to Slide 6

5 Click Slide 1 to make it active and then choose **Edit | Duplicate**. A duplicate slide appears as Slide 2.

Figure 3-6

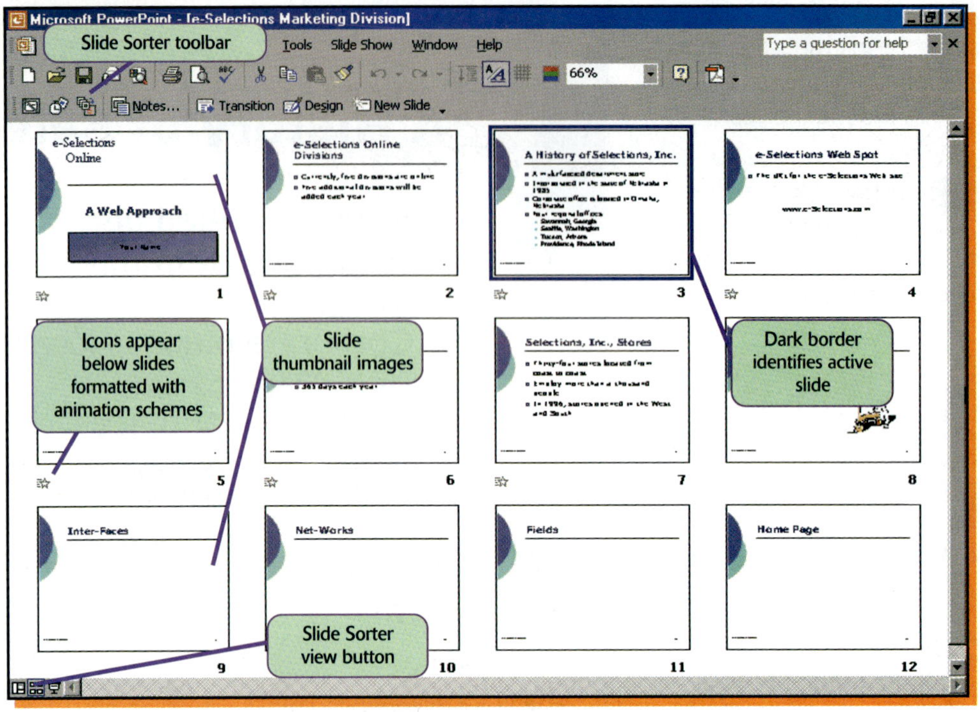

Figure 3-7

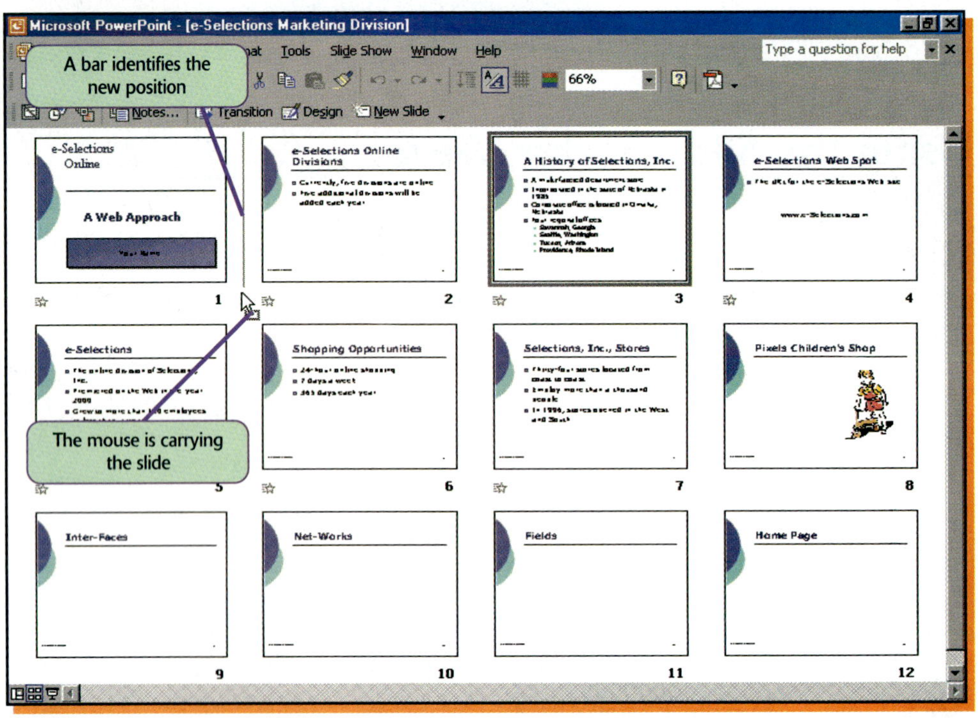

> **Other Ways**
> To duplicate a slide:
> - Press Ctrl + D.

6 Drag the new slide to the end of the presentation.

7 Click Slide 3 to make it active, press Ctrl, and then drag the slide to the end of the presentation. Save changes to the presentation.

Figure 3-8

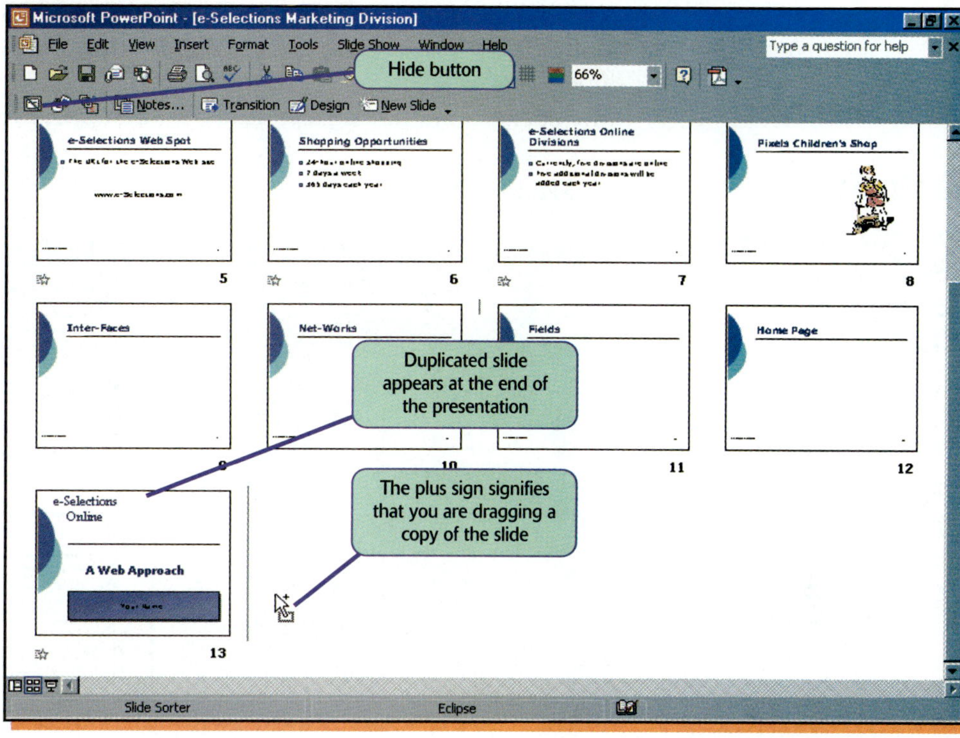

Deleting Slides

If slides become outdated and you no longer need them, you can delete them. PowerPoint offers a variety of ways to remove slides from a presentation. The active view always determines which procedure you should use and PowerPoint deletes the active or selected slide.

- Choose **Edit | Delete Slide** from any view.
- Press Delete in both the Slide Sorter and Outline views.
- Click the Cut button.

Troubleshooting To restore a slide that you accidentally delete, click the Undo button.

Task 5:
To Delete a Slide

1 Click the last slide in the presentation.

2 Press Delete.

Hiding Slides and Displaying Hidden Slides

Hiding slides enables you to include slides containing detailed information or data in your presentation but to display those slides only when the audience asks questions or when you need more details about a topic. Hidden slides remain in the background during a slide show and appear only when you access them.

Task 6:

To Hide Slides and Display Them during a Slide Show

1. Display the *e-Selections Marketing Division.ppt* presentation in **Slide Sorter** view and select Slide 3. Click the Hide Slide button on the Slide Sorter toolbar.

2. Select Slide 1 and press F5 to start the slide show. Advance to Slide 2 and then advance again. Slide 4 appears because Slide 3 is the hidden slide.

3. Press 2 and Enter to return to Slide 2. Press H to display the hidden slide. Slide 3, the hidden slide, appears.

Figure 3-9

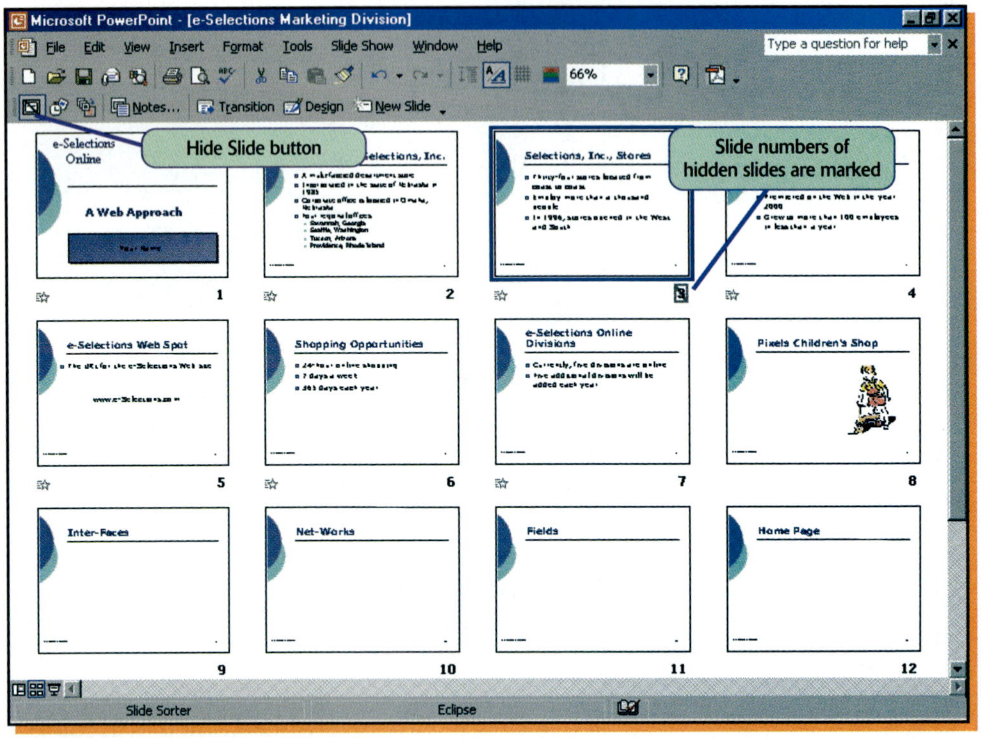

Other Ways

To hide a slide:

- Choose **Slide Show | Hide Slide** from any view.
- Right-click on any slide in Slide Sorter view and in the Slide Design pane of Normal view and select **Hide Slide**.

4 Right-click to display the slide show shortcut menu and choose **Go | Slide Navigator**.

Tip The Slide Navigator window displays a list of slide titles so that you can go directly to the slide you want to view.

Figure 3-10

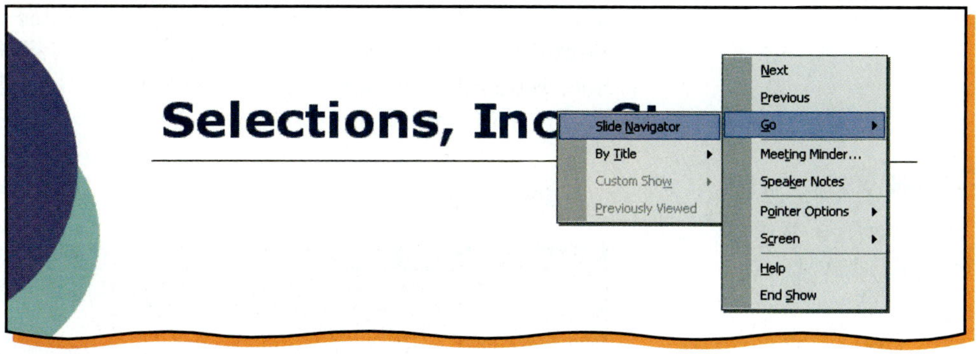

5 Review Slide Navigator features; then click **Cancel** and press Esc to end the slide show. Save changes to the presentation.

Figure 3-11

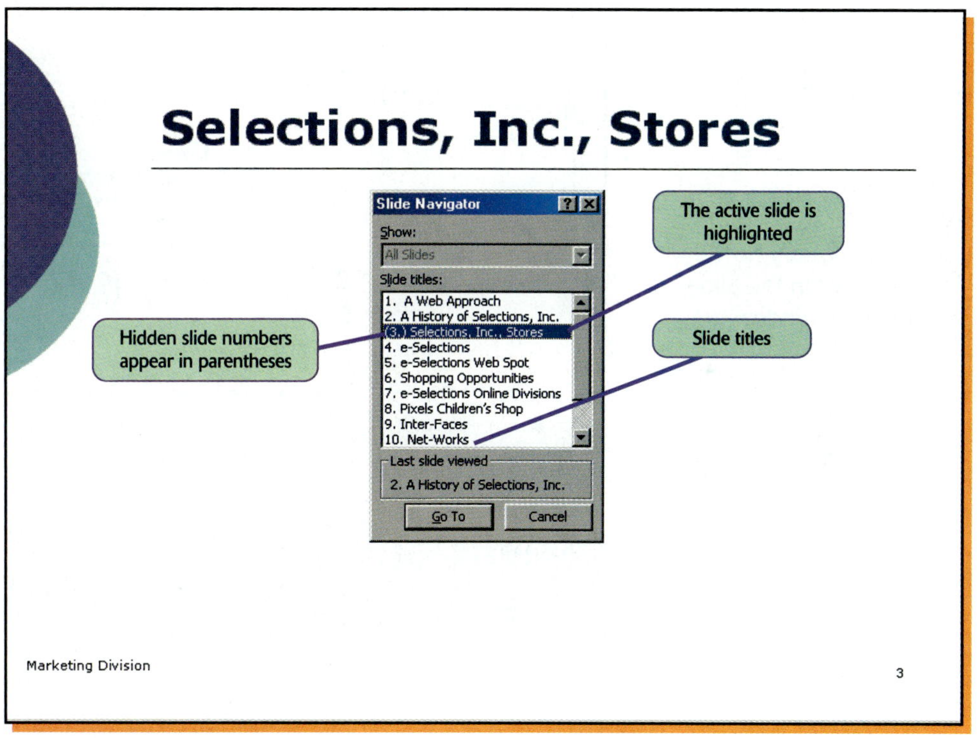

WEB TIP

You can get help developing your résumé right there on the World Wide Web. Search for *résumé* and locate some sites that provide help.

Creating Summary Slides

The PowerPoint *summary slide* feature enables you to create a new slide that contains the titles of selected slides. The new slide appears just before the first selected slide and serves as an introduction to the slides that follow. You can create a summary slide to introduce the five online Selections divisions.

Task 7: To Create a Summary Slide

1. Display the *e-Selections Marketing Division.ppt* presentation in **Slide Sorter** view.

2. Select Slide 8, press and hold down the [Shift] key, and then click Slide 12.

Troubleshooting
Change the Zoom setting, if necessary, to view all the slides in the Slide Sorter view window that you need to select.

Figure 3-12

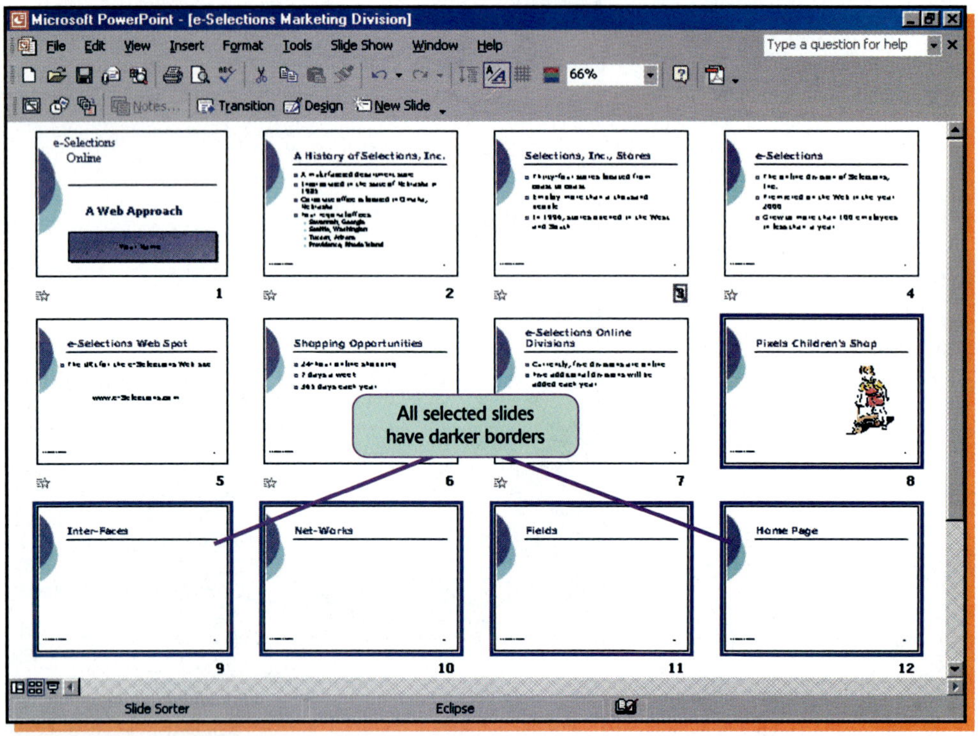

Other Ways

To select multiple slides:

- Press and hold down the [Ctrl] key and click each slide.

3 Click the Summary Slide button on the Slide Sorter toolbar to create a new slide that places selected slide titles as bulleted list items on the new slide.

4 Double-click Slide 8 to return to Normal view.

5 Select the title text and type **e-Selections Online Divisions.**

Troubleshooting
When PowerPoint capitalizes the e, click the Undo button to reverse the action.

Figure 3-13

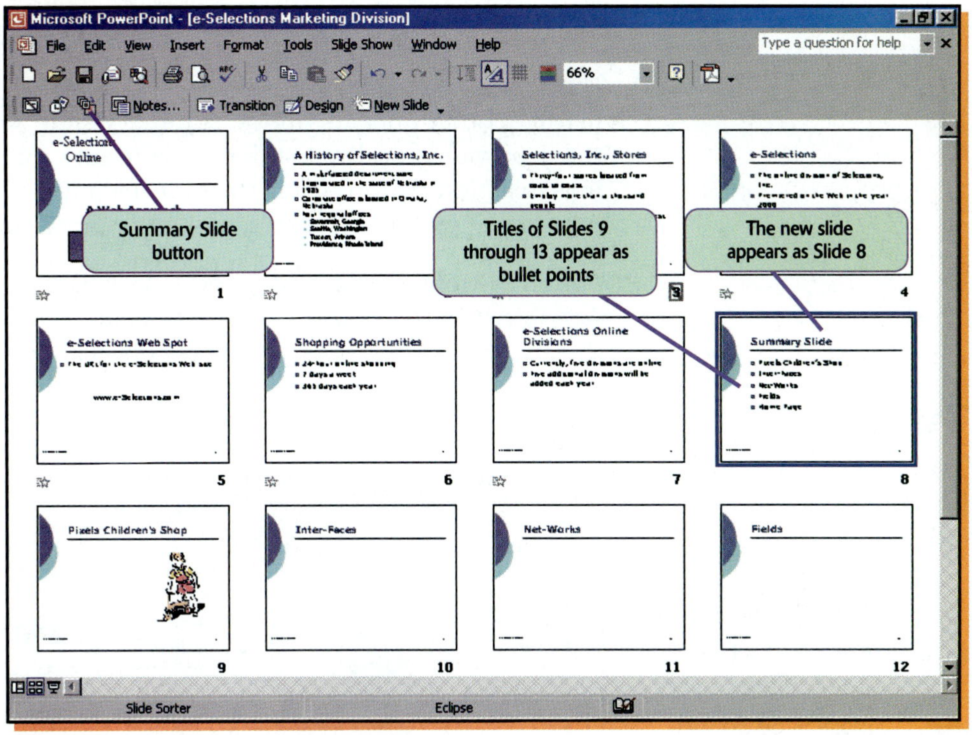

6 Display the last slide in the presentation and edit the slide to appear as shown in Figure 3-14. Save changes to the presentation.

Tip
Depending on the settings active on your computer, a light bulb may appear because of the exclamation point on this slide. Ignore it for now.

Figure 3-14

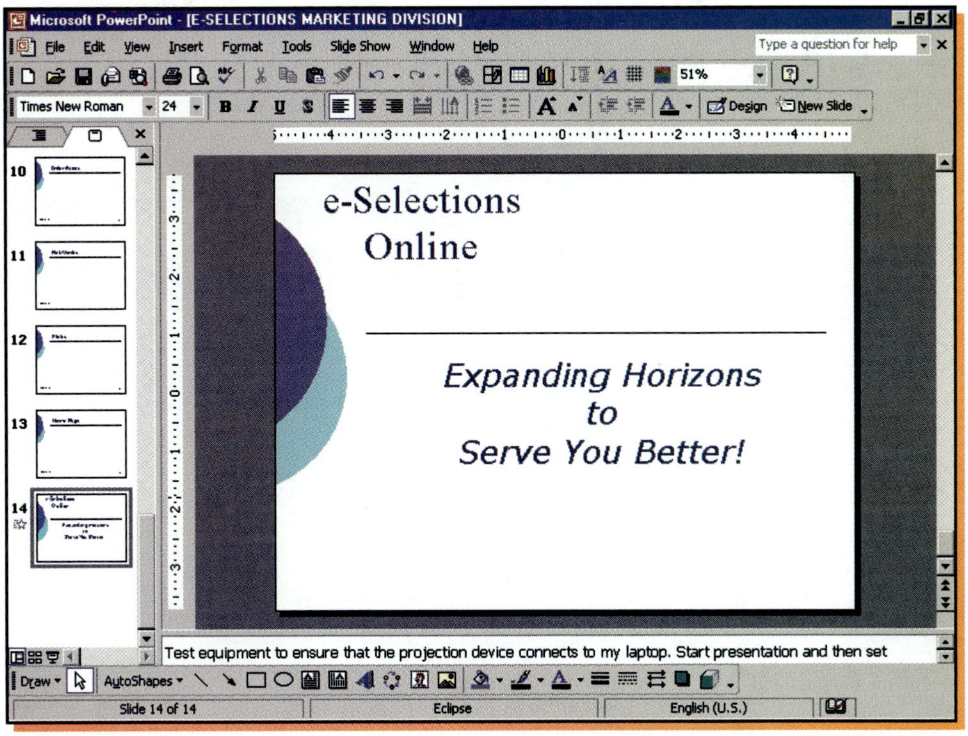

Creating Action Buttons

Action buttons enable you to control the slide that PowerPoint displays when you click the action button during a slide show. For the e-Selections Marketing Division presentation, you can create action buttons for each of the bulleted-list items that appears on the summary slide so representatives can jump to the department or division they want to find. You add text, symbols, and drawings to action buttons using the same techniques you use to add text and drawings to text boxes, rectangles, and other drawn objects.

Action buttons perform an action, so when you draw an action button, the Action Settings dialog box opens to enable you to set the action. You can set the action as you create the action buttons or go back and set the action later.

Task 8: To Create Action Buttons

1. Display Slide 8 of *e-Selections Marketing Division.ppt* in Normal view.
2. Choose **Slide Show | Action Buttons** to display the action button palette.
3. Click the Action Button: Custom □ button. The mouse pointer changes to a crosshair +.

Figure 3-15

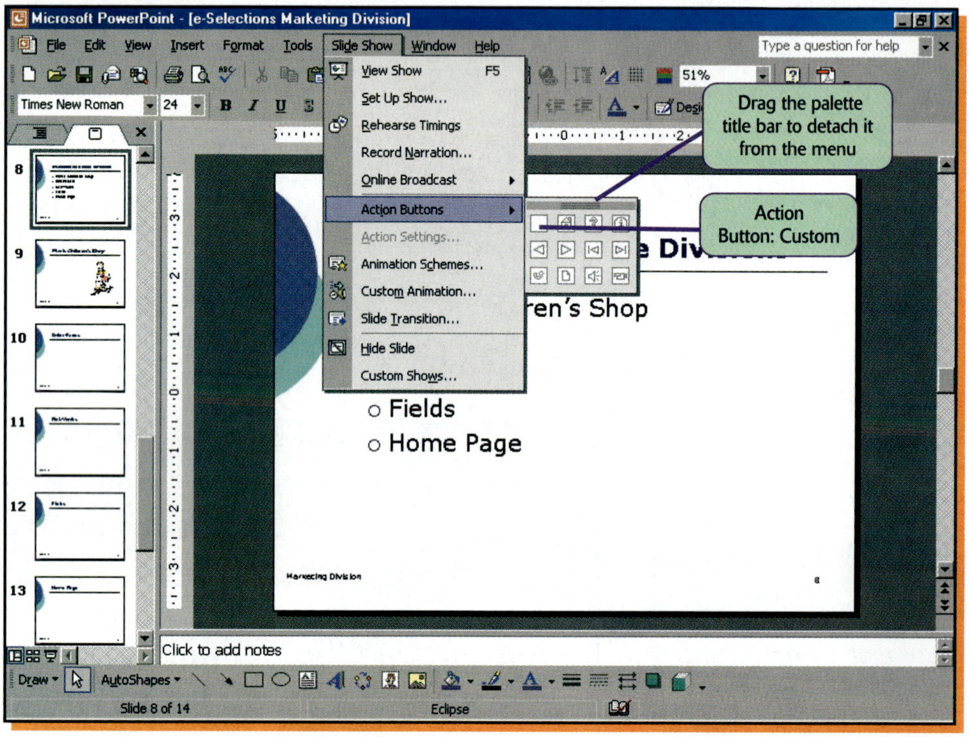

Other Ways

To display the Action Buttons palette:

- Choose **AutoShapes | Action Buttons** on the Drawing toolbar.

4 Draw a small square around the bullet for the first bulleted-list item, *Pixels Children's Shop*. The Action Settings dialog box opens.

Troubleshooting
Don't worry about the position and size of the action button—you can fix it later.

Figure 3-16

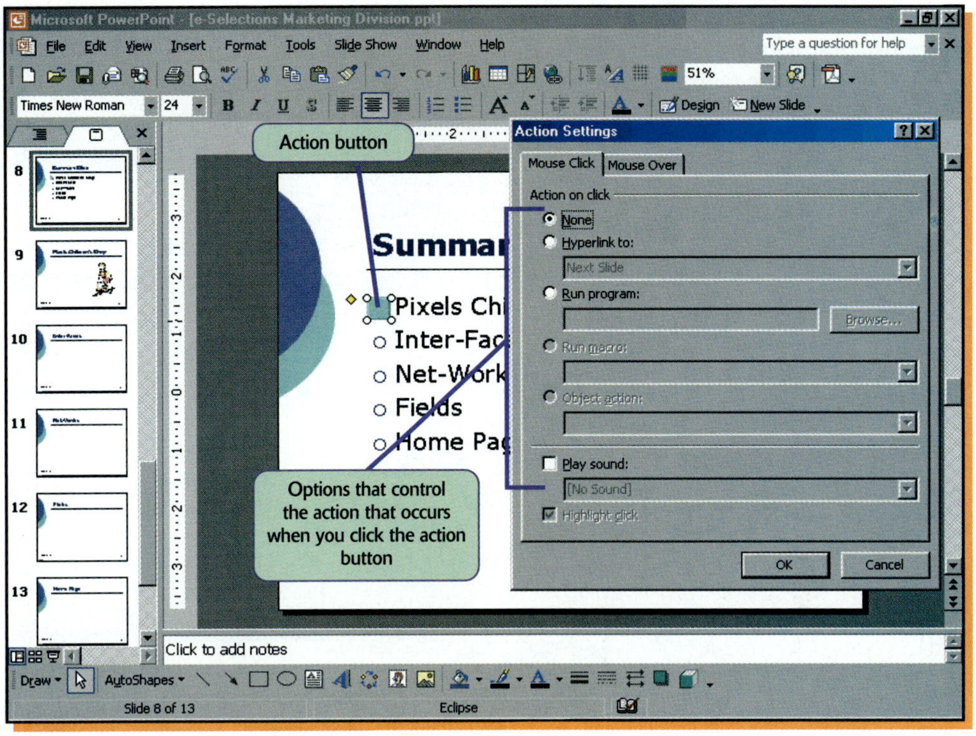

5 Click **Cancel** to close the Action Settings dialog box, right-click the action button, and select **Add Text**, to position the insertion point in the drawn shape.

Figure 3-17

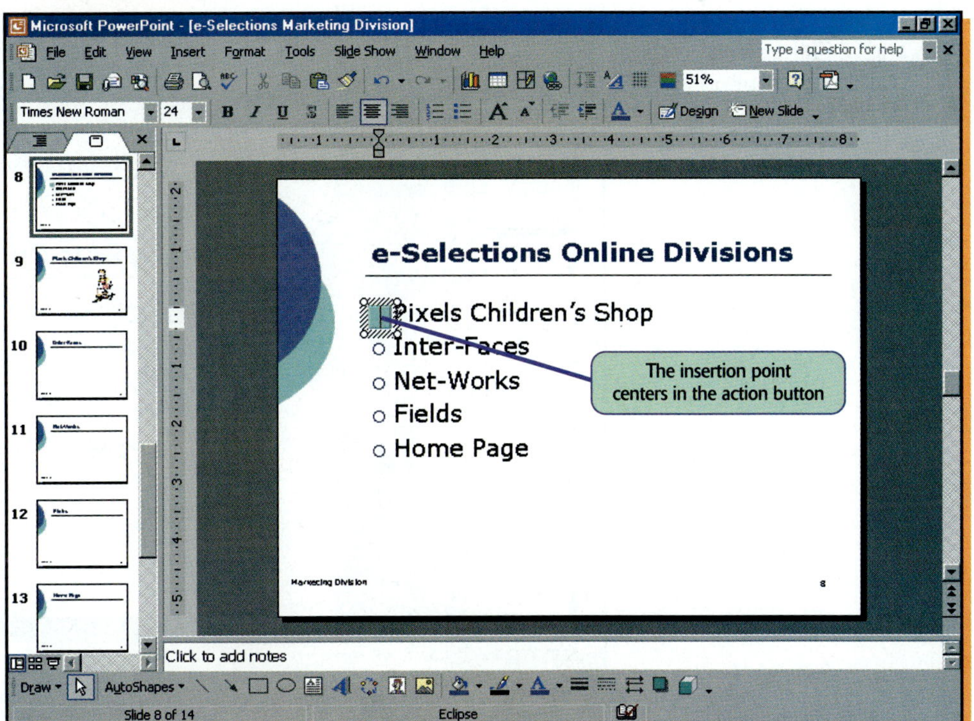

6 Choose **Insert | Symbol**. Select **Wingdings** from the Font drop-down list, select a symbol similar to the one highlighted in Figure 3-18.

7 Click **Insert**, and then **Close** to close the Symbol dialog box. The symbol appears in the drawn object beside the first bullet on the slide.

Troubleshooting
Substitute a font identified by your instructor if Wingdings is unavailable.

Figure 3-18

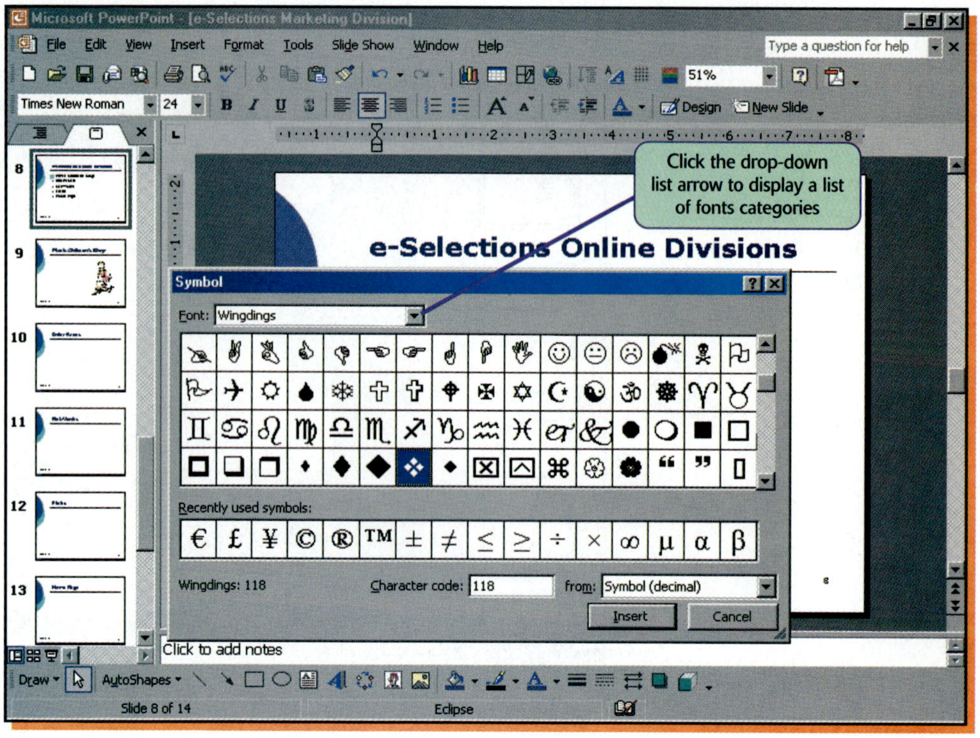

8 Click the action button border between handles to select the button, press and hold the [Ctrl] key, and then drag the button to cover the next bullet.

Figure 3-19

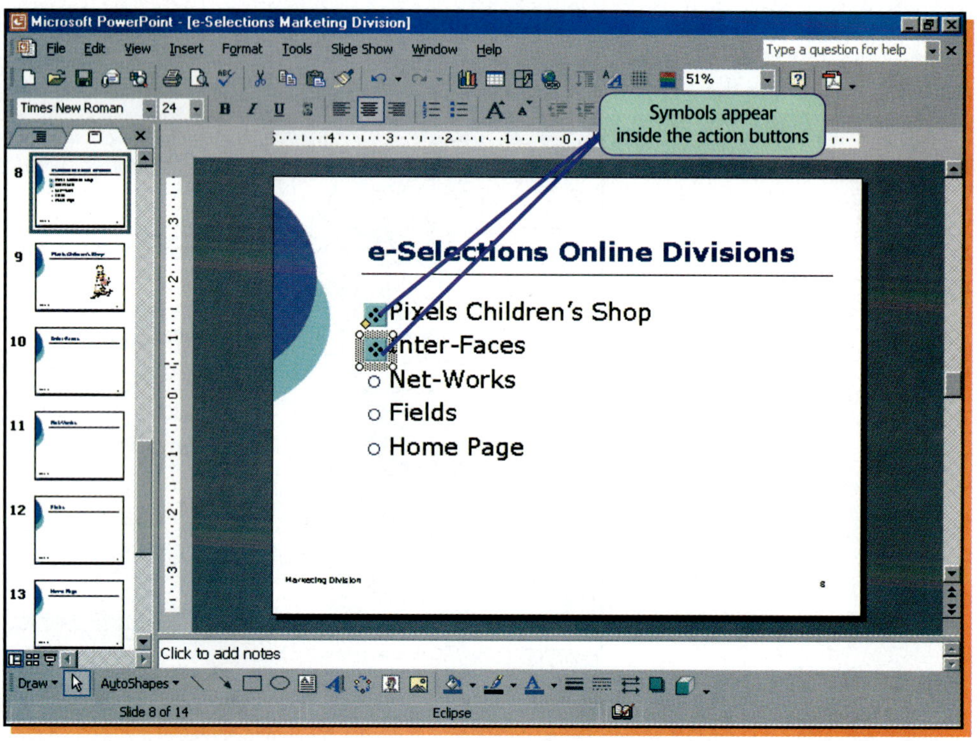

9 Repeat the procedure in Step 9 to copy action buttons to cover all five bullets.

10 Press Shift and click to select all five action buttons, and then choose **Draw | Align or Distribute | Align Right**. Save changes to the presentation.

Figure 3-20

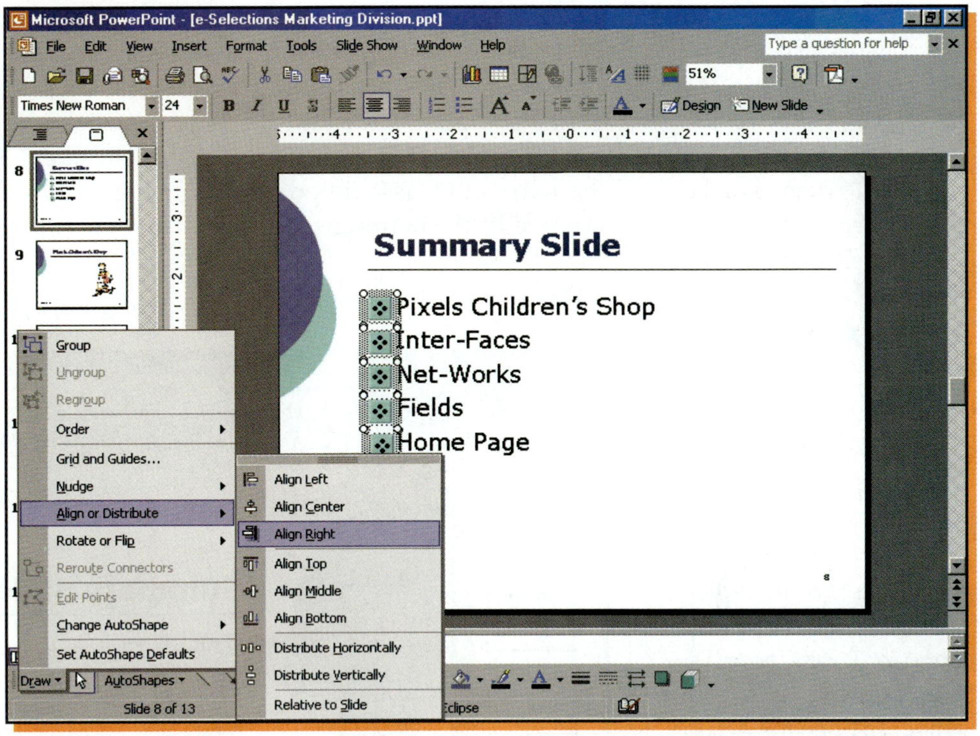

Tip Distribute options available on the Align and Distribute list enable you to space selected objects evenly. Select one of these options if your action buttons are spaced unevenly after you align them.

Creating Hyperlinks

Options contained in the Action Settings dialog box enable you to tell PowerPoint what you want to do when you click the action button during a slide show. The *Hyperlink to* option creates a link between the bulleted point on the summary slide and the slide to which it refers. During a slide show, you can click the action button to display the slide. The procedures you use to set the hyperlinks associated with an action button are also the procedures you use to edit the action associated with an action button.

Task 9:
To Set Action Button Actions

1. Click a neutral area of Slide 8 to deselect all action buttons.

2. Press Shift, right-click the edge of the action button for *Pixels Children's Shop* and select Action Settings to open the Action Settings dialog box.

Tip Pressing Shift as you click the action button ensures that the action button becomes active without positioning the insertion point for typing text inside the button.

Figure 3-21

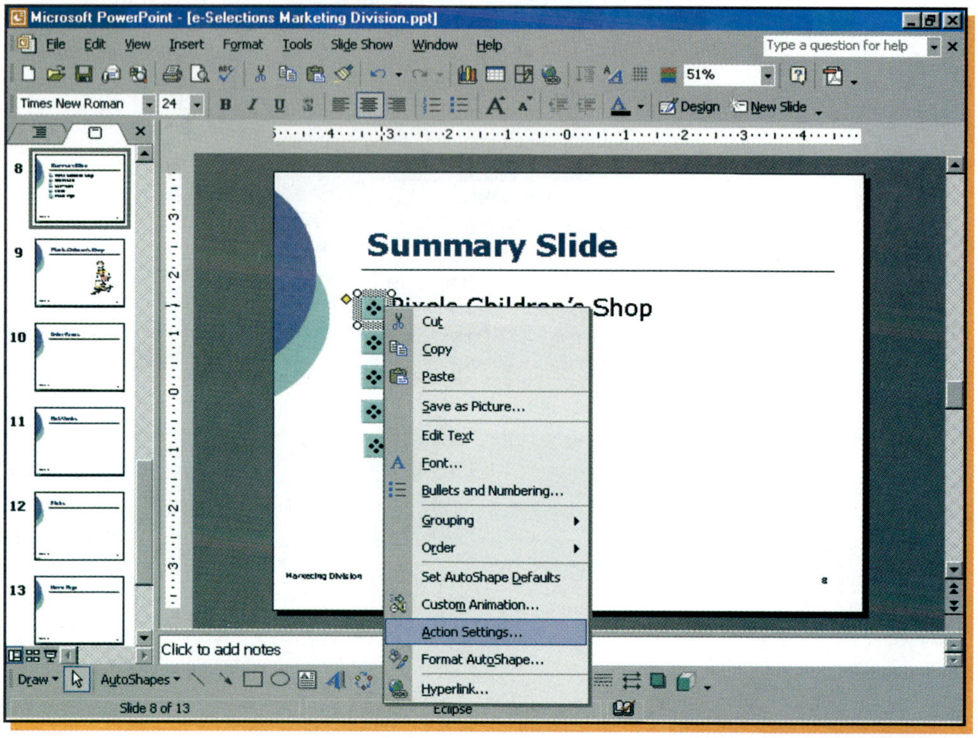

Troubleshooting If you see an insertion point in the action button, try again. Setting an action when the insertion point is active will fail.

3 Click the **Hyperlink to** option and then click the down arrow.

4 Scroll the drop-down list and click **Slide** to open the Hyperlink to Slide dialog box.

> **Tip** The Hyperlink to Slide dialog box contains a list of all slide titles for slides in the presentation.

Figure 3-22

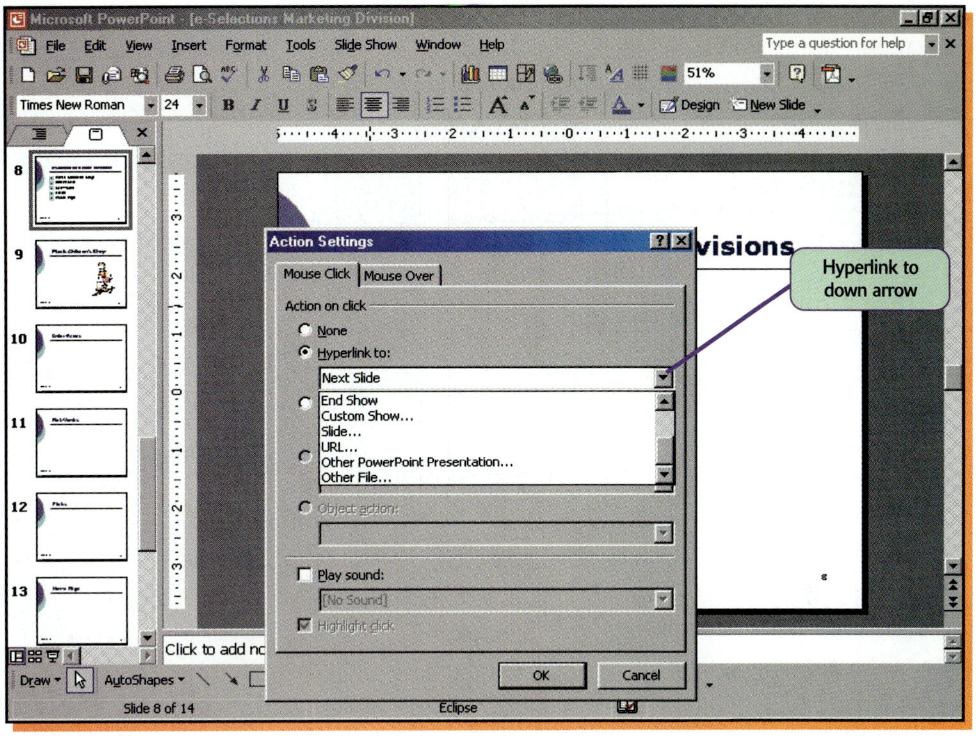

5 Select **9**. *Pixels Children's Shop*, and then click the **OK** button at the top of the Hyperlink to Slide dialog box.

6 Click the OK button at the bottom of the Hyperlink to Slide dialog box.

Figure 3-23

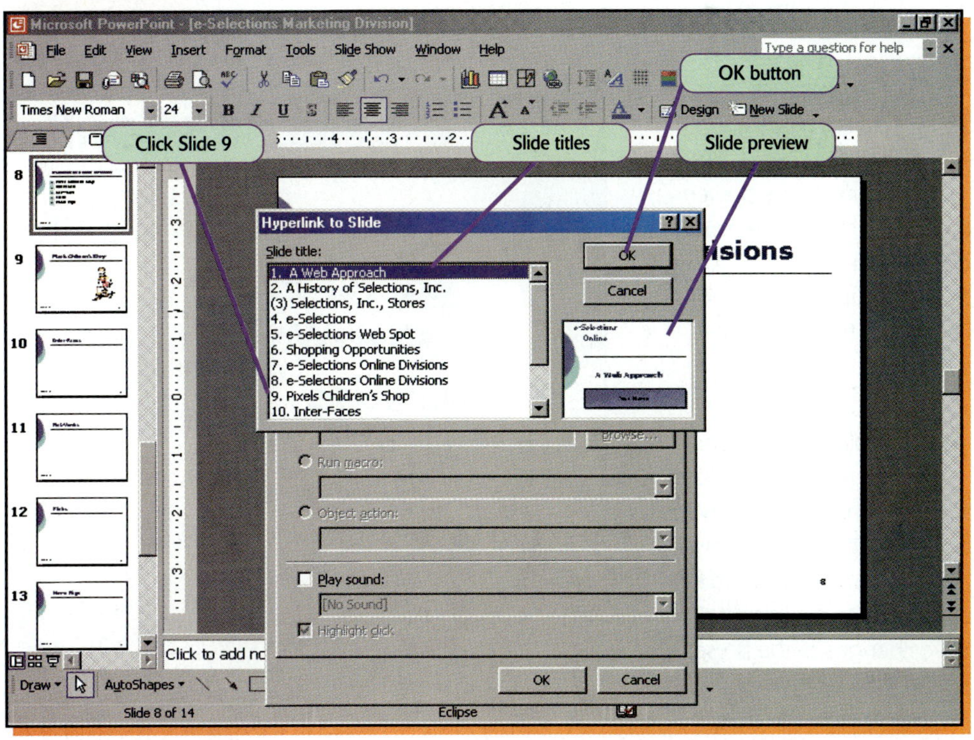

7 Click the Slide Show button to start the show with Slide 8. Slide 8 fills the screen.

Troubleshooting
Hyperlinks affect the action of the button during a slide show. As a result, setting hyperlinks appears to have no affect on the active slide.

Figure 3-24

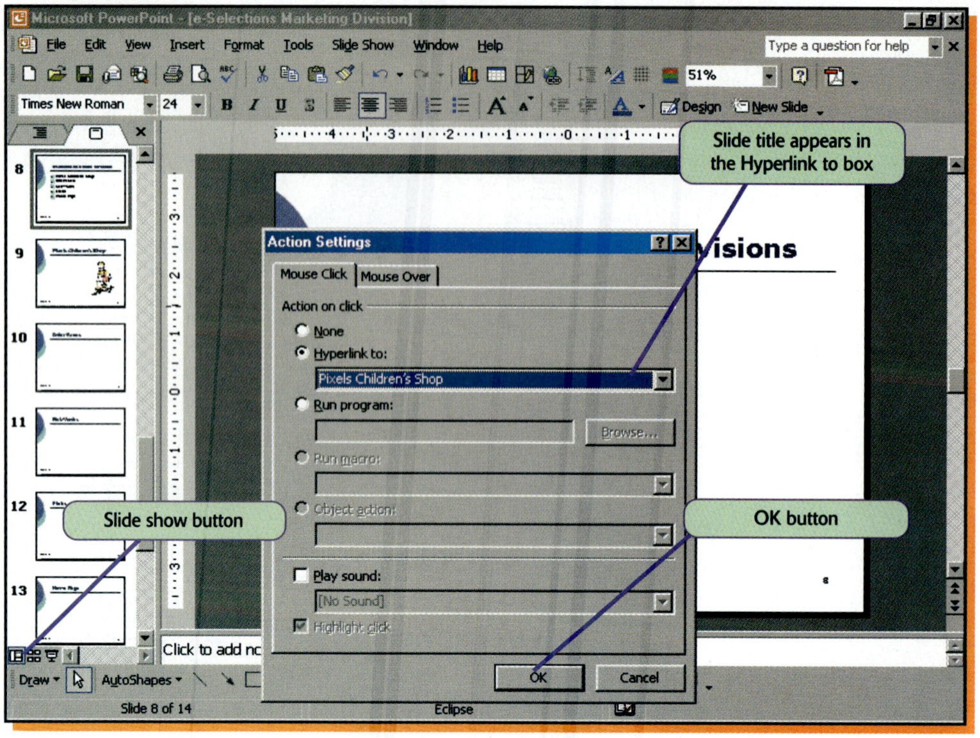

8 Position the mouse pointer on the action button for *Pixels Children's Shop*.

9 Click the action button. Slide 9 appears. Press Esc to return to the presentation and repeat the procedures in Steps 2 through 7 to link the four remaining action buttons to the appropriate slides.

10 Display the slide show and test the hyperlinks to ensure that they display the correct slide and make any adjustments necessary to link the button to the correct slide. Save changes to the presentation.

Figure 3-25

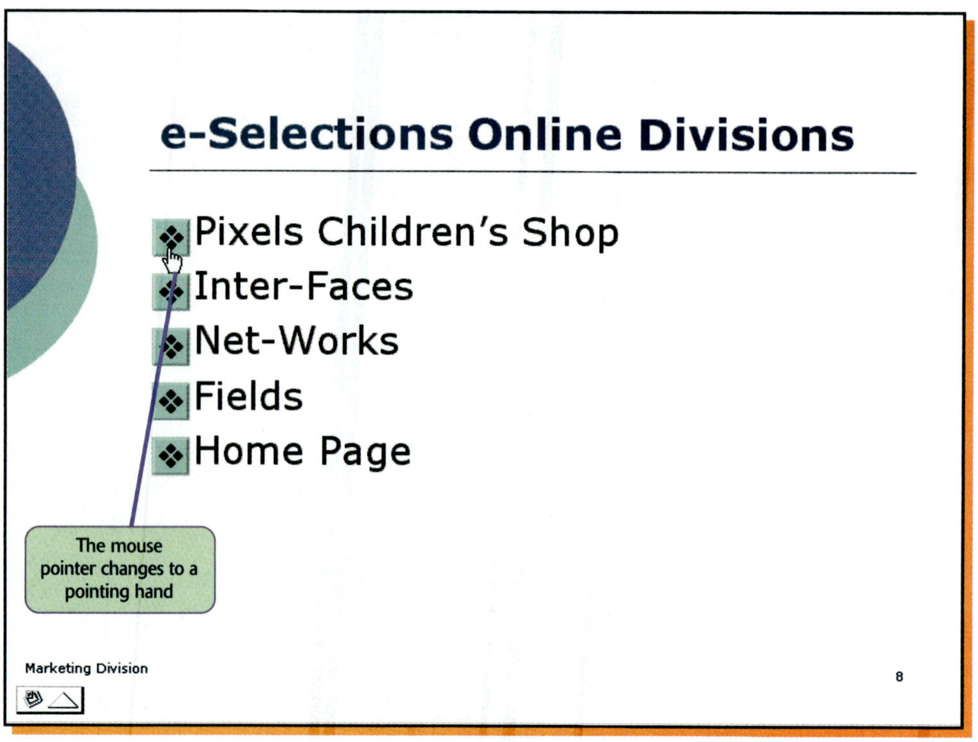

CHECK POINT

Hyperlinks can also connect bulleted-list text to slides in the presentation, alleviating the need to draw action buttons for linking. To create a hyperlink between text and slides, select the text, right-click on the selected text and choose **Hyperlink**. Then click **Place in This Document** on the Link to list and select the slide that you want hyperlinked. (You'll have an opportunity to try this technique in the end-of-project exercises.)

Applying Slide Transitions

Animation schemes enable you to control the appearance of text and other objects on slides during a slide show. Slide *transitions* control the way slides move on and off the screen during a slide show. You can use the Slide Sorter toolbar to add transitions to your slides. If slides contain animated text, the animation begins after the slide appears on screen during the show.

Task 10: To Add Slide Transitions

1. Display *e-Selections Marketing Division.ppt* in Slide Sorter view. Select Slide 1 and then click the **Transition** button on the Slide Sorter toolbar.

2. Click the **Box Out** transition for Slide 1 and select **Applause** from the Sound drop-down list.

3. Press Ctrl and select Slides 8 through 13, and select the **Random Transition** option at the bottom of the transition list.

4. Press F5 and view the entire slide show.

Apply different transitions to other slides in the presentation, adjust the speed settings for different slides, and then save changes to the presentation.

Figure 3-26

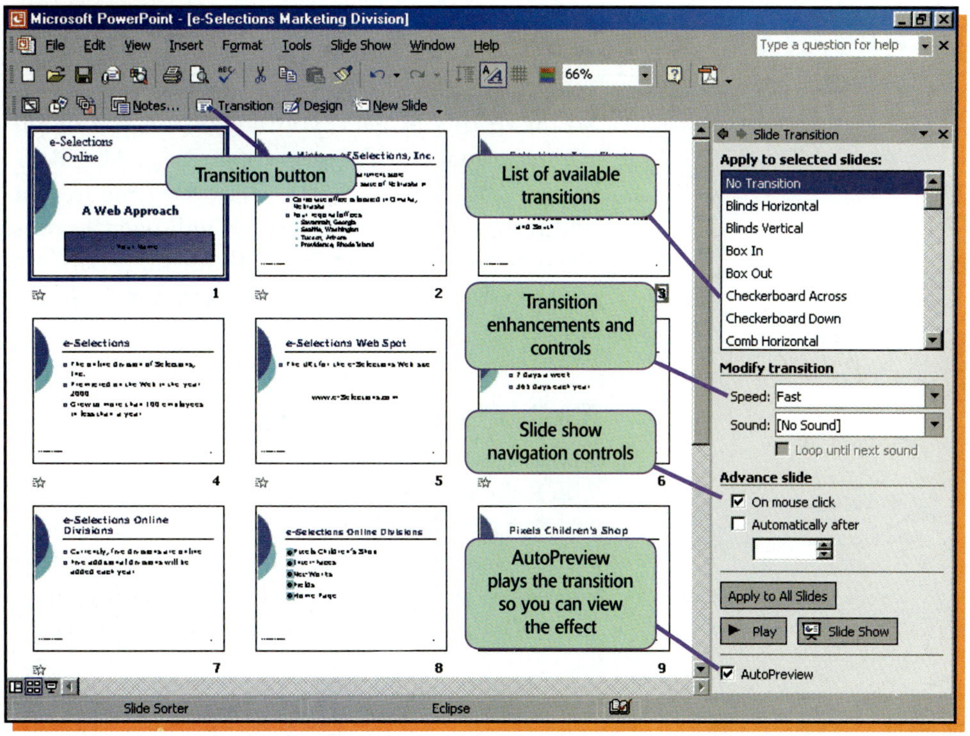

Other Ways

To display the Slide Transition task pane:

- Choose **Slide Show | Slide Transition** from any view.
- Click the down arrow on the task pane title bar and select **Slide Transition**.
- Right-click on any slide in any view and select **Slide Transition**.

Tip When you apply the Random Transition to a presentation slide, the slide will move on screen differently each time you show the presentation. For example, if you apply Random Transition to Slide 1, the first time you show the presentation, the slide may fly from the left. The next time you show the presentation, the slide may dissolve onto the screen.

WEB TIP

Have you ever considered searching the Internet for the meanings of words and phrases in other languages and cultures? It can be a fascinating pastime! For example,

- **In Chinese, Coca-Cola® translates to "Bite the wax tadpole."**
- **In Taiwan, the translated version of the Pepsi® slogan "Come Alive with the Pepsi Generation" means "Pepsi brings your ancestors back from the dead."**
- **In Brazil, a rendezvous is a place to…ahem…a bawdy house.**

Rehearsing Presentations

So far in this project, you have shown your presentation, adjusted it, created special effects, and tested hyperlinks. Mr. McGuffee indicated that marketing representatives often have a limited time in which to deliver a presentation. In addition, some representatives will use the presentation at trade shows where viewers will review slides without manually advancing the slides. PowerPoint features will help set up the presentation to meet Mr. McGuffee's requirements.

Rehearsing Timings

The Rehearse Timings feature enables you to practice your presentation delivery and track the time required to present each slide and bullet point. You can repeat delivery of information for each slide as often as necessary to get an accurate timing for the slide. When you finish the presentation, you can have PowerPoint automatically apply practiced timings to each slide.

Task 11:

To Use the Rehearse Timings Feature

1 Display *e-Selections Marketing Division.ppt* in Slide Sorter view.

2 Click the Rehearse Timings button on the Slide Sorter toolbar.

Other Ways

To start the rehearsal:

- Choose **Slide Show | Rehearse Timings** from any view.

Figure 3-27

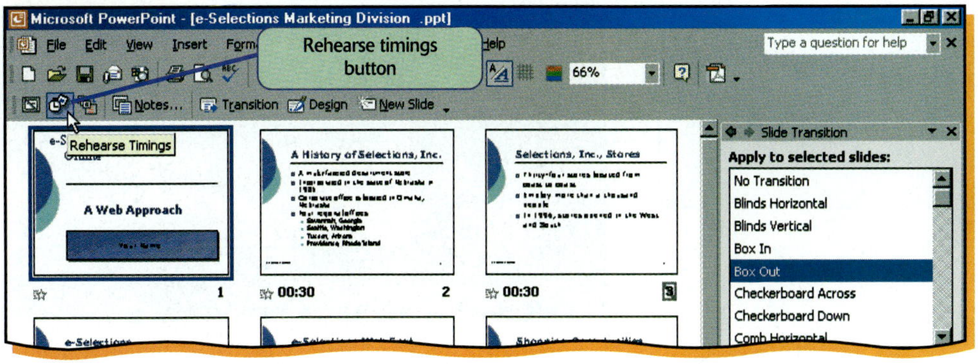

3 Click the Next button twice.

4 Read the information contained on Slide 2 and then click the Repeat button to reset the timing for the active slide.

5 Continue clicking the Next button and reading information on the slides until the presentation is complete.

Figure 3-28

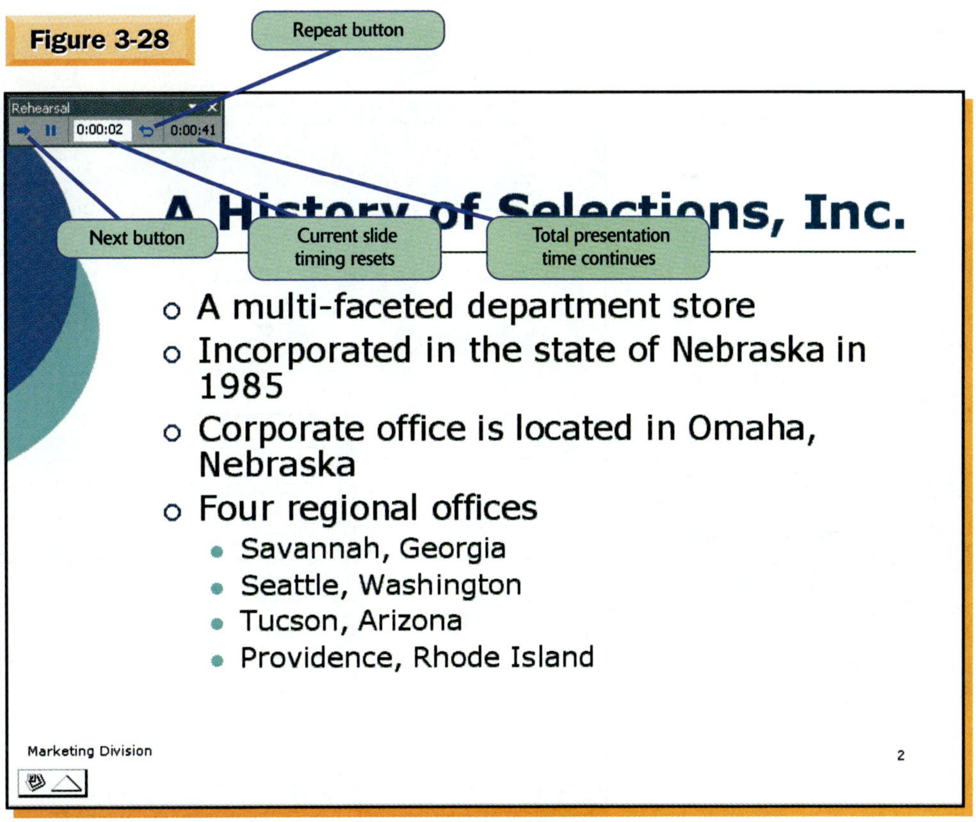

6. Click **No** to discard the timings.

Tip You can also advance the presentation using traditional techniques.

Figure 3-29

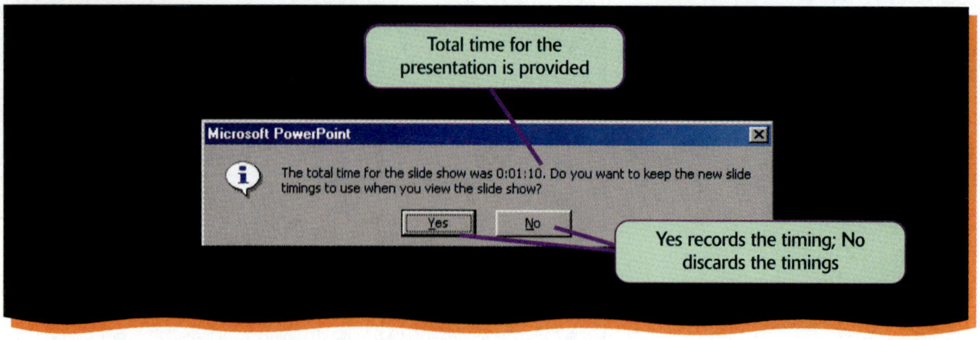

Setting Slide Timings

Setting timings manually for each slide is a beneficial way to set up presentations that viewers will review at their leisure. Many presenters apply slide timings manually when they are setting up their presentation at trade shows, kiosks, and other locations. When setting timings manually, it is a good idea to read through text on a slide at least twice before advancing to the next slide so that viewers who are unfamiliar with slide contents have time to read the information.

Task 12: To Set Slide Timings Manually

1. Display *e-Selections Marketing Division.ppt* in Slide Sorter view.

2. Click the Transition [Transition] button on the Slide Sorter toolbar.

Tip If you accept the rehearsed timings, the timings set for the active slide appear in the Slide Transition task pane.

Figure 3-30

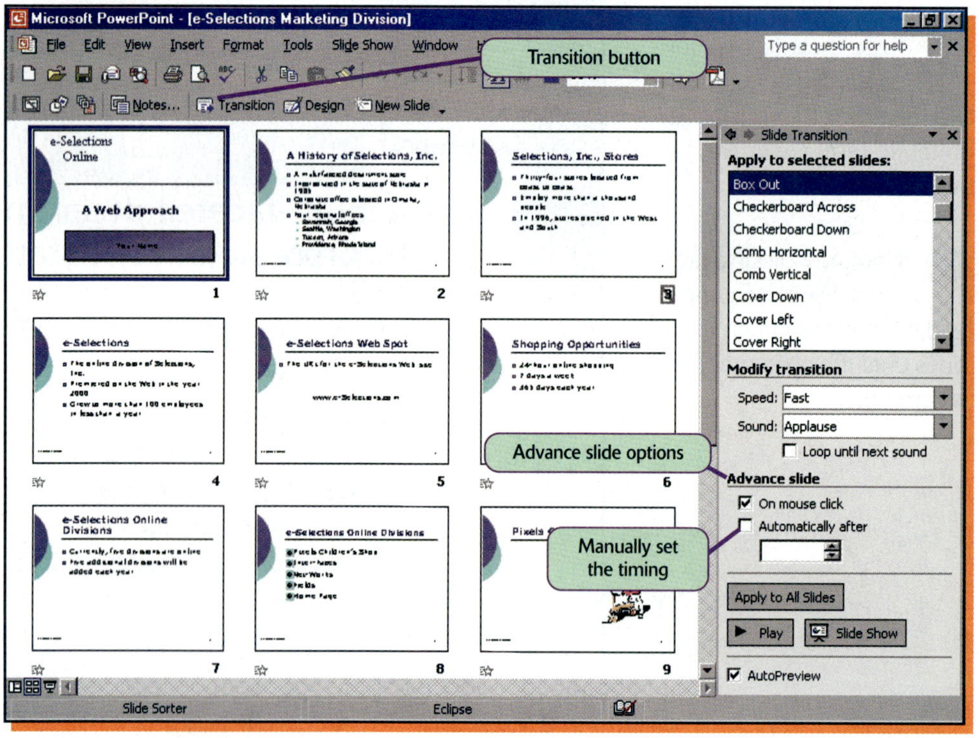

3 Select Slide 1 and choose the **Automatically after** option, as shown in Figure 3-31. Click the value spinner until the timing is set as shown in Figure 3-31.

4 Repeat the procedures from Step 3 to set timings for other slides in the presentation.

5 Start the slide show and let the show advance automatically to determine whether slide timings are adequate.

6 Make necessary adjustments to slide timings and save changes to the presentation.

Figure 3-31

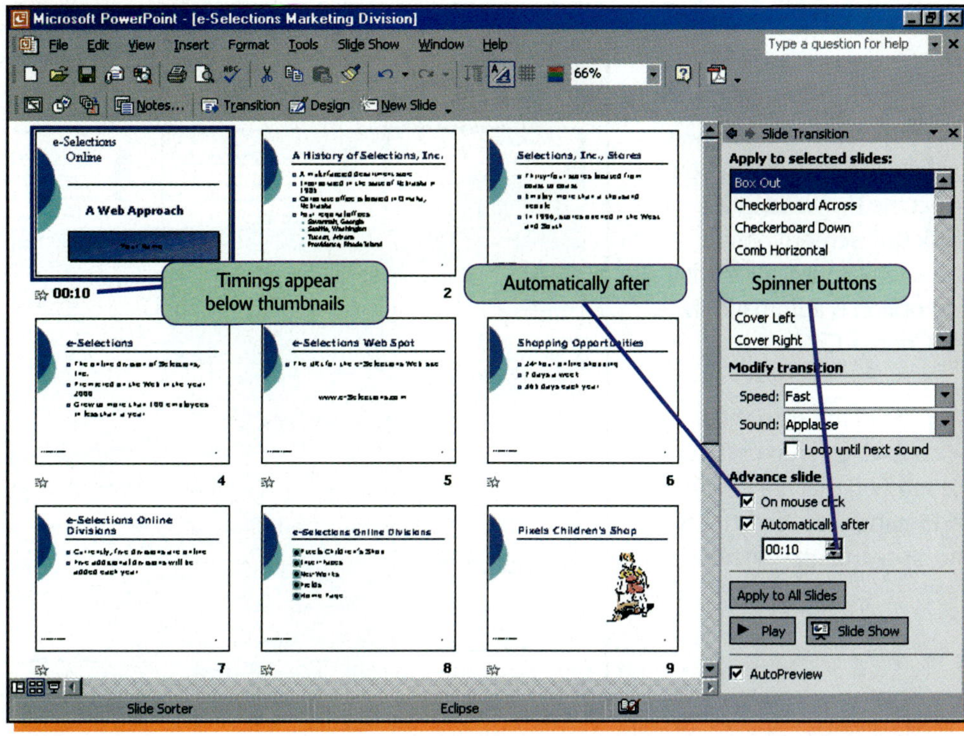

Setting Up Slide Shows

Setting presentations to run automatically is a great way to communicate information without having to start and stop a slide show manually. PowerPoint contains features that enable you to set the presentation to run without interruption and to start again after the last slide. Because you have set the presentation to run automatically, most controls are unavailable to viewers, so you don't have to worry about viewers changing or corrupting the presentation. For slides to advance automatically, you must assign timings to each slide.

Task 13:

To Set a Show to Run Automatically

1. Choose **Slide Show | Set Up Show** to open the Set Up Show dialog box. Select the **Browsed at a kiosk (full screen)** option. The Loop continuously until 'Esc' option is automatically set. Choose **OK**.

2. Start the slide show and let it run until you are satisfied that the timings and settings are correct. Save and close the presentation.

Figure 3-32

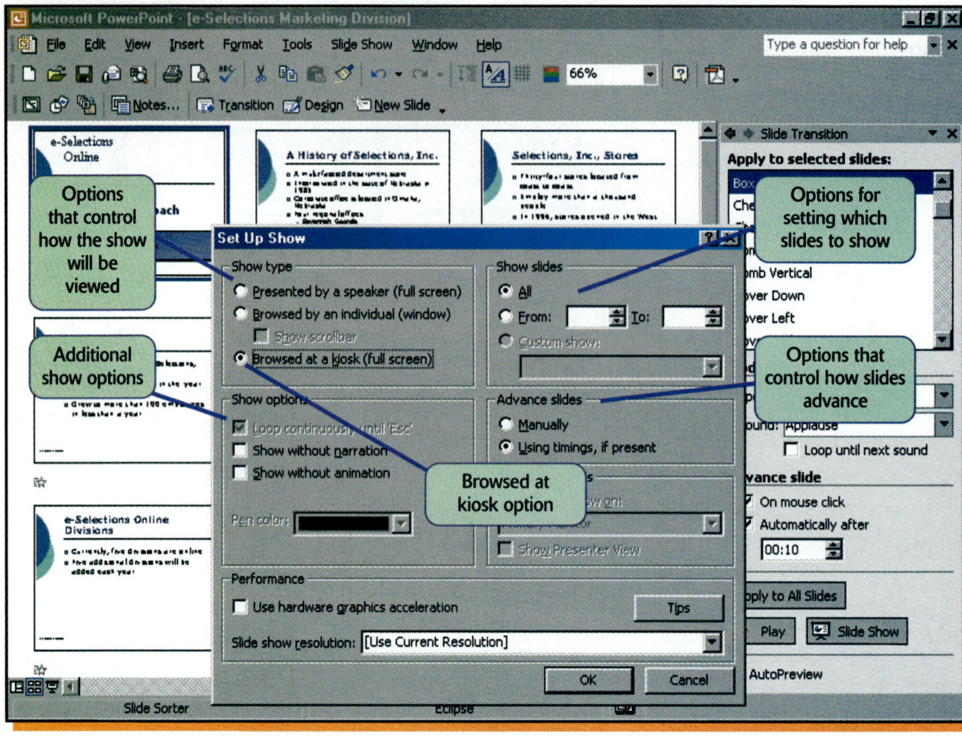

Tip

The Set Up Show dialog box is a busy dialog box that presents a number of options that control animation effects, the slides that users will view, and whether slides will advance manually or automatically. In addition, you can set the Loop continuously until 'Esc' option to restart the show automatically after the last slide is shown. When you set this option, you can stop the show at any time by pressing the Esc key.

SUMMARY AND EXERCISES

SUMMARY

- You can format slides in a presentation for on-screen viewing or for use with a projector or other audiovisual screen or flat surface as you present a report to an audience.
- Use Slide Sorter view to make final changes to the organization of the presentation—moving slides is as simple as dragging and dropping.
- Viewing your presentation as a slide show can make it come to life.
- You can use both the keyboard and mouse to move among slides in a presentation during a slide show.
- The slide show shortcut menu displays commands for navigating the slide show and controlling on-screen features.
- You can draw annotations directly on slides during a presentation without permanently affecting slide contents. PowerPoint automatically erases annotations when the slide moves off the screen; however, you can easily erase them manually as well.
- You can copy or duplicate slides so that they appear more than once in a presentation.
- Summary slides compile the titles of selected slides as bulleted-list points on the slide. Summary slides appear just before the first selected slide.
- Action buttons enable you to hyperlink to other slides during a presentation. You can copy the action buttons to other slides.
- Slide transitions create special effects as your slides move on and off the screen during a slide show.
- You can hide additional slides in case the audience asks questions or you need to present more details about a topic.
- You can add timings to slides by having PowerPoint automatically apply timings to each slide after you have rehearsed the presentation delivery or by manually assigning time to each slide.
- Setting a presentation to run automatically is a great way to communicate information without having to start and stop a slide show manually.

KEY TERMS & SKILLS

KEY TERMS

action button (p. 3-16)
annotations (p. 3-8)
hyperlink (p. 3-4)
transitions (p. 3-23)

SKILLS

Add slide transitions (p. 3-23)
Annotate slides during a slide show (p. 3-8)
Copy and duplicate slides (p. 3-9)
Create action buttons (p. 3-16)
Create summary slides (p. 3-14)
Delete slides (p. 3-11)
Hide slides and display hidden slides (p. 3-12)
Rearrange presentation slides using Slide Sorter view (p. 3-9)
Rehearse presentation delivery (p. 3-24)
Set action button actions (p. 3-20)
Set action button hyperlinks (p. 3-20)
Set presentations to run automatically (p. 3-27)
Set slide timings (p. 3-26)
Use mouse and keyboard techniques to navigate a slide show (p. 3-7)
Use the Slide Show shortcut menu (p. 3-7)
View a presentation as a slide show (p. 3-6)

STUDY QUESTIONS

MULTIPLE CHOICE

1. Which view displays miniature images of the slides?
a. Outline view
b. Slide Sorter view
c. Slide view
d. Notes view

2. Which is not a procedure used to launch a slide show?
a. Press F6.
b. Choose **View | Slide Show**.
c. Choose **Slide Show | View Show**.
d. Click the Slide Show button.

3. Which feature would you use to rearrange slides in your presentation?
a. Slide preview
b. Arrange view
c. Slide Sorter
d. View toolbar

4. When you want a slide to appear in more than one position in a presentation, you should
   a. duplicate the slide.
   b. move the slide.
   c. copy the slide.
   d. both a and c

5. Which buttons enable you to control the next slide for PowerPoint to display when you click the button during a slide show?
   a. Superlink buttons
   b. Action buttons
   c. Slide control buttons
   d. Slide show buttons

6. To return to the previous slide in a slide show using the mouse,
   a. left-click and select Previous.
   b. use the left arrow key.
   c. click the left mouse button.
   d. right-click and select Previous.

7. Which menu should you use to display commands for navigating a slide show?
   a. Standard toolbar menu
   b. Slide Show shortcut menu
   c. Navigation menu
   d. Slide Show commands menu

8. Which view should you use to add transition effects to your slides?
   a. Slide Sorter view
   b. Outline view
   c. Slide view
   d. Transition view

9. Which option from the Slide Transition effects list would you choose to make each bulleted list appear with different transition effects?
   a. Many Transitions
   b. Blinds Horizontal
   c. Random Transition
   d. Checkerboard Across

10. To create a type of "introductory" slide to precede a series of related slides, create a(n)
   a. contents slide.
   b. summary slide.
   c. introductory slide.
   d. title slide.

SHORT ANSWER

1. What option is useful to ensure that the audience focuses on you if discussion ensues while presenting a slide show?
2. How can you display hidden slides during a presentation?
3. Why would you want to hide slides in your presentation?
4. How do you add transition effects to a slide?
5. In Slide Sorter view, how will you know which slide is active?
6. What options can you use to stop a slide show?
7. What are the four different techniques you can use to start a Slide Show?
8. How can you advance to the next slide in a slide show using the keyboard?
9. What is the easiest way to insert a slide that you want to appear more than once in a presentation?
10. How do you tell PowerPoint how long to leave a slide on screen during a self-running presentation?

FILL IN THE BLANK

1. Slide Sorter view prevents slide ______________.
2. PowerPoint creates a(n) ______________ to a slide to enable you to jump to a specific area of the presentation.
3. To create a duplicate slide, use the ______________ command.
4. Slide Sorter view displays miniature, or ______________, images of the slides.
5. Use either the keyboard or the______________ to move among slides during a slide show.
6. ______________ slides enable you to include slides to be shown if you need more information or details about a topic.
7. You will find that the ______________ view makes organizing your presentation easier.
8. Viewing your presentation as a(n) ______________ makes it come to life.
9. Slide ______________ create special effects as your slides move on and off screen during a slide show.

    ______________ are drawings made on slides during a slide show.

DISCUSSION

1. List the four ways to launch a slide show.
2. What option allows you to set a presentation to run without interruption, and how do you set the option to view a full screen?
3. Why would you create a summary slide in your presentation?
4. How can you format specific slides in your presentation to jump to specific slides?
5. How can you control which slide appears first during a slide show?

GUIDED EXERCISES

1 PLAYING A SHOW

Remember the lemonade stands you set up when you were kids? Well, the concept of "making lemonade" has changed in recent years. The presentation *Making Lemonade.ppt* provides a good overview of the new meaning attached to the phrase. Follow these steps to view the presentation as a slide show:

1. Open the presentation *Making Lemonade.ppt*.
2. Press F5 to start the presentation as a slide show.
3. Advance through the slides, practicing your navigation techniques to move among presentation slides.
4. Close the presentation after it ends.

2 BACKTRACKING TO THE SUMMARY SLIDE

Now that you have discovered the wonderful advantage offered by hyperlinking action buttons to appropriate slides, you can put the finishing touches on the Marketing Division presentation. Add action buttons to the five division slides that return the viewer to the summary slide. Here's how:

1. Open *e-Selections Marketing Division.ppt* and display Slide 9 in Normal view.
2. Choose **Slide Show | Action Buttons | Action Button: Return** and draw a small button at a convenient location on the slide, displaying the Action Settings dialog box.
3. Select **Slide** from the **Hyperlink to** drop-down list and then select **8 e-Selections Online Divisions**.
4. Click **OK** twice to return to the slide.
5. With the action button selected, click the Copy button.
6. Display Slide 10 and click the Paste button.
7. Repeat the procedures in Step 6 to paste the button on Slides 11 through 13.
8. View the presentation as a slide show and test the action buttons.

9. Save changes to the presentation and e-mail the presentation to your instructor.
10. Close the presentation.

3 PLAYING PRESENTATION ENHANCEMENTS

Adding movies and sounds to presentations enhances the on-screen presence of the slides contained in a presentation. The *e-Selections Media.ppt* presentation contains a number of special features that play during a slide show. Follow these steps to view the presentation and play the enhancements:

1. Open the *e-Selections Media.ppt* presentation.
2. Display Slide 7, start the slide show with Slide 7, and notice that the sound starts playing as soon as the slide appears on screen.
3. Advance through the bullet points of the slide until the next slide appears. Notice that the sound stops when Slide 8 appears.
4. Click the graphic on Slide 8 to play the movie file.
5. Save and close the presentation.

4 PREPARING THE NOTEBOOK PRESENTATION FOR INDIVIDUAL VIEWING

The *e-Selections Notebook.ppt* presentation contains valuable information that employees can reference as needed. The presentation is currently a hodgepodge collection of slides that appear in a completely random order. To make the presentation more useful, Ms. Wright wants you to organize the presentation, create a table of contents for the presentation, and link items on the presentation to the appropriate slide. Before creating the table of contents and hyperlinks, you need to rearrange the slides. Figure 3-33 displays the slide titles in the correct order.

Figure 3-33

e-Selections Employee Handbook
Your Name
General Contents
Handbook Updates
Nature of Employment
Equal Employment Opportunity
Harassment
Three Types of Harassment
Forms of Harassment
Reporting Harassment
Employment Categories
Work Hours and Breaks
Job Transfers
General Attendance Policies
Electronic Technology
Basic Electronic Principles
Payment for Work
Scheduled Holidays

Follow these instructions to complete your task:

1. Open the *e-Selections Notebook.ppt* presentation and switch to Slide Sorter view.
2. Move the slides into the order shown in Figure 3-33.
3. Create a summary slide that displays the titles of Slides 2 through 6 and 10 through 17.

Tip PowerPoint distributes the bulleted-list items on multiple slides when they won't fit comfortably on one slide.

4. Switch to Normal view and display Slide 2.
5. Select the text for the first bulleted-list item (*General Contents*), right-click the selected text, and choose **Hyperlink** to display the Insert Hyperlink dialog box.
6. Click the Place in This Document button on the **Link to** list, select Slide 4, and click **OK**.
7. Repeat the procedures found in Steps 5 and 6 to create hyperlinks for all the other bulleted-list items on Slides 2 and 3.
8. Show the presentation as a slide show and test the hyperlinks.
9. Make the necessary adjustments to the hyperlinks, save the presentation, and pack the presentation to go.

ON YOUR OWN

The difficulty of these case studies varies:
are the least difficult; *are more difficult; and* *are the most difficult.*

1 PLAYING A PRESENTATION

Ms. Wright has asked you to review the *e-Selections Web Online.ppt* presentation and determine what links to add to slides in the presentation to make navigating to topics easy. Open the presentation and display it as a slide show. Make notes about what links would help viewers navigate the presentation to access the topic they want to view. Type the action button notes in the Notes pane for the slides to which you plan to add the action buttons. Then print a copy of the Note Pages containing the information. Save changes to the presentation.

2 SUMMARIZING THE CATALOG

The *e-Selections Web Online.ppt* presentation contains separate "catalog" pages for each of the online divisions. Create a summary slide that summarizes the various presentation slides listing items for sale at each division. Print a copy of the summary slide and save changes to the presentation.

3 SCHEDULING A TOUR

The travel club at your university is planning a series of tours next year and they have asked you to create a presentation that they can place on the Web to provide information for those interested in joining one of the tours. Your task is to define the structure for the presentation and create the needed slides and hyperlinks. The list of tours appears in Figure 3-34.

Figure 3-34

Travel Club Tours

Alaska, Land of Enchantment

Australia, Land Down Under

Greece and the Floating Islands

Spain and Portugal, Europe's Playground

Vive la France!

The British Isles in Springtime

Create a new presentation named *Your University Next Year Travel Club Tours.* Then create separate slides for each of the tours listed in Figure 3-34. Apply an appropriate template to the presentation and create a summary slide that links each bulleted-list item to the corresponding tour slide. Save changes to the presentation and e-mail the presentation to your instructor.

4 SEARCHING THE WEB FOR INFO

The *Making Lemonade.ppt* presentation contains information about a popular writer but fails to divulge the name of this writer. Search the Internet using information provided in the presentation until you can identify the writer. Then add the writer's name to the final slide in the presentation and list one other famous work by the writer. Save changes to the presentation and print a copy of the last presentation slide.

5 DINING SOUTHERN STYLE

From North Carolina to Florida and across the southern United States to California, you'll find some of the most unique cuisine anywhere. Dishes range from traditional southern fried chicken and spicy Creole dishes of south Louisiana to southwestern Mexican fare and even Asian cuisine. The *Southern Cuisine.ppt* presentation contains slides that describe a number of different types of cuisine. Your task is to arrange the slides in order by the type of food or the restaurant they describe. Then create a new slide that appears after the title slide and lists the different types of foods/restaurants described in the presentation. Then create summary slides for each type of food/restaurant in the newly created list slide. Link bulleted-list items on each summary slide to the specific food/restaurant slides. Finally, create hyperlinks from the new slide at the beginning of the presentation that accesses appropriate summary slides. When you're finished, you should have a presentation that enables the viewer to select a specific food type on Slide 2 that links to the food type/restaurant summary slide. From the food type/restaurant summary slide, the viewer can then access a specific slide. Save changes to the presentation and pack the presentation to go.

6 BUILDING A GAME SHOW

The game show craze continues to infiltrate countries all over the world. One of the most popular game shows in recent years is *Who Wants to be a Millionaire* with host Regis Philbin. The structure of the question and answer sequence from the show is easy to emulate using PowerPoint and setting action buttons. Create a new presentation that contains at least three slides: one slide to contain the question and four possible answers related to PowerPoint, one slide to indicate a wrong answer, and one slide to indicate the correct answer. Add action buttons that properly hyperlink among the slides. Then arrange the items on the question slide so that it appears as shown on the sample slides in Figure 3-35. Apply a template to the presentation, download appropriate graphics from the Internet to format your slides, or create the graphic using PowerPoint tools. When you're finished, save the presentation using the file name *<Your Initials> Game Show Craze*. Send the presentation to your instructor.

Figure 3-35

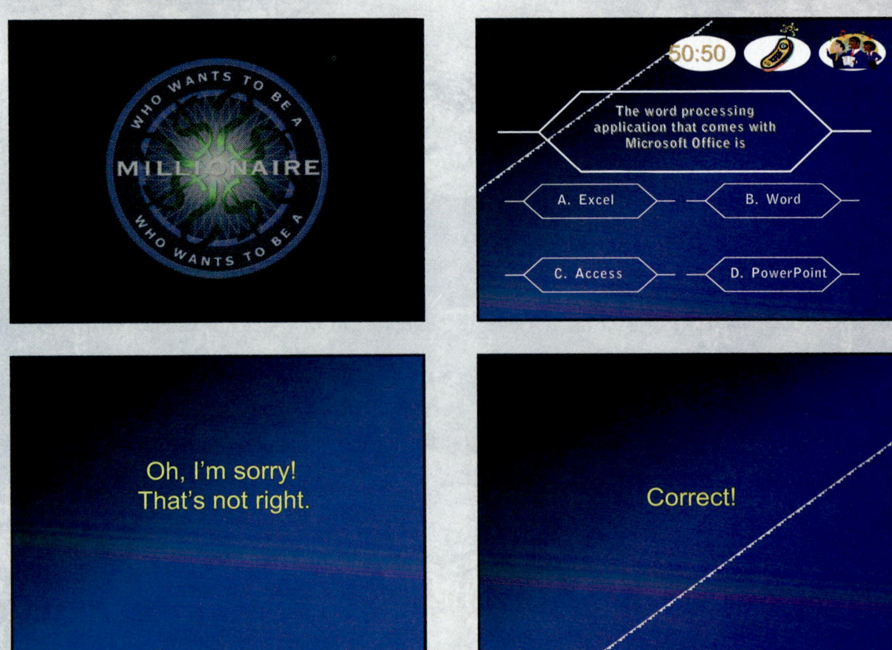

Photospread credits pages 3-2 & 3-3

©CORBIS, ©R.W. Jones/CORBIS; ©Tony Stone: ©Chuck Keeler; ©Pearson Education, ©Lorraine Castellano

FROM THE FILES

You Will Need

- ✔ e-Selections Employee Guide.ppt
- ✔ e-Selections Web.ppt
- ✔ Travel Tours.ppt
- ✔ Selections Overview.ppt
- ✔ Cuisine of the Southern US.ppt

PROJECT 4

Working with Visual Elements

PowerPoint visual elements extend beyond projecting presentations from a computer onto a screen. Special tools in PowerPoint now make sharing presentations via the Web easier than ever. Enhancements made to many of PowerPoint's advanced tools will have you sending out presentations for review and compiling reviewer comments as well as broadcasting presentations much more frequently. In this project, you explore these extended capabilities by saving presentations as Web pages, publishing them to the Web, broadcasting presentations on an Intranet, and compiling comments from presentation reviewers.

OBJECTIVES

After completing this project, you will be able to:

- *Save presentations as Web pages*
- *Publish presentations*
- *Set up a presentation review cycle*
- *Send presentations for review*
- *Compile reviewer comments*
- *Work with presentation broadcasts*

e-selections Running Case

The features you are discovering in PowerPoint 2002 seem unending. You've just been asked to format a presentation for the Web, send out two of the presentations to a number of other e-Selections employees, and combine the reviewers' comments and edits with your original so that Ms. Wright can review them and make the final edits to the presentations. At first, these tasks may seem overwhelming, but you're about to discover some PowerPoint features that will help.

Weaving eMeetings on the Web

A new concept for bringing people from all over the world together for a meeting has evolved into a new millennium approach where no one leaves home but where everyone is able to attend the same presentation at the same time. This new concept is known as an eMeeting—or electronic meeting. Thanks to Internet technology and a few key visionary companies, it is now possible for businesses to share information with everyone in their company—no matter where—in a fast, more convenient, less expensive communication environment. eMeetings are fascinating to new users. Here's how they work...

The Networked eMeetings

Two companies—one a pioneer in multimedia projectors, and the other an industry leader in advanced teleconferencing solutions—share a vision of combining their two technologies to create the ultimate networked meeting. They call their concept *eMeetings*. EMeetings are not only user-friendly but also have significantly more impact and are much less expensive than traditional meetings that require people to be flown in from all over the country.

The eMeeting concept simply requires a projector developed by one company, Web-based meeting and presentation hardware from the other company, and a full-duplex teleconferencing system.

With these new eMeeting solutions, companies can arrange internal or external Microsoft PowerPoint presentations over IP (Internet Protocol). The presenter merely feeds a PowerPoint presentation into the system connected to a host server, and uses a user-friendly remote-control device to cycle through the slides as usual. The attendees, using a Web browser, connect to the meeting by logging in to the IP address, and along with the telephone audio, are now ready to receive the visual as well as audio presentation.

Companies that use eMeetings frequently purchase the Web-based meeting and presentation hardware, so they do not have to pay a "per-use" fee. Companies that use eMeetings less frequently can "rent" space on which to host an Internet meeting.

<internet protocol>

A New Solution

eMeetings now enable an entire group to convene virtually. Playing the presentation through a projector for full-screen projection can expand collaborative group meetings. The only limitation to attendance is the size of the room. Interactive conversations occur via the telephone connection. Using this eMeeting solution, up to 25 simultaneous sites—either individual or meeting room nodes—can be logged on and participate in the information exchange. Each presentation in the eMeeting model can have a moderator or team leader organizing the session and making sure participants are logged in and running smoothly.

With additional videoconferencing components an eMeeting can successfully display both video and data seamlessly. With new video and audio streaming technologies enabled by increased bandwidth, new products will continue to emerge that allow for a fully-integrated, Web-based eMeeting.

This integrated approach presents an entirely new solution for corporate presenters, trainers, educators, resellers and others who want to increase retention, improve interaction and build teamwork. Tools such as digital projectors, teleconferencing stations, and eMeeting hardware are destined to be key convergence tools for the new millennium way of doing business.

An ambitious goal of eMeeting producers is to make their solutions part of the basic toolkit for virtual presenters. Companies with the vision and determination to join the eMeeting revolution are already leading the way.

PROJECT 4

Working with Visual Elements

The Challenge

Many of the presentations on which you have been working will eventually be placed on the e-Selections Web site. Looking ahead, Ms. Wright has asked you to format the presentations for the Web so that she can review them and see how they will appear on the Web. In addition, she would like to have the contents of the presentations reviewed before finalizing the presentations. After she receives feedback and comments from the reviewers, she would like to hold an online discussion about the presentations.

The Solution

The Web formatting and broadcasting tools found in PowerPoint make Ms. Wright's requests much easier to complete. You will be able to save the presentations as Web pages, send the presentations for review, and schedule an online broadcast using features built into PowerPoint. Figure 4-1 displays the title page for the *e-Selections Employee Guide.ppt* presentation. The title page is shown as it would appear formatted for the Web.

Figure 4-1

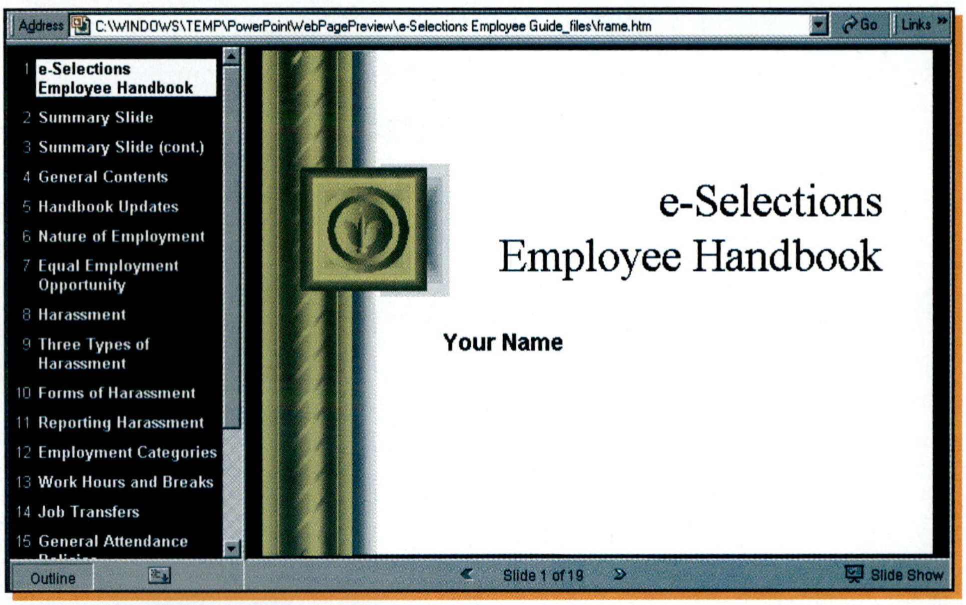

Saving Presentations as Web Pages

Each of the Office XP applications contains commands for saving files as Web pages. This feature makes converting your presentation to a format that can be displayed on the World Wide Web a snap! When you save a presentation as a Web page, PowerPoint creates a new folder in which it stores the slides and any other files required for displaying the presentation on the Web.

Tip To prevent unwanted loss of data, it's a good idea to save new presentations as PowerPoint files before you save them as Web pages.

Task 1:
To Save a Presentation as a Web Page

1. Open the *e-Selections Employee Guide.ppt* presentation.

2. Choose **File | Save as Web Page**.

Troubleshooting
If you have no access to the Internet from the computer you are using, the Save as Web Page option may be unavailable. Follow the direction of your instructor to proceed.

Figure 4-2

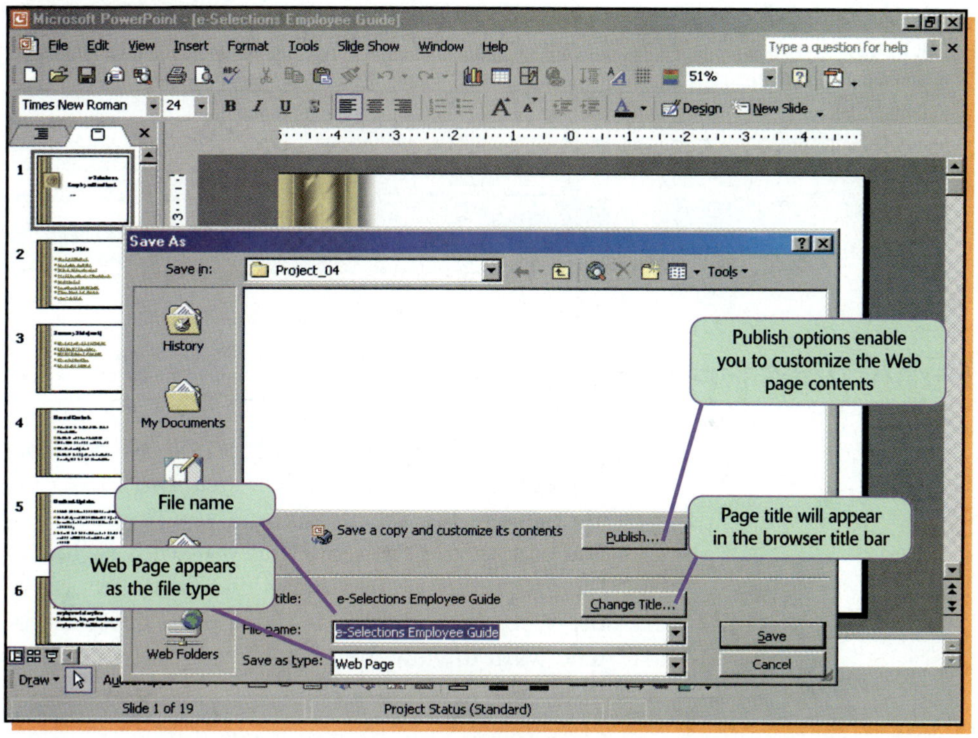

Tip The title that appears in the Page Title area appears at the top of the browser window when you view the file using a Web browser. It has no affect on the presentation contents or file name.

3. Click **Change Title**.

4. Type e-Selections Employee Guide as the Web page title, if necessary, and click **OK**.

5. Open the folder in which you want to save the Web page, if necessary, and then click Save.

Tip PowerPoint saves the file as a Web page, but the presentation appears unchanged in the PowerPoint window. PowerPoint saves the new file with an .htm extension.

Figure 4-3

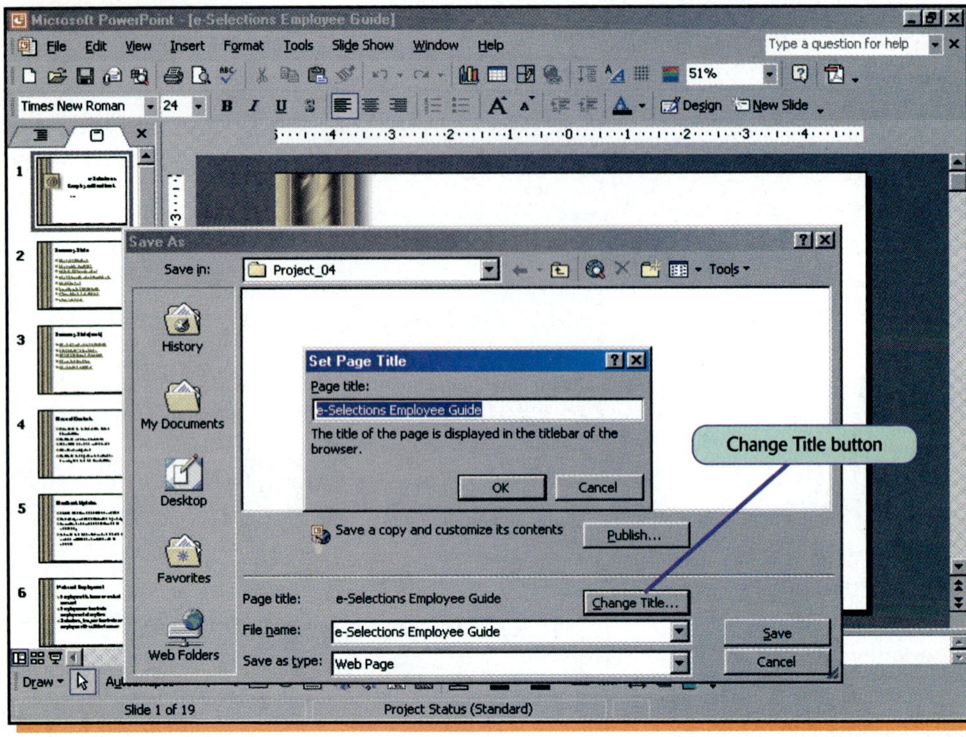

Publishing Presentations

Options available in the Publish dialog box enable you to publish copies of a presentation at different Web locations, save only selected slides as a Web page, and set the browser for which you are formatting the Web page. In addition, you can set the elements that you want included on the Web when you publish the presentation. To *publish presentations* to the Web, you must have access to the Web site to which you are publishing the presentation. In addition, those who want to view the presentation must also have access to the Web site.

Task 2:
To Publish a Presentation

1. Open the *e-Selections Employee Guide.htm* file and choose **File | Save As**. The Save As dialog box displays the same options that are displayed when saving Web pages.

2. Click **Publish** to open the Publish as Web Page dialog box and set the options identified in Figure 4-4.

3. Type C:\Temp\e-Selections Guide or the location identified by your instructor in the **File name** field, select the **Open published Web page in browser** option.

4. Click **Web Options** and select the **Show slide animation while browsing** option.

Troubleshooting
Because installations on lab computers vary, your instructor may have you set additional options. Follow the direction of your instructor before continuing.

Tip If time permits, examine the options available on each page of the Web Options dialog box. Knowing the options you can set may prove useful in the future.

Figure 4-4

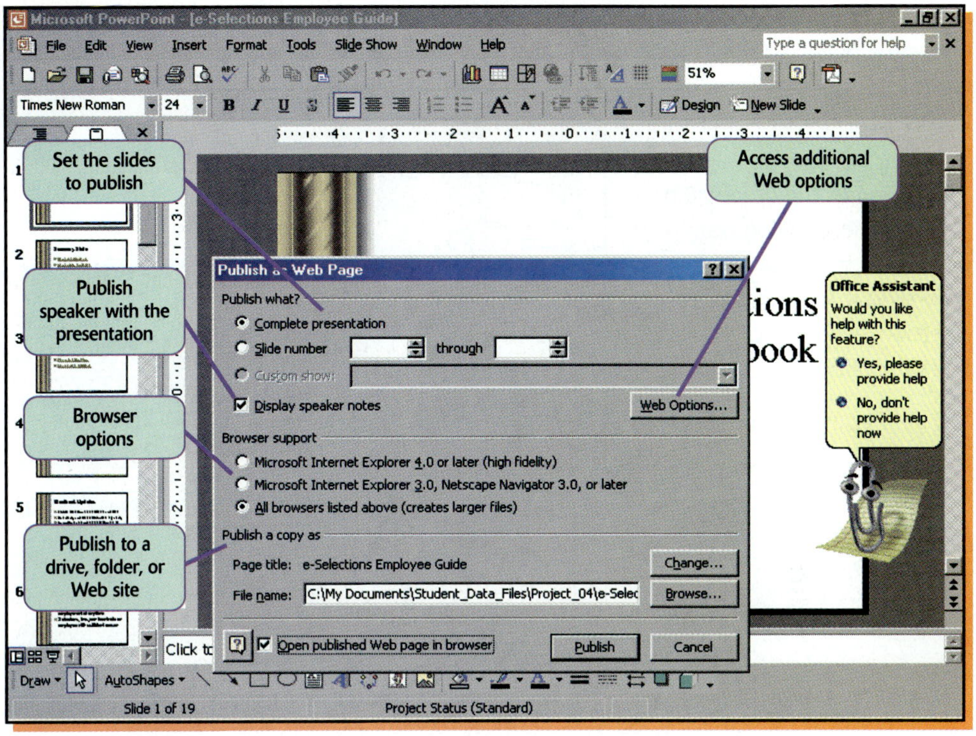

Figure 4-5

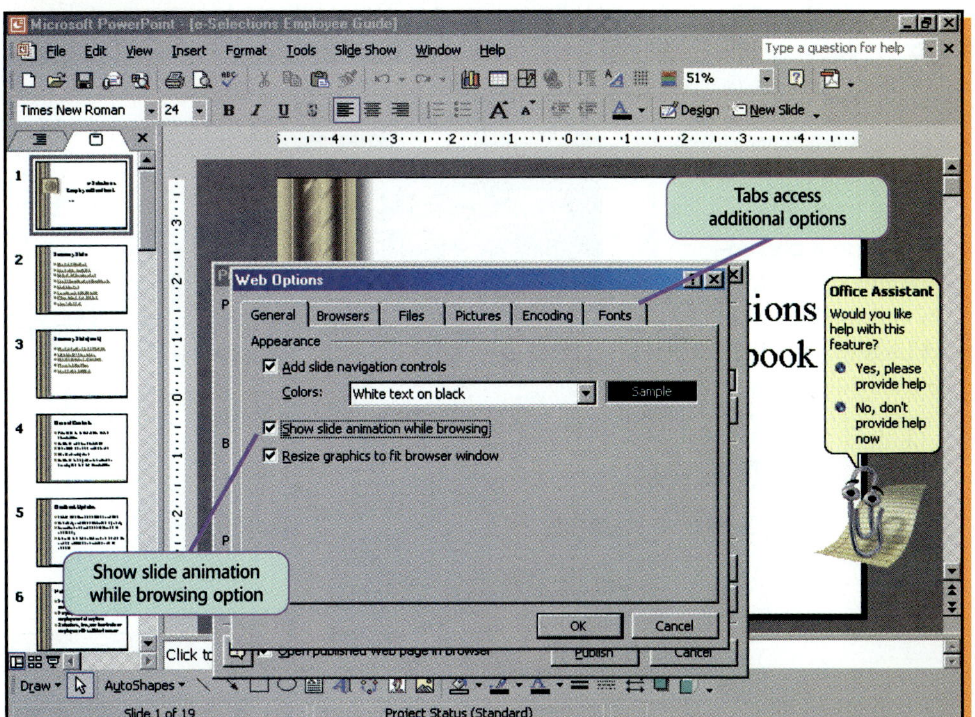

5 Click the **Browsers** tab and select **Microsoft Internet Explorer 4.0, Netscape Navigator 4.0, or later** from the Target Browsers drop-down list.

6 Review the other Web Options dialog box pages, set the options according to your instructor's direction, and then click **OK** and click Publish.

Figure 4-6

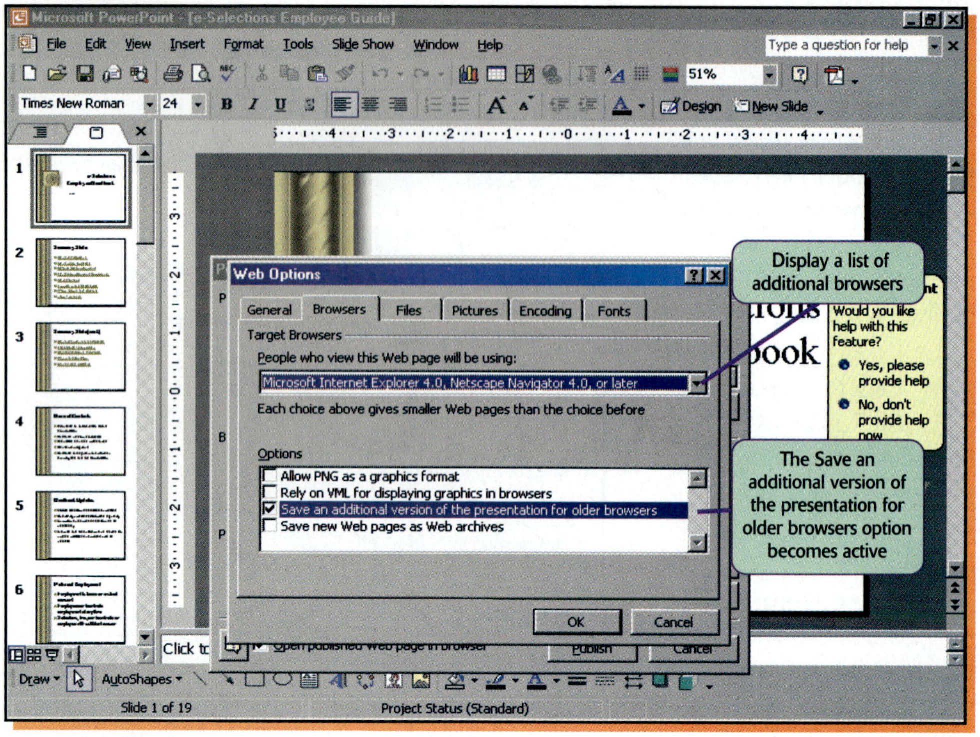

7 Close the browser window and close the presentation.

Figure 4-7

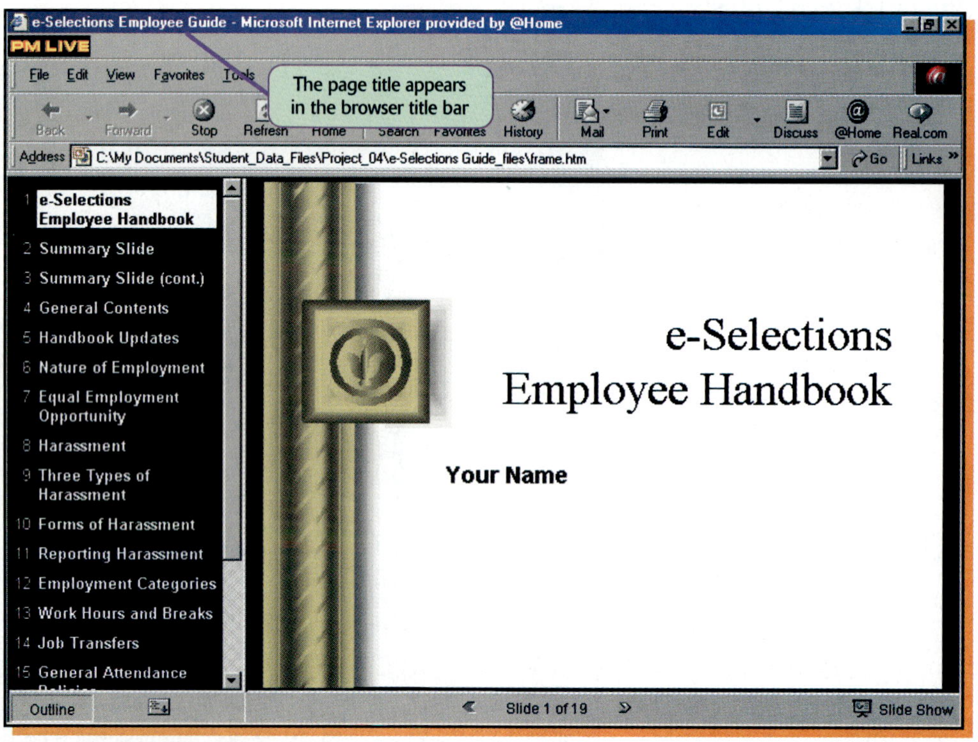

WEB TIP

If you have access rights to save and edit files on real Web sites, try publishing a presentation to the Web site. Then e-mail the site address to your friends so that they can see the work you're doing.

Setting Up a Presentation Review Cycle

PowerPoint features streamline the process of sending a presentation to other users for review. You can, in fact, send the presentation to reviewers and then combine the comments and edits from all reviewers with your original presentation before reviewing the changes and deciding which changes to implement.

Sending Presentations for Review

Troubleshooting
If you are using a program other than Outlook as your e-mail program, some of these options available may be unavailable. Follow the direction of your instructor to proceed.

PowerPoint offers two different techniques for distributing presentations for review:

- Distribute the presentations to single or multiple reviewers via Outlook e-mail so that all reviewers receive their own copy of the presentation at the same time, review and edit the presentation, and return the edited presentation to you.
- *Route* the presentation using Outlook e-mail from one recipient to another so that each reviewer adds edits and comments to the same copy of the presentation. Routing the presentation to reviewers one after another lets each reviewer see the edits and comments made by those who have already reviewed the presentation and reduces the redundancy of the edits.

You can use both of these techniques to distribute the presentations Ms. Wright wants reviewed.

Task 3: To E-Mail Presentations for Review

1. Open the *e-Selections Employee Guide.ppt* presentation.

2. Choose **File | Send To | Mail Recipient (for Review)**.

Troubleshooting
If Outlook Express is installed on your computer and you are using an e-mail program other than Outlook, Outlook Express may launch when you complete Step 2. Follow the direction of your instructor to proceed.

Figure 4-8

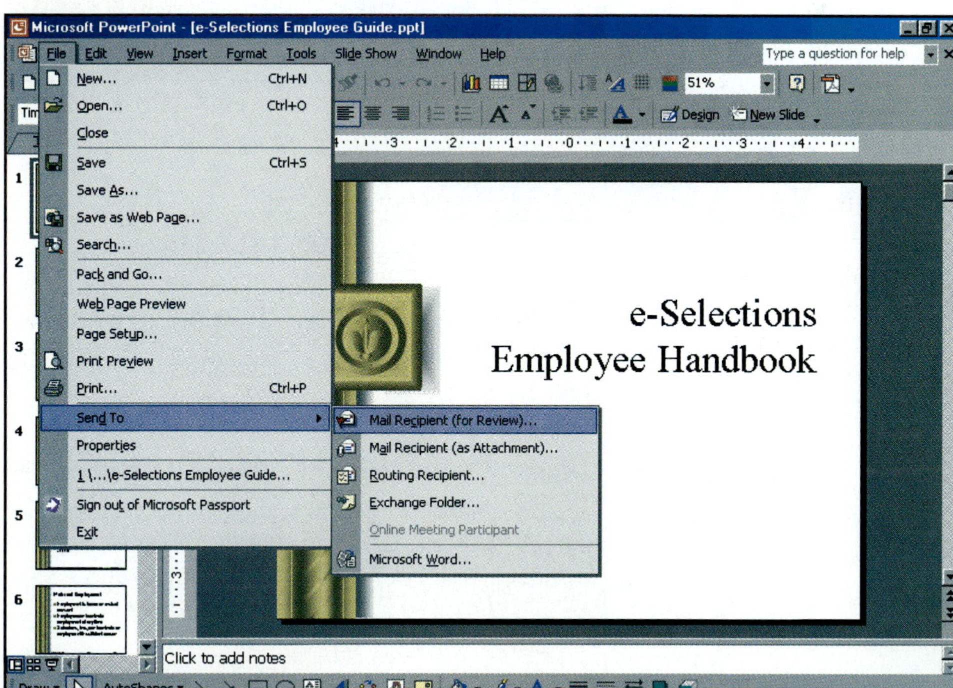

3 Obtain the e-mail address of another student and address the message to the student, your instructor, and yourself.

4 Type the following message in the message area:
Please review the presentation for format and feature placement. Make any necessary edits and suggestions directly on the presentation file and return the edited file to me.

5 Click **Send** and close the presentation. Outlook distributes a copy of the presentation to each person.

Figure 4-9

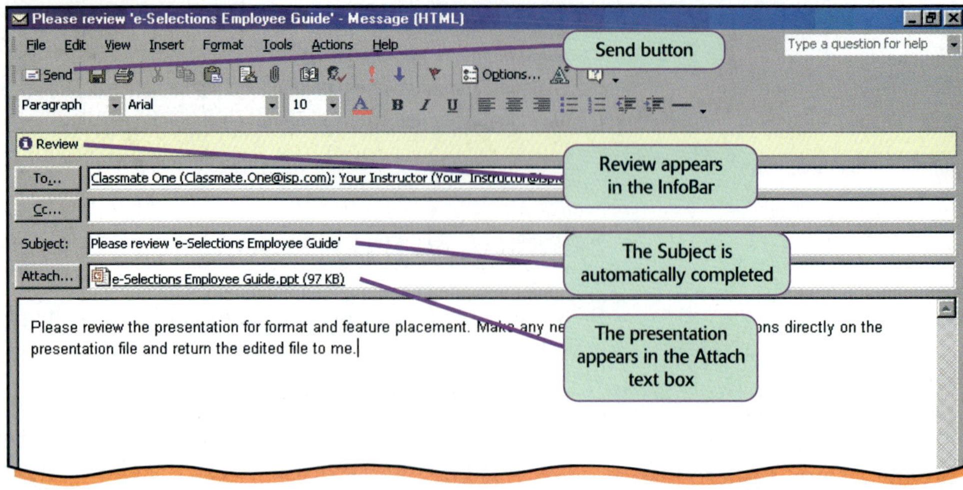

Troubleshooting As you work between PowerPoint and Outlook, a Microsoft Outlook message might appear advising you that another program is trying to access your Outlook address book. This message is designed to prevent unauthorized users from accessing your Outlook address book. Because you are the person accessing the address book, click Yes to close the message when it appears.

Tip You can also save the copies of the presentation to a public folder and then send each reviewer a message that identifies the name of the file each reviewer should review. In addition, you can copy each reviewer's file to a floppy disk and distribute each disk to the appropriate reviewer.

CHECK POINT

If you are using an e-mail program other than Microsoft Outlook, you need to approach the task of sending presentations for review a bit differently. Save a separate copy of the presentation for each reviewer so that:

- The reviewer name is part of the file name.
- The Save as type is Presentation for Review.
- All reviewer copies are saved in the same folder.

Send separate e-mail messages to each reviewer and attach each reviewer's copy of the presentation to be reviewed along with a request that they review the presentation and return their edited copy to you.

Task 4:

To Route Presentations for Review

1. Open the *e-Selections Web.ppt* presentation.

2. Choose **File | Send To | Routing Recipient**.

3. Click **Address**.

> **Troubleshooting**
> As you work between PowerPoint and Outlook, a Microsoft Outlook message might appear advising you that another program is trying to access your Outlook address book. This message is designed to prevent unauthorized users from accessing your Outlook address book. Because you are the person accessing the address book, click Yes to close the message when it appears.

4. Select one of the names in the **Name** list, press Ctrl and select your instructor's name, and then click **To**. Selected names and e-mail addresses appear in the list on the right in the order in which you selected them.

5. Click **OK**.

Figure 4-10

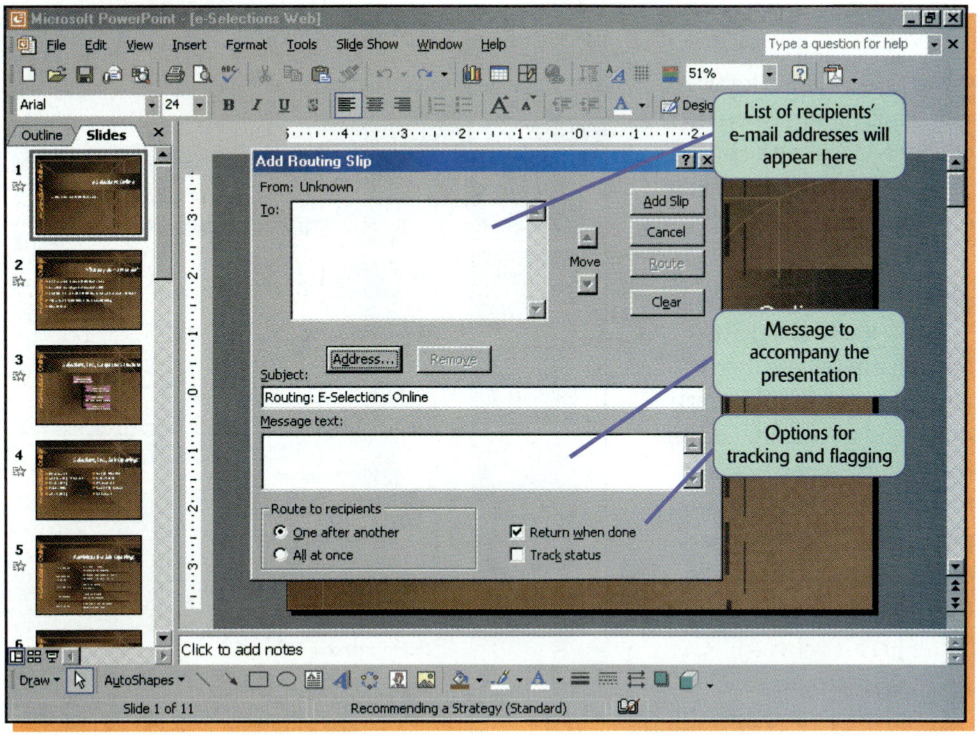

Figure 4-11

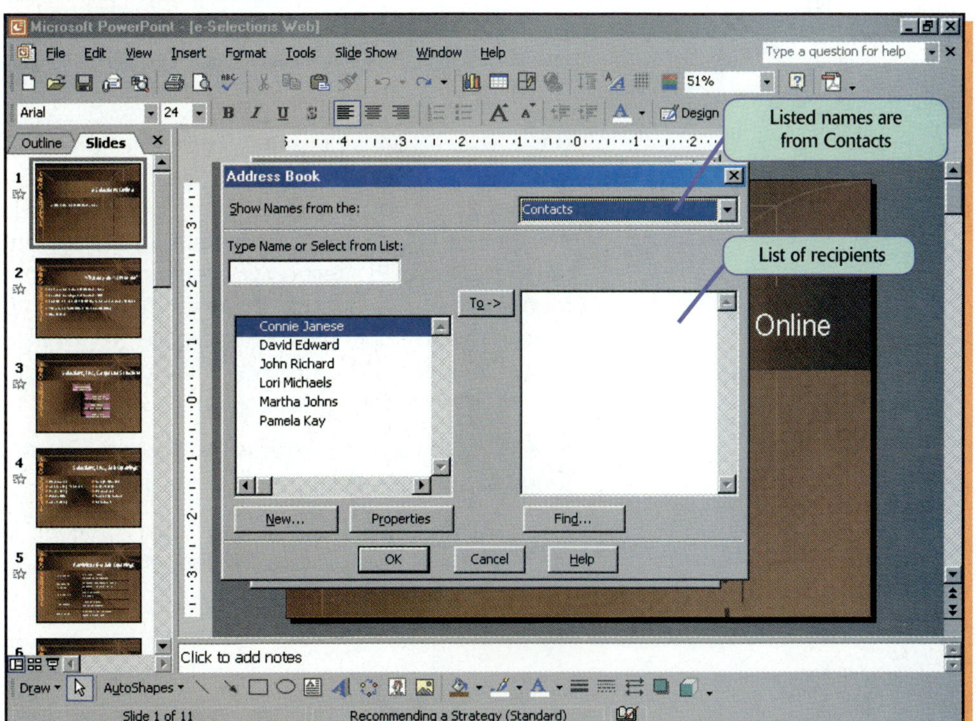

6 Select the first person listed in the **To** list and click the **Move** down arrow.

7 Select the **Track status** and **Return when done** options and make sure that you have the **One after another** routing option selected.

8 Type the following text in the **Message text** box: **Please review the attached presentation and make any necessary edits or comments. When you are finished with your review, please save your changes and route this message to the next recipient.**

9 Click **Route**, save changes and then close the presentation.

Figure 4-12

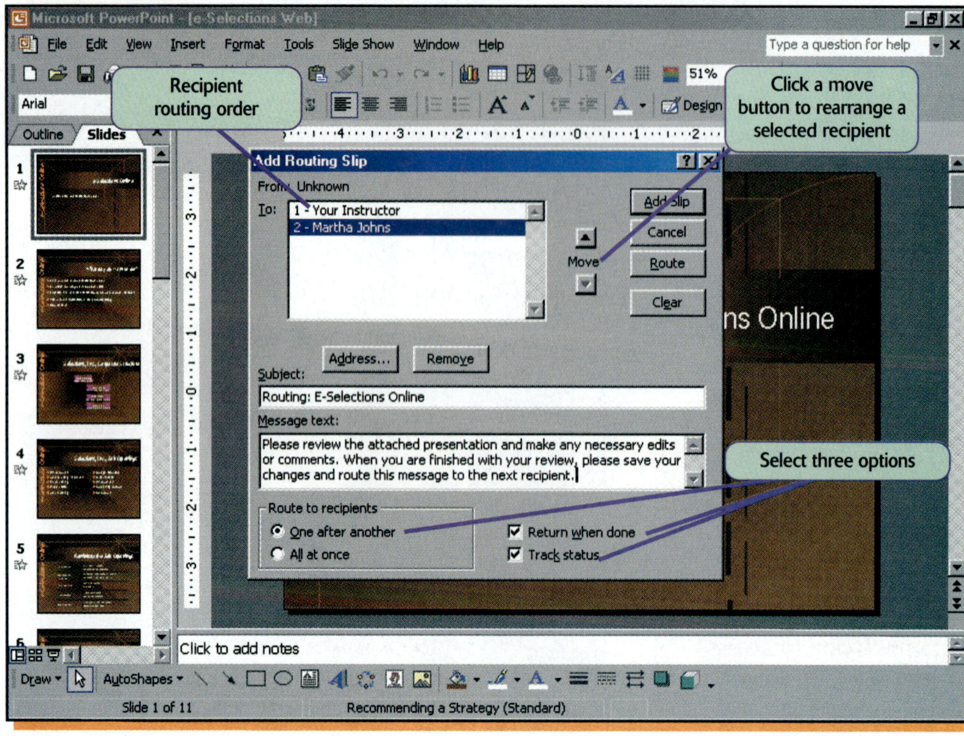

Tip

The routing slip is saved with the presentation so that you can check the presentation to see a list of those you included in the presentation routing. The routing process can take quite a long time to complete.

CHECK POINT

When you receive a presentation file that someone has asked you to review, your task is to edit the file, insert comments, and then return the edited file to the original sender or pass it along to the next routing recipient so that your edits and opinions can be considered in finalizing the presentation. The message to which the presentation is attached will contain a statement telling you that there is a routing slip attached to the message. As a result, you can simply double-click the attachment and open it. Then make the necessary edits, save changes, and close the presentation. When you close the presentation, a message appears that asks if you want to send the presentation on to the next recipient.

If you click **No** when this message appears, you should choose **File | Send To | Original Sender** (or appropriate selection).

If you use an e-mail program other than Outlook, you should open and edit the file that you've been asked to review, save changes to the file, and then notify the author that you have completed your review and attach the edited copy of the presentation, if appropriate.

Combining Edited Presentations with the Original

After they have completed their reviews and saved their edits, reviewers return edited copies of the presentation to you. In most cases, regardless of what e-mail program the reviewer used to return the presentation, the edited presentation appears as an attachment to the e-mail message. When you receive messages to which the reviewer has attached a presentation, you should save each reviewed copy of the presentation using a unique file name and then merge the presentation with your original copy. Each reviewer's edits are identified by color-coded markers that display a short description of the change when you point to them. PowerPoint even identifies conflicting edits!

Task 5:
To Combine Reviewed Presentations with the Original

1. Open the e-mail messages from your instructor that have *Edited PowerPoint Presentation* and *PowerPoint Edits* as their subjects.
2. Save the presentation attached to each message in the folder identified by your instructor.
3. Open your original copy of the *e-Selections Employee Guide.ppt* presentation.
4. Choose **Tools** | **Compare and Merge Presentations.**

Figure 4-13

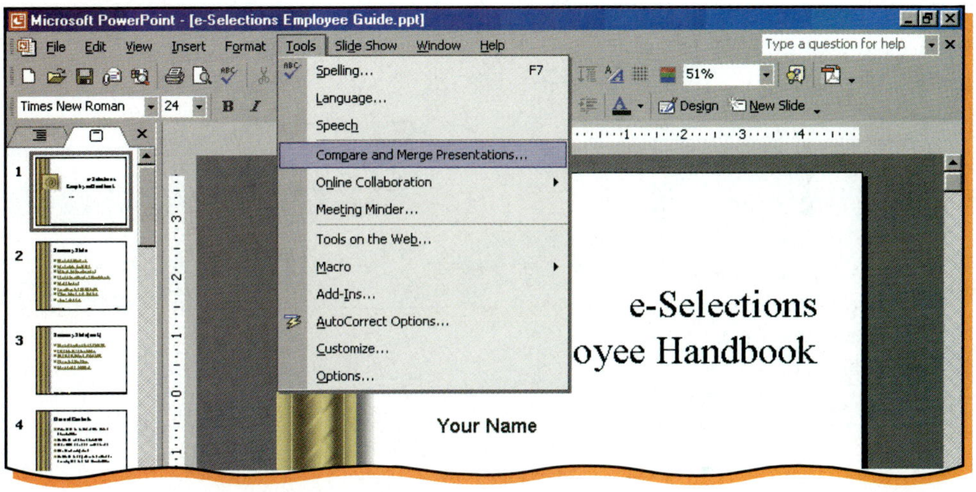

Troubleshooting The e-mail attachments sent to you by the instructor are numbered to make them easy to differentiate when you save them. Saving reviewed files in the same folder is good file management practice. Because files stored in the same folder require unique file names, numbering the attachments as you receive them is a good way to maintain the original file name and yet make each file name unique. Adding the reviewer's initials to the file name is also a good way to differentiate presentations.

5 Select the *1 e-Selections Employee Guide.ppt* and *2 e-Selections Employee Guide.ppt* files.

Tip To select multiple files, press and hold Ctrl as you click each file name.

6 Click **Merge** to add reviewer comments and edits contained in the two files to your original presentation file.

Tip PowerPoint marks each reviewer's comments using a different color so that you can tell which reviewer made each change or added a comment.

Figure 4-14

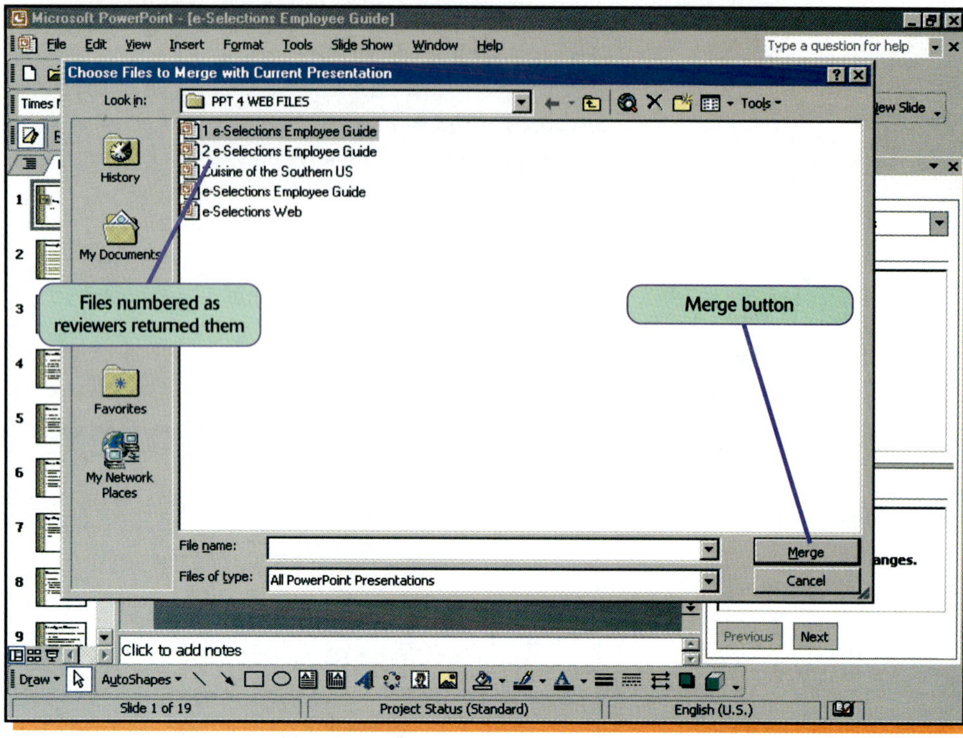

7 Point to the Comment icon on the slide.

8 Click **Next** at the bottom of the Revisions Pane.

Troubleshooting

Because the icons on the Reviewing toolbar are different from most Next and Previous icons, point to each button on the toolbar and review the screen tip until you locate the appropriate button.

Figure 4-15

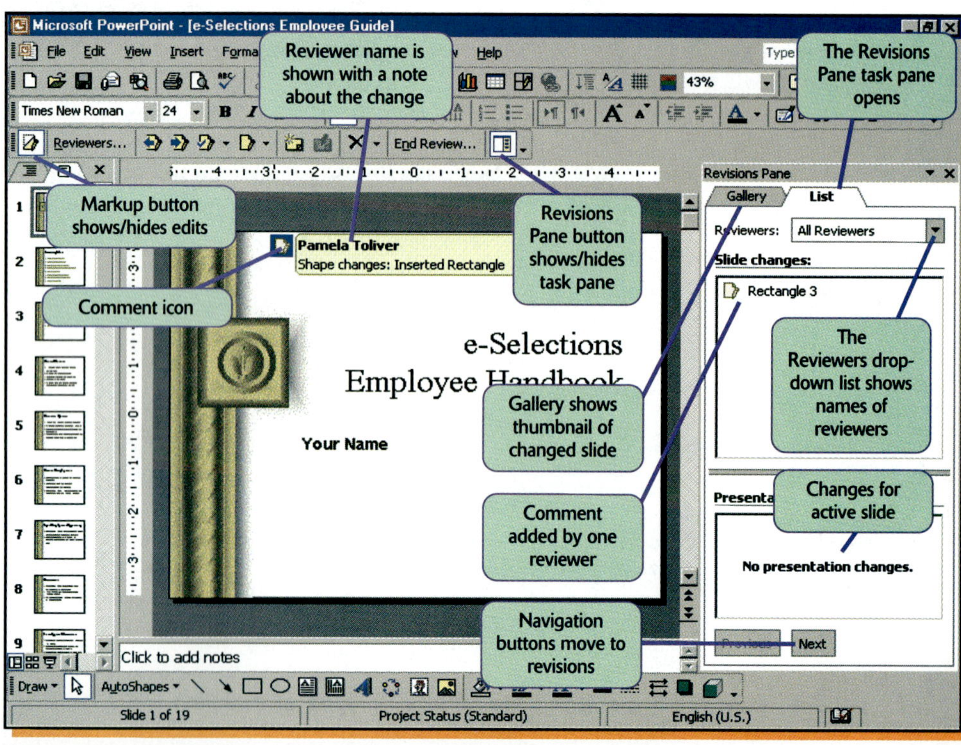

9 Point to the **Edit** icon and review the change.

Tip Three points of spacing equals only 1/4 line. While this may seem to be very little spacing, it serves to set off the paragraph appropriately.

10 Click **Next** and continue to review changes made by different reviewers until you reach the last edit.

11 Save the merged presentations using the file name *Merged Guide*.

Figure 4-16

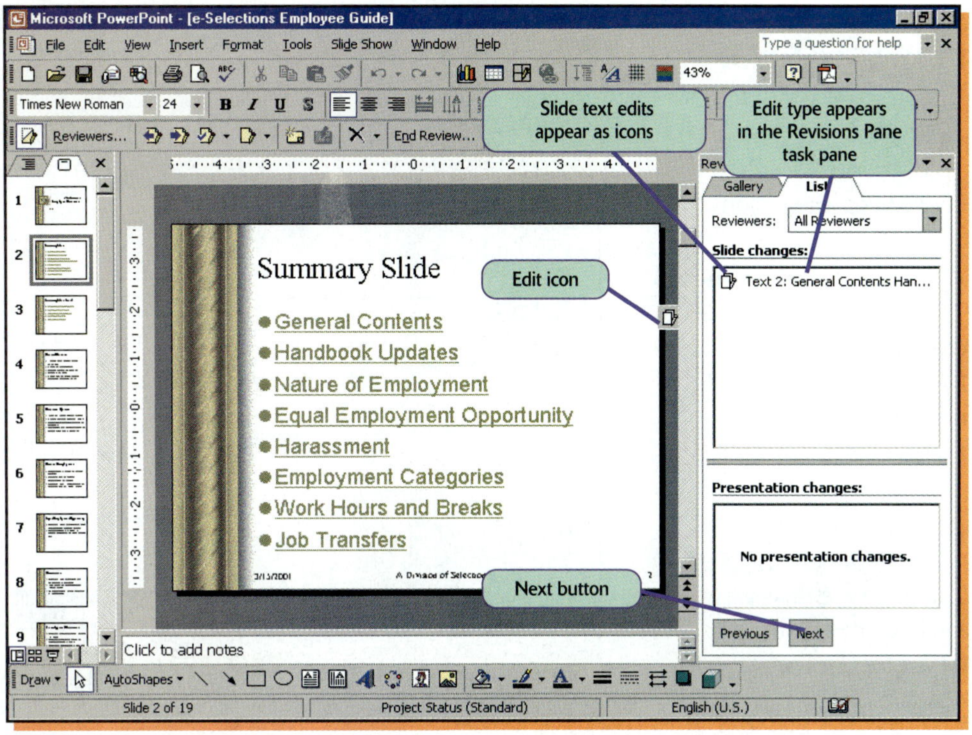

Accepting and Rejecting Reviewer Changes

As you review the changes, you decide which changes you want to incorporate and those that you want to ignore or discard. After you have completed your review and have accepted or rejected all edits, you can save changes to the presentation.

Tip The name of the Delete button on the Reviewing toolbar changes, depending on the type of change made to the slide. Sometimes the button name shown on the screen tip is Delete Marker and at other times the name shown on the screen tip is Delete Comment.

Task 6:

To Review, Accept, and Reject Reviewer Edits

1. Display Slide 1 of the merged *Merged Guide.ppt* presentation.

2. Select the **Rectangle 3** item listed in the Slide changes area of the Revisions Pane task pane. Figure 4-17 identifies different ways to accept or reject the edit.

3. Click the Delete Comment button on the Reviewing toolbar. The comment marker disappears from the slide.

4. Display Slide 2, click the edit marker, and then point to the edited text.

Figure 4-17

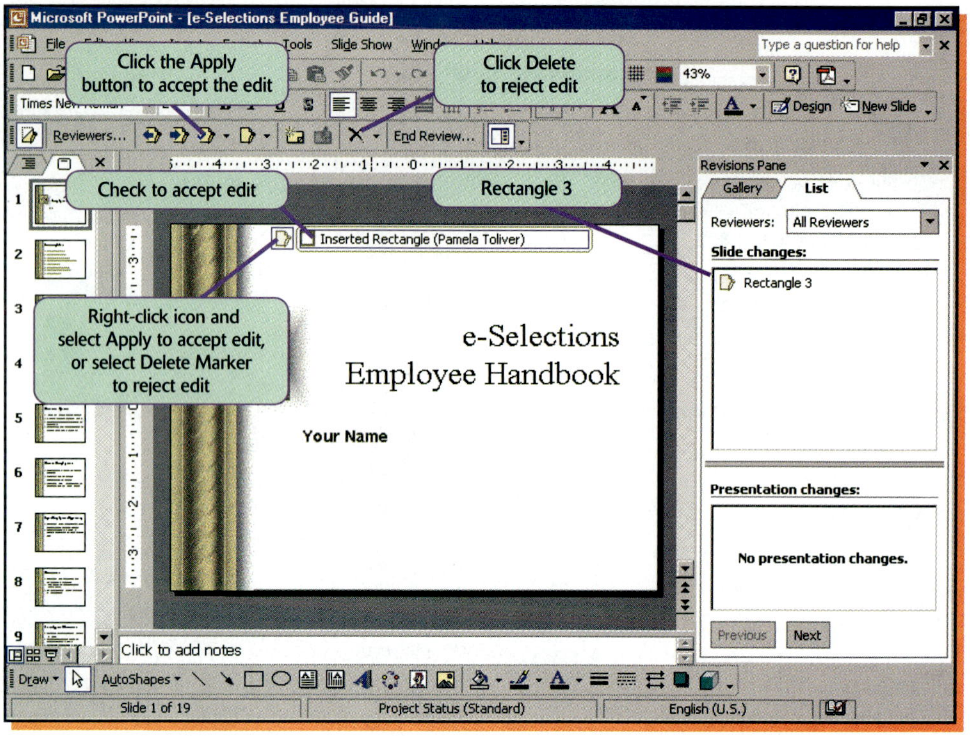

Figure 4-18

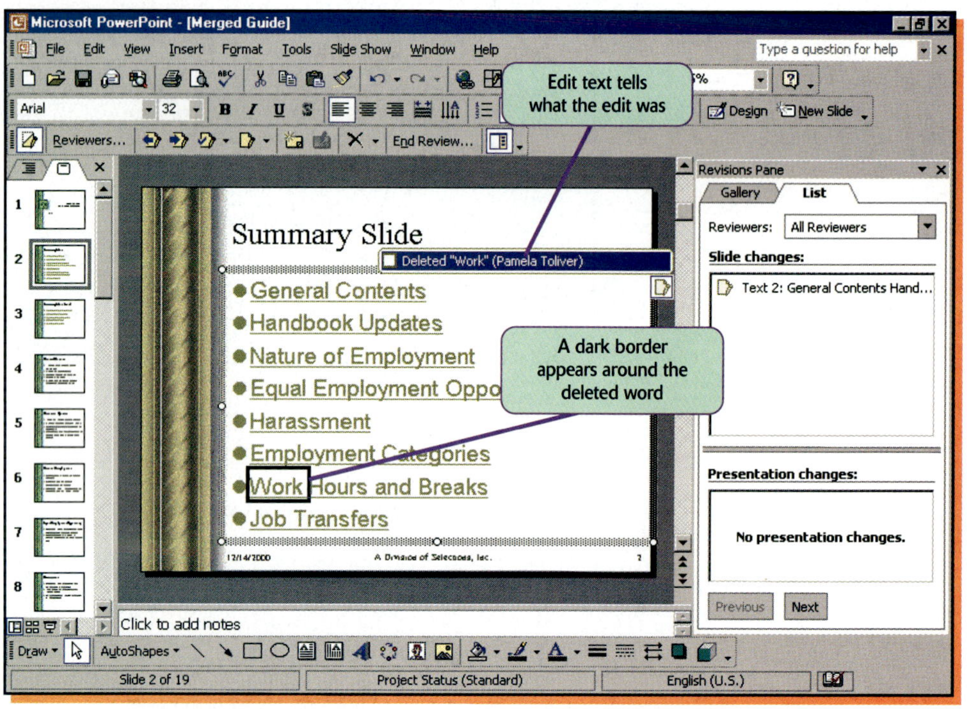

5 Click the Delete Comment button and display Slide 5.

Tip Notice the two different icon colors for comments and changes listed in the task pane? Each color identifies a comment or edit added by a separate reviewer. To determine which color is associated with each reviewer, click the Reviewers button on the Reviewing toolbar and review the list of reviewers.

Figure 4-19

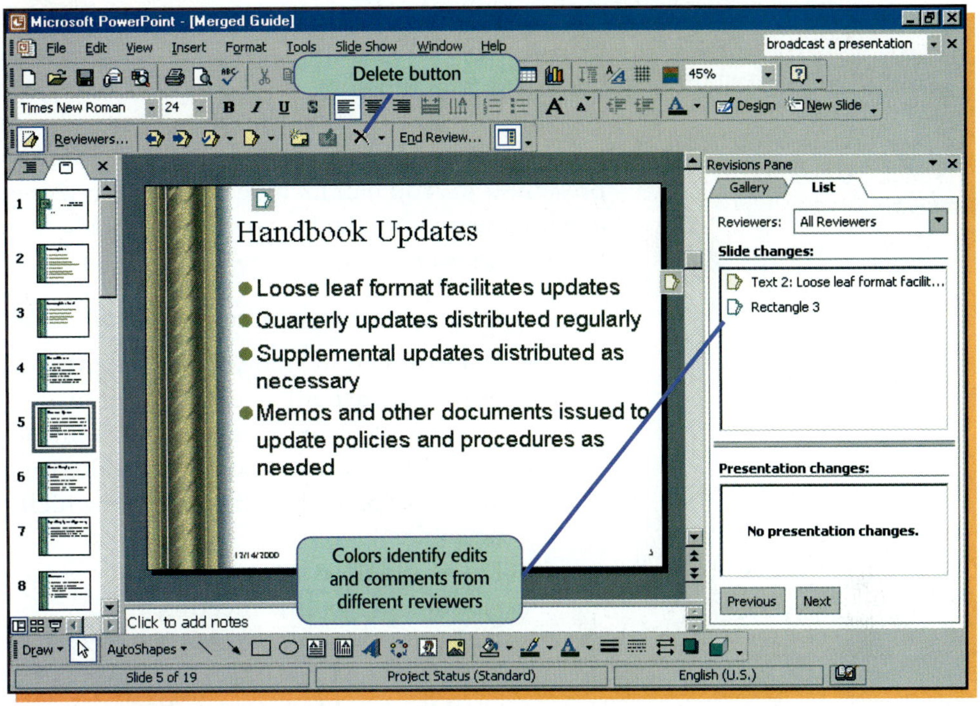

6 Select the **Text 2** item and then click the Apply button on the Reviewing toolbar.

7 Review all other changes and reject them.

8 Save changes to the presentation and close it.

Figure 4-20

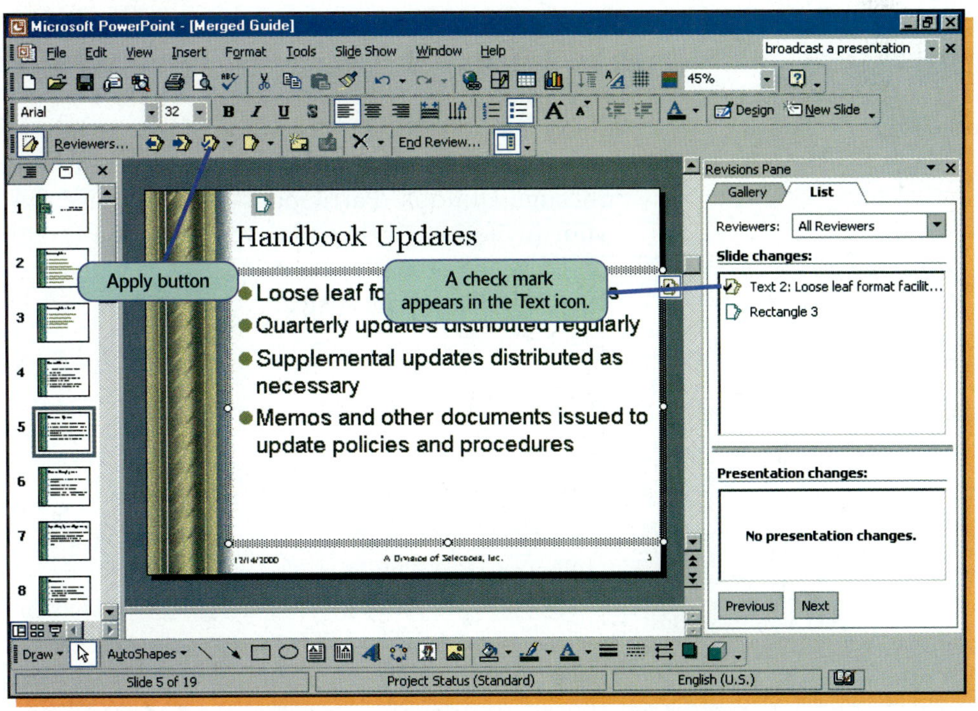

Setting Up and Scheduling an Online Broadcast

Troubleshooting
Online broadcast features are NOT designed to deliver LIVE online broadcasts over the Internet.

Broadcasting presentations is a feature that is unique to PowerPoint. Broadcasting presentations enables you to conduct an online presentation, save the broadcast, and store it where others can access and view the presentation. Those who want to view the broadcast live must have access to the intranet server (as opposed to an Internet site) from which you are broadcasting the presentation. You can include audio input using microphones and video input using cameras attached to your computers. When the broadcast is complete, PowerPoint saves it as a video file that you can open and review later.

Before setting up and scheduling a *presentation broadcast*, consider the following:

- Determine how many computers the participants who take part in the broadcast will use. Standard broadcast procedures restrict the number of computers that can connect to a LIVE broadcast to 10.
- Identify a *shared* location—a folder on an intranet server to which all participants have access—on which to store the presentation, if possible.
- Use Outlook to set up and schedule an online broadcast just as you would other online meetings.
- If the presentation you plan to broadcast isn't complete, schedule the broadcast anyway. The presentation is not distributed to participants until the broadcast starts. You can even schedule a presentation broadcast using a blank presentation and replace the blank presentation with the one you want to broadcast at the time of the broadcast.

Scheduling a Presentation Broadcast

PowerPoint works with Outlook to schedule presentation broadcasts. When you schedule the broadcast, PowerPoint sends notices of the broadcast through Outlook. Participants can then use the e-mail message to respond to your invitation. If they plan to attend the broadcast, Outlook places the event on their calendars and reminds them when it's time to connect to the broadcast. What could be easier?

Task 7:
To Set Up and Schedule a Live Presentation Broadcast

1. Open the *e-Selections Web.ppt* presentation.

2. Choose **Slide Show** | **Online Broadcast** | **Schedule a Live Broadcast**.

Troubleshooting A message box may appear informing you that the broadcast features are not currently installed on your computer. If this box appears, follow the direction of your instructor to continue.

3. Click **Settings**.

Figure 4-21

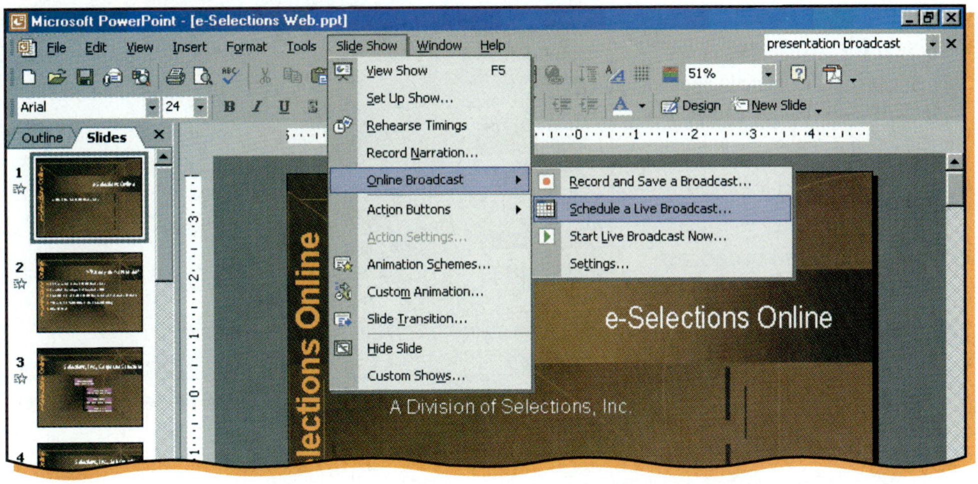

Tip Default options set on the Advanced page of the Broadcast Settings dialog box are fine for broadcasting to ten participants or fewer. Valid file locations must include a server name and follow the path structure *\\servername\foldername*.

Figure 4-22

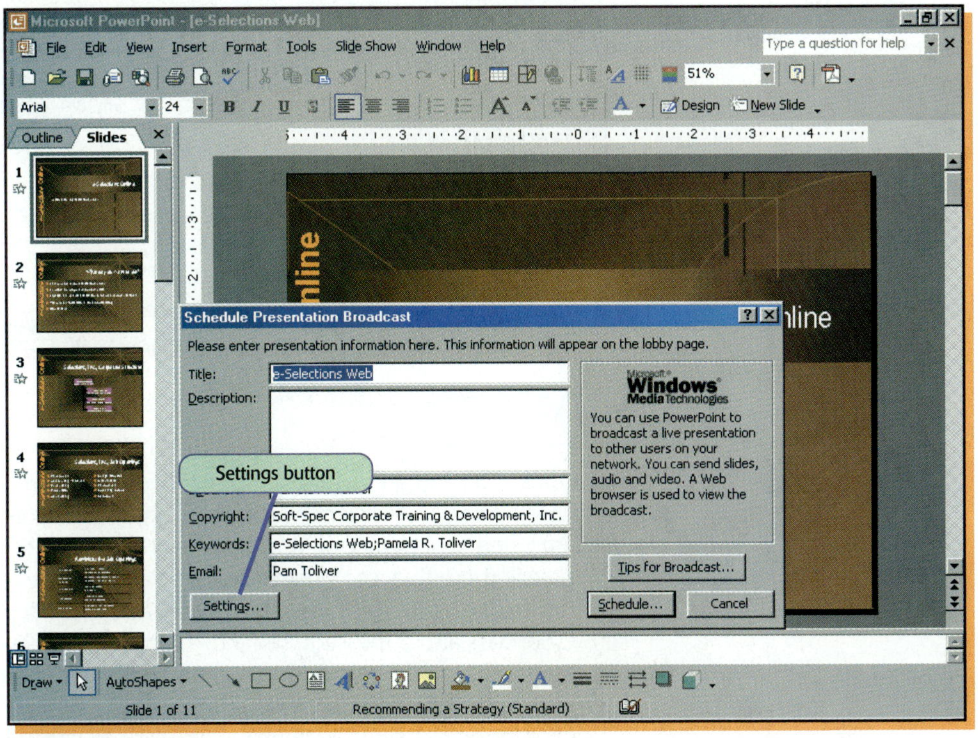

4 Set the following options according to your instructor's direction:

- Select the **Audio/Video** option for the media features available on your computer.
- Select a shared location for storing the presentation you plan to broadcast and for recording the broadcast.
- Select **Full Screen** from the Slide Show mode drop-down list.

Figure 4-23

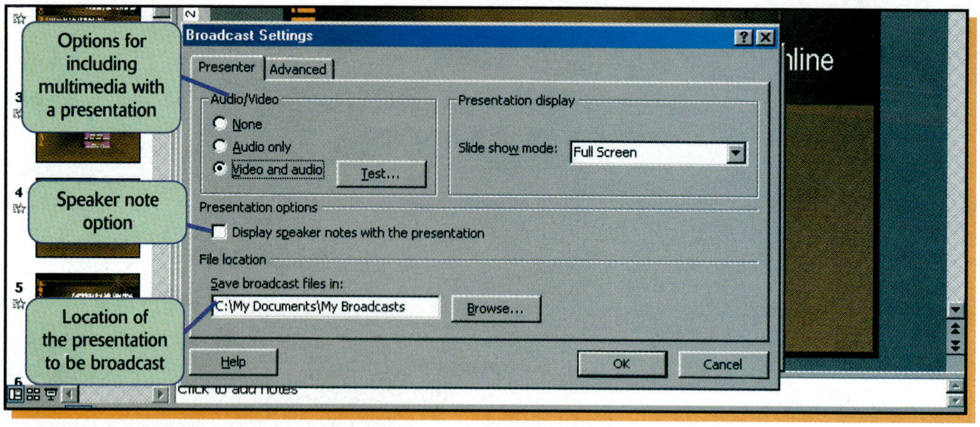

5 Click **OK**, click **Schedule** and select or type the e-mail address of your class partner in the **To** field.

6 Schedule a time for your broadcast that is mutually convenient for you and your class partner.

7 Click **Send** and then click **OK**.

Figure 4-24

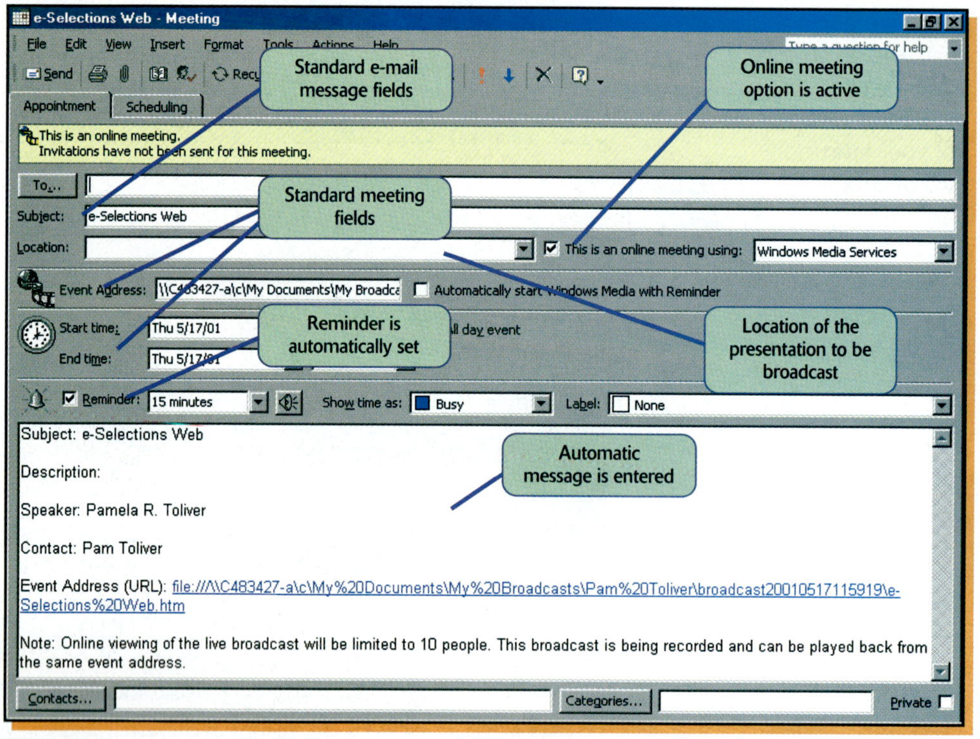

CHECK POINT

After you send an invitation to an online broadcast, those you invited to the broadcast receive an e-mail message advising them of the broadcast. If the participants are using Outlook 2002 as their e-mail program, buttons on their message toolbar enable them to accept, reject, or tentatively accept your invitation to the broadcast. If they accept the invitation, the broadcast time is scheduled in their Outlook Calendars and a message reminds them 15 minutes before the broadcast so that they can log on to the network (intranet server) and connect to the presentation. When participants respond to the meeting invitation, you receive a message in your inbox to help you identify who plans to participate in the broadcast.

SUMMARY AND EXERCISES

SUMMARY

- Each of the Office XP applications contains a Save as Web Page command for saving files as Web pages.
- When you save a presentation as a Web page, PowerPoint creates a new folder in which it stores the slides and any other files required for displaying the presentation on the Web.
- You can launch the default Web browser or display presentations saved as Web pages directly from PowerPoint.
- Presentation Web pages are saved with an .htm file extension.
- You can find options for selecting the slides to publish to the Web, the Web browsers for which you want to format the presentation, and other Web options in the Publish dialog box.
- PowerPoint contains features that enable you to send a presentation to reviewers and then combine the comments and edits from all the reviewers with your original presentation. You can then review the changes and decide which changes to implement.
- You can distribute presentations to a single reviewer or to multiple reviewers via Outlook e-mail so that each reviewer receives his or her own copy of the presentation at the same time.
- You can also route the presentation using Outlook e-mail from one recipient to another so that each reviewer's edits and comments are added to the same copy of the presentation.
- After reviewers have sent their edited copies of the presentation back to you, you can combine their presentations with your original presentation and view all comments and changes at the same time.
- Each reviewer's edits are identified by color-coded markers that display a short description of the change when you point to them.
- Online broadcasts enable multiple broadcast participants to view presentations online at the same time.
- When the broadcast is complete, PowerPoint saves it as a video file that can be opened and reviewed later.

KEY TERMS & SKILLS

KEY TERMS

distribute (p. 4-9)
participant (p. 4-22)
presentation broadcast (p. 4-18)
presentation review cycle (p. 4-9)
presenter (p. 4-2)
publish presentations (p. 4-6)
route (p. 4-9)
shared (p. 4-18)

SKILLS

Combine reviewer edits with the original (p. 4-13)
Conduct an online broadcast (p. 4-18)
Join and participate in an online broadcast (p. 4-12)
Open and respond to a presentation broadcast (p. 4-18)
Present an online broadcast (p. 4-18)
Publish presentations (p. 4-6)
Review, accept, and reject reviewer changes (p. 4-15)
Route presentations for review (p. 4-11)
Save presentations as Web pages (p. 4-5)
Schedule a presentation broadcast (p. 4-18)
Send presentations for review (p. 4-9)
Set up a presentation broadcast (p. 4-18)
Set up a presentation review cycle (p. 4-9)
View a recorded online broadcast (p. 4-26)

STUDY QUESTIONS

MULTIPLE CHOICE

1. You can find the command used to format presentations for the Web on what menu?
- a. File
- b. Edit
- c. View
- d. Insert

2. The command used to format presentations for the Web is
- a. Save.
- b. Save As.
- c. Save As HTML.
- d. Save As Web Page.

3. To view a presentation as it would appear in a Web browser,
- a. you must launch the Web browser.
- b. choose **File | Web Page Preview**.
- c. click the Print Preview button.
- d. simply open the presentation.

4. Presentations formatted for the Web are saved with what extension?
- a. .htm
- b. .html
- c. .pot
- d. .ppt

5. Publishing a presentation to the Web enables you to do all the following *except*
- a. change the page title.
- b. select the browser on which to view the presentation.
- c. set show animation options.
- d. view the presentation in the selected browser.

6. Review cycles can be set up to
- a. send a separate copy of the presentation for review to each reviewer.
- b. distribute multiple copies of the same presentation to one reviewer who then passes it on the another reviewer.
- c. enable the reviewer to combine his edits with your original presentation.
- d. none of the above

7. Routing presentations enables you to
   a. send a presentation for review as an attachment to an e-mail message.
   b. route a presentation for review so that it moves from one reviewer to the next and eventually comes back to you.
   c. route a presentation to multiple reviewers at the same time so that each receives a separate copy of the presentation.
   d. both b and c

8. To distribute a presentation for review using an e-mail program other than Outlook,
   a. save the presentation as a Web page.
   b. save the presentation as a Presentation for Review file type.
   c. save the presentation as a Word file.
   d. publish the presentation to the Web.

9. After reviewers have returned their copies of the presentation, you can
   a. open and review each reviewed presentation online.
   b. print copies of each reviewed presentation and compare presentation edits.
   c. merge edits with your original and view all edits at the same time.
   d. all of the above

10. To remove an edit marker from a merged presentation,
   a. click the Delete Comments (Delete Marker) ✖ button.
   b. click the item in the task pane.
   c. press Delete.
   d. none of the above

SHORT ANSWER

1. What pane appears when you merge edited presentations with your original?
2. How do the comments added by reviewers appear after they are merged with your original presentation?
3. How are different reviewer edits distinguished on screen?
4. What toolbars appear on screen after you merge edited presentations with the original?
5. Where must you store presentations that are to be broadcast?
6. To use Microsoft Media Services, presentations are limited to how many broadcast participants?
7. To broadcast a presentation to more than 15 computers, what program must you use?
8. Can presentation broadcasts be set up if the participant is using an e-mail program other than Outlook?
9. Describe two different ways to view a presentation as a Web page.
10. Where does the page title you assign to a presentation that you save as a Web file appear when you view the file in the browser window?

FILL IN THE BLANK

1. PowerPoint works with ____________ to schedule presentation broadcasts.
2. Online broadcasts can be set up to broadcast ____________ and ____________ if the required peripherals are available on the broadcasting system.

3. To tell the presenter of an online broadcast that you plan to attend the broadcast, click the ____________ button on the Outlook 2002 message toolbar.
4. The person conducting an online broadcast is called the ____________.
5. A person viewing an online broadcast is called a ____________.
6. Presentation Web pages are saved with a(n) ____________ file extension.
7. To send the same copy of a presentation to reviewers, one after the other, you should ____________ the presentation.
8. The command used to merge edited presentations with your original is found on the ____________ menu.
9. The ____________ toolbar opens after you merge edited presentations with your original.
10. Click the ____________button to accept a reviewer's edit.

DISCUSSION

1. What is the difference between saving a presentation as a Web page and publishing the presentation to the Web?
2. Describe the actions required by participants in an online broadcast starting with receipt of the broadcast invitation.
3. Describe the different ways to accept or reject reviewer edits.
4. Discuss the techniques you would use at your school to successfully conduct an online broadcast.

GUIDED EXERCISES

1 BUILDING A PRESENTATION

It has been proven that asking everyone on a team to contribute to decisions and information disseminated from the team enhances the success of a project. The *Selections Overview.ppt* presentation contains a few slides that provide a basic overview of Selections, Inc. Additional information needs to be included in the presentation, but you are running out of time to complete the presentation and decide to have your team members add slides containing the information for you. You decide to route the presentation to three different team members and ask each of them to complete the information on one presentation slide. Follow these steps to get the process started:

1. Open the *Selections Overview.ppt* presentation.
2. Choose **File | Send To | Routing Recipient**.
3. Type the e-mail addresses of three of your class team members and click **Send**.

As you receive each routed presentation from your team members, add comments to the existing slides and complete the information for a different slide that contains only a title so that the presentation for each team member will be different. Add your name in a comment on the slide that you complete. Then save the presentation and pass it along to the next recipient.

2 MERGING AND REVIEWING PRESENTATIONS

Being part of a team is a great way to accomplish the task of building an awesome presentation efficiently. After you receive the copy of *Selections Overview.ppt* that you routed with all the slides completed, you can merge the routed presentation with your original and complete the final presentation. Here's how:

1. Launch Outlook and open the e-mail messages containing the routed presentation.
2. Save the presentation attached to the e-mail message as a separate file.
3. Launch PowerPoint and open your original copy of *Selections Overview.ppt*.
4. Choose **Tools | Compare and Merge Presentations**.
5. Select the presentation edited by your team members and click **Merge**.
6. Review each slide's edits and comments, rejecting and accepting comments appropriately, leaving only the comments containing the team member name on the slides that each completed.
7. Save changes to the presentation and e-mail it to your instructor as an attachment.

3 TAKING CUISINE ONLINE

Posting menus and other restaurant information on the Web provides a great way for connoisseurs to locate a restaurant that serves the type of food they like. As a result, the number of restaurants advertising on the Web has exploded. Food critics are even beginning to post their reviews of restaurants online. You've worked with a presentation that identifies restaurants serving southern cuisine—let's see how it appears when you save it as a Web page. Follow these instructions:

1. Open the presentation *Cuisine of the Southern US.ppt*.
2. Choose **File | Save as Web Page**.
3. Change the page title to *Southern Cuisine* and click **Save**.
4. Choose **File | Web Page Preview** and review each of the presentation slides, testing the links as you go and making notes about changes that need to be made to the original presentation.

5. Open the original presentation and edit the presentation appropriately.
6. Save changes to the presentation and e-mail the presentation to your instructor.

4 SCHEDULING TO BROADCAST CUISINE FAR AND WIDE

Reviewing other people's presentations is an effective way to gather ideas and information for your own personal use. It's also a great way to gauge how well received your work will be. Before actually posting your *Cuisine of the Southern US.ppt* presentation online, you can schedule a broadcast and then conduct a dry run of the broadcast with other members of your team. Here's how:

1. Open the *Cuisine of the Southern US.ppt* presentation.
2. Choose **Slide Show** | **Online Broadcast** | **Schedule a Live Broadcast**.
3. Set the appropriate **Settings** options for your presentation as directed by your instructor.
4. Schedule the presentation for 15 minutes from the current time, set a reminder for 5 minutes before the broadcast, and send invitations to your class team members.
5. Respond to any invitations to broadcasts that you receive.
6. When the broadcast reminder opens, click **View Windows Media** and start the broadcast.
7. Deliver the presentation broadcast, explaining how the presentation is set up and designed, how the hyperlinks work, and how the buttons at the bottom of each slide help you to navigate.
8. When the presentation broadcast is complete, make a note of the broadcast location and title and then send this information to your instructor.

ON YOUR OWN

The difficulty of these case studies varies:
⚑ *are the least difficult;* ⚑⚑ *are more difficult; and* ⚑⚑⚑ *are the most difficult.*

1 TAKING FAMILY ONLINE

⚑ One way to share family information is to post it on a Web site. If you have not yet done so, create a presentation named *My Family* that outlines at least the last three generations of your family tree. If you already have a family tree presentation, open it and save the presentation using the file name *My Family*. Then save the presentation as a Web page. Preview the presentation in your default browser, make any necessary changes or adjustments to the presentation file, and resave it as a Web page. Then e-mail the Web page presentation file to your instructor.

2 TRAVEL THE WORLD THROUGH THE WEB

⚑ It's rare for people to be able to pick up and fly off to far away places at the drop of a hat. Travel today is quite expensive and takes careful planning. As more and more travelers turn to the Web to locate exciting travel packages, the number of travel agencies posting tours is increasing. Publish the *Travel Tours.ppt* presentation as a Web page, formatting the presentation for both browsers and changing the page title to *Your First Name Tour Packages*. Then store the Web presentation in a folder on the Web or in a public folder to which your instructor has access.

3 TOYS: THEN AND NOW

Toys have changed dramatically through the ages. Some toys popular half a century ago are still popular today while others have disappeared. Search the Internet for toys that were popular in 1950 and locate at least five toys that are still popular today. Then create a new presentation named *Toys of the Century,* which includes slides that identify the toys, the toy manufacturers, and the toys' histories. Be sure to include pictures of the toys then and now. When you're finished, save the presentation as a Web page and print a copy of the presentation as handouts with two slides per page.

4 REVIEWING CENTURY CARS

Now that the new century is well under way, it's fun to review how some of the items that we are accustomed to seeing every day have changed over the last century. Connect to the Internet and gather pictures and information about automobiles from each decade of the 1900s. Then create a new presentation titled *Decades of Automobiles* that outlines the progression of automotive development through the decades. Include features unique to cars in each decade and pictures that illustrate these features. Finally, add information to the end of the presentation that describes what automakers did to introduce their cars for the year 2000. Then send your presentation for review to at least two of your team members, merge their edited copies of your presentation with your original presentation, and accept and reject changes appropriately. Then pack the presentation to go and submit it to your instructor.

5 PUTTING YOURSELF ONLINE

As you progress through your college experience, you will eventually begin to interview for jobs. Whether the positions for which you apply are temporary part-time jobs while you're in school or full-time positions after you graduate, you will eventually be asked to tell the interviewer something about yourself. A great way to help prepare yourself for this type of interview question is by practicing—and what better way to practice than by delivering a presentation broadcast using your résumé! Open your résumé presentation or create a new presentation using information from your résumé. The presentation should contain slides that outline your accomplishments, your education, special skills, and so forth, things that you believe are important or have molded the person you have become. Then schedule and deliver a presentation broadcast. Orient your broadcast to responding to the "tell me about yourself" approach used by many interviewers. View your broadcast and repeat it until you are satisfied with the broadcast. Then send the broadcast location and number to your instructor for review.

Photospread credits pages 4-2 & 4-3

FROM THE FILES

You Will Need

- ✔ e-Selections.jpg
- ✔ Automotive Template.pot

PROJECT 5

Building New Masters

Enhancing presentations with text, art, graphs, and graphics and showing presentations with style using transitions and special effects introduced you to the basic tasks associated with building presentations. Presentation masters provide tools for creating your own special presentation design. Presentation masters form the skeleton of a presentation. As a result, the masters should support the presentation just as our skeletons support our bodies.

OBJECTIVES

After completing this project, you will be able to:

- *Display presentation masters*
- *Format the slide background*
- *Customize a color scheme*
- *Select font and bullet formats*
- *Apply animation effects*
- *Insert and format graphics on Slide Masters*
- *Create Title Masters*
- *Save presentation designs as templates*
- *Preserve existing masters*

e-selections Running Case

You've learned a great deal about PowerPoint as well as about the design elements required for creating effective presentations. It's time to put your creative talents to work designing masters for a new presentation template...from scratch!

Picture This...

Einstein said, "If I can't 'see' it, I don't understand it".

Sounds as if Mr. Einstein was a visual learner, doesn't it? With the advent of electronic presentations, formatting and displaying information on slides appropriately can make or break your presentation. Remember that slides in an electronic presentation are, in and of themselves, visuals. Here are some visual "do's" to keep in mind when you're creating slides and adding visual elements to an electronic presentation.

- **Keep slides simple**. It's easy to go overboard with visual enhancements. Slides that are cluttered with graphics and other business make it difficult to focus on the real meat of the message. Slide text should be limited to six bullet points per slide and six words per bullet point—and you don't always need a picture!

- **Focus each slide on one basic point.** Crowding too many topics into one slide creates confusion and leaves the audience wondering where you're going next in the presentation. Adding additional levels of bullet points provide a hint that you've included too much information on a slide. Leave the main bullet point but then create an additional slide that expands the topic.

- **Limit slides containing text only to six consecutive sides.** Varying the format of slides in the presentation prevents boredom.

- **Make sure text can be viewed from the back of the room.** Font sizes less than 18 points are difficult to read. Avoid typing text in all UPPERCASE letters. You don't want the audience to think you're SHOUTING at them!

Avoid mixing types of visuals

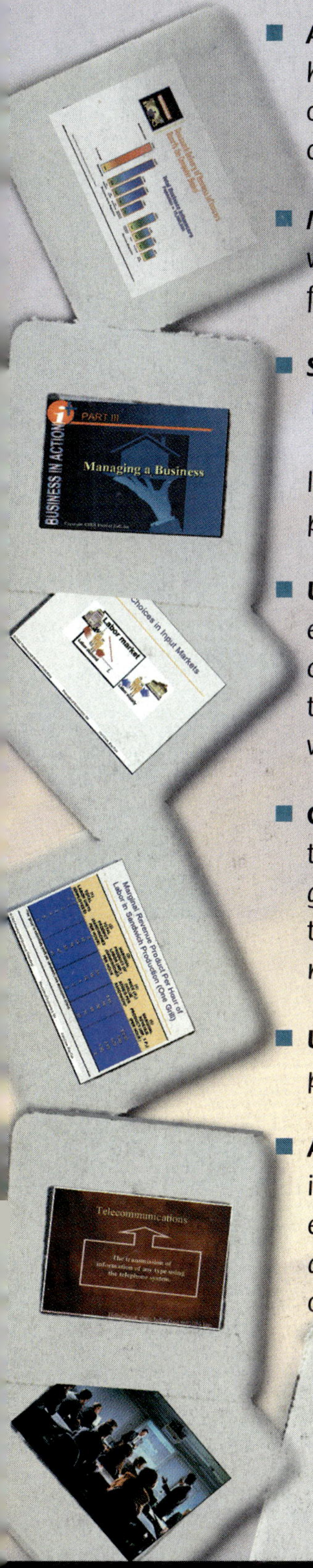

- **Avoid typos and spelling errors**—this goes without saying. But it happens—frequently. A human eye catches small mistakes often overlooked by electronic spell-checkers. Remember how you liked to point out misspelled words to your teachers? Don't let it happen to you!
- **Maintain consistency.** Templates provide a cohesive impression—especially when you pull information from different presentations. End punctuation, font, and alignment are important. Mixing them detracts from the message.
- **Select an appropriate format for each slide that best displays the type of information being presented.** For example, to show a trend in performance, use a bar, line, or trend graph; to summarize information, use bulleted lists; to show hierarchical information, use an organization chart; to show proportion of a whole, use a pie chart.
- **Use a variety of different media**—sound, video, graphics, and so forth—to enhance presentation slides and make the media pertinent to the information contained on the slide. Then sprinkle enhanced slides throughout the presentation rather than grouping them together. While the slide itself is a visual, you want to get the most from each slide in the presentation.
- **Choose high-quality graphics.** Graphic quality is extraordinarily important to presentations, but be sure they display quickly on screen. High-quality graphics are often large, and when displayed during an electronic presentation, they may appear after you've made your point and want to move to the next slide.
- **Use clip art with discretion.** Remember, clip art may not be appropriate for professional audiences.
- **Avoid mixing types of visuals.** While a good mix of visual elements should be included on slides in an electronic presentation, it's best to avoid mixing electronic presentations with other media such as flip charts, overhead projectors, and transparencies. Watching you move from the computer to a flip chart to the overhead projector adds confusion to the smooth flow of your presentation.

Last, but certainly not least, remember that you, too, are a visual. Be sure to dress appropriately!

PROJECT 5

Building New Masters

The Challenge

Mr. Ronald Carroll, Vice President of the e-Selections division of Selections, Inc., has decided that e-Selections needs a corporate template to help company employees standardize their presentations and project a professional corporate image. He has sketched a layout for the set of masters shown in Figure 5-1 and would like for you to create a template that includes both his design and a set of masters that complement his design.

Figure 5-1

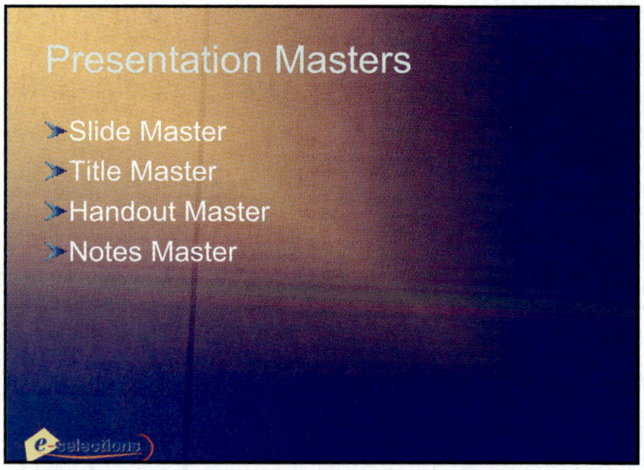

The Solution

Mr. Carroll has done an excellent job sketching out his ideas for formatting the designs for masters in the presentation template. You can start from scratch—with a blank presentation—and build the presentation from the ground up. You'll implement a five-step approach to building the first set of masters:

1. Format the background.
2. Define the color scheme.
3. Select fonts and bullets.

4. Add consistent animation.
5. Add logos or elements to appear on each slide.

After you complete the set of masters designed by Mr. Carroll, you'll have him review them, and then you'll make the necessary edits and create the second set of masters.

Displaying Presentation Masters

Each presentation you create contains slides formatted with a *template* that contains design elements, such as background color, text placeholder format, and graphics. These design elements are stored in layouts called *masters*. Each template contains a separate master for formatting each type of presentation material (slides, notes, and handouts).

Each PowerPoint 2002 template comes with at least one set of masters—even the Blank template. You can edit existing masters, add new masters to the template, or remove masters from the template. The two master layouts that make up each set of masters include:

- A *Slide Master* design is applied to slides formatted using all slide layouts except the Title slide layout.
- The *Title Master* design is applied to slides formatted using the Title slide layout.

To create the presentation design Mr. Carroll requested, you will start with blank masters and build each set of template masters so that they contain the presentation design elements. To access the masters that you want to use as a starting point, you must first create a presentation formatted using the template that contains the masters—in this case, a blank presentation.

Task 1:

To Display the Presentation Slide Master

1 Launch PowerPoint, create a new blank presentation, and close the task pane. The new slide appears in Normal view.

2 Choose **View** | **Master** | **Slide Master** to open the master view.

Figure 5-2

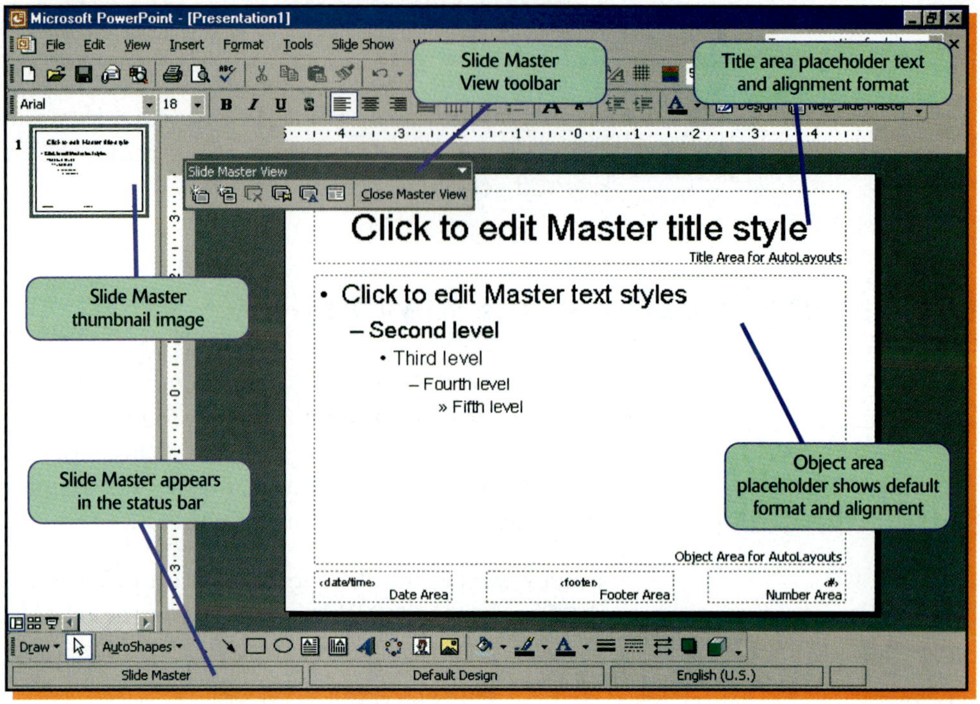

Other Ways

To display Masters:

- Hold down the Shift key and click a PowerPoint view button.

Formatting the Slide Master Background

The *slide background* for the template master contains a color design that provides the backdrop for all text and objects you place on presentation slides. As a result, adding or changing the background *color scheme* often affects the colors of title text, bulleted-list text, colors displayed in charts, and other objects you add to slides. When you like the colors you have set, you can leave the color scheme intact and simply lighten and format the background color.

Task 2:
To Format the Slide Background

1. Choose **Format | Background** to open the Background dialog box.

Figure 5-3

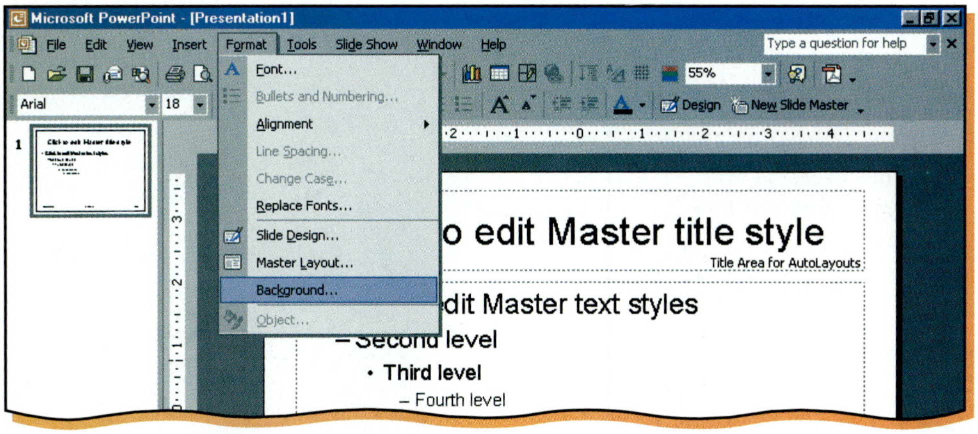

2. Click the **Background fill** down arrow.

3. Select **Fill Effects.**

Tip Changes in background color that you make to Masters affect background color of all slides except those you format individually.

Figure 5-4

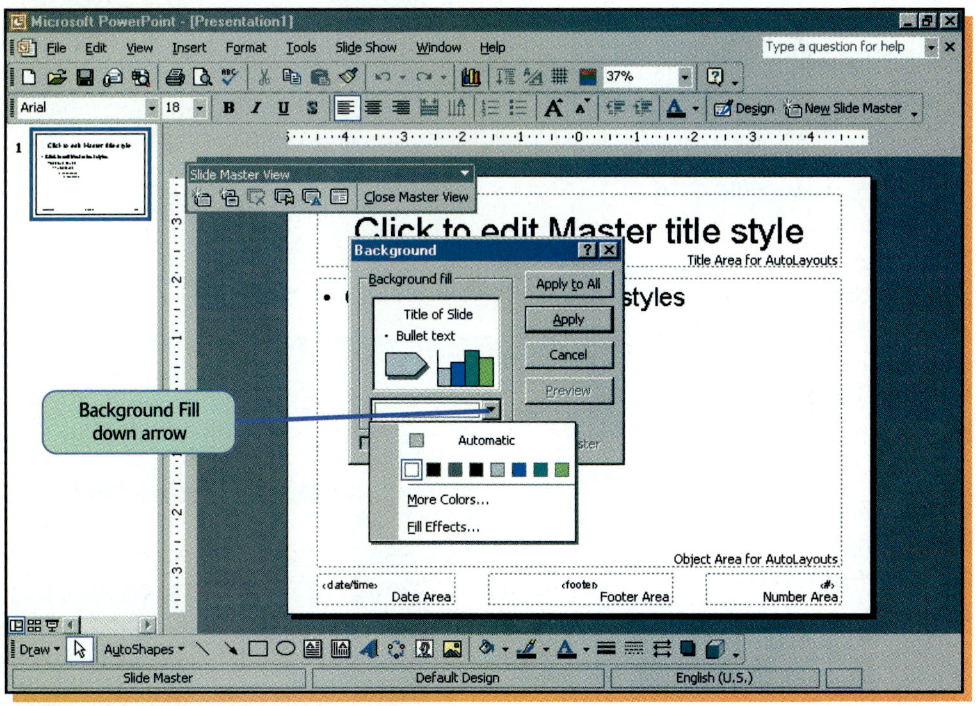

Tip As time permits, you may want to explore special effects available in the Background dialog box.

4 Select the **Two colors** option and select the settings shown in Figure 5-5.

Troubleshooting
The Color 2 box becomes available only after you select the Two colors option.

Tip
Preset color schemes designed for special effects such as sunsets and deserts are available when you select the Preset option. Explore the preset design colors by selecting the Preset option and selecting different presets from the Preset colors drop-down list.

Figure 5-5

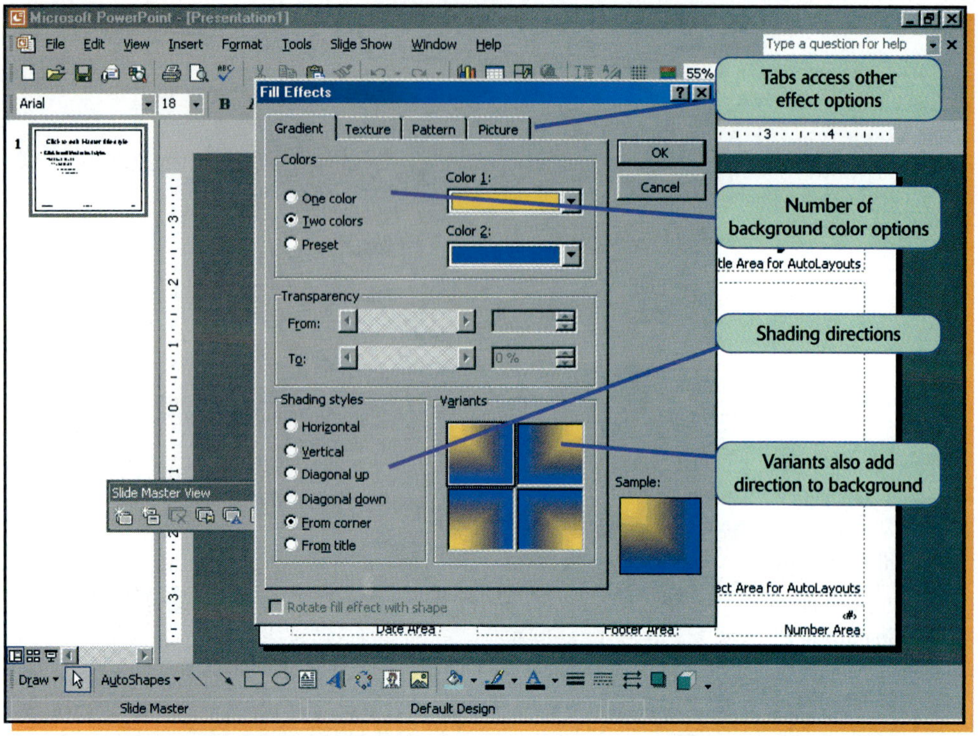

5 Click **OK** to close the Fill Effects dialog box, and then click **Apply to All** to format all slide types with the background.

6 Save the presentation using the file name *Your Initials e-Selections Design*.

Figure 5-6

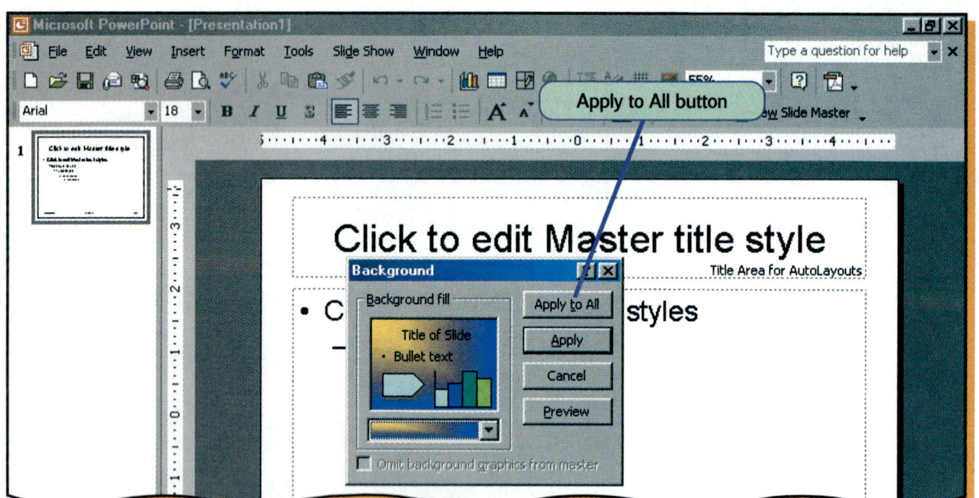

Customizing a Master Color Scheme

Each template was designed with specific colors for title text and bulleted-list text. Lines, background, fill, and accent colors have also been included in each template design. The combination of these colors is called a *color scheme*. Graphic artists designed the color schemes used in PowerPoint templates for visual effect and to complement other colors. When you need to adjust the colors displayed for different objects on your slides to better suit your needs, you can edit the individual object colors by customizing the color scheme.

Task 3:

To Customize a Color Scheme

1 Click the Design **Design** button and click the **Color Schemes** link in the task pane.

Other Ways

To display the Slide Design task pane:

- Right-click a blank area of the slide window and select **Slide Design.**
- Choose **View | Task Pane** and select **Slide Design** from the task pane drop-down list.

2 Click the **Edit Color Schemes** link at the bottom of the task pane.

3 Click the **Standard** tab, click the color scheme that most closely fits the colors you want to use for the presentation, and then click the **Custom** tab.

4 Select the item from the **Scheme colors** list you want to change and then click **Change Color**.

Figure 5-7

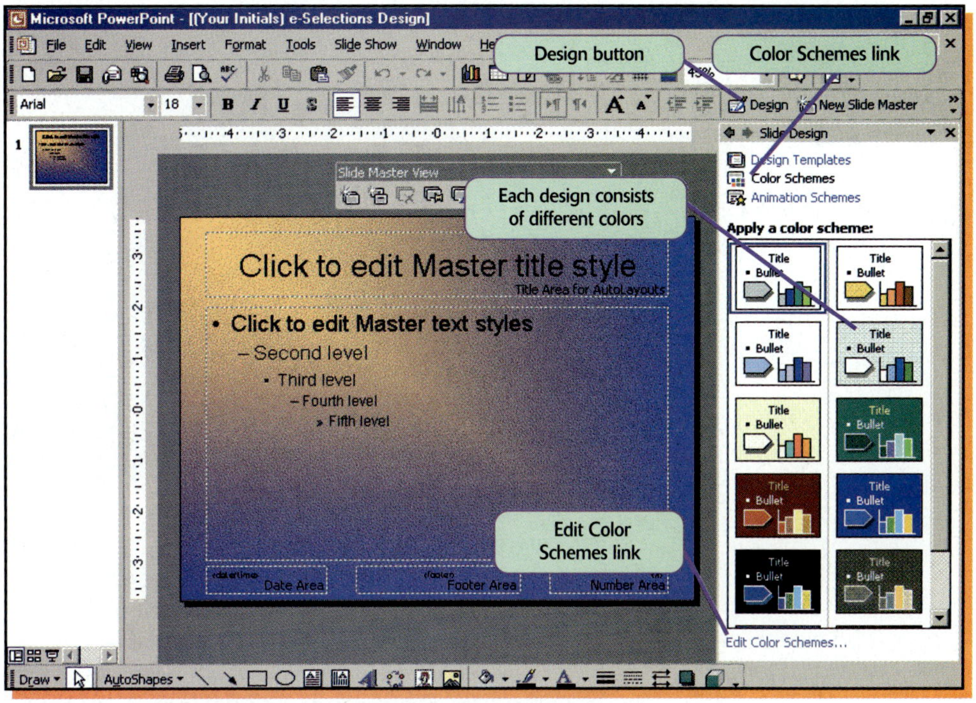

Figure 5-8

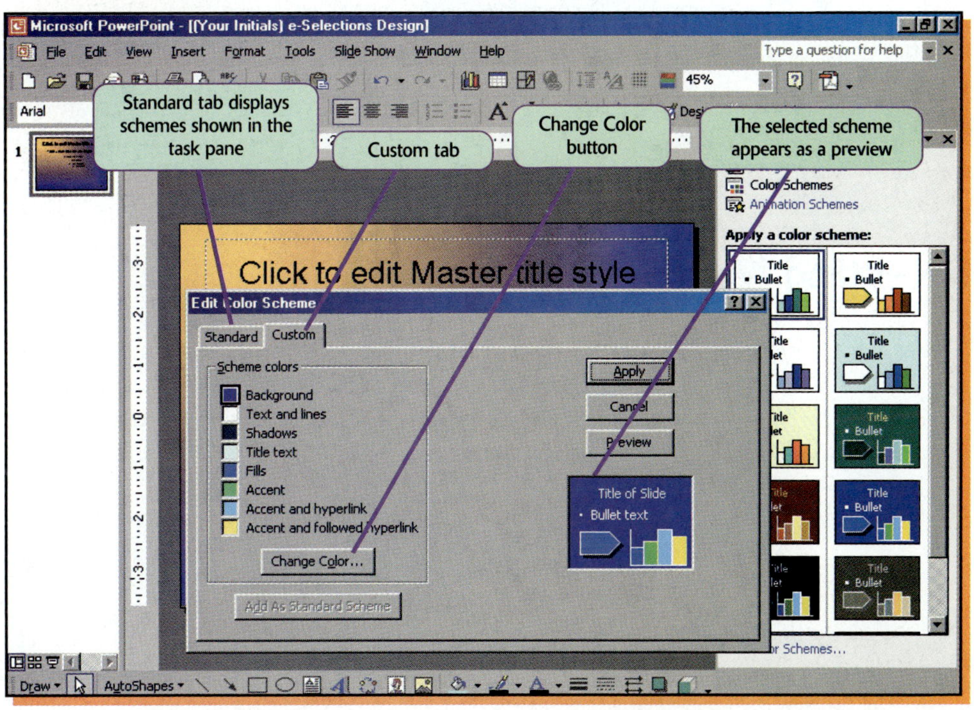

5 Click the Standard tab, select a color for the item and click **OK**. The selected color appears in the color box on the Scheme colors list.

6 Click **Apply** to apply the color change to the presentation Slide Master.

7 Close the task pane.

Figure 5-9

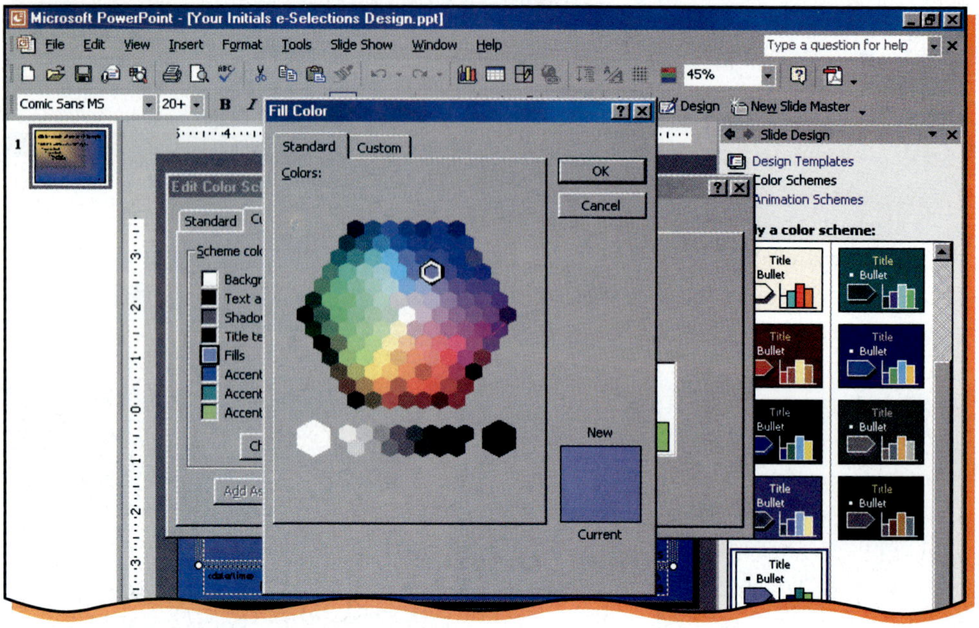

Tip You would want to leave the background color set as it is after spending so much time creating a gradient fill. Pick one of the other components. You have free reign to be creative when it comes to customizing your color schemes. You might want to take advantage of it. You can always go back and change it if it doesn't look right.

CHECK POINT

If you choose to create a custom color, you can select a position on the Custom color palette or enter values for hue, saturation, and luminescence, as well as values for depth of green, red, and blue, to create the color you want. Experiment with these values to see how they affect the color.

Selecting Master Font

To ensure that slide text style and size remain consistent on all slides in the presentation, you can change the text format and *alignment* in text placeholders on the masters. Then you can adjust text size and alignment on individual slides within a presentation as necessary.

Tip When you change the appearance and alignment of text on the Slide Master of an existing presentation, none of the text on slides that you formatted individually will be affected.

Task 4:

To Change Text Style and Alignment on the Slide Master

1. Display the **Slide Master**, if necessary.

2. Press Shift, click the *Title Area for AutoLayouts* placeholder, and then click the *Object Area for AutoLayouts* placeholder on the Slide Master.

3. Click the Align Left button on the Formatting toolbar. All placeholder text aligns to the left of the placeholder.

Figure 5-10

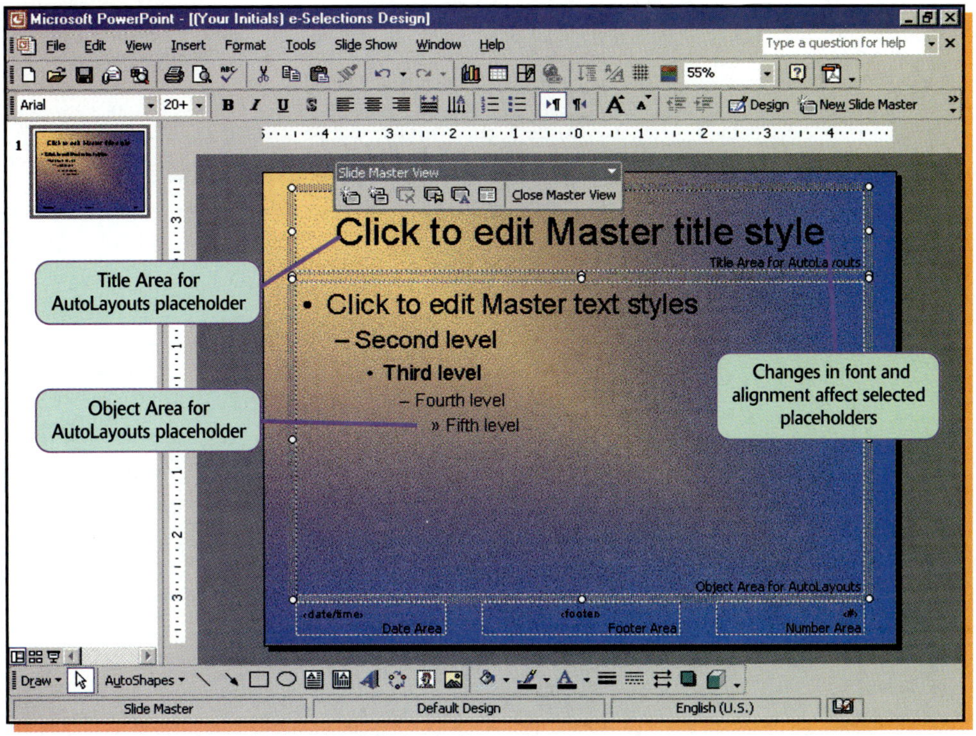

4. Click the **Font** down arrow on the Formatting toolbar and select **Comic Sans MS** font.

5. Save changes to the presentation and close the task pane.

Tip Pressing Shift as you click the placeholder ensures that you select the placeholder rather than placeholder text.

Figure 5-11

Troubleshooting If the Comic Sans MS font is not available, select a script style font such as Cataneo BT or Lucida Sans.

CHECK POINT

If you accidentally delete a placeholder from a master, you can restore it quickly and easily. Simply display the master from which the placeholder was deleted and click the Master Layout button on the Slide Master View toolbar and check the box for the missing placeholder. Placeholder options are available only for those items that someone deleted and placeholders that are active are grayed out. Be sure to click **OK** when you are finished.

Formatting Bullets

Bullet styles for each bulleted-list text level can be formatted using different characters. The format for the bullet is built into the template design and can easily be altered. When you change the *bullet format* for bullet levels on the Slide Master, the new bullet shape changes for the selected level on all slides in the presentation. PowerPoint contains a variety of text categories from which you can choose your bullet shapes. You can also select a picture bullet.

CHECK POINT

When you change the bullet format on the Slide Master of an existing presentation, bullets you have formatted individually on slides are not changed. You can also change the bullet format for a specific bullet level on the Slide Master or for a bulleted list on an individual slide to number when appropriate. Just select the level or bullet points you want to change and click the Numbering button on the Formatting toolbar.

Task 5:
To Change the Master Bullet Format for a Text Level

1 Point to the second bullet level line in the *Object Area for AutoLayouts* and right-click.

2 Select **Bullets and Numbering** from the shortcut menu to open the Bullets and Numbering dialog box.

Figure 5-12

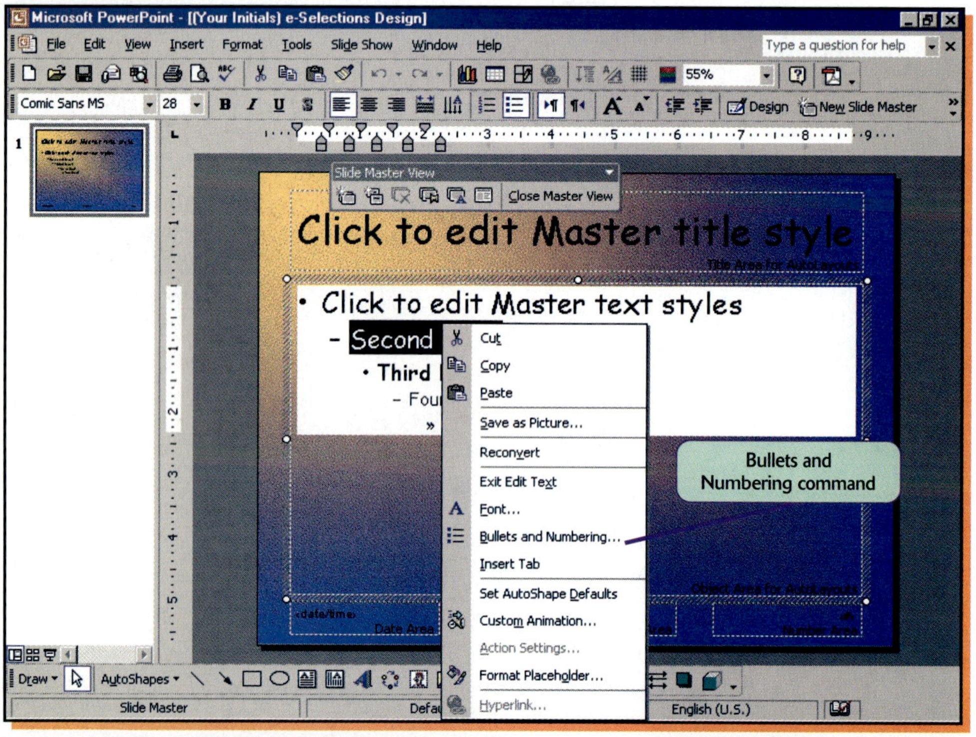

3 Click **Picture** in the Bullets and Numbering dialog box to open the Picture Bullet dialog box shown in Figure 5-13.

4 Scroll the bullet pictures, click the bullet you want to use, and click **OK**.

> **Tip** If you have a special picture that you want to use as a bullet, click the Import button at the bottom of the Picture Bullet dialog box to open the Add Clips to Organizer dialog box, locate the picture you want to use, and click the Add button.

Figure 5-13

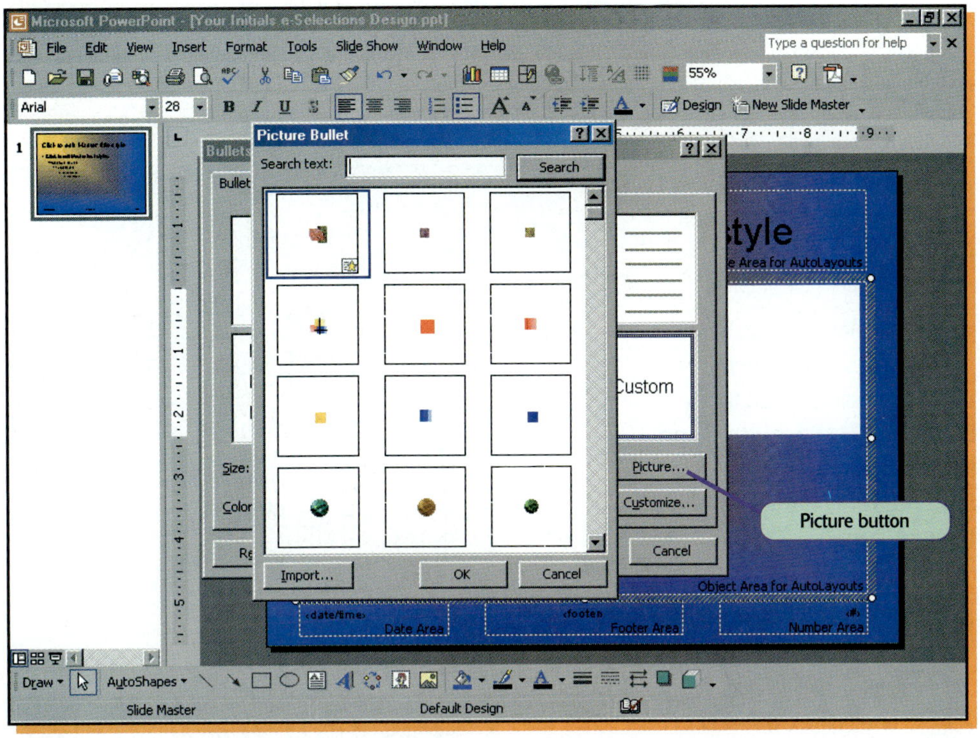

5 Change the bullet format for the first bullet level to a picture of your choice.

6 Save changes to the presentation.

Figure 5-14

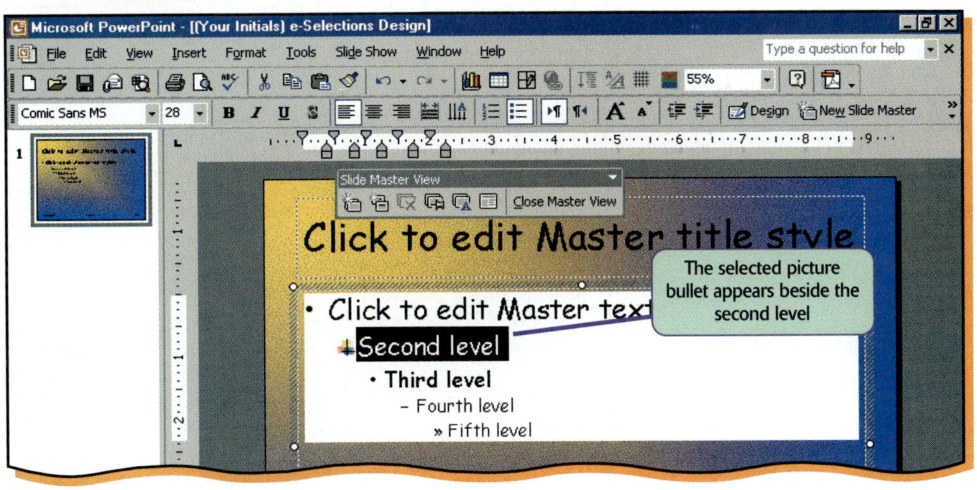

Applying Animation Effects to Masters

As you already know, PowerPoint is equipped with animation schemes that make animating slide placeholder text a snap! In PowerPoint 2002, you can set placeholders on each slide to animate individually or set all the slides in the presentation to animate using the same scheme. You can also create custom animations that enable you to set the animation of the title and then animate bulleted-list text to present each bulleted item individually. Rather than moving to each presentation slide and setting the animation scheme for each placeholder, you can set the animation scheme on the master so that each slide you add to the presentation is automatically animated.

Task 6:
To Apply Custom Animation Schemes to Masters

1. Display the masters, if necessary, select the title placeholder, click the Design **Design** button, and then click the **Animation Schemes** link at the top of the task pane.

2. Select the **Dissolve in** scheme.

3. Select the **Bulleted List** placeholder, display the Slide Transitions task pane, and select **Random Transition** from the **Slide Transition** list.

4. Choose **Slide Show | Custom Animation** to open the Custom Animation task pane.

Figure 5-15

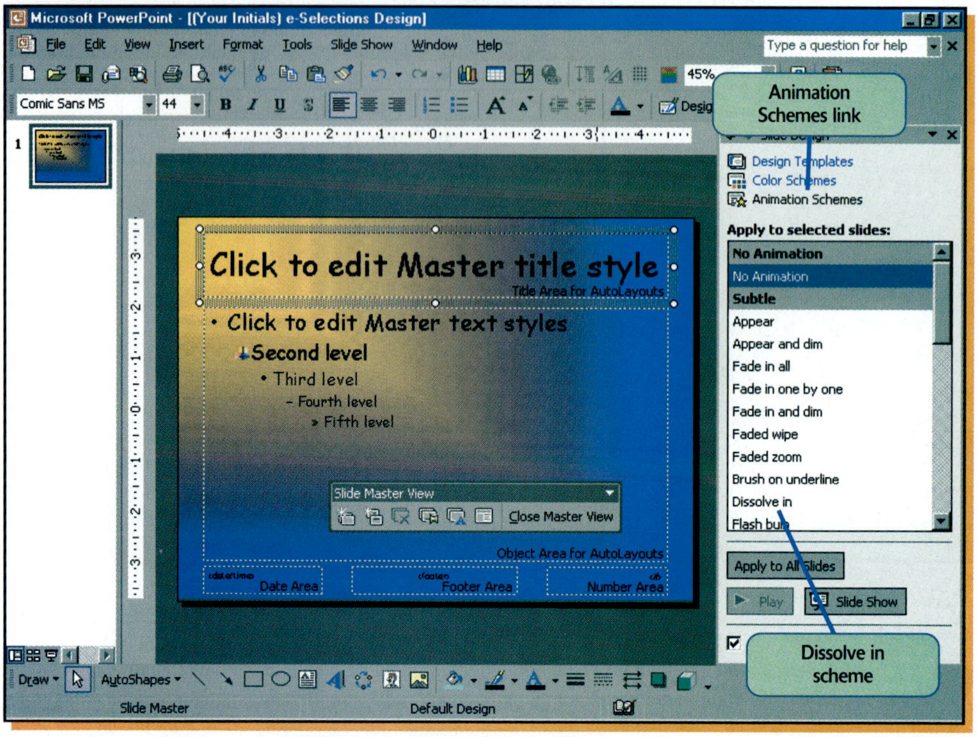

Figure 5-16

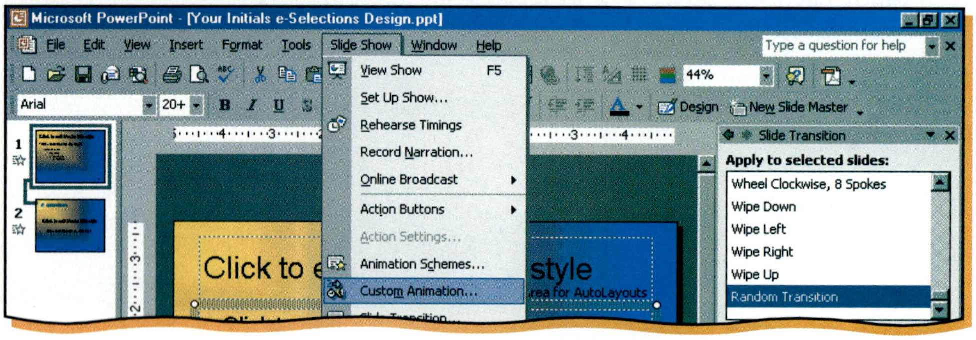

5 Click **Add Effect** | **Entrance** | **More Effects**

Figure 5-17

6 Select **Random Effects** and click **OK**.

Troubleshooting

The schemes listed in the **Recently Used** area may be different from those displayed in Figure 5-18. Listed items change as you explore different schemes.

Figure 5-18

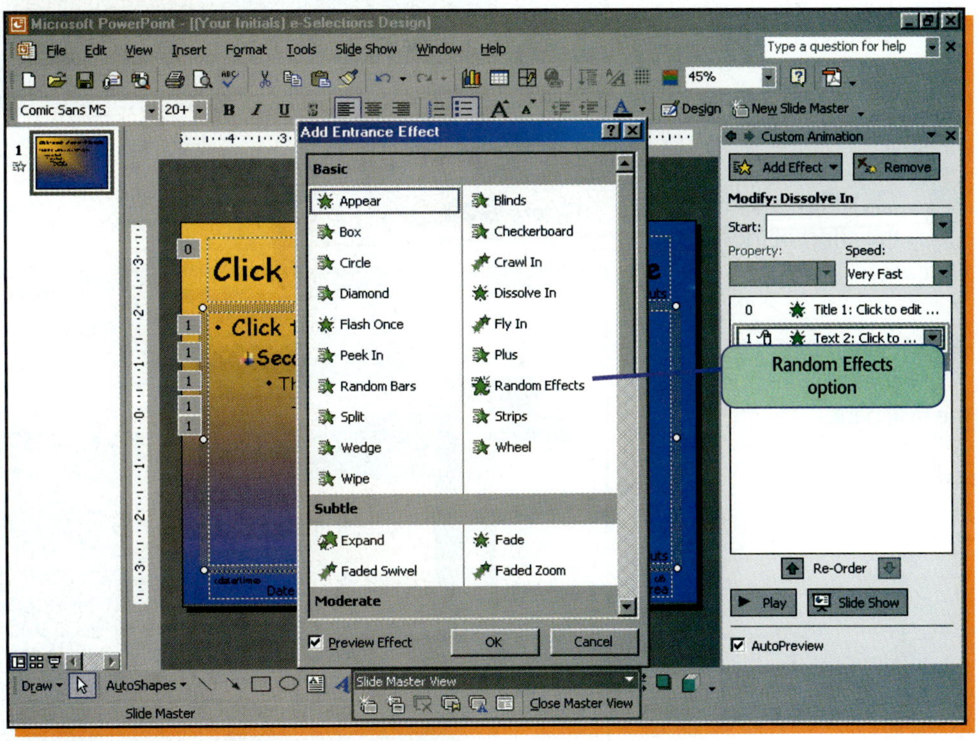

7. Click the **Start** drop-down list arrow, and select **With Previous**.

8. Click the **Text 2** item down arrow and select **Effect Options**.

9. Click the **Text Animation** tab, select **By 4th level paragraphs** from the **Group text** drop-down list, and click **OK**.

Figure 5-19

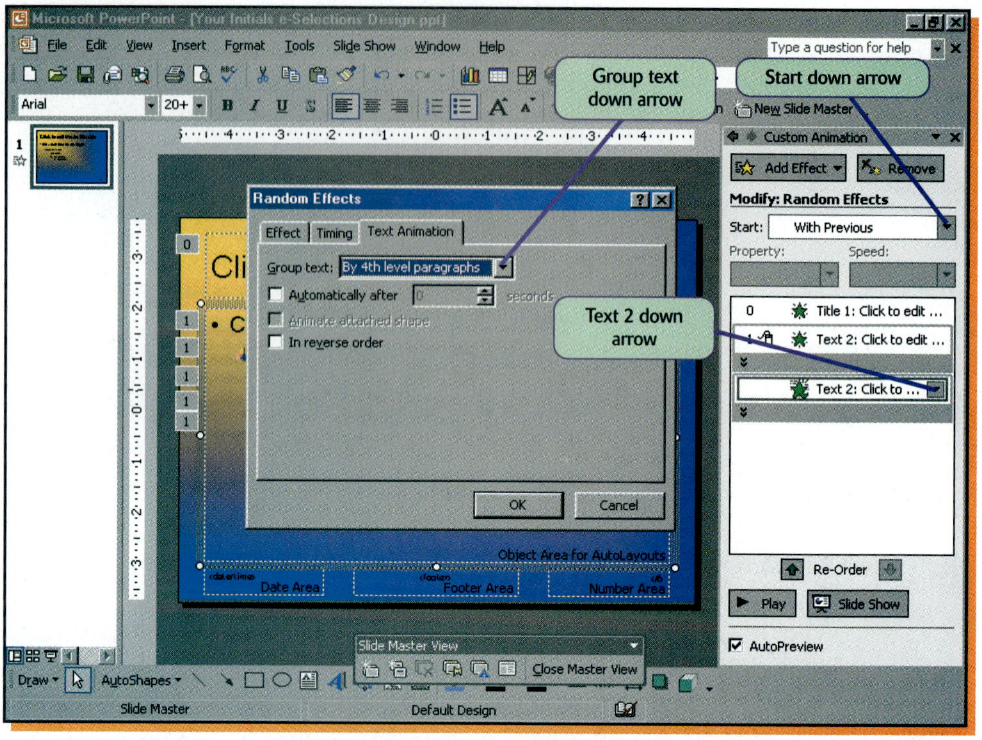

10. Click **Play** to preview the effect of the animation.

11. Save changes to the presentation and close the task pane.

Figure 5-20

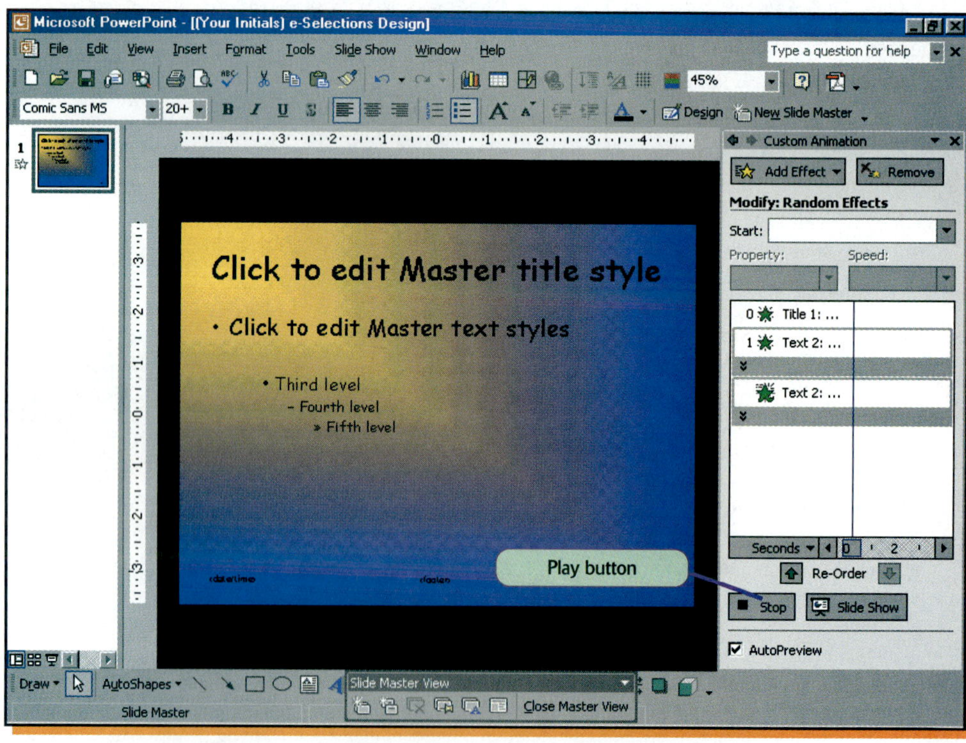

CHECK POINT

When you apply Random Effects to a placeholder on a master, PowerPoint controls the effect used to present each placeholder and bullet point. As a result, each time you show a presentation created and formatted using the template, placeholders and bullet points will appear on screen differently. PowerPoint starts the presentation of random effects with the effect immediately following the last effect used and moves through the list of available effects alphabetically. As a result, when you use a template to create a new presentation, it may be necessary to apply specific effects to slides in the presentation to control the movement of the text or object. Since PowerPoint starts its random effects with the effect immediately following the effect last used, applying a specific effect to one item will control the random effect PowerPoint uses for the next slide object.

Inserting and Formatting Graphics on Slide Masters

You're almost finished with one of the masters for the special template Mr. Carroll requested. All you have left is to add the e-Selections logo graphic to the presentation design. You can use the same procedures to insert graphics on masters that you use to insert graphics on slides.

Task 7:

To Insert and Format a Graphic on a Slide Master

1. Display the **Slide Master**, if necessary.
2. Choose **Insert | Picture | From File**, open the folder that contains the *e-Selections.jpg* graphic, and double-click *e-Selections.jpg*.

Figure 5-21

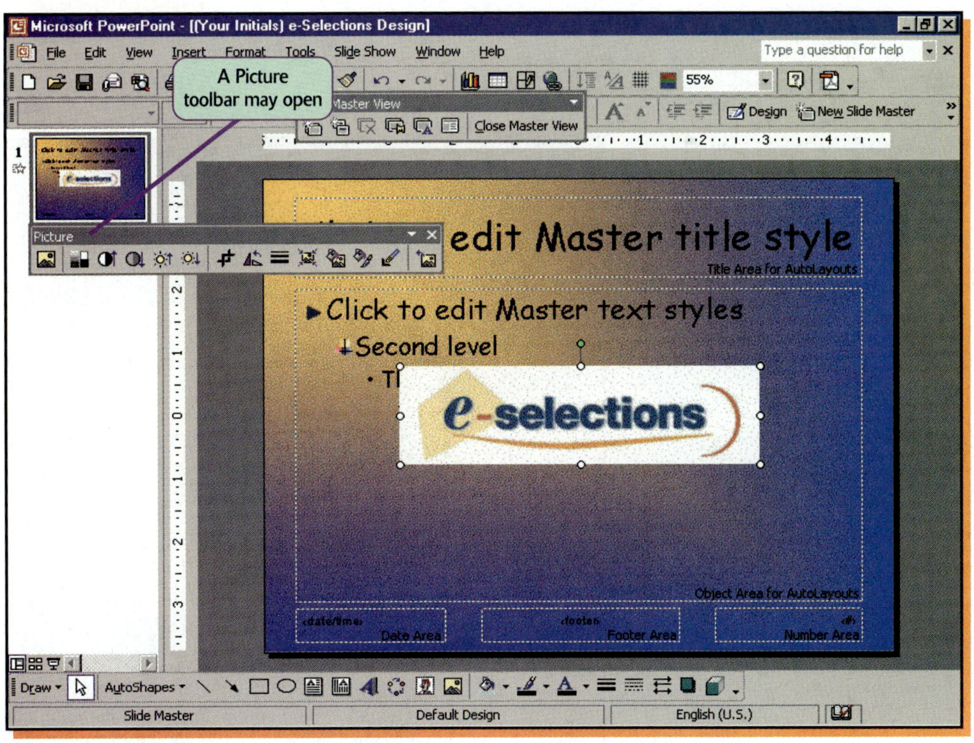

3 Move and size the graphic so that it appears as shown in Figure 5-22.

> **Tip** To size the picture without distorting the picture, drag a corner handle. To move the picture, point to the center of the picture and drag it to the position shown.

Figure 5-22

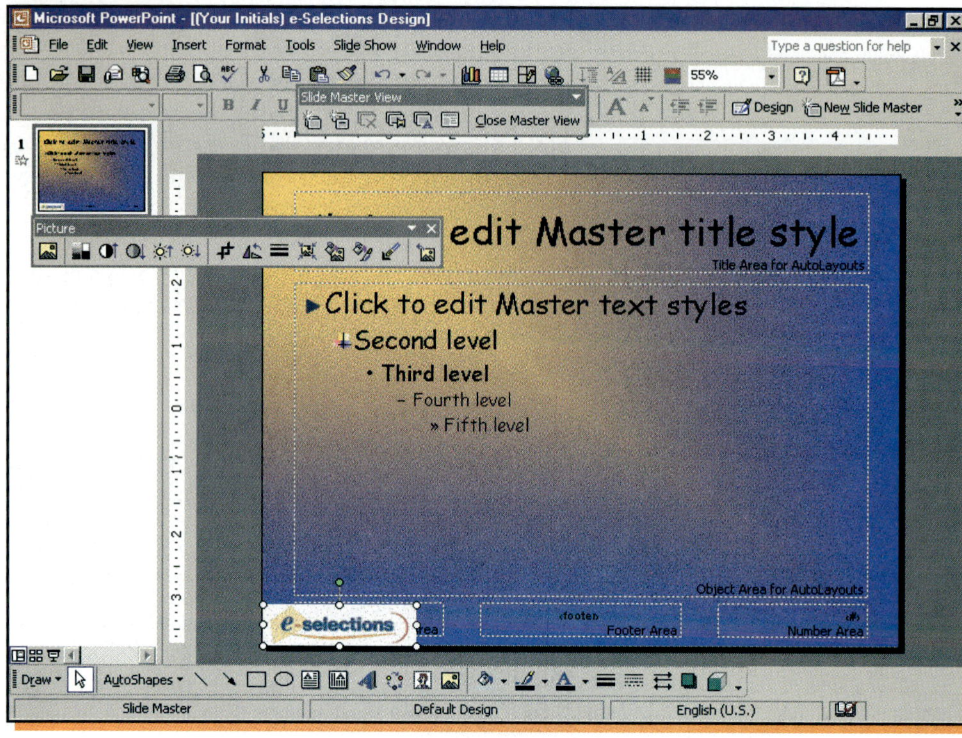

4 Select the graphic, display the Picture toolbar, if necessary, and click the Set Transparent Color button on the Picture toolbar.

> **Tip** When you click the Set Transparent Color button, the mouse pointer appears to carry a wand brush with an arrow tip.

Figure 5-23

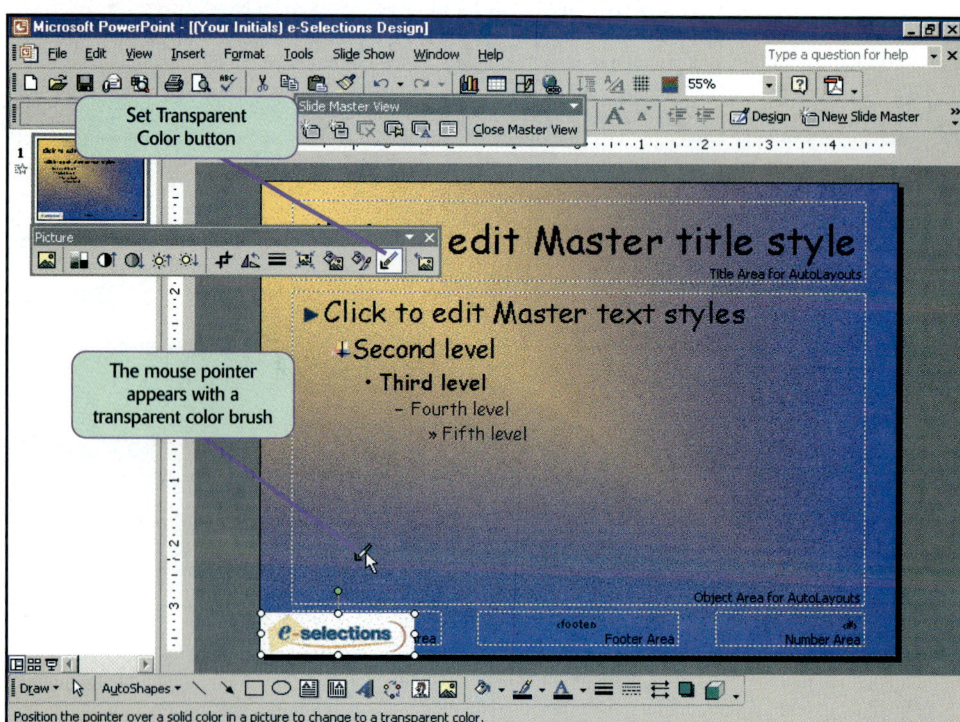

5 Click a white corner of the graphic.

6 Save changes to the presentation.

Tip Be careful when you click the picture--if you click a different area of the picture, the wrong portion of the picture becomes transparent.

Figure 5-24

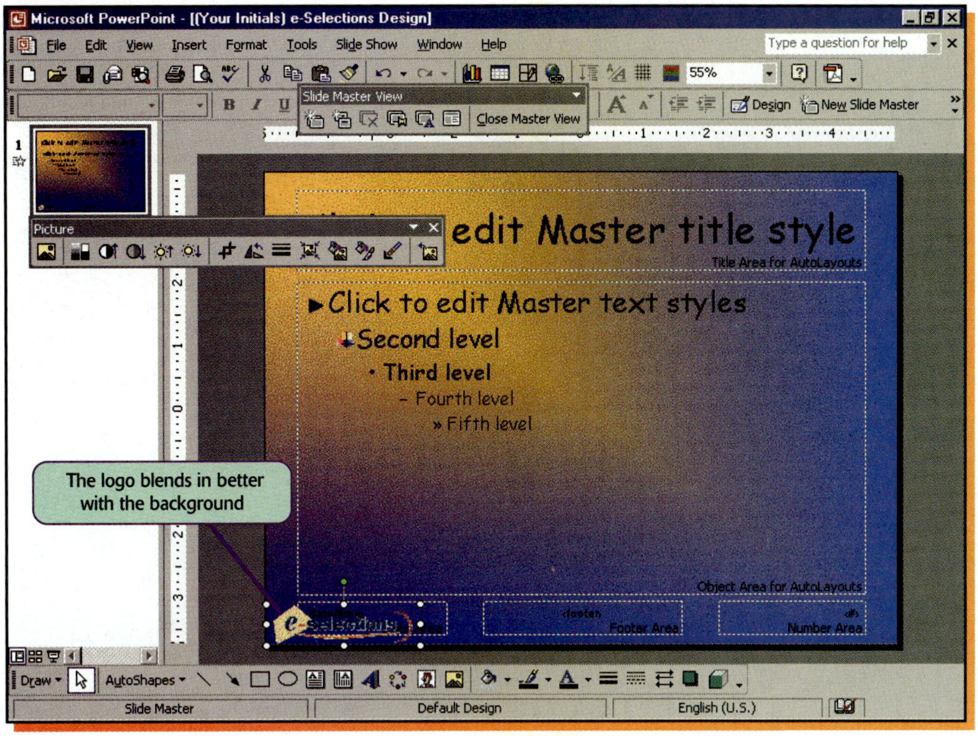

WEB TIP

Want to remember some oldies but goodies? Visit Life Magazine's "Places We Remember" and browse through the collective life of the Beatles.

Creating Title Masters

Slide Masters contain design features that are applied to all slides in the presentation except title slides. Because text on the title slide is often arranged differently from text on other slides in a presentation, you may want to adjust the layout and design for title slides using the Title Master. PowerPoint applies Title Master format to all slides in a presentation formatted using the Title slide layout.

Task 8:

To Create a Presentation Title Master

1 Display the presentation masters and then click the Insert New Title Master button on the Slide Master View toolbar.

Figure 5-25

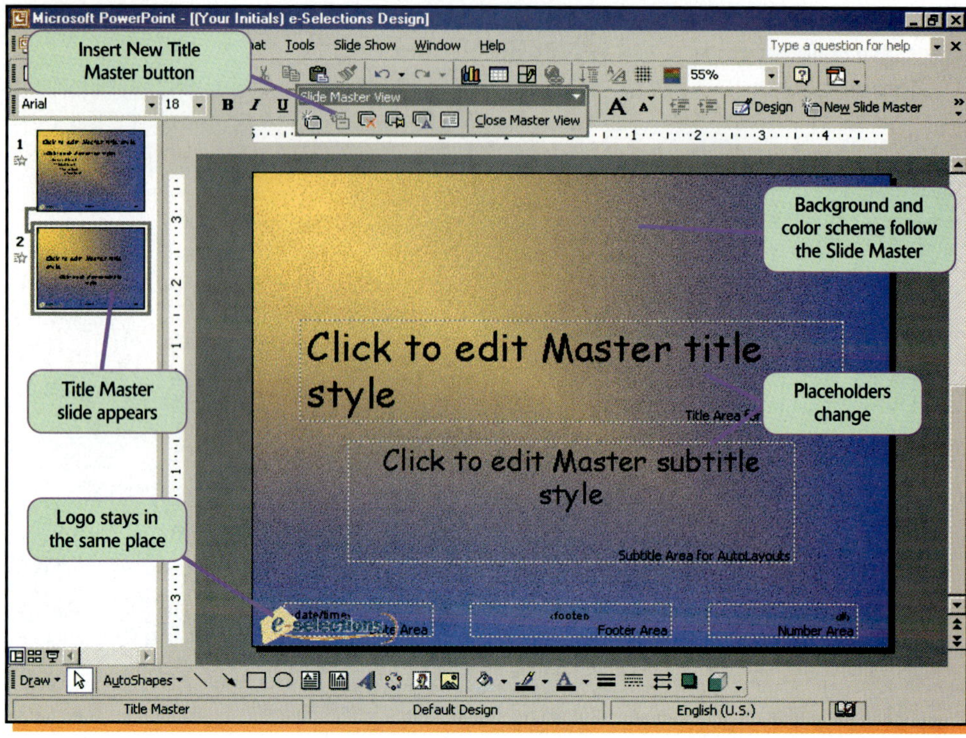

CHECK POINT

How many title masters can you create for a slide master?

Each slide master can have only one title master. As a result, if you have already formatted a title master for a given slide master, you must create a new slide master before creating another title master.

2 Center the text in the Title placeholder, and then select and size the graphic to appear as shown in Figure 5-26.

Tip To remove unwanted placeholders from masters, select the placeholder and press the Delete key.

Figure 5-26

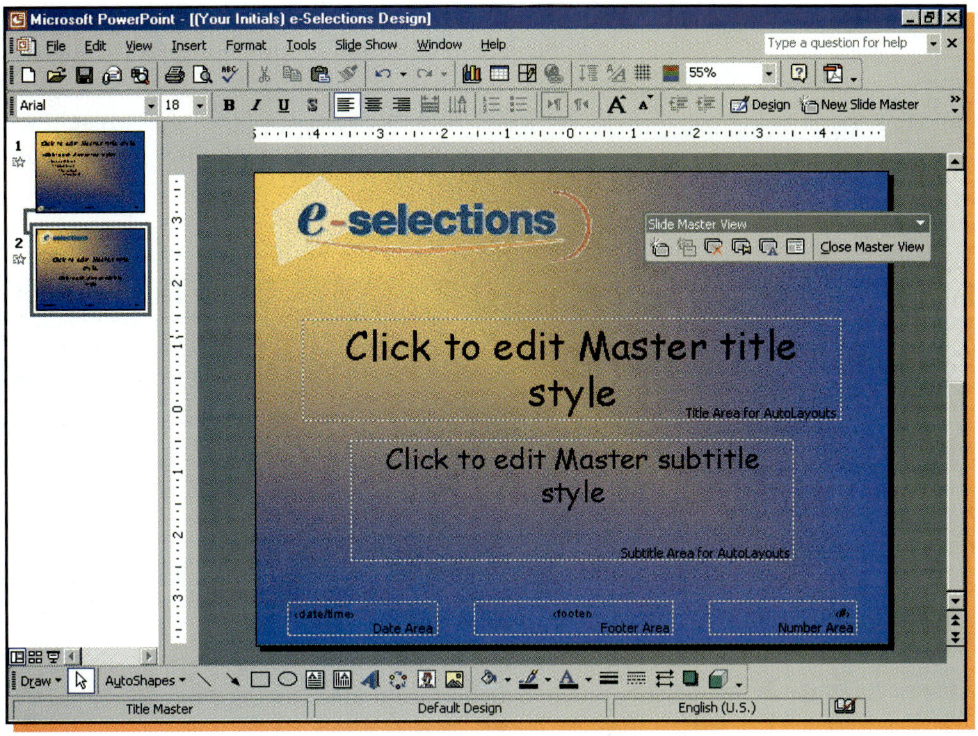

3 Display the Picture toolbar, if necessary, and then click the Color button on the Picture toolbar.

4 Select **Grayscale** and view the affect, then change the image color back to **Automatic** by selecting it from the Color list on the Picture toolbar.

5 Close the Picture toolbar, click **Close Master View** on the Slide Master View toolbar, and save changes to the presentation.

Figure 5-27

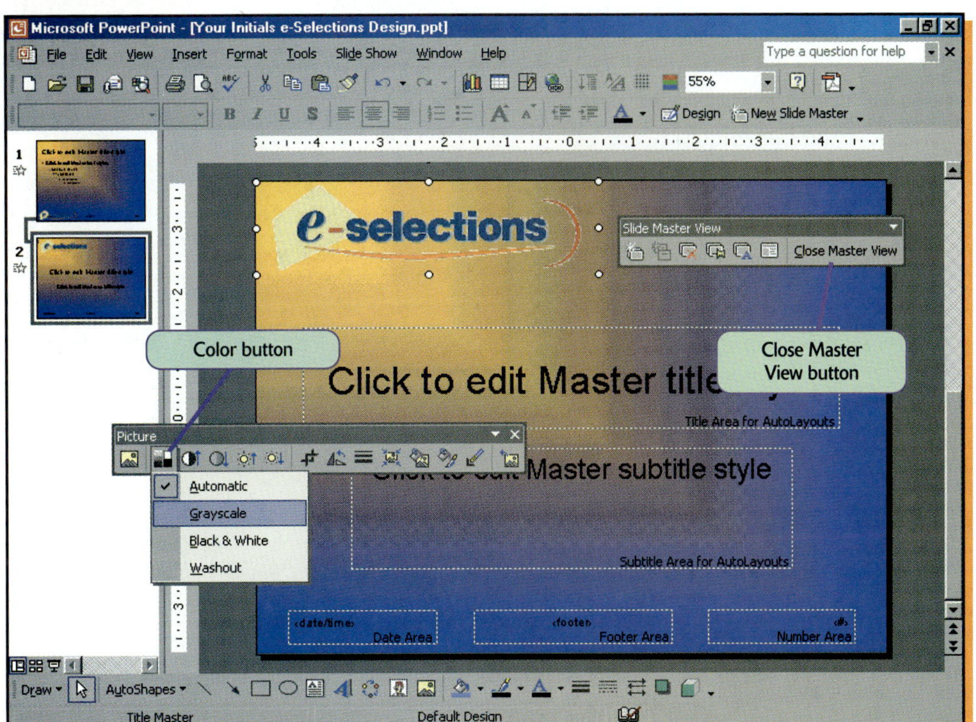

Saving Presentation Designs as Templates

Designing a presentation template for company or personal use often takes hours. As you've been working with your design, you've saved the file as a presentation to preserve your work. Saving your design as a template preserves the work in a format that you can apply to new presentations or use to reformat existing presentations. Templates store master designs and objects added to the masters.

Task 9:
To Save a Presentation Design as a Template

1. Switch to **Normal** view and choose **File | Save As.** The Save As dialog box opens.
2. Click the **Save as type** drop-down list arrow and select **Design Template**.
3. Type ***Your Initials*** **e-Selections Design** in the File name text box and press Enter. The template name appears in the presentation title bar.
4. Close the presentation template.

Figure 5-28

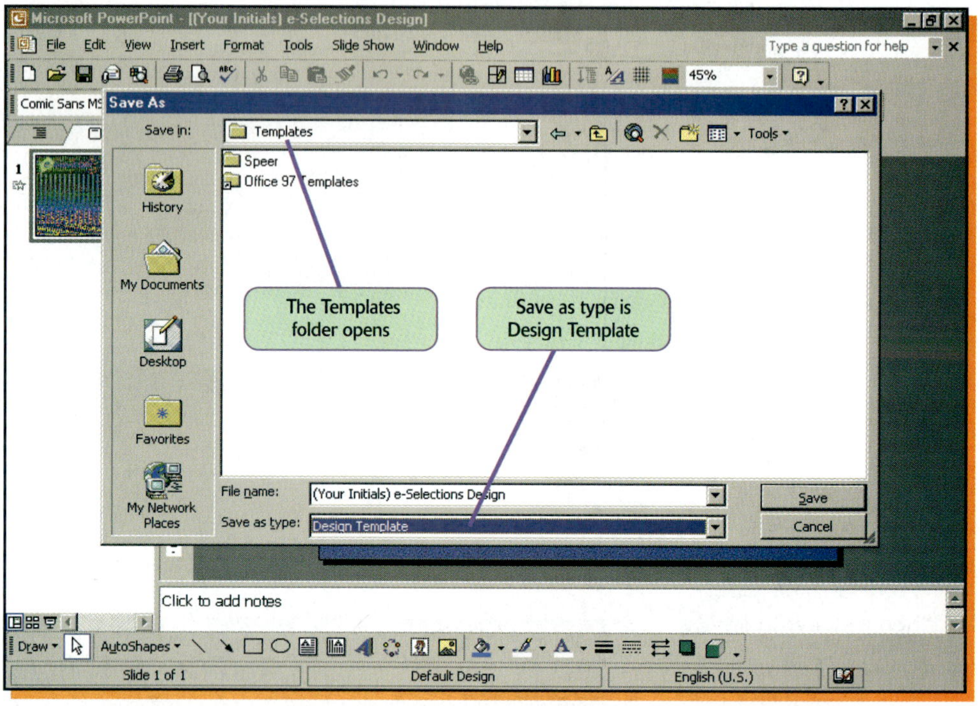

Troubleshooting To ensure that your presentation design is listed on the pages of the New Presentation dialog box when you choose **File | New**, PowerPoint automatically displays the template folder in which you need to save the template. On individual computers that require no logging in, that folder is contained on the hard disk. If you're logging onto a network, check with your instructor to find out where to save your template.

5 Choose **File** | **New**, click the **General Templates** link on the task pane, and then click the **General** tab.

6 Select your template name and press Enter. A new presentation containing a title slide formatted with the custom Title Master design is automatically created.

Figure 5-29

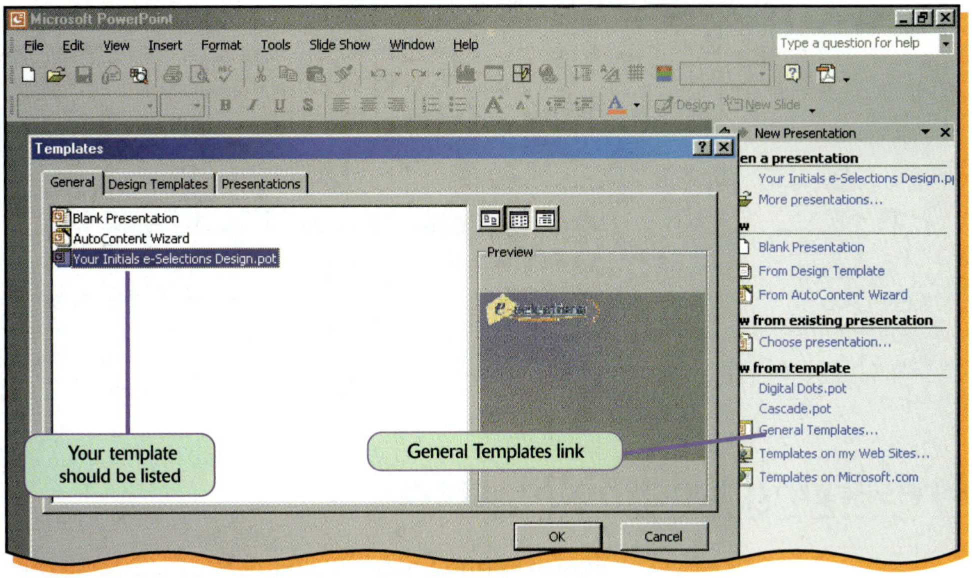

Troubleshooting If you saved the template file to a different disk or folder, open the folder containing your template. You should also see your template among those shown on the Slide Templates task pane.

7 Type **My New Title Master** in the title placeholder of the slide and type your name in the subtitle placeholder.

8 Create a new bulleted-list slide titled Presentation Masters that contains the following bullet points:

- Slide Master
- Title Master
- Handout Master
- Notes Master

9 Save the presentation using the file name *Working with Masters* and print a copy of the presentation as handouts with two slides per page.

Figure 5-30

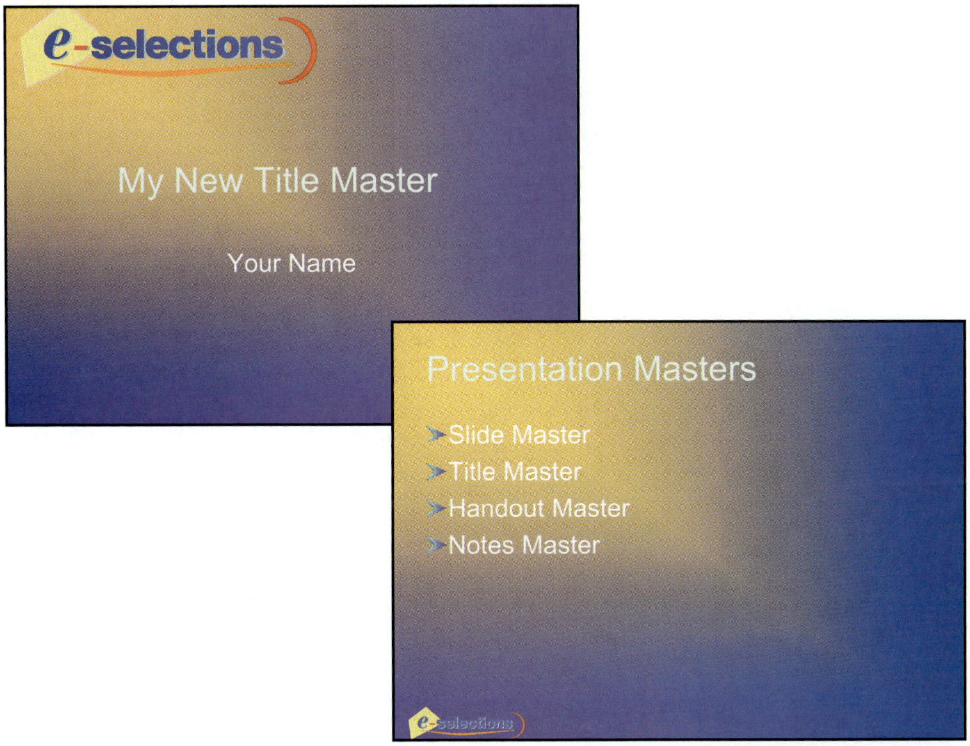

CHECK POINT

You can open the template and edit the template design. Choose **File | Open**, select **Design Templates** from the Files of type list, open the **Presentation Designs** subfolder in the Templates folder, if necessary, and double-click the template name. Changes you make to the presentation template and text you add while the template is open automatically become part of the presentation design.

If you have already created a presentation and have altered or edited the colors or format of text in the presentation, you can use this presentation as a basis for creating a new presentation template. Be sure, when you use an existing presentation to create a template, that you delete all slide text before saving the presentation as a template; and be sure to choose **File | Save As** before saving the presentation as a template. You should leave the original presentation intact!

Preserving Existing Masters

PowerPoint automatically deletes masters from templates when all presentation slides formatted using the master are removed from a presentation or when you apply a different template to the presentation. To prevent PowerPoint from automatically deleting unused masters, you can set the preserve feature for the master. When one master in a Title/Slide Master pair is preserved, PowerPoint preserves both masters in the pair.

Troubleshooting While PowerPoint preserves masters from automatic deletion, other users can manually delete preserved masters.

Task 10:
To Preserve Masters

1. Display the **Slide Master**, if necessary, and select one of the pair of master thumbnails you want to preserve.

2. Click the Preserve Master button on the Slide Master View toolbar.

3. Click **Close Master View** on the Slide Master View toolbar and save and close the file.

Figure 5-31

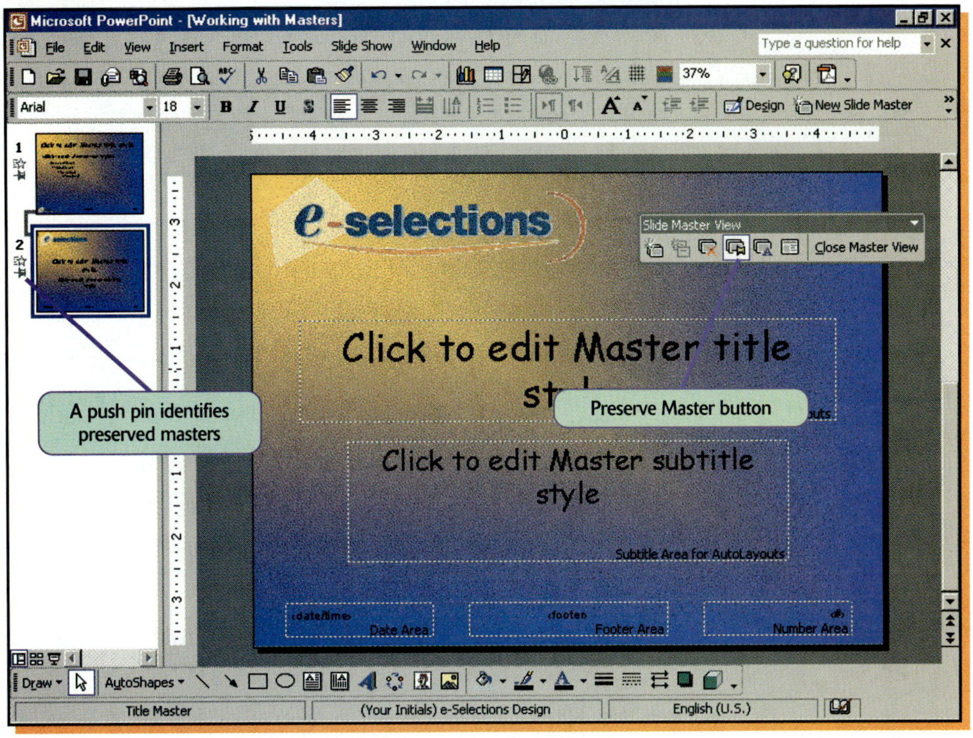

WEB TIP

Search the Internet for companies that market "policing" programs. Then create a Word document that identifies at least two products and descriptions of the programs.

SUMMARY AND EXERCISES

SUMMARY

- Masters enable you to make changes to text placeholder formats so that the changes appear on all slides in the presentation.
- The same techniques used to change the Slide Master are used to change the format and design of Title Masters, Notes Pages Masters, and Handouts Masters.
- Changes made to the Slide Master apply to slides formatted using all slide layouts *except* the Title slide layout.
- Format changes made to the Title Master affect only those slides formatted using the Title slide layout.
- Format changes you make to individual slides are unaffected by changes made to masters.
- PowerPoint provides a variety of different text categories that contain bullet shapes and formats that you can apply to bullet levels.
- You can change the appearance of a presentation template by changing the slide background color. Different features enable you to create special effects with the background fill.
- When you create a presentation design that you want to save and use again, you can save the design as a template. When you save the template in the Templates/Presentation Designs folder, the name you assign to the template appears alphabetically on the General page of the New Presentation dialog box.
- Slides formatted with the Title slide layout format will follow the color design of the Slide Master unless you create a special Title Master for the presentation template.
- Multiple masters can be added to a presentation template in PowerPoint 2002.
- To prevent PowerPoint from automatically deleting unused masters associated with a template, preserve the master. If you preserve one master in a master pair, PowerPoint automatically preserves the other master in the pair.

KEY TERMS & SKILLS

KEY TERMS

alignment (p. 5-10)
bullet format (p. 5-12)
color scheme (p. 5-6)
master (p. 5-5)
Slide Master (p. 5-5)
template (p. 5-5)
Title Master (p. 5-5)

SKILLS

Apply custom animation schemes to masters (p. 5-13)
Change bullet formats on Slide Masters (p. 5-12)
Change text style and alignment on Slide Masters (p. 5-11)
Create Title Masters (p. 5-19)
Customize a color scheme (p. 5-8)
Display presentation masters (p. 5-5)
Format the slide background (p. 5-6)
Insert and format graphics on Slide Masters (p. 5-17)
Preserve existing masters (p. 5-25)
Save a presentation design as a template (p. 5-22)

STUDY QUESTIONS

MULTIPLE CHOICE

1. You can display the presentation Slide Master by
   a. clicking the **Master** shortcut icon on the desktop.
   b. choosing **View | Master | Slide Master**.
   c. choosing **Slide Master** from the Slide Show menu.
   d. displaying a slide and pressing Enter.

2. Format changes you make to the Slide Master
   a. affect every slide in the presentation.
   b. affect every slide in the presentation except title slides.
   c. affect every slide in the presentation except title slides and slides that have been individually formatted.
   d. affect only the slide that was active when you displayed the Slide Master.

3. Area placeholders, such as page number, appear, by default, in the
   a. header area of a slide.
   b. footer area of masters.
   c. header and footer area of masters.
   d. margin of slides.

4. Information you want to add to the footer area of slides must be "turned on" from the
   a. Slide Master.
   b. Title Master.
   c. Header and Footer dialog box.
   d. individual presentation slides.

5. The area of a slide behind slide objects is called the
   a. mat.
   b. background.
   c. color scheme.
   d. template.

6. To change the color of the slide background,
   a. select the color from the Fill Color palette.
   b. double-click the slide background and set the color.
   c. select the color from the color palette in the Background dialog box.
   d. select a different template.

7. PowerPoint templates are stored
  a. in the Inbox.
  b. in the My Documents folder.
  c. in the root directory of drive C.
  d. in the Templates folder.

8. To save a presentation design as a template,
  a. choose **File | Save As**, select **Design Template** from the **Save as type** list, and type a name for the design.
  b. click the Save button.
  c. choose **File | Close**, and answer **Yes** when asked whether you want to save your work.
  d. delete the presentation and then save the template.

9. To copy a graphic from the Slide Master to the Title Master,
  a. drag the graphic to the Title Master.
  b. copy the graphic to the clipboard and paste it in the Title Master.
  c. you must redraw or insert the graphic on the Title Master.
  d. when the graphic appears on the Slide Master, it appears in the same position on the Title Master so there is no need to copy it.

SHORT ANSWER

1. From what menu do you display the Masters?
2. What Masters are available for formatting slides in a presentation?
3. What is the term associated with varying the shading of a slide background or filled object?
4. To change the direction of the shading on a slide background, what do you select?
5. What folder contains template designs?
6. What effect does changing the template design in one presentation have on existing presentations formatted using the same template?
7. How do you change the position of the slide number on a slide?
8. How do you display the Header and Footer dialog box?

FILL IN THE BLANK

1. Presentation masters form the ____________ of a presentation.
2. Template design usually follows a basic ____________-step process.
3. Pictures that are usually associated with a particular business or company are called ____________ and make great graphics on corporate templates.
4. Design elements are stored in layouts called ____________.
5. A ____________ design is applied to slides formatted using all slide layouts except the Title slide layout.
6. The ____________ design is applied to slides formatted using the Title slide layout.
7. The ____________ for the template master contains a color design that provides the backdrop for all text and objects you place on presentation slides.
8. The combination of colors for each different item that appears on a master is called a ____________.

9. Bullets for _____________ different text levels can be customized.
10. _____________ effects can be set on slides to affect the way all slides in a presentation move on and off the screen.

FOR DISCUSSION

1. What characteristics and features of slides in a presentation do you need to review after customizing template designs?
2. What is the difference between a slide layout and a Slide Master layout?
3. What are the steps required to open a template so that you can edit it?
4. How does the footer area of a Slide Master differ from the footer area of a Word document?

GUIDED EXERCISES

1 MASTERING MASTER CREATION

Each template you create in PowerPoint 2002 can contain numerous sets of masters. Now that you have completed the first set of masters for e-Selections Division of Selections, Inc., you can add another set of masters to the template, as Mr. Carroll requested. The second set of masters for the template appears in Figure 5-32.

Figure 5-32

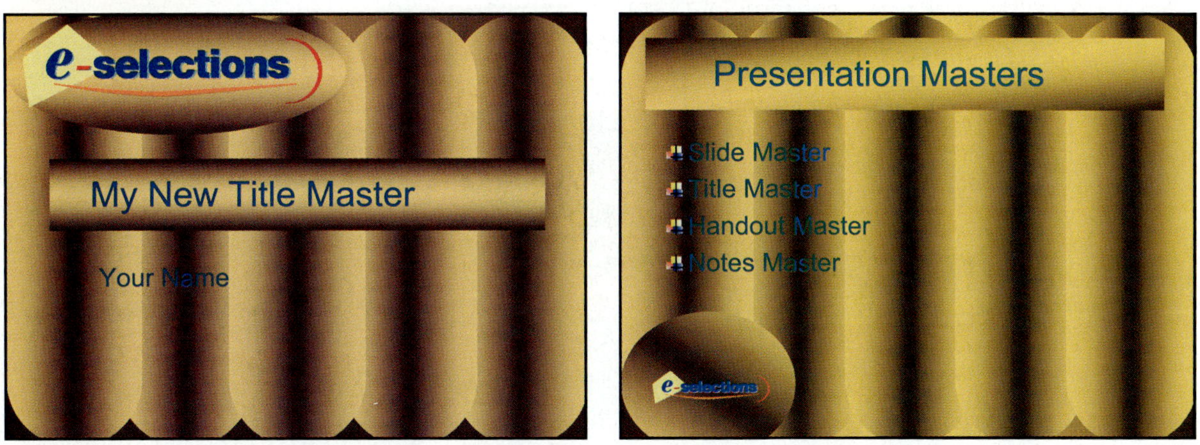

Follow these directions to create the second set of masters:

1. Open the PowerPoint presentation template *Your Initials e-Selections Design.pot*, and choose **View | Master | Slide Master**.

2. Click the Insert New Slide Master button on the Slide Master View toolbar.

3. Follow the five-step process to format the Slide Master background, bullets, font, and graphics to create the design shown in Figure 5-32.

> **Tip** The template contains numerous drawn objects. Draw the first vertical oval and then copy it to create identical ovals. Feel free to use your imagination and create a custom template if your instructor approves. Refer to Common Elements Project 3 for more detailed information about creating drawn objects.

4. Click the Insert New Title Master button on the Slide Master View toolbar.
5. Create the Title Master shown in Figure 5-32.
6. Save changes to the template and apply the masters to the presentation *Working with Masters.ppt.*
7. Print a copy of each presentation slide and e-mail the presentation to your instructor.

2 FORMATTING SLIDE MASTER PLACEHOLDERS

As you completed the tasks in this project, you learned how to format the background of templates. Placeholders are, in effect, simply drawn objects. As a result, you can apply the same basic techniques you used to format the background to format the master placeholders and add depth to the template design, as shown in Figure 5-33.

Figure 5-33

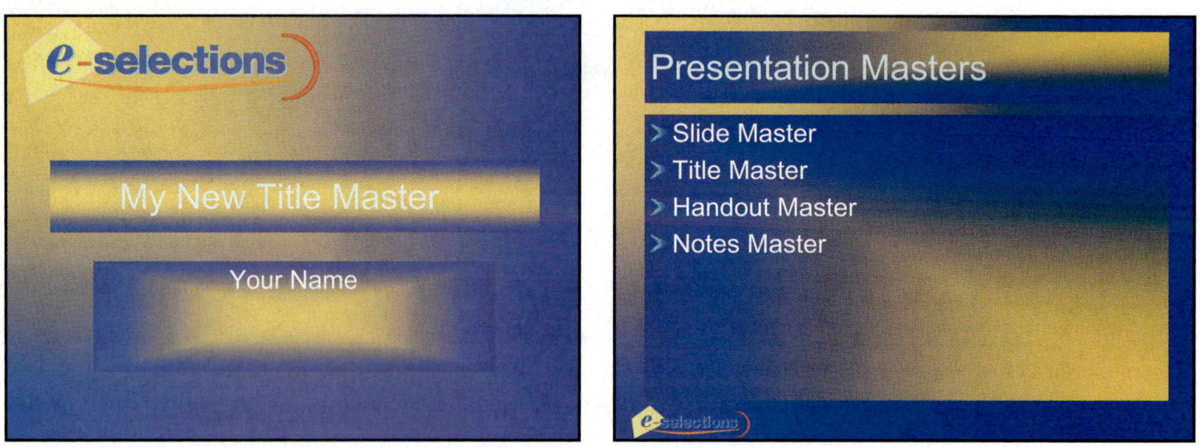

Use the following techniques to change the template design:

1. Open the template *Your Initials e-Selections Design.pot*.
2. Display the blue Slide Master, press Shift, and click the *Object Area for AutoLayouts* placeholder.

3. Delete bullet-list levels 4 and 5.
4. Display the **Drawing** toolbar, if necessary, click the Fill Color button on the Drawing toolbar, and select **Fill Effects**.
5. Select a **Shading style** and **Variant** that is different from the style and variant of the background and resembles the format shown in Figure 5-33.
6. Click **Preview** in the Fill Effects dialog box to view the effect, reselect a style and variant until you achieve the special effect, and then click **OK**.
7. Select the *Title Area for AutoLayouts* placeholder and apply a similar shading style and variant to the placeholder.
8. Save changes to the presentation template.
9. Repeat the procedures outlined in Steps 2 through 8 to format the master title and subtitle placeholders and save changes to the template.
10. Apply the new template design to the presentation *Working with Masters.ppt* and e-mail a copy of the presentation to your instructor.
11. Save and close the presentation.

3 HANDING OUT MASTERS

As you've discovered, each item that appears on a slide contains a special format and color set on masters in the template. Now that you have the template Slide and Title Masters completed, you can focus your attention to formatting the masters for other presentation materials to complement the presentation Slide and Title Masters. A sample of a Handout Master with two slides is shown in Figure 5-34.

Figure 5-34

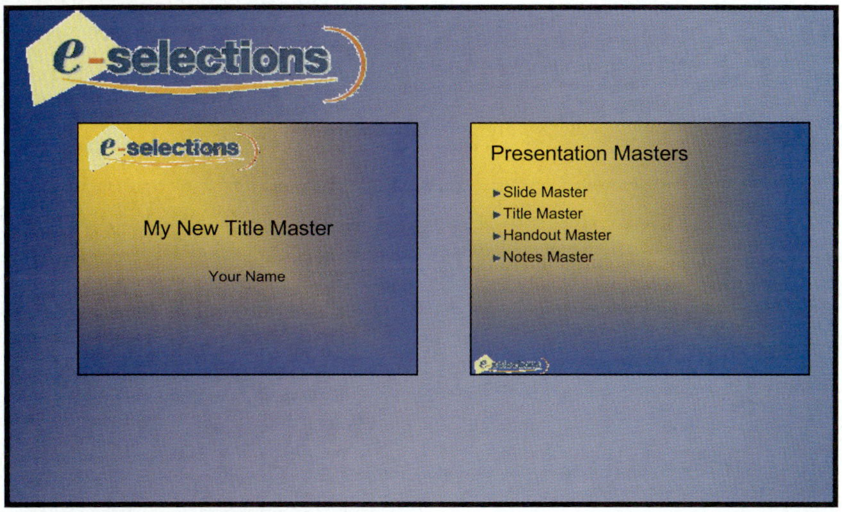

Follow these steps to format the handouts.

1. Open the *Your Initials e-Selections Design.pot* template.
2. Press and hold Shift and click the Slide Sorter View button at the bottom of the presentation window.
3. Click the **Show positioning of 6-per-page handouts** button.
4. Format the Handout Master background using the same techniques you used to format the background for the Slide Master. Select a fill and variant that complement the Slide and Title Masters.
5. Delete the Header Area placeholder and add the *e-Selections.jpg* graphic to the upper left corner of the master, sizing and formatting it appropriately.
6. Save changes to the template, print a copy of the Handouts Master, and e-mail the template to your instructor.

ON YOUR OWN

The difficulty of these case studies varies:

(1 flag) are the least difficult; (2 flags) are more difficult; and (3 flags) are the most difficult.

1 BEING CREATIVE

PowerPoint comes equipped with quite a variety of different templates that you can apply to presentations. Select one of the presentation templates that you would like to edit and change the background color, bullet formats, and font for the Slide Master. Save the template using the file name *Your Initials Customized Template Name*. Then e-mail the template to your instructor.

2 REINVENTING THE WHEEL—NOT!

The auto industry is in desperate need of a new customized design for their presentations. The only trouble is that they need the template in two hours! Building a presentation template from scratch when time is limited can be a challenge. Scratch templates, in most instances, are also unnecessary—especially when another template already exists that contains many of the features and coloring that you want to include in the new template. The template named *Automotive Template.pot* contains wheels, the perfect start to the presentation design the auto industry needs. Edit and format the design to create the template shown in Figure 5-35. Remember that you may have to adjust the layers of graphics and placeholders to display text in front of graphics. You may also have to ungroup items on the template and group items you draw or rearrange. Save your design as a new template named *Your Initials Automotive Industry*. E-mail your edited template to your instructor.

Figure 5-35

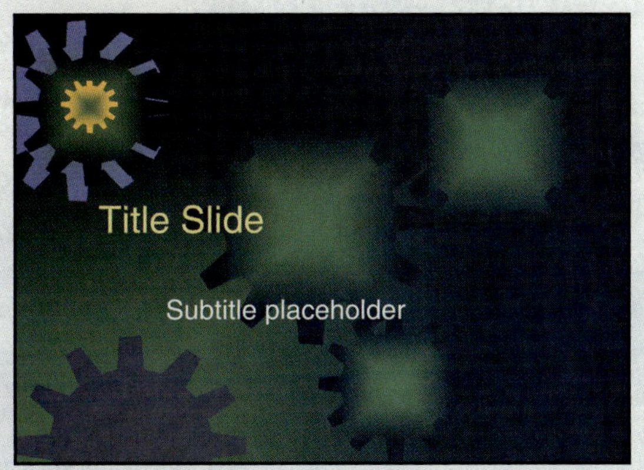

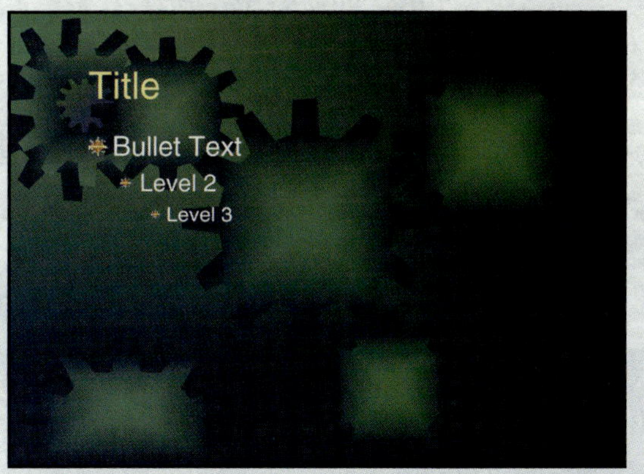

Tip See Common Elements Project 3 for detailed information about grouping and ungrouping drawn objects

3 AMUSING YOURSELF

The number of amusement parks found in the United States and abroad has grown over the last several years. From Disneyland© to HERSHEYPARK©, it seems as if everyone has their own special amusement park that they enjoy visiting. In many cases, they return to the park time and time again. Create a set of masters for the amusement park you enjoy visiting the most. Your masters should include:

- A graphic downloaded from the park's Web site to include on the masters.
- A Title Master with the downloaded graphic centered prominently and formatted with Washed Out color.
- A customized background.

Save the presentation using the file name *Your Initials Park Name* and send a copy of the template to your instructor.

4 REFORMATTING THE GOVERNMENT

Isn't there something about a governmental agency that you've always wanted to change? Well, here's your chance! Go online and locate the Web page for the agency you want to change. Review the features contained on their Web page, identify graphics associated with the agency and download those that you want to include in the template. Then create and design a template that projects the agency image that you believe the agency should project. Your template should contain one complete set of masters (all four masters) for the agency. Save the template using the file name *Your Initials Agency Name*. Print a copy of the Title, Slide, Handout, and Notes Pages Masters and e-mail a copy of the template to your instructor.

5 PERSONALIZING A TEMPLATE

Just as templates designed for companies should contain graphics, logos, and other features that project a professional image, the template you apply to your résumé should reflect your personality as well as the profession for which you are preparing and your credentials. Design a template that meets these requirements and that includes at least one Slide Master and at least four Title Masters—one for each section of your résumé. Save the design as a template using the file name *Your Initials Résumé*. Then apply the template to a presentation that contains your résumé. Adjust the text contained on each presentation slide to meet good presentation design format. Save the presentation using the file name *Your Initials Résumé*. Print a copy of the presentation as handouts with six slides per page.

6 MOVING INTO MOVIES

New movies are released every week—movies that vary in content from hilarious to deep drama. Identify a movie that was released during the current semester that you particularly enjoyed or identified with. Create a template named *Your Initials Movie Name*. Format the template background so that it reflects the nature of the movie. Include a graphic that creatively identifies the theme of the movie. Then create a presentation using the template that includes at least four slides:

- A title slide that identifies the movie title and your name along with the premier date.
- A slide that identifies the producer(s) and director(s).
- A slide that contains the word *Starring* in the title placeholder and the names of the lead actors/actresses as bullet points.
- A slide that names supporting actors/actresses.

Include additional slides as directed by your instructor to include a chronological synopsis of movie scenes and events, movie high point, movie low point, critique of actor/actress performances, suggestions for ways to improve the impact of the move. Save the presentation using an appropriate file name and send a copy of the presentation to your instructor.

Photospread credits pages 5-2 & 5-3

FROM THE FILES

You Will Need

- ✔ e-Selections.jpg
- ✔ e-Selections Online Web.ppt

PROJECT 6

Diagramming Information

The PowerPoint table and organization chart features add structured data to PowerPoint presentations. In addition to the basic table and hierarchical layouts these features offer, PowerPoint contains an extensive charting and graphing feature that enables you to graphically plot values to show relationships between different groups of data. In this project, you explore the PowerPoint graphing tool and learn how to use other diagramming tools to graphically depict information. You'll also edit and save organization charts as graphics.

e-selections Running Case

By now, it's beginning to seem as if the powers of PowerPoint are never ending! You dabbled with tables and organization charts and used those features to enter some simple structured data. Now it's time to explore the extended capabilities of PowerPoint diagrams and take a look at PowerPoint's true charting capabilities.

OBJECTIVES

After completing this project, you will be able to:

- *Work with Microsoft Graph*
- *Enter data in datasheets*
- *Format charts*
- *Animate charts*
- *Create diagrams*
- *Format diagrams*
- *Reorganize diagrams*
- *Animate diagrams*
- *Edit and save organization charts as graphics*

Don't Let Your Presentation Go Down with the Ship...

Jim Endicott, Owner/Manager of Distinction Communication compares creating templates to watching the movie *Titanic!* He says, "If you've seen the movie *Titanic*, it's pretty tough not to be overwhelmed with the visual magnitude of everything your eyes are taking in—it's mind boggling to say the least. From expansive shipyard panoramas to the decadent interiors, most of us found ourselves drawn deeply into the era." He points out that the director never once betrayed the fact that much of what we saw was created from the minds of some very creative computer graphic artists. That's right—the exterior ship images, the shipyard, the big blue Atlantic—many of the things you saw came right out of a computer!

Companies spend millions of dollars each year to create and project a corporate image—an image that is unique to their company—an image with a catchy phrase or theme song that we automatically associate with the company and its products.

Thousands of times every day marketing representatives, salespeople, and corporate executives stand in front of their clients, and potential clients, and deliver presentations that contain supporting graphics that bear no resemblance to their corporate identities. This paradigm is changing . . . business professionals are finally realizing that their presentations need to present as cohesive a corporate image as their brochures, jingles, and slogans do. Presentations to potential clients are, in fact, the first chance many companies have to make a good impression—and, as they say, you never get a second chance to make a good first impression! Here are some tips for projecting your corporate image through the use of standardized corporate templates for all your presentations:

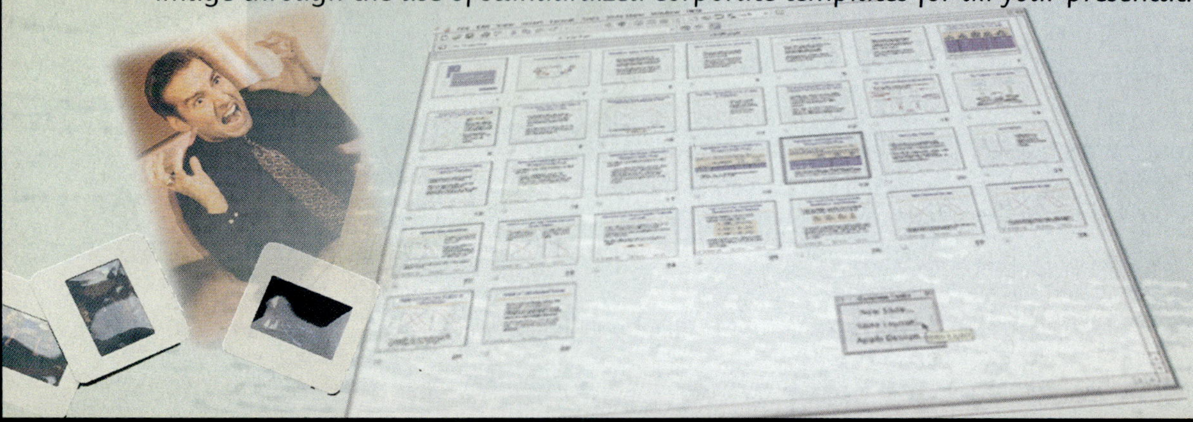

- Set standards for company colors, logo usage, and supporting images.
- Create backgrounds using a paint program, such as PhotoShop, to enhance the template design and elegance.
- Limit your font usage to increase readability and follow corporate standards.
- Define a set of colors that others can use to create presentations more easily.
- Format and align text fields that allow two-line titles.
- Review the rules for formatting and limiting slide text, and then create several sample slides that reinforce these rules.
- Identify and obtain professional graphic elements.

Remember—to be a good presenter is to be a good communicator. If designing your own presentation template simply overwhelms you, seek out a design firm with specific expertise in presentation graphics. It's worth the extra mile…and the extra dollars!

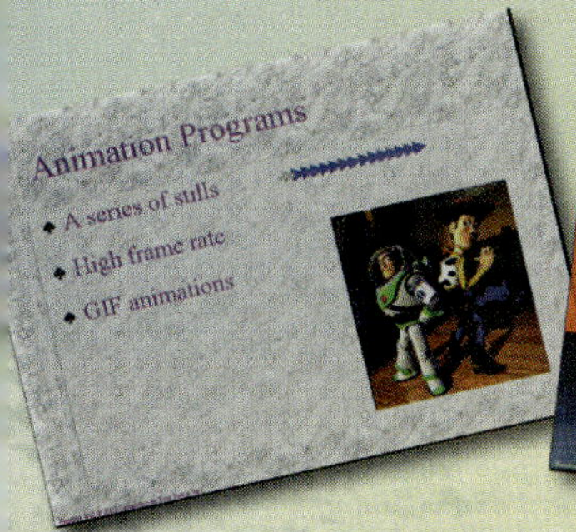

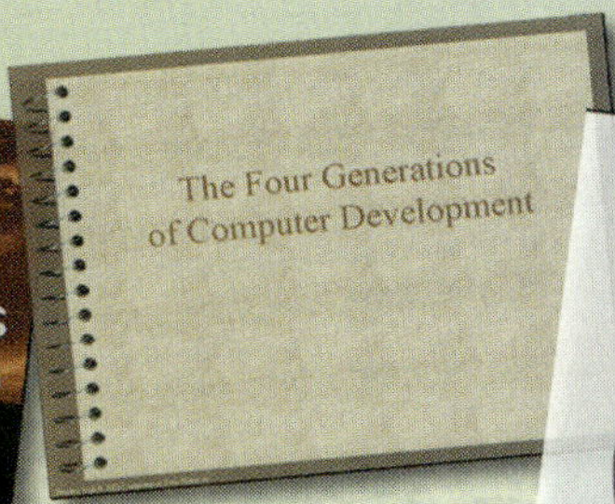

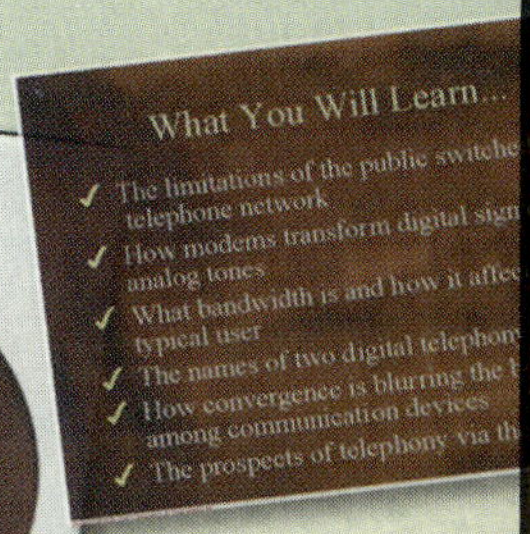

PROJECT 6

Diagramming Information

The Challenge

As e-Selections division Administrative Vice President, Mr. Ronald Carroll has the responsibility of submitting a report on division sales data to the corporate headquarters of Selections, Inc., in Omaha, Nebraska, at the end of each quarter. This year, the company president wants to impress the Board of Directors with the success of their online division and has asked Mr. Carroll to appear at the meeting and deliver a presentation about the division to the Board at its meeting next week. Mr. Carroll wants to make a great impression on the Board and has asked you to collect the sales data for each e-Selections region for last year as well as year-to-date information for the current year. He also wants to ensure that the charts will reflect last-minute changes made to the data. In addition, Mr. Carroll wants you to create a diagram that shows the departments that are currently online and expand the organization chart created in another presentation to display additional levels. After you have collected the data, he would like you to create new slides similar to those displayed in Figure 6-1 to effectively display the data.

Figure 6-1

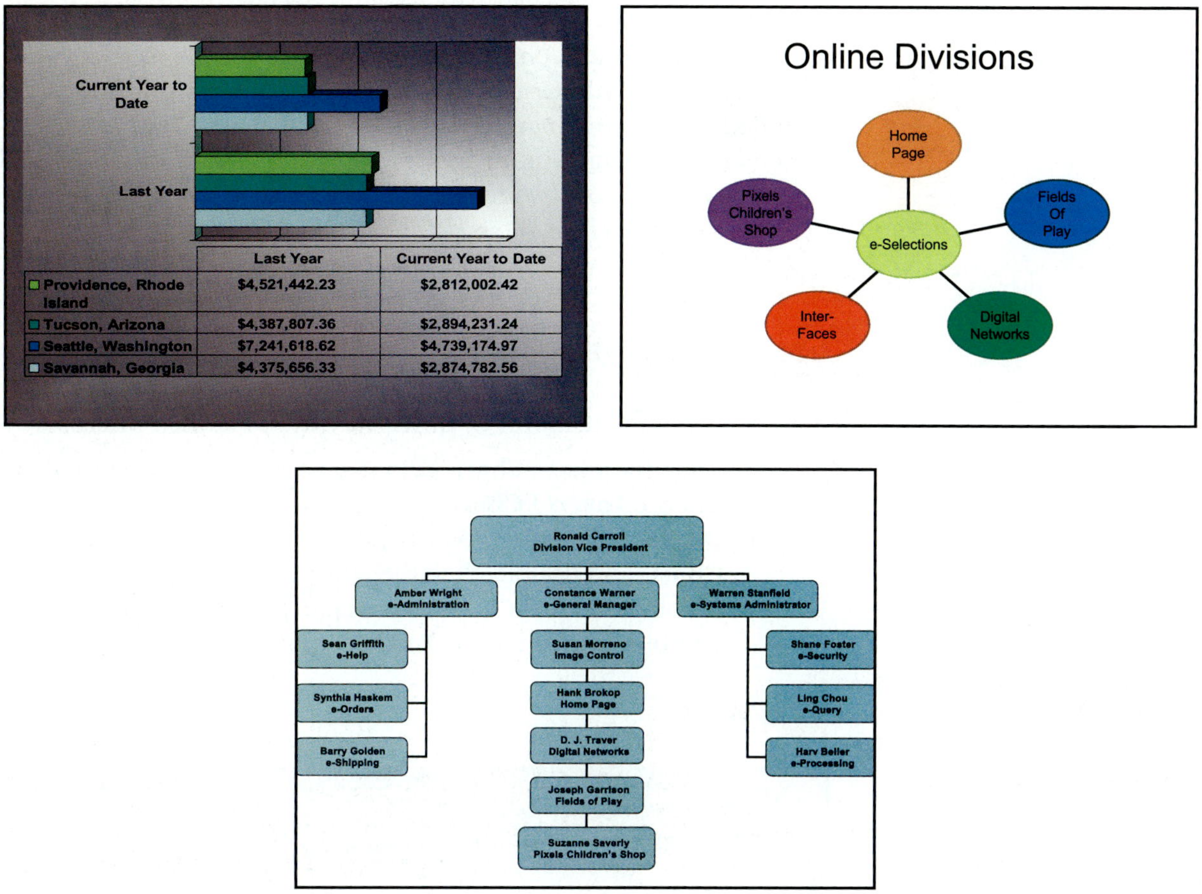

The Solution

Using PowerPoint charting tools, you can easily develop and plot the data Mr. Carroll wants to include in his presentation. Not only can you edit the existing organization chart to display additional levels, you can use the Microsoft Graph program to chart the sales data and create the diagrams using PowerPoint's new diagramming features. By creating diagrams on PowerPoint slides, you can quickly update the diagram on the slide as new departments come online. Because you'll store the sales data graph in PowerPoint, PowerPoint will automatically update the graph as you make changes to the sales data. You'll also discover how animating graphs and diagrams can wow the audience when Mr. Carroll delivers the presentation to the Board!

Working with Microsoft Graph

Charts graphically plot values to show data relationships to other data. One efficient way to add a chart to a PowerPoint slide is to use a special charting program. Microsoft Graph is a separate application that is automatically installed when you install PowerPoint. You can launch Microsoft Graph directly from PowerPoint to create charts and graphs. When you add a chart to a slide using Microsoft Graph tools, the chart becomes part of the presentation. No separate chart file is created.

Launching Microsoft Graph

PowerPoint offers a couple of different ways to launch Microsoft Graph:

- Click the Insert Chart button on the Standard toolbar.
- Choose **Insert | Chart**.
- Display the **Slide Layout** task pane, select a layout that contains a **Chart**, and double-click the chart object.
- Display the **Slide Layout** task pane, select a layout that contains a **Content**, and click the **Insert Chart** object.

Task 1:
To Launch Microsoft Graph

1. Launch PowerPoint and create a new blank presentation.
2. Display the **Slide Layout** task pane, apply the **Content** slide layout to the new slide, and close the task pane.
3. Point to the Insert Chart button.

Figure 6-2

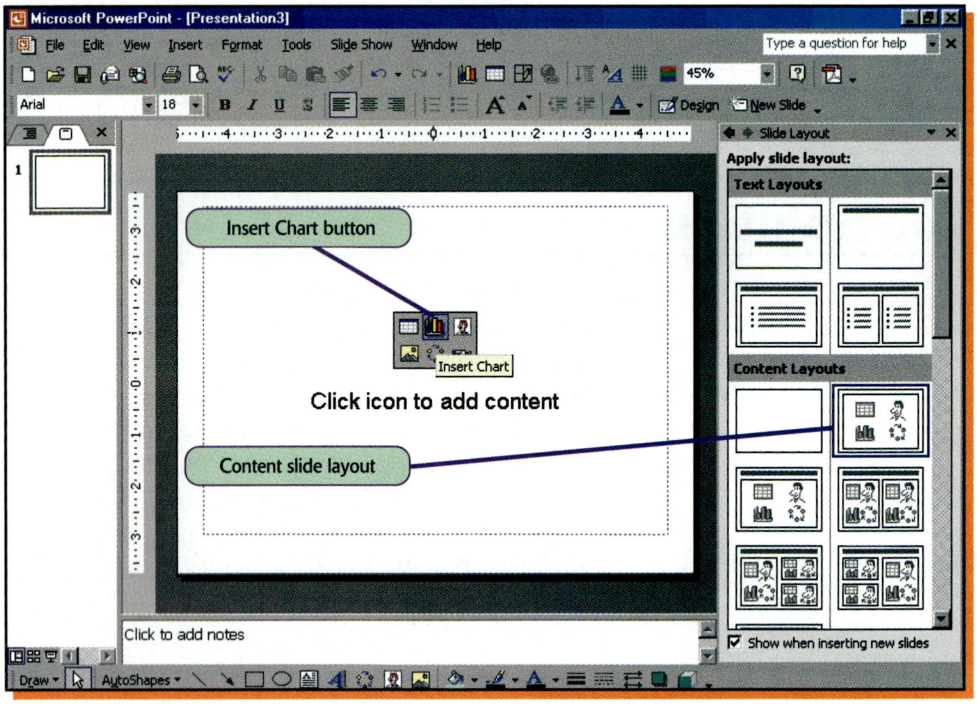

4 Click the Insert Chart icon button in the content placeholder.

> **Troubleshooting**
> If you accidentally click an area outside the graph or datasheet, Microsoft Graph closes and the chart appears on the PowerPoint slide. Simply double-click the chart to launch Microsoft Graph.

Figure 6-3

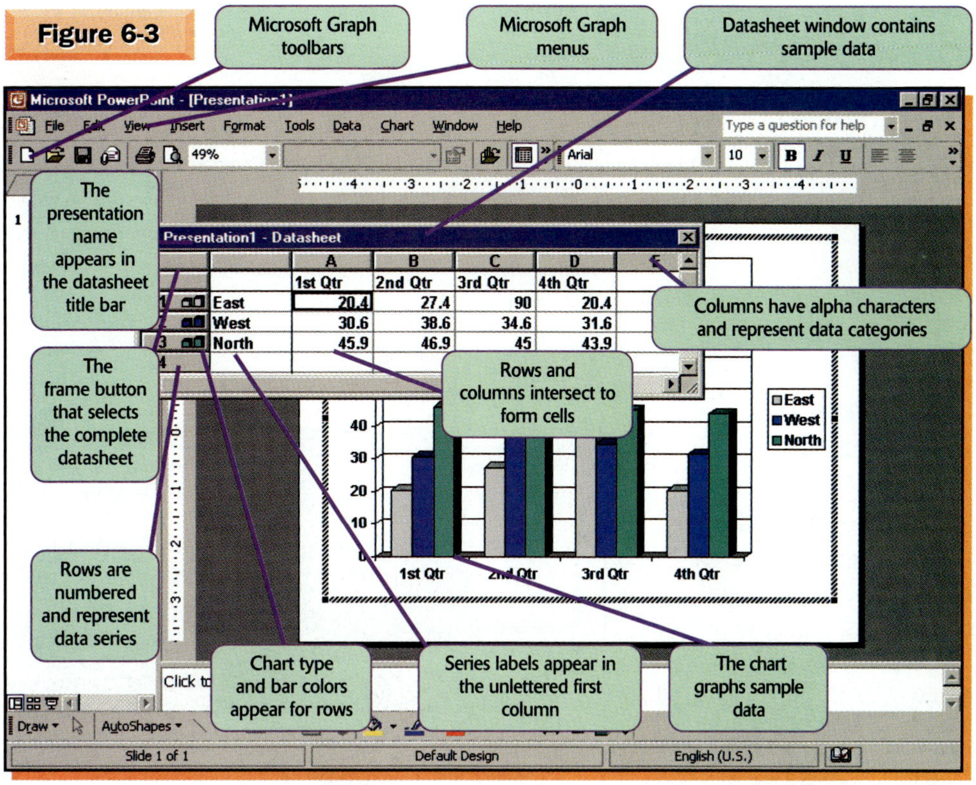

Entering Data in Datasheets

Datasheets contain the data and values that you want to graph. The techniques you use to work in the datasheet are similar to the techniques you use to edit worksheet data in Excel Access tables, or table data in Word and PowerPoint. However, the terminology associated with datasheets more closely resembles terminology associated with Excel, as described in Table 6-1.

Table 6-1 Datasheet Terminology

Term	Description
Columns	Consist of a vertical arrangement of cells containing categories of data and are identified by alphabetic characters, such as B.
Rows	Horizontal arrangement of cells that contain a series of data and are identified by numbers, such as 3.
Cells	The intersections of columns and rows that contain one piece of information.
Cell Address	Consists of the column letter and row number that intersect, such as B3.
Frame	The border that contains the column letters and the row numbers. You can click a frame button to select a column, a row, or the entire datasheet.

WEB TIP

A number of different companies provide graphing and charting programs that you can download from the Internet—many of these programs are available for a free trial! Search for the programs and download the ones that sound interesting for a trial. Compare the capabilities of the free programs to the features found in Microsoft Graph.

Task 2:
To Create the Datasheet

1. Click **Select All** in the upper left corner of the frame. The complete datasheet is highlighted.

Tip Selecting the complete datasheet ensures that all cells containing data are selected.

2. Press Delete to remove all datasheet data.

Figure 6-4

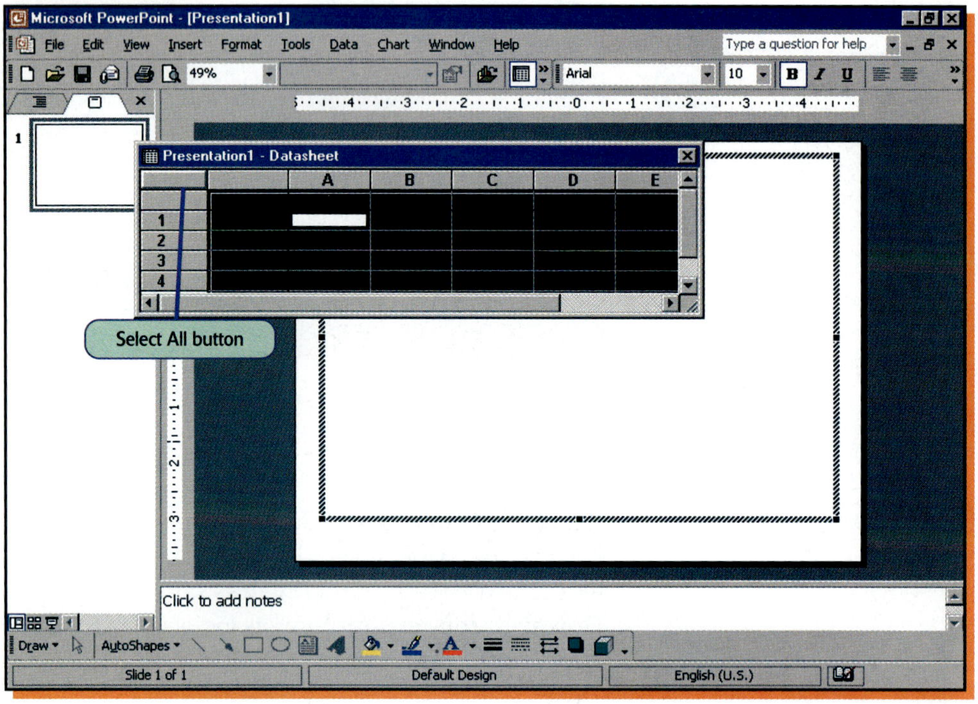

3 Type the sales data into datasheet cells so that the datasheet appears as shown in Figure 6-5.

4 Double-click the borders between the columns to size the columns and display the series label text and data.

5 Click the Save button and save the presentation containing the graph as *e-Selections Board Report*.

Figure 6-5

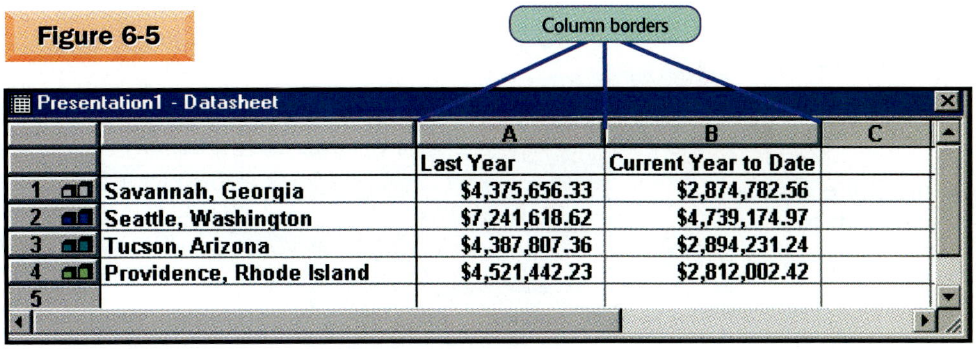

Formatting Charts

Now that you have the data entered in the datasheet, you can work on formatting the chart so that it appears as Mr. Carroll directed. Each item on the chart is a separate object that you can format individually using tools on the Microsoft Graph toolbars.

Task 3: To Format the Chart

1 Click the Chart Type list arrow on the Microsoft Graph Standard toolbar.

Troubleshooting
If the Chart Type button is hidden, display the toolbars on two lines or click the More Buttons arrow on the Microsoft Graph Standard toolbar and click the Chart Type button.

2 Click the 3-D Bar Chart button from the list and close the datasheet.

Figure 6-6

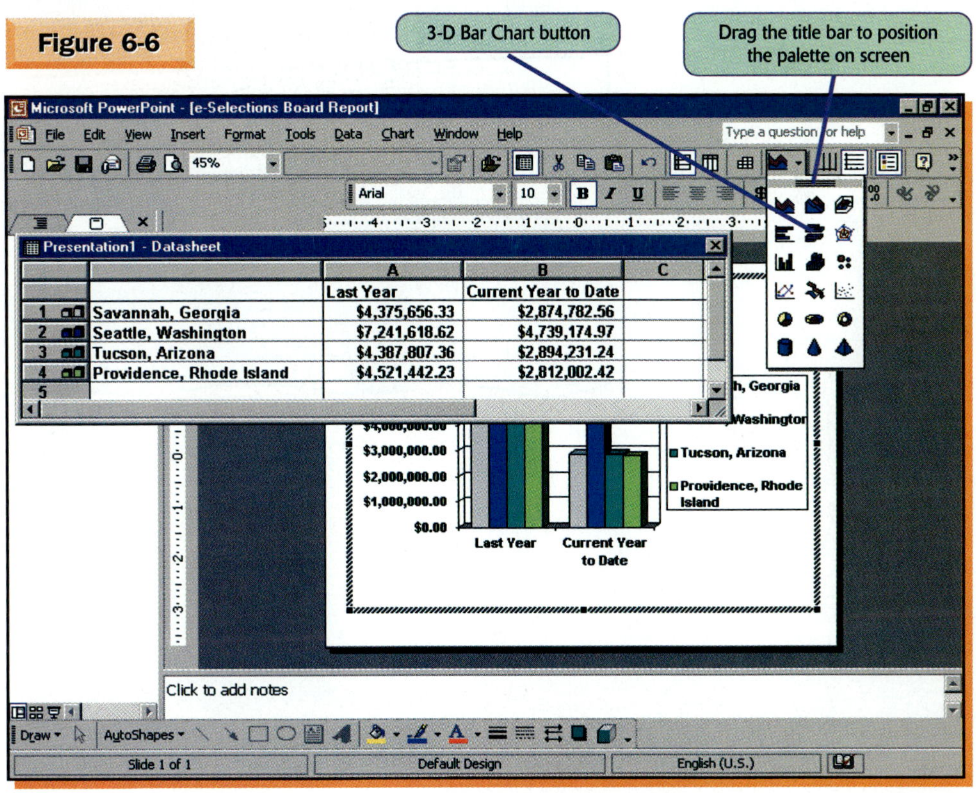

3 Choose **Chart** | **Chart Options**.

Troubleshooting
If the Office Assistant opens, hide it.

Figure 6-7

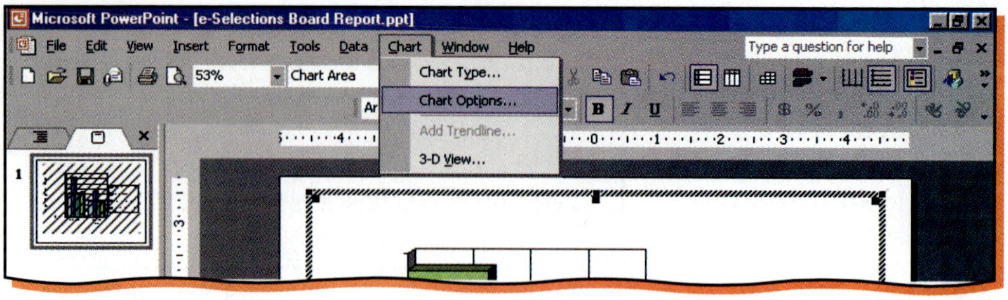

Other Ways
To open the Chart Options dialog box:
- Right-click the chart close to the outside border and select Chart Options from the shortcut menu.

4 Click the **Legend** tab and clear the check mark from the **Show legend** option.

Figure 6-8

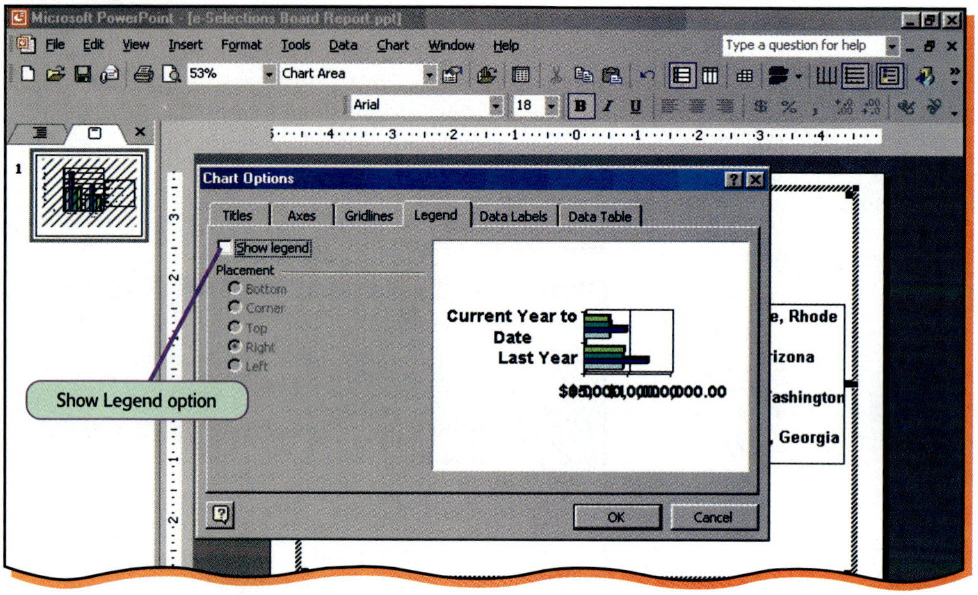

Other Ways

To remove the chart legend:

- Click the legend and press Delete.
- Right-click the legend and select **Clear.**

5 Click the **Data Table** tab. Select the **Show Data Table** option and ensure that the **Show Legend Keys** option is also checked.

Figure 6-9

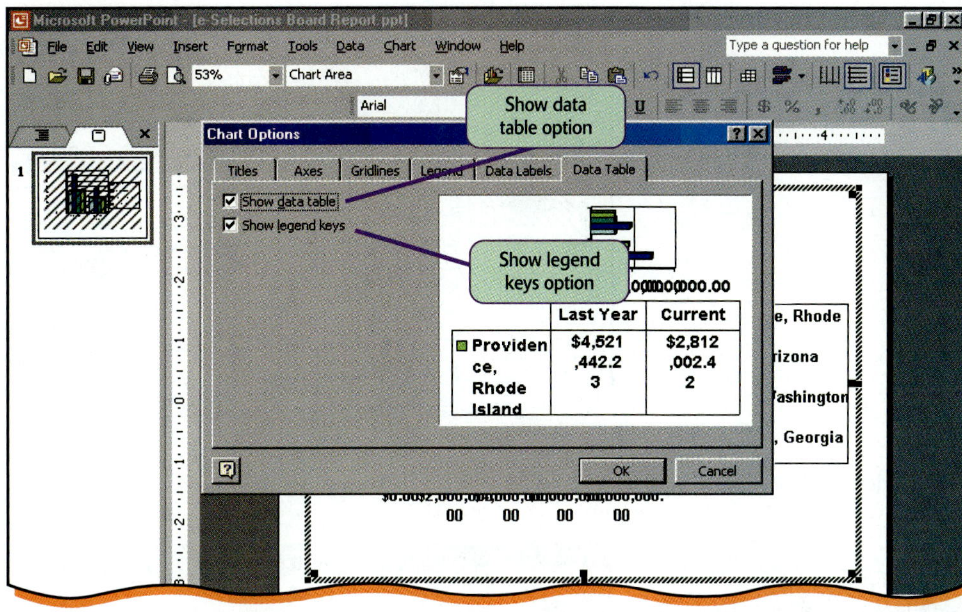

6 Click the **Axes** tab, clear the **Value (Z) axis** option, and then click **OK**.

Figure 6-10

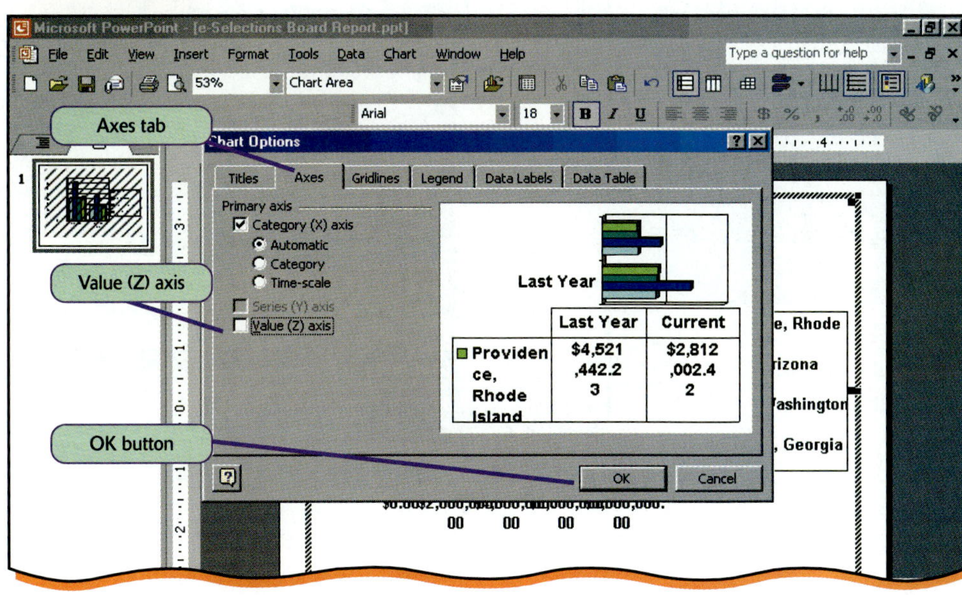

7 Right-click the area behind the bars.

Figure 6-11

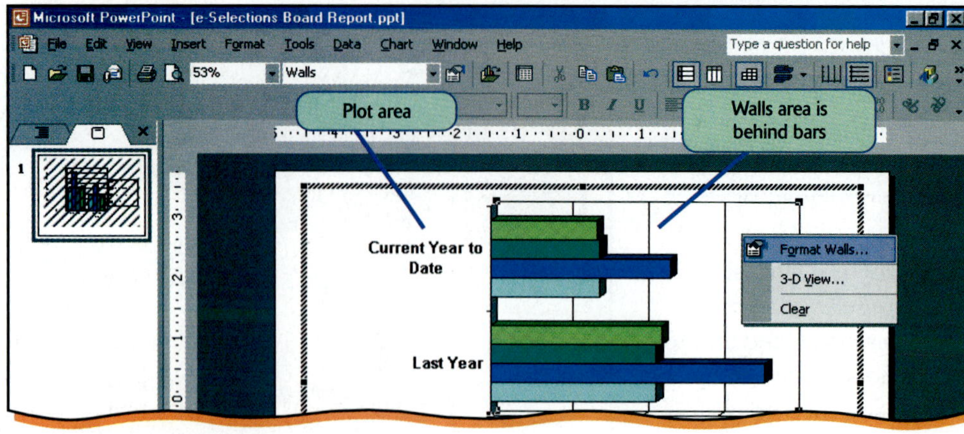

8 Select **Format Walls**.

Tip As you point to different parts of the chart, a screen tip identifies the active area. To format walls, for example, you would position the mouse pointer and pause until you see *Walls* as the screen tip. To format plot area, point to different areas until you see *Plot Area* as the screen tip.

9 Click the Fill Effects button.

Figure 6-12

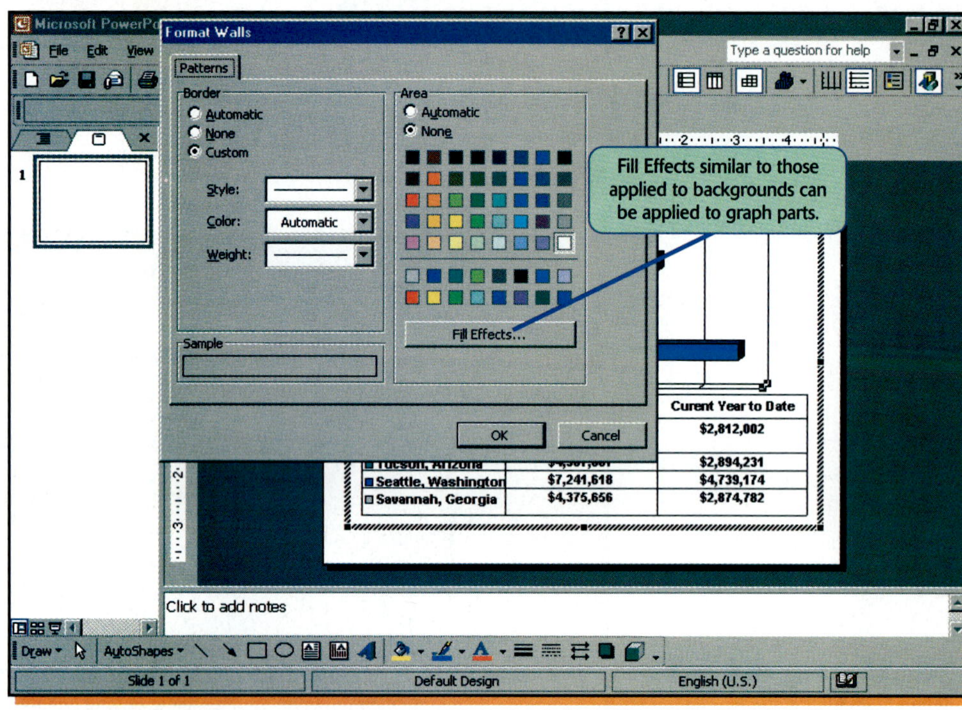

10 Select the options and colors shown in Figure 6-13, then double-click the **Plot Area** and apply a fill effect similar to that shown in Figure 6-13.

11 Click the PowerPoint slide outside the graph and datasheet area to position the graph on the slide and then save changes to the presentation.

Figure 6-13

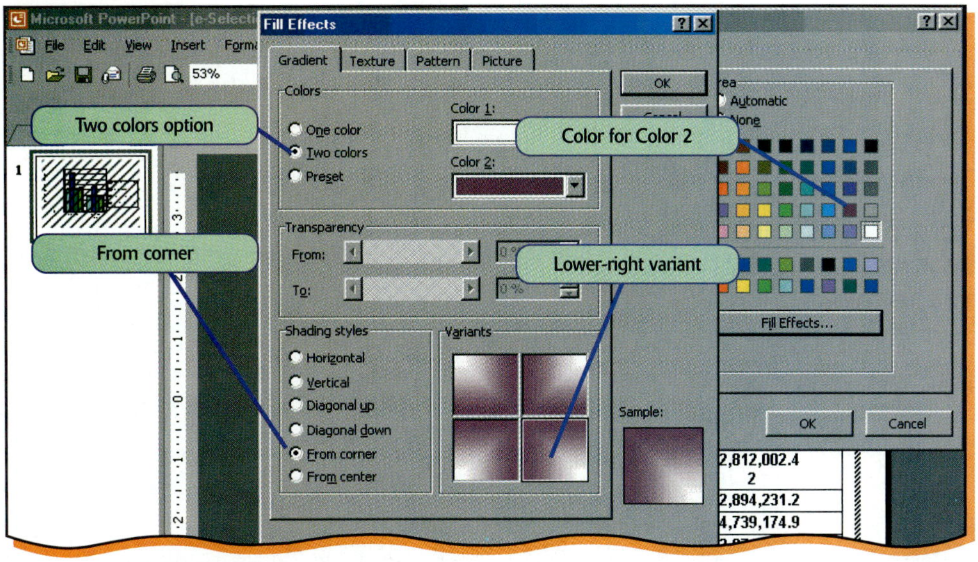

CHECK POINT

Did you know that you can change the *elevation* and angle at which charts appear on slides? It's actually quite easy to create different effects using the *3-D View* dialog box. To display the dialog box, select a 3-D format for the chart and then choose **Chart | 3-D View**.

Figure 6-14

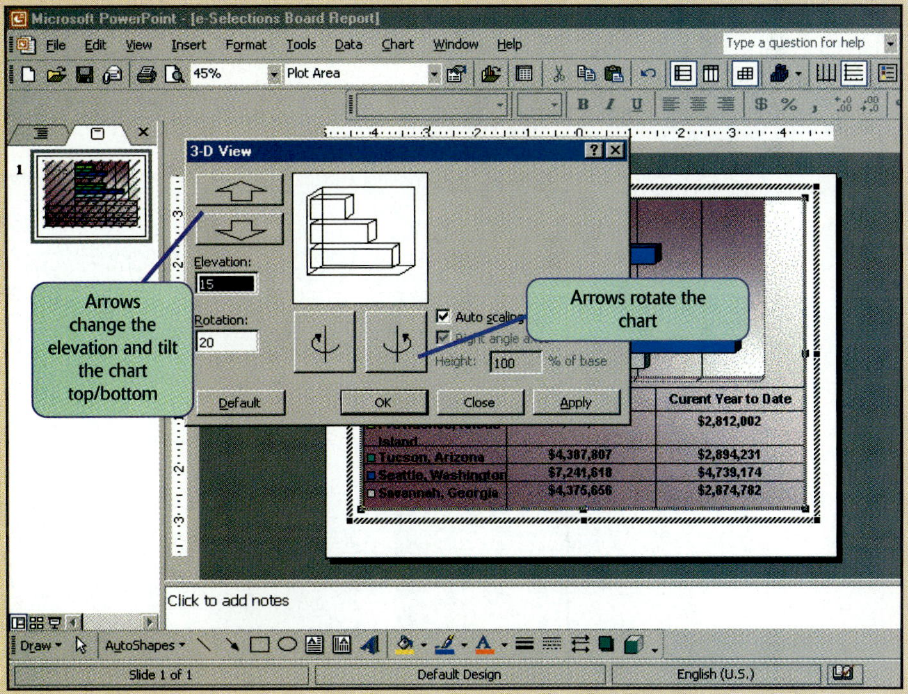

Play with some of the features found in this dialog box to create interesting angles.

Animating Charts

You can create special effects by animating slide text, charts, and diagrams. You can also apply animation effects to bars and other shapes on graphs—element by element—so that the bars and shapes appear to grow. By changing the order in which each element appears, you can create some surprise effects.

Task 4:

To Apply Animation Effects to Chart Elements

1. Right-click the chart area on the slide and select **Custom Animation**.

Other Ways To display the Custom Animation task pane:

- Choose **Slide Show | Custom Animation.**
- Click the task pane down arrow and select **Custom Animation.**

Figure 6-15

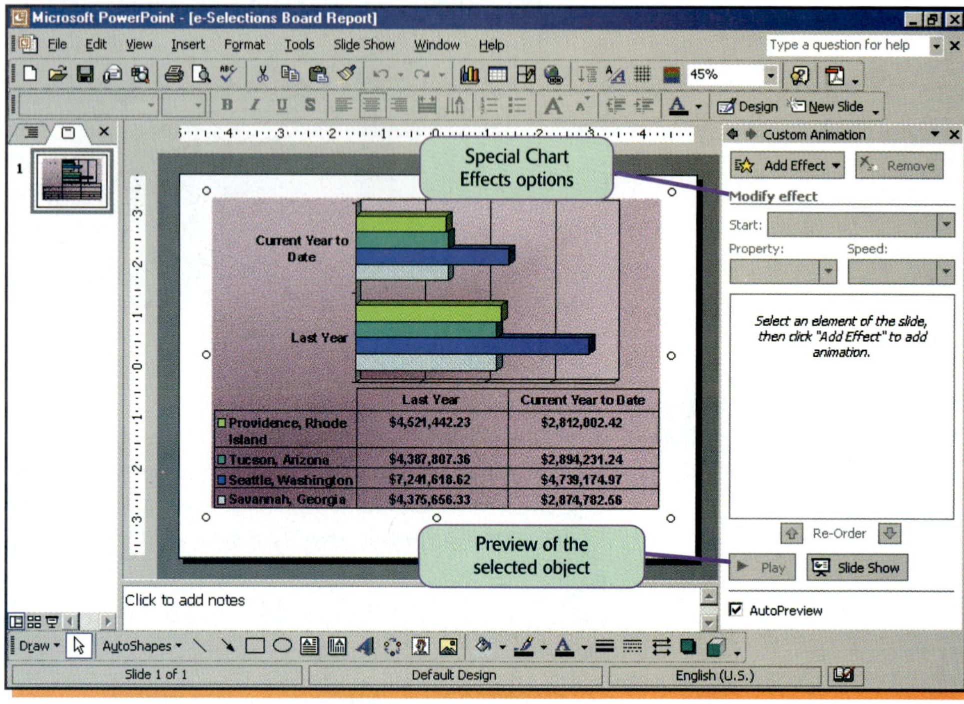

2. Click **Add Effect**, select **Entrance | More Effects | Wipe**, and click **OK**.

Figure 6-16

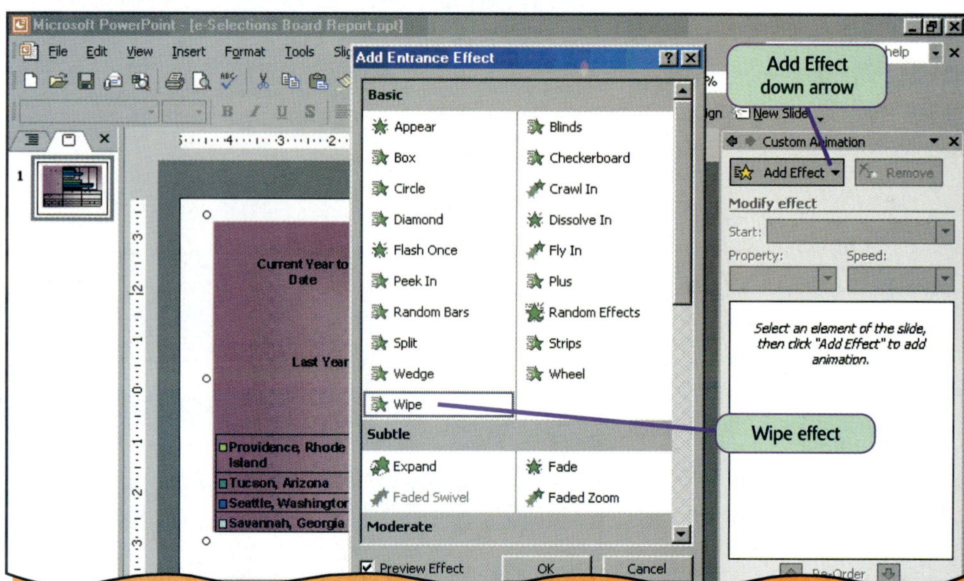

3 Click the **Chart #** down arrow and select **Effect Options**.

4 Select **Whoosh** from the **Sound** drop-down list and click the **Chart Animation** tab.

Figure 6-17

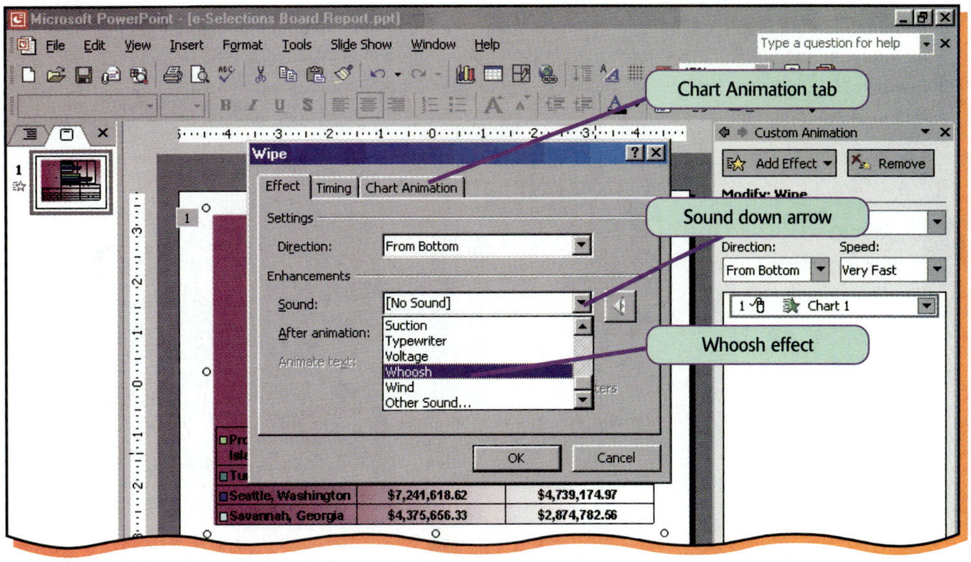

5 Select **By element in category** from the **Group Chart** drop-down list and click **OK**.

Figure 6-18

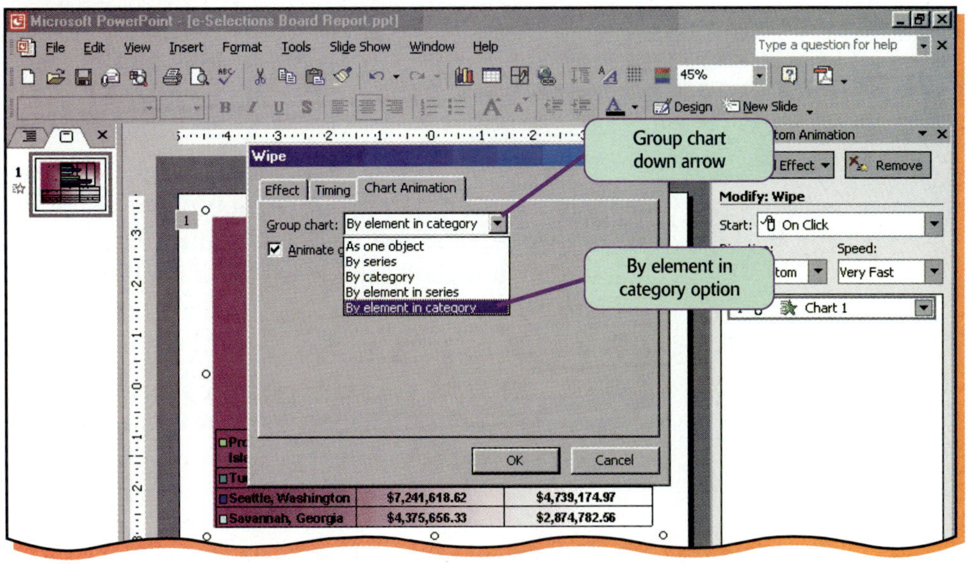

6. Select **From Left** from the **Direction** drop-down list in the task pane.

7. Press F5 to start the slide show and view the animation effects.

8. Save changes to the presentation.

Figure 6-19

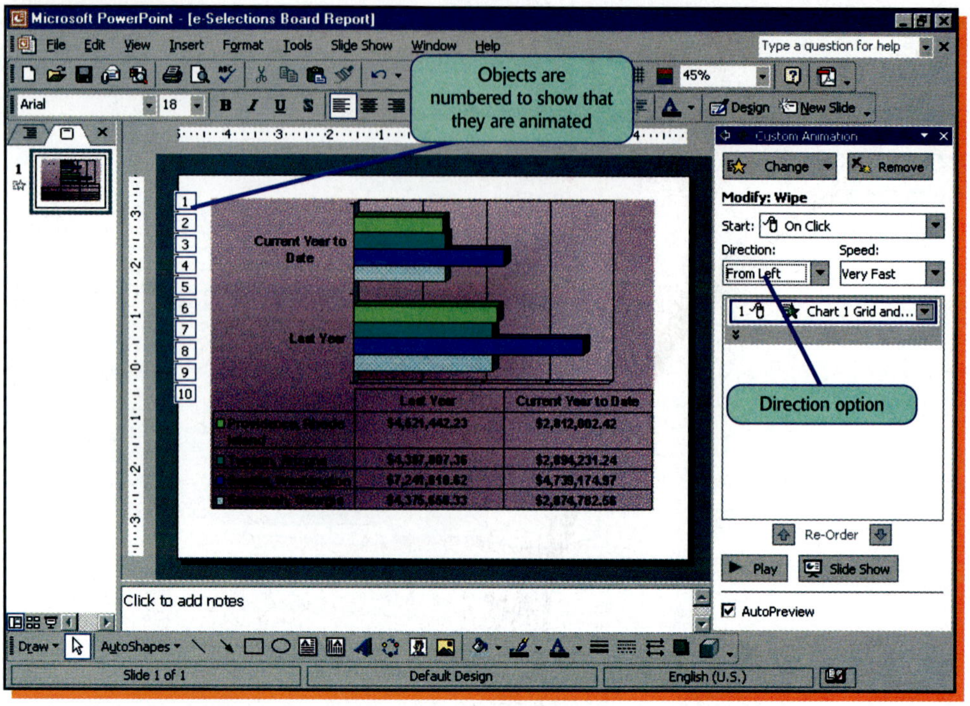

Creating and Formatting Diagrams

Charts are one type of diagram that you can add to PowerPoint slides to present data and other information using visual enhancements. PowerPoint also provides some special diagramming features that you can use to present information and data that doesn't lend itself to displaying in the organization charts or in the standard charts you've created in this Project. You can create:

- *Cycle diagrams* to show a process that has a continuous cycle.
- *Target diagrams* to show steps toward a goal.
- *Radial diagrams* to show relationships of elements to a core element.
- *Venn diagrams* to show areas of overlap between and among elements.
- *Pyramid diagrams* to show foundation-based relationships.

These diagrams illustrate conceptual data and enliven documents and presentations with information that is text-based rather than number-based.

WEB TIP

If you've updated your virus scanning software recently and have scanned your computer for infections, you probably think you're safe for the time being, right? Well computer viruses and the flu have a lot in common—they are both annoying and they are both easy to catch. The Web's interconnection allows e-fections to linger just as the flu so often does. Be sure to keep your virus vaccines up to date.

Creating Diagrams

The procedures used to create diagrams are the same regardless of what type of diagram you want to create. You can use the diagram format to create the second chart Mr. Carroll has requested.

Task 5:
To Create a Diagram

1. Create a new slide, format it using the Title and Content layout, and close the task pane.
2. Click the Insert Diagram or Organization Chart button on the content placeholder.
3. Double-click the **Radial Diagram** icon.

Figure 6-20

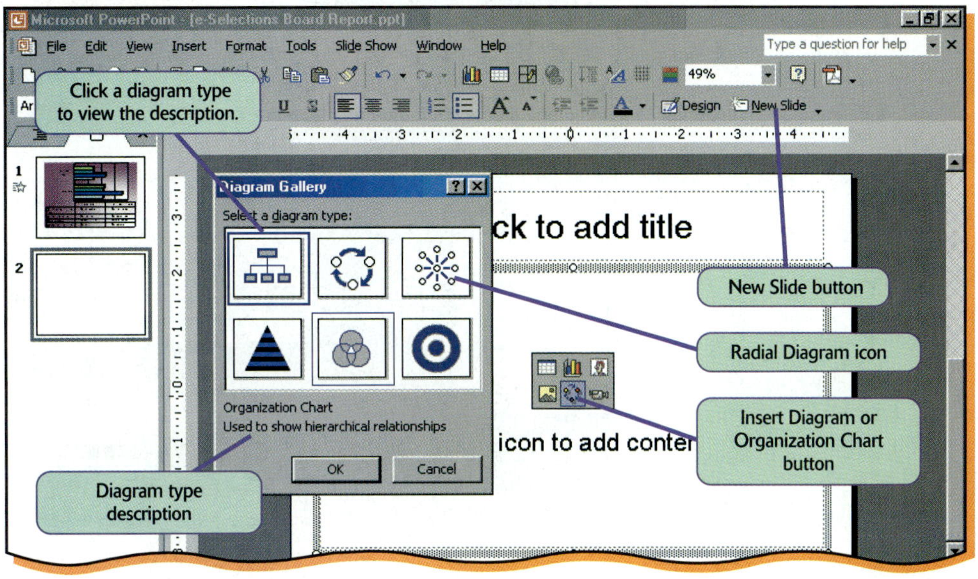

4. Click the center circle and type **e-Selections.**

Figure 6-21

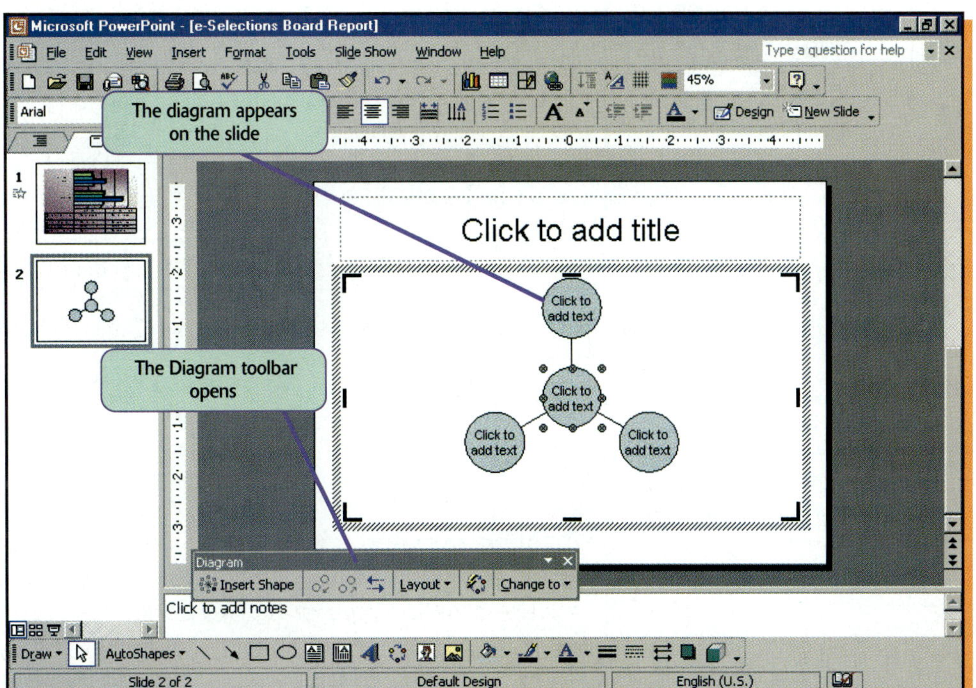

5 Click the Insert Shape button on the Diagram toolbar twice to create two additional circles on the radial diagram.

Figure 6-22

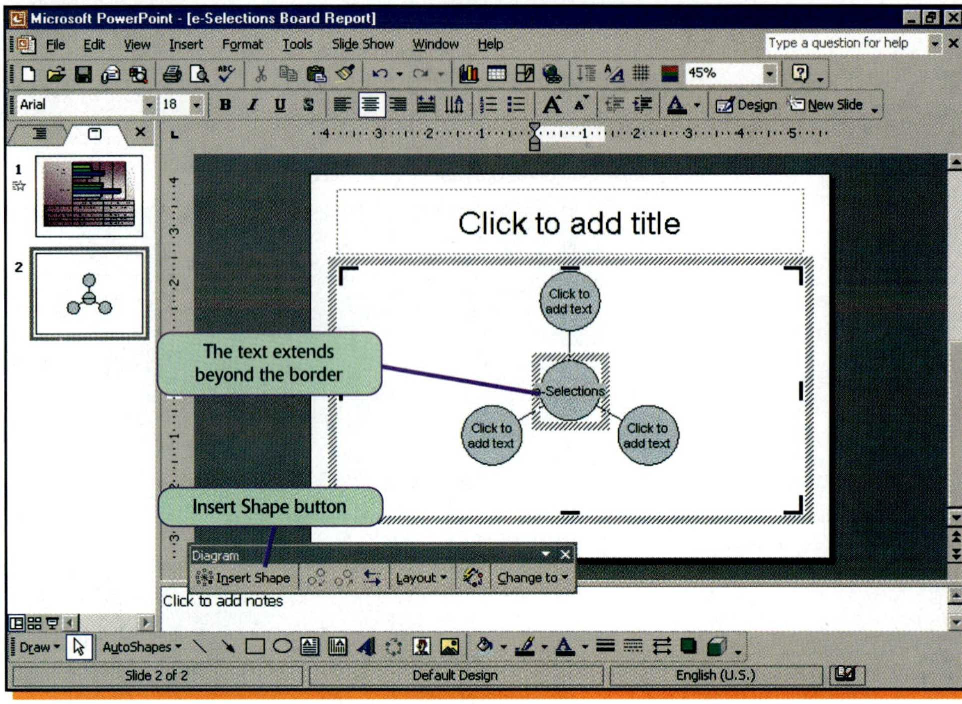

6 Click each of the circles on the diagram and type the text shown in Figure 6-23 to identify the online divisions, pressing Enter to start new lines.

7 Save changes to the presentation.

Figure 6-23

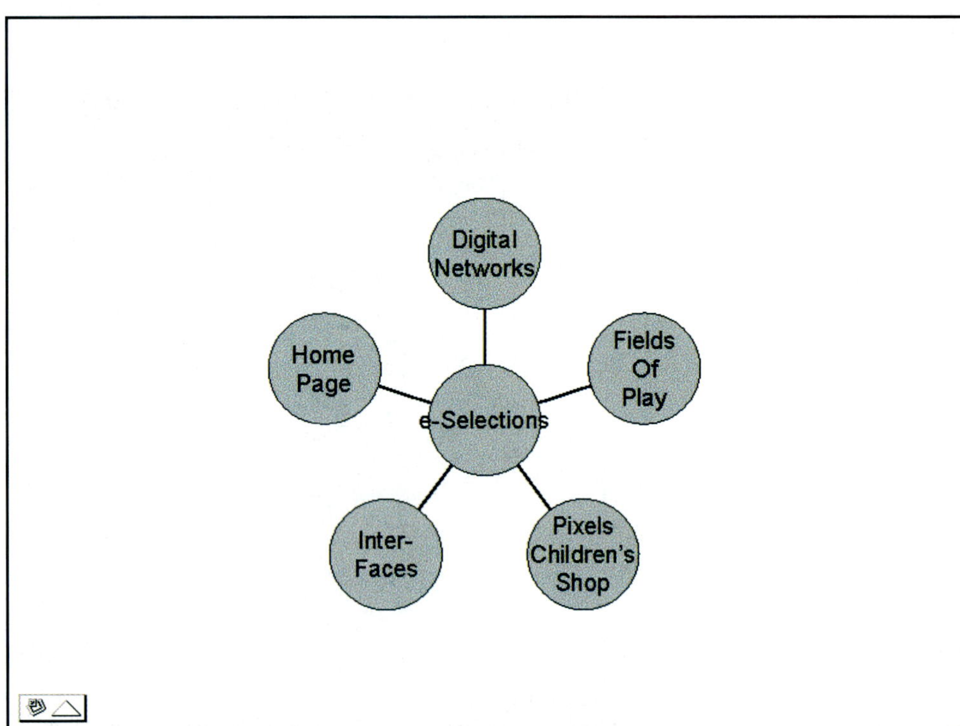

Formatting Diagrams

As you've discovered, the shapes on the radial diagram maintain their size and shape even when the text you type extends beyond the shape borders. In addition, the color of the shapes is a bit dull for the presentation Mr. Carroll wants. You need to format the diagram to change the object colors, the font size, and the overall size of the diagram.

Task 6: To Format the Radial Diagram

1. Click the diagram to select it and then click the AutoFormat button on the Diagram toolbar.
2. Select **Primary Colors** from the Select a Diagram Style list and click **Apply**

Figure 6-24

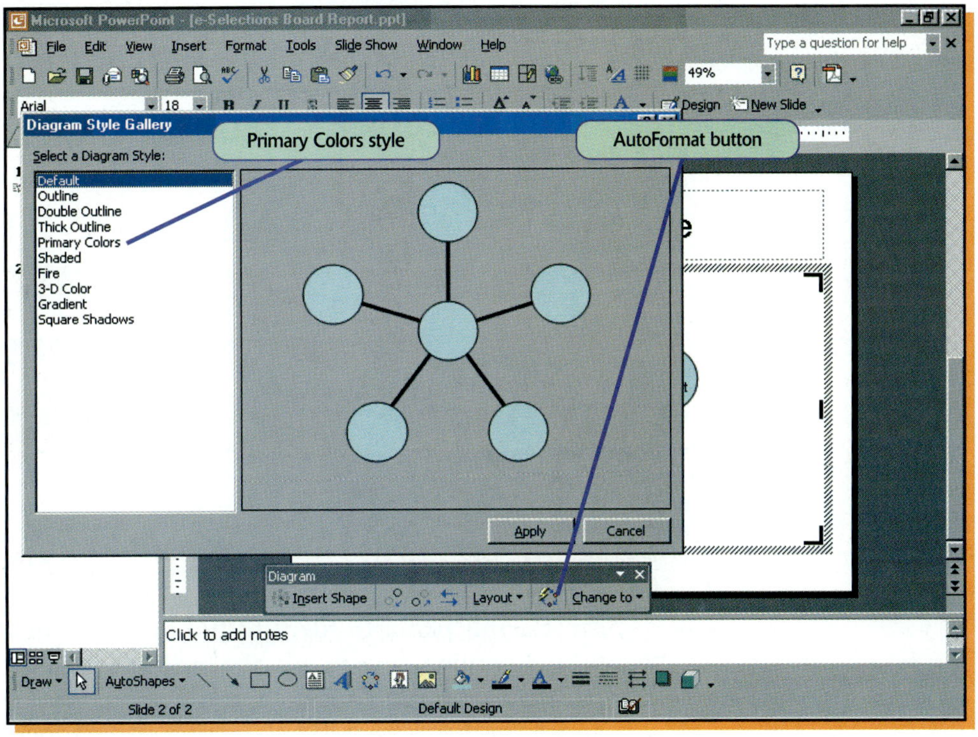

3. Click **Layout** on the Diagram toolbar and select **Scale Diagram**.

Figure 6-25

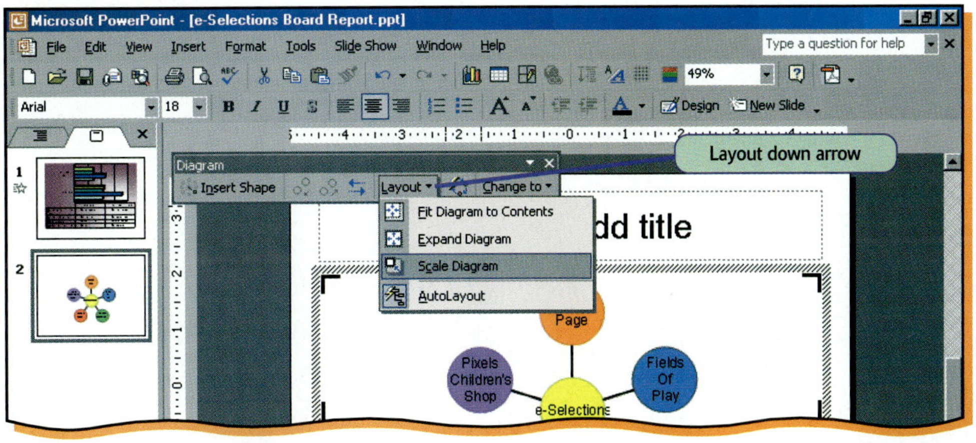

4 Press and hold the Ctrl key and drag a side handle to size the diagram to appear as shown in Figure 6-26.

5 Click **Layout** on the Diagram toolbar and select **Fit Diagram to Contents**.

6 Type the title **Online Divisions** in the title placeholder and save changes to the presentation.

Figure 6-26

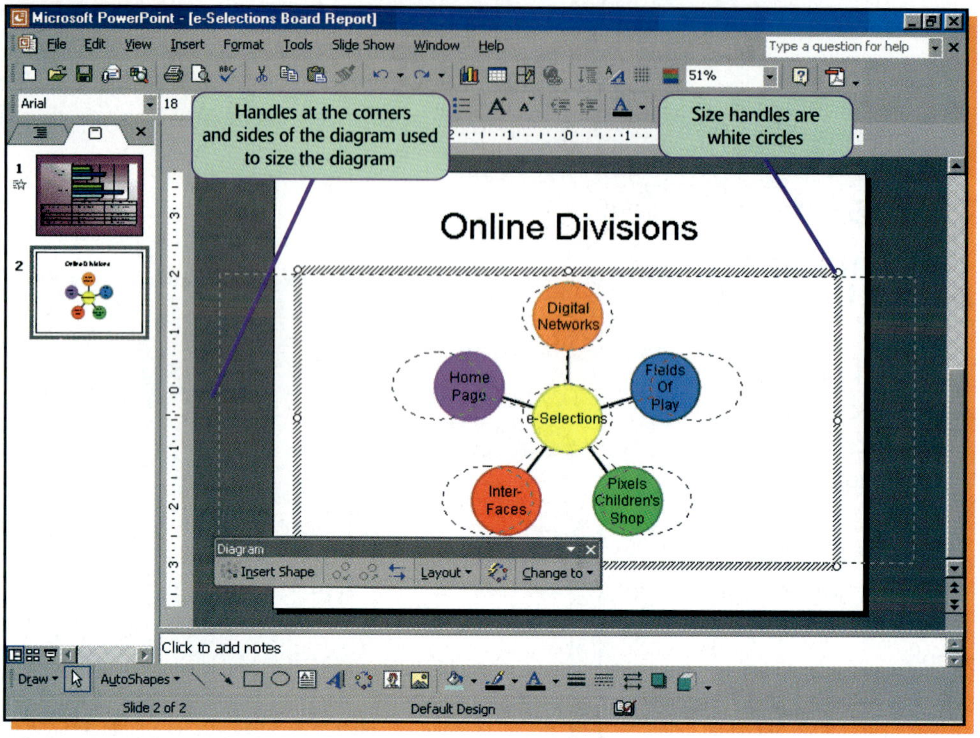

Reorganizing the Diagram Shapes

Mr. Carroll plans to identify the divisions in the order in which they were brought online. As a result, the order in which the circles appear is important. Before you animate the diagram, you need to reposition the circles so that they appear in the correct order starting at the top and moving clockwise.

Task 7:
To Reorganize Diagram Shapes

1. Select the *Digital Networks* circle and click the Move Shape Forward button on the Diagram toolbar.

2. Select the *Pixels Children's Shop* circle and click the Move Shape Backward button. The shape moves one position counterclockwise.

Figure 6-27

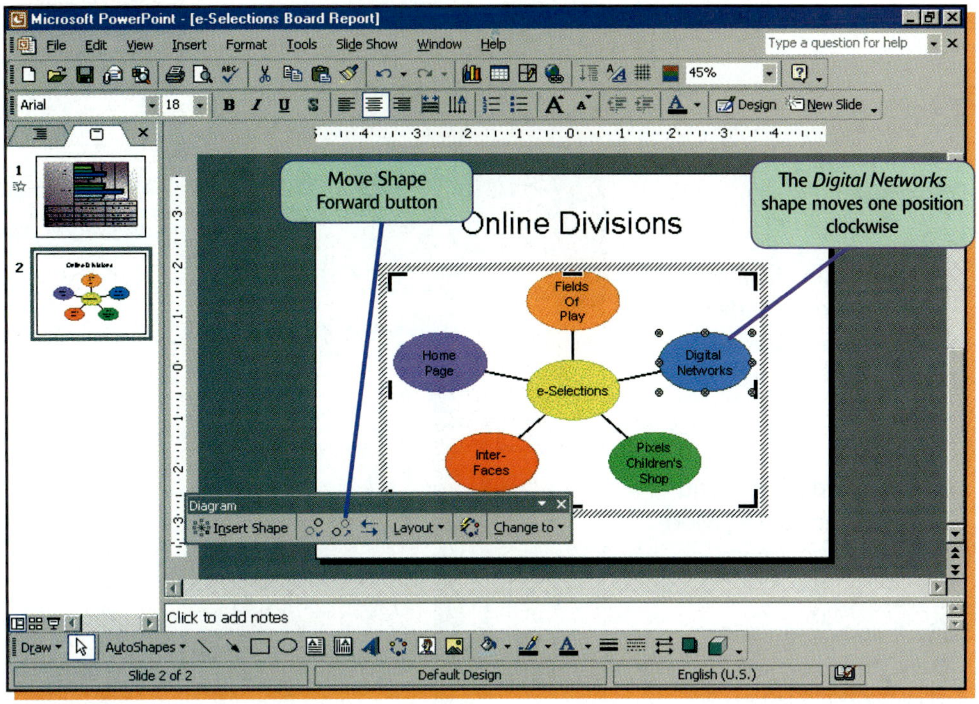

3. Repeat the procedures outlined in Steps 1 and 2 to position the shapes as shown in Figure 6-28.

Figure 6-28

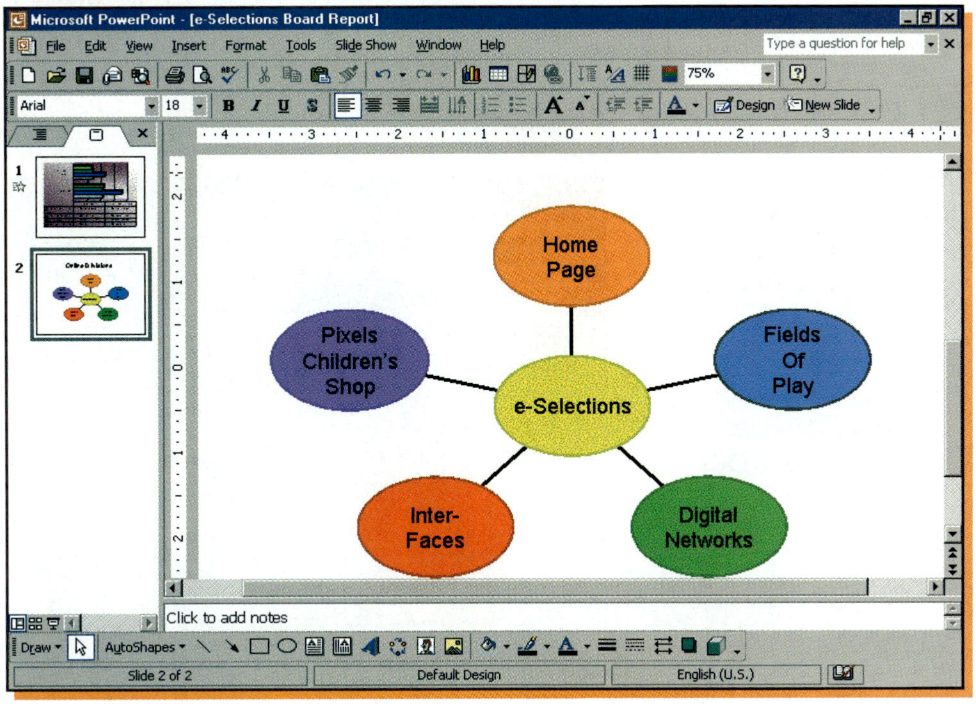

Animating Diagrams

The diagram is almost complete. All you need to do now is to animate the diagram so that each circle appears on screen individually during the slide show.

Task 8:

To Animate the Diagram

1. Select the diagram and choose **Slide Show | Custom Animation**. The Custom Animation task pane opens.

2. Click **Add Effect** and select **Entrance | More Effects**.

3. Select **Spinner** from the Moderate effect list and click **OK**. Diagram 2 appears in the Custom Animation list.

Figure 6-29

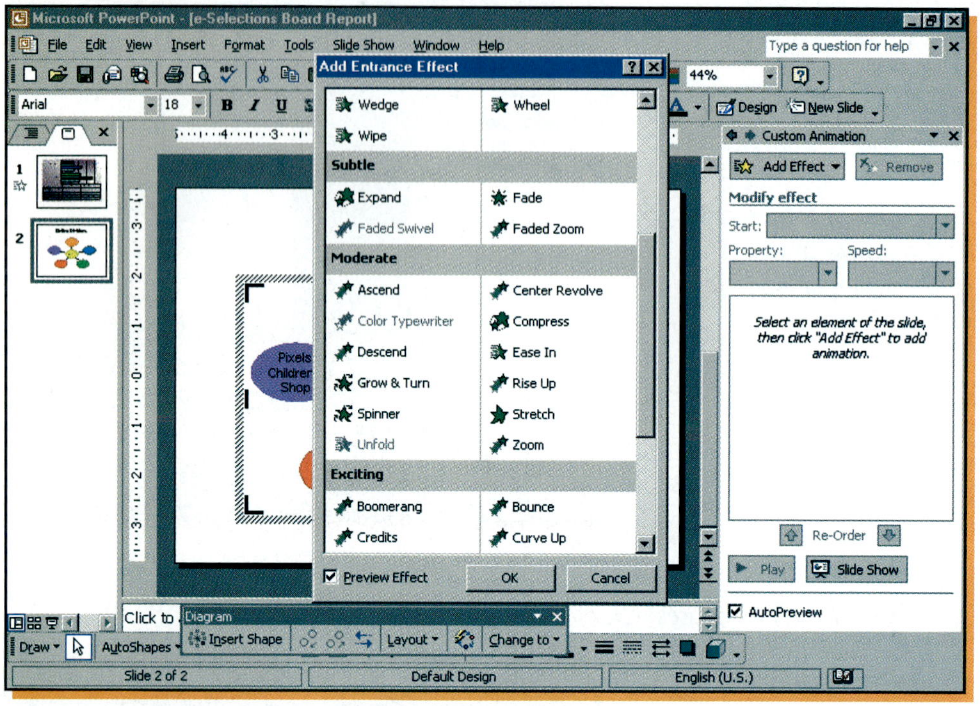

4. Click the **Diagram 2** down arrow, select **Effect Options**, click the **Diagram Animation** tab, and select **Clockwise–Outward** from the **Group Diagram** list.

5. Click the **Timing** tab, set the **Delay** value to **3** seconds, and click **OK**.

Figure 6-30

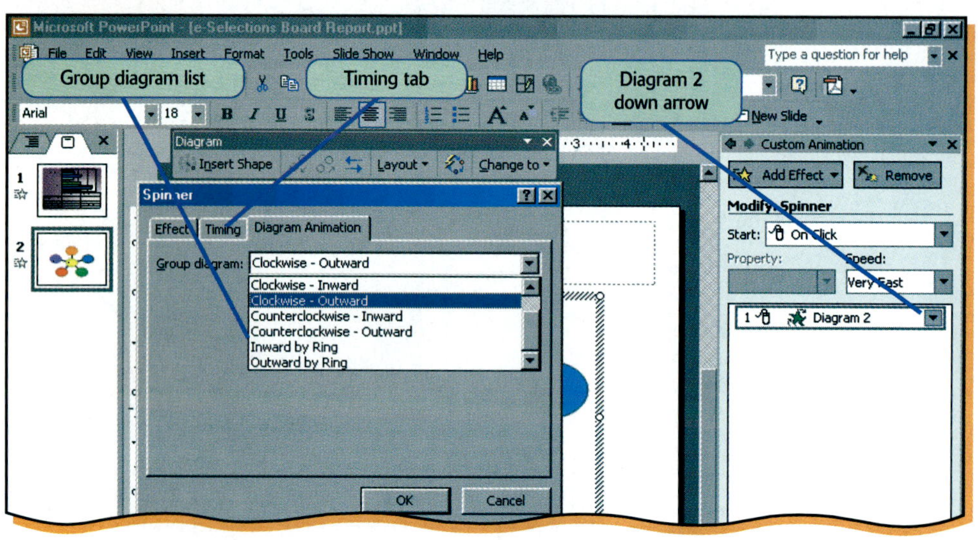

6 Click **Play** on the task pane to view the animation effects. The delay between circles will give Mr. Carroll time to introduce each division.

7 Save changes to the presentation.

Figure 6-31

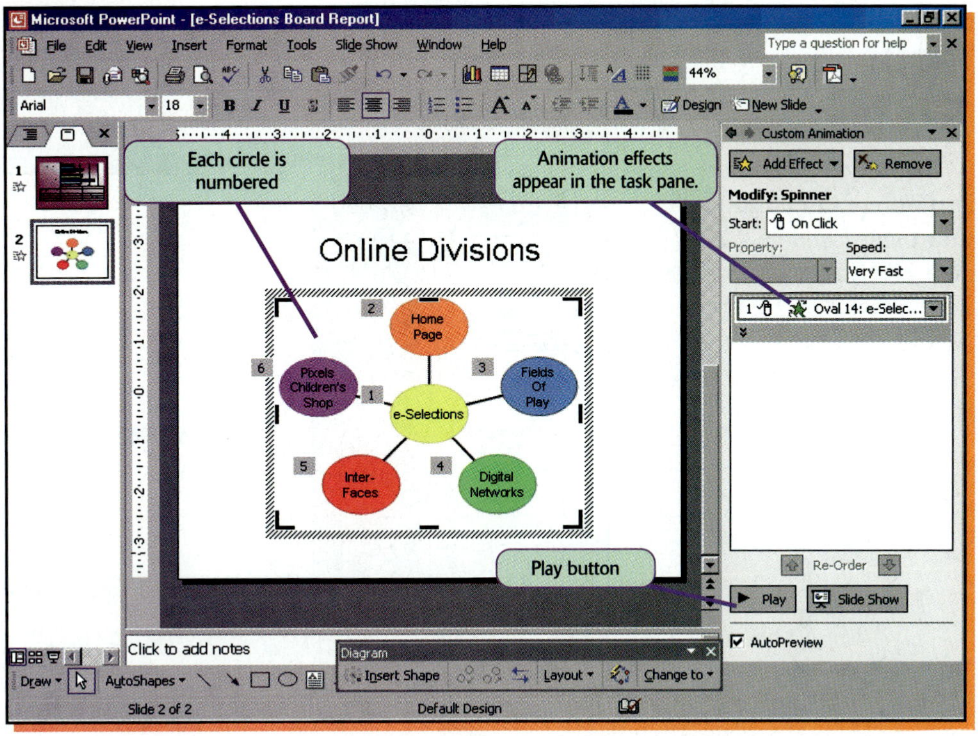

Editing and Saving Organization Charts

The basic structure of Selections, Inc., was added to a presentation Mr. Carroll had you develop earlier. Now he wants you to expand the levels of the organization chart to show the extent to which the division has grown. After making the edits, you can save the chart as a graphic so that it can be used in other files and documents.

Tip All diagram types can be saved as graphics—not just the organization chart.

Task 9:

To Edit and Save Organization Charts

1 Create a new slide, apply the **Title and Diagram or Organization Chart** slide layout to the slide, and close the task pane.

Figure 6-32

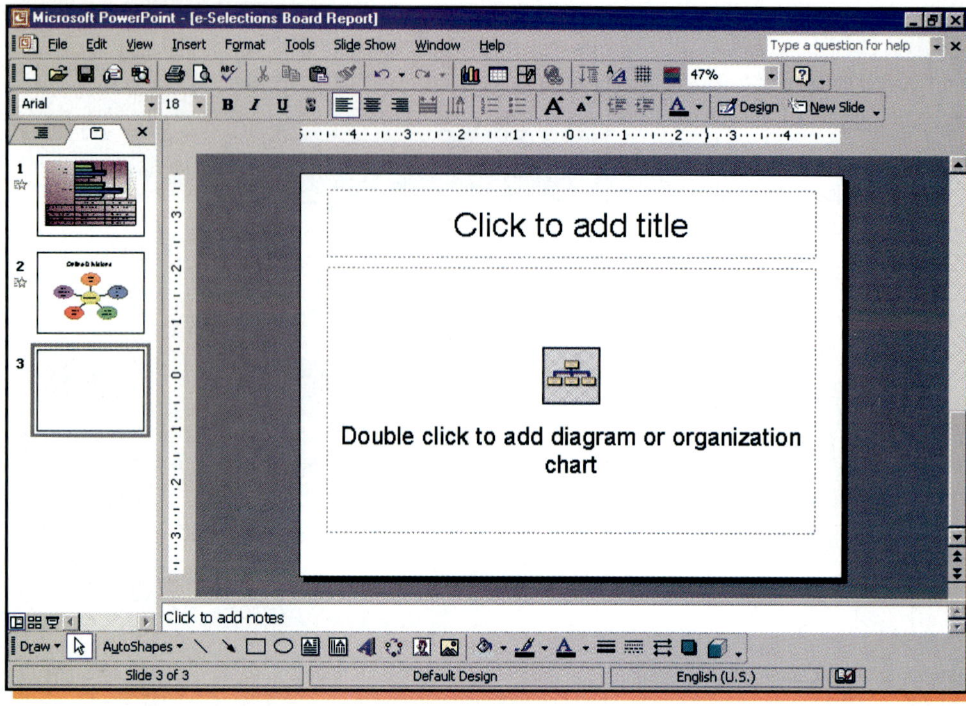

2 Double-click the object placeholder and then double-click the **Organization Chart** diagram icon.

Figure 6-33

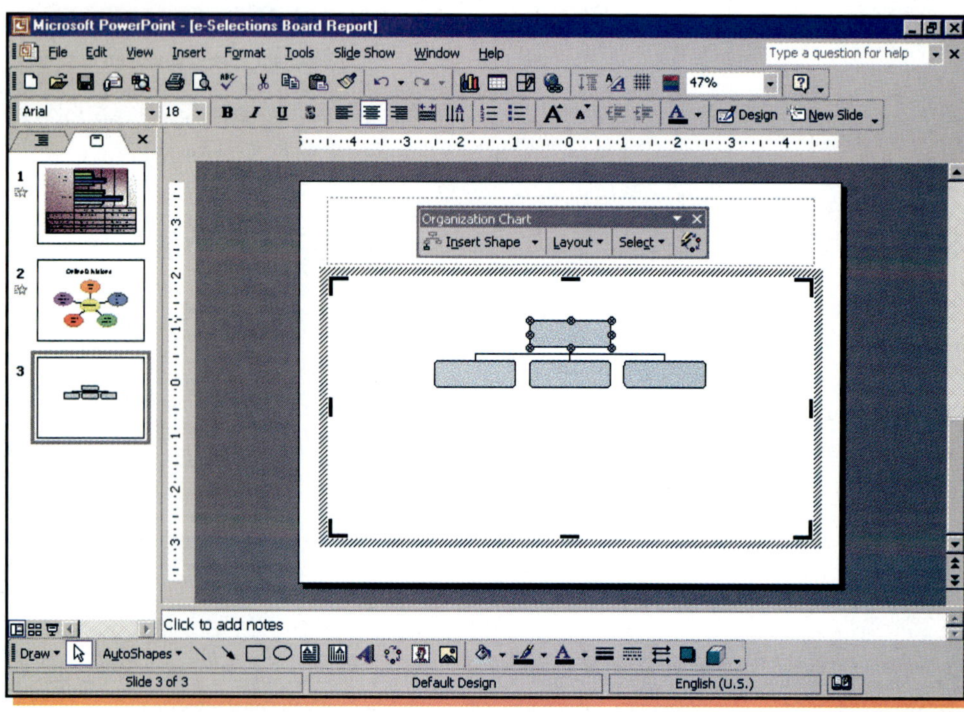

3 Delete the title placeholder and create the organization chart displayed in Figure 6-34 using the techniques you used to edit the radial diagram.

Figure 6-34

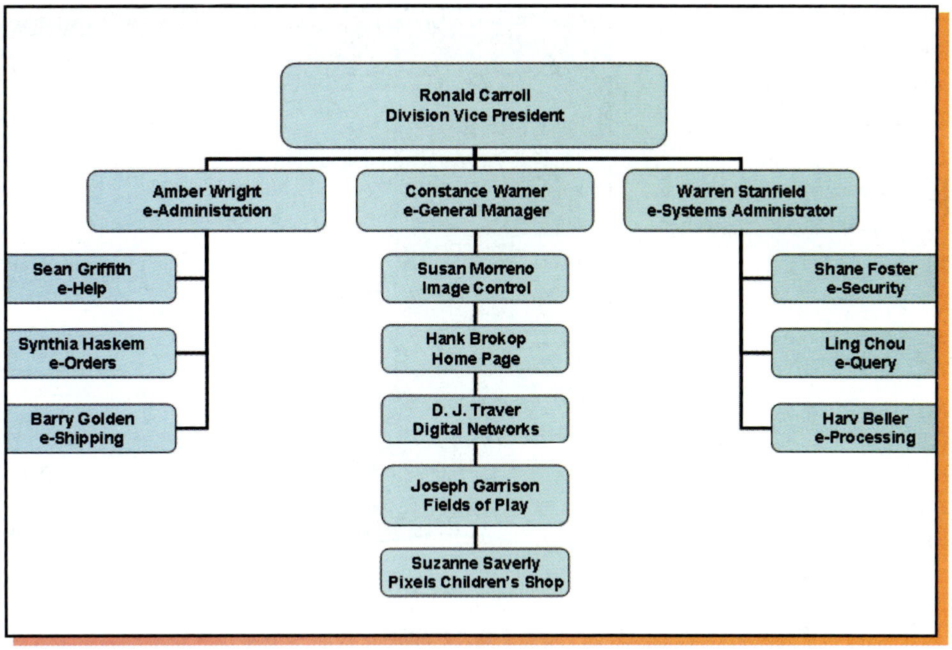

4 Right-click the organization chart and choose **Save as Picture**. The Save As Picture dialog box opens.

Figure 6-35

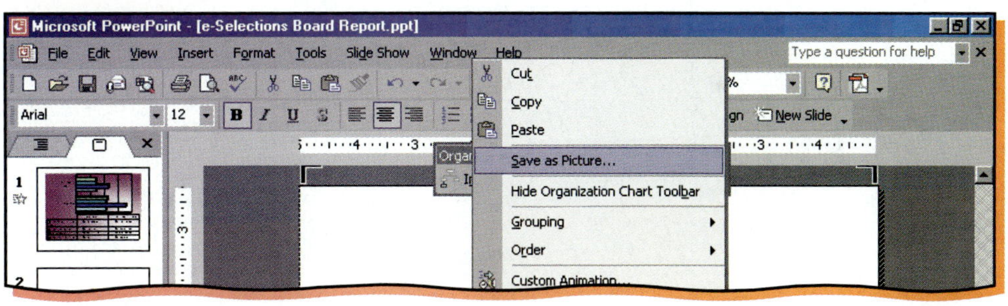

5 Open the folder into which you want to save the chart and save the chart using the file name *e-Selections Division Organization Chart*.

6 Save changes to the presentation, close the file.

Figure 6-36

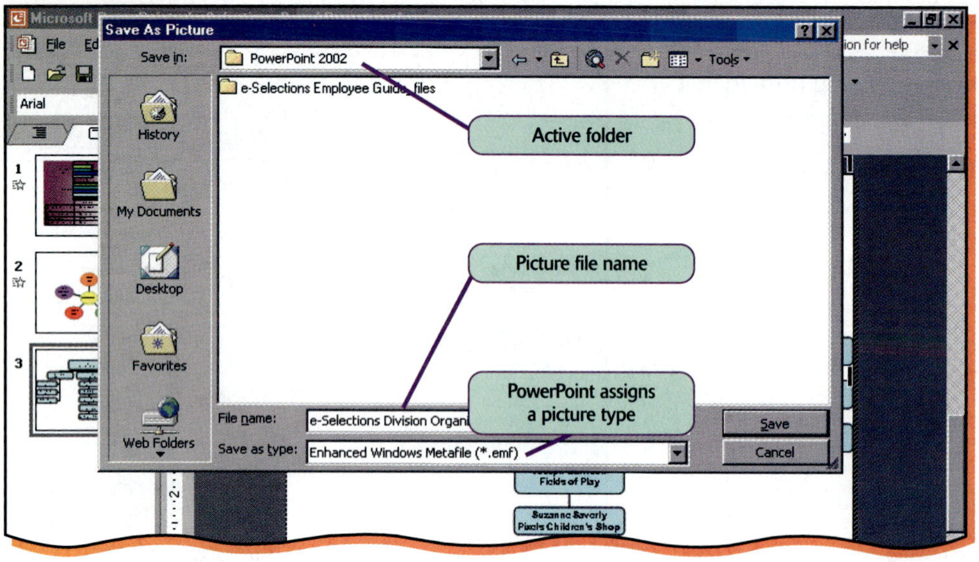

SUMMARY AND EXERCISES

SUMMARY

- PowerPoint contains an extensive charting and graphing feature that enables you to graphically plot values to show relationships between different groups of data.
- Charts graphically plot values to show relationships between different groups of data.
- PowerPoint offers a number of different ways to launch Microsoft Graph.
- Datasheets contain data and values that you want to graph.
- The datasheet displays default data each time you launch Microsoft Graph.
- Each item on the chart is a separate object.
- You can change the elevation and angle at which charts appear on slides.
- Animation effects applied to bars and other shapes on graphs can be set so that the bars and shapes to appear to grow.
- You can select the order in which elements appear.
- Cycle diagrams show a process that has a continuous cycle.
- Target diagrams show steps toward a goal.
- Radial diagrams show relationships of elements to a core element.
- Venn diagrams show areas of overlap between and among elements.
- Pyramid diagrams show foundation-based relationships.
- Diagrams illustrate conceptual data and enliven documents and presentations.
- Shapes on diagrams maintain their size and shape even when the text you type extends beyond the shape borders.
- All diagram types can be saved as graphics.

KEY TERMS & SKILLS

KEY TERMS

3-D View (p. 6-13)
cell address (p. 6-7)
cells (p. 6-7)
column (p. 6-7)
cycle diagram (p. 6-16)
datasheets (p. 6-7)
elevation (p. 6-13)
frame (p. 6-7)
pyramid diagram (p. 6-16)
radial diagram (p. 6-16)
row (p. 6-7)
target diagram (p. 6-16)
Venn diagram (p. 6-16)

SKILLS

Animate the diagram (p. 6-22)
Apply animation effects to bars and other shapes on charts (p. 6-14)
Change the chart type (p. 6-9)
Change the elevation and angle at which charts appear on slides (p. 6-14)
Create a datasheet (p. 6-8)
Create diagrams (p. 6-16)
Edit and save organization charts (p. 6-23)
Format diagrams (p. 6-16)
Launch Microsoft Graph (p. 6-6)
Reorganize the diagram shapes (p. 6-20)

STUDY QUESTIONS

MULTIPLE CHOICE

1. The most efficient way to graphically add a chart that displays data that does not exist in another application on a PowerPoint slide is to
   a. create a new slide and format the slide using the Content slide layout.
   b. launch Excel, enter the data, and create a chart that you can copy to the PowerPoint slide.
   c. use PowerPoint drawing tools to graph the data.
   d. create the data in Word, chart the data in Excel, and place it on the PowerPoint slide using the drag technique.

2. When you use a Content slide layout to create a chart,
   a. Microsoft Graph launches automatically when you apply the layout.
   b. you cannot edit the chart type or design.
   c. you can double-click the icon for the chart you want to create in the object placeholder access tools that will help you create the chart.
   d. you have to copy and paste the chart to place it on the slide.

3. To place a chart on a slide when the chart you are creating is complete,
   a. press Esc.
   b. choose **File | Send To | PowerPoint** slide.
   c. choose **Edit | Paste Special**.
   d. click the slide outside the chart area.

4. To change the type of chart used to display data,
   a. choose **Data, By Row** or **Data, By Column**.
   b. select the type from the Chart Type palette.
   c. use the default chart type and edit the graphics.
   d. switch to a different computer, create the data, and then copy it onto the slide.

5. If you accidentally click the PowerPoint slide outside the chart borders before the chart is complete,
   a. you have to create the chart all over again.
   b. double-click the chart to access the datasheet and Microsoft Graph tools again.
   c. nothing happens.
   d. the chart is saved and can be imported onto the slide.

6. Entering data in datasheets is similar to all the following *except*
   a. entering data in Excel worksheets.
   b. entering data in Word tables.
   c. entering data in Access tables.
   d. entering data in PowerPoint placeholders.

7. To animate objects on a chart or diagram so that each object appears individually,
   a. select the appropriate grouping option from the **Chart/Diagram Animation** dialog box.
   b. select each object on the chart or diagram and set an animation effect.
   c. create multiple slides to add individual items.
   d. apply the **Animate** slide layout.

8. An effective use of a Venn diagram would be to show
   a. the start and end times of each employee on a given day.
   b. the continuous flow of an employee's work schedule.
   c. the time when two employees who work different schedules are at work at the same time.
   d. a comparison of total hours worked by all employees.

9. Diagrams are used to show
   a. numeric data.
   b. conceptual ideas.
   c. data flow.
   d. textual information.

10. Organization charts show
   a. data flow.
   b. value comparisons.
   c. business animation.
   d. hierarchical structure.

SHORT ANSWER

1. Which application tools are available for adding and charting new data on a PowerPoint slide?
2. What window contains the figures you want to chart when you add a chart to a PowerPoint slide?
3. What do the rows and columns of data values represent on a chart?
4. What new menu items appear in PowerPoint while you are charting data?
5. How can you tell which object on a chart you are selecting?
6. How do you change the size of the diagram after the chart is placed on the PowerPoint slide?
7. What pages of options are available for formatting a chart when you choose **Chart | Chart Options** on the Microsoft Graph menu?
8. What happens if you double-click a chart object instead of clicking the object once to select it?
9. What happens to the chart when you close the datasheet?
10. What is the difference between data series and data categories and which of the two traditionally appears in the chart legend?

FILL IN THE BLANK

1. Vertical ____________ appear in Microsoft Graph datasheets.
2. The point at which columns and rows intersect is called a ____________.
3. The column letter and row number are known as the ____________.
4. Column letters and row numbers appear in the datasheet ____________.
5. The tilt of a chart on a slide is known as the chart ____________.
6. Changes to the tilt of a chart on a slide are made using features contained in the ____________ dialog box.
7. ____________ are used to create processes that have a continuous cycle.
8. Datasheet rows represent ____________.
9. Datasheet columns represent ____________.
10. Datasheet ____________ run horizontally.

DISCUSSION

1. What other AutoLayout formats are available for adding special types of objects to PowerPoint slides?
2. How do menu commands in PowerPoint change when Microsoft Graph is active?
3. What special techniques do you use to format and edit text contained on tables and charts added to PowerPoint slides?

GUIDED EXERCISES

1 PLOTTING SIDEWAYS

Sometimes, one of the best ways to get someone's attention is to create a chart that is formatted so uniquely that it immediately captures the audience. Of course, it's also important to ensure that the graph presents the information in an easy-to-read-and-understand format. Take, for example, the plotting of temperatures in such a way that you can see the low for the day, the high for the day, and the range in between. You could effectively plot the data and create the chart shown in Figure 6-37.

Figure 6-37

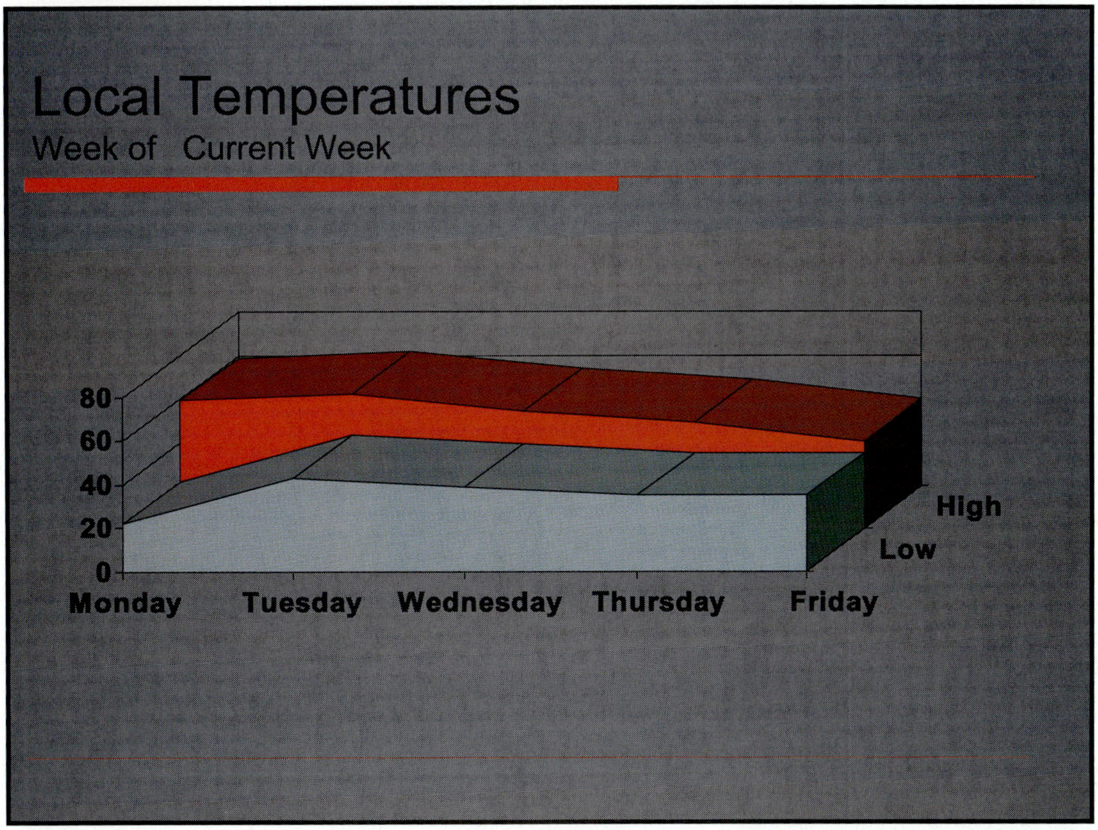

Follow these directions to create the chart:

1. Create a new presentation and change the format of the title slide to **Title and Content**.

2. Click the **Insert Chart** icon in the Content placeholder and record the data shown in Figure 6-38 in the datasheet.

Figure 6-38

Presentation2 - Datasheet

		A	B	C	D	E
		Monday	Tuesday	Wednesda	Thursday	Friday
1	Low	22	43	39	35	35
2	High	59	62	54	49	40
3						
4						

3. Choose **Chart | Chart Type**, select **Area** from the Chart type list, select **Area with 3-D visual effect** from the Chart sub-type list, and click **OK**.

4. Choose **Chart | Chart Options**, click the **Legend** tab and clear the **Show legend** option, click the **Data Labels** tab, select the **Series name** option, and click **OK**.

5. Click the slide title placeholder and type the title shown in Figure 6-30, then apply the template of your choice to the slide.

6. Save the presentation using the file name *Local Temperatures,* print a copy of the slide and close the file.

2 GRAPHING GRAPHICS

When the numbers you are plotting are a bit boring, try adding a graphic to better convey the chart's message. Figure 6-39 provides an example of the types of images you can create by doubling up graphic presentations.

Figure 6-39

Follow these steps to create the slide:

1. Create a new presentation and apply the **Title Only** slide layout to the first slide.
2. Format the slide background using a gradient color and then format the placeholder with a reverse gradient.
3. Search the Internet for a picture of a computer diskette, download the picture, and insert it using the **Insert | Picture | From File** command

4 Deselect the graphic, choose **Insert | Chart**, and type the data shown in Figure 6-40 in the datasheet.

Figure 6-40

Presentation3 - Datasheet

		A
		Billions
1	1998	207
2	1999	234
3	2000	260
4		

5 Type the slide title, save the presentation using the file name *Leasing Business Equipment*, and print a copy of the slide.

3 SNOWBALLS A VENN!

Venn diagrams provide a great way to show overlapping values and data—even when the information you want to show is amounts of snow cities have in common. The diagram shown in Figure 6-41 creates an effect designed to reach out and grab everyone's attention.

Figure 6-41

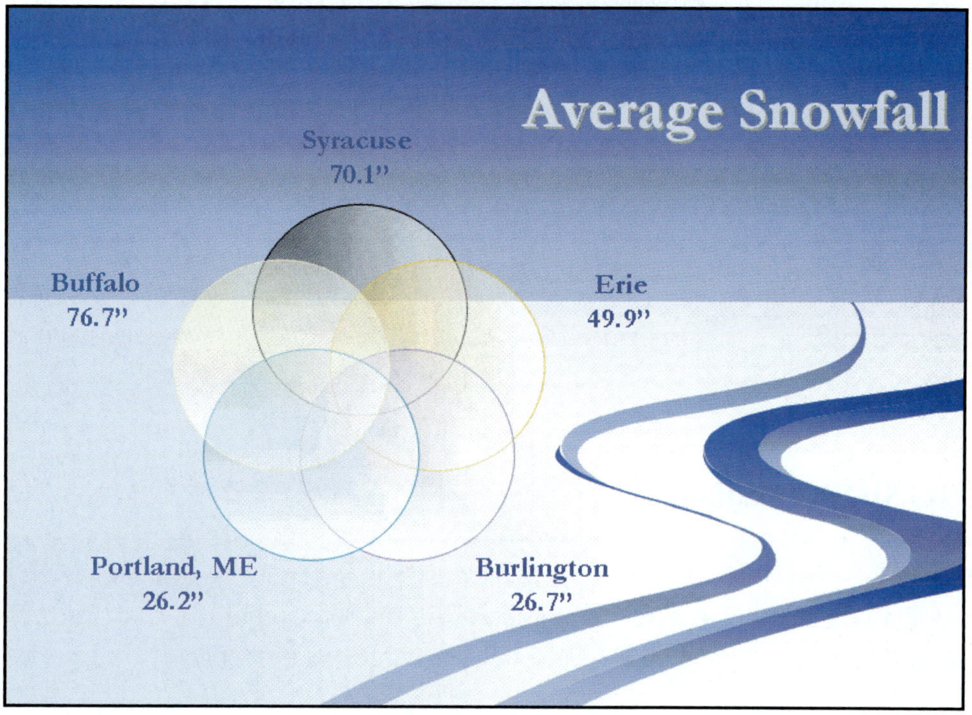

Create the diagram by following these steps:

1. Create a new presentation, format it using the template of your choice, and apply the **Title and Content** slide layout to the first slide.
2. Create a new Venn diagram, enter the text and values shown in Figure 6-41, size the diagram and text to fit appropriately on the slide.
3. Save the presentation using the file name *Overlapping Snowballs* and print a copy of the slide.

ON YOUR OWN

The difficulty of these case studies varies:

are the least difficult; *are more difficult; and* *are the most difficult.*

1 PLOTTING SIDE BY SIDE

Presenting two different charts side by side on a slide is a creative way of showing two different data sets so that viewers can compare the results. Create the chart shown in Figure 6-42 and save the presentation using the file name *Pros vs College*. Then print a copy of the slide.

Figure 6-42

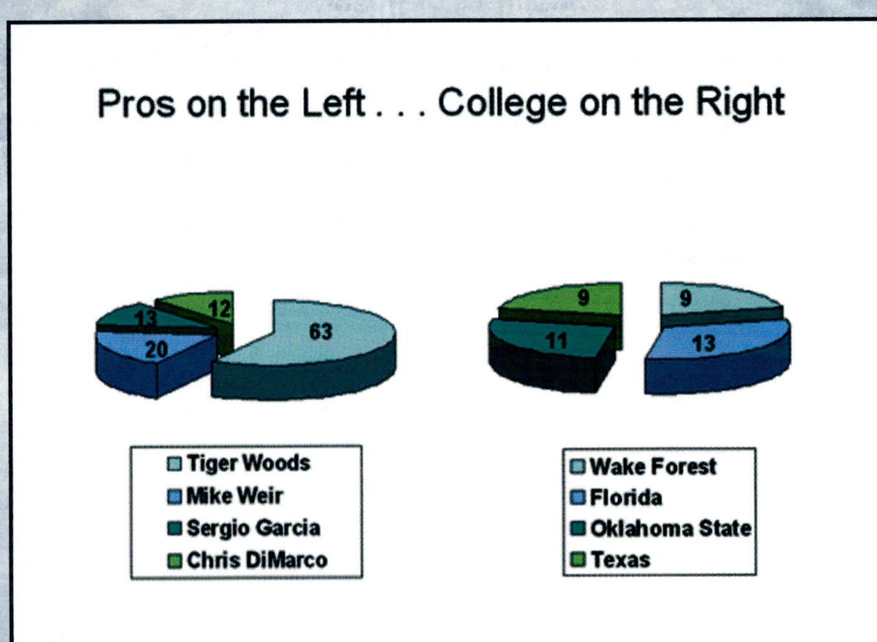

2 LIFE OF A PAYCHECK

The cycle diagram makes it easy to diagram a multistep, repeating process. The life cycle of a bank account is a great way to illustrate the monthly cycle by which many people live. Create a cycle diagram that contains at least five stages in the life of a bank account from receiving a monthly check to depletion. Save the presentation using the file name *Riches to Rags* and print a copy of the slide.

3 CHILDREN CAUGHT IN THE NET

It's fascinating to read some of the innocent ways children today are being caught unawares while they are online. Parents, teachers, and other responsible adults tell children not to give out their name, phone number, or address to strangers while they are online. But what about those seemingly innocent questions strangers online ask to learn what they want to know from children (and adults!) online. A recent survey of online users discovered that kids are willing to give out seemingly innocent information to strangers on the net. Create a chart to plot the following percentages of children who gave out:

Name of favorite store	65%
Name of parent's favorite store	54%
Type of car family drives	44%
Amount of allowance	39%
What parents do on the weekend	26%

Add an appropriate title to the presentation, format it using a template, and save the presentation using the file name *Online Queries*. Then print a copy of the slide.

4 EXTRACTING PIECES OF PIE

Pie charts are one of the easiest types of charts for the reader to understand and interpret. When pieces of the pie are too small to adequately portray their share of the pie, you can sub-divide the chart and display a bar chart that breaks down one piece of the pie. Create the chart shown in Figure 6-43 by entering data into the datasheet so that the bar chart shows the distribution of domestic funds into large, midsized, and small company funds. Save the chart as *Fund Distribution* and print a copy of the slide.

Figure 6-43

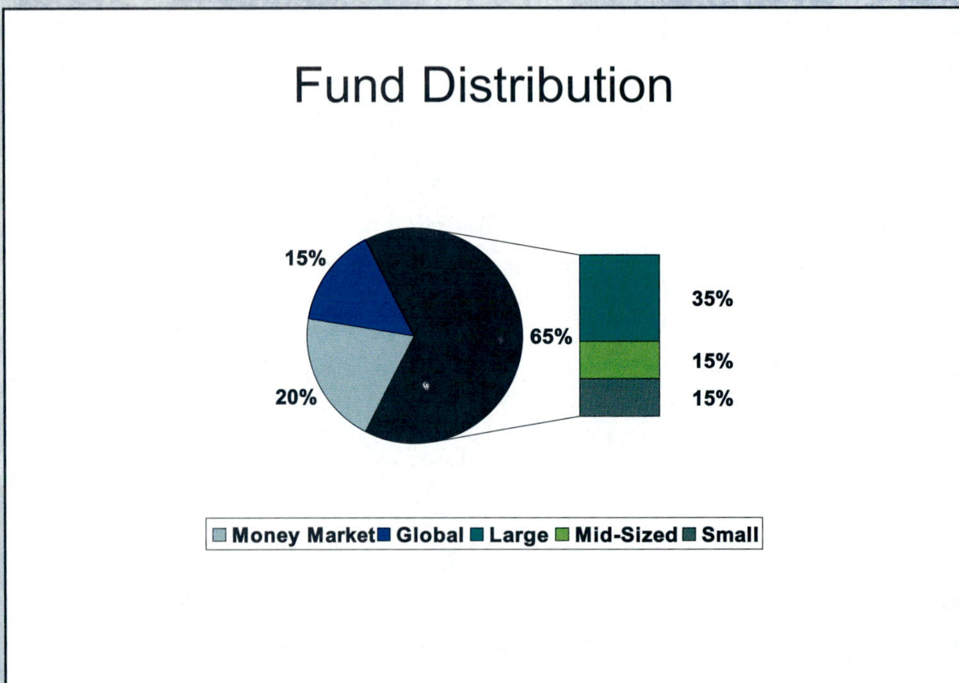

5 GAS FLOATS ON OIL

Sometimes, the chart tool is one of the most effective ways to create custom effects that you want to convey during a presentation. Because each item on a chart created using Microsoft Graph is a separate object, you can format each data element or series using a different view or object. Create a bar chart that plots the values displayed in Figure 6-44. Then convert the format of the chart to display a bar for one type of oil and a line for the other. Then remove chart walls, data labels, and all chart objects except the series labels along the x-axis. Apply a template to the slide, and add your name and date to the footer area. Add an appropriate title to the slide and save the presentation using the file name *Heating Prices*. Print a copy of the slide.

Figure 6-44

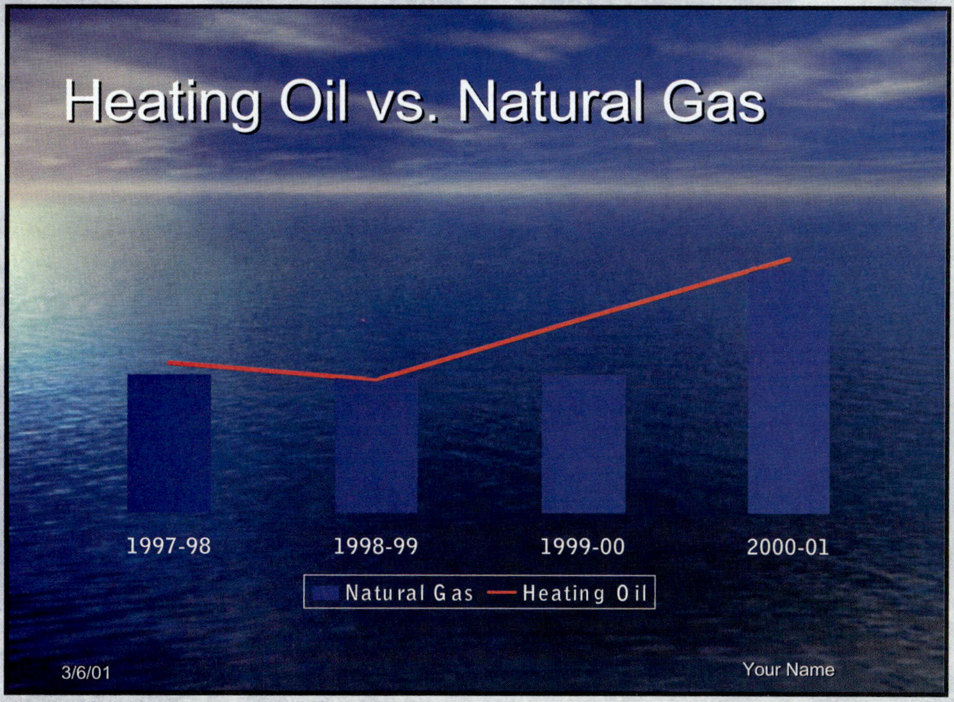

6 WEBBE CHARTS

The Web is a great source for locating and evaluating charts, graphs, and diagrams. Search the Web, locate at least three charts and three diagrams of different types, and download the charts and diagrams. Then create a new presentation named *Webbe Charts* and place each chart/diagram on a different slide. Then create a slide for each chart/diagram that summarizes the information portrayed in the chart/diagram. Finally, add another slide for each chart/diagram that contains the same information plotted using a different chart type or diagram type. Print copies of your slides as handouts with three slides per page so that each page contains the slides that relate to one chart/diagram.

Photospread credits pages 6-2 & 6-3

FROM THE FILES

You Will Need

- ✔ Cuisine of the Southern US.ppt
- ✔ e-Selections Online Web.ppt
- ✔ e-Selections Board Report.ppt
- ✔ e-Selections Notebook.ppt
- ✔ Travel Specials.ppt
- ✔ Travel Tours.ppt

PROJECT 7

Setting Up and Delivering Presentations—Advanced Techniques

By now, you've learned some of the basic techniques associated with showing your presentation as a slide show—hiding slides, adding timings, and so forth. PowerPoint offers a number of advanced slide show features that you also can include in your presentation. In this project, you learn how to insert presentation slides from other presentations, work with custom shows, and use some of the slide show tools to record information during a show.

OBJECTIVES

After completing this project, you will be able to:

- *Insert slides from other presentations*
- *Create, edit, and show custom shows*
- *Create branches to other shows*
- *Record narration*
- *Set sound items to play automatically*
- *Add speaker notes during a slide show*
- *Use the Meeting Minder*
- *Save presentations as shows*
- *Run PowerPoint shows*

e-selections Running Case

As you've worked with PowerPoint and explored its many features, you've undoubtedly come across a few features about which you are curious. Along the way, you most likely have identified tasks you were uncertain how to perform in PowerPoint. You have created some pretty fancy presentations for Mr. Carroll and want to be prepared for questions Mr. Carroll may ask about delivering the presentations. It's time to explore some of the advanced slide show techniques available in PowerPoint.

Never Let Them See You Sweat!

Sir Winston Churchill, a great orator, once said, "First tell them what you are going to talk about, then tell them, then tell what it was you told."

This is sound advice for organizing your speeches. By now, most of us have mastered the art of talking. It follows, naturally, that we all could be effective speakers, right? Well, consider the difference between *talking* and *speaking*. Talking is the natural tendency to verbalize our thoughts. Now take talking and add a few people to the room. Voila! You have *speaking*. Where *talking* involves give and take, *speaking* often seems to be more give, give, give.

Experts say that the key to effective speaking is planning and preparing and, of course, delivering! It's the planning and preparing that people often forget and, unfortunately, their forgetfulness is quite evident in their delivery.

One of Toastmasters' Top 10 tips for successful public speaking is to know your material. Material? No one ever told you that you need material? Sounds as if some planning is definitely in order.

Planning

It's to be assumed (uh-hem) that you know at least something about the topic on which you plan to speak. Beyond choosing a topic for a presentation, deciding the tools you plan to use during the delivery is part of the planning process. Choosing the right supplements help carry off the delivery and add pizzazz to your presentation. Here are some things to consider:

- **Overhead projectors and transparencies**—while these might seem primitive, they are great for informal presentations to give your audience a break from a monotonous speech.
- **35mm slides**—best used for formal presentations. Consider using them for the extremely important points that you want your listeners to remember.
- **Videotapes and films**—good options for formal presentations that don't require or invite interaction. Try to keep

And don't forget to practice!
At home as you're preparing—practice.
On your way to the assembly hall—practice. Even while the MC is introducing you—practice. Then take to the podium and smile, no matter what happens!

the video less than 20 minutes in length. After that point, viewers might lose interest and begin to get fidgety.

- **Computers**—permit you to go online during a meeting to showcase your Web site or dissect your competitors' sites. Computer presentation graphics offer dynamic effects that enhance film and video, such as fade-out transitioning between frames.
- **Interactive Digital Presentations**—such as digital whiteboards, are taking presenters beyond the laptop/projector/screen age to a new presentation environment.

Check out the market for the latest and greatest in electronic tools before deciding which visual aid best meets your presentation needs.

Delivery

Even the most seasoned of speakers can feel uneasy or anxious when they walk out to give their presentation. Answering some questions about effective delivery will have the audience on their feet when you sit down.

- How do you look and how do you feel?
- Do you find yourself more concerned with the computer that is running your presentations than your audience?
- Are you *preaching* or *speaking?*
- Are you involving and encouraging audience participation?
- What are your stance, facial expressions, arm movements, and silences telling your audience?
- Are you using the podium as a crutch?

PROJECT 7

Setting Up and Delivering Presentations—Advanced Techniques

The Challenge

Mr. Ronald Carroll, e-Selections division Administrative Vice President, has approved the format of the slides you created for his report to the Board of Directors. Now he would like you to add those slides to his basic presentation and create a custom show using specific slides from the presentation. In addition, he wants to run the show without the audience seeing the program screens during the presentation. He'd also like you to show him how to record narration for the presentation so he can distribute copies of the show to members of the Board. He also wants to add speaker notes as he practices the presentation. Finally, he asks you if there is a feature available in PowerPoint that provides tools for recording questions and requests by Board members that arise during his presentation. As you complete this project, you'll automatically add the two new slides shown in Figure 7-1 to the presentation.

Figure 7-1

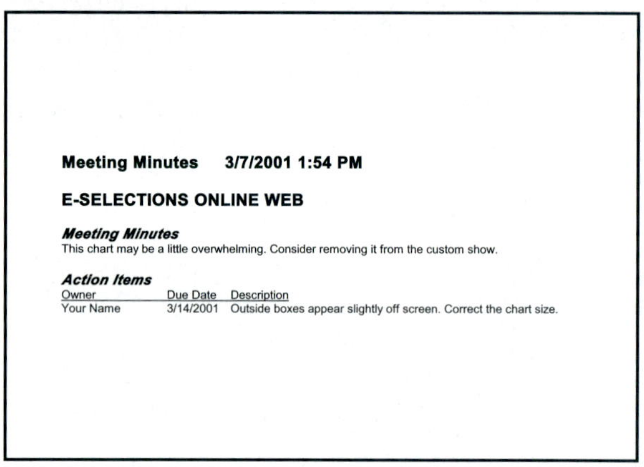

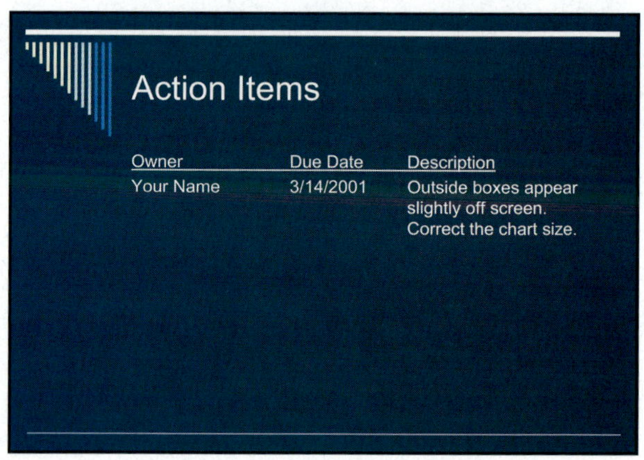

The Solution

PowerPoint contains a number of special features that will have Mr. Carroll off and running at the Board of Directors meeting next week. You can use these tools to add the chart and diagram slides to his comprehensive presentation and create a custom show designed specifically for the Board meeting. By saving the presentation as a slide show, you can show Mr. Carroll how to start the show without launching PowerPoint in the background. Before showing Mr. Carroll how to record narration and notes during the presentation, you need to bone up on the techniques that you believe will be easiest for him to use. Then you can demonstrate the techniques for Mr. Carroll and assist him as he practices the presentation delivery.

Polishing the Presentation

A number of tasks need to be completed to fine-tune Mr. Carroll's presentation so he can take it on the road. PowerPoint contains the tools you'll need to insert the slides containing the sales data, the diagram, and the organization chart and to set up the show for Mr. Carroll.

Inserting Slides from Other Presentations

Often, slides you create for one presentation can be used in a different presentation. You can insert slides from one presentation into another presentation using a couple of different techniques:

- Display the presentation containing the slides in **Slide Sorter** view, select the slides, and copy them to the Clipboard. Then open the presentation into which you want to place the slides and paste them in.
- Display the presentation into which you want to place the slides and insert slides from a different file. You can insert all slides from a file or select only the specific slides you want to include.

Task 1:

To Insert Slides from a File

1 Launch PowerPoint, open the *e-Selections Online Web.ppt* presentation, and switch to **Slide Sorter** view.

> **Tip** You can insert slides from other files from any view--inserting them from Slide Sorter view makes them easier to position. If you insert slides from a file in Normal view, be sure to display the slide you want the new slides to follow before inserting them.

Figure 7-2

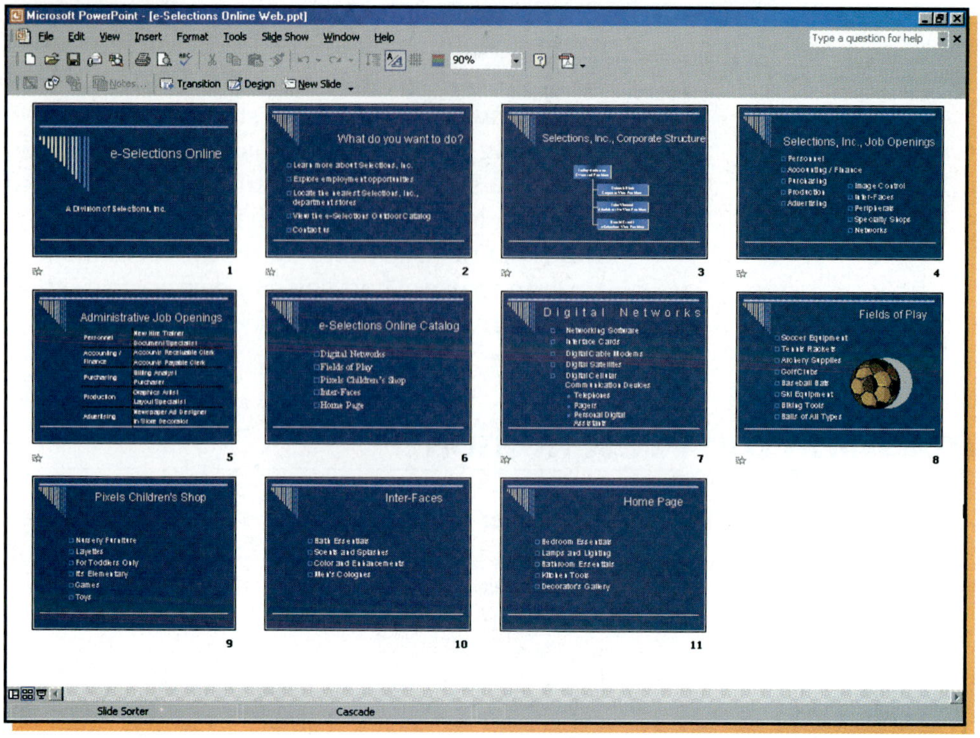

2 Position the insertion point at the end of the presentation and choose **Insert | Slides from Files** to open the Slide Finder dialog box.

Figure 7-3

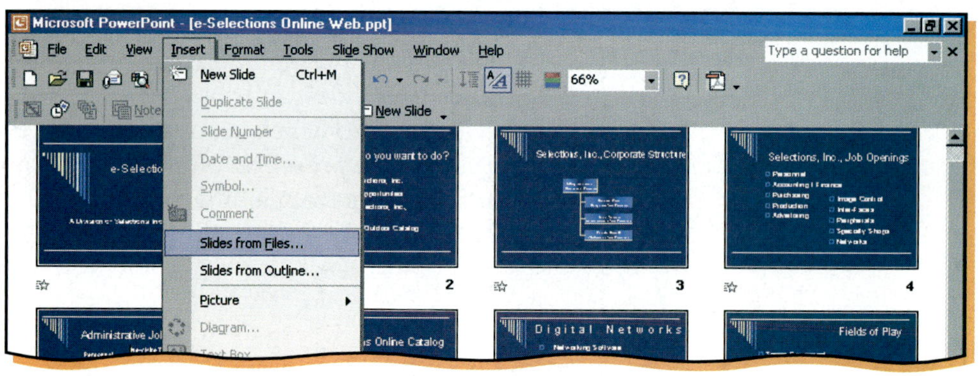

3 Click **Browse**, open the folder containing your student files, and open the *e-Selections Board Report.ppt* file.

Troubleshooting
If the thumbnail images are hidden, click the **Display** button.

4 Click **Insert All** to add all slides in the e-Selections Board Report presentation to the e-Selections Online Web presentation and then click **Close** in the Slide Finder dialog box.

Figure 7-4

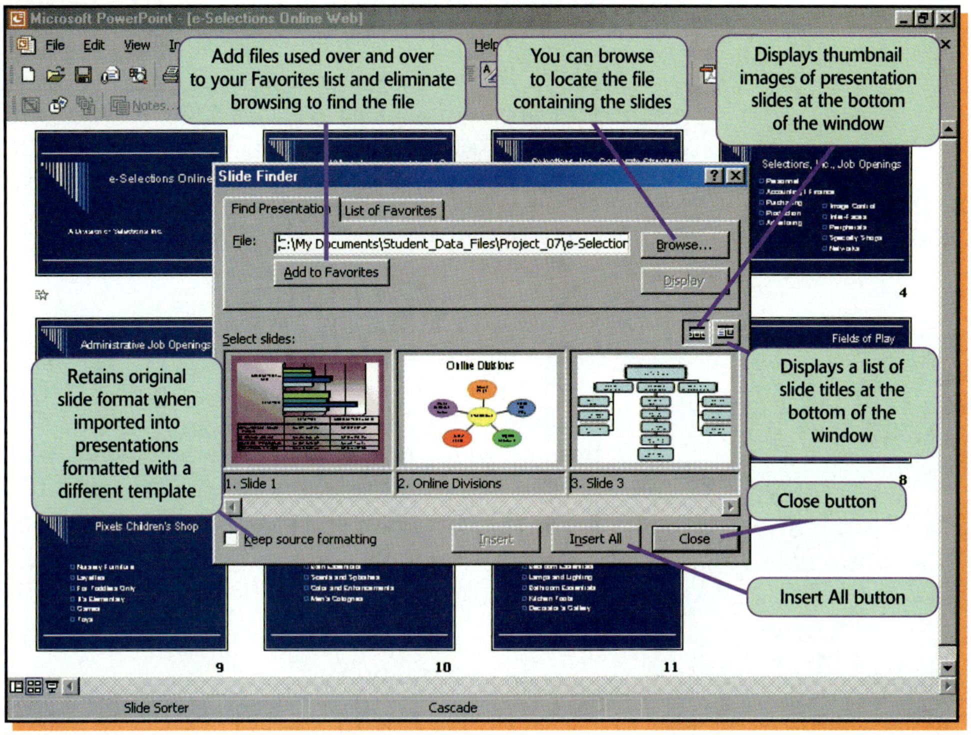

Tip
Slides added to presentations take on the color and format of the presentation template of the presentation to which you add them unless you check the Keep source formatting option in the Slide Finder dialog box.

5 Display Slide 12 in Normal view, double-click the chart to open it in Microsoft Graph, and change the format of the plot area and walls to **Automatic**.

6 Save changes to the presentation.

Figure 7-5

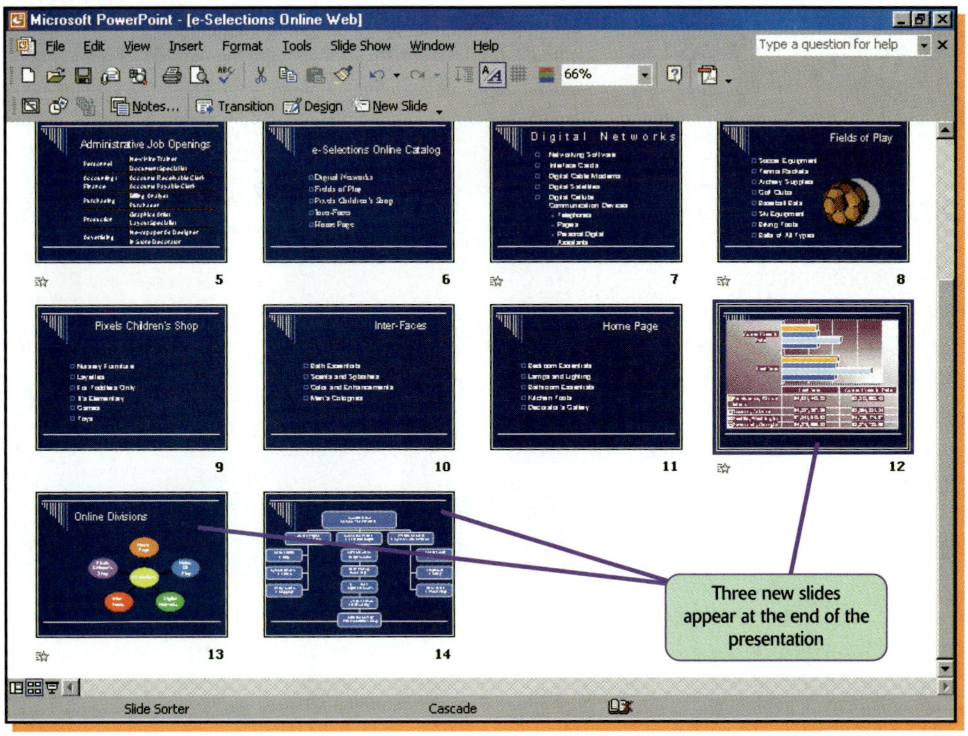

CHECK POINT

Slides you added to the *e-Selections Online* presentation were the only slides contained in the *e-Selections Board Report* presentation. There will be times when the slides you need to add to another presentation are just a few among many in the source presentation. You can insert specific slides from the source presentation by selecting them in the *Slide Finder* dialog box. Hold down the [Ctrl] key and click the thumbnail for each slide you want to insert, and then click **Insert** at the bottom of the Slide Finder dialog box.

Tip To include a slide in a custom show, the slide must be contained in the presentation in which you are creating the custom show. To add a slide from another presentation to a custom show, copy or insert the slide in the presentation containing the custom show.

Creating, Editing, and Showing Custom Shows

Because of the limited amount of time Mr. Carroll has to deliver his presentation, he wants to focus on specific slides within the presentation. Deleting or hiding the slides he wants to skip means editing the main presentation or rebuilding the deleted slides. PowerPoint's *custom shows* feature enables you to store numerous slides in the same presentation and then select the slides you want to show to a specific audience. Custom shows features:

- Custom shows consist of slides contained within a particular presentation.
- Custom shows are embedded within presentation files and no separate file is created.

Creating Custom Shows. Using the custom shows feature, you can select the slides that Mr. Carroll wants to include in his presentation and create *branches*—or links—to other custom shows so he can access them when questions arise.

Task 2:
To Create Custom Shows

1 Display Slide 1 of the *e-Selections Online Web.ppt* presentation in **Normal** view and choose **Slide Show | Custom Shows** to open the Custom Shows dialog box.

Figure 7-6

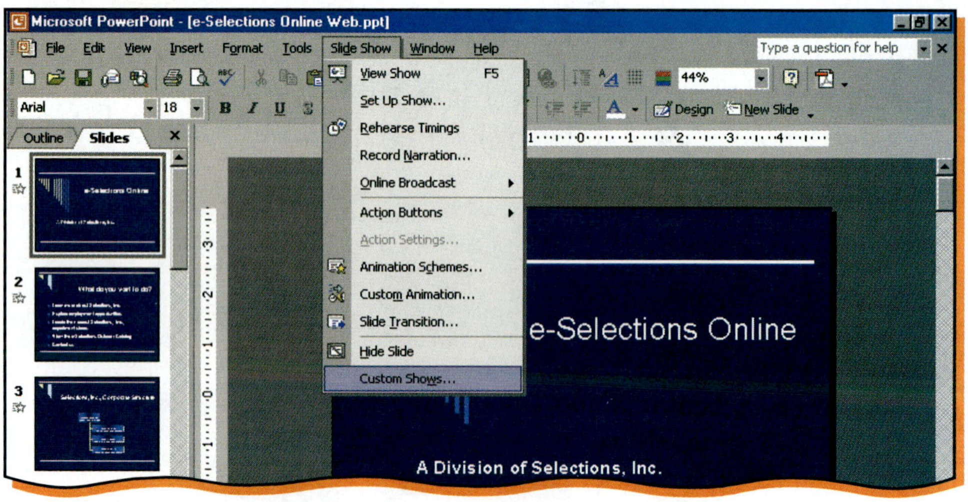

2 Click **New** to open the Define Custom Show dialog box.

Figure 7-7

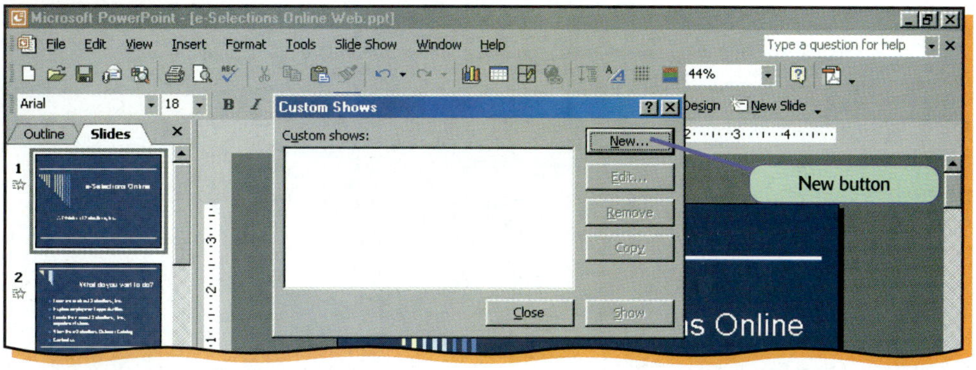

3 Type Board Meeting in the **Slide show name** text box and then double-click Slides 1, 3, 4, 12, 13, and 14 to add the slides to the custom show.

4 Click **OK**.

Tip

To select consecutive slides in the Slides in presentation list and add them to the Slides in custom show list, select the first slide you want to add, press Shift and click the last slide you want to add.

To select non-consecutive slides and add them to the custom show, press Ctrl as you click each slide.

Figure 7-8

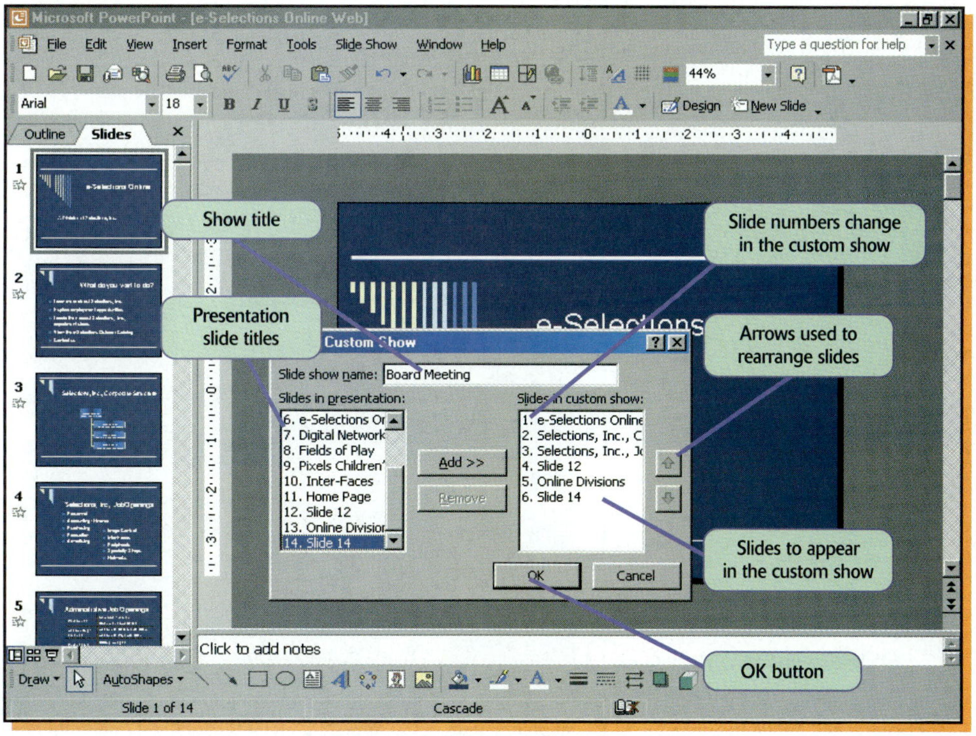

5. Click **Show** and review the show.

6. Create another new custom show, type **e-Selections Online Divisions** in the **Slide show name** text box, and add Slides 6 through 11.

7. Click **OK**, click **Close**, and save changes to the presentation file.

Figure 7-9

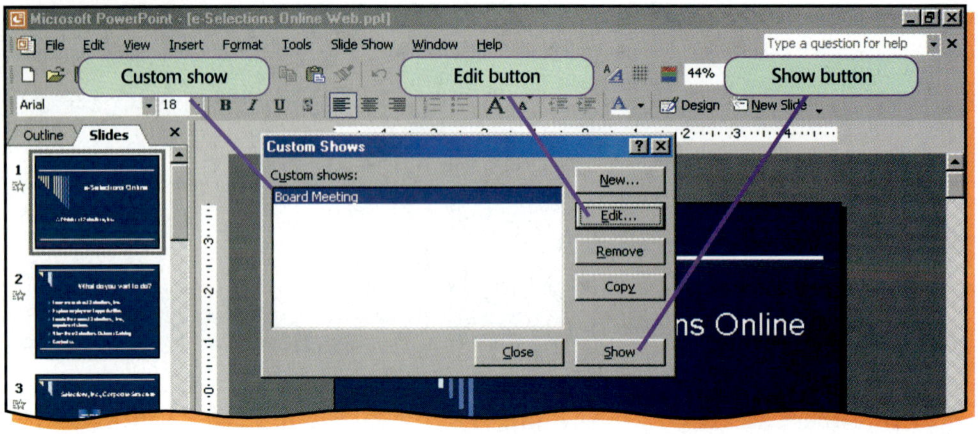

Editing Custom Shows. Edits to slide content are made directly to the slides in the presentation file. Edits made to the arrangement and slides selected for inclusion in a custom show are made using the Custom Shows dialog box.

Task 3: To Edit a Custom Show

1. Display Slide 1 of the *e-Selections Online Web.ppt* presentation in **Normal** view, choose **Slide Show | Custom Shows**, select the *Board Meeting* show, and click **Edit**.

2. Select Slide 3 in the **Slides in custom show** list and click **Remove**. The Selections, Inc., Job Openings slide no longer appears in the custom show list.

Figure 7-10

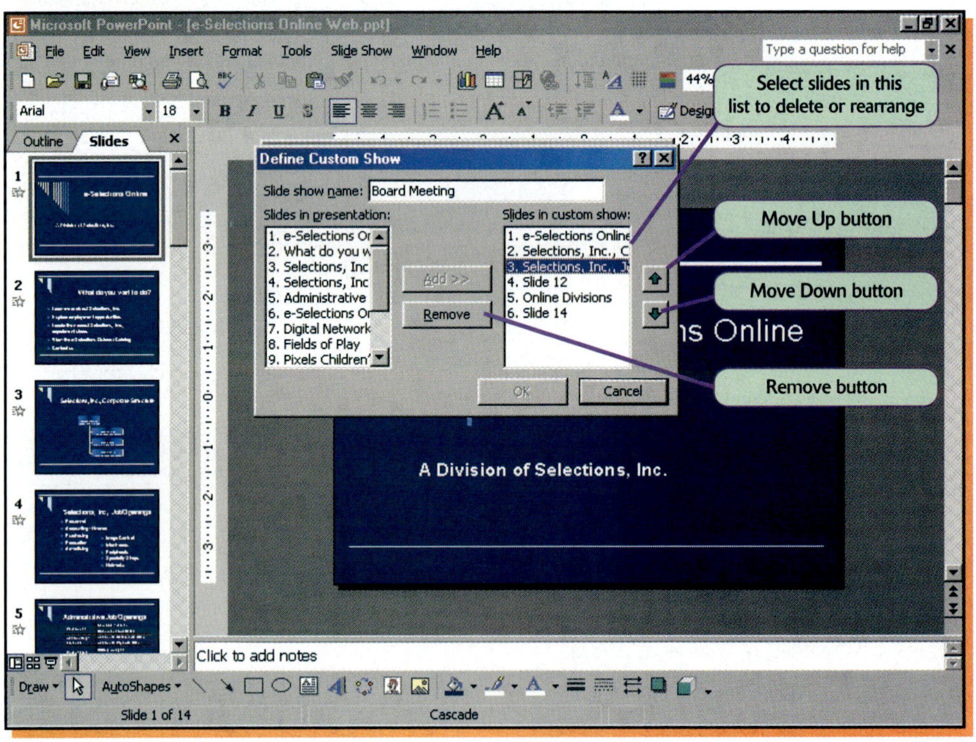

Tip Slides removed from custom shows remain part of the presentation file.

3 Select Slide 4 in the show list and click the Move Up button to position the slide as Slide 3.

4 Select Slide 4 in the show and click the Move Down button to position it as Slide 5 in the show.

5 Click **OK** and then click **Close**.

Troubleshooting
Sometimes slides you have repositioned in the show must be moved several times as your organize the Slides in custom show list.

Figure 7-11

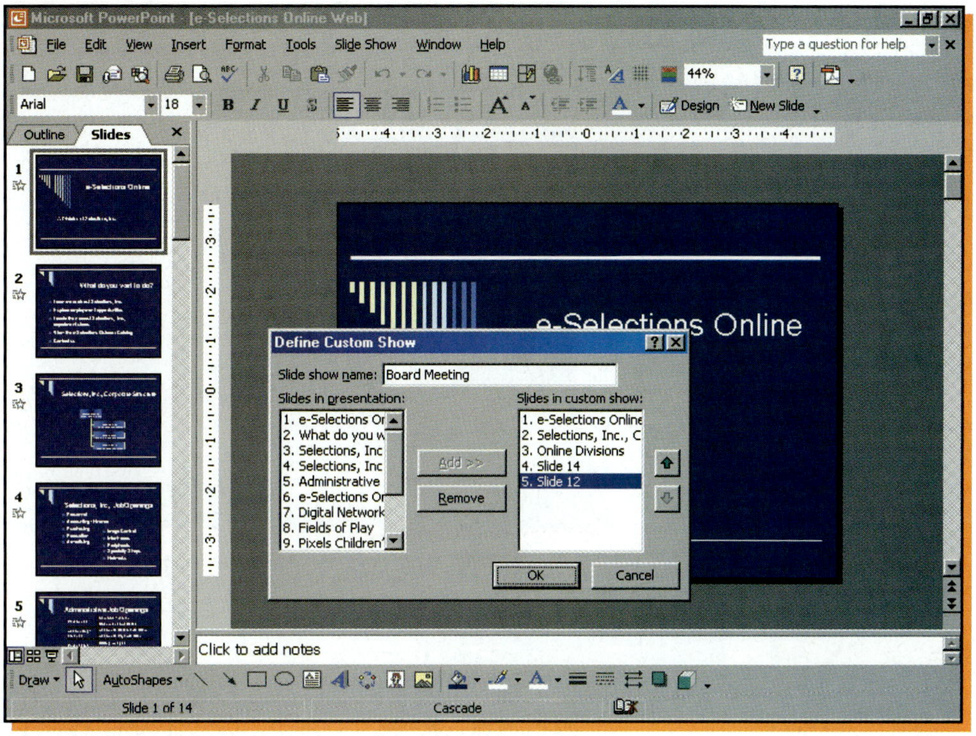

Showing Custom Shows. Because custom shows are stored as part of a presentation file, you run the custom show from the presentation Custom Shows dialog box or select the show from the Set Up Show dialog box. Settings selected in the Set Up Show dialog box are saved with the presentation so that the custom show automatically starts for Mr. Carroll.

Task 4:
To Show a Custom Show

1 Display the *e-Selections Online Web.ppt* presentation in any view and choose **Slide Show | Set Up Show** to open the Set Up Show dialog box.

Figure 7-12

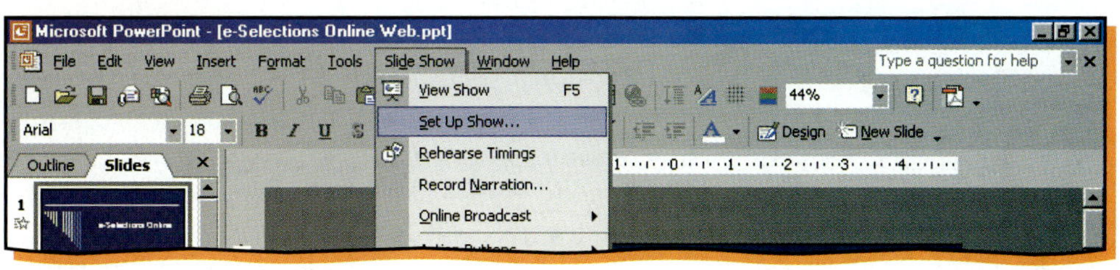

2 Select the **Custom show** option in the **Show slides** area, click the **Custom show** down arrow, and select the *Board Meeting* show.

3 Set additional options shown in Figure 7-13, click **OK**, and start the slide show. Slide 1 of the custom show appears on screen as a slide show.

4 Review the presentation and save changes to the presentation file.

Figure 7-13

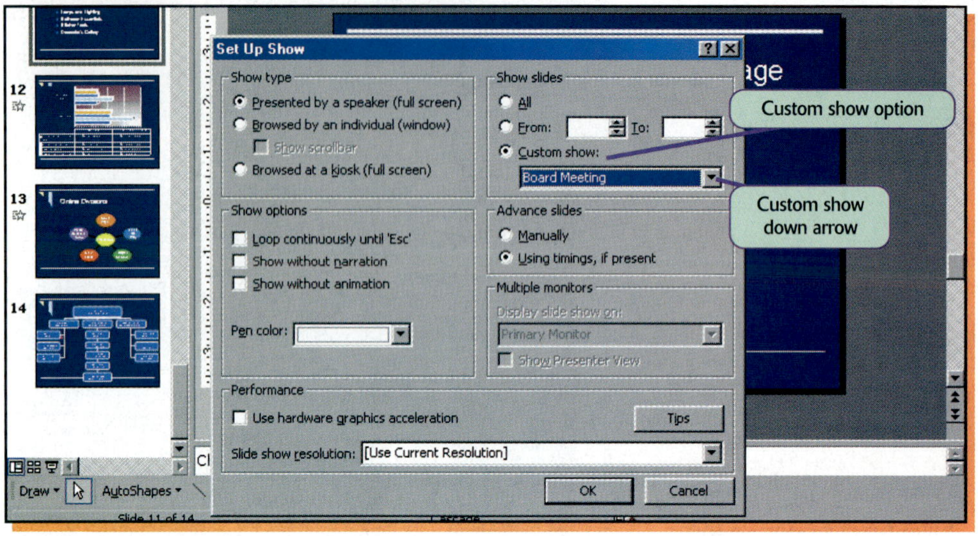

CHECK POINT

When you have recorded narration and saved it as part of a presentation that you plan to deliver live, it's easy to find yourself "butting in" on yourself. Settings in the Set Up Show dialog box make changing the settings for your live delivery easy. Choose **Slide Show | Set Up Show** to display the dialog box. Under the Show options area, you can select the option for showing the presentation without narration, without animations, or to loop (run) continuously until you stop the show. Explore other features in this dialog box to discover what you can—and cannot—do.

Tip If you consider the whole presentation as the trunk, it's easy to see how each custom show you create in a presentation can act as branch that stems from the trunk.

Creating Branches to Other Shows

Creating multiple shows, each containing slides that relate to a specific topic or adapted for a specific audience, is a great way to connect to topic-related information when questions arise during a presentation. By adding action buttons or creating hyperlinks to custom shows that link to other custom shows, you can quickly and seamlessly branch to another show during a presentation without leaving the show or fumbling with the PowerPoint program window. You can create a link between the two custom shows in the *e-Selections Online Web* presentation so that Mr. Carroll can access the online divisions show from the *Board Meeting* show.

Task 5:
To Create a Link to Branch to Another Show

1 Display Slide 13 in the *e-Selections Online Web.ppt* presentation in **Normal** view.

Troubleshooting
If the outline is displayed in the Outline/Slide Design pane in Normal view, click the Slide Design tab.

Figure 7-14

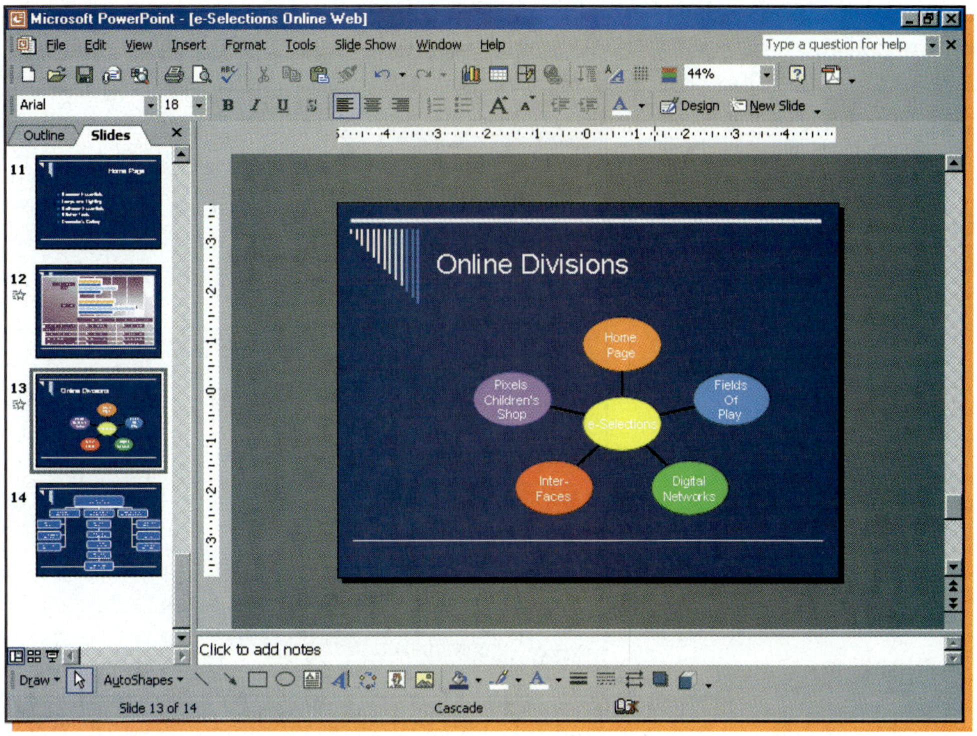

2 Right-click the title placeholder, and select **Hyperlink** to open the Insert Hyperlink dialog box.

Other Ways
To display the Hyperlink to dialog box:
- Choose **Insert | Hyperlink**

3 Click the Place in This Document icon in the **Link to** list.

Figure 7-15

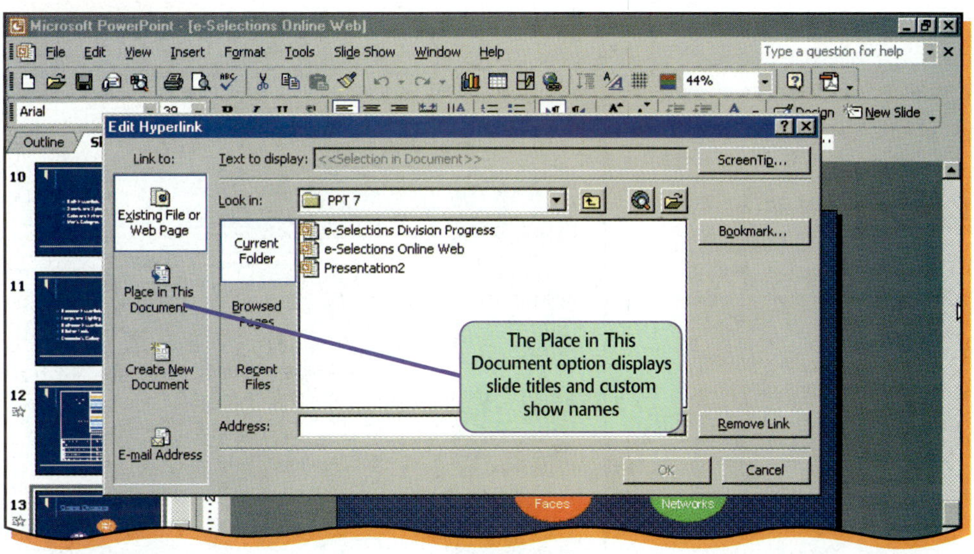

Tip
The files listed in Figure 7-15 depend on the folder you have open. As a result, the list of files you see may be different from those shown here.

4 Select the *e-Selections Online Divisions* show and select the **Show and return** option.

5 Click **OK**.

Tip The Show and return option tells PowerPoint that you want to display another show and return to the current position in the original show after the last slide in the branch shows.

Figure 7-16

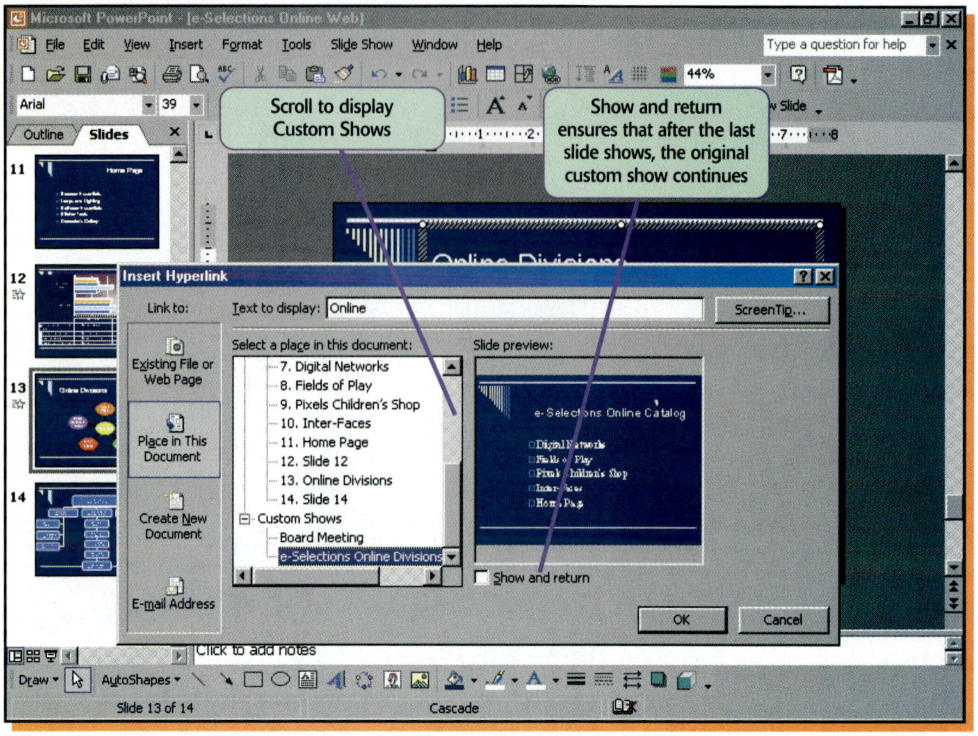

6 Click the Slide Show (from current slide) button to view the slide and click the slide title to display the other custom show and to test the link.

7 Save changes to the presentation.

Tip Because you hyperlinked the custom show to the text in the title placeholder, the placeholder text appears underlined. When you point to the title text, the mouse pointer appears as a pointing hand to indicate that if you click, PowerPoint will hyperlink to the whatever is set as the hyperlink.

Figure 7-17

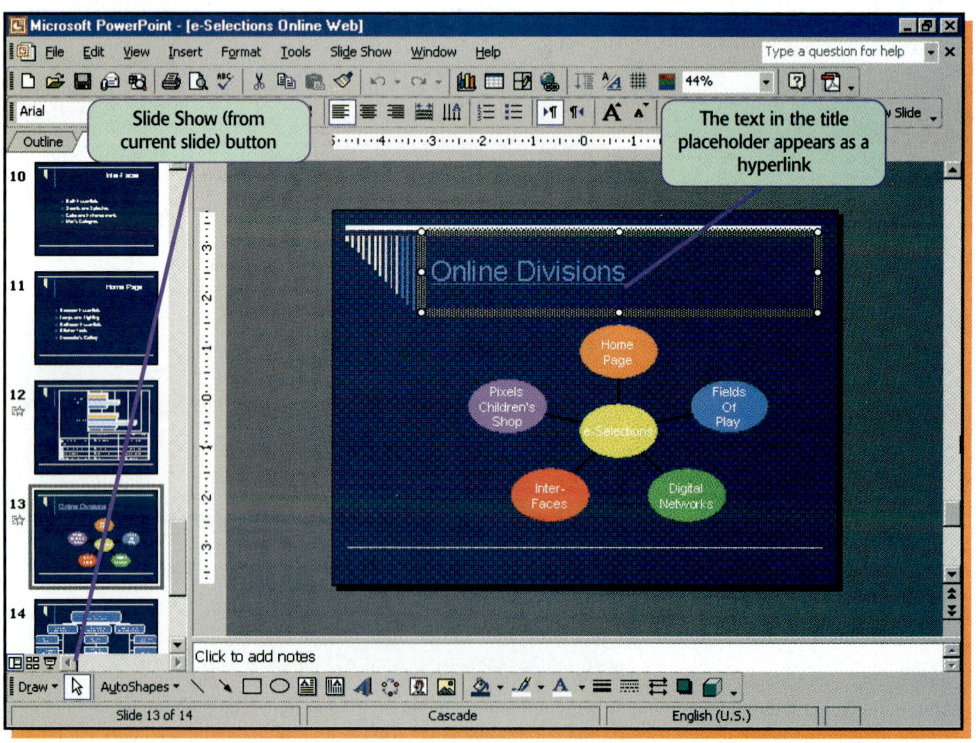

Working with Slide Show Tools

WEB TIP

The most common format for music you download from the Internet is .mp3. These files are about one-tenth the size of a song on a commercial audio CD. As a result, files that would normally occupy 8 megabytes of hard disk space in .wav format require only 800 kilobytes in .mp3 format. While the quality of downloaded music is not as high as commercial CDs, you can conserve space and reduce presentation size by adding .mp3 files instead of .wav files to PowerPoint slides.

PowerPoint contains a number of tools to quickly and easily add narration, create speaker notes, set up appointments, and create meeting reports. To get the most from some of these tools, you'll need to have a sound card, a microphone, and a pair of speakers set up and working properly.

Recording Narration

PowerPoint comes equipped with a feature that automatically stores recorded *narration* with individual slides in the presentation. As a result, you can display each slide contained in a custom show and record the narration for that slide—sometimes over and over again—until you get it right. Then you can move on to the next slide and record the narration. Mr. Carroll mentioned that he would like to add his speech to slides in the presentation so that when he distributes the presentation to Board members, his narrative will be included for future reference. Before Mr. Carroll starts his narration, you will show him how to test the system so that his narration is recorded.

Tip To preserve the presentation that Mr. Carroll will use during the meeting, you need to make a copy of the presentation to use for recording the narration.

Task 6:
To Record Narration

1 Display the *e-Selections Online Web.ppt* presentation in **Normal** view and save the presentation as a new file named *e-Selections Division Progress*.

2 Display the first slide to contain narration and choose **Slide Show | Record Narration** to open the Record Narration dialog box.

Figure 7-18

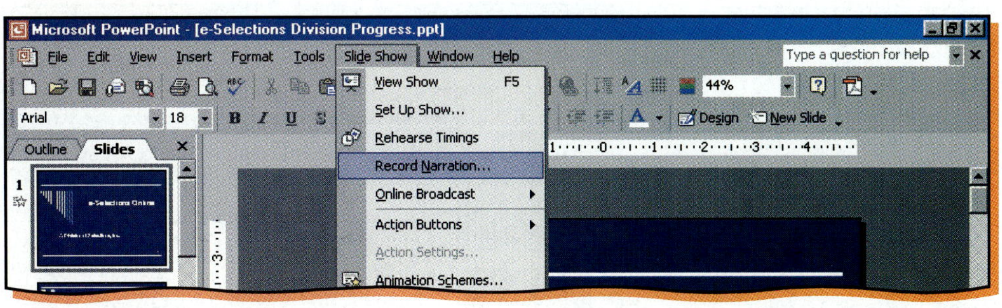

3 Click **Set Microphone Level** and read the sample phrase contained in the dialog box to test the microphone.

4 Click **OK**.

Troubleshooting

Sometimes, when microphones are connected after a computer is already up and running, PowerPoint does not recognize the microphone. If your microphone is connected but no green bar appears as you read the sample text, read the text several times. If you still see no green bar, it may be necessary for you to reboot your computer. Contact your instructor if you continue to have problems.

Figure 7-19

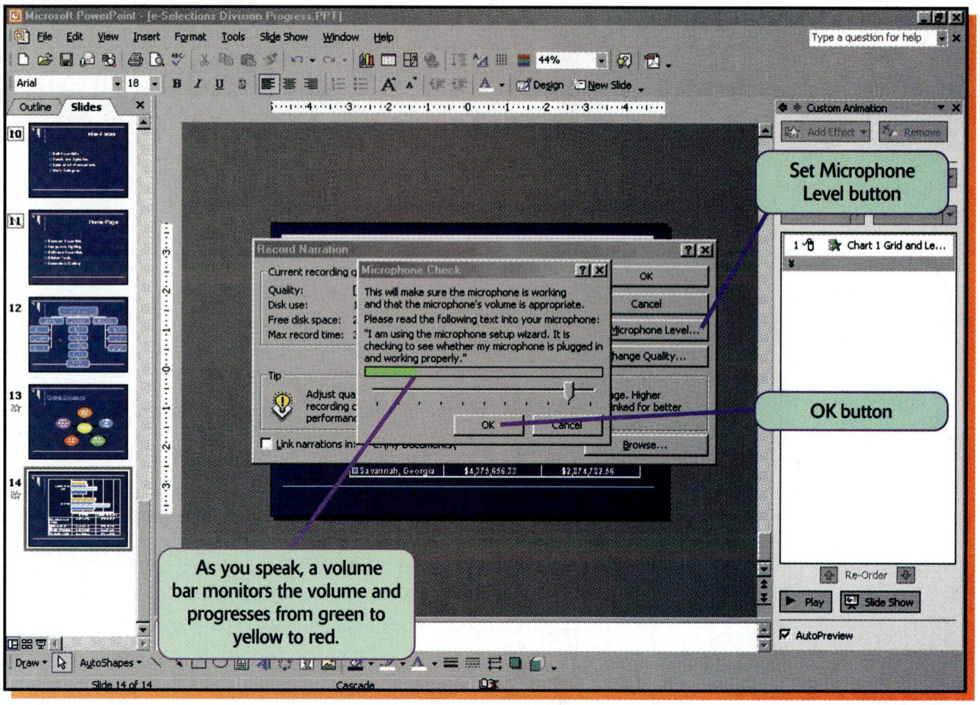

5 Select the **Link narration in** option to store the narration in the active folder, click **OK**.

Tip

PowerPoint automatically adjusts the microphone level for the voice of the speaker. Testing the microphone simply ensures that the microphone is operating properly.

Figure 7-20

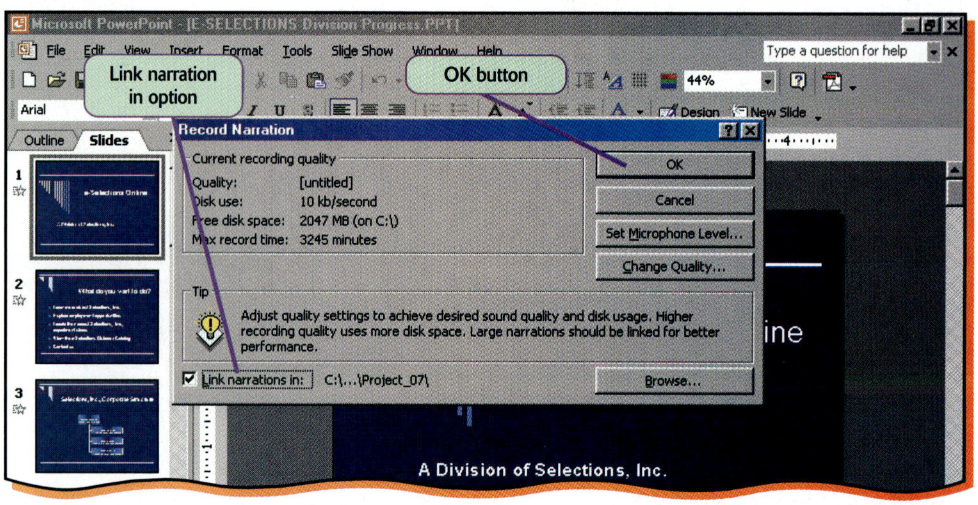

6 Show the first slide while you record the narration for it, and then press Esc.

7 Click **Don't Save**.

8 Repeat the procedures contained in Steps 2 through 6 to record narration for each slide in the *Board Meeting* custom show.

9 Show the complete presentation as a slide show and identify the slides for which you want to change the narration.

10 Repeat the procedures contained in Steps 2 through 6 to re-record the narration for those slides you identified as you reviewed the slide show.

11 Save changes to the presentation.

Figure 7-21

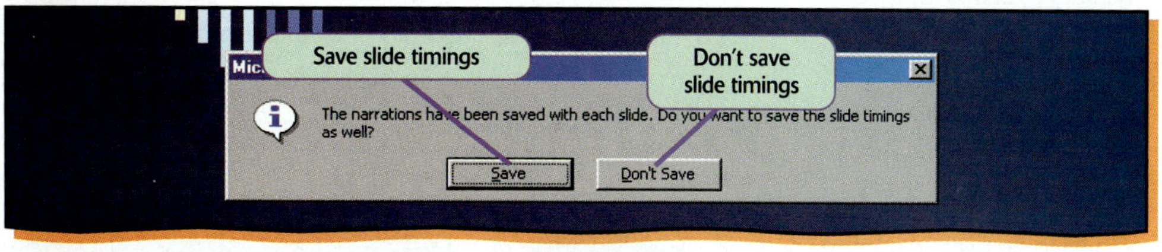

Figure 7-22

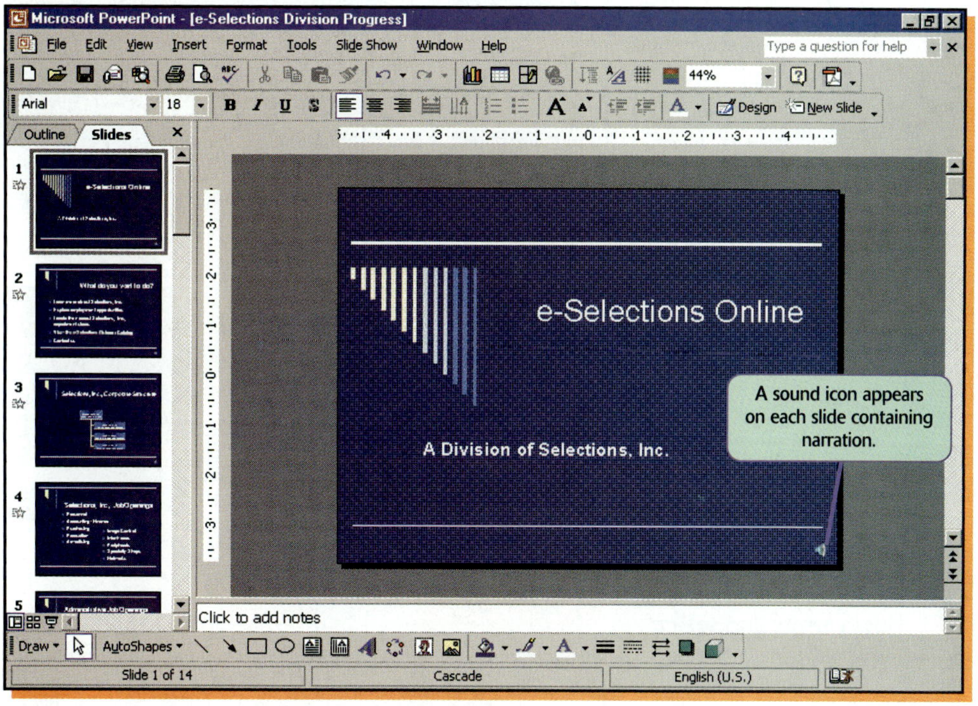

Setting Sound Items to Play Automatically

A sound icon appears on each slide on which you recorded narration. You can either click the icon to play the narration or set the narration to play automatically. Because Mr. Carroll plans to distribute the presentation to each Board member, it's important that the sound items are set to play automatically.

Task 7:
To Set Sound Items to Play Automatically

1. Display Slide 1 (the first slide containing a sound icon), right-click the sound icon, and select **Custom Animation**.

Figure 7-23

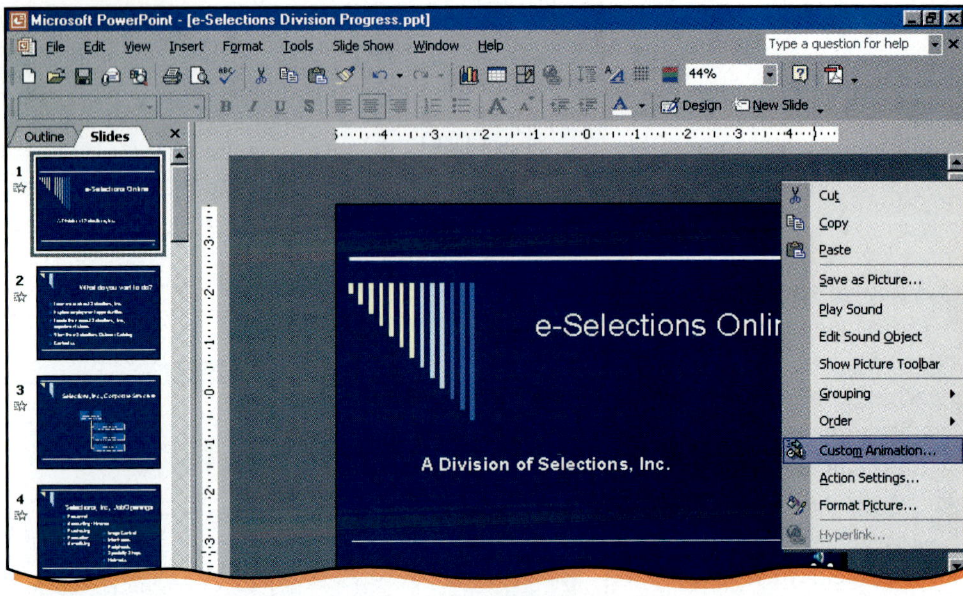

Tip

Options on the Media # drop-down list control when the animation starts:

- **On click** starts the animation when you click the mouse
- **With previous** starts the animation at the same time the previous items starts
- **After previous** starts the animation after the previous item completes its animation

2. Click the **Media #** down arrow and select **Start with Previous**.
3. Click **Play** on the task pane to test the settings.
4. Show the presentation as a slide show and make necessary adjustments to slide timings, animations, and sound item settings.
5. Save and close the presentation.

Figure 7-24

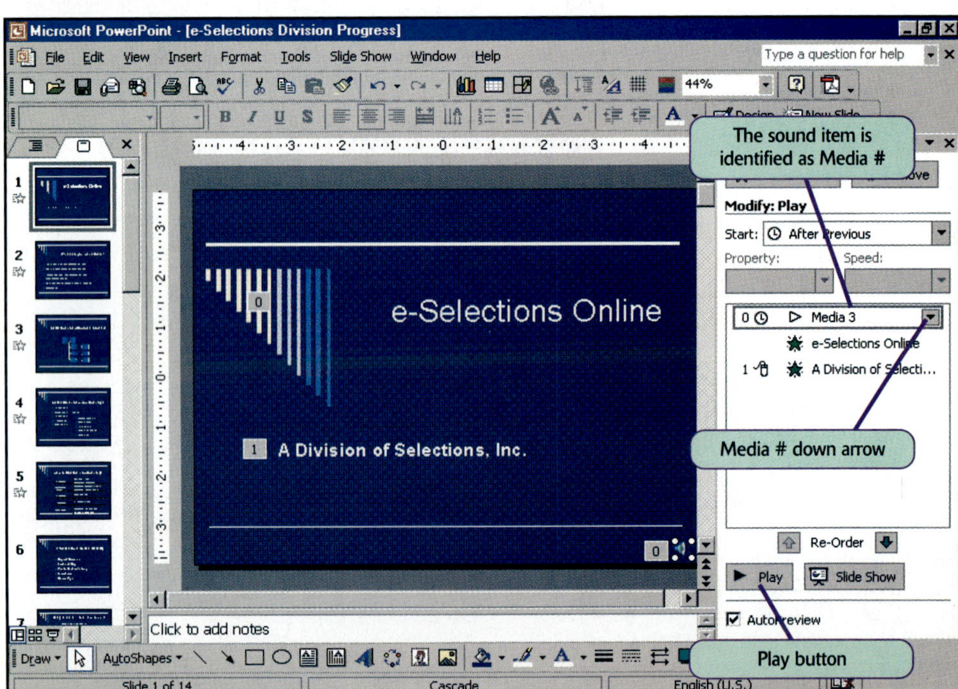

Adding Speaker Notes During a Slide Show

Practicing your presentation is a great way to identify pieces of information that you want to be sure to mention. PowerPoint's *speaker notes* feature is a great tool for jotting down your ideas as you practice. Text added to speaker notes during a slide show appear in the Notes pane of the presentation window for the slide that was active when you recorded the speaker notes.

Task 8:
To Create Speaker Notes During a Slide Show

1. Open *e-Selections Online Web.ppt* and start the *Board Meeting* custom show.

Figure 7-25

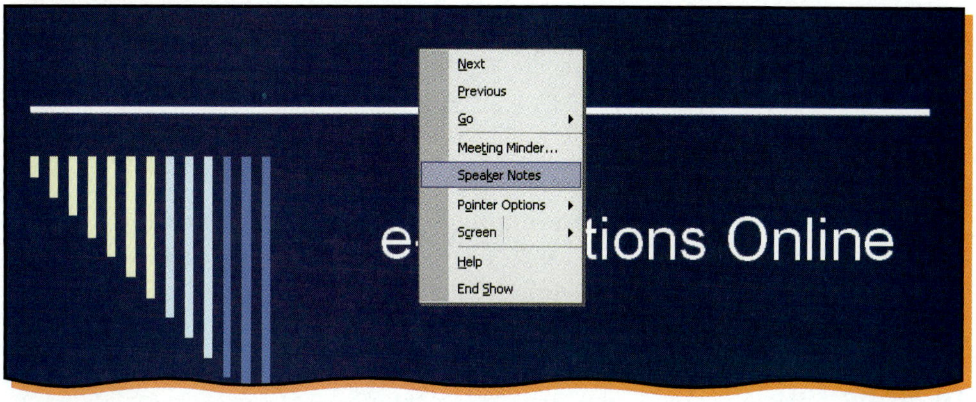

2. Right-click the title Slide 1 and select **Speaker Notes**.

3. Type the following text in the **Speaker Notes** dialog box.

One advantage of being on the cutting edge of corporate innovations is seeing the excitement associated with branching out into untapped fields.

Another advantage is watching the company grow and maximize its success.

Figure 7-26

4. Click **Close** and press Esc to stop the slide show.

5. Start the *Board Meeting* custom show again and add speaker notes to other slides in the show.

6. Save changes to the presentation.

Troubleshooting
If you are using an e-mail and calendaring program other than Outlook, you may be unable to schedule appointments using the Meeting Minder. Follow the direction of your instructor to complete that portion of the task.

Using the Meeting Minder

The *Meeting Minder* is a tool that you can use from any PowerPoint view to schedule appointments in Microsoft Outlook, add *action items* for follow-up tasks, and record questions and other notes in the form of minutes during a live presentation. After the presentation, you can use the Meeting Minder to generate *meeting minutes* and create a slide of action items. Items you record in the Meeting Minder dialog box are saved as part of the presentation.

Accessing the Meeting Minder. You can display the Meeting Minder dialog box from any PowerPoint view as well as from a slide show:

- From Normal, Slide Sorter, or Notes Pages view, choose **Tools | Meeting Minder**.
- From a slide show, right-click and select **Meeting Minder** from the shortcut menu.

Scheduling Appointments During a Slide Show. The integration of PowerPoint with Outlook enables you to create and schedule an appointment during a slide show and record the appointment in the Outlook Calendar.

Task 9: To Schedule Appointments during a Slide Show

1. Open the *e-Selections Online Web.ppt* presentation and show the *Board Meeting* custom show.
2. Right-click on the title slide, select **Meeting Minder**, click **Schedule**.

Figure 7-27

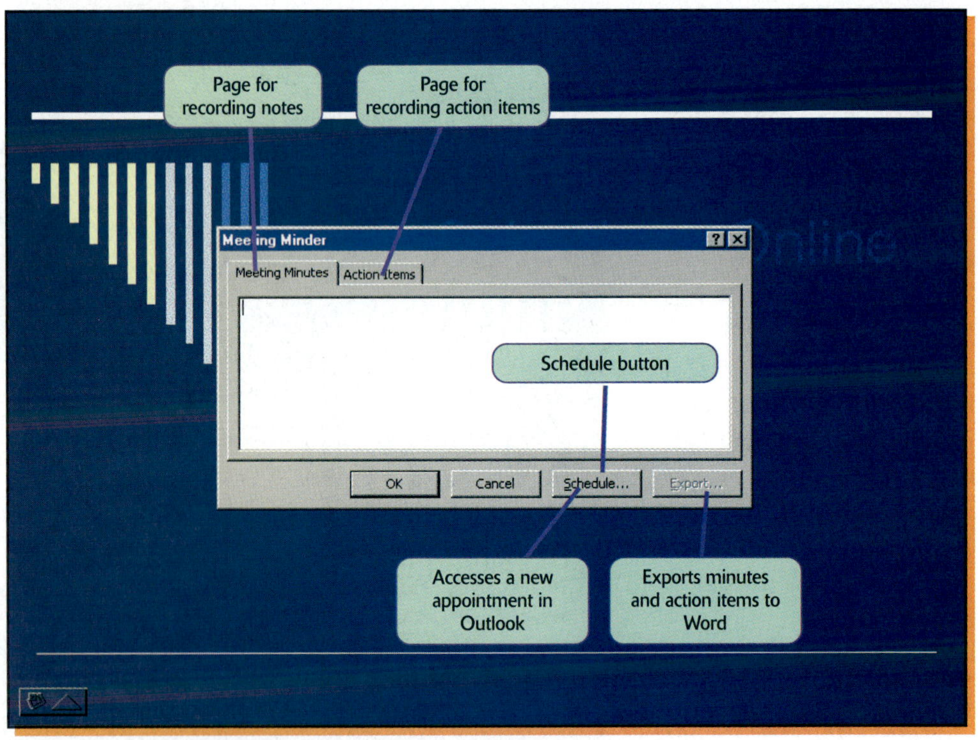

3 Record the appointment information displayed in Figure 7-28.

4 Click the Save and Close **Save and Close** button. The Meeting Minder dialog box remains open in the slide show.

5 Click **OK** to close the Meeting Minder and display Slide 2 in the custom show.

Tip Meeting minutes and action items are stored with the presentation when you save it. As a result, be sure to remove such items before showing the presentation to the next audience.

Figure 7-28

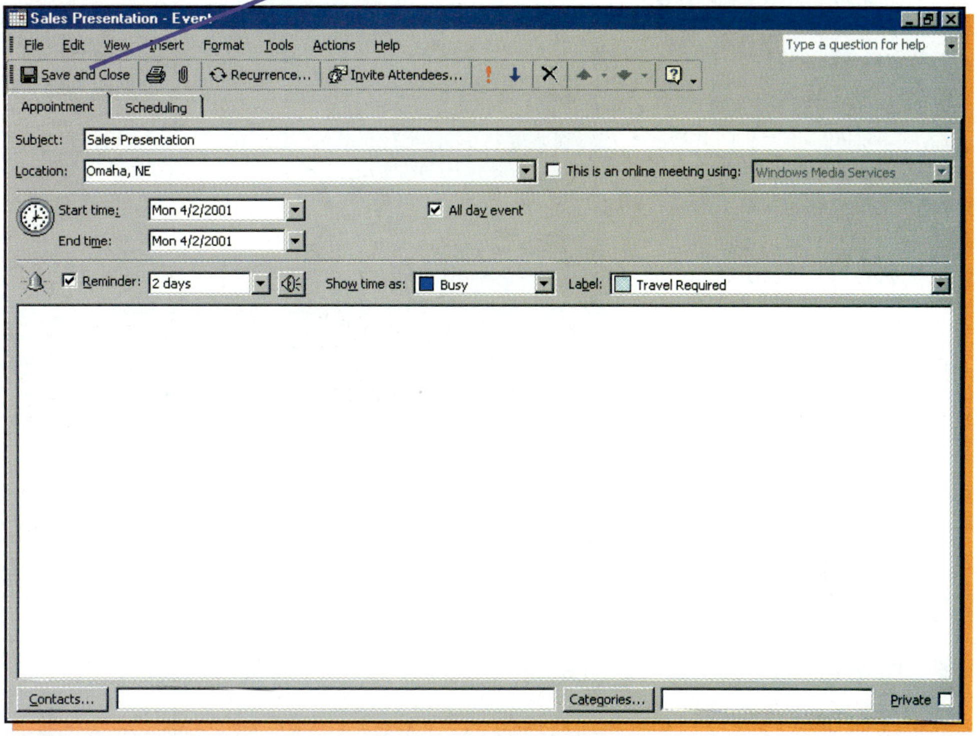

Recording Meeting Minutes and Action Items in the Meeting Minder. Action items you record in the Meeting Minder dialog box are recorded as you type them onto new slides that PowerPoint adds to the end of the presentation. Action item slides make great review slides and provide a quick overview of tasks that need to be completed as a result of presentation discussion. Notes you record on the Meeting Minutes page of the Meeting Minder dialog box can be exported to a Word document along with the items recorded on the Action Items page.

WEB TIP

The new .mu domain type is becoming popular for bands and other music organizations that want to set up Web domains. It stands for music and offers relief for music groups from the crowded .com domain names.

Task 10:

To Record Meeting Minutes and Action Items

1. Display Slide 4 of the *Board Meeting* custom show, display the **Meeting Minder** dialog box, and click the **Action Items** tab.

2. Type the following information in fields of the dialog box:
Description: Outside boxes appear slightly off screen. Correct the chart size.
Assigned To: Your Name
Due Date: *Next Wednesday*

3. Click **Add** to add the item to the task to the action items list.

4. Click the **Meeting Minutes** tab.

Figure 7-29

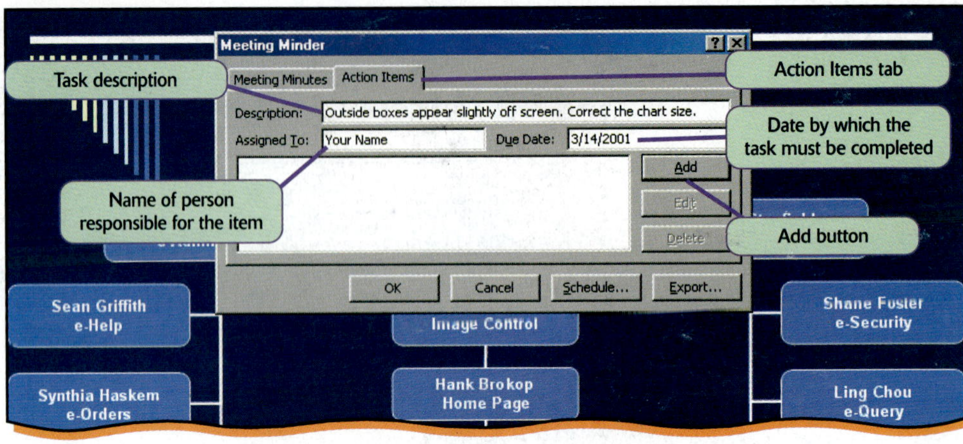

Tip Substitute next Wednesday's date for *Next Wednesday*.

Figure 7-30

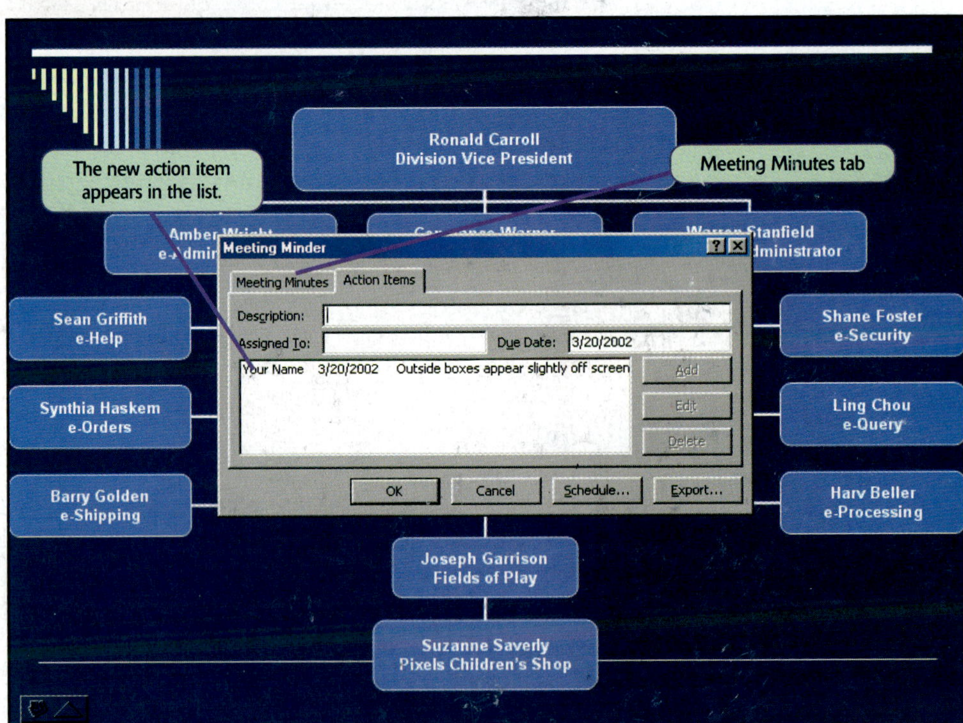

5 Type the following text in the Meeting Minutes box and click OK:

This chart may be a little overwhelming. Consider removing it from the custom show.

Figure 7-31

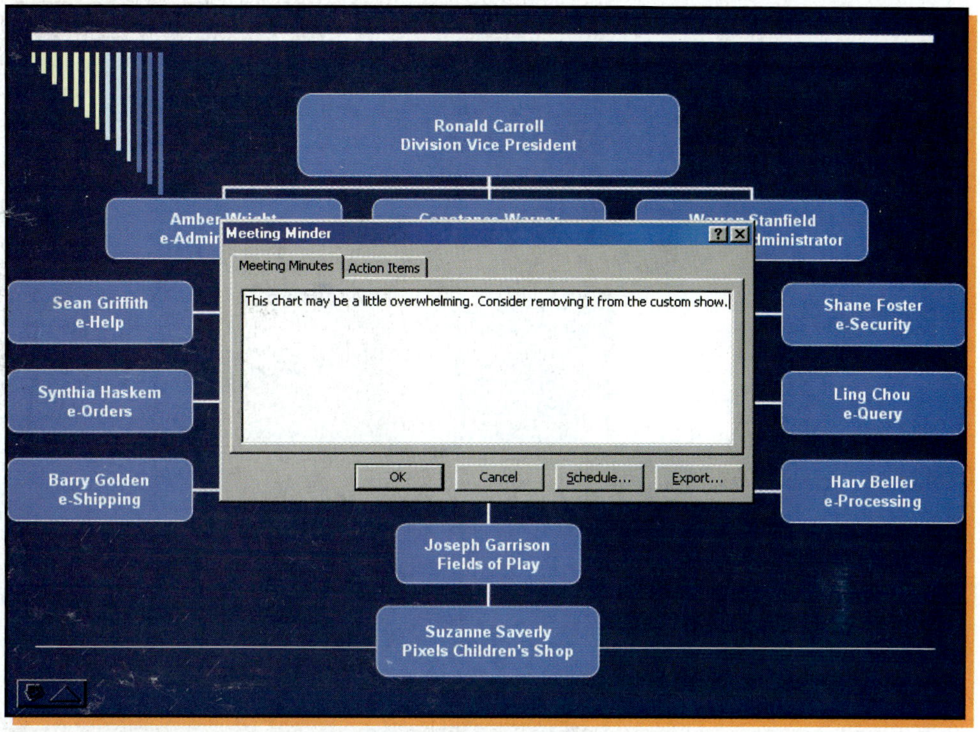

6 Continue showing the presentation until the last slide appears on screen.

7 Complete the slide show and save changes to the presentation.

Tip PowerPoint creates multiple action items slides when necessary to record the action items you create. These slides are saved as part of the presentation file. Before showing the presentation to another audience, you may need to remove the action items slides.

Figure 7-32

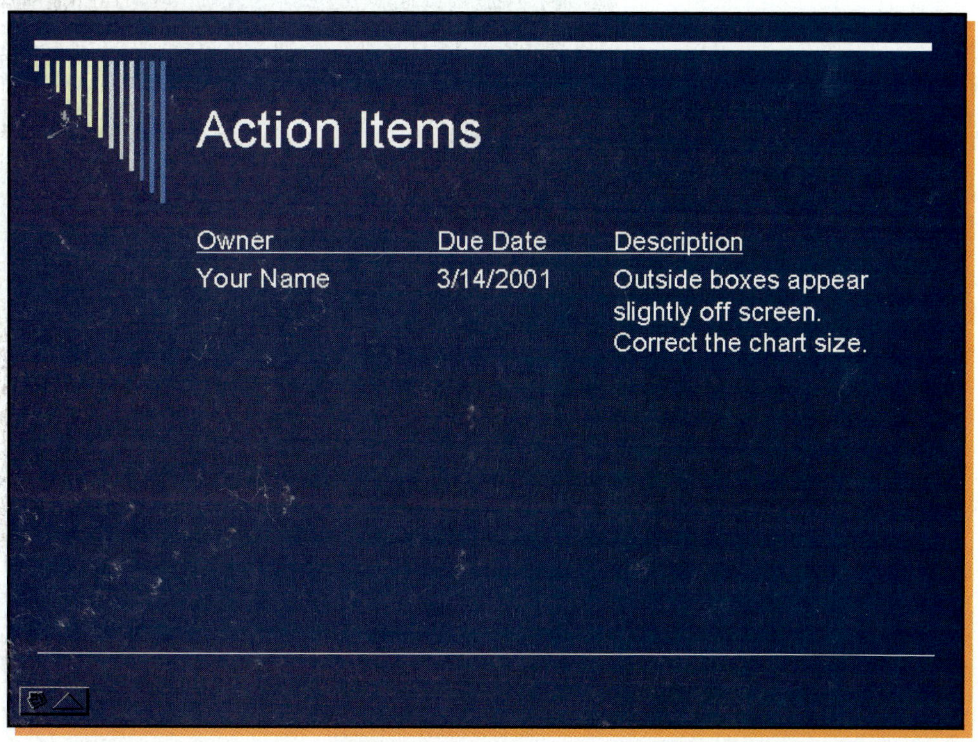

Exporting Meeting Minutes and Action Items. Meeting minutes and action items recorded during a presentation practice or a live presentation are saved as part of the presentation file so that you can access and review them later. The easiest way to get the meeting minutes and action items into a document is to *export* them using tools available in the Meeting Minder dialog box.

Task 11: To Export Meeting Minutes and Action Items

1. Display the presentation *e-Selections Online Web.ppt* in **Normal** view, choose **Tools | Meeting Minder**, and click **Export** to open the Meeting Minder Export dialog box.

2. Select both options and click **Export Now**.

Figure 7-33

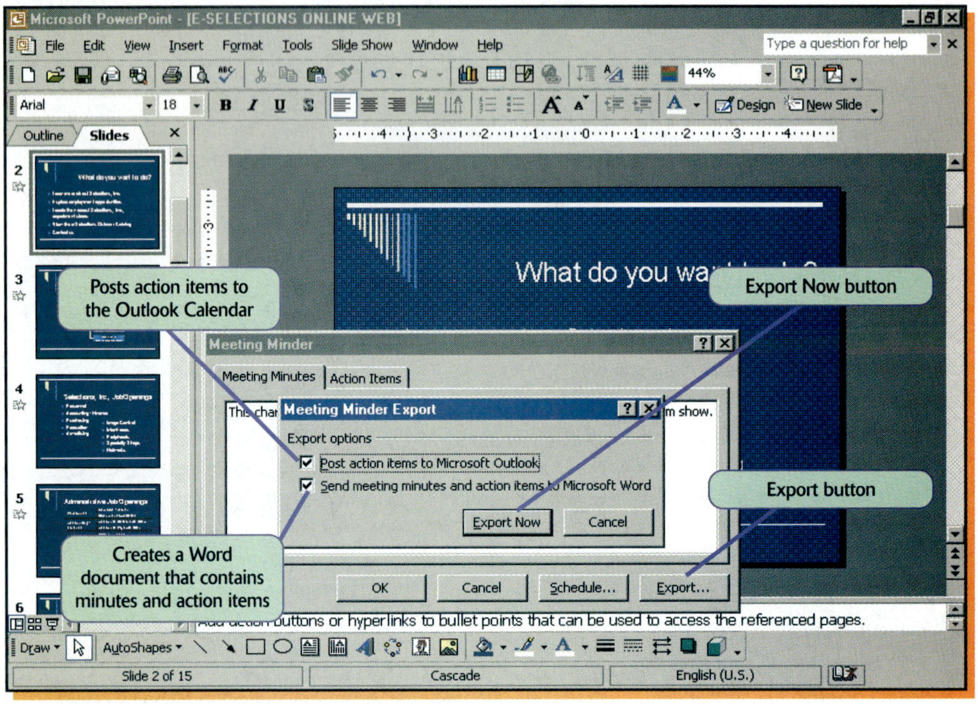

3. Click the Save and Close button to save the action item in Outlook, if necessary.

Troubleshooting If you are using a program other than Outlook, PowerPoint may bypass step 3.

Figure 7-34

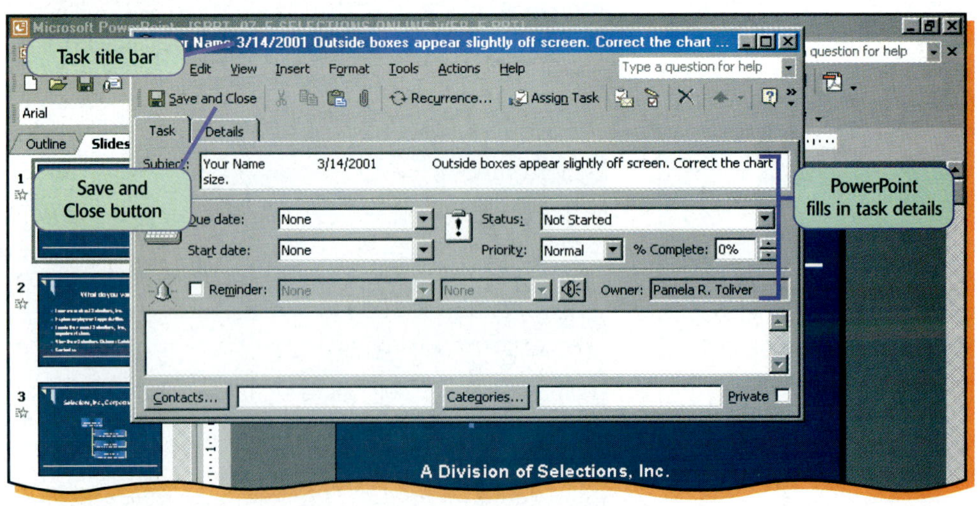

4 Save the document as *Board Meeting Show Notes*, close the document and Word, and save changes to the presentation. Leave the presentation open.

Figure 7-35

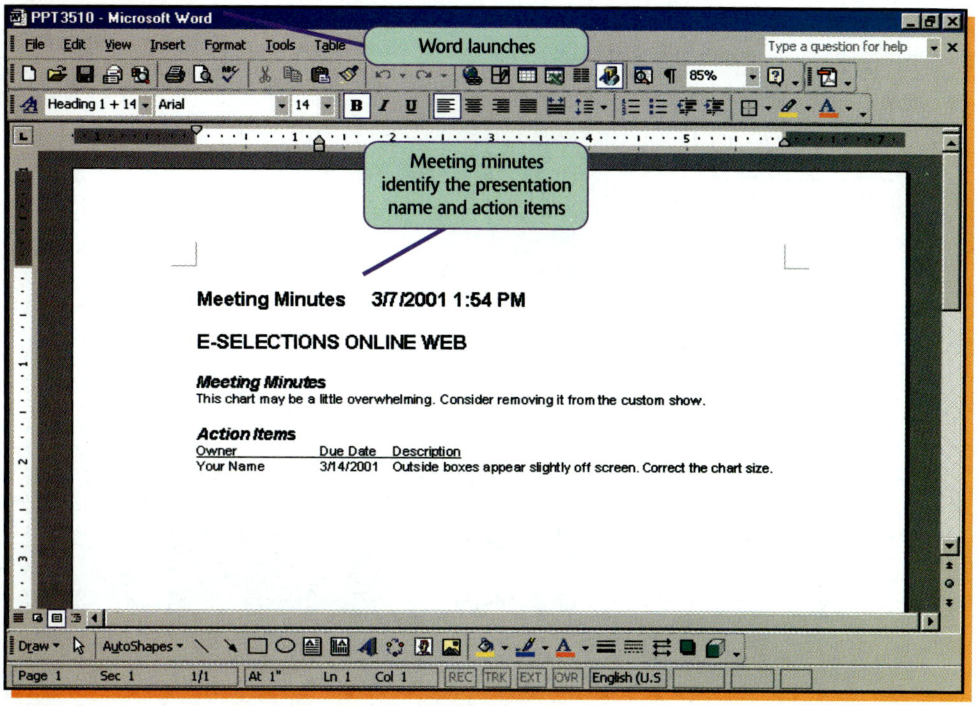

Troubleshooting When you export meeting minutes to Word, Word creates a temporary file named PPT to identify PowerPoint as the application that generated the file followed by a multi-digit number and the .rtf extension. The extension identifies the file as a Rich Text Format file that can be opened in a wide variety of applications. Word stores the file in the default Temp folder for your login ID. To name the file using a more descriptive file name and store the file in a different folder to make it easier to find, use the **File | Save As** command.

Saving Presentations as Shows

If you have access to e-mail, you may have received an e-mail message with a PowerPoint show attached. There are a number of different shows circulating. One of the most popular was the show that pictured New Year's celebrations around the world when January 1, 2000, arrived. Saving presentations as shows enables you to start the slide show without first launching PowerPoint. *PowerPoint shows* automatically launch as slide shows. This format will be great for Mr. Carroll's presentation to the Board.

Task 12:
To Save a Presentation as a Show

1. Display *e-Selections Online Web.ppt* in **Normal** view and choose **File | Save As**.

Tip You can display the presentation you are saving in any view—using Normal view in this task ensures that your screen matches those shown in this book.

2. Click the **Save as type** down arrow, and select **PowerPoint Show**.

3. Click the **Save in** down arrow and select **Desktop** so that a shortcut to the presentation show will appear on the desktop.

4. Click **Save** and then close all presentations and exit PowerPoint.

Figure 7-36

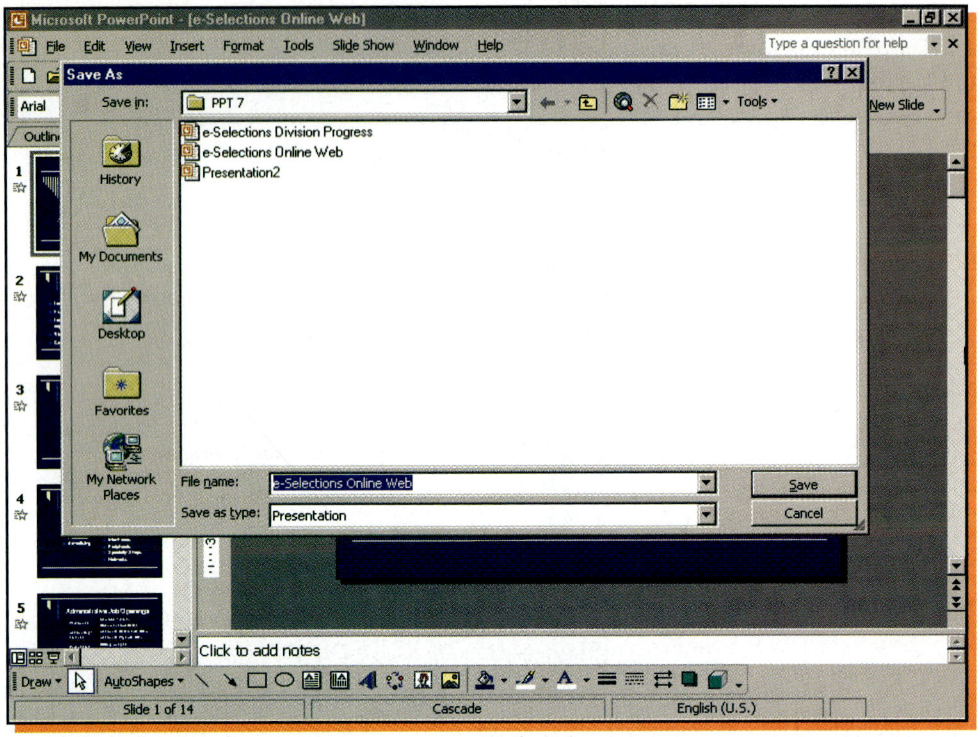

Tip PowerPoint saves the presentation as a show with a .pps extension. The icon PowerPoint uses to identify shows is different from presentation icons. By saving the file to the desktop, it's easier to see how you can run the show without first launching PowerPoint and opening a folder, etc. Although you can open the PowerPoint show as a presentation in PowerPoint, PowerPoint shows are designed specifically to be self-running. As a result, the show launches automatically when you double-click the icon.

SUMMARY AND EXERCISES

SUMMARY

- You can insert slides from one presentation into another presentation using the copy/paste procedure or the **Insert | Slides from Files** command to select and insert slides.
- Slides inserted into presentations from other presentations take on the color and format of the presentation template of the receiving presentation unless you check the Keep source formatting option in the Slide Finder dialog box.
- You can insert specific slides from the source presentation by selecting them in the Slide Finder dialog box.
- PowerPoint's custom shows feature enables you to store numerous slides in one presentation and then select the slides you want to show to a specific audience.
- Custom shows consist of slides contained within a single presentation.
- Custom shows are embedded within presentation files and no separate file is created.
- Using the custom shows feature, you can create branches to other custom shows, presentations, or files.
- Edits to slide content are made directly on the presentation slides. Edits made to the arrangement and slides selected for inclusion in a custom show are made using the Custom Shows dialog box.
- Slides removed from custom shows remain part of the presentation file.
- Because custom shows are stored as part of a presentation file, you run the custom show from the presentation Custom Shows dialog box or use the Set Up Show dialog box to set the show to run.
- Settings selected in the Set Up Show dialog box are saved with the presentation.
- PowerPoint contains tools for adding narration, creating speaker notes, setting up appointments, and creating meeting reports.
- A sound card, microphone, and speakers are required for recording narration.
- A sound icon appears on each slide on which you record narration.
- PowerPoint's Speaker Notes feature is a great tool for jotting down ideas as you practice delivering a presentation.

- The Meeting Minder is a tool that you can use from any PowerPoint view to schedule appointments in Outlook, add action items for follow-up tasks, and record questions and other notes in the form of minutes during a live presentation.
- Items you record in the Meeting Minder dialog box are saved as part of the presentation.
- You can display the Meeting Minder dialog box from any PowerPoint view as well as from a slide show
- The integration of PowerPoint with Outlook enables you to create and schedule an appointment during a slide show and record it in the Outlook Calendar.
- Action items you record in the Meeting Minder dialog box are recorded, as you type them, on new slides that PowerPoint adds to the end of the presentation.
- Notes you record on the Meeting Minutes page of the Meeting Minder dialog box can be exported to a Word document along with the items recorded on the Action Items page.
- PowerPoint shows automatically launch as slide shows.
- PowerPoint saves presentation shows with a .pps extension.
- A PowerPoint Show icon that is different from the presentation icon identifies shows.

KEY TERMS & SKILLS

KEY TERMS

action items (p. 7-20)
branches (p. 7-8)
custom shows (p. 7-8)
export (p. 7-24)
Meeting Minder (p. 7-20)
minutes (p. 7-20)
narration (p. 7-15)
Slide Finder (p. 7-8)
sound card (p. 7-15)

SKILLS

Create branches to other shows (p. 7-13)
Create custom shows (p. 7-8)
Create speaker notes during a slide show (p. 7-19)
Edit a custom show (p. 7-10)
Export meeting minutes and action items (p. 7-24)
Insert slides from other presentations (p. 7-5)
Record meeting minutes and action items (p. 7-22)
Record narration (p. 7-15)
Save presentations as shows (p. 7-25)
Schedule appointments during a slide show (p. 7-20)
Set sound items to play automatically (p. 7-17)
Show a custom show (p. 7-11)
Using the Meeting Minder (p. 7-20)

STUDY QUESTIONS

MULTIPLE CHOICE

1. PowerPoint contains tools for accomplishing all the following tasks except
   a. hiding slides.
   b. adding slide timings.
   c. narrating shows.
   d. recording CDs.

2. To copy slides from one presentation into another,
   a. copy the slides from Slide Sorter view and paste them in the new presentation.
   b. you must first create a new presentation and then choose **File | Insert**.
   c. create a custom show and paste the slides into it.
   d. none of the above

3. When you use the **Insert | Slides from Files** command,
   a. the Open dialog box appears.
   b. the Slide Finder dialog box opens.
   c. the Custom Shows dialog box opens.
   d. the Browse for File dialog box opens.

4. When you insert slides from other presentation files,
   a. all slides in all presentations on your hard disk appear in the Slide Finder dialog box.
   b. you can select the file containing the slides you want to use in the Slide Finder dialog box.
   c. all slides in the presentation you select from the Open dialog box are automatically inserted into the active presentation.
   d. all slides in the active presentation are saved as graphics.

5. The two options available for inserting slides from one presentation into another are
   a. All and None.
   b. All and Selected.
   c. Insert All and Insert.
   d. Insert All and Insert Selected.

6. Slides added to custom shows are limited to
   a. a maximum of 10.
   b. infinity.
   c. slides contained in the presentation file.
   d. a maximum of 100.

7. To create a branch to access another custom show,
   a. create a hyperlink.
   b. use the **Create Branch** command in the **Custom Show** dialog box.
   c. embed the second custom show within a slide on the active show.
   d. you must create an action button.
8. Recording narration in a slide show requires all of the following *except*
   a. speakers.
   b. a microphone.
   c. a sound card.
   d. a player.
9. The Meeting Minder dialog box contains tools for recording
   a. speaker notes, meeting minutes, and action items.
   b. narration, speaker notes, and action items.
   c. meeting minutes, action items, and Outlook appointments.
   d. meeting minutes, action items, and narration.
10. Saving presentations as PowerPoint shows offers all the following advantages *except*
    a. showing the presentation without launching PowerPoint.
    b. reducing the amount of disk space required for the file.
    c. automatically launching the show from a computer desktop.
    d. identifying the show file by its file name extension—.pps.

SHORT ANSWER

1. How do you access the Slide Finder dialog box?
2. How do you access the Custom Shows dialog box?
3. How do you access the Record Narration dialog box?
4. How do you select the file containing the slides you want to insert from the Slide Finder dialog box?
5. How do you insert only a few slides into the active presentation?
6. Do you have to save a presentation as a separate file before recording narration?
7. If you record narration in a presentation file, how do you show the presentation live without the narration?
8. After you record narration, what do you have to do to ensure that the narration starts at the right time?
9. What button on the Meeting Minder dialog box do you use to create an appointment in the Outlook Calendar?
10. What happens to action items you record in the Meeting Minder?

FILL IN THE BLANK

1. Information recorded in the ____________ dialog box during a slide show appears in the Notes pane of Normal view.
2. Images that appear at the bottom of the Slide Finder dialog box are called ____________.
3. Links created between custom shows are often referred to as ____________.
4. Self-running presentations are saved as ____________.
5. Special groupings of slides within a presentation are saved as ____________.
6. PowerPoint shows are saved with a ____________ file name extension.
7. A voice recording saved with a presentation is referred to as ____________.
8. To send meeting minutes and action items to a Word document, click the ____________ button.
9. When you use the Meeting Minder to record information during a slide show, ____________ appear(s) on new slides PowerPoint creates at the end of the presentation.
10. A ____________ appears on each slide for which narration is recorded.

DISCUSSION

1. What is the difference between the speaker notes you record during a slide show and meeting minutes?
2. When recording narration for a presentation, how is the narration for slides set?
3. What are the two different procedures you can use to show a custom show and in what ways do they differ?
4. Discuss the difference between creating hyperlinks from one slide in a presentation to other slides in the presentation and setting up custom shows and branching to other custom shows.

GUIDED EXERCISES

1 PINPOINTING SLIDE MANAGEMENT

Presentations you create from scratch are often built to address specific needs or to address a particular audience. As a result, users of PowerPoint often find that they have the same information stored in a number of different presentation files. The tools available in PowerPoint are designed to help you improve your file management techniques. You can use these tools to create a "directory" of slide titles. After you get a good look at the repetition found in the slide titles, you'll have a better idea about which presentations you need to consolidate.

Figure 7-37

Follow these directions to create the title directory:

1. Launch PowerPoint and create a new blank presentation.
2. Display the **Slide Finder** dialog box, click **Browse** and select the following presentations:
   - *Cuisine of the Southern US.ppt*
   - *e-Selections Notebook.ppt*
   - *e-Selections Online Web.ppt*
   - *Travel Specials.ppt*

Although only the last file selected appears in the Files text box, other files are listed on the Files list. Be sure all four files are selected before continuing.

> **Tip** Remember the Shift + click and Ctrl + click techniques for selecting multiple files?

3. Select the first slide, select the **Keep source formatting** option, and click **Insert**. The slide appears as Slide 2 in the new presentation.
4. Click the **Files** down arrow, select the next file in the list, and click **Display**.
5. Repeat Steps 3 and 4 to insert the title slide for each presentation into the new presentation.
6. Click **Close** and delete the blank first slide from the presentation.
7. Save the presentation using the file name *Presentations Directory*.

2 MOVING RESTAURANTS

The *Cuisine of the Southern US.ppt* presentation contains a number of different types of restaurants grouped linearly in the presentation. It makes a great test of the custom shows feature. You can create several custom shows with each show containing slides for a particular type of restaurant. Then you can edit the links on the presentation summary page to access the custom show instead of a slide.

Follow these directions to complete this activity:

1. Launch PowerPoint and open *Cuisine of the Southern US.ppt*.
2. Display the **Custom Shows** dialog box and create the following custom shows containing the slide numbers identified:

Custom Show Name	Slide Numbers
Southwestern	3, 4, 5
Southern Country	6, 7, 8
Cajun	9, 10
Asian	11, 12, 13, 14
Seafood	15, 16, 17

3. Close the **Custom Shows** dialog box and display Slide 2 in **Normal** view.
4. Right-click on **Southwestern**, select **Edit Hyperlink**, select the *Southwestern* custom show, and click **OK**.

Troubleshooting Sometimes PowerPoint identifies the correct hyperlink automatically. However, it's always a good idea to check the links to be certain that they are accurate.

5. Repeat the procedures identified in Step 4 to edit the hyperlinks for each bullet point on Slide 2.
6. Save changes to the presentation, view the slide show to test the hyperlinks, and make necessary adjustments to the custom shows and hyperlinks.
7. Save changes to the presentation and close it.

3 SOUTHERN DRAWL

Have you ever noticed how people from the South tend to speak a bit slower than people from the North? Wouldn't it be fun to record narration for a presentation with a Southern accent? Follow these steps to record the narration for the presentation *Cuisine of the Southern US.ppt*. And don't forget to put your "southern flair" into the narrative.

1. Open the presentation *Cuisine of the Southern US.ppt*.
2. Choose **Slide Show | Record Narration**, test the microphone, and click **OK**.
3. Display each presentation slide and record narration (with a southern flair) about the information contained on the slide. Save the slide timings with the narration.
4. Show the narrated presentation as a Slide Show and make notes about your accent and the content of your narration. Then re-record the narration for slides you identify.
5. Save changes to the presentation and e-mail a copy of the presentation to your instructor for review.

ON YOUR OWN

The difficulty of these case studies varies:
one flag are the least difficult; two flags are more difficult; and three flags are the most difficult.

1 TRAVELING EASY

A bulletin has just arrived that outlines some travel specials. Because you already have a presentation developed that identifies travel tours available, you can add the new bulletin to the presentation. The bulletin is contained in a presentation named *Travel Specials.ppt* and the file into which you need to place it is *Travel Tours.ppt*. After the presentation is complete, save changes to the presentation and print a copy of the presentation as handouts with six slides per page.

2 SHOWING OFF THE TRAVEL TOURS

PowerPoint shows offer a great venue for distributing information about your travel opportunities—whether you send them by e-mail, display them during a travel show, or deliver the presentation live. Open your latest copy of *Travel Tours.ppt* and save the presentation as a PowerPoint Show. Then e-mail the presentation to your instructor.

3 CUTTING THE FAT

Editing presentations is an important part of presentation development. Sometimes, however, when time is running short, presentations are "finalized" before they've been fine-tuned. Show the *Cuisine of the Southern US.ppt* and review all slides in the show. As you view the show, record notes and action items that identify corrections, changes, and improvements that, in your opinion, need to be made to the presentation. Schedule time in Outlook to make the edits and mark the due dates of all action items and edits to your next class period.

4 SUBDIVIDING A PRESENTATION

Early in your PowerPoint 2002 training, you learned how to group slides related to a certain topic together in a presentation. In this project, you learned how to create custom shows that provide another way to group related slides. Use the custom show feature to group slides related to different sections of the *e-Selections Notebook.ppt* presentation and create branches that enable you to access all other custom shows from every custom show. Save changes to the presentation and send the presentation to your instructor.

5 WEB WORDS

As you've already discovered, the World Wide Web can be a great source of graphics, photos, and other information related to many different topics. Outline a presentation about a topic related to your major field of study. Then search the Web for images—photos and other graphics—related to the presentation that follows the flow of your outline. Download at least ten graphics and references containing the names of photographers and other artists whose work you download. Create a presentation containing only graphic picture slides (properly referenced, of course), practice the presentation, and then record your presentation delivery as narration. Save the file as a PowerPoint show using the file name *Your Name Your Field of Study*. E-mail the show to your instructor.

6 SELLING YOURSELF LIVE

You may have already created a résumé presentation. If not, then here's your chance to create and dress up your résumé presentation using features explored in this project. Create or open your résumé presentation and save it using the file name *Interview*. Edit the new copy of your presentation so that it contains each of the following elements:

- A custom template
- Text and object animation
- At least three appropriate graphics or photos
- The date and page number on each slide
- A chart or diagram
- Three custom shows organized so that all slides fit into at least one custom show
- Links in all custom shows that branch to all other custom shows

After you've edited and saved the presentation, practice delivering the presentation and add speaker notes as you practice the slide show. Finally, add narration to your presentation and save the narrated copy as a separate file named *Narrated Interview*. Print a copy of the *Interview.ppt* presentation as notes pages and e-mail the narrated file to your instructor.

Photospread credits pages 7-2 & 7-3

©Tony Stone: ©Michael Rosenfeld; ©Masterfile: ©Bill Frymire-3 Dimensional Graphics, ©Jim Craigmyle; ©Pearson Education; ©Lorraine Castellano

FROM THE FILES

You Will Need

- ✔ e-Selections Division Organization Chart.wmf
- ✔ e-Selections Inventory.ppt
- ✔ e-Selections Overstock Inventory.mdb
- ✔ e-Selections Overstock.doc & .xls
- ✔ e-Selections Web Online.ppt
- ✔ Etch-a-Sketch.doc & .pot
- ✔ Executive Overview.doc
- ✔ Facts.doc & Myths.ppt
- ✔ New Year's Eve Travel Specials.doc
- ✔ Online Sale Items.doc
- ✔ Selections Managers.mdb
- ✔ Top Ten Sellers.xls
- ✔ Travel Specials.ppt

PROJECT 8

Sharing Information

PowerPoint 2002 is part of the Microsoft Office XP suite that includes a number of compatible programs. One of the advantages of using applications that are part of an Office suite is that you can share data among the applications and eliminate the need to re-enter data that already exists in another application file. In this project, you learn how to integrate data among the four major products included in the Office suite—Word, Excel, Access, and PowerPoint. You'll also learn how to share outlines between Word and PowerPoint to create new files and how to create links between files using graphics.

e-selections Running Case

Now that you are well versed in PowerPoint, you've been reassigned to the e-Selections finance department to work on a special project. As you address the requirements of the project, you'll learn some fascinating advanced features associated with all four Office applications.

OBJECTIVES

After completing this project, you will be able to:

- *Identify differences between linking and embedding*
- *Embed a Word table on a PowerPoint slide*
- *Link data from Excel to a PowerPoint slide*
- *Create a Word document from a PowerPoint outline*
- *Save a PowerPoint slide as a graphic*
- *Insert slides from a Word outline*
- *Add an organization chart graphic to a PowerPoint presentation*
- *Change organization chart graphic colors*
- *Create a hyperlink between PowerPoint and Access*

Survivor?

Surviving the jungle out there takes careful planning. The new reality television shows that became so popular at the turn of the century illustrate this. While many viewers didn't plan to, they became *Survivor* junkies! Perhaps one of the draws to these shows is what viewers learned about themselves, human nature, the craftiness of others, and, of course, audiences.

Jim Endicott, Owner/Manager of Distinction, came up with some real lessons learned by watching some of the reality television shows that were broadcast during that time.

Americans have a real hunger for what's "real"

While the series was artificial, Americans tuned in by the millions because there was an element of unpredictable human drama.

- Would Sue's scheming finally do her in?
- Would Richard's planning ever pay off?
- Would Kelly get the boot if she didn't keep winning immunity?

Endicott points out that there are two basic approaches frequently seen with presentations:

- Presenters create very canned content consisting of predictable presentation elements delivered in a predictable fashion by a single presenter.
- Presenters add a touch of realism to presentation content by stretching themselves a bit.

Be a little unpredictable, if you dare

During the course of a presentation, introduce graphical elements that are a little nonstandard. Perhaps a couple screen captures of a Web site. If you have some good quality video, introduce 30-40 seconds of well-chosen digital video. Digitize a voice-over from an industry expert, embed the sound with the person's photo, and animate in a text-quote highlight.

Include "real" interaction with your audience

Take a detour from your prepared delivery and enlist your audience, at select times, as copresenters by

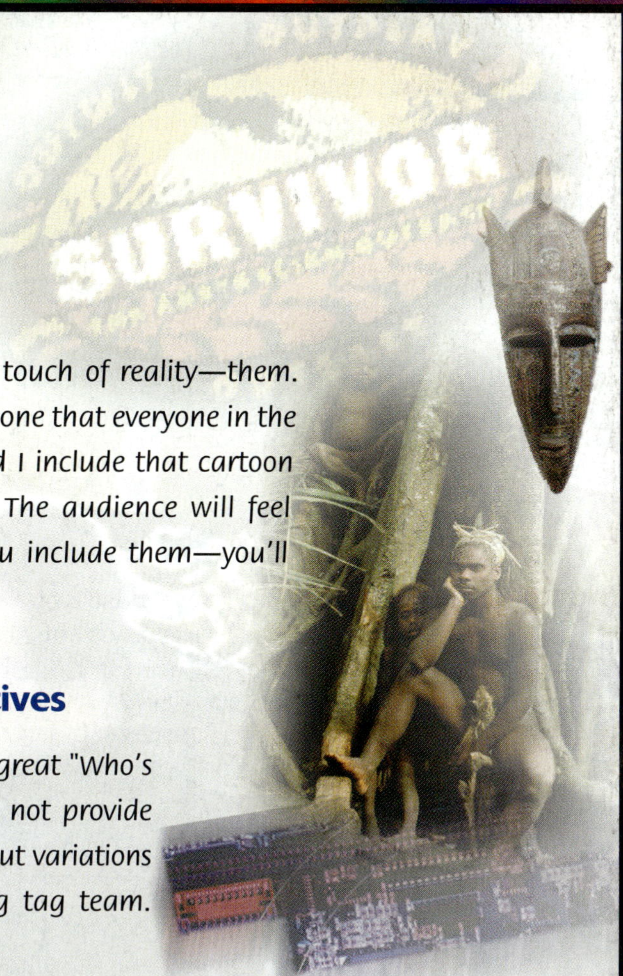

posing a question or soliciting feedback. You've just included a touch of reality—them. Include a cartoon or screen saver of an unusual character or someone that everyone in the audience can relate to. Then pose the question, "Now why would I include that cartoon in my presentation?" Audience feedback is real. Bottom line: The audience will feel like your presentation is free to explore and more real when you include them—you'll 'survivor' them.

Copresenting introduces several unique perspectives

Think of the memorable copresenters Abbott and Costello and their great "Who's on First" routine immediately comes to mind. Copresenting may not provide standalone presenters with the ego gratification they are seeking, but variations in the personalities and delivery styles can create a compelling tag team. Imagine if Survivor Island only had one person for thirteen weeks!

Be real with your audiences

After the first *Survivor* series ran, a post-*Survivor* interview revealed that the American viewing audience had actually wanted Rudy to win the million dollars and the title. That's right, old, cantankerous, feisty, and painfully blunt Rudy. Fifty-million people did not necessarily share his views on life and lifestyles, but they appreciated his blunt honesty in a world that's calculated, canned, and contrived, and he became the hometown boy. People (and audiences) appreciate honesty and candor. They appreciate responses that are not always crafted, massaged, and read.

Reality is pretty compelling stuff. The most reality many presentation audiences get is when a presenter's laptop locks up and they are treated to a few minutes of spontaneous human drama. It's clear that there's a hunger for real human interaction. Stale, artificial experiences just don't cut it. Maybe it's time to take a new look at the presentations you've been delivering.

PROJECT 8

Sharing Information

The Setup

Because you're using multiple applications in this project, you need to review your setup to ensure that your screen will match the figures pictured in this project. Make sure the settings shown in Table 8-1 are active.

Table 8-1

Application Settings	Feature Setting
Office Assistant	Hide the **Office Assistant.**
View	Word: Display **Print Layout** view. Excel: Ensure that both the formula bar and the status bar are displayed. PowerPoint: Display **Normal** view.
Toolbars	Word, Excel, and PowerPoint: Ensure that both the Standard and Formatting toolbars are active and that the toolbars are displayed on two rows. If you don't see both of them, choose **View | Toolbars,** and then select them. Close all other active toolbars.
Zoom	Word: Set the zoom to **Page Width**. Excel: Set the zoom to **100%**. PowerPoint: Set the zoom to **33%**.
Ruler	Word: Display the **Ruler**. PowerPoint: Display the **Ruler**.
Task Panes	Close the task panes in all applications as you launch them.

The Challenge

Synthia Haskem, e-Orders manager, and Socia Newburgh, e-Administration manager in charge of maintaining the online inventory database, have identified a use for your special talents. First, they want you to complete an inventory presentation by adding the slides shown in Figure 8-1 to the presentation. After the presentation is complete, they want you to create a Word document using the presentation outline, and add an organization chart that was created for another presentation to the new presentation. Finally,

Ms. Newburgh wants to be able to launch her Access overstock inventory database while she is showing the presentation. Figure 8-1 identifies some of the files you will create as you complete these tasks.

Figure 8-1

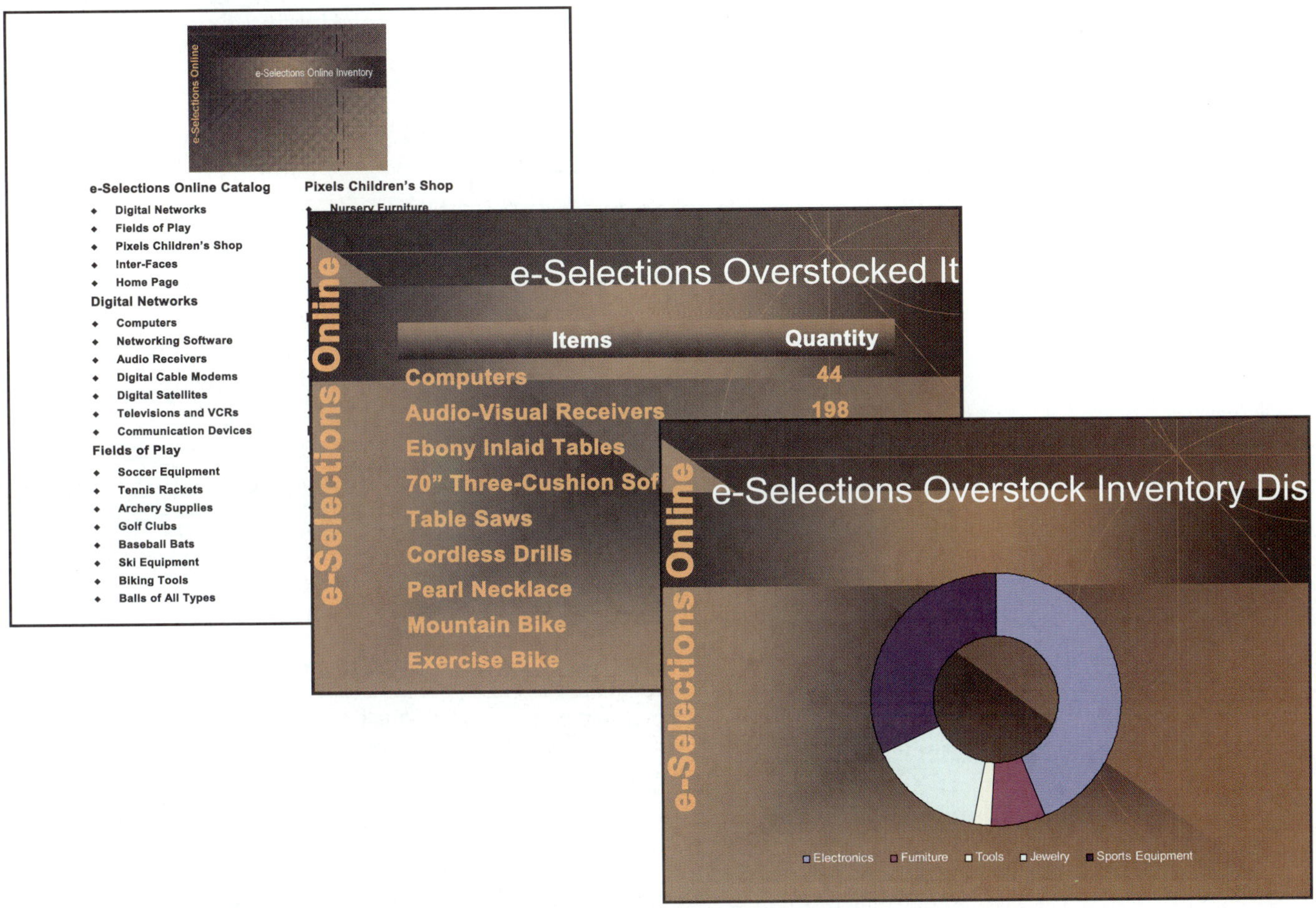

The Solution

When information, such as the table on the first slide in Figure 8-1 already exists in another file, you can copy it and paste it into PowerPoint as an embedded object. When the data contained in the chart shown on the second slide in Figure 8-1 is added to a presentation, it is often helpful to create a link between the files from which you take the data and the PowerPoint presentation. Creating a link between the two files enables you to update the chart each time you show the presentation, if necessary. Some of the information in slides to be added to the presentation already exists in a Word document. You can insert the new slides using the Word document and avoid retyping the info. After the presentation is complete, you can create the Word document shown in Figure 8-1 directly from the presentation outline. By saving Slide 1 as a graphic, you can insert a picture of the slide in the Word document. Because the data required for the new presentation is based on information contained in a Word file, you can use that file to create the new presentation and add the organization chart as a graphic. Last, you can link the slide containing the Online Products List to the Access database that contains the full inventory so that Ms. Newburgh can access the inventory to check product availability if she needs to while showing the presentation. Before you begin, however, you need to know some of the terminology used for sharing data.

Identifying Differences between Linking and Embedding

If the data you want to include in a file already exists in another file—even if that file was created in another application—you can open the file in its original application and copy the data to a new file. The procedure you use to copy the data depends on whether you want the information to reflect the most up-to-date information or to remain constant. Table 8-2 identifies the terms associated with sharing information among Office XP applications.

Table 8-2 Linking and Embedding Terminology

Term	Description
Source file	The file containing the information you want to use in a new file.
Source application	The application used to create the source file.
Target file	The file receiving information that is currently stored in the source file.
Target application	The application used to create the target file.
Embedded objects	Data, graphics, or other objects placed in target files and saved with the file. Embedded objects remain constant when they are added to files, even if the original (source) file changes. Files with embedded objects are often much larger than files containing linked objects.
Linked objects	Data, graphics, charts, or other objects placed in target files with a reference and attachment to the source file. When you create a link between the source file and the target file, the target file recognizes that there are linked files and each time you open the target file, the target application asks you whether you want to update the links. You can choose to update the target file or keep the data the way it appears.

You've already embedded items in the files you've created. When you added graphics, WordArt, and other items to your files, they were embedded and saved with the file. You'll use both embedding and linking to create the files in this project. Here are some basic considerations for choosing whether to link or embed objects in your new file:

- Are you going to use the document with different data or updated information at a later date? If so, consider linking the data to the document file you plan to reuse.
- How is your memory? Your computer memory, of course. If it is limited, you might want to link the files. Embedding graphics and data files increases the size of the file, which can sorely tax limited resources.

- Are you planning to copy the file to a floppy disk or use the target file away from the computer that contains the source files? If so, consider embedding so that you are sure to have everything you need when you reach your destination. Unless you're very careful, linked files are often left behind.

Embedding a Word Table in a PowerPoint Slide

Although the table feature in PowerPoint is very similar to the table feature in Word, the data you want to add to the slide in the *e-Selections Inventory* presentation has already been added to a report created in Word. Copying the information from Word into PowerPoint employs the same basic techniques you used to copy data between Word and Excel and between other Windows-based applications.

CHECK POINT

You could also drag data between Word and PowerPoint to embed the table. To drag data between applications, you need to arrange the application windows so that you can see the data in one application and the position where you want to place it in the other window. An easy way to arrange the windows is to tile them. Maximize the two windows you want to use and minimize all other application windows. Next, right-click a blank area of the taskbar and select **Tile Windows Vertically**. Then display the portion of each application window you need to access, select the data to copy in the source file, press and hold the Ctrl key and drag the data to the position in the target file. If you forget the Ctrl key, you'll move the data—you can use Undo to reverse the action. Of course, if all else fails, you can create the table from scratch directly in PowerPoint.

Task 1:

To Copy Data from Word to PowerPoint

1. Launch PowerPoint, close the task pane, and open *e-Selections Inventory.ppt* in **Normal** view.

2. Create a new **Title Only** slide at the end of the presentation and type the title shown in Figure 8-2 in the title placeholder.

Troubleshooting
If you place the slide in the wrong location, display Slide Sorter view and reposition it or drag the thumbnail slide image in the Slide Design pane or Normal view to the correct location.

3. Launch Word, close the task pane, and open *e-Selections Overstock.doc* in **Print Layout** view.

4. Click the Select Table icon to select the complete table and click the Copy button.

Figure 8-2

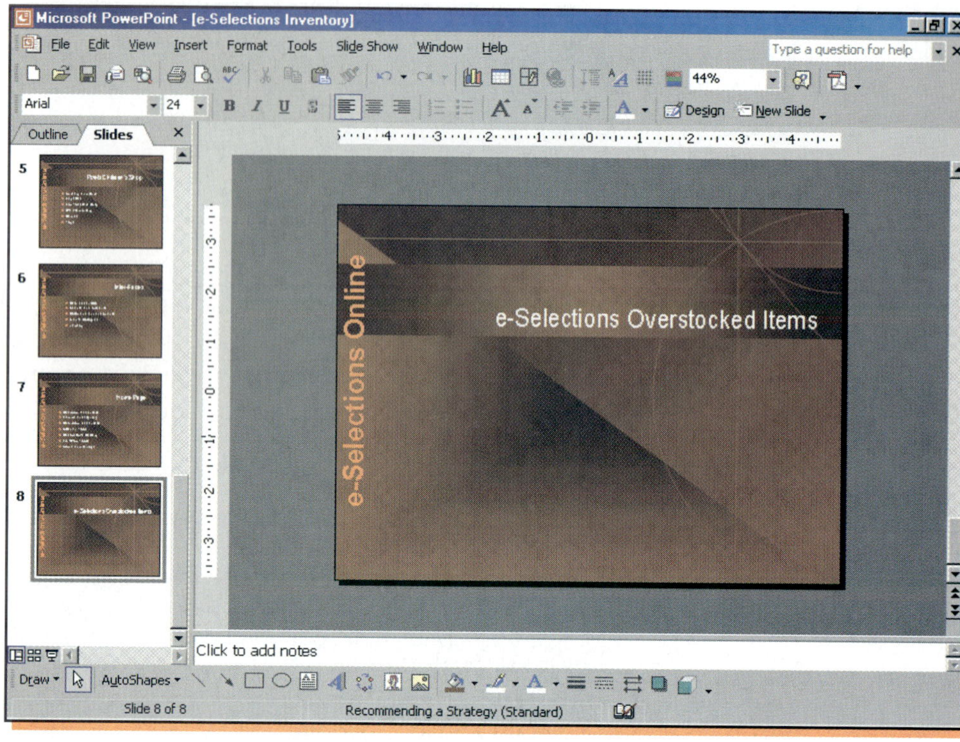

Figure 8-3

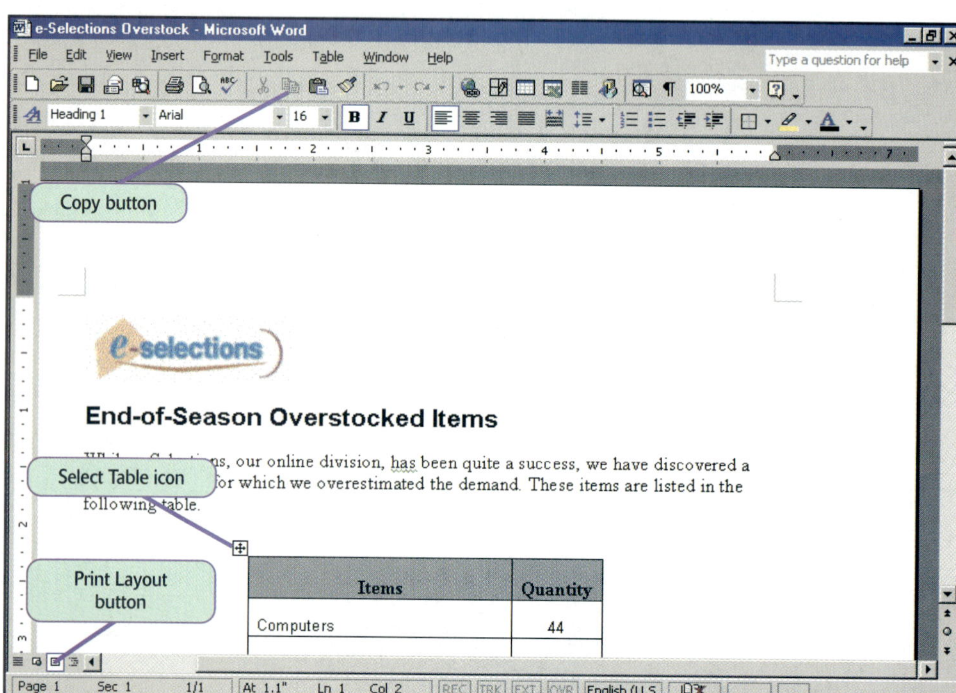

5 Switch to PowerPoint and click the Paste button to paste the table on the slide.

Tip The Tables and Borders toolbar may open. You can close it or move it out of the way.

Figure 8-4

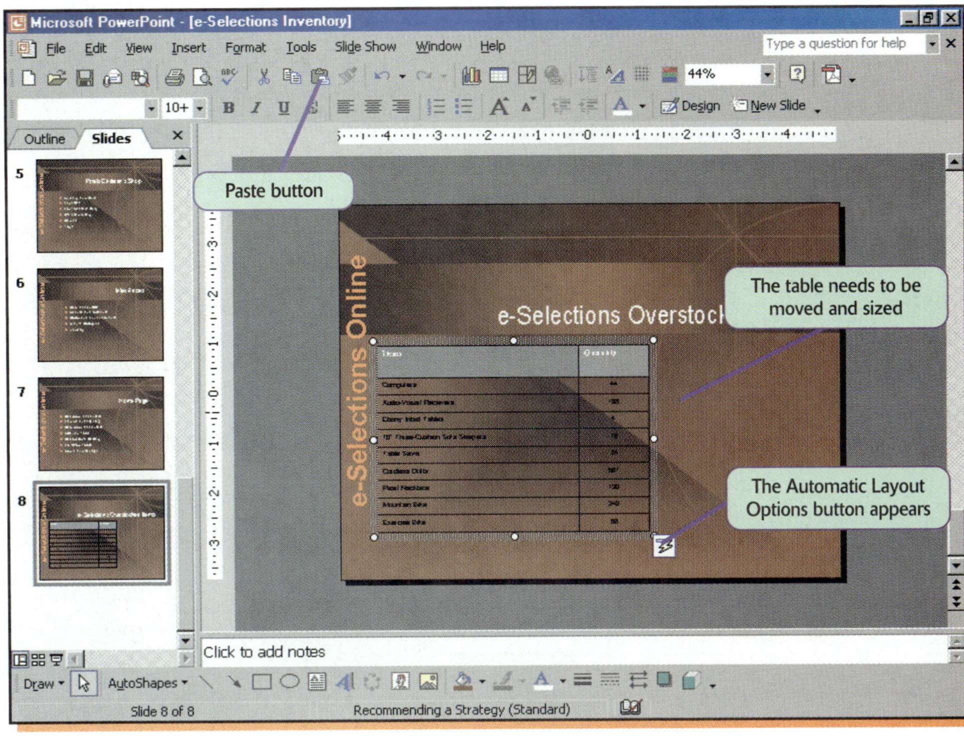

6 Format, align, adjust font size and color, and apply background color to the table so that is appears as shown in Figure 8-5.

Tip Several steps are required to format the table so that it appears as shown in the figure. Size the table on the slide by dragging a corner handle. Then select the title row of the table, center the text, and change the font size and color. Finally, select the remaining table rows and change the font size and font color.

7 Save changes to the presentation.

8 Exit Word and leave PowerPoint open.

Figure 8-5

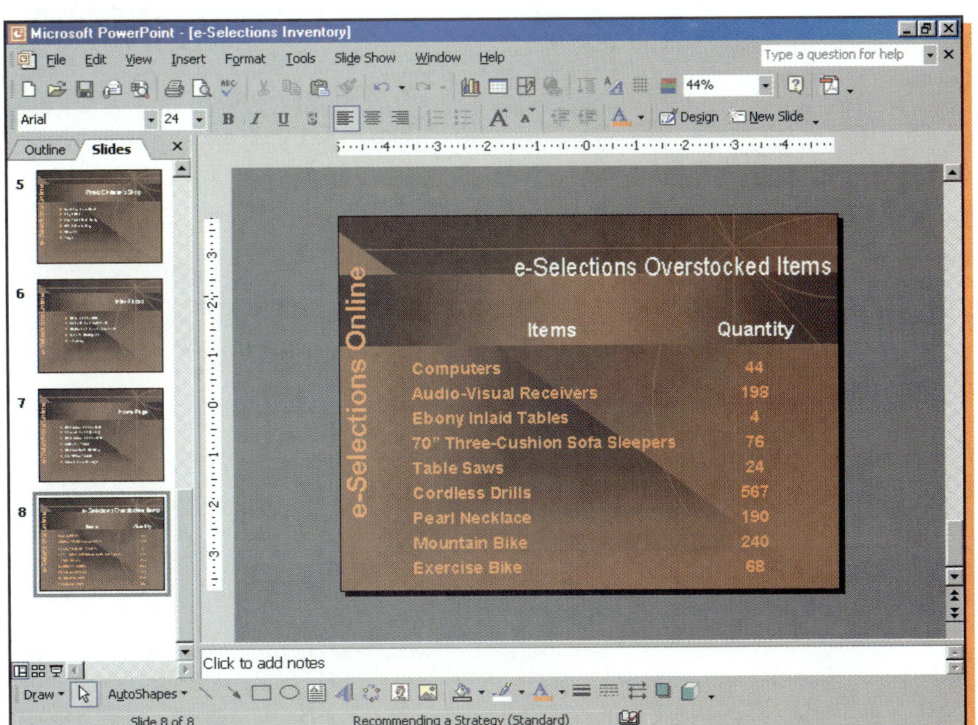

Linking Data from Excel to a PowerPoint Slide

The data for the second new slide you are to create already exists in an Excel worksheet. Thus, you can copy the data from the Excel workbook and place it on the PowerPoint slide. Linking the data ensures that PowerPoint will always display the most recent information, in the event that the Excel source file is changed.

Task 2:
To Link Data from Excel to a PowerPoint Slide

1. Display Slide 8 in *e-Selections Inventory.ppt*, if necessary, create another new **Title Only** slide, and type the title shown in Figure 8-6 in the title placeholder.

Figure 8-6

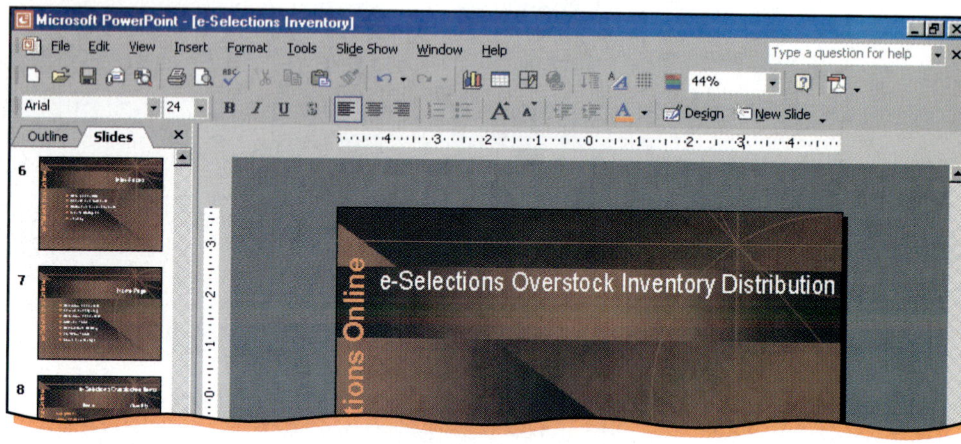

2. Launch Excel, open *e-Selections Overstock.xls*, and display the *Overstocked Inventory Value* worksheet.

3. Click the white area of the chart to select the chart and click the Copy button.

Figure 8-7

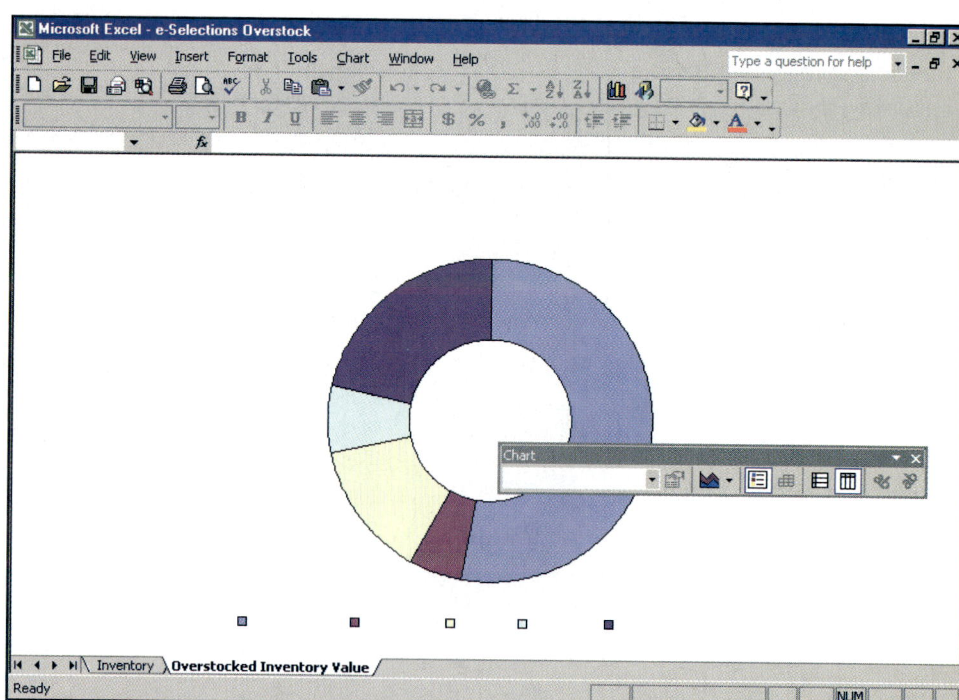

Tip By placing the chart on the clipboard, you can create a link between the chart and the target file when you paste the chart on the slide.

4 Switch to PowerPoint and choose **Edit | Paste Special** to open the Paste Special dialog box.

Figure 8-8

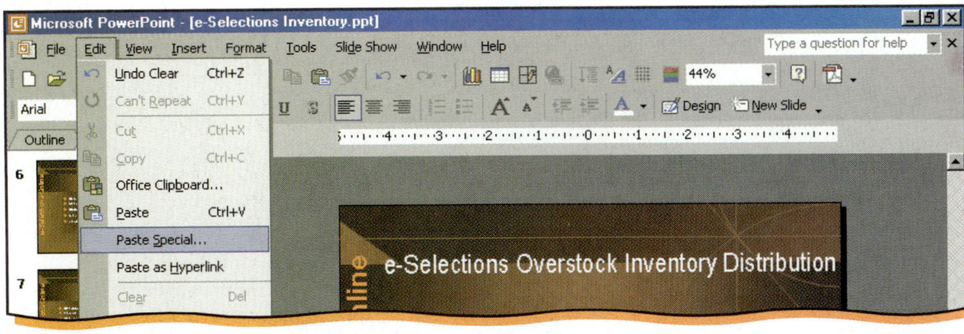

CHECK POINT

Do you recall the difference between linking and embedding?

Embedded files become part of the file in which you place them and remain static. To change or update the file, you must remove the current file and replace it with an updated file.

Linking, on the other hand, maintains a tie to the original file so that you can update the file object each time you open the file containing the link. As a result, the data contained in the linked object can reflect up-to-the minute data from the original file.

5 Choose **Paste link**, ensure that **Microsoft Excel Chart Object** is selected, and click **OK**.

Figure 8-9

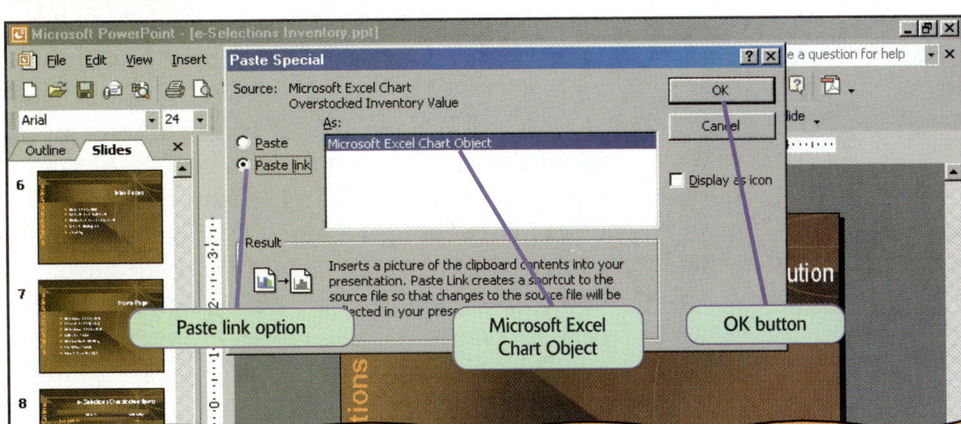

Troubleshooting

The object types listed in the As box vary, depending on the object contained on the clipboard and the programs you have installed on your computer. As a result, you may see additional objects listed.

6 Adjust the size and position of the chart and title placeholder on the slide as shown in Figure 8-10.

7 Save changes to the presentation and print a copy of the two new slides.

8 Close the workbook and exit Excel but leave PowerPoint open.

Troubleshooting
Because the Excel file contains values that must recalculate each time you open the file, a message box may open, asking if you want to save changes to the file. Click **Yes**.

Figure 8-10

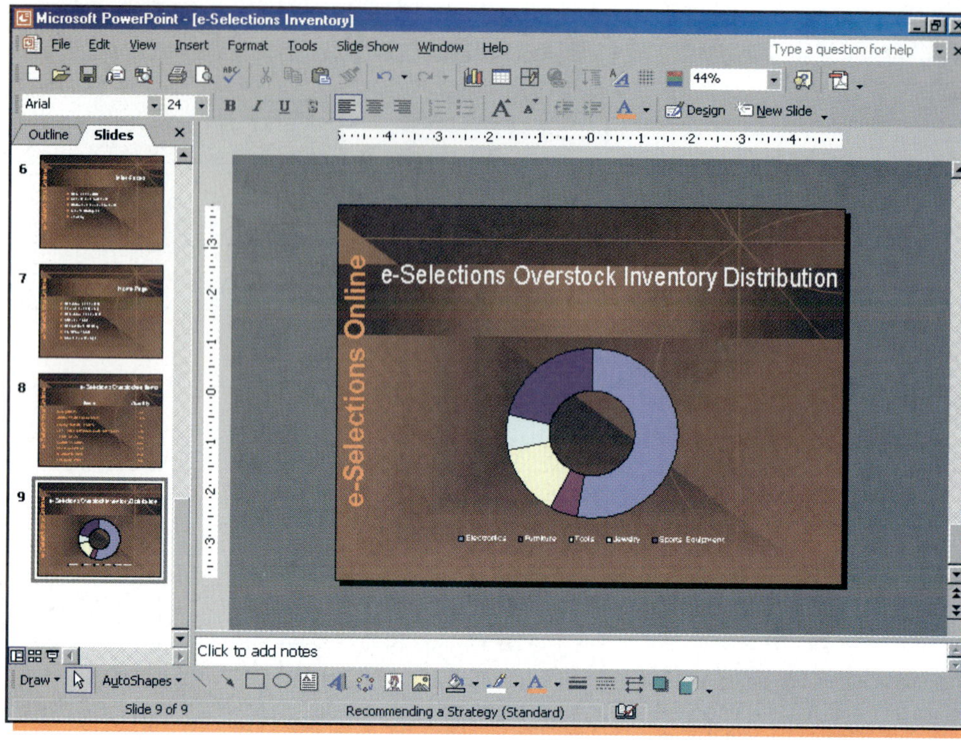

Creating a Word Document from a PowerPoint Presentation Outline

Outlines from PowerPoint presentations are effective guides for developing Word reports that parallel the presentation. Although you can print handouts and outlines with slide images directly from PowerPoint, you can send the outline to Word and get a more document-like outline that you can then embellish with additional report text, if needed. PowerPoint contains tools that enable you to send the presentation outline directly to Word with just the touch of a button! What's more, you can even choose a format for the Word document. Because the document Ms. Newburgh wants contains only the information contained in the presentation as it stands now, you can create the document before inserting the additional slides.

Task 3:

To Create a Word Document from a PowerPoint Presentation Outline

1 Display Slide 1 of *e-Selections Inventory.ppt*, if necessary, and click the **Outline** tab on the Outline/Slide pane.

2 Choose **File | Send To | Microsoft Word.**

Tip Sending a presentation outline to Word enables you to develop a written report that parallels the presentation.

Figure 8-11

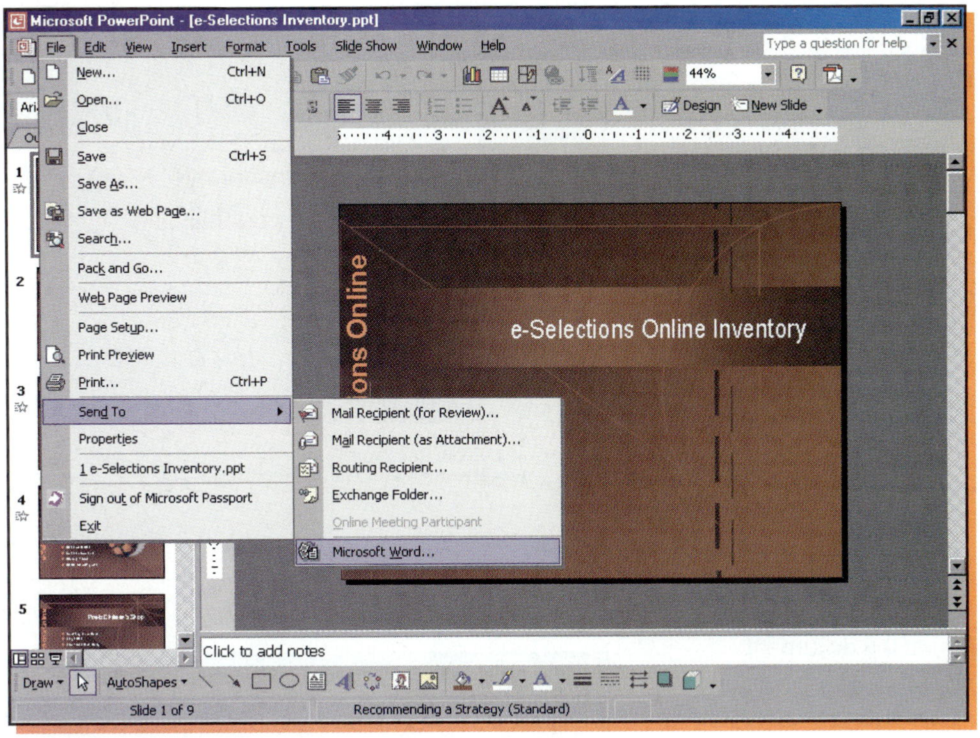

3 Click **Outline only** and then click **OK**. The outline appears in a new Word document.

Tip As you review the options available in this dialog box, you may identify formats that you can use. For example, you can use options in this dialog box to print audience handouts that contain slides as well as lines for notetaking.

Figure 8-12

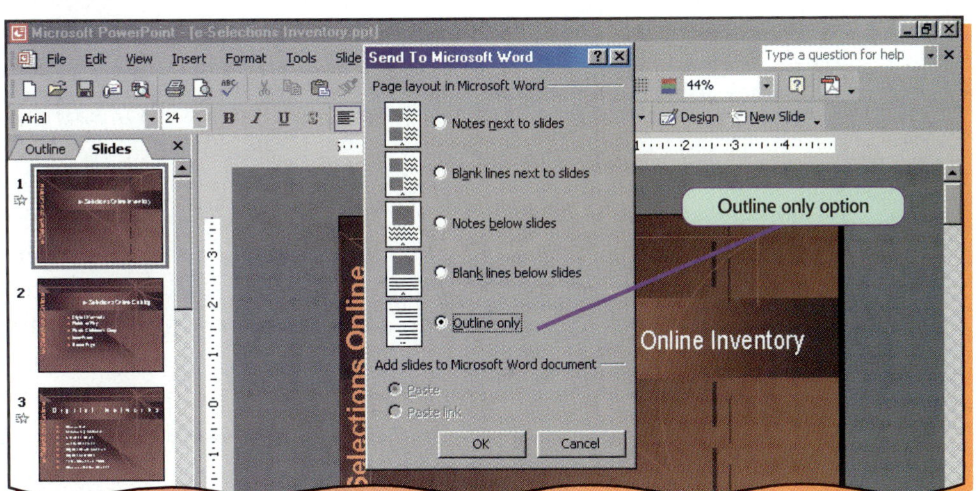

4 Select the paragraph containing the text **Networking Software**, click the **Style** box on the Formatting toolbar, type your first name and press Enter. You've just created a new style!

5 Apply the style to all bullet points in the document.

Figure 8-13

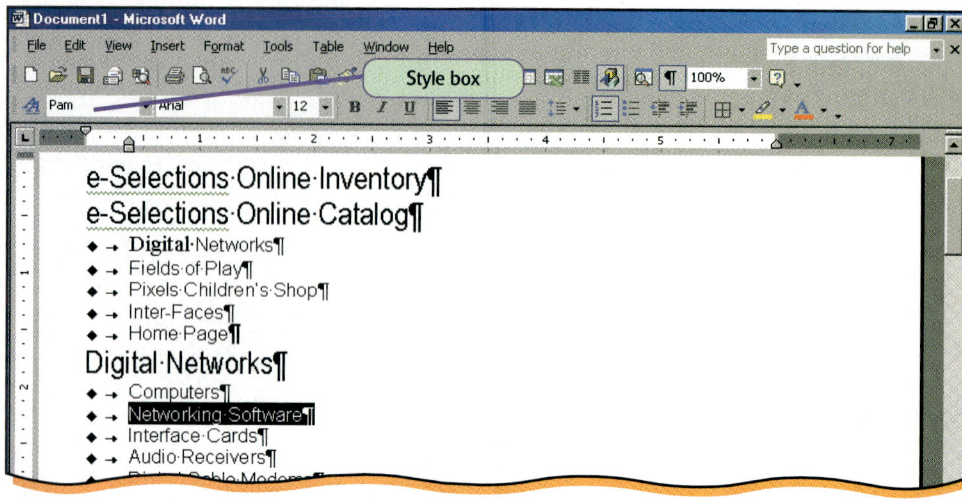

6 Make the following additional changes to format the document:

- Left-align all text
- Delete the last two text lines.
- Delete the first text line.
- Delete *Interface Cards*.
- Insert a continuous section break at the top of the document.
- Format the text below the section break into two columns.

Figure 8-14

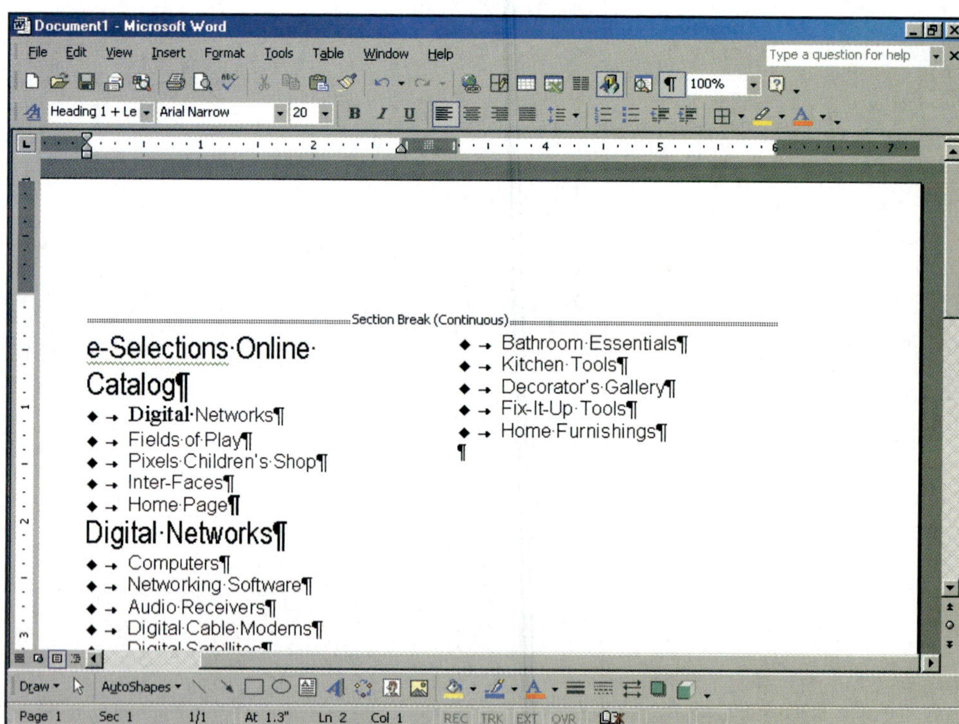

Troubleshooting If the outline slips onto page 2 when you insert the section break, check the style you created to ensure that the **Keep with Next** option is turned off. You can quickly check the format by choosing **Format | Paragraph | Line and Page Breaks**. Then clear the check mark from the **Keep with Next** option if it's checked. Monitor size and zoom settings active on your computer may change the number of text lines that appear in the second column. That's okay—you'll fix it later.

7 Choose **File** | **Page Setup** and click the **Layout** tab.

8 Click the **Vertical alignment** down arrow, select **Center**, and click **OK**.

9 Click the Print Preview button.

Tip Selecting Center from the Vertical alignment list centers text between the top and bottom margins.

Figure 8-15

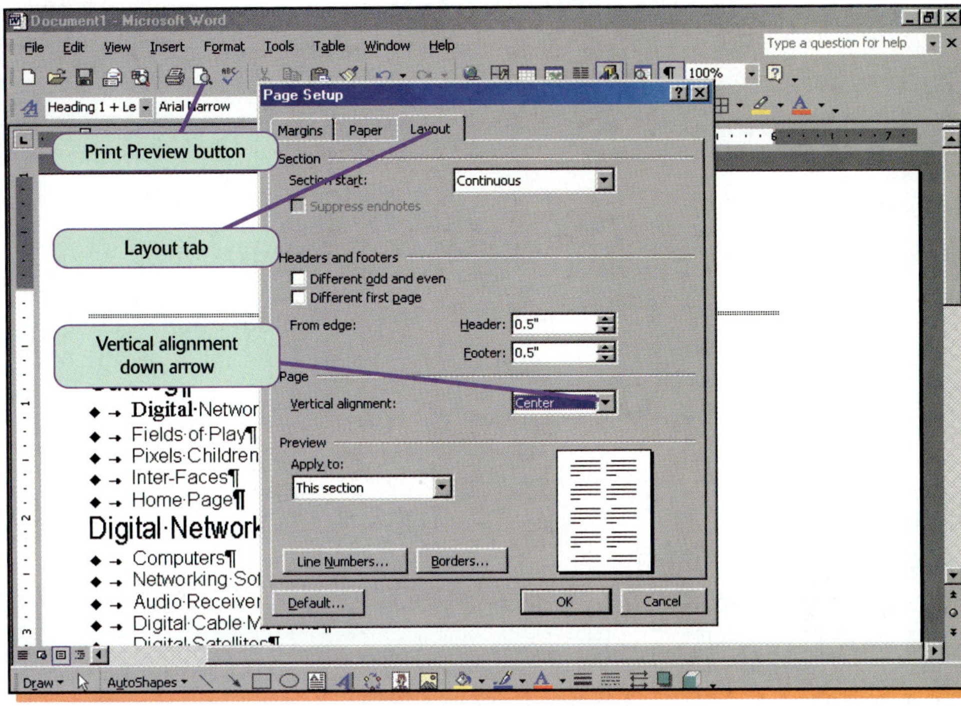

10 Click Close on the Preview toolbar.

Troubleshooting Be sure to click the Close button on the Print Preview toolbar to close the view rather than the document close button.

11 Save the Word document using the file name *e-Selections Online Catalog Outline*.

Figure 8-16

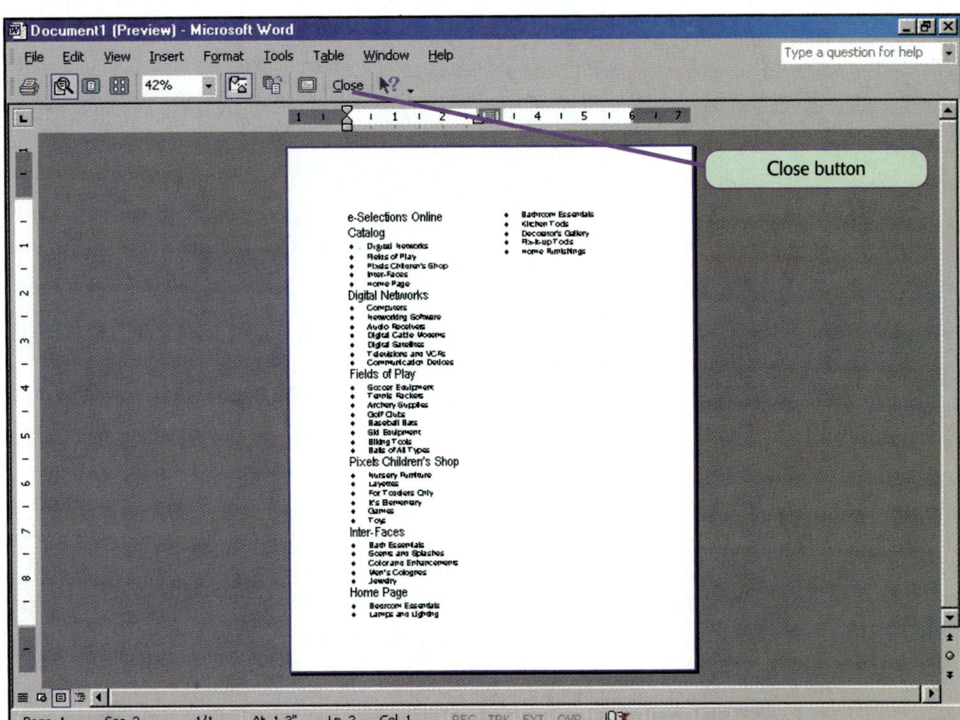

CHECK POINT

Consider different alternatives for sharing data using the techniques addressed in Task 3. Do you suppose that you can also send a Word outline to PowerPoint and create a new presentation? (Check out Guided Exercise 1 in the end-of-project section for the answer.)

Saving a PowerPoint Slide as a Graphic

Another way to share data among Office XP applications is to capture information from one application as a graphic and place it into a file in another application. PowerPoint slides make effective graphics that not only enhance a document, but also relay a message. PowerPoint includes file options that enable you to save your slides in the most popular image formats.

Task 4:

To Save a PowerPoint Slide as a Graphic and Add It to a Word Document

1. Launch Word, if necessary, and open *e-Selections Online Catalog Outline.doc* and display the document in **Print Layout** view.

2. Launch PowerPoint, if necessary, open *e-Selections Inventory.ppt*, and display Slide 1 in **Normal** view.

3. Choose **File | Save As**. The Save As dialog box opens.

4. Open the drive and folder you want to use to store the graphic, and then click the **Save as type** down arrow.

Figure 8-17

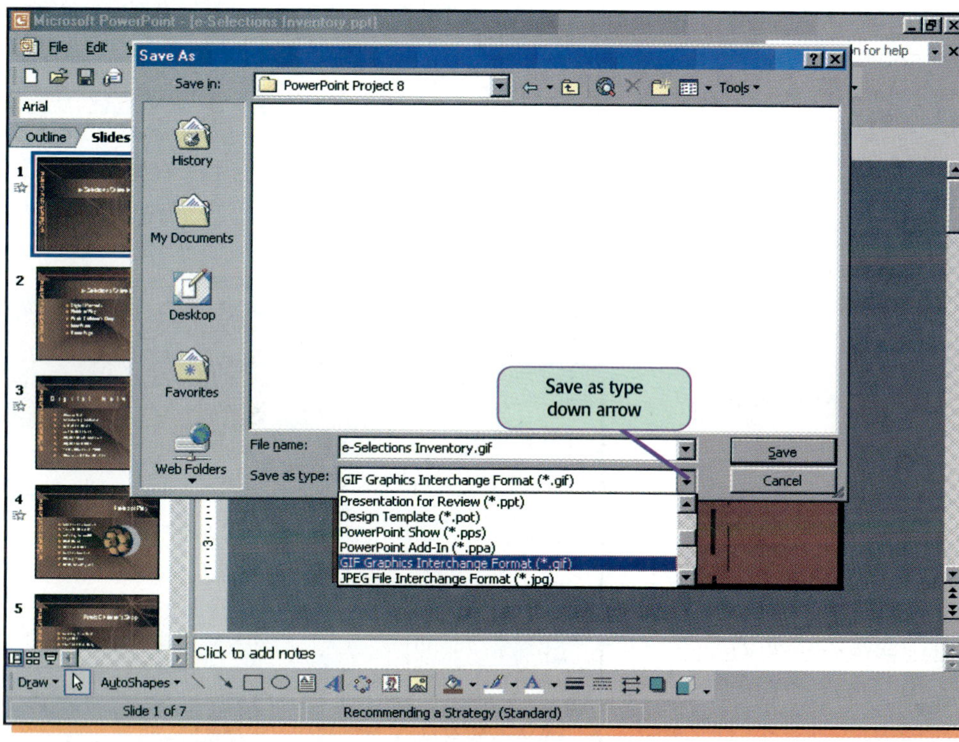

Tip

PowerPoint offers a wide variety of different graphics formats you can use to save slides as pictures. Experiment with several of the formats when you have time to determine which formats work better in your presentations.

5 Select **GIF Graphics Interchange Format** and click **Save**. The Microsoft PowerPoint message windows opens so that you can tell PowerPoint whether you want to save only the current slide or all presentation slides.

6 Click **Current Slide Only** to export only Slide 1, close the presentation, and exit PowerPoint.

WEB TIP

When the graphic files will be added to documents you save on the Web, save the graphics in either .gif (pronounced like "jiff") or .jpg (often called "jay peg") format.

Figure 8-18

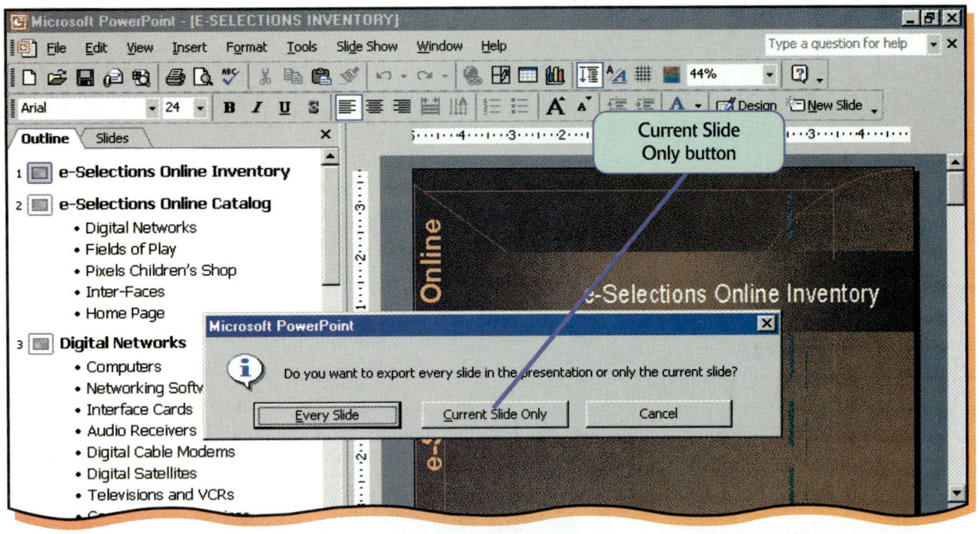

Tip If you save every slide in the presentation as graphics, PowerPoint creates a folder and names the folder the presentation name. Then PowerPoint saves each slide individually in the selected file format, naming each slide sequentially as Slide1, Slide2, and so on.

7 Switch to Word and position the insertion point at the top of the outline before the section break.

8 Choose **Insert | Picture | From File** and insert the *e-Selections Inventory.gif* graphic at the top of the document. Center, size, and position the graphic as shown in Figure 8-19.

Tip Changing the size of the figure controls the number of text lines that appear in each column.

9 Save changes to the document, print a copy of the document, and then exit Word.

Figure 8-19

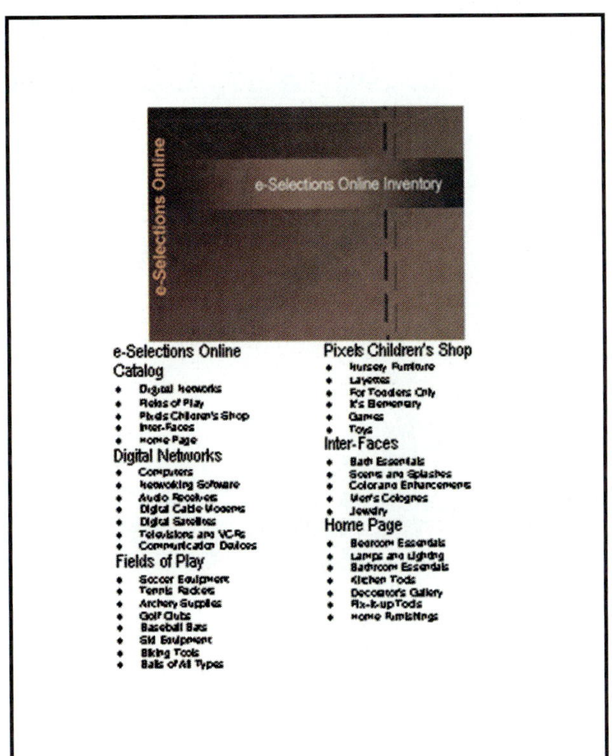

Inserting Slides into a PowerPoint Presentation from a Word Outline

When the information you want to use to create a presentation already exists in a Word file, you can either send the Word document to PowerPoint and create a new presentation or insert slides into an existing presentation using information from the Word file. You can insert a list of items from the different Selections, Inc., department stores that will be listed for sale online. These items are currently listed in a Word document.

Task 5:

To Insert Slides from a Word Outline

1. Open *e-Selections Inventory.ppt*, display the last slide in **Normal** view, and click the Slides tab in the Outline/Slide Design pane.

2. Choose **Insert | Slides from Outline**. The Insert Outline dialog box opens.

3. Open the folder containing your student files, select the *Online Sale Items.doc*, and click **Insert**.

Tip The **Insert | Slides from Outline** command is similar to the **Insert | Slides from File** command.

Figure 8-20

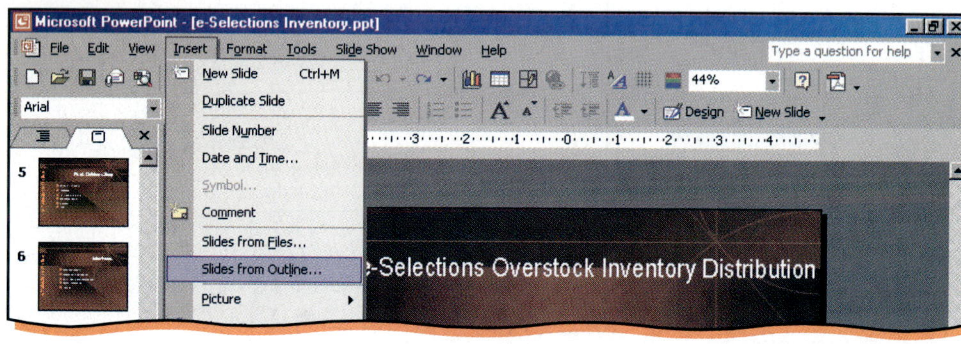

Figure 8-21

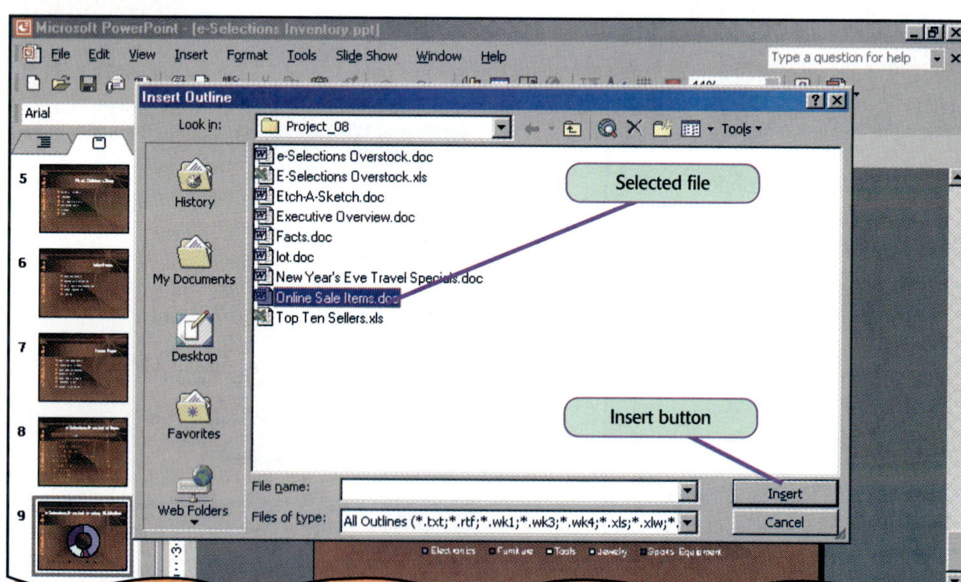

4 Size the bullet placeholder on each new slide and adjust the font size for bullet points to make them easier to read.

5 Save changes to the presentation.

Figure 8-22

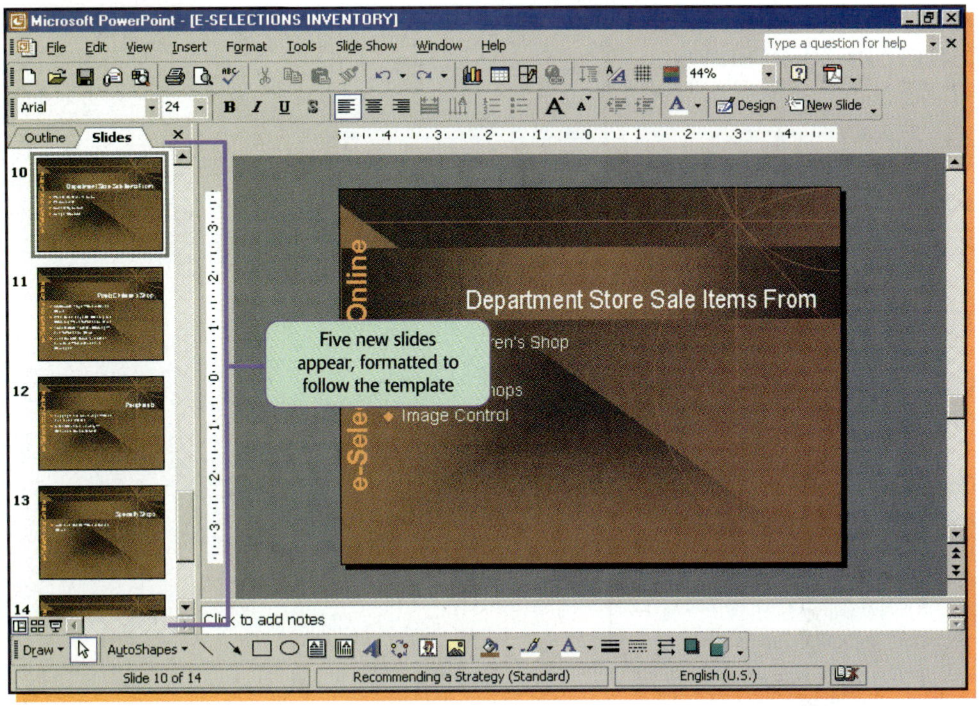

WEB TIP

Implementation of the Digital Archives has satisfied the dream of President Franklin Roosevelt. His dream? Making the records of the past available for the use of men and women of the future. See if you can locate the Franklin D. Roosevelt Library & Digital Archives online and discover some very interesting facts.

Adding an Organization Chart Graphic to a PowerPoint Presentation

Slides are not the only objects that you can save as pictures using PowerPoint. You can save charts, diagrams, and organizational charts as well. You can add an organization chart saved as a graphic to the presentation and size and position the graphic as you would other objects you add to slides. Ms. Newburgh wants the chart to be part of the presentation so that she can reference it if necessary.

Task 6:
To Add an Organization Chart Graphic to a Slide

1. Open *e-Selections Inventory.ppt*, if necessary, and display Slide 14 in **Normal** view.

2. Create a new slide, format the slide using the **Blank** slide layout and close the task pane.

Tip The blank slide appears with items contained on the slide master. As a result, the slide does not appear to be blank but there are no placeholders on the slide.

3. Choose **Insert | Picture | From File**, open your student folder, and double-click *e-Selections Division Organization Chart.wmf*.

4. Size and position the graphic as it appears in Figure 8-24 and save changes to the presentation.

Troubleshooting Be sure to drag a corner handle on the organization chart to prevent text distortion.

Figure 8-23

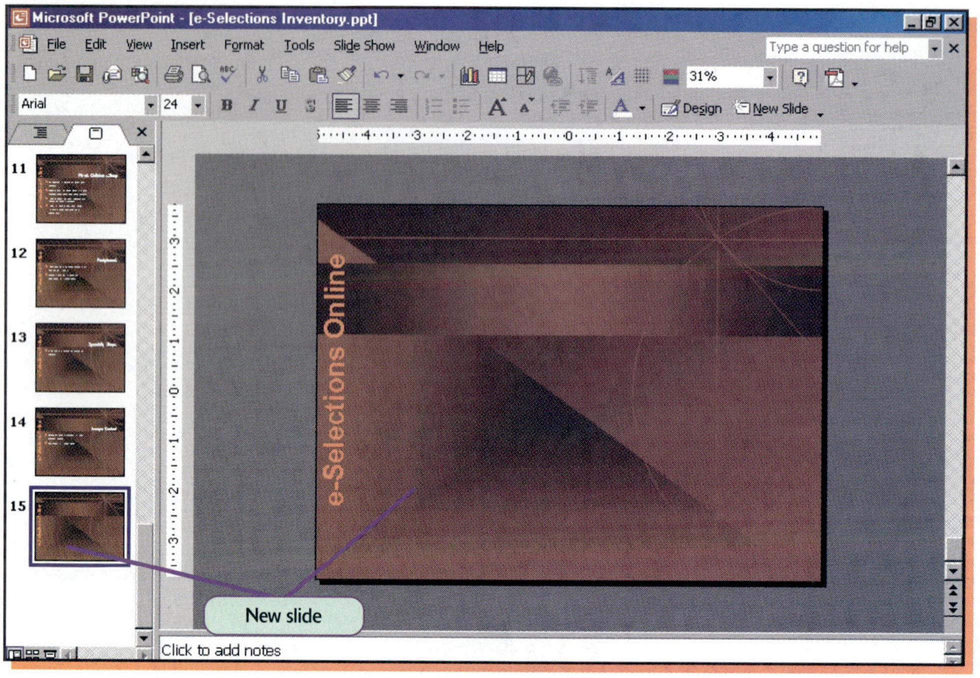

Figure 8-24

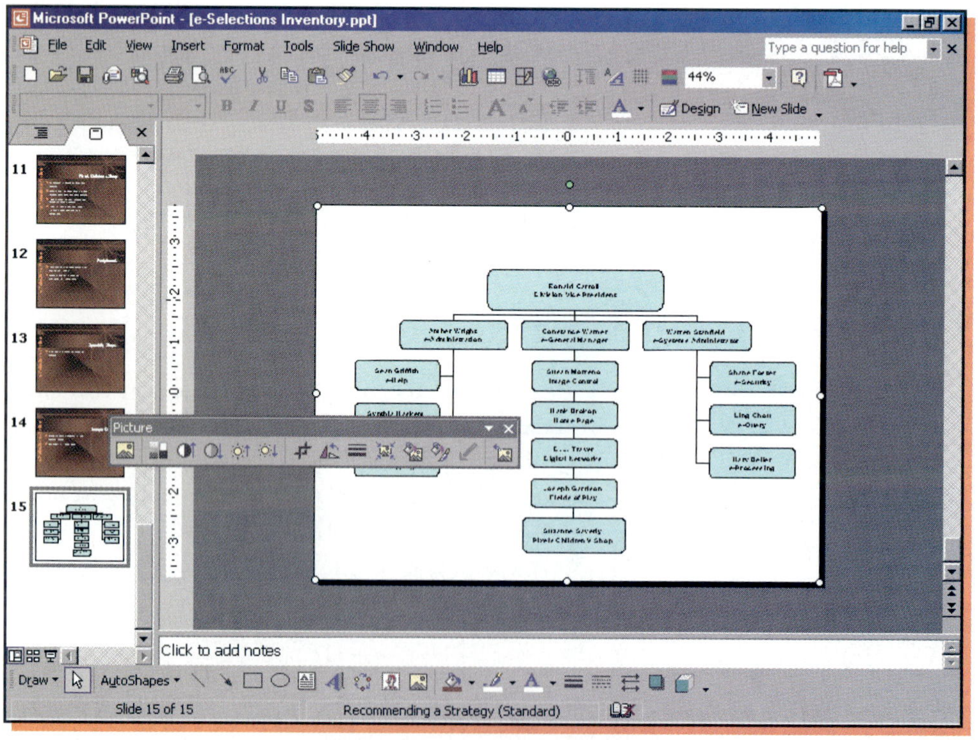

Changing Organization Chart Graphic Colors

To improve the appearance of the organization chart, the colors need to be changed so that the chart blends in with the presentation template. Adding the organization chart as a graphic makes editing the colors possible.

Task 7:

To Recolor the Organization Chart Graphic

1. Display Slide 15 of *e-Selections Inventory.ppt*, double-click the organization chart object, and click **Recolor** to open the Recolor Picture dialog box.

Figure 8-25

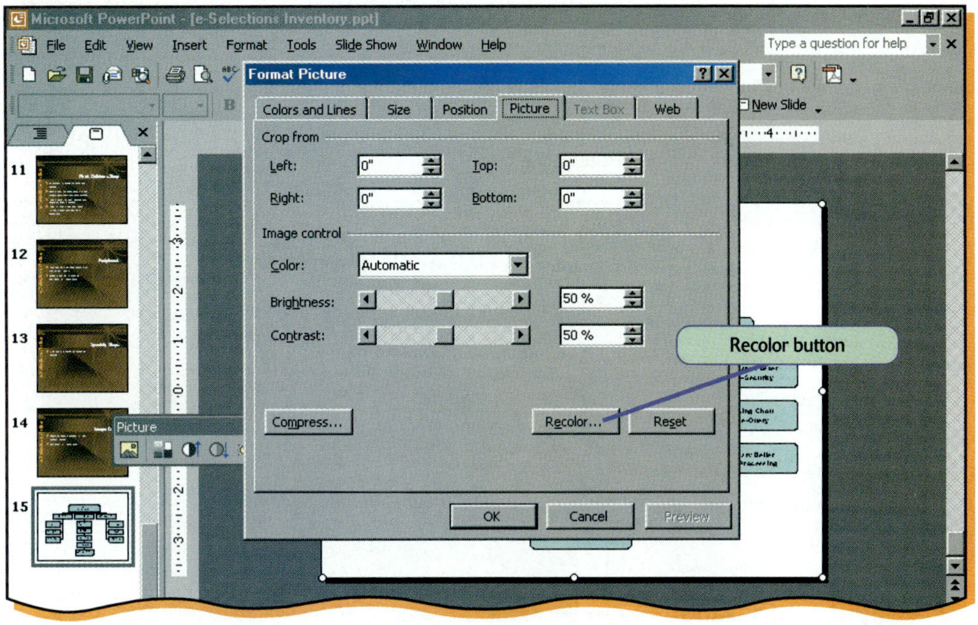

2. Select all options in the Original column and select the options and colors shown in Figure 8-26.

3. Click **OK** twice and save changes to the presentation.

Tip Text color follows the color of the lines, which is the top color in both columns. Check with your instructor to see if it's all right to customize the colors.

Figure 8-26

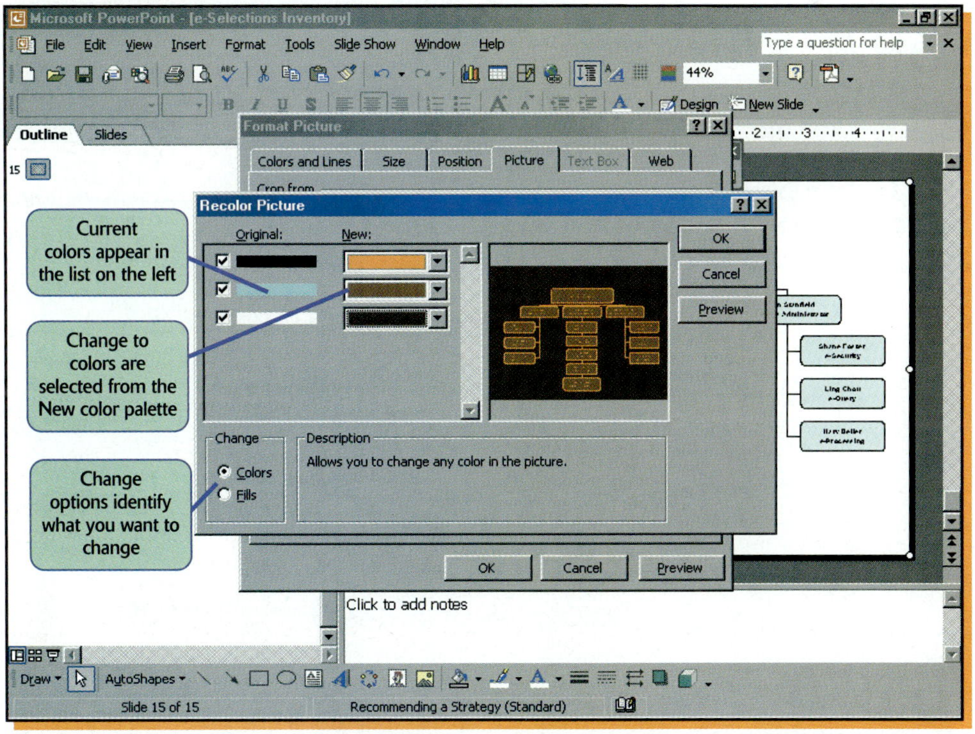

Creating a Hyperlink Between a PowerPoint Presentation and an Access Database

Two of the new slides you added to the presentation contain data from Word and Excel that is based on information from an Access database table. To provide Ms. Newburgh with additional information about the overstocked items, she would like for you to link the data to Access so that she can provide requested information while she is presenting the slide show. You can create a hyperlink from the presentation that automatically launches Access and opens the database table.

Task 8:

To Create a Hyperlink between PowerPoint and Access

1. Launch PowerPoint, open *e-Selections Inventory.ppt*, display Slide 8 in **Normal** view. The slide containing the overstocked items list appears.

2. Display the **Drawing** toolbar, if necessary, choose **AutoShapes | Action Buttons**, and create a blank **Custom** button, positioning it in the lower-right corner of the slide.

3. Click the **Hyperlink to** option and select **Other File** from the **Hyperlink to** drop-down list to open the Hyperlink to Other File dialog box.

Figure 8-27

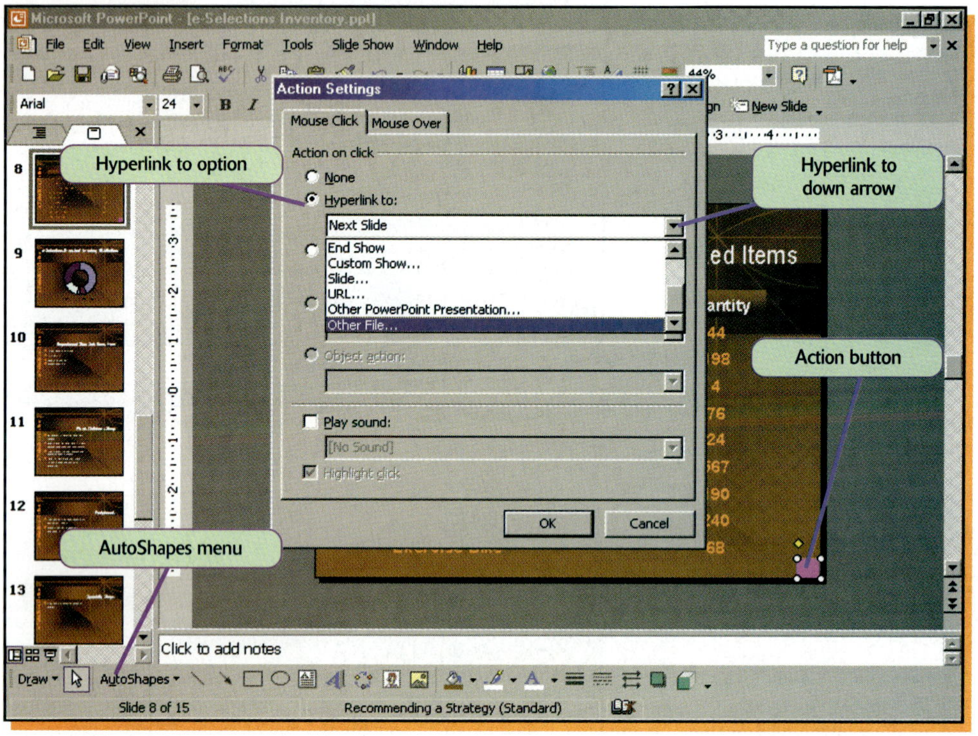

Tip

Notice the variety of different objects you can set the action button to hyperlink to. While many of the items listed hyperlink to different slides in the presentation, you can also set hyperlinks to URLs and other presentations. Hyperlinking to another file sets hyperlinks to most other file types. However, if the application used to create the file you set as the hyperlink, the file may not open.

4 Locate and select the *e-Selections Overstock Inventory.mdb*, and then choose **OK**.

Tip Notice that All Files (*.*) appears in the Files of type text box and many different file types appear in the Hyperlink to Other File dialog box. Because PowerPoint does not know what file you plan to set as the hyperlink, if presents all files in the active folder.

Figure 8-28

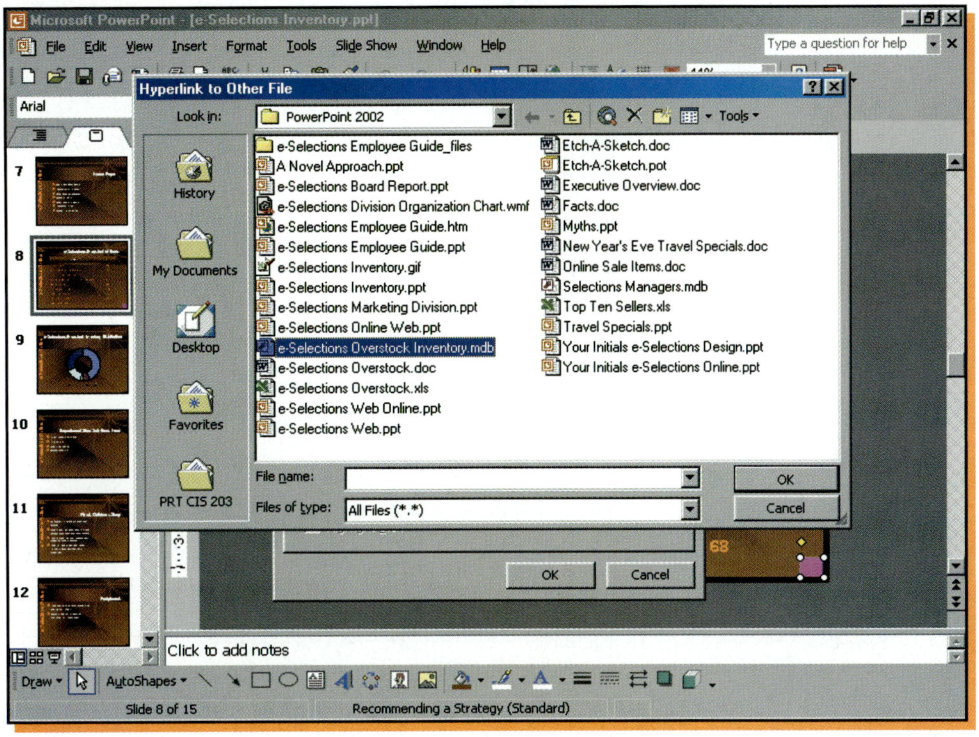

5 Choose **OK** again to close the **Action Settings** dialog box and format the custom animation button to blend into the background of the slide.

6 Save changes to the presentation, and start the slide show with the current slide.

7 Click the custom action button in the lower-right corner of the slide. Access launches and opens the linked database. With the database open, you can open any database object and review the data.

8 Close **Access**, end the slide show, and exit **PowerPoint**.

Figure 8-29

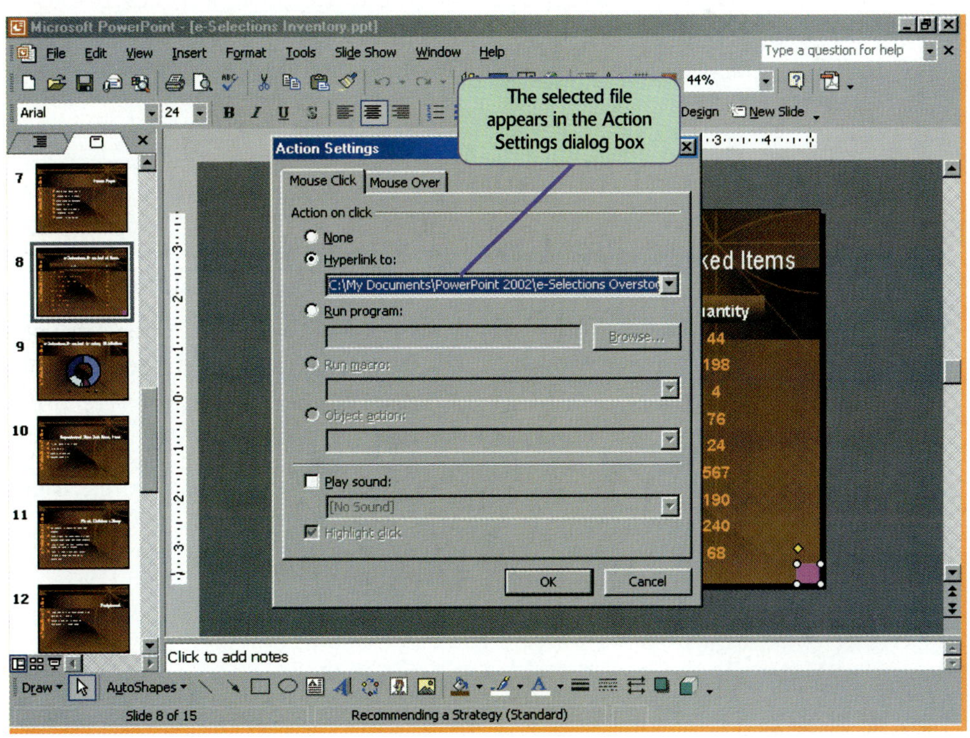

SUMMARY AND EXERCISES

SUMMARY

- You can copy and paste data from Office XP applications to other applications.
- Many of the tools you use to create and format information are available in all Office XP applications. As a result, learning to use the tools in one application means you will know how to apply features in other applications.
- The **File | Send To** command displays a number of different commands you can use to share information among Office XP applications.
- Saving files as graphics enables you to enhance other files by inserting the graphics.
- Hyperlinks enable you to open files in one application while you are working in another.
- Source files are files containing the information you want to use in a new file.
- Target files are files receiving information that is currently stored in another file.
- Embedded objects include data, graphics, or other objects placed in target files and saved with the file.
- Embedded objects remain constant when they are added to files, even if the original (source) file changes.
- Files with embedded objects are often much larger than files containing linked objects.
- Linked objects include data, graphics, charts, or other objects placed in target files with a reference and attachment to the source file.
- When you create a link between the source file and the target file, the target file recognizes that there are linked files and each time you open the target file, the target application asks you whether you want to update the links.
- An easy way to arrange the windows is to tile them.

- You can either send a Word document to PowerPoint to create a new presentation or insert slides into an existing presentation using information from a Word file.
- You can save charts, diagrams, and organizational charts as graphics.
- Colors of graphic objects such as charts and diagrams can be changed to blend in with the presentation template.
- Text of recolored charts and diagrams follows the color of the object lines.

KEY TERMS & SKILLS

KEY TERMS

embedded objects (p. 8-6)
linked objects (p. 8-6)
linking (p. 8-6)
source application (p. 8-6)
source file (p. 8-6)
target application (p. 8-6)
target file (p. 8-6)

SKILLS

Add an organization chart graphic to a PowerPoint presentation (p. 8-19)
Create a hyperlink between a PowerPoint presentation and an Access database (p. 8-22)
Create a Word document from a PowerPoint presentation slide (p. 8-13)
Embed a Word table in a PowerPoint slide (p. 8-7)
Identify differences between linking and embedding (p. 8-6)
Insert slides into a PowerPoint presentation from a Word outline (p. 8-18)
Link data from Excel to a PowerPoint slide (p. 8-10)
Recolor an organization chart graphic (p. 8-21)
Save a PowerPoint slide as a graphic (p. 8-16)

STUDY QUESTIONS

MULTIPLE CHOICE

1. To send a PowerPoint outline to Word, use the
   a. File menu.
   b. Edit menu.
   c. Tools menu.
   d. Insert menu.
2. You can use all the following techniques to place Excel data in PowerPoint files *except*
   a. dragging the data from Excel to PowerPoint.
   b. cutting the data from the Excel worksheet and choosing **Edit | Paste Special** to paste it into PowerPoint.
   c. copying the Excel data to the Clipboard and pasting it into PowerPoint.
   d. retyping the data from Excel into PowerPoint.
3. To create a link between data from Access and PowerPoint,
   a. press Ctrl as you drag.
   b. press Enter.
   c. choose **Edit | Paste Special**.
   d. choose **File | Export**.
4. When you want to create a new table using tools in PowerPoint, you can
   a. choose **Insert | Table**.
   b. use the drag technique to copy it from Word.
   c. use the Clipboard.
   d. choose an AutoLayout format that contains the object placeholder you want to add.
5. When you create a new object in a PowerPoint presentation using tools from another application,
   a. the object is embedded in the presentation.
   b. the object becomes a separate file.
   c. the source application opens as a button on the toolbar.
   d. you can't create new data in a PowerPoint slide.
6. When you add a Word table to a PowerPoint slide, the toolbars that are visible include
   a. PowerPoint default toolbars.
   b. Word and PowerPoint Formatting toolbars.
   c. Word Standard and Formatting toolbars.
   d. none of the above

7. To access a linked or embedded object copied from another application and add it to a PowerPoint slide,
   a. close the presentation and exit PowerPoint.
   b. launch the source application and open the file.
   c. press Enter.
   d. double-click the object.

8. To save a slide as a graphic, choose
   a. **File | Save as** and select a graphic format from the Save as type list.
   b. **Insert | Picture | From File**.
   c. **File | Send To**.
   d. **Edit | Paste Special**.

9. To place a slide graphic in a Word document, choose
   a. **File | Save as** and select a graphic format from the Save as type list.
   b. **Insert | Picture | From File**.
   c. **File | Send To**.
   d. **Edit | Paste Special**.

10. Adding information to a file that is copied from another file in such a way that you can update the file when information in the original file changes is known as
    a. linking.
    b. embedding.
    c. importing.
    d. exporting.

SHORT ANSWER

1. What option do you choose from the Paste Special dialog box to create a link between the source and target files?
2. What appears on graphic objects to enable you to change the size of the graphic?
3. What dialog box appears when you send a PowerPoint presentation outline to Word?
4. How do you access the shortcut menu for an object in a presentation slide?
5. Where does data have to be to enable you to use the Paste Special feature?
6. How many slides in a presentation can you save as graphics at the same time?
7. How do you edit an object from another application that is embedded or linked to a file in another application?
8. On what menu does the hyperlink command appear?
9. What types of objects can you save as graphics?

FILL IN THE BLANK

1. ______________ objects are stored with the file and increase the size of the file.
2. To ensure that information created in one application can be updated when the information is added to a file in another application, ______________ the files.
3. Save graphics that will be used on the Internet or Web sites in ______________ or ______________ format.
4. The ______________ command on the File menu of Word and PowerPoint enables you to share files between the two applications.
5. Use the ______________ command on the Edit menu when you want to link data between files.
6. The ______________ icon helps you capture the complete table in Word.
7. The ______________ icon appears automatically when you paste a table from Word onto a PowerPoint slide
8. Adding an object to a slide so that it is saved with the presentation is known as ______________
9. The file that contains an object or text to be added to another file is called the ______________.
10. The application used to create the file into which information is copied is called the ______________.

FOR DISCUSSION

1. How do you create a new document using a presentation outline?
2. What is the difference between linked files and hyperlinked files?
3. What techniques do you use to ensure that a link is created when you add data from Word or Excel or Access to a PowerPoint slide?
4. Discuss the benefits of hyperlinking files to other files.

GUIDED EXERCISES

1 SHARING FILES

Software programs that are part of a suite are designed to work together as a team. Therefore, it makes no difference whether you create a document in Word or a presentation in PowerPoint—you can use the files from one application to create a file in the other application. In this exercise, you use a Word outline to create a new PowerPoint presentation and then format the presentation using a custom template.

1. Launch Word, if necessary, and open *Etch-a-Sketch.doc*.
2. Choose **File | Send to | Microsoft PowerPoint**.

Figure 8-30

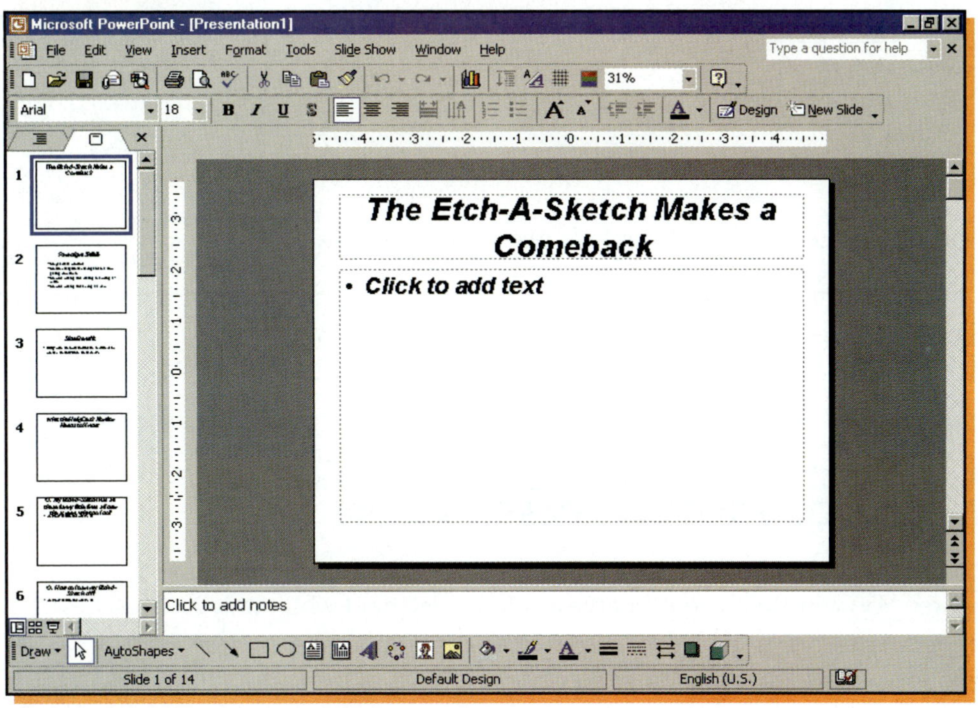

3. Click the Design **Design** button on the Formatting toolbar and then click **Browse** at the bottom of the task pane. The Apply Design Template dialog box opens.
4. Open the folder containing your student files and double-click the *Etch-a-Sketch.pot* template file.

Figure 8-31

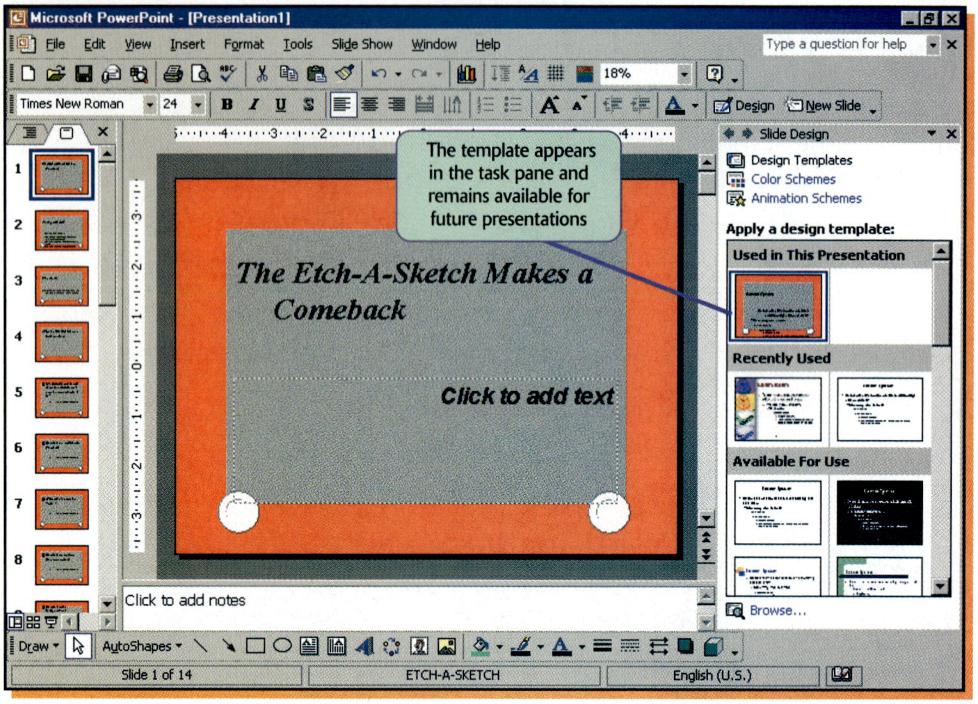

5. Make the necessary adjustments to text on each slide and apply animation effects to each slide.

6. Save the presentation using the file name *A Technological Comeback*.

2 LINKING AND HYPERLINKING EXCEL WORKSHEET DATA TO A POWERPOINT PRESENTATION

Hyperlinks can be attached to files to launch any application installed on a computer. You can even use it to access a full worksheet when only a portion of the data from the worksheet is linked to another file. In this exercise, you will add the slide pictured in Figure 8-32 to the presentation *e-Selections Web Online.ppt* by linking the data from the Excel worksheet *Top Ten Sellers.xls* to the slide. After formatting and sizing the data appropriately, you will create an action button that launches Excel and opens the *Top Ten Sellers.xls* worksheet when you click on it.

Figure 8-32

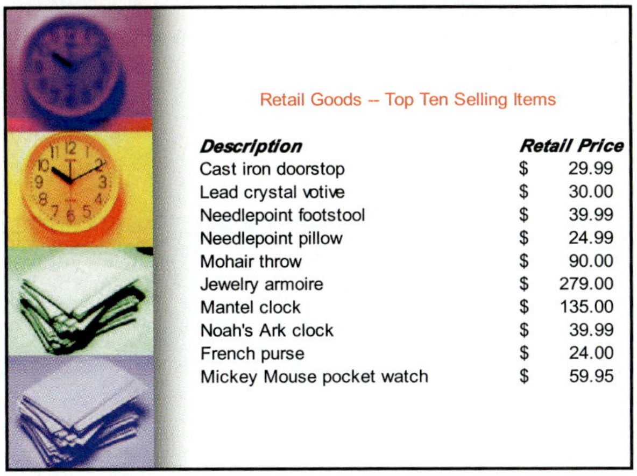

Follow these instructions to complete the exercise:

1. Open *e-Selections Web Online.ppt* in PowerPoint and create a new blank slide at the end of the presentation.
2. Open *Top Ten Sellers.xls* in Excel, select cells A1-B13, copy the data to the Clipboard.
3. Switch back to PowerPoint, choose **Edit** | **Paste Special** | **Paste Link**, and click **OK**.
4. Size and position the table as shown in Figure 8-32.
5. Select the table, and choose **Insert** | **Hyperlink**.
6. Locate and double-click the *Top Ten Sellers.xls* file.
7. Save changes to the presentation and print a copy of the new slide.
8. Show the presentation as a slide show and test the hyperlink. Make necessary adjustments to the file, save changes, and close all open files.

ON YOUR OWN

The difficulty of these case studies varies:
are the least difficult; *are more difficult; and* *are the most difficult.*

1 COPYING AND LINKING A WORD TABLE TO A NEW SLIDE

You've explored the techniques for linking an Excel worksheet to a PowerPoint presentation. Apply those techniques to this exercise. Create a new title only slide at the end of the *Travel Specials.ppt* presentation and add the title shown in Figure 8-33. Copy the table contained in *New Year's Eve Travel Specials.doc* and link it to the new slide. Position the table as shown in Figure 8-33. Save changes to the presentation and print a copy of the new slide.

Figure 8-33

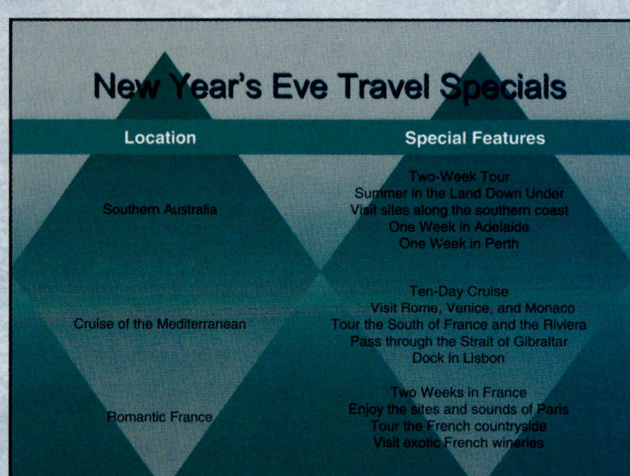

2 CREATING, FORMATTING, AND HYPERLINKING

The *Executive Overview.doc* document contains the structure you want to use for a new presentation. Create a new presentation from the Word outline, format the presentation using an appropriate template, and save the presentation using the file name *Executive Overview*. Then add hyperlinks between the bullet-point text that appears on Slide 2 and the appropriate slide in the presentation. Create a hyperlink between Slide 9 (Packet Information and Content) and the *Selections Managers.mdb* file. Save changes to the presentation and pack the presentation to go. Be sure to include linked files and the Access database file in the package you create.

3 PICTURING ACCESS DATA—MISSION *NOT* IMPOSSIBLE!

Data contained in Access databases can be portrayed graphically by linking the data to a PowerPoint presentation, formatting the presentation, and saving presentation slides as graphics. Your task in this exercise, should you choose to accept it, is multifaceted:

- Locate a new PowerPoint template on the Microsoft Web site, download the template, customize the template, and apply it to a new presentation.
- Search the Internet for the names of two primary actors and actresses from five different shows that aired during each of the last five decades. Research the actors and actresses and gather as much information about them as you can. Then create a database named *Decades of Performers* and record at least five fields of information about each actor and actress in the database. Create a form in the database that displays individual information about each actor and actress.
- Download pictures of the ten actors and the ten actresses from the Internet.
- Create a new PowerPoint presentation named *Decades of Performers* formatted using your customized template. Add a slide for each actor and actress whose picture you download from the Internet. Insert the picture on the appropriate slide and create a hyperlink between the picture and Access.
- Add animation to the presentation.
- As a bonus, see if you can create the hyperlink in such a way that it opens the specific actor's or actress's record form in Access.

When you have completed the presentation and database, e-mail both the presentation and the database to your instructor.

4 DISTINGUISHING MYTHS FROM FACTS

Have you ever heard people from older generations make statements that they believed to be factual that had you wondering how in the world they came up with such ideas? Many of these statements are based on time-tested observation—others have been handed down through several generations. Myths are known to exist in the business *world* as well as in the business of *life*. These common misperceptions cost you, the consumer, thousands of dollars each year. These myths have been identified in a PowerPoint presentation; the facts are stored in a Word document. By interspersing the facts as slides in the presentation with the myths you'll discover that one myth is not countered by fact. Search the Internet for stories related to the missing fact and identify at least three arguments to support the fact. Insert the information contained in the *Facts.doc* file into the *Myths.ppt* file. Then organize the slides containing the facts so that each fact slide appears immediately after the myth to which it refers. Format the fact slides using a different master to distinguish them. Save the file as a new presentation named *Myths & Facts* and print the presentation as handouts with two slides per page. Close the presentation and exit all open applications.

Photospread credits pages 8-2 & 8-3
©CORBIS: ©R.W. Jones/CORBIS; ©FPG: ©Telegraph Colour Library 1998, ©Mark Adams 1999; ©Tony Stone: ©James Strachan; ©Pearson Education; ©Lorraine Castellano

Glossary

3-D view The angle at which a 3-dimensional object is positioned to show height, width, and depth.

Action button A button created on a slide that controls the action PowerPoint takes when you click the button during a slide show. You can set the action button to display a specific slide, to open an Office file, or to start a different presentation.

Action item A task identified during a slide show that is added to the Action Items page of the Meeting Minder dialog box and is also added to the slide that appears at the end of a slide show.

Alignment The position of text within a placeholder: left, center, or right.

Animation Special visual or sound effects added to text and other slide objects to control how text or objects appear on screen during a slide show.

Animation Effects Same as Animation

Animation order The order in which slide objects appear when the slide is on screen during a slide show.

Animation scheme A collection of animation effects that, when applied to slide objects, control the movement of objects both on and off the screen.

Annotation Temporary text, marks, and drawings added to slides on screen during a slide show.

Audience The participants in a presentation conference.

AutoContent Wizard A PowerPoint feature that helps the user to build an outline for a specific type of presentation by providing options for specific pieces of information about the presentation.

AutoFit A PowerPoint feature that automatically sizes text contained in slide placeholders to fit within the boundaries of the placeholder.

AutoFormat A collection of predefined layouts, colors, and arrangements of organization chart boxes.

Background The underlying color, texture, pattern, or image that is applied to the complete slide to form the underlying base for other slide objects.

Black screen A blank black screen presented during a slide show to shift the focus of the audience to the presenter.

Border style The format of the line—bold, broken, dashed, and so forth—drawn around boxes, graphic objects, and paragraphs on slides.

Branches Links created in a presention to access groups of slides saved as a custom show within a presentation or separate presentations stored outside the active presentation.

Bullet format The shape, color, size, and indentation of the bullet that precedes bulleted items.

Category Data represented by columns on a Microsoft Graph datasheet that is graphically presented.

Cell The intersection of a column and a row on a Microsoft Graph datasheet.

Cell address The column letter and row number of a cell.

Chart A graphic presentation of numeric data.

Chart type The shape of the object—bar, pie wedge, line, and other types—used to present numeric data in a chart.

Clip Organizer A set of media clips—clip art images, sound files, and so forth—supplied by Microsoft and used to enhance presentations.

Clipboard A Windows feature used to hold one cut or copied snippet of information.

Color scheme A set of complementary colors used for the background, text, and other components in a presentation or template.

Column Vertical areas of Microsoft Graph chart datasheets that are labeled alphabetically and represent data categories.

Comments Notes added to slides by reviewers or the presentation author to hold reminder notes, questions, or comments about the slide.

Computer address Internet Protocol locations identified by the Presentation Conference Wizard that enable the presenter of the presentation to connect to audience participants.

Custom animation Special effects added to animation settings using the Custom Animation dialog box.

Custom show A slide show created within a presentation that is made up of selected slides contained in the existing presentation.

Cycle diagram A diagram layout used to show a repeating process in a continuous cycle.

Datasheet A spreadsheet-like layout that contains data and labels to be included on a Microsoft Graph chart.

Demote To change slide title text to a bullet list point or an existing bullet point to a lower level bullet point.

Distributed Increasing the space between characters of text so that the text expands the width of the placeholder.

Effects Settings applied to text and other slide objects to control the way they appear on screen during a slide show.

Elevation The angle at which a chart is displayed.

Embedded objects Data added to a slide saved as part of the PowerPoint presentation file.

Export Send information to another location—specifically, to send conference or meeting minutes to Word or to schedule appointments in Outlook.

Flip object Turn a graphic or other object so that it faces the opposite direction.

Footer The area at the bottom of a slide that contains information—page number, name, and so forth—that appears on screen for every slide in the presentation.

Frame The outside border buttons on a chart datasheet that can be used to select rows or columns.

Graphics Visuals in the form of pictures and drawings added to Office files.

Grayscale Display presentation slides in black and white and shades of gray rather than in full color.

Group Combine multiple drawn or graphic objects into one.

Handouts PowerPoint presentation materials printed with multiple slide images on each page and optional lines for note taking.

Header Text that is set to appear at the top of each presentation slide.

Hidden slide A slide included in a presentation to provide supplementary information that is marked to show only when specifically accessed.

Hierarchical structure A graphic presentation that outlines a top-down or bottom-up organizational structure, such as the structure of the management levels within an organization.

Hypertext Markup Language (HTML) A format used to save PowerPoint presentation files for use on the Web.

Hyperlink An invisible connection between text or slide objects for navigating to specific slides, opening other files, and/or performing other actions by clicking the hyperlinked item during a slide show.

Images Graphic pictures added to slides.

Internet Protocol (IP) address A specific location on the Internet that an active connection holds. In PowerPoint, IP addresses are identified by the Presentation Conference Wizard and are used when audience participants are trying to join a presentation conference.

Label Information included in a Microsoft Graph datasheet that can be used to identify data. Label information often appears in the legend of a chart.

Landscape Paper orientation that prints with the long side of the paper as the top of the document.

Legend Information that appears on a Microsoft Graph chart to explain the meaning of data bars, lines, or pie wedges.

Linked objects Objects stored outside the presentation file that are connected to a slide in the presentation in such a way that they updated each time you open the presentation file.

Line spacing The setting that controls the amount of space (such as single, double, and so forth) between lines of text.

Loop A term used to indicate that an action is supposed to repeat until a condition is met or until the action is stopped by a user.

Master The layout and design elements and features, such as background color, text placeholder format, and graphics used to format slides in a presentation.

Meeting Minder A PowerPoint feature used to take minutes (notes) during a slide show, record tasks that need to be completed as action items, and schedule meetings based on discussion that takes place during a presentation.

Microsoft Graph A software application that can be used to graph numeric data in PowerPoint.

Minutes The notes taken during a slide show to record meeting or conference activities.

Multimedia The elements and objects—graphics, sound, movies, and so forth—added to presentations to enhance slides and make presentations more entertaining.

Narration The live recording of narrative for each slide in a presentation that can be saved as part of the presentation file.

Normal view The default tri-pane view that includes a presentation outline/slide pane, slide image, and notes area.

Office Clipboard An Office XP feature designed to hold up to 24 snippets of cut or copied information from different Office applications.

On-screen show A PowerPoint presentation designed for viewing on a computer monitor or projected from a computer onto a screen.

Online broadcast A presentation delivered, formatted, and saved for posting to a Web site so that others can view it.

Organization Chart A chart that displays boxes in such a way that the hierarchical organization of box contents is identified.

Orientation The position of information on paper—portrait and landscape.

Outline view The on screen display of slide placeholder text in the outline/slide pane.

Pack and Go A PowerPoint feature that compresses presentation files into a format to fit on a single disk that can be easily transported to another computer.

Participant A person who participates in an online presentation as part of the audience.

Placeholder A predefined area outlined on a slide that is designed to hold specific items, such as text, bulleted lists, graphs, tables, and charts.

Play options Options that control when multimedia elements contained in a presentation play, how long they play, and the order in which they play.

Portrait Paper orientation that is taller than it is wide.

Presentation A collection of slides all related to the same topic and stored together in a single file.

Presentation Broadcast An online meeting conducted using tools in PowerPoint to review a presentation file.

Presentation review cycle The routine review process that starts when a presentation is distributed for review, reviewers respond to the presentation with comments, and the comments are compiled for final edits.

Presenter The person who sets up a presentation conference and controls the activities that occur during a conference.

Progress bar A "grow" bar that tracks the progress of a slide show, indicates whether the current slide has been on screen too long or too short a time, and tracks the length of a slide show to indicate whether the presentation is progressing too quickly or too slowly.

Promote To change bulleted text to a slide title or a lower level bullet point to a higher level bullet point

Publish presentations Format presentations so that they can be posted to a Web site.

Pyramid diagram A triangular-shaped diagram used to show foundation-based layers.

Radial diagram A diagram layout used to display the relationships of items and values to a core element.

Replace Fonts Change the font of text throughout a presentation by identifying a substitute font.

Rotate Adjust the tilt or angle of a graphic or other object.

Route Send presentations for review from one person to the next in such a way that the comments and notes added by one person can be viewed by others during the routing process.

Row Horizontal areas of Microsoft Graph datasheets that are identified by numbers and hold series data.

Scanned image A graphic image that is captured and formatted through the use of a scanner to be recognized by a computer.

Series Data that is grouped on a Microsoft Graph datasheet in such a way that information that pertains to the same item appears in a datasheet row.

Shadow Faint outlines that can be placed behind drawn objects, text, and other slide elements to create special effects.

Shared A common location on a server or on the Internet that users can access.

Slide The basic unit of a presentation similar to a page in a Word document or a worksheet in an Excel workbook. Presentations typically consist of numerous slides.

Slide background The color scheme and pattern that forms the backdrop for all text and objects on presentation slides.

Slide Finder A dialog box used to insert slides from one presentation into another presentation.

Slide Layout A PowerPoint slide format that contains object placeholders.

Slide Master The master layout for all presentation slides except slides formatted using the Title slide layout.

Slide Notes The pane that appears at the bottom of the Normal view and holds presentation notes to assist the presenter during a slide show.

Slide Show The display of slides in a presentation window without the PowerPoint toolbars, title bar, and status bar so that each slide fills the screen as it is accessed.

Slide Sorter view The PowerPoint view that displays small images (often called thumbnail images) of each slide in a presentation so that you can review the flow of the presentation and easily reorganize the presentation.

Slide view The PowerPoint view that expands the slide pane of the Normal view and reduces the size of the outline pane.

Sound card A piece of hardware added to a computer that is used to project sound from the computer.

Source The program or file from which information originates.

Style Checker A PowerPoint feature used to identify slide text structure and notify you when set options are violated.

Subordinate A person who reports to another person (supervisor) and whose box appears on a lower level of the organization chart than the supervisor.

Table slides Slides formatted to contain tables in columns and rows.

Target The program or file into which information from another program or file is placed.

Target diagram A diagram layout used to show steps toward a projected goal.

Task pane A separate pane that opens on the right side of the PowerPoint window and displays formats and other items used to format and build presentations.

Template A professionally developed slide design that you can apply to presentations to give a consistent look to all slides in the presentation.

Text category A list of character sets which contain items that can be used to format bullets.

Thumbnails The small images of graphics and template designs in the task pane, and miniature slide images in the PowerPoint Slide Sorter view.

Title Master A special master that contains settings for slides formatted using the Title slide layout.

Transitions Special effects that appear as slides move on and off the screen during a slide show.

Transparent color A see-through color used to blend graphics with the slide background color so that text appears.

Ungroup To separate a graphic or drawn object into the individual pieces that make up the complete image.

Update To make current so that the object contains the most recent information.

Venn diagram A diagram layout in which there are areas of overlap between data elements.

View The different ways to display slides on screen to make working with slides and slide features during development of a presentation more efficient.

Visual Clarity A PowerPoint feature that checks your presentations for font suitability and legibility of slide titles and body text.

Windows metafile One type of graphic file format that PowerPoint uses to save presentation slides and slide objects as graphics.

Index

Q-R

S

U-V

W-X-Y-Z